Fodor's 06

ALASKA

Where to Stay and Eat for All Budgets

Must-See Sights and Local Secrets

Ratings You Can Trust

Fodor's Travel Publications New York, Toronto, London, Sydney, Auckland
www.fodors.com

FODOR'S ALASKA 2006
Editor: Heidi Leigh Johansen

Editorial Production: Tom Holton
Editorial Contributors: Emmanuelle Alspaugh, Carissa Bluestone, Satu Hummasti, Sue Kernaghan, Brian Kluepfel, Don Pitcher, Tom Reale, Bill Sherwonit
Maps: David Lindroth Inc.; Mark Stroud, Moon Street Cartography, *cartographers*; Bob Blake and Rebecca Baer, *map editors*
Design: Fabrizio La Rocca, *creative director*; Guido Caroti, *art director*; Moon Sun Kim, *cover design*; Melanie Marin, *senior picture editor*
Production/Manufacturing: Colleen Ziemba
Cover Photo (Denali National Park): Larry Ulrich Stock Photograghy

COPYRIGHT

ISBN 1–4000–1561–8

ISSN 0271–2776

SPECIAL SALES
Fodor's Travel Publications are available at special discounts for bulk purchases for sales promotions or premiums. Special editions, including personalized covers, excerpts of existing guides, and corporate imprints, can be created in large quantities for special needs. For more information, contact your local bookseller or write to Special Markets, Fodor's Travel Publications, 1745 Broadway, New York, NY 10019. Inquiries from Canada should be directed to your local Canadian bookseller or sent to Random House of Canada, Ltd., Marketing Department, 2775 Matheson Boulevard East, Mississauga, Ontario L4W 4P7. Inquiries from the United Kingdom should be sent to Fodor's Travel Publications, 20 Vauxhall Bridge Road, London SW1V 2SA, England.

AN IMPORTANT TIP & AN INVITATION
Although all prices, opening times, and other details in this book are based on information supplied to us at press time, changes occur all the time in the travel world, and Fodor's cannot accept responsibility for facts that become outdated or for inadvertent errors or omissions. So **always confirm information when it matters,** especially if you're making a detour to visit a specific place. Your experiences—positive and negative—matter to us. If we have missed or misstated something, **please write to us.** We follow up on all suggestions. Contact the Alaska editor at editors@fodors.com or c/o Fodor's at 1745 Broadway, New York, NY 10019.

PRINTED IN THE UNITED STATES OF AMERICA

10 9 8 7 6 5 4 3 2 1

Be a Fodor's Correspondent

Your opinion matters. It matters to us. It matters to your fellow Fodor's travelers, too. And we'd like to hear it. In fact, we *need* to hear it.

When you share your experiences and opinions, you become an active member of the Fodor's community. That means we'll not only use your feedback to make our books better, but we'll publish your names and comments whenever possible. Throughout our guides, look for "Word of Mouth," excerpts of your unvarnished feedback.

Here's how you can help improve Fodor's for all of us.

Tell us when we're right. We rely on local writers to give you an insider's perspective. But our writers and staff editors—who are the best in the business—depend on you. Your positive feedback is a vote to renew our recommendations for the next edition.

Tell us when we're wrong. We're proud that we update most of our guides every year. But we're not perfect. Things change. Hotels cut services. Museums change hours. Charming cafés lose charm. If our writer didn't quite capture the essence of a place, tell us how you'd do it differently. If any of our descriptions are inaccurate or inadequate, we'll incorporate your changes in the next edition and will correct factual errors at fodors.com *immediately.*

Tell us what to include. You probably have had fantastic travel experiences that aren't yet in Fodor's. Why not share them with a community of like-minded travelers? Maybe you chanced upon a beach or bistro or B&B that you don't want to keep to yourself. Tell us why we should include it. And share your discoveries and experiences with everyone directly at fodors.com. Your input may lead us to add a new listing or highlight a place we cover with a "Highly Recommended" star or with our highest rating, "Fodor's Choice."

Give us your opinion instantly at our feedback center at www.fodors.com/feedback. You may also e-mail editors@fodors.com with the subject line "Alaska Editor." Or send your nominations, comments, and complaints by mail to Alaska Editor, Fodor's, 1745 Broadway, New York, NY 10019.

You and travelers like you are the heart of the Fodor's community. Make our community richer by sharing your experiences. Be a Fodor's correspondent.

Happy traveling!

Tim Jarrell

Tim Jarrell, Publisher

CONTENTS

MAPS

CLOSEUPS

ABOUT THIS BOOK

Our Ratings

Sometimes you find terrific travel experiences and sometimes they just find you. But usually it's up to you to select the right combination of experiences. That's where our ratings come in.

As travelers we've all discovered a place so wonderful that its worthiness is obvious. And sometimes that place is so experiential that superlatives don't do it justice: you just have to be there to know. These sights, properties, and experiences get our highest rating, **Fodor's Choice,** indicated by orange stars throughout this book.

Black stars highlight sights and properties we deem **Highly Recommended,** places that our writers, editors, and readers praise again and again for consistency and excellence.

By default, there's another category: any place we include in this book is by definition worth your time, unless we say otherwise. And we will.

Disagree with any of our choices? Care to nominate a place or suggest that we rate one more highly? Visit our feedback center at www.fodors.com/feedback.

Budget Well

Hotel and restaurant price categories from **¢** to **$$$$** are defined in the opening pages of each chapter. For attractions, we always give standard adult admission fees; reductions are usually available for children, students, and senior citizens. Want to pay with plastic? **AE, DC, MC, V** following restaurant and hotel listings indicate if American Express, Diner's Club, MasterCard, and Visa are accepted.

Restaurants

Unless we state otherwise, restaurants are open for lunch and dinner daily. We mention dress only when there's a specific requirement and reservations only when they're essential or not accepted—it's always best to book ahead.

Hotels

Hotels have private bath, phone, TV, and air-conditioning and operate on the European Plan (a.k.a. EP, meaning without meals), unless we specify that they use the Continental Plan (CP, with a Continental breakfast), Breakfast Plan (BP, with a full breakfast), or Modified American Plan (MAP, with breakfast and dinner) or are all-inclusive (including all meals and most activities). We always list facilities but not whether you'll be charged an extra fee to use them, so when pricing accommodations, find out what's included.

Many Listings

- ★ Fodor's Choice
- ★ Highly recommended
- ✉ Physical address
- ✥ Directions
- 📫 Mailing address
- ☎ Telephone
- 📠 Fax
- 🌐 On the Web
- 📧 E-mail
- 🎟 Admission fee
- ⏲ Open/closed times
- ⚑ Start of walk/itinerary
- Ⓜ Metro stations
- 💳 Credit cards

Hotels & Restaurants

- 🏨 Hotel
- 🛏 Number of rooms
- 👍 Facilities
- 🍽 Meal plans
- ✕ Restaurant
- ✍ Reservations
- 👔 Dress code
- 🚬 Smoking
- 🍷 BYOB
- ✕🏨 Hotel with restaurant that warrants a visit

Outdoors

- 🏌 Golf
- ⛺ Camping

Other

- 👶 Family-friendly
- ℹ Contact information
- ⇨ See also
- ✉ Branch address
- ☞ Take note

WHAT'S WHERE

ANCHORAGE

With nearly half the state's population, Anchorage is Alaska's biggest city and the state's only true metropolis. You'll find a varied selection of ethnic restaurants, a performing arts center, theater groups, an opera company, and an orchestra here. The Anchorage Museum of History and Art houses an outstanding collection of historic and contemporary Alaskan art. The Alaska Native Heritage Center celebrates the rich diversity of the state's original inhabitants. At nearby Lake Hood—the largest seaplane base in the world—the Alaska Aviation Heritage Museum preserves examples of rare and restored planes.

For all the attractions Anchorage offers, most visitors spend little time here, using it as a jumping-off point for excursions into less-settled parts of the state or merely as a place to catch a plane home. But there's plenty to do and see if you are passing through—and the occasional moose ambling down a city bike trail or a hawk passing through will remind you of the vast stretches of wilderness just outside the city borders.

SOUTH CENTRAL ALASKA

South Central encapsulates nearly all that the state has to offer: great fishing, hiking, rafting, and wildlife viewing, much of it easily accessible. Using Anchorage as a base, you could spend several vacations in this region and still be left wanting more. Especially well visited are the towns of Seward and Homer on the Kenai Peninsula. Kodiak, 100 mi offshore in the gulf of Alaska, is known as the Emerald Island for its green-carpeted mountains. The biggest terrestrial carnivore on Earth, the Kodiak brown bear, makes its home here. Even areas not readily reachable by road are within a short, easy flight by small plane, and dozens of charter outfits compete for your business. Although the summer crowds can be daunting in some of the most popular spots, a little research and effort can take you to areas where you can experience true wilderness solitude.

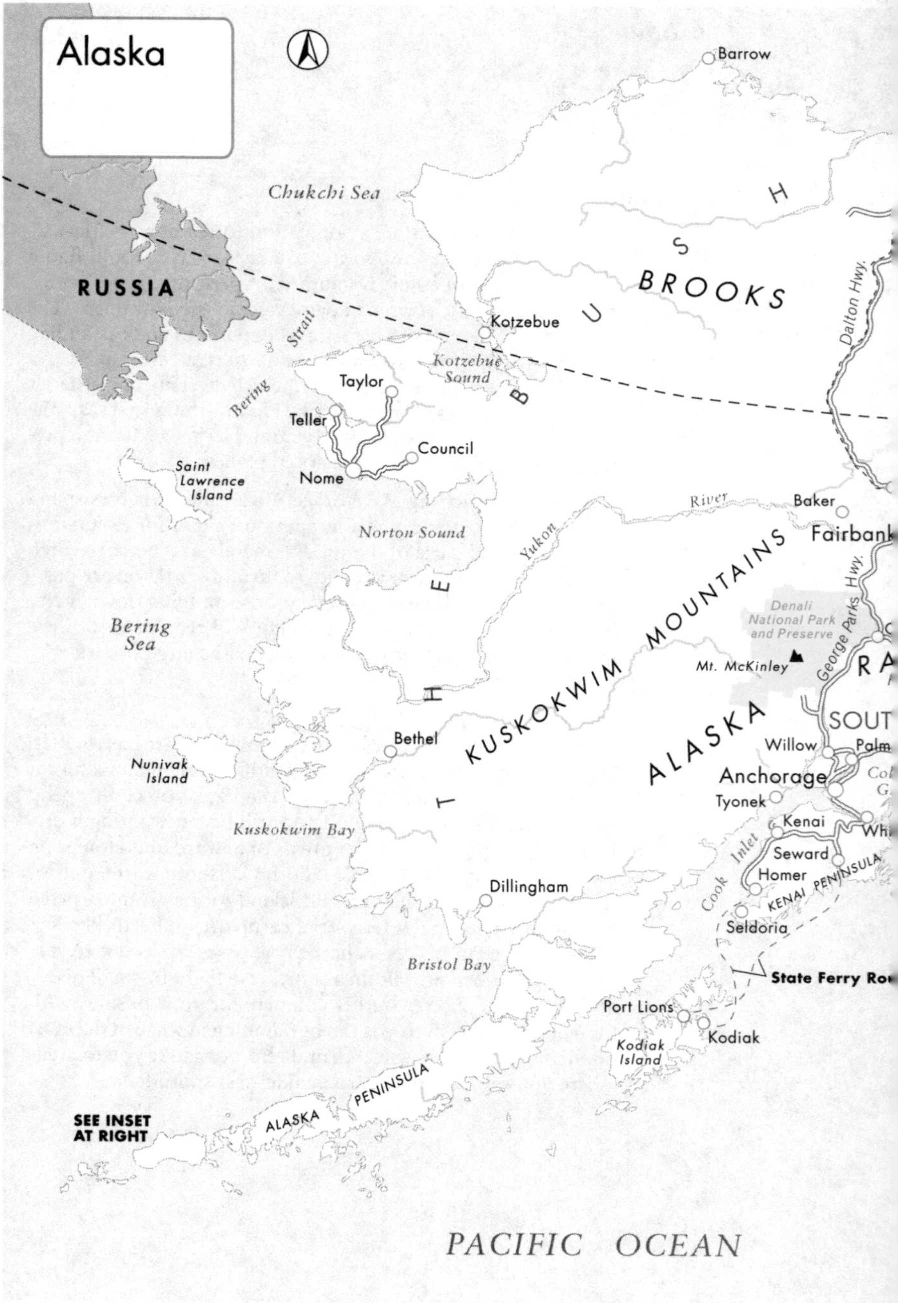

Alaska
Barrow
Chukchi Sea
RUSSIA
T H E B U S H
BROOKS
Dalton Hwy.
Kotzebue
Kotzebue Sound
Bering Strait
Taylor
Teller
Council
Nome
Saint Lawrence Island
Norton Sound
Yukon River
Baker
Fairbank
Bering Sea
Denali National Park and Preserve
George Parks Hwy.
Mt. McKinley
KUSKOKWIM MOUNTAINS
ALASKA
RA
SOUT
Willow
Palm
Anchorage
Tyonek
Kenai
Seward
Homer
Cook Inlet
KENAI PENINSULA
Seldoria
State Ferry Ro
Bethel
Nunivak Island
Kuskokwim Bay
Dillingham
Bristol Bay
Port Lions
Kodiak
Kodiak Island
ALASKA PENINSULA
SEE INSET AT RIGHT
PACIFIC OCEAN

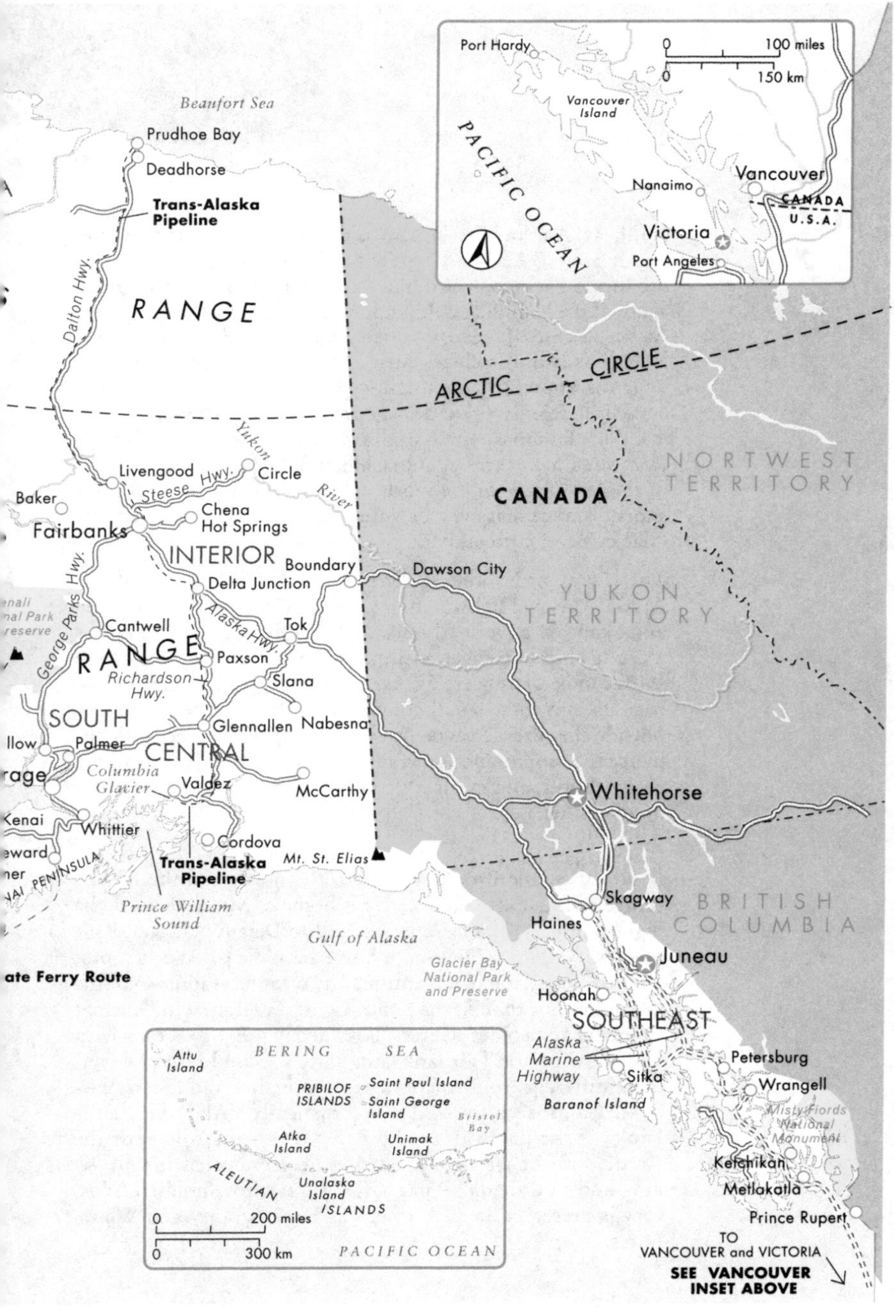
Port Hardy
0
100 miles
0
150 km
Vancouver Island
PACIFIC OCEAN
Nanaimo
Vancouver
CANADA
U.S.A.
Victoria
Port Angeles
Beaufort Sea
Prudhoe Bay
Deadhorse
Trans-Alaska Pipeline
Dalton Hwy.
RANGE
ARCTIC CIRCLE
Yukon River
NORTWEST TERRITORY
CANADA
Livengood
Steese Hwy.
Circle
Baker
Chena Hot Springs
Fairbanks
INTERIOR
Boundary
Dawson City
Delta Junction
George Parks Hwy.
YUKON TERRITORY
Cantwell
Alaska Hwy.
Tok
RANGE
Paxson
Richardson Hwy.
Slana
SOUTH
Nabesna
Glennallen
Palmer
CENTRAL
Columbia Glacier
Valdez
McCarthy
Whitehorse
Kenai
Whittier
Cordova
Trans-Alaska Pipeline
Mt. St. Elias
Prince William Sound
Skagway
Haines
BRITISH COLUMBIA
Gulf of Alaska
Juneau
Glacier Bay National Park and Preserve
Hoonah
SOUTHEAST
Alaska Marine Highway
Petersburg
Sitka
Wrangell
Baranof Island
Misty Fiords National Monument
Ketchikan
Metlakatla
Prince Rupert
TO VANCOUVER and VICTORIA
SEE VANCOUVER INSET ABOVE
Attu Island
BERING SEA
PRIBILOF ISLANDS
Saint Paul Island
Saint George Island
Bristol Bay
Atka Island
Unimak Island
ALEUTIAN ISLANDS
Unalaska Island
0
200 miles
0
300 km
PACIFIC OCEAN

SOUTHEAST ALASKA

Southeast Alaska (also known as the Panhandle or more commonly among Alaskans simply as "Southeast") encompasses the Inside Passage—more than a century ago the traditional route to the Klondike goldfields and today the centerpiece for Alaskan cruises. Juneau, the state's water-locked capital, is here, as well as fishing villages such as Petersburg and Ketchikan, which is known for its totem-pole carving. An onion-dome cathedral accents Sitka, the onetime capital of Russian America. Each fall up to 4,000 eagles gather just outside Haines to feast on salmon at the Alaska Chilkat Bald Eagle Preserve. One of the few places in the world where you can inspect from a short distance massive tidewater glaciers is the justly famous Glacier Bay National Park.

The towns of Southeast Alaska are linked by air and the Alaska Marine Highway (the state ferry system); only Haines and Skagway have road links to "the Outside." If you're not a cruise-ship passenger, visiting towns serviced by the cruise ships can be disconcerting, as the ships disgorge thousands of tourists into these small communities. However, the scenery outside the often-crowded towns is phenomenal: long fjords pierce the mountainous terrain, timbered slopes plunge to the rocky shores, and marine life abounds, from tiny sea birds to multi-ton whales.

THE INTERIOR

Bounded by the Brooks Range to the north and the Alaska Range to the south, the Interior is home to Mt. McKinley, the highest peak in North America, and to Denali National Park & Preserve, a 6-million-acre home to some of Alaska's best wildlife, scenery, and adventure. The weather is more extreme in the Interior than in the South Central region, with warmer summers and colder winters. Founded in 1901 by a merchant and a prospector, Fairbanks, the state's second-largest city, is quite different from Anchorage: it is smaller and less sophisticated and is considered more rustically "Alaskan." Fairbanks is the gateway to the Far North—the towns of the Arctic and the Bering Coast that are connected mainly by air—and to Canada's Yukon Territory, whose gold-rush history is preserved in such towns as Dawson City and Whitehorse.

THE BUSH

The Bush, more a spirit than a place, is the last frontier of the Last Frontier. From Nome to Barrow, much of the ground is permanently frozen, and for months at a time the sun never sets—or rises. In the Arctic are the hardy Eskimo people and the Prudhoe Bay oil fields, near Barrow, America's northernmost community. Prospectors still pan for gold on the beach in Nome, where they are occasionally joined by a wandering polar bear. Only one road leads up to the Arctic, the Dalton Highway. Otherwise, the only link between these outposts of civilization is by air or sea—unless you happen to have a sled-dog team, a snowmobile, or a Rollagon (a vehicle specially designed for crossing tundra).

The Bush offers brown-bear viewing in Katmai National Park, steaming volcanoes on the Alaska Peninsula and the Aleutian Islands, and the Bering seacoast's more than 100,000 square mi of watery wilderness. If you're planning an unguided Bush visit, keep in mind the planning and research involved, not to mention the primitive facilities you'll find here. Many of the smaller villages don't have any visitor amenities such as hotels, restaurants, or public transportation. However, if you can get past the logistical barriers, exploring the Bush is true adventuring. You're miles from civilization, without of the conveniences of modern life; self-reliance and creativity go a long way in making your stay safe and enjoyable.

QUINTESSENTIAL ALASKA

Seafood & Sourdough

Alaska's primary claim to gastronomic fame is seafood. The rich coastal waters produce prodigious quantities of halibut, salmon, crab, and shrimp, along with such specialties as abalone, sea urchin, herring roe, and sea cucumbers. If you haven't yet tasted fresh Alaskan salmon, do so here—there's nothing quite like a barbecued Copper River king salmon.

Sourdough bread, pastries, and pancakes are a local tradition, dating back to the gold-rush days. Prospectors and pioneers carried a stash of sourdough starter so that they could always whip up a batch of dough in short order. The old-timers became known as sourdoughs, a title that latter-day Alaskans earn by living here for 20 years.

After you return from your outdoor adventure, indulge your cravings with the best of Alaskan culinary delights. Start with sourdough pancakes for breakfast; for lunch go for smoked salmon spread on sourdough bread; top it off with a dinner of fresh halibut and wild-berry cobbler. Then you can consider yourself an honorary Alaska sourdough.

Kayaking

Sea kayaking is big among Alaskans. It was the Aleuts who invented the kayak (or *bidarka*) to fish and hunt sea mammals. When early explorers encountered the Aleuts, they compared them to sea creatures, so at home did they appear on their small ocean craft. Kayaks have the great advantage of portability. More stable than canoes, they also give you a feel for the water and a view from water level. Oceangoing kayakers will find plenty of offshore Alaskan adventures, especially in the protected waters of the Southeast, Prince William Sound, and Kenai Fjords National Park.

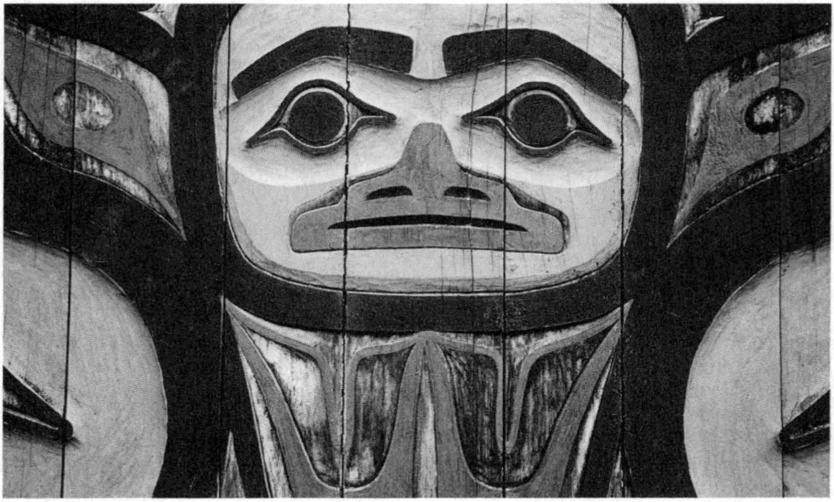

The variety of Alaskan marine life that you can view from a sea kayak is astonishing. It's possible to see whales, seals, sea lions, and sea otters, as well as bird species too numerous to list. Although caution is required when dealing with large stretches of open water, the truly Alaskan experience of self-propelled boating in a pristine ocean environment can be a life-changing thrill.

Native Crafts

Alaska's rich Native culture is reflected in its abundance of craft traditions, from totem-pole carving to handwoven baskets and detailed carvings. Alaska has adopted two symbols that guarantee the authenticity of crafts made by Alaskans: a hand symbol indicates the item was made by one of Alaska's Native peoples; a polar bear marks an item as made in Alaska.

Each of Alaska's Native groups is noted for particular skills. Eskimo art includes animal carvings of walrus ivory, spirit masks, dance fans, baskets made of baleen, and jewelry. Also be on the lookout for mukluks (seal- or reindeer-skin Eskimo boots). The Tlingit of Southeast Alaska are known for their totems and carvings, as well as for baskets and hats woven from spruce root and cedar bark. Tsimshian Indians also work with spruce root and cedar bark, and Haida Indians are noted basket makers and carvers. Athabascans specialize in fur garments and beadwork. The Aleuts' grass basketry is considered among the best in the world.

WHEN TO GO

Because Alaska is so big, each region experiences a different climate, and seasons come and go at different times of the year. In summer, the sun does not set for more than 2½ months in Barrow, north of the Arctic Circle. Even as far south as Juneau, you can see a glow of twilight in the sky at midnight. In winter, the situation is reversed, and the sun does not rise for more than two months in Alaska's northernmost regions. Anchorage gets about 5½–6 hours of daylight in mid-December.

Alaska is not a land of perpetual ice and snow—97% of the state is snow-free during those long summer days. With fair weather comes an onslaught of tourists and peak season prices. Summer, particularly late June through July, brings on plagues of mosquitoes. July and August are also the rainiest months throughout South Central and Interior Alaska. Fortunately, in perpetually wet Southeast Alaska, these months are the driest portion of the year. To avoid the summer crowds and prices, go during spring or fall.

Winter is the season for skiing, sledding, ice-skating, dog mushing, ice-fishing, and other sports. The long nights are also ideal for viewing the northern lights.

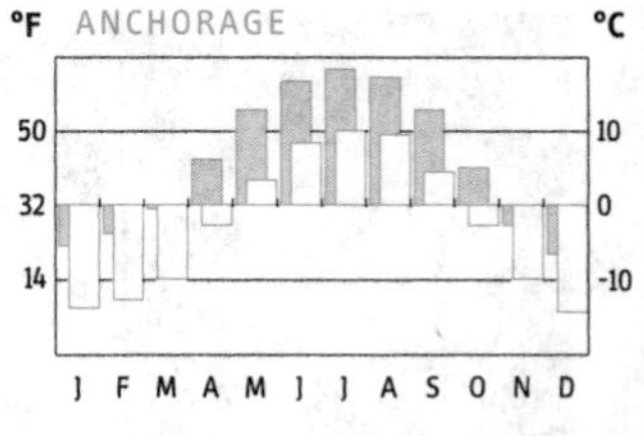

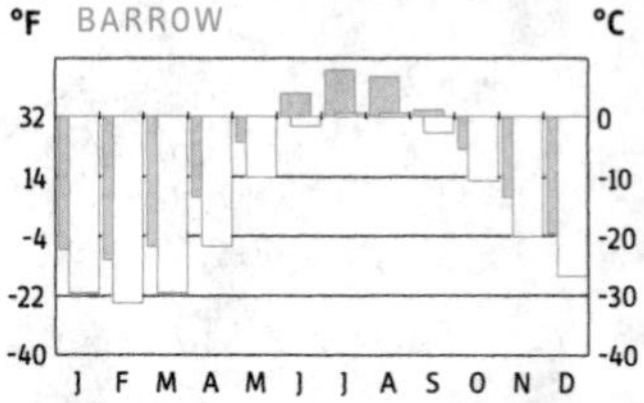

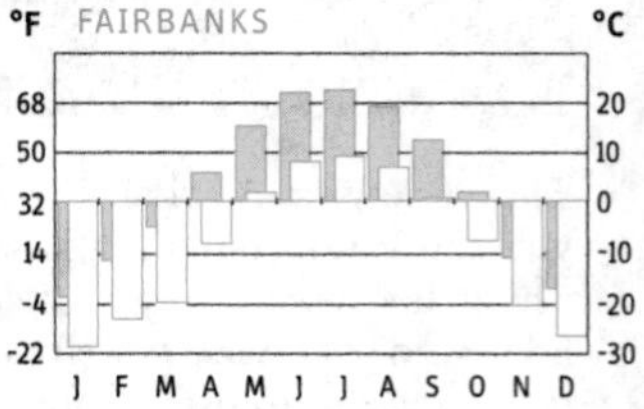

Climate

These charts list the average daily maximum and minimum temperatures for several Alaskan cities.

Forecasts **Weather Channel Connection** ☎ 900/932-8437 95¢ per minute from a Touch-Tone phone 🌐 www.weather.com.

Time Zones

Numbers below vertical bands relate each zone to Greenwich Mean Time (0 hrs).
Local times frequently differ from these general indications, as indicated by light-face numbers on map.

Anchorage **2**
Atlanta **20**
Bogotá **23**
Buenos Aires **27**
Caracas **24**
Chicago **10**
Dallas **11**
Denver **8**
Edmonton **4**
Halifax **17**
Honolulu **1**
Juneau **3**
Lima **25**
Los Angeles **7**
Mexico City **13**
Miami **21**
Minneapolis **9**
Montevideo **28**
Montréal **16**
New Orleans **12**
New York City **18**
Ottawa **15**
Rio de Janeiro **30**
San Francisco **6**
San José (CR) **22**
Santiago **26**
São Paolo **29**
Toronto **14**
Vancouver **5**
Washington, D.C. **19**

IF YOU LIKE

Museums

A superb way to learn about Alaskan history and heritage is to hit any one of these museums, whose exhibits and treasures range from ceremonial blankets and Native masks to gold-rush history pieces and Eskimo singing concerts.

- **Alaska Native Heritage Center, Anchorage.** Enjoy the 26 acres of grounds while you receive an introduction to the diverse Native cultural groups that populate Alaska. Five village exhibits encircle a small lake.
- **Anchorage Museum of History and Art, Anchorage.** In addition to a fine collection of historical items, this museum features contemporary Alaskan art, guided tours, great meals (courtesy of Marx Brothers' Cafe), and a classy gift shop.
- **Living Museum of the Arctic, Kotzebue.** You can experience Eskimo culture firsthand at this unique museum: Listen to a storyteller, watch a ceremonial dance, and bounce high on a blanket toss—an ancient practice whereby hunters were launched high in the air from blankets of walrus or seal hide to scan the seas for game.
- **University of Alaska Museum of the North, Fairbanks.** A must-see for all visitors to the Interior, the museum gives an excellent overview of Alaska's human and natural history, including the state's largest display of gold, and Blue Babe, a mummified steppe bison.

Bicycling

Biking can be a rewarding adventure in accessible parts of the state. The paved-road system is straightforward, and traffic is usually light. However, the road shoulders can be narrow, and people tend to drive fast in rural areas. Unpaved highways are bikable but are tougher going. Use caution when it comes to traffic, weather, and wildlife.

- **Anchorage, Alaska.** Anchorage has an excellent bike-trail system. Biking this city is a good way to appreciate its setting as a metropolis perched on the edge of vast wilderness—but beware the occasional furry creature sharing the bike trail with you!
- **Denali National Park & Preserve.** Take your mountain bike on the Alaska Railroad and bike Denali. Although the park road is largely unpaved, it has a good dirt surface and only light traffic. This immense preserve has some of the best wildlife viewing in the state.
- **The Interior.** Mountain biking has become a hot sport here. Fairbanks has miles of scenic bike paths along the Chena River. Most roads have wide shoulders and those incredible Alaska views. Trails used in winter by mushers, snowmobilers, and cross-country skiers are taken over by mountain bikers when the snow melts.
- **Southeast Alaska and the Ferry System.** You can bring your bike on Alaska's ferry system at an extra charge. Use it to explore the Southeast's charming communities and surrounding forests, but come prepared for heavy rain.

Creature Comforts

Alaska isn't only tundra hiking, grizzly-bear watching, and salmon fishing. If you know where to look, it's possible to spend your vacation pampering yourself, enjoying fine dining and a great wine selection, and still experiencing hearty outdoor adventures in the "real" Alaska.

As with many activities in Alaska, accessibility is a primary consideration. Lodging properties can be divided into those on the road system, and those that require a boat or air journey. In Southeast Alaska, many lodges can be reached by boat from a nearby town or village, while properties elsewhere in the state usually require a flight in a small plane.

- **Alaska's Capital Inn, Juneau.** Luxury meets history in this gracious hilltop bed-and-breakfast with upscale services, delicious breakfasts, and period furnishings from the early 1900s.
- **Alyeska Prince Hotel, Girwood.** An hour south of Anchorage, this luxurious hotel offers plenty of opportunities for spoiling yourself silly. The crown jewel of the resort is the Seven Glaciers Restaurant, a 7-minute tram ride up Mt. Alyeska. There you can enjoy the stunning view of the valley and the namesake glaciers; knowledgeable diners consider the restaurant to be among Alaska's finest.
- **Chena Hot Springs Resort, Chena Hot Springs.** If you are in or near Fairbanks, some thermal soaking is a must. Here you can spend the day enjoying a wide range of outdoor activities, followed by a long soak in the hot-springs-warmed hot tubs, topped off by an exceptional dinner.
- **Kachemak Bay Wilderness Lodge, Homer.** Across Kachemak Bay from Homer, and accessible by boat or float plane, you can fill your days with hiking, fishing, guided-boats tours, and sightseeing in this pristine setting, followed by delicious seafood dining. The owners are long-time Alaskans who know how to cater to nature lovers, and the attentive and professional staff can meet your every need.
- **Kenai Princess Wilderness Lodge, Cooper Landing.** Charming bungalows with fireplaces and vaulted ceilings of natural-finish wood make up this sprawling complex on a bluff overlooking the Kenai River. Flightseeing, fishing, and hiking on the nature trail near the lodge are among the possible activities.
- **Pearson's Pond Luxury Inn and Adventure Spa, Juneau.** Yoga in the morning; wine and cheese in the evening; whirlpool tubs with rain showers; private balconies; and a well-stocked breakfast nook—all are among the luxurious amenities that define this B&B, situated on a small pond near Mendenhall Glacier.
- **Seven Seas Mariner, Seven Seas Cruises.** Cordon Bleu cuisine, a luxurious spa, and impeccable service make this all-suites, all-balcony ship a top choice for relaxing in the lap of luxury while cruising amidst dramatic Alaskan scenery.

Scenic Drives

You'll be hard-pressed to find a drive in Alaska that isn't scenic. Spectacular mountain ranges, sweeping marine panoramas, and mile upon mile of open tundra are possible backdrops. Besides world-class scenery, there's always the potential for wildlife encounters, so the wise motorist is always on alert for something furry darting—or strolling, in the case of the regal moose—out of the roadside brush. Keep in mind that many roads are not plowed in winter, and heavy rain can create hazardous conditions. To obtain Alaskan road reports, call the State Department of Transportation in Fairbanks.

- **Glenn Highway, South Central.** Passing between the Chugach and Talkeetna mountains and past numerous glaciers, this highway heading east out of Anchorage is especially scenic in late summer and early fall.
- **Kalifornsky Beach Road, South Central.** Near Soldotna, this 20-mi-long loop off the Sterling Highway is parallel to the coastline along Cook Inlet. The peaks of the Alaska Range are visible, and the active volcanoes Mt. Iliamna and Mt. Redoubt are across the inlet. Boats ply the waters here, and bald eagles and beluga whales are common sights.
- **George Parks Highway, South Central and Interior.** Connecting Fairbanks and Anchorage, and passing by Denali National Park, the George Parks offers views of Mt. McKinley on a clear day. Heading south, the mountain seems to loom over you as you drive towards Talkeetna.
- **Richardson Highway, South Central and Interior.** The first highway built in Alaska, this 364-mi road between Fairbanks and the port of Valdez will offer you farm country, vast tundra, and mountain vistas.
- **Taylor Highway, South Central and Interior.** Winding along mountain ridges and through valleys of the Fortymile River is a 160-mi stretch of narrow, rough, gravel highway. This road will transport you to another era when gold was the main reason folks from the Lower 48 made it into the Interior. It remains one of the few places to see active mining without leaving the road system.
- **Denali Highway, Interior.** For a rustic drive, try this road between Paxson and Cantwell. The gravel road is 135 mi of semi-tough sledding for highway vehicles; if you've got a well-equipped ride, it's worth the effort. You'll find open tundra, views of the Alaska Range, lakes and streams, and miles of land that moose, caribou, grizzlies, wolves, and numerous species of birds call home sweet home.
- **Dalton Highway, Interior and the Bush.** More than 400 mi of road, the Dalton Highway connects Interior Alaska to the shores of the Arctic Ocean. Winding, exhilarating, and varied, it's a true Alaskan motor trek. Built as a hauling road, there are still plenty of 18-wheelers that will share the highway with you as you cross through the Brooks Range into the Arctic Plains.

ON THE CALENDAR

WINTER	Top seasonal events include the Anchorage Fur Rendezvous in February, the Iditarod Trail Sled Dog Race in March, Juneau's Alaska Folk Festival in April, and Sitka's Alaska Day Celebration in October.
December	The offbeat Talkeetna Winterfest (☎ 907/733–2330) combines competitive athletic events for women in the Wilderness Women Contest, with competitive bidding for eligible mountain-man bachelors at the Bachelor Society Ball.
January	Bethel's Kuskokwim 300 (☎ 907/543–3300 🌐 www.k300.org) is one of the state's premier sled-dog races. At Seward's Polar Bear Jump Off (☎ 907/224–5230 🌐 www.sewardak.org) bare skin meets barely above-freezing water. Spread over two weekends, the Anchorage Folk Festival (☎ 907/566–2334 🌐 www.anchoragefolkfestival.org) at the University of Alaska Anchorage features hundreds of performers and musical workshops.
Mid-January–February	Sled-Dog Racing (☎ 907/562–2235) season in Anchorage begins with sprints every weekend.
February	Tent City Winter Festival (☎ 800/367–9745 🌐 www.wrangellchamber.org) in Wrangell captures the flavor of Alaska's early days. At the Cordova Iceworm Festival (☎ 907/424–7260 🌐 www.iceworm.org) a 140-foot iceworm parades through city streets. Other events include a talent show and fun fair. Participants in the Yukon Quest International Sled Dog Race (☎ 907/452–7954 🌐 www.yukonquest.com) mush their way between Whitehorse, the Yukon Territory, and Fairbanks. Anchorage's Fur Rendezvous (☎ 907/277–8615 🌐 www.furrondy.net) delivers more than 150 events—from snowshoe softball to the Open World Championship Sled Dog Races.
SPRING	
March	The World Ice Art Championships and Winter Carnival (☎ 907/452–1105 🌐 www.icealaska.com) brings the finest ice artists to downtown Fairbanks. The Iditarod Trail Sled Dog Race (☎ 907/376–5155 or 800/545–6874 🌐 www.iditarod.com) stretches 1,049 mi from Anchorage to

	Nome. More than 70 dog teams compete in the world's premier sled-dog race. The **Bering Sea Ice Golf Classic** (☎ 907/443–5535 ⊕ www.nomealaska.org) is played with orange golf balls on the pack ice of the Bering Sea near Nome during the Iditarod. The seasonal "Nome National Forest" (150 or so abandoned Christmas trees) provides forest cover.
April	The three-day **Camai Dance Festival** (☎ 907/543–1977 ⊕ www.bethelarts.com) in Bethel attracts dance groups from throughout Alaska and also from outside the state. The **Alaska Folk Festival** (☎ 907/463–3316 ⊕ www.juneau.com/aff) in Juneau is a laid-back mix of music, handmade crafts, and foods. The **Alyeska Spring Carnival** (☎ 907/754–2259 or 800/880–3880 ⊕ www.alyeskaresort.com) holds court at the Alyeska Resort & Ski Area, 40 mi southeast of Anchorage. The featured event is the Slush Cup, in which skiers and snowboarders attempt to ski across a slushy pond at the base of the mountain. The **World Free Skiing Championship** (☎ 206/933–2809 ⊕ www.cmfvaldez.com) lures the world's top daredevil skiers to snowy Thompson Pass near Valdez. It's part of the **Chugach Mountain Festival,** which also includes a mountain-bike race, backcountry ski race, and film festival.
Late April–early May	During the **Copper River Delta Shorebird Festival** (☎ 907/424–7260) in Cordova, there are tours to beaches to witness the migration of millions of shorebirds.
May	The **Little Norway Festival** (☎ 907/772–4636 ⊕ www.petersburg.org) in Petersburg salutes the town's Scandinavian heritage. The **Kodiak Crab Festival** (☎ 907/486–5557 ⊕ www.kodiak.org) brings good food, a parade, a footrace, a survival-suit race, and the blessing of the fleet. **Juneau Jazz 'n Classics** (☎ 907/463–3378 ⊕ www.juneau.com/music) features performances by regionally and nationally known classical and jazz musicians over a 10-day period.
SUMMER	
June	The **Sitka Summer Music Festival** (☎ 907/747–6774 ⊕ www.sitkamusicfestival.org) is a monthlong series of chamber music performances.

	The Midnight Sun Baseball Game (☎ 907/451–0095 🌐 www.goldpanners.com) celebrates the longest day of the year, in Fairbanks. The game begins at 10:30 PM with no need for stadium lights.
July	The Mt. Marathon Race (☎ 907/224–8051 🌐 www.sewardak.org) in Seward is a rugged and often bloody race up the 3,000-foot mountain. The best vantage point is right below the trail's starting line.
	The World Eskimo–Indian Olympics (☎ 907/452–6646 🌐 www.weio.org) in Fairbanks tests participants in such skills as ear pulling, the knuckle hop, and the blanket toss.
	The popular KBBI Concert on the Lawn (☎ 907/235–7721 🌐 www.kbbi.org) transforms Homer with a mini-Woodstock mélange of live bands and good food.
August	Southeast Alaska State Fair (☎ 907/766–2476 🌐 www.seakfair.org) brings exhibits, music, and other fun-filled activities to the Haines Fairgrounds.
Late August–early September	The Alaska State Fair (☎ 907/745–4827 or 800/850–3247 🌐 www.alaskastatefair.org) in Palmer is the state's big end-of-summer blowout. Don't miss the famous 90-pound cabbages and other gargantuan vegetables.
FALL	
October	The Alaska Day Celebration (☎ 907/747–5940 🌐 www.sitka.com) brings out the whole town of Sitka to celebrate October 18, the day the United States acquired Alaska from Russia. The weeklong festival includes a period costume ball and a parade.
	Held in conjunction with the annual Alaska Federation of Natives convention, the Quyana Alaska Native Dance Festival (☎ 907/274–3611 🌐 www.nativefederation.org) in Anchorage provides a taste of the state's Native culture.
November	The Athabascan Old Time Fiddling Festival (☎ 907/452–1825) enlivens Fairbanks with traditional Native music.
	The Carrs Great Alaska Shoot-out (☎ 907/786–1230 🌐 www.shootout.net) takes place at Sullivan Arena in Anchorage, where some of the best college basketball teams in the country compete.

GREAT ITINERARIES

HIGHLIGHTS OF ALASKA

8 to 11 days

Sprawling national parks, wildlife viewing in Kenai Peninsula, breathtaking views from the overlooks of the Chugach Mountains outside Anchorage: Alaska begs to be experienced. Besides seeing natural wonders, you can gain a sense of the state's culture from the communities that dot its limited highway system. Start or end this survey with two or three days in Anchorage.

2 or 3 days: Seward

Surrounded by lush mountains at the head of Resurrection Bay, Seward is the primary gateway to Kenai Fjords National Park. You can join a coastal wildlife tour; walk to the icy snout of Exit Glacier; or explore massive cold-water tanks at Alaska SeaLife Center.

1 or 2 days: Kenai & Soldotna

The sportfishing hubs of South Central, these sister cities lie along the world-famous Kenai River. Five species of Pacific salmon spawn here each summer, including the mighty king, which may weigh 90 pounds or more. You can take a stroll through Kenai's old town, which includes a Russian Orthodox Church, or dig clams at Clam Gulch, 24 mi south of Soldotna.

2 or 3 days: Homer

This end-of-the-road coastal town calls itself the halibut capital of the world, but it also has a thriving community of artists and writers. Take a water taxi to nearby Kachemak Bay State Park, a rugged coastal wilderness of rain forest, jagged mountains, pale blue glaciers, and abundant wildlife. Visit the Pratt Museum, which has a saltwater aquarium, wildflower garden, and natural history displays.

1 day: Talkeetna

Mountaineers congregate at this rural community before flying into the Alaska Range. Denali National Park's entrance area is another 140 mi up the highway, but if you're pressed for time or can't get a bus reservation in the park, you can book a flightseeing trip here, and land on a glacier if you're so inclined.

2 days: Fairbanks

Born as a gold-mining camp at the start of the 20th century, the Golden Heart of Alaska's Interior is the starting point for trips into much of northern Bush Alaska. Near town, you can hike the nature trails in Creamer's Field Migratory Waterfowl Refuge. Or visit Pioneer Park, a theme park with museums, Native displays, and a gold-rush exhibit.

10 TO 16 DAYS: WILDERNESS ALASKA

Grizzly bears and herds of caribou, placid bays and white-water rapids, stretches of tundra and spruce forests: Alaska's wildlands are an outdoor playground. Though some areas are remote and expensive to visit, you can access several of the state's premier parks, refuges, and other public lands from the highway system and nearby gateway communities.

3 or 4 days: Denali National Park & Preserve

Larger than the state of Massachusetts, Alaska's oldest and most famous parkland is a wilderness of high mountains, glacial rivers, northern forest, and expansive tundra plains. Mt. McKinley rises 20,320 feet into the heavens, while grizzly bears roam alpine meadows and wolves hunt caribou, moose, and Dall sheep. You'll find plentiful opportunities for camping, hiking, and river rafting here.

1 or 2 days: Denali State Park

Little Denali, as it is sometimes called, has some of South Central Alaska's best tundra hikes, along the Curry-Kesugi Ridge. The park's spectacular views of Mt. McKinley are among the finest anywhere. At Byers Lake you can camp or stay in public-use cabins.

2 or 3 days: Chugach State Park

Anchorage's ½-million-acre backyard wilderness includes 3,350-foot Flattop Mountain, Alaska's most-climbed peak. Dozens of glaciers, jagged spires, tundra meadows, forested valleys, and plenty of wildlife populate this natural expanse.

1 or 2 days: Chugach National Forest

Sprawling across much of the Kenai Peninsula and Prince William Sound, this 6-million-acre national forest has vast wooded lowlands, glacially carved mountains, and pristine coastal areas. While visiting, you can stay in campgrounds or the public-use cabins.

1 or 2 days: Kenai National Wildlife Refuge

Covering nearly 2 million acres, the Kenai refuge encompasses part of the vast Harding Icefield as well as rugged peaks and forested lowlands inhabited by moose, black bears, and grizzlies.

2 or 3 days: Kenai Fjords National Park

Tidewater glaciers, rugged fjords, heavily crevassed Exit Glacier, and a variety of ocean life are highlights of this spectacular coastal parkland. Explore the park's perimeters on coastal wildlife tours based in Seward. You can also fly in, stay in public-use cabins, and travel by kayaks in bays devoid of other humans.

SMART TRAVEL TIPS

Finding out about your destination before you leave home means you won't spend time organizing everyday minutiae once you've arrived. You'll be more streetwise when you hit the ground as well, better prepared to explore the aspects of Alaska that drew you here in the first place. The organizations in this section can provide information to supplement this guide; contact them for up-to-the-minute details, and consult the A to Z sections that end each chapter for facts on the various topics as they relate to Alaska's many regions. Happy landings!

AIR TRAVEL

Alaska Airlines is the flagship carrier to Alaska, with year-round service from Seattle to Anchorage, Juneau, Fairbanks, Ketchikan, and towns around the state. In addition, the airline has nonstop flights linking Anchorage with Chicago, Dallas, Denver, Las Vegas, Los Angeles, and Portland, Oregon. Alaska Airlines and its subsidiary, Horizon Air, fly to many other North American cities from their Seattle hub, with nonstop Alaska flights to Boston, Denver, Washington, D.C., Miami, Newark, Orlando, and various Mexican cities. Continental, Delta, and United have year-round flights to Anchorage from Seattle. Other year-round nonstop flights to Anchorage are aboard America West from Phoenix, Continental from Houston, Northwest from Minneapolis–St. Paul, and Delta from Salt Lake City. Hawaiian Vacations has year-round charters between Anchorage and Honolulu.

Several airlines provide summer-only nonstop Anchorage flights from Lower 48 cities: Alaska Airlines from Phoenix; American from Dallas; Delta from Los Angeles; Frontier from Denver; Northwest from Detroit; and United from Chicago and Denver. Sun Country Airlines has seasonal charters connecting Anchorage with Minneapolis.

International travel connections to Anchorage include nonstop flights from a number of cities in Asia and Europe. Year-round service is offered from Seoul on Korean Air. In summer Alaska Airlines and

Air Canada have flights from Vancouver, China Airlines has flights from Taipei, Thomas Cook Condor Airlines flies from Frankfurt (some flights stop in Whitehorse, Yukon Territory), and Magadan Airlines flies from Petropavlovsk, in Russia. Both Japan Airlines and Alaskan Vacations have summer service between Tokyo and Anchorage.

Thomas Cook Condor Airlines flies into Fairbanks in summer from Frankfurt with a stop in Whitehorse, Yukon. Air North connects Whitehorse with Juneau and Fairbanks year-round. Japan Airlines offers a few nonstop flights from Tokyo to Fairbanks during the winter for travelers in search of northern lights. Other Fairbanks air connections include a stop in Anchorage.

If you are traveling from Britain, Continental Airlines flies from Gatwick, Birmingham, or Manchester via Newark and Seattle; Delta from Gatwick to Cincinnati or Salt Lake City; and United from Heathrow via San Francisco or Chicago. Travelers from Australia and New Zealand can take Qantas into Los Angeles out of Sydney, Melbourne, or Auckland. Air New Zealand flies from Sydney and Auckland to Los Angeles. United flies from Sydney to Los Angeles and San Francisco, and to Los Angeles from Melbourne and Auckland.

Commercial air travel to major towns in Alaska is usually by jet or turboprop. Scheduled air-taxi and air-charter services provide access to smaller towns and remote locales, using propeller-driven Bush aircraft that land on wheels, on floats, or on skis. Helicopters are increasingly popular for flightseeing and fast transport.

WITHIN ALASKA

Air travel within Alaska can be quite expensive, particularly for routes to Bush destinations where flying is the only option. A round-trip flight between Anchorage and Dutch Harbor typically costs more than $800—more than a flight from Anchorage to Hong Kong!

The workhorses of the north are the six-passenger Beavers, most of which were built in the 1950s and are still flying. The cost of an "air taxi" flight between towns or backcountry locations depends upon distance and the type of plane used, the number of people in your group, the length of the flight in each direction (including the time the pilot flies back empty after dropping you off), and the destination. Typical hourly rates are approximately $515 for a Beaver, with room for up to six people and gear; or $310 for a Cessna 185, with room for three people and gear.

Small planes have played a legendary part in the state's history: Bush pilots have helped explore Alaska and have been responsible for many dramatic rescue missions. But be aware that small planes cannot transport more than a limited amount of gear and cannot fly safely in poor weather. Your drop-off and pickup flights are therefore subject to delays, which are sometimes counted in days, not hours. When traveling in remote areas away from any towns or villages, be sure to carry extra food. Although most villages have general stores, fresh produce tends to be expensive and sometimes unavailable. Note also that some items are not allowed on commercial aircraft. This includes camp-stove fuel and the so-called "bear mace" (pepper spray) sold in camping-goods stores.

Contact the following airlines for flights within Alaska: Bering Air for flights from Nome or Kotzebue to smaller communities of the Far North; Era Aviation for flights to Cordova, Homer, Iliamna, Kenai, Kodiak, Valdez, and 17 western Alaska villages; and Frontier Flying Service from Anchorage to Fairbanks, along with many Bush villages. Contact Warbelow's Air Ventures and Larry's Flying Service for flights out of Fairbanks to Interior destinations. Peninsula Airways (PenAir) covers western Alaska, including Aniak, Dutch Harbor, McGrath, Dillingham, King Salmon, Sand Point, St. Paul, and St. George. Wings of Alaska serves several Southeast Alaska towns, including Juneau, Skagway, Haines, and Gustavus.

BOOKING

When you book, look for nonstop flights and remember that "direct" flights stop at least once. Try to avoid connecting flights, which require a change of plane. Two airlines may operate a connecting flight jointly, so ask whether your airline operates every segment of the trip; you may find that the carrier you prefer flies you only part of the way. To find more booking tips and to check prices and make online flight reservations, log on to www.fodors.com.

CARRIERS

Major Airlines **Air Canada** ☎ 888/247-2262 🌐 www.aircanada.com. **Air New Zealand** ☎ 800/262-1234, 800/063-385 in Australia, 0800/737-000 in New Zealand 🌐 www.airnz.com. **Alaska Airlines** ☎ 800/426-0333 🌐 www.alaskaair.com. **America West Airlines** ☎ 800/235-9292 🌐 www.americawest.com. **American Airlines** ☎ 800/433-7300 🌐 www.aa.com. **China Airlines** ☎ 800/227-5118 🌐 www.china-airlines.com. **Continental Airlines** ☎ 800/525-0280, 0800/776-464, 01293/776-464 in U.K. 🌐 www.continental.com. **Delta** ☎ 800/221-1212, 0800/414-767 in U.K. 🌐 www.delta.com. **Frontier Airlines** ☎ 800/432-1359 🌐 www.frontierairlines.com. **Japan Airlines** ☎ 800/525-3663 🌐 www.jal.com. **Korean Air** ☎ 800/438-5000 🌐 www.koreanair.com. **Northwest** ☎ 800/225-2525 🌐 www.nwa.com. **Qantas** ☎ 800/227-4500, 800/112-121 in Australia, 800/808-767 in New Zealand 🌐 www.qantas.com. **Thomas Cook Condor Airlines** ☎ 800/524-6975 🌐 www.thomascook.us. **United** ☎ 800/241-6522, 800/722-5243 in Canada, 0800/888-555 in U.K., 131-777 in Australia 🌐 www.ual.com.

Smaller Airlines **Air North** ☎ 867/668-2228, 800/764-0407 in U.S., 800/661-0407 in Canada 🌐 www.flyairnorth.com. **Bering Air** ☎ 907/443-5464 or 800/478-4111 🌐 www.beringair.com. **Era Aviation** ☎ 907/266-8394 or 800/866-8394 🌐 www.eraaviation.com. **Frontier Flying Service** ☎ 907/474-0014 or 800/478-6779 🌐 www.frontierflying.com. **Hawaiian Vacations** ☎ 907/243-2323 or 800/969-2700 🌐 www.hawaiianvacations.com. **Larry's Flying Service** ☎ 907/474-9169 🌐 www.larrysflying.com. **Magadan Air** ☎ 907/248-2994. **PenAir** ☎ 907/243-2323 or 800/448-4226 🌐 www.penair.com. **Regal Air** ☎ 907/243-8535 🌐 www.alaska.net/~regalair. **Rust's Flying Service** ☎ 907/243-1595 or 800/544-2299 🌐 www.flyrusts.com. **Sun Country Airlines** ☎ 800/359-6786 🌐 www.suncountry.com. **Warbelow's Air Ventures** ☎ 907/474-0518 or 800/478-0812 🌐 www.warbelows.com. **Wings of Alaska** ☎ 907/789-2021 🌐 www.wingsofalaska.com.

CHECK-IN & BOARDING

Always **find out your carrier's check-in policy.** Plan to arrive at the airport about two hours before your scheduled departure time for domestic flights and 2½ to 3 hours before international flights. You may need to arrive earlier if you're flying from one of the busier airports or during peak air-traffic times. To avoid delays at airport-security checkpoints, try not to wear any metal. Jewelry, belt and other buckles, steel-toe shoes, barrettes, and underwire bras are among the items that can set off detectors.

Assuming that not everyone with a ticket will show up, airlines routinely overbook planes. When everyone does, airlines ask for volunteers to give up their seats. In return, these volunteers usually get a several-hundred-dollar flight voucher, which can be used toward the purchase of another ticket, and are rebooked on the next available flight out. If there are not enough volunteers, the airline must choose who will be denied boarding. The first to get bumped are passengers who checked in late and those flying on discounted tickets, so get to the gate and check in as early as possible, especially during peak periods.

Always **bring a government-issued photo ID** to the airport; even when it's not required, a passport is best.

CUTTING COSTS

The least expensive airfares to Alaska are often priced for round-trip travel and must usually be purchased in advance. Airlines generally allow you to change your return date for a fee; most low-fare tickets, however, are nonrefundable. It's smart to call a number of airlines and check the Internet; when you are quoted a good price, book it on the spot—the same fare may not be available the next day, or even the next hour. Always check different routings and look into using alternate airports. Also, price off-peak flights and red-eye, which may be significantly less expensive than others. Travel agents, especially low-fare specialists (⇨ Discounts & Deals), are helpful.

Consolidators are another good source. They buy tickets for scheduled flights at reduced rates from the airlines, then sell them at prices that beat the best fare available directly from the airlines. (Many also offer reduced car-rental and hotel rates.) Sometimes you can even get your money back if you need to return the ticket. Carefully read the fine print detailing penalties for changes and cancellations, purchase the ticket with a credit card, and confirm your consolidator reservation with the airline.

The Internet is an increasingly important source for discount travel information. Three helpful sites are Travelocity, Expedia, and Orbitz. If you have flexibility in your travel dates, check airline Internet sites for special last-minute deals. Alaska Airlines and some other carriers have specials to and from Alaska. These generally allow only a maximum one-week stay but sometimes cost less than half the going rate. Some of the shorter and more popular air routes within Alaska can be quite competitive; an Internet fare from Anchorage to Homer typically costs around $110 each way. In general, prices are lowest when booked two weeks ahead, but Web fares often pop up with lower rates.

Consolidators **AirlineConsolidator.com** ☎ 888/468-5385 🌐 www.airlineconsolidator.com; for international tickets. **Best Fares** ☎ 800/880-1234 🌐 www.bestfares.com; $59.90 annual membership. **Cheap Tickets** ☎ 800/377-1000 or 800/652-4327 🌐 www.cheaptickets.com. **Expedia** ☎ 800/397-3342 or 404/728-8787 🌐 www.expedia.com. **Hotwire** ☎ 866/468-9473 or 920/330-9418 🌐 www.hotwire.com. **Now Voyager Travel** ✉ 1717 Avenue M, Brooklyn, NY 11230 ☎ 212/459-1616 📠 718/504-4762 🌐 www.nowvoyagertravel.com. **Onetravel.com** 🌐 www.onetravel.com. **Orbitz** ☎ 888/656-4546 🌐 www.orbitz.com. **Priceline.com** 🌐 www.priceline.com. **Travelocity** ☎ 888/709-5983, 877/282-2925 in Canada, 0870/111-7061 in the U.K. 🌐 www.travelocity.com.

ENJOYING THE FLIGHT

State your seat preference when purchasing your ticket, and then repeat it when you confirm and when you check in. For more legroom, you can request one of the few emergency-aisle seats at check-in, if you're capable of moving obstacles comparable in weight to an airplane exit door (usually between 35 pounds and 60 pounds)—a Federal Aviation Administration requirement of passengers in these seats. Seats behind a bulkhead also offer more legroom, but they don't have underseat storage. Don't sit in the row in front of the emergency aisle or in front of a bulkhead, where seats may not recline. SeatGuru.com has more information about specific seat configurations, which vary by aircraft.

Ask the airline whether a snack or meal is served on the flight. If you have dietary concerns, request special meals when booking. These can be vegetarian, low-cholesterol, or kosher, for example. It's a good idea to pack some healthful snacks and a small (plastic) bottle of water in your carry-on bag. On long flights, try to maintain a normal routine, to help fight jet lag. At night, get some sleep. By day, eat light meals, drink water (not alcohol), and **move around the cabin** to stretch your legs. For additional jet-lag tips consult *Fodor's FYI: Travel Fit & Healthy* (available at bookstores everywhere).

All flights to and within Alaska are smoke-free, including charter flights and flights into the Bush. Many scheduled flights to Bush communities are on small planes, most of which seat 6–15 passengers. Turbulence is not uncommon, which can leave you white-knuckled and green in the face after a particularly harrowing trip. Fortunately, most flights are uneventful, though the scenery below makes them memorable.

FLYING TIMES

Average travel time is 3½ hours from Seattle to Anchorage, 8 hours from Chicago, 7 hours from Dallas, and 6 hours from Los Angeles. Travel times from other destinations depend on your connection, since you'll need to route through other cities to get to Anchorage. Many of the low-fare flights out of Anchorage depart around 1 AM, so be sure you are at the airport on the correct day when flying just after midnight!

HOW TO COMPLAIN

If your baggage goes astray or your flight goes awry, complain right away. Most carriers require that you **file a claim immediately.** The Aviation Consumer Protection Division of the Department of Transportation publishes *Fly-Rights,* which discusses airlines and consumer issues and is available online. You can also find articles and information on mytravelrights.com, the Web site of the nonprofit Consumer Travel Rights Center.

Airline Complaints **Aviation Consumer Protection Division** ✉ U.S. Department of Transportation, Office of Aviation Enforcement and Proceedings, C-75, Room 4107, 400 7th St. SW, Washington, DC 20590 ☎ 202/366-2220 🌐 airconsumer.ost.dot.gov. **Federal Aviation Administration Consumer Hotline** ✉ for inquiries: FAA, 800 Independence Ave. SW, Washington, DC 20591 ☎ 800/322-7873 🌐 www.faa.gov.

RECONFIRMING

Check the status of your flight before you leave for the airport. You can do this on your carrier's Web site, by linking to a flight-status checker (many Web booking services offer these), or by calling your carrier or travel agent.

AIRPORTS

Anchorage's airport is the main hub for Alaska. Vancouver, in Canada, is the starting point for some Alaskan cruises that make their first stop in Ketchikan, Alaska's southernmost town.

Airport Information **Ted Stevens Anchorage International Airport** (ANC) ☎ 907/266-2525 🌐 www.dot.state.ak.us/anc. **Vancouver International Airport** (YVR) ☎ 604/303-3603 🌐 www.yvr.ca.

ALASKA PUBLIC LANDS OFFICES

Get details on Alaska's vast public lands from Alaska Public Lands Information centers in Ketchikan, Tok, Anchorage, and Fairbanks or on the Internet at 🌐 www.nps.gov/aplic.

Alaska Public Lands Information Center ✉ 605 W. 4th Ave., Anchorage 99501 ☎ 907/271-2737 ✉ 250 Cushman St., Suite 1A, Fairbanks 99701 ☎ 907/456-0527 📠 907/456-0154 ✉ 50 Main St., Ketchikan 99901 ☎ 907/228-6214 ✉ Mile 1314, Alaska Hwy., Tok 99780 ☎ 907/883-5667. **Southeast Alaska Discovery Center** ✉ 50 Main St., Ketchikan 99901 ☎ 907/228-6220 📠 907/228-6234.

BEARS

If you're lucky—and careful—the sight of one of these magnificent creatures in the wild can be a highlight of your visit. By respecting bears and exercising care in bear country, neither you nor the bear will suffer from the experience. Remember that bears don't like surprises. Make your presence known by talking, singing, rattling a can full of gravel, or tying a bell to your pack, especially when terrain or vegetation obscures views. Travel with a group, which is noisier and easier for bears to detect. If possible, walk with the wind at your back so your scent will warn bears of your presence. And avoid bushy, low-visibility areas whenever possible.

Give bears the right-of-way—lots of it—especially sows with cubs. Don't camp on animal trails; they're likely to be used by bears. If you come across a carcass of an animal or detect its odor, avoid the area entirely; it's likely a bear's food cache. Store all food and garbage away from your campsite in airtight or specially designed bear-proof containers. The Park Service supplies these for hikers in Denali and Glacier Bay national parks and requires that backcountry travelers use them. If a bear approaches you while you are fishing, stop. If you have a fish on your line, cut your line.

If you do encounter a bear at close range, don't panic, and, above all, don't run. You can't outrun a bear, and by fleeing you could trigger a chase response from the bear. Talk in a normal voice to help identify yourself as a human. If traveling with others, stand close together to "increase your size." If the bear charges, it could be a bluff; as terrifying as this may sound, the experts advise standing your ground. If a brown bear actually touches you, then drop to the ground and play dead, either flat on your stomach or curled in a ball with your hands behind your neck. If you don't move, a brown bear will typically break off its attack once it feels the threat is gone. If you are attacked by a black bear, you are probably better off fighting back with rocks, sticks, or anything else you find, since black bears are more likely to attack a person intentionally. Polar bears can be found in remote parts of the Arctic, but tourists are highly unlikely to encounter them in summer.

For more information on bears, ask for the brochure "Bear Facts: The Essentials for Traveling in Bear Country" from any of the Alaska Public Lands offices. Bear safety information is also available on the Internet at www.state.ak.us/adfg.

BIKE TRAVEL

The main highways are heavily trafficked in the summer, and the shoulders are often not particularly wide. Bikers traveling between such crowded routes as Anchorage to Seward are risking their lives. A better bet would probably be to choose less-traveled roads and trails. Mountain bikes are available for rent in the larger Alaskan towns. Ferry travelers pay a small extra charge to transport bikes. Pick up an Alaska cycling guidebook, such as *Alaska Bicycle Touring Guide* by Pete Praetorius (Denali Press) or *Mountain Bike Alaska* by Richard Larson (Glacier House Publications), for further details. Mountain-bike rentals are available in most larger Alaskan towns for around $30 per day or $15 for three hours. The Arctic Bicycle Club organizes races and tours, and its Web site is a good source of details on riding in Alaska.

Bike Rentals & Tours **Arctic Bicycle Club** Box 230130, Anchorage 99523-0130 907/566-0177 www.arcticbike.org. **Downtown Bicycle Rental** 333 W 4th Ave., Suite 206, Anchorage 907/279-5293 www.alaska-bike-rentals.com. **Mountain Bike Alaska** Box 6754, Palmer 99645 907/745-5014 or 866/354-2453 www.mountainbikealaska.com.

BIKES IN FLIGHT

Most airlines accommodate bikes as luggage, provided they are dismantled and boxed; check with individual airlines about packing requirements. Some airlines sell bike boxes, which are often free at bike shops, for about $20 (bike bags can be considerably more expensive). International travelers often can substitute a bike for a piece of checked luggage at no charge; otherwise, the cost is about $100. Most U.S. and Canadian airlines charge $40–$80 each way.

BOAT & FERRY TRAVEL

If you are looking for a casual alternative to a luxury cruise, **travel as Alaskans do, aboard the ferries of the Alaska Marine Highway System.** When planning your trip, ask about special onboard programming. Forest Service naturalists ride the larger ferries in summer, providing a running commentary on sights. In addition, the Arts-on-Board Program presents educators and entertainers on selected summer sailings. The Alaska Marine Highway ferries travel within Alaska and between Bellingham, Washington, and the towns of the Inside Passage. The Marine Highway also links up with British Columbia Ferries in Prince Rupert, and, as of 2004, a speedy catamaran ferry offers vehicle and passenger service connecting Juneau with Sitka and Petersburg. In addition, the Inter-Island Ferry Authority serves Southeast Alaska's Prince of Wales Island with the towns of Ketchikan, Wrangell, and Petersburg.

CUTTING COSTS

The AlaskaPass allows unlimited travel on bus, ferry, and rail lines in Alaska, along with bus and ferry travel in British Columbia and the Yukon. Passes are available for 15 consecutive days of travel ($829), as well as for 8 days of travel in a 12-day period ($699) or 12 days of travel in a 21-day period ($849). There is a $75 booking fee. Most travelers book their entire itinerary in advance; if you don't have a car, there is usually room on ferries for those without prebookings.

AlaskaPass 206/463-6550 or 800/248-7598 206/463-6777 www.alaskapass.com.

FARES & SCHEDULES

Make reservations for ferry travel by calling the Alaska Marine Highway System. They will mail the tickets, or you can pick them up from the ferry office at your starting point. Request a copy of its printed schedule over the phone, or download it from the Internet at www.ferryalaska.com. Online reservations are also available.

PAYING

You can pay for ferry travel by cash, credit card (American Express, Discover, MasterCard, or Visa), cashier's check, money order, certified check, or personal check from an Alaskan bank.

Boat & Ferry Information **Alaska Marine Highway** ✉ 6858 Glacier Hwy., Juneau 99801-7909 ☎ 907/465-3941 or 800/642-0066 ☎ 907/277-4829 🌐 www.ferryalaska.com. **B.C. Ferries** ✉ 1112 Fort St., Victoria, British Columbia V8V 4V2 ☎ 250/386-3431, 888/223-3779 in B.C. ☎ 250/381-5452 🌐 www.bcferries.bc.ca. **Inter-Island Ferry Authority** ✉ Box 495, Craig 99921 ☎ 907/826-4848 or 866/308-4848 ☎ 907/826-2829 🌐 www.interislandferry.com.

BUS TRAVEL

Greyhound Lines of Canada serves Vancouver, with service as far north as Whitehorse in the Yukon. Two companies provide onward bus service into South Central and Interior Alaska from Whitehorse. Alaska Direct Bus Lines operates year-round van service connecting Anchorage and Fairbanks with Glennallen, Delta Junction, Skagway, and Tok in Alaska, along with Whitehorse in the Canadian Yukon. Alaska/Yukon Trails provides year-round bus service between Anchorage and Fairbanks, plus seasonal service connecting Fairbanks with Dawson City in the Yukon.

Denali Overland Transportation has frequent van service in the summer between Anchorage, Talkeetna, and Denali National Park. The Alaska Park Connection has summertime bus service between Seward and Anchorage, continuing north to Denali National Park. Homer Stage Line provides year-round service between Anchorage and Homer, plus summertime service connecting Seward with Anchorage and Homer. Quick Shuttle bus service runs between Vancouver and Seattle. Green Tortoise buses provide a casual alternative way to travel north, with funky classic buses that are popular with young backpackers. Smoking is prohibited on all Alaska buses or vans. Contact the individual companies for their scheduled service.

CUTTING COSTS

The AlaskaPass allows unlimited travel on ferry, rail lines, and Holland America buses (Whitehorse to Fairbanks only) in Alaska and the Yukon (*see* Cutting Costs *in* Boat & Ferry Travel).

PAYING

Accepted forms of payment vary among the bus companies, but all accept MasterCard and Visa, along with traveler's checks.

RESERVATIONS

Reservations are generally not needed for bus transportation around Alaska, but it is always a good idea to call ahead if your travel dates are not flexible.

Bus Information **Alaska Direct Bus Lines** ✉ Box 100501, Anchorage 99510 ☎ 907/277-6652 or 800/770-6652. **Alaska Park Connection** ✉ Box 22-1011, Anchorage 99522 ☎ 907/245-0200 or 800/266-8625 🌐 www.alaskacoach.com. **Alaska/Yukon Trails** ✉ Box 84278, Fairbanks 99708 ☎ 907/457-2034 or 800/770-7275 🌐 www.alaskashuttle.com. **Denali Overland Transportation** ✉ Box 330, Talkeetna 99676 ☎ 907/733-2384 or 800/651-5221 🌐 www.denalioverland.com. **Green Tortoise** ✉ Box 84278, San Francisco, CA 94133 ☎ 415/956-7500 or 800/867-8647 🌐 www.greentortoise.com. **Greyhound Lines of Canada** ☎ 604/482-8747 or 800/661-8747 🌐 www.greyhound.ca. **Homer Stage Line** ✉ Box 1912, Homer 99603 ☎ 907/235-7090 or 907/399-1847 ☎ 907/235-0565 🌐 www.homerstageline.com. **Quick Shuttle** ☎ 604/244-3744 or 800/665-2122 🌐 www.quickcoach.com.

BUSINESS HOURS

Most Alaskan stores are open weekdays from 9 AM to 5 PM, though many have longer hours and remain open on weekends. All the larger towns have at least one convenience store that stays open all the time. In small Bush villages, the general store may be open just a few hours per day and closed on Sunday, whereas in larger cities the grocery stores remain open 24 hours a day, seven days a week.

BANKS & OFFICES

Banks and credit unions are typically open weekdays 10–5, and some have limited Saturday hours, particularly in Anchorage, Fairbanks, and Juneau. Most government and other offices are open weekdays 9–5, though some close at 4:30.

GAS STATIONS

Many Alaskan gas stations remain open until 10 PM, and in the larger towns and cities, some stay open 24 hours a day. Most are also open on weekends, particularly along the main highways. In the smallest villages gas may be available only on weekdays, but these settlements typically have only a few miles of roads.

MUSEUMS & SIGHTS

Hours of sights and attractions are denoted in the book by the clock icon, ⏲. Museums in smaller Southeast Alaska towns typically open whenever a cruise ship or ferry is in port, even if it is late on a Sunday evening. *See* specific town descriptions for more information.

PHARMACIES

Pharmacy hours vary across Alaska, but most local hospitals have a pharmacy that provides service at any hour.

SHOPS

Alaskan gift shops are typically open weekdays or whenever cruise ships are in port. Gift shops in Anchorage are generally open year-round, but in other towns many places close in October and reopen in May.

CAMERAS & PHOTOGRAPHY

Alaska is one of the world's premier spots for nature and wildlife photography. Because of the high latitude, the light remains at a low angle for many hours during long summer days, creating extraordinary photographic conditions.

Digital cameras are increasingly used by both amateurs and professional photographers, and the proliferation of Internet cafés has made it possible to e-mail digital photos to friends easily as you travel. Larger towns generally have at least one business where you can transfer these photos to CDs or output them as prints. Serious photographers often carry a laptop computer to store images and burn CDs or DVDs. If you're shooting digital, be sure to bring extra rechargeable batteries (and a charger), along with additional memory cards. Other storage options include units built around a portable hard drive with a card reader, or a laptop computer.

Photographers who shoot with film will find that an ISO 200-speed print film is sufficient for most purposes, though ISO 400 is better for low-light situations and action shots. Many professional photographers shoot color slides, using Fuji's Sensia II or Velvia, along with Kodak's Ektachrome 100SW.

A zoom lens covering 28 mm–105 mm is adequate for most Alaskan scenes, but longer telephoto lenses (200 mm and up) are useful for wildlife photos. A tripod is essential in dimly lighted situations and highly recommended for photographing wildlife with a telephoto lens.

Not everyone in Alaska appreciates being photographed, particularly in smaller Native villages where locals have sometimes been exploited by photographers. Ask for permission before taking a photograph of someone. Many museums do not allow flash or tripods, and photography is restricted or prohibited inside Russian Orthodox churches and certain Native cemeteries.

The *Kodak Guide to Shooting Great Travel Pictures* (available at bookstores everywhere) is loaded with tips.

Photo Help Kodak Information Center ☎ 800/242–2424 🌐 www.kodak.com.

EQUIPMENT PRECAUTIONS

A plastic bag or umbrella will help keep your camera dry during wet weather. Winter travelers may need to contend with extremely cold conditions, which can greatly reduce battery life, fog lenses, and even cause complete mechanical failure. Be sure to pack extra batteries for your camera, especially when heading into remote areas. Lens fogging can be lessened by storing the camera and lenses in a cool place.

Don't pack film or equipment in checked luggage, where it is much more susceptible to damage. X-ray machines used to view checked luggage are extremely powerful and therefore are likely to ruin your film. Try to ask for hand inspection of film, which becomes clouded after repeated exposure to airport X-ray machines, and keep videotapes and computer disks away from metal detectors. Always keep film, tape, and computer disks out of the sun. Carry an extra supply of batteries, and be prepared to turn on your camera, camcorder, or laptop to prove to airport security personnel that the device is real.

FILM & DEVELOPING

Print film is available almost everywhere in Alaska, but slide film is often not available outside the larger towns and cities. Both types tend to be expensive (up to $8 for a 24-exposure roll), so carry plenty. All the larger towns have film developing and printing available, and many also have one-hour photo labs. In addition, larger towns also have facilities for printing digital images, and larger stores often sell digital-camera storage cards.

CAR RENTAL

Rental cars are available in most Alaska towns. In Anchorage and other major destinations, expect to pay around $50 a day or $300 a week for a compact car with air-conditioning (not needed in Alaska), an automatic transmission, and unlimited mileage. Some of the locally owned companies offer lower rates for older cars. Rates can be substantially higher for larger vehicles, four-wheel drives, sport utility vehicles, and vans. In small towns, particularly those off the road system in Southeast Alaska or the Bush, rental rates are higher, often $65 per day and up. Also note that vehicles in these remote towns are typically several years old, and some would rate as "beaters." **Reserve well ahead for the summer season, particularly for the popular minivans and SUVs.** A 10 percent state tax is tacked on to all car rentals in Alaska, plus any local taxes.

Major Agencies **Alamo** ☎ 800/327-9633 🌐 www.alamo.com. **Avis** ☎ 800/331-1212, 800/879-2847 or 800/272-5871 in Canada, 0870/606-0100 in the U.K., 02/9353-9000 in Australia, 09/526-2847 in New Zealand 🌐 www.avis.com. **Budget** ☎ 800/527-0700 🌐 www.budget.com. **Dollar** ☎ 800/800-4000, 0800/085-4578 in the U.K. 🌐 www.dollar.com. **Hertz** ☎ 800/654-3131, 800/263-0600 in Canada, 0870/844-8844 in the U.K., 02/9669-2444 in Australia, 09/256-8690 in New Zealand 🌐 www.hertz.com. **National Car Rental** ☎ 800/227-7368 🌐 www.nationalcar.com. **Payless** ☎ 800/729-5377 🌐 www.paylesscarental.com. **Thrifty** ☎ 907/276-2855 or 800/367-2277 🌐 www.thrifty.com.

CUTTING COSTS

Discount travel Web sites such as Travelocity.com can help with finding the lowest rates for Alaska's larger cities. Be sure to ask in advance about discounts if you have a AAA or Costco card, or are over age 50.

For a good deal, book through a travel agent who will shop around. Also, price local car-rental companies—whose prices may be lower still, although their service and maintenance may not be as good as those of major rental agencies—and research rates on the Internet. Consolidators that specialize in air travel can offer good rates on cars as well (⇨ Air Travel). Remember to ask about required deposits, cancellation penalties, and drop-off charges if you're planning to pick up the car in one city and leave it in another. If you're traveling during a holiday period, also make sure that a confirmed reservation guarantees you a car.

Local Agencies **Affordable New Car Rentals** ☎ 907/243-3370, 800/248-3765 in Anchorage, 907/452-7341 in Fairbanks 🌐 www.ancr.com. **Arctic Rent-A-Car** ☎ 800/478-8696, 907/561-2990 in Anchorage, 907/479-8044 in Fairbanks 🌐 www.arcticrentacar.com. **Denali Car Rental** ☎ 907/276-1230, 800/757-1230 in Anchorage 🌐 www.denalicarrentalak.com. **U-Save Auto Rental** ☎ 907/272-8728 or 800/254-8728 in Anchorage, 907/479-7060 or 877/979-7060 in Fairbanks 🌐 www.usaveak.com.

INSURANCE

When driving a rented car you are generally responsible for any damage to or loss of the vehicle. You also may be liable for any property damage or personal injury that you may cause while driving. Before you rent, see what coverage you already have under the terms of your personal auto-insurance policy and credit cards.

For about $9 to $25 a day, rental companies sell protection, known as a collision- or loss-damage waiver (CDW or LDW), that eliminates your liability for damage to the car; it's always optional and should never be automatically added to your bill. In most states you don't need a CDW if you have

personal auto insurance or other liability insurance. However, **make sure you have enough coverage to pay for the car.** If you do not have auto insurance or an umbrella policy that covers damage to third parties, purchasing liability insurance and a CDW or LDW is highly recommended.

REQUIREMENTS & RESTRICTIONS

In Alaska you must be 21 (and no older than 99) to rent a car, and rates may be higher if you're under 25. When picking up a car, non-U.S. residents will need a reservation voucher, a passport, a driver's license (written in English), and a travel policy that covers each driver.

SURCHARGES

Before you pick up a car in one city and leave it in another, ask about drop-off charges or one-way service fees, which can be substantial. Also inquire about early-return policies; some rental agencies charge extra if you return the car before the time specified in your contract while others give you a refund for the days not used. Most agencies note the tank's fuel level on your contract; to avoid a hefty refueling fee, return the car with the same tank level. If the tank was full, refill it just before you turn in the car, but be aware that gas stations near the rental outlet may overcharge. It's almost never a deal to buy a tank of gas with the car when you rent it; the understanding is that you'll return it empty, but some fuel usually remains. Surcharges may apply if you're under 25 or if you take the car outside the area approved by the rental agency. You'll pay extra for child seats (about $8 a day), which are compulsory for children under five, and usually for additional drivers (up to $25 a day, depending on location).

CAR TRAVEL

Your driver's license may not be recognized outside your home country. International driving permits (IDPs) are available from the American and Canadian automobile associations and, in the United Kingdom, from the Automobile Association and Royal Automobile Club. These international permits, valid only in conjunction with your regular driver's license, are universally recognized; having one may save you a problem with local authorities.

Driving to Alaska is a popular alternative to flying or cruising, especially for RVers, but you'll need to **set aside plenty of time.** Though journeying through Canada on the Alaska Highway can be exciting, the trek from the Lower 48 states is a long one. It's a seven-day trip from Seattle to Anchorage or Fairbanks, covering close to 2,500 mi. From Bellingham, Washington, and the Canadian ports of Prince Rupert and Stewart, you can link up with ferry service along the Marine Highway to reach southeastern Alaska.

The Alaska Highway begins at Dawson Creek, British Columbia, and stretches 1,442 mi through Canada's Yukon to Delta Junction; it enters Alaska at Tok. The two-lane highway is paved for its entire length and is open year-round. Highway services are available about every 50 to 100 mi (sometimes at shorter intervals).

The rest of the state's roads are found almost exclusively in the South Central and Interior regions. They lie mainly between Anchorage, Fairbanks, and the Canadian border. Only one highway extends north of Fairbanks, and a couple run south of Anchorage to the Kenai Peninsula. These roads vary from four-lane freeways to nameless two-lane gravel roads and are generally open and maintained year-round. The Glenn Highway begins at Tok and travels south to Anchorage. The Richardson Highway parallels the Alaska pipeline from Fairbanks south to the port city of Valdez.

The Seward Highway heads south from Anchorage through the Kenai Mountains to Seward, with the Sterling Highway branch heading southwest to Kenai and Homer. The George Parks Highway connects Anchorage and Fairbanks, passing Denali National Park en route. The Steese Highway runs northwest of Fairbanks to the gold-rush town of Circle. The Dalton Highway begins at the end of the Elliott Highway, 73 mi north of Fairbanks, and leads 414 mi to Deadhorse, the supply center for the Prudhoe Bay oil fields. This gravel truck route presents unique challenges; **contact the Alaska Public Lands Information centers in Fairbanks, Tok, or Anchorage if you plan to drive the Dalton Highway.**

If you plan extensive driving in Alaska, join an automobile club such as AAA that offers towing and other benefits. Because of the long distances involved, you should seriously consider a plan (such as AAA Plus) that extends towing benefits to 100 mi in any direction.

The Milepost, available in bookstores or from Morris Communications, is a mile-by-mile guide to sights and services along Alaska's highways.

Alaska Public Lands Information Center ✉ 605 W. 4th Ave., Anchorage 99501 ☎ 907/271-2737 🌐 www.ak.blm.gov ✉ 250 Cushman St., Suite 1A, Fairbanks 99701 ☎ 907/456-0527 🖷 907/456-0154 ✉ 50 Main St., Ketchikan 99901 ☎ 907/228-6214 ✉ Mile 1314, Alaska Hwy., Tok 99780 ☎ 907/883-5667. ***The Milepost*** ✉ Morris Communications, 735 Broad St., Augusta, GA 30901 ☎ 907/272-6070 or 800/726-4707 🖷 907/258-5360 🌐 www.themilepost.com.

GASOLINE

Gas prices in the Anchorage area are comparable with those in the Lower 48, but expect to pay more elsewhere, such as Juneau or Ketchikan, and far more in remote areas, particularly small villages off the road network, where fuel must be flown in. Fuel prices in Canada along the Alaska Highway are also very high. Most gas stations take Visa and MasterCard, and many also accept other credit cards and debit cards.

ROAD CONDITIONS

If you are planning to drive to Alaska, come armed with patience. Road construction sometimes creates long delays on the Canadian side of the border, so don't plan a tight schedule. Also, frost damage creates dips in the road that require slower driving.

Driving in Alaska is much less rigorous than it used to be, although it still presents some unusual obstacles. Moose often wander onto roads and highways. If you come across one while you're driving, it's best to **stop your car, pull off the road, and wait for the moose to cross.** The moose will usually move on its own. Be especially vigilant when driving at dusk or night, since moose can be active at all hours. In addition, keep your eyes open for other moose in the area, since a mother will often cross the road followed by one or two calves.

Flying gravel is a hazard to watch for along the Alaska and Dalton highways, especially in summer. A bug screen will help keep gravel and kamikaze insects off the windshield, but few travelers use them. Some travelers use clear, hard plastic guards to cover their headlights. (These are inexpensive and are available from almost any garage or service station along the major access routes.) Don't cover headlights with cardboard or plywood, because you'll need your lights often, even in daytime, as dust is thrown up by traffic passing in both directions. (Headlights must be used at all times on the Seward Highway south of Anchorage.)

Unless you plan to undertake one of the remote highways (especially the Dalton Highway to Prudhoe Bay), you won't need any special equipment. But be sure that the equipment you do have is in working condition, from tires and spare to brakes and engine. Carrying spare fuses, spark plugs, jumper cables, a flashlight with extra batteries, a tool kit, and an extra fan belt is recommended.

If you get stuck on any kind of road, be careful about pulling off; the shoulder can be soft. In summer it stays light late, and though traffic is also light, one of Alaska's many good Samaritans is likely to stop to help and send for aid (which may be many miles away). In winter, pack emergency equipment—a shovel, tire chains, such high-energy food as nuts or chocolate, and extra-warm clothing and blankets to help you through the wait for aid should you need it. Never head out onto unplowed roads unless you are prepared to walk back.

Cellular phones are an excellent idea for travel in Alaska, particularly on the main roads, but check with your service provider for coverage. AAA members may also want to upgrade to the "Plus" policy, which allows for towing of up to 100 mi if you break down. Road maps are available at gas stations and grocery stores throughout Alaska.

RULES OF THE ROAD

Always strap children into approved child-safety seats and make sure all passengers use a seatbelt.

Alaska honors valid driver's licenses from any state or country, and the speed limit on most state highways is 55 mph, but much of the Parks Highway (between Wasilla and Fairbanks) and the Seward Highway (between Anchorage and Seward) is 65 mph. Unless otherwise posted, you may make a right turn on a red light after coming to a complete stop. Seat belts are required on all passengers in Alaska, and children under age five must be in child safety seats. State troopers rigorously enforce speed limits along the main highways.

State law requires that slow-moving vehicles pull off the road at the first opportunity if leading more than five cars. This is particularly true on the highway between Anchorage and Seward, where RV drivers have a bad reputation for not pulling over. Alaskans don't take kindly to being held up en route to their favorite Kenai River fishing spot.

RVS

The secret to a successful RV trip to Alaska is preparation. Expect to drive on more gravel and rougher roads than you're accustomed to. **Batten down everything**; tighten every nut and bolt in and out of sight, and don't leave anything to bounce around inside. Travel light, and your tires and suspension system will take less of a beating. Protect your headlights and the grille area in front of the radiator. Make sure you carry adequate insurance to cover the replacement of your windshield.

Most of Alaska's public campgrounds accommodate trailers, but hookups are available only in private RV parks. Water can be found at most stopping points, but it may be limited for trailer use. Think twice before deciding to drive an RV or pull a trailer during the spring thaw. The rough roadbed can be a trial.

RV Rentals **ABC Motorhome Rentals** ☎ 907/279-2000 or 800/421-7456 🌐 www.abcmotorhome.com. **Alaska Motorhome Rentals** ☎ 907/258-7109 or 800/254-9929 🌐 www.alaskarv.com. **Alaska Panorama RV Rentals** ☎ 907/562-1401 or 800/478-1401 🌐 www.alaskapanorama.com. **Alaska Superior RV** ☎ 907/561-7723 or 800/764-4625 🌐 www.goalaska.com. **Clippership Motorhome Rentals** ☎ 907/562-7051 or 800/421-3456 🌐 www.clippershiprv.com. **GoNorth RV Camper Rental** ☎ 907/479-7272 or 866/236-7272 🌐 www.gonorthalaska.com. **Great Alaskan Holidays** ☎ 907/248-7777 or 888/225-2752 🌐 www.greatalaskanholidays.com.

CHILDREN IN ALASKA

Be sure to plan ahead and involve your youngsters as you outline your trip. When packing, include things to keep them busy en route. On sightseeing days try to schedule activities of special interest to your children. Many families travel to Alaska with children in tow, and most tourist facilities—including restaurants, museums, and hotels—go out of their way to accommodate them. Note, however, that some bed-and-breakfasts cater to couples looking to escape their own or other people's children and do not allow kids, particularly those under 12. Young children may easily become bored on long bus or plane trips, and many of the more adventurous activities in Alaska such as sea kayaking, river rafting, and bear viewing are potentially dangerous for youngsters. If you are considering an adventure trip, ask about taking kids. Babysitting agencies do not exist in Alaska, but short-term care may be available at local day-care centers in the larger towns.

If you are renting a car, don't forget to arrange for a car seat when you reserve. For general advice about traveling with children, consult *Fodor's FYI: Travel with Your Baby* (available in bookstores everywhere).

FLYING

If your children are two or older, ask about children's airfares. As a general rule, infants under two not occupying a seat fly at greatly reduced fares or even for free.

But if you want to guarantee a seat for an infant, you have to pay full fare. Consider flying during off-peak days and times; most airlines will grant an infant a seat without a ticket if there are available seats.

Experts agree that it's a good idea to use safety seats aloft for children weighing less than 40 pounds. Airlines set their own policies: if you use a safety seat, U.S. carriers usually require that the child be ticketed, even if he or she is young enough to ride free, because the seats must be strapped into regular seats. And even if you pay the full adult fare for the seat, it may be worth it, especially on longer trips. Do **check your airline's policy about using safety seats during takeoff and landing.** Safety seats are not allowed everywhere in the plane, so get your seat assignments as early as possible.

When reserving, request children's meals or a freestanding bassinet (not available at all airlines) if you need them. But note that bulkhead seats, where you must sit to use the bassinet, may lack an overhead bin or storage space on the floor.

LODGING

Most hotels in Alaska allow children under a certain age to stay in their parents' room at no extra charge, but others charge for them as extra adults; be sure to find out the cutoff age for children's discounts.

Best Choices **Cascade Inn** ✉ 2035 Halibut Point Rd., Sitka 99835 ☎ 907/747-6804 or 800/532-0908 🖷 907/747-6572 ⊕ www.cascadeinnsitka.com. **Comfort Inn Ship Creek** ✉ 111 Ship Creek Ave., Anchorage 99501 ☎ 907/277-6887 or 800/228-5150 🖷 907/274-9830 ⊕ www.comfortinn.com. **Frontier Suites Airport Hotel** ✉ 9400 Glacier Hwy., Juneau 99801 ☎ 907/790-6600 or 800/544-2250 🖷 907/790-6612 ⊕ www.frontiersuites.com. **The Landing** ✉ 3434 Tongass Ave., Ketchikan 99901 ☎ 907/225-5166 or 800/428-8304 🖷 907/225-6900 ⊕ www.bestwestern.com. **Merrill Field Inn** ✉ 420 Sitka St., Anchorage 99501 ☎ 907/276-4547 or 800/898-4547 🖷 907/276-5064 ⊕ www.merrillfieldinn.com. **SpringHill Suites by Marriott** ✉ 3401 A St., Anchorage 99503 ☎ 907/562-3247 or 888/287-9400 🖷 907/562-3250 ⊕ www.springhillsuites.com. **Wedgewood Resort** ✉ 212 Wedgewood Dr., Fairbanks 99701 ☎ 907/456-3642 or 800/528-4916 🖷 907/451-8184 ⊕ www.fountainheadhotels.com.

SIGHTS & ATTRACTIONS

Places that are especially appealing to children are indicated by a rubber-duckie icon (🐤) in the margin.

CONSUMER PROTECTION

Whether you're shopping for gifts or purchasing travel services, **pay with a major credit card** whenever possible, so you can cancel payment or get reimbursed if there's a problem (and you can provide documentation). If you're doing business with a particular company for the first time, contact your local Better Business Bureau and the attorney general's offices in your state and (for U.S. businesses) the company's home state as well. Have any complaints been filed? Finally, if you're buying a package or tour, always consider travel insurance that includes default coverage (⇨ Insurance).

BBBs **Council of Better Business Bureaus** ✉ 4200 Wilson Blvd., Suite 800, Arlington, VA 22203 ☎ 703/276-0100 🖷 703/525-8277 ⊕ www.bbb.org.

CUSTOMS & DUTIES

When shopping abroad, keep receipts for all purchases. Upon reentering the country, **be ready to show customs officials what you've bought.** Pack purchases together in an easily accessible place. If you think a duty is incorrect, appeal the assessment. If you object to the way your clearance was handled, note the inspector's badge number. In either case, first ask to see a supervisor. If the problem isn't resolved, write to the appropriate authorities, beginning with the port director at your point of entry.

IN AUSTRALIA

Australian residents who are 18 or older may bring home A$900 worth of souvenirs and gifts (including jewelry), 250 cigarettes or 250 grams of cigars or other tobacco products, and 2.25 liters of alcohol (including wine, beer, and spirits). Residents under 18 may bring back A$450 worth of goods. If any of these individual allowances are exceeded, you must pay duty for the entire amount (of the group of products in which the allowance was exceeded). Members of the same family traveling together may pool their allowances.

Prohibited items include meat products. Seeds, plants, and fruits need to be declared upon arrival.

Australian Customs Service Locked Bag 3000, Sydney International Airport, Sydney, NSW 2020 02/6275-6666 or 1300/363263, 02/8334-7444 or 1800/020-504 quarantine-inquiry line 02/8339-6714 www.customs.gov.au.

IN CANADA

Canadian residents who have been out of Canada for at least seven days may bring in C$750 worth of goods duty-free. If you've been away fewer than seven days but more than 48 hours, the duty-free allowance drops to C$200. If your trip lasts 24 to 48 hours, the allowance is C$50 if the goods are worth more than C$50, you must pay full duty on all of the goods. You may not pool allowances with family members. Goods claimed under the C$750 exemption may follow you by mail; those claimed under the lesser exemptions must accompany you. Alcohol and tobacco products may be included in the seven-day and 48-hour exemptions but not in the 24-hour exemption. If you meet the age requirements of the province or territory through which you reenter Canada, you may bring in, duty-free, 1.5 liters of wine *or* 1.14 liters (40 imperial ounces) of liquor *or* 24 12-ounce cans or bottles of beer or ale. Also, if you meet the local age requirement for tobacco products, you may bring in, duty-free, 200 cigarettes, 50 cigars or cigarillos, and 200 grams of tobacco. You may have to pay a minimum duty on tobacco products, regardless of whether or not you exceed your personal exemption. Check ahead of time with the Canada Border Services Agency or the Department of Agriculture for policies regarding meat products, seeds, plants, and fruits.

You may send an unlimited number of gifts (only one gift per recipient, however) worth up to C$60 each duty-free to Canada. Label the package UNSOLICITED GIFT—VALUE UNDER $60. Alcohol and tobacco are excluded.

Canada Border Services Agency Customs Information Services, 191 Laurier Ave. W, 15th floor, Ottawa, Ontario K1A 0L5 800/461-9999 in Canada, 204/983-3500, 506/636-5064 www.cbsa.gc.ca.

IN NEW ZEALAND

All homeward-bound residents may bring back NZ$700 worth of souvenirs and gifts; passengers may not pool their allowances, and children can claim only the concession on goods intended for their own use. For those 17 or older, the duty-free allowance also includes 4.5 liters of wine or beer; one 1,125-ml bottle of spirits; and either 200 cigarettes, 250 grams of tobacco, 50 cigars, *or* a combination of the three up to 250 grams. Meat products, seeds, plants, and fruits must be declared upon arrival to the Agricultural Services Department.

New Zealand Customs Head office: The Customhouse, 17-21 Whitmore St., Box 2218, Wellington 09/300-5399 or 0800/428-786 www.customs.govt.nz.

IN THE U.K.

From countries outside the European Union, including United States, you may bring home, duty-free, 200 cigarettes, 50 cigars, 100 cigarillos, or 250 grams of tobacco; 1 liter of spirits or 2 liters of fortified or sparkling wine or liqueurs; 2 liters of still table wine; 60 ml of perfume; 250 ml of toilet water; plus £145 worth of other goods, including gifts and souvenirs. Prohibited items include meat and dairy products, seeds, plants, and fruits.

HM Customs and Excise Portcullis House, 21 Cowbridge Rd. E, Cardiff CF11 9SS 0845/010-9000 or 0208/929-0152 advice service, 0208/929-6731 or 0208/910-3602 complaints www.hmce.gov.uk.

IN THE U.S.

U.S. residents who have been out of the country for at least 48 hours may bring home, for personal use, $800 worth of foreign goods duty-free, as long as they haven't used the $800 allowance or any part of it in the past 30 days. This exemption may include 1 liter of alcohol (for travelers 21 and older), 200 cigarettes, and 100 non-Cuban cigars. Family members from the same household who are traveling together may pool their $800 personal exemptions. For fewer than 48 hours, the duty-free allowance drops to $200, which may include 50 cigarettes, 10 non-Cuban cigars, and 150 ml of alcohol (or 150 ml of perfume containing alcohol). The $200 allowance cannot be combined with other individuals' exemptions, and if you exceed it, the full value of all the goods will be taxed. Antiques, which U.S. Customs and Border Protection defines as objects more than 100 years old, enter duty-free, as do original works of art done entirely by hand, including paintings, drawings, and sculptures. This doesn't apply to folk art or handicrafts, which are in general dutiable.

You may also send packages home duty-free, with a limit of one parcel per addressee per day (except alcohol or tobacco products or perfume worth more than $5). You can mail up to $200 worth of goods for personal use; label the package PERSONAL USE and attach a list of its contents and their retail value. If the package contains your used personal belongings, mark it AMERICAN GOODS RETURNED to avoid paying duties. You may send up to $100 worth of goods as a gift; mark the package UNSOLICITED GIFT. Mailed items do not affect your duty-free allowance on your return.

To avoid paying duty on foreign-made high-ticket items you already own and will take on your trip, register them with a local customs office before you leave the country. Consider filing a Certificate of Registration for laptops, cameras, watches, and other digital devices identified with serial numbers or other permanent markings; you can keep the certificate for other trips. Otherwise, bring a sales receipt or insurance form to show that you owned the item before you left the United States.

For more about duties, restricted items, and other information about international travel, check out U.S. Customs and Border Protection's online brochure, *Know Before You Go*. You can also file complaints on the U.S. Customs and Border Protection Web site, listed below.

U.S. Customs and Border Protection ✉ for inquiries and complaints, 1300 Pennsylvania Ave. NW, Washington, DC 20229 🌐 www.cbp.gov ☎ 877/227-5551, 202/354-1000.

DISABILITIES & ACCESSIBILITY

Travelers with disabilities will find good facilities at the most popular tourist areas, particularly places that deal with large numbers of elderly cruise-ship passengers. Some Forest Service cabins are wheelchair accessible, and state ferries, trains, and most cruise ships are well set up to accommodate passengers with disabilities.

In general, Alaskan Bush villages are not at all wheelchair friendly, with rough gravel roads and minimal facilities. Travelers with disabilities may also have difficulties getting into and out of the small aircraft used to reach these villages, and many of the adventure wilderness trips may be challenging.

Access Alaska is a nonprofit independent-living center in Anchorage; individuals with disabilities can contact them for more specialized details about Alaska facilities and support. Other independent living centers are in Juneau and Fairbanks.

Alaska Welcomes You! books tours, cruises, and other trips customized to personal abilities, specializing in trips for seniors, those with special needs, and families with young children. Clients have access to their complete database of accessible accommodations, attractions, and tours.

Local Resources **Access Alaska** ✉ 121 W. Fireweed La., Suite 105, Anchorage 99503 ☎ 907/248-4777, 800/770-4488 in Alaska, 907/248-8799 TTY 📠 907/248-0639 🌐 www.accessalaska.org. **Alaska Welcomes You!** Box 91333, Anchorage 99509 ☎ 907/349-6301 or 800/349-6301 📠 907/344-3259 🌐 www.accessiblealaska.com.

LODGING

Despite the Americans with Disabilities Act, the definition of accessibility seems to differ from hotel to hotel. Some properties may be accessible by ADA standards for people with mobility problems but not for people with hearing or vision impairments, for example.

If you have mobility problems, ask for the lowest floor on which accessible services are offered. If you have a hearing impairment, check whether the hotel has devices to alert you visually to the ring of the telephone, a knock at the door, and a fire/

emergency alarm. Some hotels provide these devices without charge. Discuss your needs with hotel personnel if this equipment isn't available, so that a staff member can personally alert you in the event of an emergency.

If you're bringing a guide dog, get authorization ahead of time and write down the name of the person with whom you spoke.

All larger hotels in Alaska have at least one wheelchair-accessible room, and those hotels built in the last decade often have several such rooms. Most bed-and-breakfasts are not as wheelchair friendly; contact B&B referral agencies for those with accessible facilities. Alaska Welcomes You! can set up accessible lodging throughout the state.

RESERVATIONS

When discussing accessibility with an operator or reservations agent, ask hard questions. Are there any stairs, inside *or* out? Are there grab bars next to the toilet *and* in the shower/tub? How wide is the doorway to the room? To the bathroom? For the most extensive facilities meeting the latest legal specifications, opt for newer accommodations. If you reserve through a toll-free number, consider also calling the hotel's local number to confirm the information from the central reservations office. Get confirmation in writing when you can.

TRANSPORTATION

The U.S. Department of Transportation Aviation Consumer Protection Division's online publication *New Horizons: Information for the Air Traveler with a Disability* offers advice for travellers with a disability, and outlines basic rights. Visit DisabilityInfo.gov for general information.

Alaska Direct Bus Lines offers a 10% discount to passengers with disabilities for intercity travel. AnchorRIDES provides transportation for senior citizens and those with disabilities within the Anchorage area. You do not need to be an Alaska resident to use this service, but you should contact AnchorRIDES at least a day in advance. Hertz has hand-controlled rental cars in Anchorage. The Alaska Marine Highway System has elevators on all of its vessels and wheelchair-accessible cabins on its six vessels equipped with staterooms. ERA Helicopters has wheelchair lifts at its Juneau and Denali National Park locations, and Alaska Cab offers lift-equipped van service in Anchorage. The Alaska Railroad has cars that are accessible for people who use wheelchairs; cars also have wheelchair locks and lifts. Seward, Portage, Whittier, Anchorage, Talkeetna, Denali National Park, and Fairbanks stations all have lifts, with at least one lockdown for service on all trains.

Bus Travel **Alaska Direct Bus Lines** ✉ Box 501, Anchorage 99501 ☎ 907/277-6652 or 800/770-6652. **AnchorRIDES** ☎ 907/562-8444 🌐 www.peoplemover.org.

Car Rental **Hertz** ☎ 800/654-3131, 800/654-2280 TTY 🌐 www.hertz.com.

Ferry Travel **Alaska Marine Highway** ☎ 907/465-3941 or 800/642-0066 📠 907/277-4829 🌐 www.ferryalaska.com.

Flightseeing **ERA Helicopters** ☎ 907/266-8351 or 800/843-1947 🌐 www.eraaviation.com.

Taxis **Alaska Cab** ☎ 907/563-5353 🌐 www.alaskacabs.com.

Train Travel **Alaska Railroad** ☎ 907/265-2494 in Anchorage, 907/458-6025 in Fairbanks, 800/544-0552 📠 907/265-2323 🌐 www.alaskarailroad.com.

Information & Complaints **Aviation Consumer Protection Division** (⇨ Air Travel) for airline-related problems 🌐 airconsumer.ost.dot.gov/publications/horizons.htm for airline travel advice and rights. **Departmental Office of Civil Rights** ✉ for general inquiries, U.S. Department of Transportation, S-30, 400 7th St. SW, Room 10215, Washington, DC 20590 ☎ 202/366-4648, 202/366-8538 TTY 📠 202/366-9371 🌐 www.dotcr.ost.dot.gov. **Disability Rights Section** ✉ NYAV, U.S. Department of Justice, Civil Rights Division, 950 Pennsylvania Ave. NW, Washington, DC 20530 ☎ ADA information line 202/514-0301, 800/514-0301, 202/514-0383 TTY, 800/514-0383 TTY 🌐 www.ada.gov. **U.S. Department of Transportation Hotline** ☎ for disability-related air-travel problems, 800/778-4838 or 800/455-9880 TTY.

TRAVEL AGENCIES

In the United States, the Americans with Disabilities Act requires that travel firms serve the needs of all travelers. Some agencies specialize in working with people with disabilities.

Travelers with Mobility Problems **Access Adventures/B. Roberts Travel** 1876 East Ave., Rochester, NY 14610 800/444-6540 www.brobertstravel.com, run by a former physical-rehabilitation counselor. **Accessible Vans of America** 37 Daniel Rd. W, Fairfield, NJ 07004 877/282-8267, 888/282-8267, 973/808-9709 reservations 973/808-9713 www.accessiblevans.com. **Care-Vacations** No. 5, 5110-50 Ave., Leduc, Alberta, Canada, T9E 6V4 780/986-6404 or 877/478-7827 780/986-8332 www.carevacations.com, for group tours and cruise vacations. **Flying Wheels Travel** 143 W. Bridge St., Box 382, Owatonna, MN 55060 507/451-5005 507/451-1685 www.flyingwheelstravel.com.

Travelers with Developmental Disabilities **New Directions** 5276 Hollister Ave., Suite 207, Santa Barbara, CA 93111 805/967-2841 or 888/967-2841 805/964-7344 www.newdirectionstravel.com.

DISCOUNTS & DEALS

Be a smart shopper and compare all your options before making decisions. A plane ticket bought with a promotional coupon from travel clubs, coupon books, and direct-mail offers or purchased on the Internet may not be cheaper than the least expensive fare from a discount ticket agency. And always keep in mind that what you get is just as important as what you save.

The AlaskaPass allows unlimited travel on ferry and rail lines in Alaska, along with travel on certain buses (*see* Cutting Costs *in* Boat & Ferry Travel).

DISCOUNT RESERVATIONS

To save money, look into discount reservations services with Web sites and toll-free numbers, which use their buying power to get a better price on hotels, airline tickets (⇨ Air Travel), even car rentals. When booking a room, always **call the hotel's local toll-free number** (if one is available) rather than the central reservations number—you'll often get a better price. Always ask about special packages or corporate rates.

Hotel Rooms **Accommodations Express** 800/444-7666 or 800/277-1064. **Hotels.com** 800/246-8357 www.hotels.com. **Quikbook** 800/789-9887 www.quikbook.com. **Turbotrip.com** 800/473-7829 w3.turbotrip.com.

PACKAGE DEALS

Don't confuse packages and guided tours. When you buy a package, you travel on your own, just as though you had planned the trip yourself. Fly/drive packages, which combine airfare and car rental, are often a good deal. In cities, ask the local visitor's bureau about hotel and local transportation packages that include tickets to major museum exhibits or other special events.

EATING & DRINKING

The restaurants we list are the cream of the crop in each price category. Restaurants are indicated in the text by a knife-and-fork icon, ✕. Establishments denoted by both a knife-and-fork icon and a lodging icon, ✕🏨, stand out equally for their restaurants and rooms.

For restaurants:

CATEGORY	COST*
$$$$	over $25
$$$	$20-$25
$$	$15-$20
$	$10-$15
¢	under $10

*per person for a main course at dinner

MEALTIMES

Alaskan restaurants typically serve breakfast until 10 or 11, lunch from 11 to 2, and dinner starting around 4. Unless otherwise noted, the restaurants listed in this guide are open daily for lunch and dinner.

RESERVATIONS & DRESS

Reservations are always a good idea; we mention them only when they're essential or not accepted. Book as far ahead as you can, and reconfirm as soon as you arrive. (Large parties should always call ahead to check the reservations policy.) We mention dress only when men are required to wear a jacket or a jacket and tie.

SPECIALTIES

Alaska is best known for its seafood, particularly such stars as king salmon, halibut, king crab, and shrimp. Anchorage and Juneau have superb restaurants specializing in fresh seafood, but you will also discover seafood on the menu in virtually any coastal Alaskan town. The open-air salmon bakes in Juneau, Tok, Denali National Park & Preserve, and Fairbanks serve excellent, all-you-can-eat grilled salmon and halibut. Anchorage has the greatest diversity of restaurants, including classy steak houses, noisy brewpubs, authentic Thai and Mexican eateries, and a wide variety of other ethnic places.

WINE, BEER & SPIRITS

Alcohol is sold at liquor stores in most Alaskan towns and cities along the road system, as well as in settlements along the Inside Passage. Alcoholism is a devastating problem in Native villages, and because of this many of these Bush communities are "dry" (no alcohol allowed) or "damp" (limited amounts allowed for personal use, but alcohol cannot be sold). Be sure to check the rules before flying into a Bush community with alcohol, or you might find yourself charged with illegally importing it.

Alaska's best-known microbrew is made by Alaskan Brewing Company in Juneau. Its Alaskan Amber is available in six-packs or on draft throughout the Pacific Northwest. Anchorage is home to several popular brewpubs, and their beers are sold in local liquor stores. Homer Brewing Company in the town of Homer sells its beers in local bars or in take-away bottles. You'll also find brewpubs in Fairbanks, Haines, Skagway, and Wasilla.

ECOTOURISM

Concern for the environment has spawned a worldwide movement called ecotourism, or green tourism. Ecotourists aim to travel responsibly, taking care to conserve the environment and respect indigenous populations. The Alaska Wilderness Recreation and Tourism Association includes many of the state's wilderness-dependent businesses and promotes eco-friendly activities across the state. For information about environmental concerns peculiar to Alaska as well as a list of resources and ecotour operators, *see* Planning Your Trip *in* Chapter 1.

The Alaska Wilderness Recreation and Tourism Association ☎ 907/258-3171 🌐 www.awrta.org. **The International Ecotourism Society** 🌐 www.ecotourism.org.

GAY & LESBIAN TRAVEL

Alaska is a politically conservative state, and openly gay and lesbian travelers may not be well accepted in some towns. Although Fairbanks and Juneau both have active gay and lesbian communities, Anchorage is the real center for Alaska, with a Gay and Lesbian Community Center and two gay bars (Mad Myrna's and the Raven), along with gay-oriented travel agencies, stores, and a theater company (Out North Contemporary Art House). For gay and lesbian information, Identity Inc. produces a monthly magazine, operates a gay and lesbian help line, and runs the above-mentioned community center.

Gay- & Lesbian-Friendly Travel Agencies **Different Roads Travel** ✉ 1017 N. LaCienega Blvd., Suite 308, West Hollywood, CA 90069 ☎ 310/289-6000 or 800/429-8747 (Ext. 14 for both) 📠 310/855-0323 ✉ lgernert@tzell.com. **Kennedy Travel** ✉ 130 W. 42nd St., Suite 401, New York, NY 10036 ☎ 800/237-7433 or 212/840-8659 📠 212/730-2269 🌐 www.kennedytravel.com. **Now, Voyager** ✉ 4406 18th St., San Francisco, CA 94114 ☎ 415/626-1169 or 800/255-6951 📠 415/626-8626 🌐 www.nowvoyager.com. **Skylink Travel and Tour/Flying Dutchmen Travel** ✉ 1455 N. Dutton Ave., Suite A, Santa Rosa, CA 95401 ☎ 707/546-9888 or 800/225-5759 📠 707/636-0951; serving lesbian travelers.

Gay & Lesbian Resources **Gay and Lesbian Community Center** ✉ 2110 E. Northern Lights Blvd. ☎ 907/929-4528. **Identity Inc.** ☎ 907/258-4777 🌐 www.identityinc.org.

HEALTH

PESTS & OTHER HAZARDS

During the summer months Alaska is infamous for its sometimes-dense clouds of mosquitoes and other biting insects. They are generally the worst in Interior Alaska but can be an annoyance throughout the state. **Be sure to bring mosquito repellents containing DEET.** Also occasionally used (but less effective) is the Avon product Skin So Soft. Mosquito coils may be of some help if you are camping or staying in remote cabins. Headnets are sold in local sporting-goods stores and are a wise purchase if you plan to spend extended time outdoors, particularly in the Interior or on Kodiak Island.

HOLIDAYS

Major national holidays are New Year's Day (Jan. 1); Martin Luther King Day (3rd Mon. in Jan.); Presidents' Day (3rd Mon. in Feb.); Memorial Day (last Mon. in May); Independence Day (July 4); Labor Day (1st Mon. in Sept.); Columbus Day (2nd Mon. in Oct.); Thanksgiving Day (4th Thurs. in Nov.); Christmas Eve and Christmas Day (Dec. 24 and 25); and New Year's Eve (Dec. 31).

INSURANCE

The most useful travel-insurance plan is a comprehensive policy that includes coverage for trip cancellation and interruption, default, trip delay, and medical expenses (with a waiver for preexisting conditions).

Without insurance you'll lose all or most of your money if you cancel your trip, regardless of the reason. Default insurance covers you if your tour operator, airline, or cruise line goes out of business—the chances of which have been increasing. Trip-delay covers expenses that arise because of bad weather or mechanical delays. Study the fine print when comparing policies.

U.K. residents can buy a travel-insurance policy valid for most vacations taken during the year in which it's purchased (but check preexisting-condition coverage). British and Australian citizens need extra medical coverage when traveling overseas.

Always **buy travel policies directly from the insurance company**; if you buy them from a cruise line, airline, or tour operator that goes out of business you probably won't be covered for the agency or operator's default, a major risk. Before making any purchase, review your existing health and home-owner's policies to find what they cover away from home.

Travel Insurers In the U.S.: **Access America** ✉ 2805 N. Parham Rd., Richmond, VA 23294 ☎ 800/284-8300 📠 804/673-1469 or 800/346-9265 🌐 www.accessamerica.com. **Travel Guard International** ✉ 1145 Clark St., Stevens Point, WI 54481 ☎ 800/826-1300 or 715/345-1041 📠 800/955-8785 or 715/345-1990 🌐 www.travelguard.com.

FOR INTERNATIONAL TRAVELERS

For information on customs restrictions, *see* Customs & Duties.

CAR RENTAL

When picking up a rental car, non-U.S. residents need a reservation voucher for any prepaid reservations that were made in the traveler's home country, a passport, a driver's license, and a travel policy that covers each driver.

CURRENCY

The dollar is the basic unit of U.S. currency. It has 100 cents. Coins are the copper penny (1¢); the silvery nickel (5¢), dime (10¢), quarter (25¢), and half-dollar (50¢); and the golden $1 coin, replacing a now-rare silver dollar. Bills are denominated $1, $5, $10, $20, $50, and $100, all mostly green and identical in size; designs and background tints vary. In addition, you may come across a $2 bill, but the chances are slim. The exchange rate at this writing is US$1.82 per British pound, US$.81 per Canadian dollar, US$.77 per Australian dollar, and US$.71 per New Zealand dollar.

ELECTRICITY

The U.S. standard is AC, 110 volts/60 cycles. Plugs have two flat pins set parallel to each other.

EMERGENCIES

For police, fire, or ambulance, **dial 911** (0 in rural areas).

INSURANCE

Britons and Australians need extra medical coverage when traveling overseas.

Insurance Information In the U.K.: **Association of British Insurers** ✉ 51 Gresham St., London EC2V 7HQ ☎ 020/7600-3333 📠 020/7696-8999 🌐 www.abi.org.uk. In Australia: **Insurance Council of Australia** ✉ Level 3, 56 Pitt St., Sydney, NSW 2000 ☎ 02/9253-5100 📠 02/9253-5111 🌐 www.ica.com.au. In Canada: **RBC Insurance** ✉ 6880 Financial Dr., Mississauga, Ontario L5N 7Y5 ☎ 800/387-4357 or 905/816-2559 📠 888/298-6458 🌐 www.rbcinsurance.com. In New Zealand: **Insurance Council of New Zealand** ✉ Level 7, 111-115 Customhouse Quay, Box 474, Wellington ☎ 04/472-5230 📠 04/473-3011 🌐 www.icnz.org.nz.

MAIL & SHIPPING

You can buy stamps and aerograms and send letters and parcels in post offices. Stamp-dispensing machines can occasionally be found in airports, bus and train stations, office buildings, drugstores, and the like. You can also deposit mail in the stout, dark blue, steel bins at strategic locations everywhere and in the mail chutes of large buildings; pickup schedules are posted. You can deposit packages at public collection boxes as long as the parcels are affixed with proper postage and weigh less than one pound. Packages weighing one or more pounds must be taken to a post office or handed to a postal carrier.

For mail sent within the United States, you need a 37¢ stamp for first-class letters weighing up to 1 ounce (23¢ for each additional ounce) and 23¢ for postcards. You pay 80¢ for 1-ounce airmail letters and 70¢ for airmail postcards to most other countries; to Canada and Mexico, you need a 60¢ stamp for a 1-ounce letter and 50¢ for a postcard. An aerogram—a single sheet of lightweight blue paper that folds into its own envelope, stamped for overseas airmail—costs 70¢.

To receive mail on the road, have it sent c/o General Delivery at your destination's main post office (use the correct five-digit ZIP code). You must pick up mail in person within 30 days and show a driver's license or passport.

PASSPORTS & VISAS

The best time to apply for a passport or to renew is in fall and winter. Before any trip, check your passport's expiration date, and, if necessary, renew it as soon as possible.

When traveling internationally, carry your passport even if you don't need one. Not only is it the best form of ID, but it's also being required more and more. As of December 31, 2005, for instance, Americans need a passport to re-enter the country from Bermuda, the Caribbean, and Panama. Such requirements also affect reentry from Canada and Mexico by air and sea (as of December 31, 2006) and land (as of December 31, 2007). **Make two photocopies of the data page** (one for someone at home and another for you, carried separately from your passport). If you lose your passport, promptly call the nearest embassy or consulate and the local police.

Australian Citizens **Passports Australia** ☎ 131-232 🌐 www.passports.gov.au. **United States Consulate General** ✉ MLC Centre, Level 59, 19–29 Martin Pl., Sydney, NSW 2000 ☎ 02/9373-9200, 1902/941-641 fee-based visa-inquiry line 🌐 usembassy-australia.state.gov/sydney.

Canadian Citizens **Passport Office** ✉ to mail in applications: 70 Cremazie St., Gatineau, Québec J8Y 3P2 ☎ 800/567-6868, 866/255-7655 TTY 🌐 www.ppt.gc.ca.

New Zealand Citizens **New Zealand Passports Office** ✉ For applications and information, Level 3, Boulcott House, 47 Boulcott St., Wellington ☎ 0800/22-5050 or 04/474-8100 🌐 www.passports.govt.nz. **Embassy of the United States** ✉ 29 Fitzherbert Terr., Thorndon, Wellington ☎ 04/462-6000 🌐 usembassy.org.nz. **U.S. Consulate General** ✉ Citibank Bldg., 3rd floor, 23 Customs St. E, Auckland ☎ 09/303-2724 🌐 usembassy.org.nz.

U.K. Citizens **U.K. Passport Service** ☎ 0870/521-0410 🌐 www.passport.gov.uk. **American Consulate General** ✉ Danesfort House, 223 Stranmillis Rd., Belfast, Northern Ireland BT9 5GR ☎ 028/9038-6100 📠 028/9068-1301 🌐 www.usembassy.org.uk. **American Embassy** ✉ for visa and immigration information or to submit a visa application via mail (enclose an SASE), Consular Information Unit, 24 Grosvenor Sq., London W1A 2LQ ☎ 090/5544-4546 or 090/6820-0290 for visa information (per-minute charges), 0207/499-9000 main switchboard 🌐 www.usembassy.org.uk.

TELEPHONES

All U.S. telephone numbers consist of a three-digit area code and a seven-digit local number. Within many local calling areas, you dial only the seven-digit number. Within some area codes, you must dial "1" first for calls outside the local area. To call between area-code regions, dial "1" then all 10 digits; the same goes for calls to numbers prefixed by "800," "888," "866," and "877"—all toll free. For calls to numbers preceded by "900" you must pay—usually dearly.

For international calls, dial "011" followed by the country code and the local number. For help, dial "0" and ask for an overseas operator. The country code is 61 for Australia, 64 for New Zealand, 44 for the United Kingdom. Calling Canada is the same as calling within the United States, although you might not be able to get through on some toll free numbers. Most local phone books list country codes and U.S. area codes. The country code for the United States is 1.

For operator assistance, dial "0." To obtain someone's phone number, call directory assistance at 555–1212 or occasionally 411 (free at many public phones). To have the person you're calling foot the bill, phone collect; dial "0" instead of "1" before the 10-digit number.

At pay phones, instructions often are posted. Usually you insert coins in a slot (usually 25¢–50¢ for local calls) and wait for a steady tone before dialing. When you call long-distance, the operator tells you how much to insert; prepaid phone cards, widely available in various denominations, are easier. Call the number on the back, punch in the card's personal identification number when prompted, then dial your number.

LODGING

Assume that hotels operate on the European Plan (EP, with no meals) unless we specify that they use the Breakfast Plan (BP, with a full breakfast), the Continental Plan (CP, with a Continental breakfast), Modified American Plan (MAP, with breakfast and dinner), or the Full American Plan (FAP, with all meals).

The lodgings we list are the cream of the crop in each price category. We always list the facilities that are available—but we don't specify whether they cost extra: when pricing accommodations, always ask what's included and what costs extra.

For hotels:

CATEGORY	ANCHORAGE*	ELSEWHERE IN ALASKA*
$$$$	over $250	over $225
$$$	$200–$250	$175–$225
$$	$150–$200	$125–$175
$	$100–$150	$75–$125
¢	under $100	under $75

*All prices are for a standard double room in high season, excluding tax and service.

BED & BREAKFASTS

Bed-and-breakfasts are common across Alaska and provide a fine way to learn about the area you're in while staying with a local. Nearly every Alaskan town has at least one B&B, and dozens of choices are available in the larger cities. At last count, Anchorage had more than 175 B&Bs, including modest suburban apartments, elaborate showcase homes with dramatic vistas, and everything in between.

Reservation Services **Alaska Private Lodgings/Stay with a Friend** Box 3552, Homer 99603-3552 907/235-2148 or 888/235-2148 907/235-3773 www.alaskabandb.com. **Alaska's Mat-Su Bed & Breakfast Association** Box 873507, Wasilla 99687 www.alaskabnbhosts.com. **Anchorage Alaska Bed & Breakfast Association** Box 242623, Anchorage 99524-2623 907/272-5909 or 888/584-5147 www.anchorage-bnb.com. **Bed & Breakfast Association of Alaska** www.alaskabba.com. **Bed & Breakfast Association of Alaska INNside Passage Chapter** www.accommodations-alaska.com. **Fairbanks Association of Bed & Breakfasts** www.ptialaska.net/~fabb. **Kenai Peninsula Bed & Breakfast Association** www.kenaipeninsulabba.com.

CAMPING

Camping in Alaska needn't be a daunting experience: think of it as camping elsewhere in the Lower 48, except that the mosquitoes are worse and there's a greater likelihood of a nighttime bear visit. Some newcomers to bear country are uneasy sleeping in a tent, but encounters are rare. **Store food inside your vehicle** where it's less likely to tempt bears. The midnight sun can also keep tent campers awake. Whether you're in a tent or an RV, you'll need warm bedding, insect repellent, rain protection, and tight containers for food storage.

Public campgrounds in Alaska are operated by the U.S. Forest Service, State Division of Parks and Outdoor Recreation, National Park Service, and Bureau of Land Management. Of the national parks, only Denali has developed car-camping facilities, and these campsites fill quickly. Several other Alaskan national parks have walk-in campgrounds, and all parks allow backcountry camping. In addition to the public campgrounds, private RV parks can be found in Alaska's larger towns.

CUTTING COSTS

Alaska is an expensive place, with transportation, food, and lodging costs substantially above those in the Lower 48 states. Off-season hotel rates are often much lower, but most travelers prefer to visit Alaska in the summer, when days are long and temperatures are mild. Shoulder-season (May and September) travelers may find somewhat lower rates, but some businesses and attractions may be closed. Camping is always an option, particularly if you enjoy the great outdoors for which Alaska is so famous. Travelers willing to sleep in bunks may want to check out the state's many hostels, some of which have family rooms.

Alaska's unique Marine Highway System provides a reasonable way to travel the Inside Passage and to coastal towns in Prince William Sound, the Kenai Peninsula, Kodiak, and out to the Aleutians. Many budget travelers sleep in the covered solarium onboard these ferries, saving any extra room charges.

HOME EXCHANGES

If you would like to exchange your home for someone else's, join a home-exchange organization, which will send you its updated listings of available exchanges for a year and will include your own listing in at least one of them. It's up to you to make specific arrangements.

Exchange Clubs **HomeLink USA** ✉ 2937 NW 9th Terrace, Wilton Manors, FL 33311 ☎ 954/566-2687 or 800/638-3841 📠 954/566-2783 🌐 www.homelink.org; $75 yearly for a listing and online access; $45 additional to receive directories. **Intervac U.S.** ✉ 30 Corte San Fernando, Tiburon, CA 94920 ☎ 800/756-4663 📠 415/435-7440 🌐 www.intervacus.com; $128 yearly for a listing, online access, and a catalog; $68 without catalog.

HOSTELS

No matter what your age, you can save on lodging costs by staying at hostels. In some 4,500 locations in more than 70 countries around the world, Hostelling International (HI), the umbrella group for a number of national youth-hostel associations, offers single-sex, dorm-style beds and, at many hostels, rooms for couples and family accommodations. Membership in any HI national hostel association, open to travelers of all ages, allows you to stay in HI-affiliated hostels at member rates; one-year membership is about $28 for adults (C$35 for a two-year minimum membership in Canada, £15 in the U.K., A$52 in Australia, and NZ$40 in New Zealand); hostels charge about $10–$30 per night. Members have priority if the hostel is full; they're also eligible for discounts around the world, even on rail and bus travel in some countries.

Official Hostelling International hostels can be found in Ketchikan and Sitka. Many other Alaskan hostels are not affiliated with HI, including ones in Anchorage, Denali, Fairbanks, Girdwood, Haines, Homer, Juneau, McCarthy, Petersburg, Seward, Skagway, Slana, Sterling, Talkeetna, Tok, and Wrangell. Most of these are only open seasonally, but hostels in Anchorage, Fairbanks, Girdwood, Homer, Juneau, Skagway, and Talkeetna provide year-round lodging. Hostels.com has contact information for all Alaskan hostels.

Hostels.com 🌐 www.hostels.com. **Hostelling International–USA** ✉ 8401 Colesville Rd., Suite 600, Silver Spring, MD 20910 ☎ 301/495-1240 📠 301/495-6697 🌐 www.hiusa.org. **Hostelling International–Canada** ✉ 205 Catherine St., Suite 400, Ottawa, Ontario K2P 1C3 ☎ 613/237-7884 or 800/663-5777 📠 613/237-7868 🌐 www.hihostels.ca. **YHA England and Wales** ✉ Trevelyan House, Dimple Rd., Matlock, Derbyshire DE4 3YH, U.K. ☎ 0870/870-8808, 0870/770-8868, 0162/959-2600 📠 0870/770-6127 🌐 www.yha.org.uk. **YHA Australia** ✉ 422 Kent St., Sydney, NSW 2001 ☎ 02/9261-1111 📠 02/9261-1969 🌐 www.yha.com.au. **YHA New Zealand** ✉ Level 1, Moorhouse City, 166 Moorhouse Ave., Box 436, Christchurch ☎ 03/379-9970 or 0800/278-299 📠 03/365-4476 🌐 www.yha.org.nz.

HOTELS

Alaskan motels and hotels are similar in quality to those in the Lower 48 states. Most Alaskan motels are independent, but you'll find the familiar chains (including Best Western, Comfort Inn, Days Inn, Hampton Inn, Hilton, Holiday Inn, Marriott, Motel 6, Super 8, and Sheraton) in Anchorage. Westmark Hotels is a regional chain, owned by cruise-tour operator Holland America Westours, with 15 locations, including hotels in Anchorage, Fairbanks, Kenai, Kodiak, Sitka, and Valdez in Alaska, plus Beaver Creek and Whitehorse in Canada's Yukon Territory. Princess Tours owns a luxury hotel in Fairbanks and lodges outside Denali National Park, near Denali State Park, near Wrangell–St. Elias National Park, and on the Kenai Peninsula. All hotels listed have private bath unless otherwise noted.

Toll-Free Numbers **Best Western** ☎ 800/528-1234 🌐 www.bestwestern.com. **Choice** ☎ 800/424-6423 🌐 www.choicehotels.com. **Clarion** ☎ 800/424-6423 🌐 www.choicehotels.com. **Comfort Inn** ☎ 800/424-6423 🌐 www.choicehotels.com. **Days Inn** ☎ 800/325-2525 🌐 www.daysinn.com. **Doubletree Hotels** ☎ 800/222-8733 🌐 www.doubletree.com. **Embassy Suites** ☎ 800/362-2779 🌐 www.embassysuites.com. **Fairfield Inn** ☎ 800/228-2800 🌐 www.marriott.com. **Hilton** ☎ 800/445-8667 🌐 www.hilton.com. **Holiday Inn** ☎ 800/465-4329 🌐 www.ichotelsgroup.com. **Howard Johnson** ☎ 800/446-4656 🌐 www.hojo.com. **Hyatt Hotels & Resorts** ☎ 800/233-1234 🌐 www.hyatt.com. **La Quinta** ☎ 800/531-5900 🌐 www.lq.com. **Marriott** ☎ 800/228-9290 🌐 www.marriott.com. **Quality Inn** ☎ 800/424-6423 🌐 www.choicehotels.com. **Radisson** ☎ 800/333-3333 🌐 www.radisson.com. **Ramada** ☎ 800/228-2828, 800/854-7854 international reservations 🌐 www.ramada.com or www.ramadahotels.com. **Red Lion and WestCoast Hotels and Inns** ☎ 800/733-5466 🌐 www.redlion.com. **Sheraton** ☎ 800/325-3535 🌐 www.starwood.com/sheraton. **Sleep Inn** ☎ 800/424-6423 🌐 www.choicehotels.com. **Westin Hotels & Resorts** ☎ 800/228-3000 🌐 www.starwood.com/westin.

WILDERNESS LODGES

To really get away from it all, book a remote lodge with rustic accommodations in the middle of breathtaking Alaskan wilderness. Some of the most popular are in the river drainages of Bristol Bay, in Southeast Alaska, and along the Susitna River north of Anchorage. Most of these lodges place a heavy emphasis on fishing; a stay generally includes daily guided fishing trips as well as all meals. They can be astronomically expensive (daily rates of $250–$600 per person), so if you're not interested in fishing, you won't want to seek these out. Lodges in and near Denali National Park emphasize the great outdoors, and some even include wintertime dogsledding. Activities focus on hiking, rafting, flightseeing, horseback riding, and natural-history walks. For getting deep into the wilderness, these lodges are an excellent alternative to the hotels and cabins outside the park entrance.

MEDIA

INTERNET ACCESS

Alaska is one of the most "wired" places in America. Internet access is available in all the larger towns and cities and even in many remote Bush communities. Most Alaskan public libraries have computer terminals where you can check e-mail or surf the Web for free, and many towns also have businesses that rent computer access by the hour. In addition, hotel rooms are increasingly set up with data ports on their phones and wireless Internet (Wi-Fi) for those traveling with laptop computers. The larger and newer hotels typically have a business center with computers for Internet access, along with fax and copy machines. In addition, many smaller motels and B&Bs have at least one computer available to guests for Web access.

NEWSPAPERS & MAGAZINES

Alaska's primary statewide newspaper is the ***Anchorage Daily News*** (🌐 www.adn.com). Other papers with substantial regional coverage are the ***Fairbanks Daily News-Miner*** (🌐 www.news-miner.com) and the ***Juneau Empire*** (🌐 www.juneauempire.com). ***Alaska Magazine*** (🌐 www.alaskamagazine.com) covers the state on a monthly basis and is distributed nationally. In addition, many mid-size Alaskan towns have their own weekly newspapers.

RADIO & TELEVISION

Most larger Alaskan communities have their own commercial AM or FM radio stations. Alaska also has an extensive network of public stations, with National Public Radio/Alaska Public Radio (www.

aprn.org) affiliates based in 20 different towns. The flagship station is KSKA 91.1 FM in Anchorage, but public radio can also be heard in many of the smallest villages around the state. Native-owned KNBA 90.3 FM, in Anchorage, broadcasts a mix of music and programming (without ads) aimed at the state's large Native community.

Most Alaskan hotels and motels have cable or satellite television reception, providing a wide selection of channels. The primary Anchorage TV stations are KIMO channel 13 (ABC), KTVA channel 11 (CBS), KTUU channel 2 (NBC), KTBY channel 4 (Fox), and KAKM channel 7 (PBS). In Fairbanks they are KATN channel 2 (ABC), KTVF channel 11 (CBS and NBC), K07UU channel 7 (Fox), and KUAC channel 9 (PBS). In Juneau they are KJUD channel 8 (ABC) and KTOO channel 3 (PBS).

MONEY MATTERS

Because of its off-the-beaten-path location, Alaska has always been an expensive travel destination. Major roads link Anchorage with Fairbanks and other cities and towns in South Central and Interior Alaska, but most other parts of the state are accessible only by air or water. This is even true of Alaska's state capital, Juneau. Costs in Anchorage and Fairbanks are only slightly higher than for Lower 48 cities, and you will find discount stores such as Wal-Mart, Costco, and Fred Meyers, but as you head to more remote parts of the state, prices escalate. In Bush communities food, lodging, and transportation costs can be far higher than in Anchorage, since nearly everything must be brought in by air.

Prices throughout this guide are given for adults. Substantially reduced fees are almost always available for children, students, and senior citizens. For information on taxes, *see* Taxes.

ATMS

All the larger towns (and most places with a bank) in Alaska now have ATMs, but **don't expect to find an ATM in the remote Bush villages.** Nearly all ATMs in Alaska charge a fee (typically $1.50) if you don't have an account. Grocery stores typically accept ATM cards and will give you cash back with no surcharge.

CREDIT CARDS

Throughout this guide, the following abbreviations are used: **AE,** American Express; **D,** Discover; **DC,** Diners Club; **MC,** MasterCard; and **V,** Visa.

Reporting Lost Cards **American Express** ☎ 800/992-3404. **Diners Club** ☎ 800/234-6377. **Discover** ☎ 800/347-2683. **MasterCard** ☎ 800/622-7747. **Visa** ☎ 800/ 847-2911.

NATIONAL PARKS

Look into discount passes to save money on park entrance fees. For $50, the National Parks Pass admits you (and any passengers in your private vehicle) to all national parks, monuments, and recreation areas, as well as other sites run by the National Park Service, for a year. (In parks that charge per person, the pass admits you, your spouse and children, and your parents, when you arrive together.) Camping and parking are extra. The $15 Golden Eagle Pass, a hologram you affix to your National Parks Pass, functions as an upgrade, granting entry to all sites run by the NPS, the U.S. Fish and Wildlife Service, the U.S. Forest Service, and the Bureau of Land Management. The upgrade, which expires with the parks pass, is sold by most national-park, Fish-and-Wildlife, and BLM fee stations. A major percentage of the proceeds from pass sales funds National Parks projects.

Both the Golden Age Passport ($10), for U.S. citizens or permanent residents who are 62 and older, and the Golden Access Passport (free), for persons with disabilities, entitle holders (and any passengers in their private vehicles) to lifetime free entry to all national parks, plus 50% off fees for the use of many park facilities and services. (The discount doesn't always apply to companions.) To obtain them, you must show proof of age and of U.S. citizenship or permanent residency—such as a U.S. passport, driver's license, or birth certificate—and, if requesting Golden Access, proof of disability. The Golden Age and

Golden Access passes are available only at NPS-run sites that charge an entrance fee. The National Parks Pass is also available by mail and phone and via the Internet.

National Park Foundation ✉ 11 Dupont Circle NW, Suite 600, Washington, DC 20036 ☎ 202/238-4200 🌐 www.nationalparks.org. **National Park Service** ✉ National Park Service/Department of Interior, 1849 C St. NW, Washington, DC 20240 ☎ 202/208-6843 🌐 www.nps.gov. **National Parks Conservation Association** ✉ 1300 19th St. NW, Suite 300, Washington, DC 20036 ☎ 202/223-6722 or 800/628-7275 🌐 www.npca.org.

Passes by Mail & Online **National Park Foundation** 🌐 www.nationalparks.org. **National Parks Pass** National Park Foundation ✉ Box 34108, Washington, DC 20043 ☎ 888/467-2757 🌐 www.nationalparks.org; include a check or money order payable to the National Park Service, plus $3.95 for shipping and handling (allow 8 to 13 business days from date of receipt for pass delivery), or call for passes.

PACKING

Not all of Alaska has the fierce winters that are usually associated with the state. Winter in the Southeast and South Central coastal regions is relatively mild—Chicago and Minneapolis experience harsher weather than Juneau. It's a different story in the Interior, where temperatures in the subzero range and biting winds keep most visitors indoors.

The best way to keep warm under colder conditions is to **wear layers of clothing, starting with thermal underwear and socks.** The outermost layer should be lightweight, windproof, rainproof, and hooded. Down jackets (and sleeping bags) have the disadvantage of becoming soggy when wet; the newer synthetics (particularly wind-block fabrics) are the materials of choice. Footgear needs to be sturdy, and if you're going into the backcountry, be sure it's waterproof. Rubber boots are often a necessity in coastal areas. When wearing snow boots, be certain they are not too tight. Restricting your circulation will only make you colder.

Wherever you go in Alaska (and especially in the Southeast), **be prepared for rain.** To keep yourself dry, pack a collapsible umbrella or bring a rain slicker, as sudden storms are common. Although Alaskan summers are mild, an extra sweater or jacket for cool evenings will come in handy. UVA/UVB sunscreen, insect repellent, and sunglasses are necessities. A pair of binoculars will help you track any wildlife you encounter.

Befitting the frontier image, dress is mostly casual day and night. Bring along one outfit that is appropriate for "dress-up," if you enjoy doing so, though it's not necessary.

In your carry-on luggage, pack an extra pair of eyeglasses or contact lenses and enough of any medication you take to last a few days longer than the entire trip. You may also ask your doctor to write a spare prescription using the drug's generic name, as brand names may vary from country to country. In luggage to be checked, **never pack prescription drugs, valuables, or undeveloped film.** And don't forget to carry with you the addresses of offices that handle refunds of lost traveler's checks. Check *Fodor's How to Pack* (available at online retailers and bookstores everywhere) for more tips.

To avoid customs and security delays, carry medications in their original packaging. Don't pack any sharp objects in your carry-on luggage, including knives of any size or material, scissors, nail clippers, and corkscrews, or anything else that might arouse suspicion.

To avoid having your checked luggage chosen for hand inspection, don't cram bags full. The U.S. Transportation Security Administration suggests packing shoes on top and placing personal items you don't want touched in clear plastic bags.

CHECKING LUGGAGE

You're allowed to carry aboard one bag and one personal article, such as a purse or a laptop computer. Make sure what you carry on fits under your seat or in the overhead bin. Get to the gate early, so you can board as soon as possible, before the overhead bins fill up.

Baggage allowances vary by carrier, destination, and ticket class. On international flights, you're usually allowed to check two bags weighing up to 70 pounds (32 kilograms) each, although a few airlines allow checked bags of up to 88 pounds (40 kilograms) in first class. Some international carriers don't allow more than 66 pounds (30 kilograms) per bag in business class and 44 pounds (20 kilograms) in economy. If you're flying to or through the United Kingdom, your luggage cannot exceed 70 pounds (32 kilograms) per bag. On domestic flights, the limit is usually 50 to 70 pounds (23 to 32 kilograms) per bag. In general, carry-on bags shouldn't exceed 40 pounds (18 kilograms). Most airlines won't accept bags that weigh more than 100 pounds (45 kilograms) on domestic or international flights. Expect to pay a fee for baggage that exceeds weight limits. Check baggage restrictions with your carrier before you pack.

Airline liability for baggage is limited to $2,500 per person on flights within the United States. On international flights it amounts to $9.07 per pound or $20 per kilogram for checked baggage (roughly $640 per 70-pound bag), with a maximum of $634.90 per piece, and $400 per passenger for unchecked baggage. You can buy additional coverage at check-in for about $10 per $1,000 of coverage, but it often excludes a rather extensive list of items, shown on your airline ticket.

Before departure, itemize your bags' contents and their worth, and label the bags with your name, address, and phone number. (If you use your home address, cover it so potential thieves can't see it readily.) Include a label inside each bag and **pack a copy of your itinerary.** At check-in, make sure each bag is correctly tagged with the destination airport's three-letter code. Because some checked bags will be opened for hand inspection, the U.S. Transportation Security Administration recommends that you leave luggage unlocked or use the plastic locks offered at check-in. TSA screeners place an inspection notice inside searched bags, which are re-sealed with a special lock.

If your bag has been searched and contents are missing or damaged, file a claim with the TSA Consumer Response Center as soon as possible. If your bags arrive damaged or fail to arrive at all, file a written report with the airline before leaving the airport.

Complaints **U.S. Transportation Security Administration Contact Center** ☎ 866/289-9673 🌐 www.tsa.gov.

SAFETY

Alaska is big, wild, and not particularly forgiving, so travelers lacking outdoor experience need to take precautions when venturing away from the beaten path. If you lack backcountry skills or feel uncomfortable handling yourself if a bear should approach (⇨ Bears), take a guided trip instead or join a class at the National Outdoor Leadership School, which is based in Palmer (an hour north of Anchorage).

Education **National Outdoor Leadership School** ☎ 907/745-4047 🌐 www.nols.edu.

SENIOR-CITIZEN TRAVEL

The Alaska Railroad offers discounted rates to senior citizens during off-peak months (late September–early May), while the Alaska Marine Highway offers discounted fares year-round. Alaska Direct Bus Lines offers a 10% discount for intercity travel.

To qualify for age-related discounts, mention your senior-citizen status up front when booking hotel reservations (not when checking out) and before you're seated in restaurants (not when paying the bill). Be sure to have identification on hand. When renting a car, ask about promotional car-rental discounts, which can be cheaper than senior-citizen rates.

Educational Programs **Elderhostel** ✉ 11 Ave. de Lafayette, Boston, MA 02111 ☎ 877/426-8056, 978/323-4141 international callers, 877/426-2167 TTY 📠 877/426-2166 🌐 www.elderhostel.org. **Interhostel** ✉ University of New Hampshire, 6 Garrison Ave., Durham, NH 03824 ☎ 603/862-1147 or 800/733-9753 📠 603/862-1113 🌐 www.learn.unh.edu.

SHOPPING

The best buys in Alaska are products of local materials made by Native peoples and other artists and craftspeople living in the state. Before you buy, **make sure the local crafts are genuine.** The state has adopted two symbols that guarantee the authenticity of crafts made by Alaskans. A silver hand symbol indicates the item was made by one of Alaska's Native peoples. A polar bear verifies the item was "Made in Alaska." If some items with these tags seem more expensive than you expected, examine them closely and you'll probably find that they are handmade, one-of-a-kind pieces.

Although these symbols are designed to ensure authentic Alaskan and Native-made products, it doesn't mean that items lacking them are not authentic. This applies in particular to Native artists who may or may not go through the necessary paperwork to obtain the silver hand labels. They often come to town and sell items directly to shop owners for cash. It pays to shop around, ask questions, and learn about the different types of Native crafts from around the state.

Some Alaskan shops sell carved items made in Southeast Asia, primarily Bali, and not all of these crafts are labeled as such. When some clerks are asked about these items' origins, they may say, "We got it in Anchorage." Unfortunately, this may just mean that they picked it up at the Anchorage airport after the items were flown in from Asia. Before buying something—particularly an expensive piece—ask questions to make sure it is authentic. You can protect yourself by visiting a number of shops first to learn the differences between Alaskan handcrafted items and those that are mass-produced.

Carved walrus ivory pieces are sold in many Alaskan shops. Some of these are pieces of raw ivory carved by Native Alaskan artists, and others are fossilized ivory, which can be legally used by other carvers. Although walrus ivory is legal to own in the United States, transporting it through other countries—including Canada—requires a permit from Convention on Trade in Endangered Species (CITES).

Authenticity & Permits **Alaska's Native peoples** ☎ 907/269-6610 or 888/278-7424 www.eed.state.ak.us/aksca. **Convention on Trade in Endangered Species (CITES)** www.cites.org. **Made in Alaska** www.madeinalaska.org.

SMART SOUVENIRS

Authentic Native art is always worth looking over, even if you cannot afford the finest pieces. Alaska has an abundance of artists whose works fill local galleries. Some, such as Rie Muñoz and Barbara Lavalle, are nationally known, but you should also check out prints by Ray Troll and Evon Zerbetz in Ketchikan, unique and colorful pins by William Spear in Juneau, and the paintings of Nancy Yaki and Erik Behnke in Homer. Several towns are known for their galleries, most notably Homer, but also Sitka, Juneau, Haines, and Ketchikan. Be sure to look for items made from musk-ox wool (qiviut) in Anchorage and Palmer, along with birch syrup from **Kahiltna Birchworks** (www.alaskabirchsyrup.com); it's sold in many Alaskan gift shops and at the Anchorage Saturday and Sunday Markets.

SIGHTSEEING GUIDES

A couple of companies operate sightseeing tours statewide. For local sightseeing outfits in individual cities and towns, *see* Tours *in* regional A to Z sections.

Sightseeing-Tour Companies **Alaska Airlines Vacations** ☎ 800/468-2248 www.alaskaair.com. **Alaska Sightseeing/Cruise West** ☎ 206/441-8687 or 800/580-0072 www.cruisewest.com. **Alaska Wildland Adventures** ☎ 907/783-2928 or 800/334-8730 fax 907/783-2130 www.alaskawildland.com. **Glacier Bay Cruiselines** ☎ 206/623-7110 or 800/451-5952 www.glacierbaytours.com. **Gray Line of Alaska** ☎ 907/277-5581 or 800/544-2206 fax 907/225-9386 www.graylineofalaska.com. **Princess Tours** ☎ 206/336-6000 or 800/835-8907 fax 907/225-9386 www.princess.com.

SPORTS & THE OUTDOORS

FISHING

License fees for nonresidents are $10 for a 1-day permit, $20 for 3 days, $30 for 7 days, $50 for 14 days, and $100 for an annual license. If you're going to be fishing for king salmon, an additional stamp that doubles these costs is required. Licenses are available from the Fish and Game Web site or, in-state, from sporting-goods stores, charter-boat operators, and fishing lodges.

Information & Licenses **Alaska Department of Fish & Game** Box 25525, Juneau 99802-5525

☎ 907/465-4180 seasons and regulations, 907/465-2376 licenses 🌐 www.adfg.state.ak.us.

STUDENTS IN ALASKA

Student discounts are available at many Alaskan museums and other attractions.

IDs & Services **STA Travel** ✉ 10 Downing St., New York, NY 10014 ☎ 212/627-3111, 800/777-0112 24-hr service center 📠 212/627-3387 🌐 www.sta.com. **Travel Cuts** ✉ 187 College St., Toronto, Ontario M5T 1P7, Canada ☎ 800/592-2887 in the U.S., 416/979-2406 or 866/246-9762 in Canada 📠 416/979-8167 🌐 www.travelcuts.com.

TAXES

SALES TAX

Alaska does not impose a state sales tax, but individual cities and boroughs have their own. Anchorage has no sales tax.

TIME

Nearly all of Alaska lies within the Alaska time zone, 20 hours behind Sydney, 9 hours behind London, 4 hours behind New York City, 3 hours behind Chicago, and 1 hour behind Los Angeles and western Canada. The nearly unpopulated Aleutian Islands are in the same time zone as Hawaii, 5 hours behind the East Coast.

TIPPING

In addition to tipping waiters and waitresses, taxi drivers, and baggage handlers, tipping others who provide personalized services is common in Alaska. Tour-bus drivers who offer a particularly informative trip generally receive a tip from passengers at the end of the tour. A small amount left in your hotel room is also much appreciated by the cleaning staff. Fishing guides are commonly tipped around 10% by their clients, particularly if the guide helped them land a big one. In addition, gratuities may also be given to pilots following a particularly good flightseeing or bear-viewing trip, but the amount is up to your own discretion.

TOURS & PACKAGES

Because everything is prearranged on a prepackaged tour or independent vacation, you spend less time planning—and often get it all at a good price.

BOOKING WITH AN AGENT

Travel agents are excellent resources. But it's a good idea to collect brochures from several agencies, as some agents' suggestions may be influenced by relationships with tour and package firms that reward them for volume sales. If you have a special interest, find an agent with expertise in that area. The American Society of Travel Agents (ASTA) has a database of specialists worldwide; you can log on to the group's Web site to find one near you.

Make sure your travel agent knows the accommodations and other services of the place being recommended. Ask about the hotel's location, room size, beds, and whether it has a pool, room service, or programs for children, if you care about these. Has your agent been there in person or sent others whom you can contact?

Do some homework on your own, too: local tourism boards can provide information about lesser-known and small-niche operators, some of which may sell only direct.

BUYER BEWARE

Each year consumers are stranded or lose their money when tour operators—even large ones with excellent reputations—go out of business. So check out the operator. Ask several travel agents about its reputation, and try to **book with a company that has a consumer-protection program.** (Look for information in the company's brochure.) In the United States, members of the United States Tour Operators Association are required to set aside funds (up to $1 million) to help eligible customers cover payments and travel arrangements in the event that the company defaults. It's also a good idea to choose a company that participates in the American Society of Travel Agents' Tour Operator Program; ASTA will act as mediator in any disputes between you and your tour operator.

Remember that the more your package or tour includes, the better you can predict the ultimate cost of your vacation. Make sure you know exactly what is covered, and beware of hidden costs. Are taxes, tips, and transfers included? Entertainment and excursions? These can add up.

Tour-Operator Recommendations **American Society of Travel Agents** (⇨ Travel Agencies). **CrossSphere-The Global Association for Packaged Travel** ✉ 546 E. Main St., Lexington, KY 40508 ☎ 859/226-4444 or 800/682-8886 📠 859/226-4414 🌐 www.CrossSphere.com. **United States Tour Operators Association** (USTOA) ✉ 275 Madison Ave., Suite 2014, New York, NY 10016 ☎ 212/599-6599 📠 212/599-6744 🌐 www.ustoa.com.

FLIGHTSEEING

Although flightseeing is expensive, it's not only the best way to grasp the expansiveness and grandeur of the land but also the only way to reach remote parts of Alaska. However, it can be dangerous. Before your flight, contact the air tour operator to check how long the company has been in service, its accident/incident statistics, and its safety procedures. If possible, try to meet with and talk to your pilot before the trip. Know where you're going and how long the trip will take. Avoid trips with long stopovers in remote areas—drastic weather changes can result in the cancellation or complication of your return flight. Pay attention to the safety message at the start of the flight, especially noting the location of emergency survival gear. The long distances, mountainous terrain, and challenging weather conditions are all hazardous factors, but pilot error, due sometimes to passenger interference, is often involved. Never push a pilot to do something he or she is reluctant to do, such as circle low over a bear, and never pressure the pilot to hurry up. Missing your scheduled landing or ship departure is much better than pushing a pilot to fly in unsafe weather conditions.

For flightseeing operators, *see* regional A to Z sections.

GROUP TOURS

Among companies that sell tours to Alaska, the following are nationally known, have a proven reputation, and offer plenty of options. The classifications used below represent different price categories, and you'll probably encounter these terms when talking to a travel agent or tour operator. The key difference is usually in accommodations, which run from budget to better, and better yet to best.

Super-Deluxe **Abercrombie & Kent** ✉ 1520 Kensington Rd., Suite 212, Oak Brook, IL 60523-2156 ☎ 630/954-2944 or 800/323-7308 📠 630/954-3324 🌐 www.abercrombiekent.com.

Deluxe **Maupintour** ✉ 10650 W. Charleston Blvd., Summerlin, NV 89135-1014 ☎ 800/255-4266 📠 702/260-3787 🌐 www.maupintour.com. **Tauck World Discovery** ✉ 10 Norden Pl. 📭 Norwalk, CT 06855 ☎ 203/899-6500 or 800/788-7885 📠 203/222-7702 🌐 www.tauck.com.

Deluxe/First-Class **Globus** ✉ 5301 S. Federal Cir., Littleton, CO 80123-2980 ☎ 303/797-2800 or 866/755-8581 📠 303/347-2080 🌐 www.globusjourneys.com.

First-Class & Tourist-Range **Collette Vacations** ✉ 162 Middle St., Pawtucket, RI 02860 ☎ 401/728-9000 or 800/340-5158 📠 401/728-4745 🌐 www.collettevacations.com. **Gadabout Tours** ✉ 700 E. Tahquitz Canyon Way, Palm Springs, CA 92262-6767 ☎ 760/325-5556 or 800/952-5068 📠 760/325-5127 🌐 www.gadabouttours.com. **Mayflower Tours** ✉ 1225 Warren Ave. 📭 Box 490, Downers Grove, IL 60515 ☎ 630/435-8500 or 800/323-7604 📠 630/960-3575 🌐 www.mayflowertours.com. **Trafalgar Tours** ✉ 11 E. 26th St., Suite 1300, New York, NY 10010 ☎ 212/689-8977 or 866/544-4434 📠 800/457-6644 🌐 www.trafalgartours.com.

PACKAGES

Like group tours, independent vacation packages are available from major tour operators and airlines. Packages may include fly/drive itineraries with B&B accommodations or ferry-liner tours. The companies listed below offer vacation packages in a broad price range.

Independent Vacation Packages **Alaska Airlines Vacations** 📭 Box 68900, Seattle, WA 98168 ☎ 800/468-2248 🌐 www.alaskaair.com. **Alaska Bound** ✉ 116 Cass St., Traverse City, MI 49684 ☎ 231/439-3000 or 888/252-7527 📠 231/439-3004 🌐 www.alaskabound.com. **Alaska Tour & Travel** 📭 Box 221011, Anchorage 99522-1011 ☎ 907/245-0200 or 800/208-0200 🌐 www.alaskatravel.com. **Alaska Tours** 📭 413 G St., Anchorage 99501 ☎ 907/277-3000 📠 907/272-2532 🌐 www.alaskatours.com. **Gray Line of Alaska** ☎ 206/281-3535 or 800/544-2206 🌐 www.graylinealaska.com. **Homer Travel & Tours** 📭 435 E. Pioneer Ave., Homer, AK 99603 ☎ 907/235-7751 or 800/478-7751 www.alaskahomertravel.com. **Juneau Guide** 4541 Sawa Cir., Juneau, AK 99603 907/789-3772 or 888/658-6328 www.juneaubb.com. **Knightly Tours** Box 16366, Seattle, WA 98116 206/938-8567 or 800/426-2123 206/938-8498 www.knightlytours.com. **See Alaska Tours** Box 244744, Anchorage 99524 907/278-5704 www.alaskatours.net. **Viking Travel** Box 787, Petersburg 99833 907/772-3818 or 800/327-2571 907/772-3940 www.alaskaferry.com.

From the U.K. **Arctic Experience Ltd.** 29 Nork Way, Banstead SM7 1PB 01737/218-800 www.arctic-discover.co.uk. **Kuoni Travel** Kuoni House, Dorking RH5 4AZ 01306/744-445 www.kuoni.co.uk. **Vacation Canada** Cambridge House, 8 Cambridge St., Glasgow G3 2DZ 0990/168-215.

THEME TRIPS

Bicycling **Alaska Backcountry Bike Tours** Box 6754, Palmer, AK 99645 907/746-5018 or 866/354-2453 510/527-1444 www.mountainbikealaska.com. **Backroads** 801 Cedar St., Berkeley, CA 94710-1800 510/527-1555 or 800/462-2848 510/527-1444 www.backroads.com.

Bird-Watching **Alaska Birding and Wildlife Tours** 4300 B St., Suite 402, Anchorage 99503 877/424-5637 907/278-2316 www.alaskabirding.com. **Victor Emanuel Nature Tours** 2525 Wallingwood Dr., Suite 1003, Austin, TX 787646 512/328-5221 or 800/328-8368 512/328-2919 www.ventbird.com. **Wilderness Birding Adventures** 5515 Wild Mountain Rd., Eagle River 99577 907/694-7442 www.wildernessbirding.com. **Wings Birding Tours** 1643 N. Alvernon Way, Suite 105, Tucson, AZ 85712 520/320-9868 or 888/293-6443 520/320-9373 www.wingsbirds.com.

Canoeing, Kayaking & Rafting **Above and Beyond Alaska** Box 22083, Juneau 99802 907/364-2333 907/364-2553 www.beyondak.com. **Alaska Discovery** 5310 Glacier Hwy., Juneau 99801 907/780-6226 or 800/586-1911 907/780-4220 www.akdiscovery.com. **Alaska Outdoor Adventures** Box 770, Whittier 99693 907/472-2534 or 877/472-2534 907/472-2480 www.akadventures.com. **Alaska River Adventures** Box 725, Cooper Landing 99572 907/595-2000 or 888/836-9027 907/595-3454 www.alaskariveradventures.com. **Alaska Wildland Adventures** Box 389, Girdwood 99587 907/783-2928 or 800/334-8730 907/783-2130 www.alaskawildland.com. **Anadyr Adventures** Box 1821, Valdez 99572 907/835-2814 or 800/865-2925 www.anadyradventures.com. **Chugach Adventure Guides** Box 641, Girdwood 99587 907/783-2004 or 877/783-2004 www.alaskanrafting.com. **James Henry River Journeys** Box 807, Bolinas, CA 94924 415/868-1836 or 800/786-1830 415/868-9033 www.riverjourneys.com. **Nova** Box 1129, Chickaloon 99674 907/745-5753 or 800/746-5753 907/745-5754 www.novalaska.com. **OARS** Box 67, Angels Camp, CA 95222 209/736-4677 or 800/346-6277 209/736-2902 www.oars.com. **REI Adventures** Box 1938, Sumner, WA 98390-0800 253/437-1100 or 800/622-2236 253/395-8160 www.rei.com. **TrekAmerica** Box 189, Rockaway, NJ 07866 973/983-1144 or 800/221-0596 973/983-8551 www.trekamerica.com.

Dogsledding **Chugach Express Dog Sled Tours** Box 1396, Girdwood 99587 907/783-2266 907/783-2625. **Godwin Glacier Dog Sled Tours** Box 28038, Scottsdale, AZ 85255 907/224-8239 or 888/989-8239 907/224-2398 www.alaskadogsled.com. **IdidaRide Sled Dog Tours** Box 2906, Seward 99664-2906 907/224-8607 or 800/478-3139 907/224-8608 www.ididaride.com. **Plettner Sled Dog Kennels** Box 299136, Wasilla 99687-9136 907/892-6944 or 877/892-6944 907/892-6945 www.plettner-kennels.com. **Sourdough Outfitters** Box 90, Bettles 99726 907/692-5252 907/692-5557 www.sourdoughoutfitters.com. **Susitna Dog Tours** Box 464, Willow 99688 907/495-6324 907/495-6325 www.susitnadogtours.com.

Ferry Tours **Knightly Tours** (⇨ Packages). **Viking Travel** (⇨ Packages).

Heli-skiing **Chugach Adventure Guides** Box 641, Girdwood 99587 907/783-2004 or 877/783-2004 www.chugachpowderguides.com. **Valdez Heli-Camps** Box 2495, Valdez 99686 907/783-2004 or 877/783-2004 907/835-3291 www.valdezhelicamps.com. **Valdez Heli-Ski Guides** Box 57, Girdwood 99587 907/835-4528 800/817-4828 www.valdezhiliskiguides.com.

Hiking **Alaskan Gourmet Adventures** 11090 Hideaway Lake Dr., Anchorage 99516 907/346-1087 www.hikealaska.com. **Alaska Two-Legged Tours** Box 261, Girdwood 99587 907/317-4813 or 877/252-5344 www.twoleggedtours.com. **Mountain Travel-Sobek** 1266 66th St., Emeryville, CA 94608 510/594-6000 or 888/687-6235 510/594-6001 www.mtsobek.com. **Sourdough Outfitters** (⇨ Dogsledding).

Learning Vacations Earthwatch Institute ⊠ 3 Clock Tower Pl., Suite 100 ⌂ Box 75, Maynard, MA 01754 ☎ 978/461-0081 or 800/776-0188 ☒ 978/461-2332 ⊕ www.earthwatch.org. **National Audubon Society** ⊠ 700 Broadway, New York, NY 10003 ☎ 212/979-3000 ☒ 212/979-3188 ⊕ www.audubon.org. **Natural Habitat Adventures** ⊠ 2945 Center Green Ct., Boulder, CO 80301 ☎ 303/449-3711 or 800/543-8917 ☒ 303/449-3712 ⊕ www.nathab.com. **Nature Expeditions International** ⊠ 7860 Peters Rd., Suite F-103, Plantation, FL 33324 ☎ 954/693-8852 or 800/869-0639 ☒ 954/693-8854 ⊕ www.naturexp.com. **Naturequest** ⊠ 30872 South Coast Hwy., Suite 185, Laguna Beach, CA 92651 ☎ 949/499-9561 or 800/369-3033 ☒ 949/499-0812 ⊕ www.naturequesttours.com. **Oceanic Society Expeditions** ⊠ Fort Mason Center, Bldg. E, San Francisco, CA 94123-1394 ☎ 415/441-1106 or 800/326-7491 ☒ 415/474-3395 ⊕ www.oceanicsociety.org. **Sierra Club** ⊠ 85 2nd St., 2nd floor, San Francisco, CA 94105 ☎ 415/977-5522 ☒ 415/977-5795 ⊕ www.sierraclub.org. **Smithsonian Journeys** ⌂ Box 23293, Washington, DC 20026-3293 ☎ 202/357-4700 or 877/338-8687 ☒ 202/633-9250 ⊕ www.smithsonianjourneys.org.

Native Tours Alaska Airlines Vacations (⇨ Packages). **Alaska Heritage Tours** ⊠ 2525 C St., Suite 401, Anchorage 99503 ☎ 907/265-4500 or 877/258-6877 ☒ 907/263-5186 ⊕ www.ahtours.com. **Alexander's River Adventure** ⌂ Box 62, Nenana 99760 ☎ 907/474-3924. **Cape Fox Tours** ⌂ Box 6656, Ketchikan 99901 ☎ 907/225-4846 ⊕ www.capefoxtours.com. **Goldbelt Tours** ⊠ 9097 Glacier Hwy, Suite 100, Juneau 99801 ☎ 907/789-4183 or 800/478-3610 ☒ 907/789-9383 ⊕ www.goldbelttours.com. **Northern Alaska Tour Company** ⌂ Box 82991, Fairbanks 99708 ☎ 907/474-8600 or 800/474-1986 ☒ 907/474-4767 ⊕ www.northernalaska.com. **Sitka Tours** ⊠ 200 Katlian St., Sitka 99835 ☎ 907/747-3770 or 888/270-8687 ☒ 907/747-3770 ⊕ www.sitkatribe.org. **Tundra Tours** ⌂ Box 189, Barrow 99723 ☎ 907/852-3900 or 800/478-8520 ⊕ www.topoftheworldhotel.com.

Natural History Alaska Two-Legged Tours ⊠ Box 261, Girdwood 99587 ☎ 907/317-4813 or 877/252-5344 ⊕ www.twoleggedtours.com. **Alaska Wildland Adventures** (⇨ Canoeing, Kayaking & Rafting). **Camp Denali** ⌂ Box 67 Denali National Park AK 99755 ☎ 907/683-2290 ☒ 907/683-1568 ⊕ www.campdenali.com. **Great Alaska Adventure Lodge** ⊠ 33881 Sterling Hwy., Sterling 99672 ☎ 907/262-4515 or 800/544-2261 ☒ 907/262-8797 in summer ⊕ www.greatalaska.com. **Hallo Bay**

Wilderness Camp ⌂ Box 2904, Homer 99603 ☎ 907/235-2237 ⊕ www.hallobay.com. **Walrus Islands Expeditions** ⊠ 4828 Rochelle, Homer 99603 ☎ 907/235-9349 ⊕ www.alaskawalrusisland.com.**Wilderness Birding Adventures** (⇨ Bird-Watching).

Photography Alaska Birding and Wildlife Tours (⇨ Bird-Watching). **Alaska Photo Tours** ⌂ Box 91134, Anchorage 99509-1134 ☎ 907/339-85001 or 800/799-3051 ☒ 907/733-3052 ⊕ www.alaskaphototours.com. **Camp Denali** (⇨ Natural History). **Dolphin Charters** ⌂ 1007 Leneve Place El Cerrito, CA 94530 ☎ 510/527-9622 or 800/472-9942 ☒ 510/525-0720 ⊕ www.dolphincharters.com. **Hallo Bay Wilderness Camp** (⇨ Natural History). **Joseph Van Os Photo Safaris** ⌂ Box 655, Vashon Island, WA 99070 ☎ 206/463-5383 ☒ 206/463-5484 ⊕ www.photosafaris.com. **Naturally Wild Photo Adventures** ⌂ Box 333 Chillicothe, OH 45601 ☎ 740/774-6243 ⊕ www.naturallywild.net.

RV Tours ABC Motorhome Rentals (⇨ RV Rentals). **Alaska Motorhome Rentals** (⇨ RV Rentals). **Alaska Panorama RV Rentals** (⇨ RV Rentals). **Alaska Superior RV** (⇨ RV Rentals). **Clippership Motorhome Rentals** (⇨ RV Rentals). **Fantasy RV Tours** ⌂ 111 Camino Del Rio, Gunnison, CO 81230 ☎ 970/642-4562 or 800/952-8496 ☒ 970/642-4573 ⊕ www.fantasyrvtours.com. **GoNorth RV Camper Rental** (⇨ RV Rentals). **Great Alaskan Holidays** (⇨ RV Rentals).

Sportfishing Alaska River Adventures (⇨ Canoeing, Kayaking & Rafting). **Alaska Wildland Adventures** (⇨ Canoeing, Kayaking & Rafting). **Fishing International** ⊠ 1825 4th St., Santa Rosa, CA 95404 ☎ 707/542-4242 or 800/950-4242 ☒ 707/526-3474 ⊕ www.fishinginternational.com. **Great Alaska Adventure Lodge** (⇨ Natural History). **Rod & Reel Adventures** ⊠ 32617 Skyhawk Way, Eugene, OR 97405 ☎ 541/349-0777 or 800/356-6982 ☒ 541/338-0367 ⊕ www.rodreeladventures.com. **Sport Fishing Alaska** ⊠ 9310 Shorecrest Dr., Anchorage 99515 ☎ 907/344-8674 or 888/552-8674 ☒ 907/243-9447 ⊕ www.alaskatripplanners.com.

Wilderness High Adventures Alaska Mountain Guides ⌂ Box 1081, Haines 99827 ☎ 907/766-3366 or 800/766-3396 ⊕ www.alaskamountainguides.com. **Alaska Mountaineering School** ⌂ Box 566, Talkeetna 99676 ☎ 907/733-1016 ☒ 907/733-1362 ⊕ www.climbalaska.org. **Brooks Range Aviation** ⌂ Box 10, Bettles 99726 ☎ 907/692-5444 or 800/692-5443 ☒ 907/692-2185 ⊕ www.brooksrange.com. **Regal Air** ☎ 907/243-

8535 ⊕ www.alaska.net/~regalair/. **Rust's Flying Service** ✉ Box 190867, Anchorage 99519 ☎ 907/243-1595 or 800/544-2299 ⊕ www.flyrusts.com. **Warbelow's Air Ventures** ☎ 907/474-0518 or 800/478-0812 ⊕ www.warbelows.com. **Sourdough Outfitters** (⇨ Dogsledding).

TRAIN TRAVEL

The state-owned Alaska Railroad has service connecting Seward, Anchorage, Denali National Park, and Fairbanks. Amtrak serves Seattle and Vancouver; VIA Rail Canada serves Vancouver and Prince Rupert, British Columbia.

Travel aboard the Alaska Railroad is leisurely (Anchorage to Fairbanks is an all-day trip), so you can enjoy spectacular scenery along the way. Some cars have narration, and food is available on board in the dining car and at the café. Some private tour companies that offer a more glitzy trip between Anchorage and Fairbanks hook their luxury railcars to the train. For a less expensive alternative, ride one of the public dome cars, owned and operated by the railroad. Seating in the public cars is unassigned, and passengers take turns under the observation dome. The railroad's public cars are a great place to meet resident Alaskans.

Except for the Seward–Anchorage leg, all service operates year-round. Trains run daily in summer; service is reduced from September to late May. Dining cars are available on all trains.

For a scenic and historic trip between Skagway and Fraser, British Columbia, take the White Pass & Yukon Route, which follows the treacherous path taken by prospectors during the Klondike gold rush of 1897–98. A bus links the terminal at Fraser with Whitehorse, capital of the Yukon Territory.

CUTTING COSTS

The AlaskaPass allows unlimited travel on bus, ferry, and rail lines in Alaska; *see* Cutting Costs *in* Boat & Ferry Travel.

FARES & SCHEDULES

Tickets can be purchased in advance over the phone using a credit card. If your reservation is a month or more ahead of time, the company will mail you the ticket; otherwise travelers can pick them up at the departure station. Travel agents also sell tickets for travel aboard the Alaska Railroad.

Train Information **Alaska Railroad** ✉ Box 107500, Anchorage 99510 ☎ 907/265-2494 in Anchorage, 907/458-6025 in Fairbanks, 800/544-0552 📠 907/265-2323 ⊕ www.alaskarailroad.com. **Amtrak** ☎ 800/872-7245 ⊕ www.amtrak.com. **VIA Rail Canada** ☎ 800/561-3949 ⊕ www.viarail.com. **White Pass & Yukon Route** ✉ Box 435, Skagway 99840 ☎ 907/983-2217, 800/343-7373 in U.S. and Canada ⊕ www.whitepassrailroad.com.

PAYING

Cash, Discover, Visa, and MasterCard are accepted.

RESERVATIONS

Advance reservations are highly recommended for midsummer train travel, particularly between Seward and Anchorage and between Anchorage and Denali National Park & Preserve.

TRANSPORTATION AROUND ALASKA

Visitors to Alaska arrive by air and highway, and aboard ships and ferries. Cruise ships are a particularly popular way to travel, especially in Southeast Alaska, where many towns (including the state capital of Juneau) are not accessible by road. The Alaska Marine Highway ferry system provides car and passenger service throughout Southeast Alaska, as well as a number of towns in South Central Alaska and out to the Aleutian Islands.

The famous Alaska Highway is the primary road access into the state, starting in Dawson Creek, British Columbia, and continuing 1,390 mi to Delta Junction, Alaska. A network of two-lane highways connects the main towns and cities in South Central and Interior Alaska, including Anchorage and Fairbanks. Jet service is available to Alaska's cities and larger towns. Smaller Bush planes (sometimes on floats) are the lifeblood of more remote parts of Alaska.

TRAVEL AGENCIES

A good travel agent puts your needs first. Look for an agency that has been in business at least five years, emphasizes customer service, and has someone on staff who specializes in your destination. In addition, **make sure the agency belongs to a professional trade organization.** The American Society of Travel Agents (ASTA) has more than 10,000 members in some 140 countries, enforces a strict code of ethics, and will step in to mediate agent-client disputes involving ASTA members. ASTA also maintains a directory of agents on its Web site; ASTA's TravelSense.org, a trip planning and travel advice site, can also help to locate a travel agent who caters to your needs. (If a travel agency is also acting as your tour operator, *see* Buyer Beware *in* Tours & Packages.)

Travel agents are found in all of Alaska's cities and larger towns, and some of the state's larger travel agencies are listed below.

Local Agent Referrals **American Society of Travel Agents** (ASTA) ✉ 1101 King St., Suite 200, Alexandria, VA 22314 ☎ 703/739-2782 or 800/965-2782 24-hr hotline 📠 703/684-8319 🌐 www.astanet.com and www.travelsense.org. **Association of British Travel Agents** ✉ 68-71 Newman St., London W1T 3AH ☎ 020/7637-2444 📠 020/7637-0713 🌐 www.abta.com. **Association of Canadian Travel Agencies** ✉ 130 Albert St., Suite 1705, Ottawa, Ontario K1P 5G4 ☎ 613/237-3657 📠 613/237-7052 🌐 www.acta.ca. **Australian Federation of Travel Agents** ✉ Level 3, 309 Pitt St., Sydney, NSW 2000 ☎ 02/9264-3299 or 1300/363-416 📠 02/9264-1085 🌐 www.afta.com.au. **Travel Agents' Association of New Zealand** ✉ Level 5, Tourism and Travel House, 79 Boulcott St., Box 1888, Wellington 6001 ☎ 04/499-0104 📠 04/499-0786 🌐 www.taanz.org.nz.

Alaska Travel Agencies **Alaska Tours** (⇨ Tours & Packages: Independent Vacation Packages). **All Ways Travel** ✉ 302 G St., Anchorage 99501-2186 ☎ 907/276-3644 or 800/676-2946 📠 907/258-2211 🌐 www.alaskatripshop.com. **Easy Travel** ✉ 3120 Denali St., Suite 1, Anchorage 99503-4029 ☎ 907/562-3279 or 800/383-3279 📠 907/273-1998 🌐 www.easytravel.nu. **Explore Tours** ✉ 1415 E. Tudor Rd., Suite 102, Anchorage 99507 ☎ 907/786-0192 or 800/523-7405 🌐 www.exploretours.com. **Homer Travel & Tours** ✉ 435 Pioneer Ave., Homer 99603 ☎ 907/235-7751 or 800/478-7751 🌐 www.alaskahomertravel.com. **Navigant International/Alaska** ✉ 206 W. 34th Ave., Anchorage 99503 ☎ 907/786-3200 or 800/478-2829 📠 907/786-3298 🌐 www.navigant.com. **One Stop Travel** ✉ 1501 Huffman Rd., Suite 197, Anchorage 99515 ☎ 907/278-7006 or 800/770-4440 📠 907/565-7888 🌐 www.onestoptravel.net. **See Alaska Tours** (⇨ Tours & Packages: Independent Vacation Packages). **USTravel** ✉ 1415 E. Tudor Rd., Anchorage 99507-1033 ☎ 907/561-2434 or 800/478-2434 📠 907/786-0180 🌐 www.ustravelak.com. **Viking Travel** (⇨ Tours & Packages: Independent Vacation Packages).

VISITOR INFORMATION

Learn more about foreign destinations by checking government-issued travel advisories and country information. For a broader picture, consider information from more than one country.

The Alaska Travel Industry Association (a partnership between the state and private businesses) publishes the *Alaska Vacation Planner*, a free, comprehensive information source for statewide travel year-round. Alaska's regional tourism councils distribute vacation planners highlighting their local attractions. The official State of Alaska Web site contains additional information and links.

Statewide Information **Alaska Department of Fish and Game** 📫 Box 25526, Juneau 99802-5526 ☎ 907/465-4112, 907/465-4180 sportfishing seasons and regulations, 907/465-2376 license information 🌐 www.state.ak.us/adfg. **Alaska Division of Parks** ✉ 400 Willoughby Ave., Suite 400, Juneau 99801 ☎ 907/465-4563 🌐 www.alaskastateparks.org. **Alaska Travel Industry Association** ✉ 2600 Cordova St., Suite 201, Anchorage 99503 ☎ 907/929-2200 or 800/862-5275 to order Alaska Vacation Planners 🌐 www.travelalaska.com. **Alaska Marine Highway System** ☎ 907/465-3941 or 800/642-0066 🌐 www.ferryalaska.com. **Alaska Public Lands Information Center** 🌐 www.nps.gov/aplic.

Regional Information **Kenai Peninsula Tourism Marketing Council** ✉ 35477 Kenai Spur Hwy., Suite 1205, Soldotna 99669 ☎ 907/262-5229 or 800/535-3624 📠 907/262-5212 🌐 www.kenaipeninsula.org. **Southwest Alaska Municipal Conference** ✉ 3300 Arctic Blvd., Suite 203, Anchorage 99503 ☎ 907/562-7380 📠 907/562-0438 🌐 www.southwestalaska.com.

City Information **Anchorage** 🌐 www.anchorage.net. **Cordova** 🌐 www.cordovachamber.com. **Fairbanks** 🌐 www.explorefairbanks.com.

Haines ⊕ www.haines.ak.us. **Homer** ⊕ www.homeralaska.org. **Juneau** ⊕ www.traveljuneau.com. **Ketchikan** ⊕ www.visit-ketchikan.com. **Kodiak** ⊕ www.kodiak.org. **Matanuska-Susitna Valley** ⊕ www.alaskavisit.com. **Nome** ⊕ www.nomealaska.org/vc. **Petersburg** ⊕ www.petersburg.org. **Prince of Wales Island** ⊕ www.princeofwalescofc.org. **Seward** ⊕ www.sewardak.org. **Sitka** ⊕ www.sitka.org. **Skagway** ⊕ www.skagway.com. **Soldotna** ⊕ www.soldotnachamber.com. **Talkeetna** ⊕ www.talkeetna-chamber.com. **Wrangell** ⊕ www.wrangellchamber.org. **Unalaska/Dutch Harbor** ⊕ www.unalaska.info. **Valdez** ⊕ www.valdezalaska.org. **Whittier** ⊕ www.whittieralaska.com. **Yakutat** ⊕ www.yakutatalaska.com.

British Columbia & Yukon **Tourism British Columbia** Box 9830, Victoria, British Columbia V8W 9W5 Canada ☎ 604/435-5622 or 800/435-5622 ⊕ www.hellobc.com. **Tourism Yukon** Box 2703, Whitehorse, Yukon Territory Y1A 2C6 Canada ☎ 867/667-5340 or 800/789-8566 ☎ 867/667-3546 ⊕ www.touryukon.com.

Government Advisories **Consular Affairs Bureau of Canada** ☎ 800/267-6788 or 613/944-6788 ⊕ www.voyage.gc.ca. **U.K. Foreign and Commonwealth Office** ✉ Travel Advice Unit, Consular Directorate, Old Admiralty Building, London SW1A 2PA ☎ 0870/606-0290 or 020/7008-1500 ⊕ www.fco.gov.uk/travel. **Australian Department of Foreign Affairs and Trade** ☎ 300/139-281 travel advisories, 02/6261-1299 Consular Travel Advice ⊕ www.smartraveller.gov.au or www.dfat.gov.au. **New Zealand Ministry of Foreign Affairs and Trade** ☎ 04/439-8000 ⊕ www.mft.govt.nz.

WEB SITES

Do check out the World Wide Web when planning your trip. You'll find everything from weather forecasts to virtual tours of famous cities. Be sure to visit Fodors.com (⊕ www.fodors.com), a complete travel-planning site. You can research prices and book plane tickets, hotel rooms, rental cars, vacation packages, and more. In addition, you can post your pressing questions in the Travel Talk section. Other planning tools include a currency converter and weather reports, and there are loads of links to travel resources.

Sports & Wilderness Adventures

1

WORD OF MOUTH

"When I was younger, I almost ran off with my lover to Alaska. I always wondered what I missed."

—cigalechanta

"Now that we're back from our two-week Alaska trip, I can say quite honestly that kayaking in Alaska will not disappoint you. The place is magnificent. My best advice is to bring a barrel of money and tons of time!"

—BayouGal

"As long as you have a good pair of hiking boots treated with water repellent, you should be fine. We also brought a pair of shoes for walking, and something a little bit nicer for going out in the evening."

—Julie304

www.fodors.com/forums

By Peggy Wayburn and Mary Engel

Updated by Bill Sherwonit

IN THE ALEUT LANGUAGE, the word *Alaska* means "the Great Land"—an appropriate name for the 49th state of the United States, the one with more land in parks, wilderness areas, and wildlife refuges than all the other states combined. In fact, about one-third of Alaska's 375 million acres is set aside in protected public lands.

These are lands not only of prodigious scale but of prodigious beauty. Four great mountain ranges—and more than 30 lesser chains—sweep through Alaska: the St. Elias, Alaska, Brooks, and Chugach ranges. One is the highest coastal range in the world; another includes the highest point of the North American continent (Mt. McKinley, 20,320 feet); the third lies north of and roughly defines the Arctic Circle; and the fourth arcs through Alaska's most populous region. In between the mountains are rugged canyons, treeless valleys, flower-filled meadows, limpid lakes, blue-iced glaciers, waterfalls, deep-shadowed rain forests, and spacious tundras. Adding to this wealth are some 47,000 mi of spectacular tidal coastline.

Because of its relative inaccessibility and frequently demanding climate, most of this extraordinary area has remained largely undeveloped since it was acquired by the United States in 1867. (The United States paid Russia all of $7.2 million for this treasure.) First called Indian Country and then made a district, Alaska became a proper territory in 1912. However, except for military and federal reservations and a handful of homesites, the first extensive subdivision of Alaska did not occur until 1959, when the territory achieved statehood.

At that time Congress granted the new state 104 million acres to be selected out of more than 300 million acres of "vacant, unappropriated public land," which up to that time had been administered in Alaska by the Bureau of Land Management (or BLM, the federal agency that is charged with caring for the country's uncommitted public lands). Of that total, 91 million acres have so far been conveyed to the state. In 1970 another congressional act—the Alaska Native Claims Settlement Act (ANCSA)—gave to Alaska's Native people an additional 44 million acres to be chosen from the remaining unappropriated lands; so far, about 38 million acres have actually been selected and transferred to Native ownership. And in 1980, the Alaska National Interest Lands Conservation Act (ANILCA) established federal protection for about 104 million acres of outstanding Alaska land for the use and enjoyment of all the American people—and indeed of people throughout the world. Gaining passage of this legislation is considered by many to be the most extraordinary environmental achievement in the country's history.

Alaska's protected federal lands include nearly 55 million acres of national parks (administered by the National Park Service), 73 million acres of national wildlife refuges (administered by the United States Fish and Wildlife Service), 25 wild and scenic rivers totaling nearly 2 million acres (administered by federal agencies), and 5.8 million acres of land administered by the United States Forest Service as wilderness areas. (Forest Service "multiple use" lands total nearly 17 million acres.) Alaska's remaining vacant and unappropriated public land still administered by the BLM now totals just under 86 million acres and will continue to decline as land is allotted. Along with the federally protected lands established in Alaska by the passage of ANILCA in 1980, approximately 3.2 million acres of superb lands are set aside as state parks.

Because Alaska's public lands are as varied as they are magnificent, recreational opportunities range from such spectator activities as wildlife viewing to rigorous participatory sports such as mountaineering (thousands of mountains in this state haven't even been named, much less been climbed) and extreme skiing. Many of these lands are only partially accessible: although you can drive to some, you will more often have to go by air—usually air taxi—or boat to the area of your choice.

The state's most-visited parks are Denali National Park and Preserve, Glacier Bay National Park and Preserve, Kenai Fjords National Park, and Chugach State Park; however, this doesn't mean a backpacker or kayaker can't have a remote wilderness experience there. Parks closer to roads, and closer to Anchorage and Fairbanks, are likely to have more visitors, but that doesn't necessarily translate into the numbers encountered in parks in the Lower 48. On the other hand, if you're after a truly remote and out-of-the-way experience, you may want to try some of the least-visited places in the state, such as Wood-Tikchik State Park, where one lonely ranger patrols 1.55 million acres, or Aniakchak National Monument and Preserve, south of Katmai, where a ranger can go days or sometimes weeks without seeing a visitor.

WILDLIFE VIEWING

Alaska is one of the few places in the country where you can easily view wildlife in its natural state. It's unique among the 50 United States for its vast resource of protected wilderness and is rich in birds, animals, and fish. Alaska's wild beauty adds a powerful dimension to any wildlife-viewing experience.

Alaska's 375 million acres support more than 800 species of animals—mammals, birds, and fish. The 105 different mammals range from whales to shrews (Alaska's shrews are the smallest of North America's land mammals, weighing 1/10 ounce). The nearly 300 species of birds range from hummingbirds to bald eagles, including species found nowhere else in North America. Migrant birds come here annually from every continent and many islands to take advantage of Alaska's rich breeding and rearing grounds: its wetlands, its rivers, its shores, and its tundras. Among the 430 different kinds of fish—including five different kinds of salmon—some weigh more than 300 pounds (halibut) whereas others more commonly weigh less than a pound (arctic grayling).

The largest number of animals can be seen during periods of migration. The state is strategically positioned for creatures that migrate vast distances. Some birds, for instance, fly from the southern tip of South America to nest and rear their young on sandbars in Alaska's wild rivers. Others travel from parts of Asia to enjoy an Alaskan summer. The arctic tern is the greatest of these long-distance voyagers, coming here all the way from Antarctica. Sea mammals congregate in great numbers in the waters of Prince William Sound, the Panhandle, the Gulf of Alaska, and

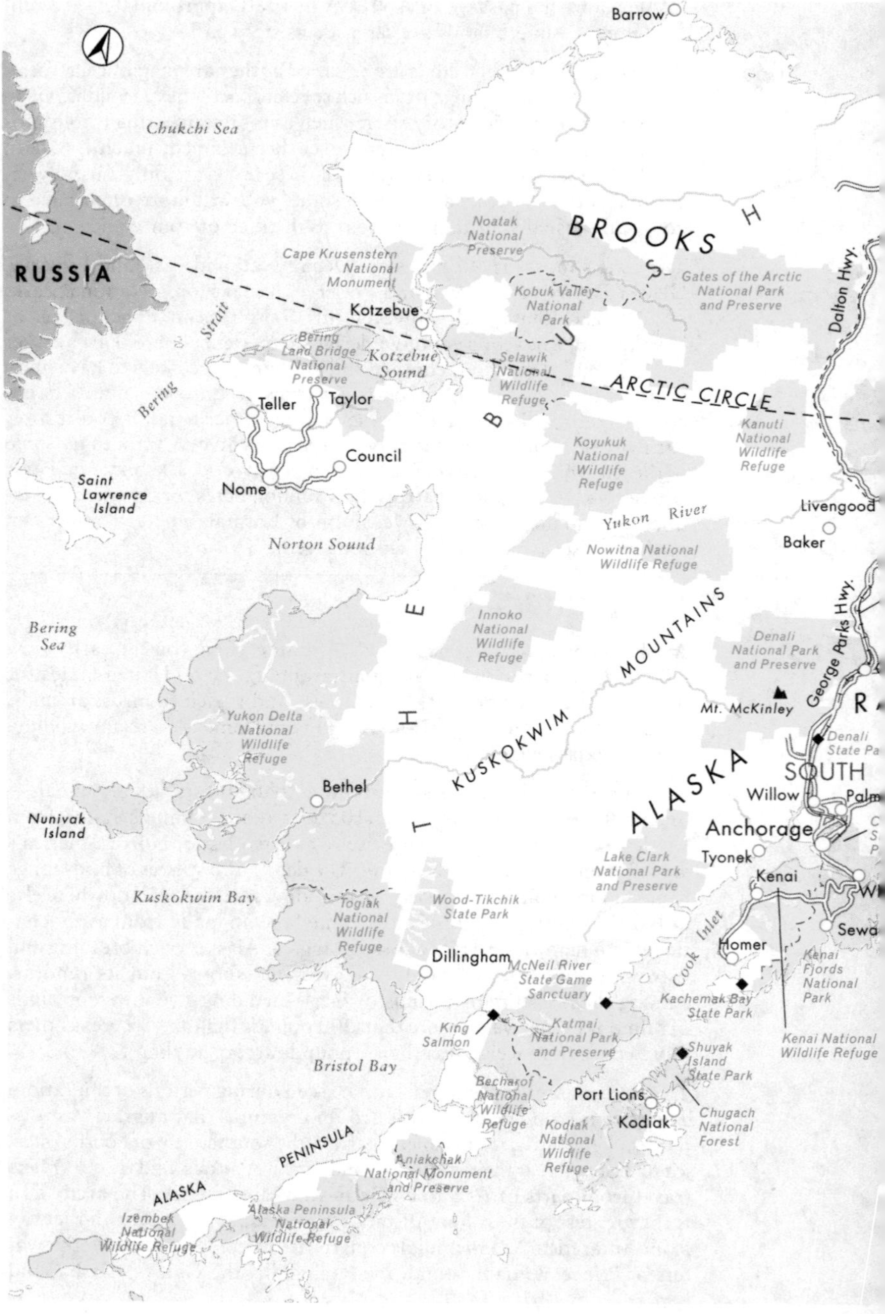
Barrow
Chukchi Sea
RUSSIA
BROOKS
Noatak National Preserve
Cape Krusenstern National Monument
Kobuk Valley National Park
Gates of the Arctic National Park and Preserve
Dalton Hwy.
Kotzebue
Bering Strait
Bering Land Bridge National Preserve
Kotzebue Sound
Selawik National Wildlife Refuge
ARCTIC CIRCLE
Teller
Taylor
Kanuti National Wildlife Refuge
Koyukuk National Wildlife Refuge
Council
Nome
Saint Lawrence Island
Yukon River
Livengood
Baker
Norton Sound
Nowitna National Wildlife Refuge
Bering Sea
Innoko National Wildlife Refuge
MOUNTAINS
Denali National Park and Preserve
George Parks Hwy.
Mt. McKinley
Yukon Delta National Wildlife Refuge
KUSKOKWIM
Denali State Pa
SOUTH
ALASKA
Bethel
Willow
Palm
Nunivak Island
Anchorage
Tyonek
Lake Clark National Park and Preserve
Kenai
Kuskokwim Bay
Togiak National Wildlife Refuge
Wood-Tikchik State Park
Cook Inlet
Sewa
Homer
Dillingham
McNeil River State Game Sanctuary
Kenai Fjords National Park
Kachemak Bay State Park
King Salmon
Katmai National Park and Preserve
Kenai National Wildlife Refuge
Shuyak Island State Park
Bristol Bay
Becharof National Wildlife Refuge
Port Lions
Kodiak
Chugach National Forest
Kodiak National Wildlife Refuge
ALASKA PENINSULA
Aniakchak National Monument and Preserve
Izembek National Wildlife Refuge
Alaska Peninsula National Wildlife Refuge

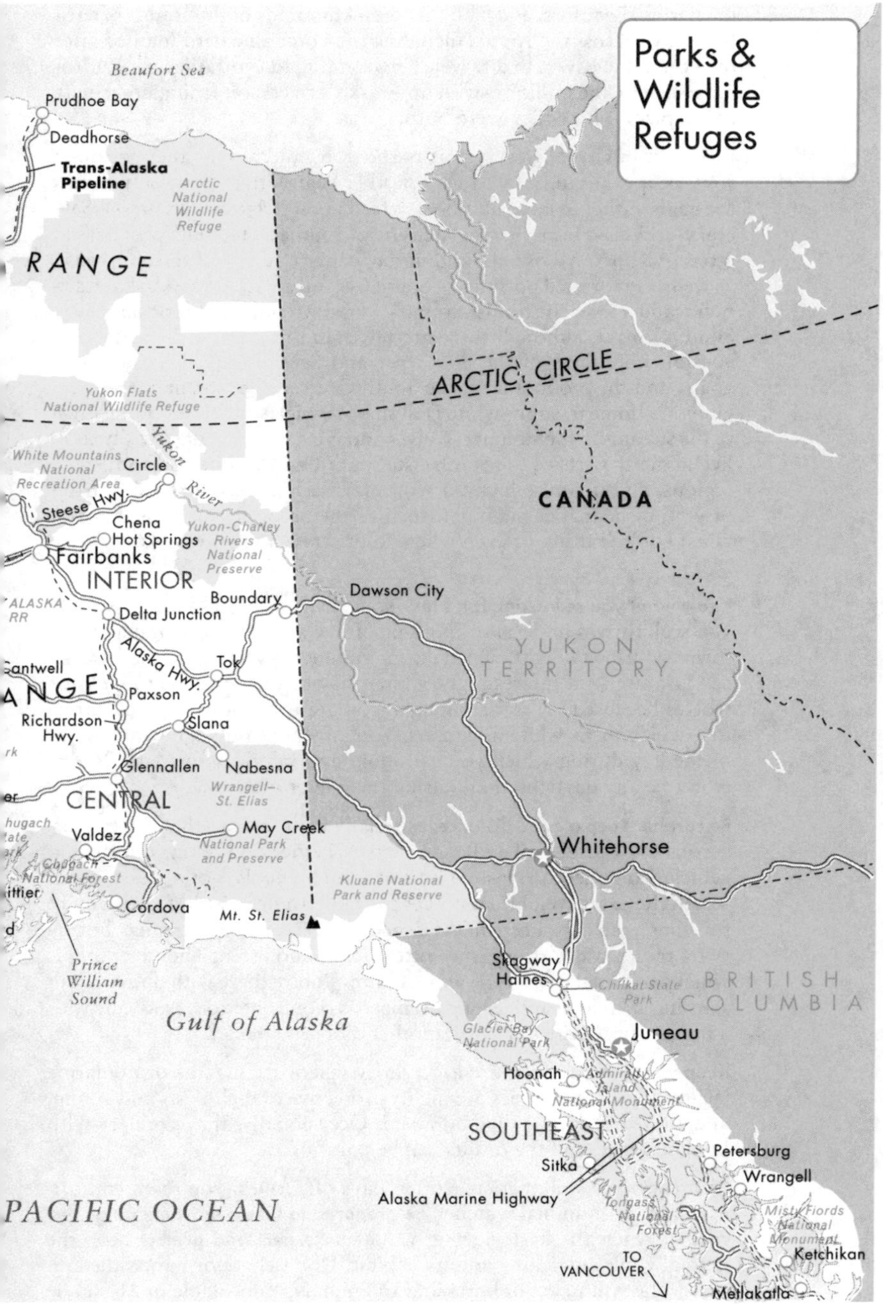
Parks & Wildlife Refuges
Beaufort Sea
Prudhoe Bay
Deadhorse
Trans-Alaska Pipeline
Arctic National Wildlife Refuge
RANGE
Yukon Flats National Wildlife Refuge
ARCTIC CIRCLE
CANADA
White Mountains National Recreation Area
Circle
Yukon River
Steese Hwy.
Chena Hot Springs
Yukon-Charley Rivers National Preserve
Fairbanks
INTERIOR
ALASKA RR
Boundary
Dawson City
Delta Junction
Alaska Hwy.
Tok
YUKON TERRITORY
Cantwell
ANGE
Paxson
Richardson Hwy.
Slana
Nabesna
Glennallen
Wrangell–St. Elias
CENTRAL
May Creek
National Park and Preserve
Valdez
Chugach National Forest
Whitehorse
Kluane National Park and Reserve
Cordova
Mt. St. Elias
Prince William Sound
Skagway
Haines
Chilkat State Park
BRITISH COLUMBIA
Gulf of Alaska
Glacier Bay National Park
Juneau
Hoonah
Admiralty Island National Monument
SOUTHEAST
Petersburg
Sitka
Wrangell
Alaska Marine Highway
PACIFIC OCEAN
Tongass National Forest
Misty Fiords National Monument
Ketchikan
TO VANCOUVER
Metlakatla

the Bering, Beaufort, and Chukchi seas. Hundreds of thousands of caribou move across the Arctic, including the Porcupine herd (named after the Porcupine River) that travels between Canada and Alaska. Anadromous fish by the millions swim up Alaska's rivers, returning unerringly to the place where they were born.

Bears live in virtually every part of the state, and though they are often solitary, it is not unusual to see a mother bear with cubs. In some areas the bears gather in large numbers to feed upon rich runs of salmon. Several world-class bear-viewing areas from Southeast to Southwest Alaska attract visitors. Moose abound in the wetter country of the Southeast, as well as in forested portions of South Central and Interior Alaska. Caribou wander over the tundra country of the Arctic, sub-Arctic, and even South Central, although there are fewer in this part of the state. The coastal mountains of the Southeast and South Central harbor wild goats, and the mountains of the South Central, Interior, and Arctic regions are home to snow-white Dall sheep, which sometimes come down to the streams in the summer. Wolves and lynx, though not so easily seen, live in many parts of the Southeast, South Central, Interior, and Arctic regions, and if you're lucky, a wolf may dash across the road in front of you, or a smaller mammal, such as the arctic fox, may watch you when you're rafting or even when you're traveling on wheels.

Strategies for Spotting Wildlife

Know what you're looking for. Have some idea of the habitat the wildlife you seek thrives in. Season and time of day are critical. You may want to view during twilight, which during summer in certain parts of Alaska can last all night. Interestingly, winter may be the best time to look for wolves because they stand out against the snow (not true for the arctic fox, which turns white in winter). You may have only a few hours out of the day during which you can look, and in northern Alaska, there won't be any daylight at all during the winter months.

Be careful. Keep a good distance, especially with animals that can be dangerous (⇨ CloseUp: The Bear Facts). Whether you're on foot or in a vehicle, don't get too close. A pair of good binoculars or a scope is well worth the extra weight. Don't get too close to or touch a fox (if you're traveling with pets, keep them leashed). The fox you admire may be carrying rabies. **Move slowly,** stop often, look, and listen. The exception is when you see a bear; let the animal know you're there with noise. Avoid startling an animal and risking a dangerous confrontation, especially with a mother bear with cubs or a mother moose with calf.

Keep your hat on if you are in territory where arctic terns or pomarine jaegers nest. Both species are highly protective of their nests and young, and they are skillful dive-bombers. Occasionally, they connect with human heads, and the results can be painful.

Be prepared to wait; patience often pays off. And if you're an enthusiastic birder or animal watcher, **be prepared to hike over some rough terrain** to reach the best viewing vantage. **Respect and protect** both the animal you're watching and its habitat. Don't chase or harass the animals. The willful act of harassing an animal is punishable in Alaska by a $1,000 fine. This includes flushing birds from their nests and purposely frightening animals with loud noises.

Don't disturb or surprise the animals, which also applies to birds' eggs, the young, the nests, and such habitats as beaver dams. It's best to let the animal discover your presence quietly, if at all, by keeping still or moving slowly (except when viewing bears or moose). If you accidentally disturb an animal, limit your viewing time and leave as quietly as possible. **Don't use a tape recorder or any device** to call a bird or to attract other animals if you're in bear country, as you might call an angry bear. And **don't feed the animals,** as any creature that comes to depend on humans for food almost always comes to a sorry end. Both state and federal laws prohibit the feeding of wild animals.

Best Viewing

Even those traveling by car in Alaska have abundant opportunity to spot wildlife. For those traveling by boat, the **Alaska Marine Highway**—the route plied by Alaska's state ferries—passes through waters rich with fish, sea mammals, and birds. Throughout the Southeast, ferries often provide sightings of whales and sea otters and virtually always of bald eagles. In **Kenai Fjords National Park,** tour boats enable you to view sea mammals and seabirds. Smaller boats and touring vessels are found in such places as **Glacier Bay National Park and Preserve,** an especially good place to spot humpback whales, puffins, seals, shorebirds, and perhaps a black or brown bear. **Denali National Park and Preserve** is known worldwide for its wildlife; you are likely to see grizzlies, moose, Dall sheep, caribou, foxes, golden eagles, and perhaps even wolves. The **Alaska Chilkat Bald Eagle Preserve** hosts the world's largest gathering of bald eagles each fall and winter. And Dall sheep that inhabit **Chugach State Park** can often be seen along the Seward Highway south of Anchorage.

BEARS You can't be absolutely sure you'll spot a grizzly bear in **Denali National Park and Preserve** (📫 Box 9, Denali National Park 99755 ☎ 907/683–2294 🌐 www.nps.gov/dena), but your chances are better than 50–50 that you'll see grizzlies digging in the tundra or eating berries. Sometimes females even nurse their cubs within sight of the park road. Talk with the staff at the visitor center near the park entrance when you arrive.

Katmai National Park (📫 Box 7, King Salmon 99613 ☎ 907/246–3305 🌐 www.nps.gov/katm), on the Alaska Peninsula, has an abundance of bears—on average more than one brown bear per square mile, among the highest densities of any region in North America. In July, when the salmon are running up Brooks River, bears concentrate around Brooks River Falls, resulting in a great view of these animals as they fish, and the spectacle of hundreds of salmon leaping the falls.

Kodiak National Wildlife Refuge (✉ 1390 Buskin Rd., Kodiak 99615 ☎ 907/487–2600 🌐 www.kodiak.fws.gov), on Kodiak Island, is an excellent place to see brown bears, particularly along salmon-spawning streams.

The **McNeil River State Game Sanctuary,** on the Alaska Peninsula, hosts the world's largest gathering of brown bears—as many as 70 have been counted at one time at McNeil Falls—and thus affords unsurpassed photographic opportunities. Peak season, when the local salmon are running, is early June through mid-August. Much-sought-after reservations are available by a lottery conducted in March by the **Alaska Department of Fish and Game** (✉ 333 Raspberry Rd., Anchorage 99518 ☎ 907/267–2182 🌐 www.wc.adfg.state.ak.us/mcneil/index.cfm).

At **Pack Creek,** on Admiralty Island, you'll see brown bears (the coastal equivalents of grizzlies) fishing for spawning salmon—pink, chum, and silver. To get here, you can fly (air charter) or take a boat from Juneau. If you time your visit to coincide with the salmon runs in July and August, you will almost surely see bald eagles and flocks of gulls, too. Permits are required to visit during the peak bear-viewing period; contact **Admiralty Island National Monument** (✉ 8461 Old Dairy Rd., Juneau 99801 ☎ 907/586–8790 🌐 www.fs.fed.us/r10/tongass/districts/admiralty/packweb/packhome.html).

The **Silver Salmon Creek Lodge** (📫 Box 3234, Soldotna 99669 ☎ 888/872–5666 🌐 www.silversalmoncreek.com) conducts a bear-viewing program along the shores of western Cook Inlet, near Lake Clark National Park, with lodging, meals, and guide services for both bear viewing and sportfishing.

BIRDS If you come on your own, try the following sure and easily accessed bets for bird spotting. In **Anchorage,** walk around Potter Marsh or Westchester Lagoon or along the Coastal Trail for shorebirds, waterfowl, and the occasional bald eagle. Songbird enthusiasts are likely to see many species in town or neighboring Chugach State Park. The **Anchorage Audubon Society** (☎ 907/338–2473) has a bird-report recording.

In **Juneau,** visit the Mendenhall Wetlands State Game Refuge, next to the airport, for ducks, geese, and swans (there are trails and interpretive signs). In **Fairbanks,** head for the Creamer's Field Migratory Waterfowl Refuge on College Road. Here, if you're lucky, you might see sandhill cranes in summer and spectacular shows of ducks and geese in spring.

Great crowds of bald eagles visit the Chilkat River, near **Haines** in Southeast Alaska, each November and December. In the summer, rafting on almost any Alaskan river brings the near certainty of sighting nesting shorebirds, arctic terns, and merganser mothers trailed by chicks. Approximately 200 species of birds have been sighted on the **Pribilof Islands,** but you will almost certainly need to be part of a guided tour to get there.

CARIBOU The migrations of caribou across Alaska's Arctic regions are wonderful to watch, but they are not always easy to time because of annual variations in weather and routes that the herds follow. The U.S. Fish and Wildlife Service and Alaska Department of Fish and Game will have the best guess as to where you should be and when. Or you can settle for seeing a few caribou in places such as Denali National Park.

MARINE ANIMALS At **Round Island,** outside Dillingham in the Southwest, bull walruses by the thousands haul out during the summer. Part of the Walrus Islands State Game Sanctuary, Round Island can be visited by permit only. For details, contact the **Alaska Department of Fish and Game** (📫 Box 1030, Dillingham 99576 ☎ 907/842–2334 🌐 www.wildlife.alaska.gov/index.cfm?adfg=refuge.rnd_is). Access is by floatplane or, more commonly, by

THE BEAR FACTS

ALASKA IS SOMETIMES CALLED "BEAR COUNTRY," *and for good reason. It is the only one of the nation's 50 states to be inhabited by all three North American ursine species: the polar bear, black bear, and brown bear (also known as grizzly). The statewide population of each species thrives, thanks largely to Alaska's abundance of wild, remote, and undeveloped regions.*

You'll find few places in Alaska where bears don't inhabit the landscape. Even Anchorage, with its urban developments and large human population, is visited by black and brown bears. Wherever you venture in Alaska, keep in mind these tips for travel in bear country:

Avoid sudden encounters. *Whenever possible, travel in open country, during daylight hours, and in groups. Make noise—talking or singing is preferable to carrying "bear bells"—and leave your dog at home. Most attacks occur when a bear is surprised at close quarters or feels threatened.*

Stay alert. *Look for signs of bears, such as fresh tracks, scat, matted vegetation, or partially consumed salmon.*

Choose your tent site carefully. *Pitch the tent away from trails, streams with spawning salmon, and berry patches. Avoid areas that have a rotten smell or where scavengers have gathered; these may indicate the presence of a nearby bear cache, and bears aggressively defend their food supplies.*

Keep food away from campsites. *Cook meals at least 100 feet from tents, and store food and other odorous items away from campsites. Hang food between trees where possible, or store your food in bear-resistant food containers. Avoid strong-smelling foods, and clean up after cooking and eating. Store garbage in airtight containers or burn it, and pack up the remains.*

If you encounter a bear:

Identify yourself. *Talk to the bear, to identify yourself as a human. Don't yell. And don't run. Running will trigger a bear's predatory instincts, and a bear can easily outrun you. Back away slowly, and give the bear an escape route. Don't ever get between a mother and her cubs.*

Bigger is better. *Bears are less likely to attack a larger target. Therefore, increase your apparent size. Raise your arms above your head to appear larger and wave them slowly, to better identify yourself as a human. With two or more people, it helps to stand side by side. In a forested area it may be appropriate to climb a tree, but remember that black bears and young grizzlies are agile tree climbers.*

As a last resort, play dead. *If a bear charges and makes contact with you, fall to the ground, lie flat on your stomach or curl into a ball, hands behind your neck, and remain passive. If you are wearing a pack, leave it on. Once a bear no longer feels threatened, it will usually end its attack. Wait for the bear to leave before you move. The exception to this rule is when a bear displays predatory behavior. Instead of simply charging, a bear hunting for prey will show intense interest while approaching at a walk or run and it may circle, as if stalking you. But remember that such circumstances are exceedingly rare and most often involve black bears, which are much smaller and less aggressive than grizzlies (and can be driven off more easily).*

boat. Expect rain, winds, and the possibility of being weathered in. Rubber boots are essential, as are a four-season tent, high-quality rain gear, and plenty of food.

It's easier, but expensive (more than $1,000 for travel and tour) to visit the remote **Pribilof Islands**—where about 80% of the world's northern fur seals and 200 species of birds can be seen—but you may also encounter fog and Bering Sea storms. Tours to the Pribilofs leave from Anchorage. Contact the **Alaska Maritime National Wildlife Refuge** (✉ 95 Sterling Hwy., Suite 1, Homer 99603 ☎ 907/235–6546 or 907/235–6961 🌐 www.r7.fws.gov) for information about wildlife viewing.

Whale-Watching Cruises

Fodor's Choice ★ A close encounter with whales in their natural environment can be a thrilling experience. Hearing the resonant whoosh of a whale exhaling and witnessing such acrobatics as "spy-hopping" (a whale poking its head straight out of the water for a look around), breaching, and skimming, you can't help but feel amazed and humbled by their awesome presence.

It's possible to see migrating whales along much of Alaska's coast from March through September: from the Southeast region's Inside Passage to South Central's Prince William Sound, Kodiak Archipelago, and Kenai Fjords National Park, and then north through the Bering, Chukchi, and Beaufort seas in Arctic waters. The whales most commonly seen on whale-watching trips are orcas (or killer whales) and humpbacks.

Whale watching is not the average spectator sport. It's more like a seagoing game of hide-and-seek. Whales are unpredictable, so be prepared to wait and watch patiently, scanning the water for signs. Sometimes it seems that the whales don't want to be watched; other times they might rub up against the boat. Also unpredictable are the weather and sea conditions. You can get wet and chilled, and possibly seasick.

Most cruises travel in or through waters that attract several species, although some focus on a particular type of whale. If you **ask when the best time to take a specific trip is,** you may find out that the sighting record is better during some months than others. You have to weigh the pros and cons of traveling on small versus large boats. Make sure you know what kind of boat is used for the trip you are considering. A trip with 15 people is certain to be quite different from one with 150. The larger boats can handle stormy seas much better than the smaller boats and offer much better indoor accommodations when the weather turns nasty. The smaller boats should appeal to those who want to steer clear of crowds; plus you feel closer to the surrounding seascape. More flexible itineraries are another benefit of small boats.

Tour Companies

Glacier Bay Cruiseline. Multiday tours through the Inside Passage provide opportunities to view whales and other marine life, such as sea otters, porpoises, seals, and seabirds. Trips into Glacier Bay National Park run from the dock at Bartlett Cove, near Glacier Bay Lodge. Watching for whales, as well as calving glaciers, is part of the daily routine. Naturalists on board provide local expertise. ✉ *2101 4th Ave., Suite*

2200, Seattle, WA 98121 ☎ *800/451–5952* 🖷 *206/623–7809* 🌐 *www.glacierbaycruiseline.com.*

Mariah Tours. Seward's small-boat trips offer whale-watching and glacier tours into Kenai Fjords National Park. Its two boats carry no more than 16 guests each. Mariah runs 9- to 9½-hour tours into the park, including a "captain's choice" that goes where the wildlife action is. Tours run from mid-May through early September. Besides orcas and humpback whales, you're likely to see bald eagles, sea otters, sea lions, seals, and thousands of seabirds. 📫 *2525 C St., Suite 405, Anchorage 99503* ☎ *907/777–2805 or 877/777–2805* 🖷 *907/777–2888* 🌐 *www.alaskaheritagetours.com.*

★ **Kenai Fjords Tours.** Part of the Native-owned Alaska Heritage Tours, this company's tours include those that explore Resurrection Bay and Kenai Fjords National Park in South Central Alaska. They range from three-hour natural-history tours to five-hour gray-whale-watching tours (late March to early May only) and full-day cruises to Aialik Bay or Northwestern Fjord. Prime whale-watching time for orcas and humpback whales is June through August. Most of the company's boats are 75 feet–95 feet long, with room for 90–150 passengers, but it also has a smaller vessel with a 22-passenger limit. Overnight packages can also be arranged. ✉ *2525 C St., Suite 405, Anchorage 99503* ☎ *907/777–2805 or 877/777–2805* 🖷 *907/777–2888* 🌐 *www.alaskaheritagetours.com.*

SPORTS & OUTFITTERS

Vacationing in Alaska can be a lot more than viewing glaciers. An increasing number of trips and tours now make it possible to spend a week or two (or more) learning—and performing—feats from horsepacking within sight of Mt. McKinley to mushing through some of the state's most challenging landscapes, including Gates of the Arctic National Park, far above the Arctic Circle. Below you'll find some recommended trips, questions to consider, and suggestions to help you choose the right program.

Dogsledding

"Hike!" commands a musher as he releases a brake. They don't call it "mushing" for nothing. The word is from the French *moucher,* which means "to go fast." And the dogs do. On command, a team of surprisingly small but amazingly strong huskies charges off, howling and yowling excitedly. Of all the wild sporting adventures out there, dogsledding may be the wildest—you're literally out in the wild with pack animals, just like a polar explorer.

Dogsledding is not for everyone. For one thing, you have to like the cold. You also have to like roughing it. Even the nicest accommodations are only a step or two removed from camping, and with camping out comes cooking out. Most important, you have to like dogs—a lot. Contrary to the romantic image you may have of sled dogs, they're not all cuddly, clean Siberian huskies. They're often mutts—that is, mixed-breed Alaskan huskies—and often not particularly well groomed. Most mushers, including the people who run dogsled tours, take very good care of their dogs, but the dogs are working dogs, not show dogs or pets.

Here are some facts to consider when choosing your trip: on some mushing trips, participants travel by cross-country skiing or snowshoeing, rather than actually mushing, for at least part of the trip; some introduction to these sports is usually included in your orientation. **If you're not interested in skiing or snowshoeing, make sure you'll be given a sled.** It's always smart to **get a good idea of how strenuous the outfitter's pace is.** If you're expecting a relaxing vacation, make sure you don't pick an outfitter who will have you doing everything from hitching up the dogs to pitching tents.

Outfitters

There's usually enough snow on the ground for dogsled runs from October or November through March or April.

Chugach Express Dog Sled Tours. Year-round mushing tours pass through a valley surrounded by the Chugach Mountains, about an hour's drive south of Anchorage. The one-hour tours include a visit to the kennel of the owner, a former Iditarod musher, and you can learn about dog care, feeding, breeding, and equipment. You can also drive the team. *Box 1396, Girdwood 99587 907/783–2266, 907/783–7669 (for reservations).*

Redington Sled Dog Rides. Raymie Redington, son of the Iditarod Trail Sled Dog Race's founding father, Joe Redington Sr., leads half-hour to overnight mushing trips along the historic Iditarod Trail in the Susitna Valley north of Anchorage. *Mile 12.5, Knik Rd. Box 877653, Wasilla 99687 907/376–6730.*

★ **Sourdough Outfitters.** From February through April, 4- to 11-day sledding expeditions are organized within the Gates of the Arctic National Park and the North Slope, among the world's last great wilderness areas. Sourdough Outfitters also leads day trips in and around the community of Bettles, where the outfit is based. The owners provide all camping gear plus special boots, heavy-hooded parkas, insulated windproof mittens, and snowshoes. *Box 26066, Bettles Field 99726 907/692–5252 www.sourdoughoutfitters.com.*

Glacier Trekking

An estimated 100,000 glaciers flow out of Alaska's mountains, covering 29,000 square mi—or 5% of the state. These slow-moving "rivers of ice" concentrate in the Alaska Range, Wrangell Mountains, and the state's major coastal mountain chains: the Chugach, St. Elias, Coast, and Kenai ranges. Alaska's largest glacier, the Bering, covers 2,250 square mi—twice the size of Rhode Island.

Glaciers are formed where annual snowfall exceeds melting. As it accumulates, snow is buried and recrystallized. Eventually it becomes compacted into dense, airless ice, sometimes thousands of feet thick. Where glaciers reach tidewater, as at Glacier Bay and Kenai Fjords National Parks, they may calve immense icebergs.

Many glaciers can be approached from Alaska's road system or coastal waters—but don't try to walk on them, or even get too close, without the proper gear and training. Large chunks of ice sometimes fall from a glacier's snout with no forewarning; unwitting sightseers have been killed by such ice blocks when standing too close. Unprepared trekkers have also slipped and fallen to their deaths in the glacier's crevasses. If you're an adventurous backcountry traveler, glaciers present icy avenues into the remote corners of several premier mountain wilderness areas, including Denali, Wrangell–St. Elias, and Kenai Fjords national parks and Chugach and Kachemak Bay state parks.

Glacier travel should be attempted only after you've been properly trained. Glacier terrain includes a mix of ice, rock debris, and often-deep surface snow; sometimes frigid pools of meltwater collect on the surface or icy rivulets flow across the glacier. Most dangerous are glacier crevasses. Sometimes hidden by snow, especially in spring and early summer (a popular time for glacier trekking), these cracks in the ice may present life-threatening traps for unwary travelers. Though some are only inches wide, others may be several yards across and hundreds of feet deep. If you haven't been taught proper glacial travel and crevasse-rescue techniques, **hire a backcountry guide** to provide the necessary gear and expertise. Some companies offer day or half-day hikes onto glaciers that don't have the same physical demands as longer treks but that still require proper equipment and training. For instance, St. Elias Alpine Guides takes hikers of all ages and abilities on one of its glacier walks.

Outfitters

Alaska Mountaineering School. Whether it's on mountaineering expeditions to 20,320-foot Mt. McKinley or less extreme treks into the Alaska Range or other mountains, this company takes wilderness explorers on glacier treks through pristine backcountry. You can also learn the region's natural and human history while exploring rugged mountain landscapes. The mountaineering school can provide training before you go. *Box 566, Talkeetna 99676* *907/733–1016* *907/733–1362* *www.climbalaska.org*.

★ **St. Elias Alpine Guides.** Based in the town of McCarthy, within Wrangell–St. Elias National Park, St. Elias Alpine Guides conducts day hikes to nearby glaciers and also leads extended glacier treks into the wild backcountry of this "mountain kingdom." *Box 92129, Anchorage 99509* *888/933–5427 or 907/554–4445* *907/554–4409* *www.steliasguides.com*.

Hiking & Backpacking

From Southeast coastal rain forest to Interior mountain meadows with spectacular views of Mt. McKinley and alpine tundra in the high Arctic, Alaska presents some of the continent's finest landscape for wilderness hiking and backpacking. Or, if remote backcountry is not your preference, it's possible to travel well-maintained and well-marked trails on the edges of Alaska's largest city and still get a taste of the wild. Many of the "frontcountry" trails in road-accessible parklands, refuges, and forests are well maintained and cross terrain that is easy for novice hikers, the elderly, and families with children.

Chugach State Park, along Anchorage's eastern edge, has dozens of trails, many of them suited for frontcountry explorers. And though it is best known for its "trail-less wilderness," Denali National Park has several easy-to-hike trails near the park entrance, while nearby "Little Denali"—Denali State Park—has the 36-mi-long Kesugi Ridge Trail, within easy reach of the Parks Highway. These, however, are exceptions to the rule. Most of Alaska remains pristine wilderness, with few or no trails. In such areas it's best to be with an experienced backcountry traveler who understands the dangers and challenges of trail-less wilderness terrain: how to behave in bear country, how to navigate using map and compass techniques, and how to cross glacial streams.

Terrain

FORESTS Forest trails are often wet, especially in coastal lowlands, and they may be soggy or potholed—sometimes they're even blocked with beaver dams. Trails through forested lands are difficult to maintain. The ground stays wet much of the time, and brush grows back quickly after it is cut. Especially nasty is devil's club, a large, attractive plant with greenish flowers that eventually become a cluster of bright red berries; it's also thickly armored with stinging needles. Virtually all hiking country in the Southeast is part of the 17-million-acre Tongass National Forest, administered by the U.S. Forest Service. Several popular trails have also been built within Chugach National Forest and Chugach State Park in South Central Alaska. Although the Forest Service does not consider trail maintenance a top priority, it is a good source for checking the latest condition of backcountry roads and paths.

RIVERS Crossing Alaska's rivers requires care. Many are swift, glacial, silty streams that are harder to read than clear-water streams. Many flow over impermeable bottoms (either rock or permafrost), which means a good rain can raise water levels a matter of feet, not inches, in just a short time. Warm days can also dramatically increase the meltwater from glaciers. Be aware of weather changes that might affect the ease of river crossings. Look for the widest, shallowest place you can find, with many channels. This may entail traveling up- or downstream. A guide who knows the region is invaluable at such times.

A sturdy staff—your own or made from a handy branch—is useful to help you keep your balance and measure the depths of silty water. You should unbuckle your pack when crossing a swift stream; you can then shed it if you need to. Avoid wearing a long rain poncho; it can catch the water like a sail catches wind and tip you off your feet. For added stability it may help for two or more people to link arms when crossing. Hikers debate the best footwear for crossing Alaskan rivers. Some take along sneakers and wear them through the water; others take off their socks so they will remain dry and can comfort cold feet on the opposite shore. But bear in mind that Alaskan waters are probably frigid, and the bottom is usually rough; bare feet are not advised. One school even advocates wearing your boots—socks and all—and continuing your hike with wet feet.

TUNDRA Tundra hiking—especially in higher alpine country—can be a great pleasure. In places, the ground is so springy you feel like you're walking on a trampoline. In the Arctic, however, where the ground is underlaid with permafrost, you will probably find the going as wet as it is in the Southeast forests, particularly at lower elevations. The summer sun melts the top, often a thin layer above the permafrost, leaving puddles, small lakes, and marshy spots behind. Comfortable waterproof footgear can help when traversing such wet landscapes. Tundra travel can require the skill of a ballet dancer if the ground is tufted with tussocks (mushroom-shape clumps of grass, making slippery, unstable hummocks). Tussocky tundra can quickly tire those not used to such terrain and it slows the pace of even the most experienced hikers.

Outfitters

Alaska Mountaineering School. Though perhaps best known for its mountaineering expeditions on Mt. McKinley, this company also leads custom-designed backcountry expeditions in the Alaska Range and other mountain chains around the state. The company emphasizes a "holistic" approach to its trips, which entails learning about the natural and human history of the area, from the wildflowers and native birds to the early explorers; "getting there" is not simply about reaching the destination or summit. *Box 566, Talkeetna 99676* *907/733–1016* *907/733–1362* *www.climbalaska.org.*

Alaska Nature Tours and Backcountry Outfitters. This company in Southeast Alaska leads hiking trips into the Alaska Chilkat Bald Eagle Preserve near Haines from May through September, with an emphasis on the area's natural history. Outings range from beach walks and rainforest hikes to more strenuous alpine hikes. *Box 491, Haines 99827* *907/766–2876* *907/766–2844* *www.kcd.com/aknature.*

★ **Arctic Treks.** Wilderness hiking and backpacking trips, sometimes combined with river trips, explore areas throughout the Arctic region's Brooks Range, including two of North America's most remote and ruggedly beautiful wildlands: Gates of the Arctic National Park and the Arctic National Wildlife Refuge. *Box 73452, Fairbanks 99707* *907/455–6502* *907/455–6522* *www.arctictreksadventures.com.*

St. Elias Alpine Guides. For more than a quarter century, this outfitter has been taking people into a part of Alaska that some people call North America's mountain kingdom: the St. Elias and Wrangell mountain ranges. Based in the town of McCarthy, within Wrangell–St. Elias National Park, St. Elias Alpine Guides leads a full spectrum of day activities, including ghost-town tours of the Kennicott Mine, glacier walks, mountain hikes, and nature tours. The company also guides mountain ascents and extended backpacking expeditions. *Box 92129, Anchorage 99509* *888/933–5427 or 907/554–4445* *907/554–4409* *www.steliasguides.com.*

Horsepacking

There are no traffic jams and no overcrowded campgrounds on horsepacking vacations. The farther into the wilderness you go, the more untouched and spectacular the landscape. You can also cover a lot more ground with less effort than you can while backpacking.

To minimize a horsepacking group's impact on the environment, most are limited to 12 riders. Some go down to just three or four. Most outfits post at least two wranglers for 12 guests, and some bring along another person who serves as cook and/or assistant wrangler. All outfitters who operate on federal lands are required to have a permit.

It's a good idea to **find out how much time is spent in the saddle** each day and how difficult the riding is. Six hours is a long day in the saddle, and although some outfitters schedule that much, most keep the riding time to about four hours. Most trips move at a walk, but some trot, lope, and even gallop. As with many other guided adventures, special expertise is not required for horsepacking.

On trips into the wilderness, expect the food to be straightforward cowboy fare, cooked over a campfire or cookstove. Although a cook goes along on some trips, guides often pull double duty in the kitchen, and often a little help from group members is willingly accepted. **If you have any dietary restrictions, make arrangements beforehand.** For lodging, don't allow yourself to be surprised: **find out what the rooms are like** if you're going to be staying in motels or cabins, and if the trip involves camping, **ask about the campsites** and about shower and latrine arrangements.

Outfitters

Castle Mountain Outfitters. Based in the Matanuska Valley below towering mountains, this outfitter conducts a variety of trips ranging from guided hour-long horseback rides to one-week horsepacking expeditions. *Box 115, Chickaloon 99674 907/745–6427 907/745–6428.*

Wrangell Outfitters. This husband-wife team takes visitors on horsepacking trips into the alpine heart of Wrangell–St. Elias National Park, for activities that range from hiking and camping to photography and wildlife viewing. *1680 Wolverine La., Fairbanks 99709 907/479–5343 907/479–5344 www.wrangelloutfitters.com.*

River Rafting

From the Southeast Panhandle to the far reaches of the Arctic, Alaska is blessed with an abundance of wild, pristine rivers. The federal government has officially designated more than two dozen of Alaskan streams as "wild and scenic rivers," but hundreds more would easily qualify for that description. Some meander gently through forests or tundra. Others, fed by glacier runoff, rush wildly through mountains and canyons.

Because so much of Alaska is roadless wilderness, rivers often serve as the best avenues to explore the landscape and view wildlife. This is especially true in several of Alaska's premier parklands and refuges. Here, as elsewhere, rivers are ranked according to their degrees of difficulty. Class I rivers are considered to be "easy" floats with minimal rapids; at the other extreme, Class VI rivers are extremely dangerous and nearly impossible to navigate. Generally only very experienced river runners should attempt anything above Class II on their own. Also be aware that river conditions change considerably from season to season and sometimes day to day. **Always check ahead to determine a river's current condition.** Do-it-yourselfers would be wise to consult two books on Alaska's rivers: *Fast & Cold: A Guide to Alaska Whitewater* (Skyhouse), by Andrew Embick (though intended primarily for white-water kayakers, it has good information for rafters as well), and *The Alaska River Guide: Canoeing, Kayaking, and Rafting in the Last Frontier* (Alaska Northwest Books), by Karen Jettmar.

Fortunately you don't have to be an expert river runner to explore many of Alaska's premier waterways. Experienced rafting companies operate throughout the state. Some outfits emphasize extended wilderness trips and natural-history observations, whereas others specialize in thrilling one-day (or shorter) floats through Class III and IV white water that will get your adrenaline pumping. And some combine a little of both.

Be certain that the guide gives you a safety talk before going on the water. It's important to know what you should do if you do get flipped out of the raft or if the boat overturns. Also find out what gear and clothing are required. Ask if you'll be paddling or simply riding as a passenger. Reputable rafting companies will discuss all of this, but it never hurts to ask.

Outfitters

Alaska Discovery. This outfitter leads 9- to 12-day trips down two of North America's wildest rivers, the Tatshenshini and Alsek. The river trips begin in Canada and end in one of Alaska's premier parklands, Glacier Bay, as rafters float between peaks nearly 3 mi high and through valleys inhabited by grizzlies, moose, and sometimes wolves. The company also does 10- to 12-day combined rafting and hiking trips in the Arctic National Wildlife Refuge and on the Noatak River, which runs through Gates of the Arctic National Park. ✉ *5310 Glacier Hwy., Juneau 99801* ☎ *907/780–6226 or 800/586–1911* 📠 *907/780–4220* 🌐 *www.akdiscovery.com.*

Denali Raft Adventures. River trips are conducted on the glacially fed, white-water Nenana River, which skirts the eastern boundary of Denali National Park. Trips vary from two-hour Class I–II scenic floats or white-water canyon trips with big rapids to all-day floats. The two-hour scenic and canyon trips can also be combined. 📫 *Drawer 190 DRA, Denali Park 99755* ☎ *907/683–2234 or 888/683–2234* 📠 *907/683–1281* 🌐 *www.denaliraft.com.*

★ **Nova.** This outfitter has been rafting Alaska's rivers since 1975. For most of that time, the company has specialized in full-, part-, or multiday white-water trips down the Matanuska, Chickaloon, and Talkeetna rivers in South Central Alaska. Over the past decade, Nova has expanded its reach and now also leads multiday float trips through Wrangell–St. Elias National Park and part-day trips on the Kenai Peninsula's Six-Mile River. White-water ratings range from Class I to Class V. ✉ *Mile 76, Glenn Hwy.* 📫 *Box 1129, Chickaloon 99674* ☎ *907/745–5753 or 800/746–5753* 📠 *907/745–5754* 🌐 *www.novalaska.com.*

Wilderness Birding Adventures. The owners are both experienced river runners and expert birders. Among their trips is a rafting, hiking, and birding expedition through one of the world's last great wilderness areas, the Arctic National Wildlife Refuge. ✉ *5515 Wild Mountain Rd., Eagle River 99577* ☎📠 *907/694–7442* 🌐 *www.wildernessbirding.com.*

Sea Kayaking

Fodor's Choice ★ Sea kayaking can be as thrilling or as peaceful as you make it. More stable than a white-water kayak and more comfortable than a canoe, a sea kayak—even one loaded with a week's worth of gear—is maneuverable enough to poke into hidden crevices, explore side bays, and beach on deserted spits of sand.

Anyone who doesn't mind getting a little wet and has an average degree of fitness can be a sea kayaker. The basic stroke is performed in a circular motion with a double-bladed paddle: you pull one blade through the water while pushing forward with the other through the air. Most people pick it up with a minimal amount of instruction. Don't assume, though, that if you've done 10 minutes without tipping over you'll be adequately prepared to circumnavigate Glacier Bay National Park. There's a lot to learn, and until you know your way around tides, currents, and nautical charts, you should go with an experienced guide who also knows what and how to pack and where to pitch a tent. A reputable outfitter can supply such a guide.

It is important for you to **honestly evaluate your own tolerance for cold, dampness, and high winds.** Nothing can ruin a trip faster than pervasive discomfort. Always **ask whether the outfitter stocks a variety of boats,** so you can experiment until you find the kayak that best fits your weight, strength, ability, and paddling style.

Outfitters

★ **Alaska Discovery.** One of Alaska's oldest outfitters, this company has been running low-impact, nature-oriented adventure trips since 1972. Experienced guides know Southeast Alaska intimately, and they emphasize both sea-kayaking skills and safety in their instruction. Destinations include Tracy Arm, Glacier Bay, Icy Bay, Point Adolphus (an excellent spot for whale watching), Admiralty Island (with bear viewing at Pack Creek), and Granite Fjord. Alaska Discovery also now leads an inn-to-inn paddling trip through the Kenai Peninsula's Kachemak Bay. ✉ *5310 Glacier Hwy., Juneau 99801* ☎ *907/780–6226 or 800/586–1911* 🖷 *907/780–4220* 🌐 *www.akdiscovery.com.*

Spirit Walker Expeditions, Inc. This veteran Southeast company offers guided wilderness sea-kayaking trips that combine a mix of scenery, wildlife, solitude, and paddling within the Inside Passage. Guides prepare meals, offer instruction, and provide all needed paddling gear. Beginners are welcome. 📫 *Box 240, Gustavus 99826* ☎ *907/697–2266 or 800/529–2537* 🖷 *907/697–2701* 🌐 *www.seakayakalaska.com.*

Sunny Cove Sea Kayaking Company. Extended trips in and around Kenai Fjords National Park in South Central Alaska include five nights of camping at Northwestern Fjord or three nights in Aialik Bay; at both locales kayakers can paddle among icebergs, seals, and seabirds as tidewater glaciers calve in the distance. Day and overnight trips navigate within Resurrection Bay, near Seward. Tours include kayaking equipment and instruction, meals, and lots of chances to see wildlife. Combination tours with Kenai Fjords Cruises are also offered. 📫 *Box 3332, Seward 99664*

☎ *907/224–8810, 800/770–9119 reservations* 🖷 *907/224–881* 🌐 *www.sunnycove.com.*

Skiing

It may not have the reputation of several other western states, but Alaska offers plenty of skiing terrain for both Nordic skiers and downhill racers. Three of Alaska's largest cities—Anchorage, Fairbanks, and Juneau—have nearby alpine ski areas, complete with equipment rentals, ski schools, and other amenities. Many of Alaska's towns, both large and small, have regularly maintained trails for cross-country skiers. Anchorage's trail system is considered among the nation's finest and has hosted world-class races.

For those who are more ambitious, Alaska's wilderness areas present unlimited opportunities—and lots of challenges. Unless you are knowledgeable in winter backcountry travel, camping techniques, and avalanche dangers, the best strategy is to hire a guide when exploring Alaska's backcountry on skis. Given the extremes of Alaska's winters, your primary concern should be safety: **be sure your guide has had avalanche-awareness and winter-survival training.** Conditions can change quickly, especially in mountainous areas, and what began as an easy cross-country ski trip can suddenly become a survival saga if you're not prepared for the challenges of an Alaska winter.

When you are prepared, the rewards of backcountry skiing are well worth the hardships and challenges: immense solitude and quiet, sparkling skies; fantastic landscapes; and, if you're lucky, a display of northern lights or perhaps the distant howling of wolves.

Outfitters

Alaska Mountaineering School. Custom cross-country ski trips of varying lengths and degrees of difficulty can be arranged, primarily through Denali national and state parks, with an emphasis on natural history as well as backcountry exploration and the challenges of winter travel. 📫 *Box 566, Talkeetna 99676* ☎ *907/733–1016* 🖷 *907/733–1362* 🌐 *www.climbalaska.org.*

Alaska Nature Tours and Backcountry Outfitters. This company in Southeast Alaska rents ski gear and, from December through March, leads five-hour Nordic ski trips into the Alaska Chilkat Bald Eagle Preserve near Haines. If you visit in early winter, you are likely to see many of the bald eagles that visit the preserve annually. 📫 *Box 491, Haines 99827* ☎ *907/766–2876* 🖷 *907/766–2844* 🌐 *www.kcd.com/aknature.*

★ **Ultima Thule Outfitters.** Based at a fly-in-only lodge on the Chitina River within Wrangell–St. Elias National Park, Ultima Thule leads guided activities in the surrounding mountains, including alpine treks and Nordic and telemark skiing. Other adventures include mushing, wildlife viewing, rafting, and mountain climbing. A longtime presence in the St. Elias Mountains, Ultima Thule is known as much for its family-style hospitality as its scenic backcountry adventures. 📫 *Box 109, Chitina 99566* ☎ *907/258–0636* 🖷 *907/278–2292* 🌐 *www.ultimathulelodge.com.*

Sportfishing

Filled with hundreds of species of fish, including many highly prized catches, Alaska's more than 3 million lakes, innumerable streams, and thousands of miles of coastal waters are an angler's paradise. All five species of Pacific salmon (king, silver, sockeye, pink, and chum) spawn in Alaska's waters, alongside ample quantities of rainbow trout, steelhead, arctic char, Dolly Varden char, arctic grayling, northern pike, and halibut.

A few fish reach huge proportions: for example, a world-record king salmon weighing 97¼ pounds was caught in Alaska's Kenai River, and halibut exceeding 300—and occasionally 400—pounds are annually caught in Pacific Ocean waters. But some anglers will tell you that bigger isn't necessarily better. Sockeye, among the smallest salmon, are considered by many to be both the best tasting and best fighting, pound for pound, of any fish. And though the arctic grayling commonly weighs a pound or less, it is a favorite among fly fishermen.

Roadside fishing for salmon, trout, char, and grayling is possible in South Central and Interior Alaska. In fact, Alaska's best-known salmon stream, the Kenai River, is road accessible. But in most of the state, prime fishing waters can be reached only by boat or air. Not surprisingly, hundreds of fishing charters and dozens of sportfishing lodges operate statewide, attracting anglers from around the world. Southwest Alaska, in particular, is known for its fishing, but many of its prime spots are remote and expensive to reach.

You should be aware that sportfishing regulations vary widely from area to area. Licenses are required for both fresh- and saltwater fishing. To learn more about regulations, contact the **Alaska Department of Fish and Game** (Box 25526, Juneau 99802-5526 907/465-4180 sportfishing seasons and regulations, 907/465-2376 licenses www.adfg.state.ak.us).

Outfitters & Charters

When hiring a guide, **ask what species are likely to be caught, catch limits, and any special equipment or clothing needs.** Normally, all necessary fishing gear is provided and the guides will teach you the appropriate fishing techniques. In some cases, catch-and-release ethics may be emphasized.

Alaskan Fishing Adventures. Anglers are guided in several areas of the Kenai Peninsula south of Anchorage, including Resurrection Bay, Cook Inlet, and the Kenai River, home of the famous "Kenai Kings," salmon that may reach 90 pounds or more. Among the other species they catch are halibut, sockeye and silver salmon, and rainbow trout. Boats have a four-person limit on rivers, six-person limit on salt water. *Box 2457, Soldotna 99669 800/548-3474 907/262-0827 www.alaskanfishing.com.*

Central Charter Booking Agency. In Homer, this company can arrange fishing trips in outer Kachemak Bay and Lower Cook Inlet, areas known for excellent halibut fishing. Though most charters focus on halibut, some also fish for salmon. Boat sizes vary considerably; some have a 6-person limit, whereas others can take up to 16 passengers. *4241 Homer*

Spit, Homer 99603 ☎ 907/235–7847 or 800/478–7847 📠 907/235–2895 🌐 www.centralcharter.com.

Great Alaska Adventure Lodge. Fishing packages are among the adventure trips run out of this Kenai River lodge. Trips include fly-in fish camps, river floats, and saltwater charters. Expert guides can get you into king, silver, and pink salmon; halibut; rainbow trout; and grayling. Stories are traded at happy hour and during dinner in the lodge. *✉ 33881 Sterling Hwy., Sterling 99672 ☎ 907/262–4515 in summer, 360/697–6454 in winter, 800/544–2261 year-round 📠 907/262–8797 🌐 www.greatalaska.com.*

Alaska's Top Fish & Their Sources

SPECIES	COMMON NAME	WHERE FOUND
Arctic Char (F, S)	Char	SC, SW, NW, I, A
Arctic Grayling (F)	Grayling	SE, SC, SW, NW, I, A
Brook Trout (F)	Brookie	SE
Burbot (F)	Lingcod	SC, SW, NW, A
Chinook (F, S)	King Salmon	SE, SC, SW, I
Chum Salmon (F, S)	Dog Salmon	SE, SC, SW, NW, I
Coho Salmon (F, S)	Silver Salmon	SE, SC, SW, NW, I
Cutthroat Trout (F, S)	Cutthroat	SE, SC
Dolly Varden (F, S)	Dolly	SE, SC, SW, NW, I, A
Lake Trout (F)	Laker	SC, SW, NW, I, A
Northern Pike (F)	Northern	SC, SW, NW, I
Hammerhandle Pacific Halibut (S)	Halibut	SE, SC, SW, NW
Pink Salmon (F, S)	Humpie	SE, SC, SW, NW, I
Smelt (F, S)	Smelt	SE, SC, SW, NW, I, A
Rainbow Trout (F)	Rainbow	SE, SC, SW, I
Sheefish (F)	Shee, Inconnu	NW, I
Sockeye Salmon (F, S)	Red Salmon	SE, SC, SW, NW, I
Steelhead (F, S)	Steelie	SE, SC, SW

(F) = *Freshwater*
(S) = *Saltwater*
A = *Arctic*
SC = *South Central*
I = *Interior*
SE = *Southeast*
NW = *Northwest*
SW = *Southwest*

PLANNING YOUR TRIP

It's best to plan your trip to Alaska months, or even a year, in advance, particularly to Alaska's most popular destinations, such as Denali and

CloseUp

IMPORTANT WILDERNESS SAFETY TIPS

IN ADDITION TO ALL OF THE RESEARCH *and planning that will go into your Alaskan adventure, keep in mind these notable safety concerns and tips.*

Preparation & Organization

Be sure you're in good shape before venturing into backcountry—or travel with an experienced guide. Prepare yourself for the type of landscape you'll be visiting. If you are traveling by boat along the coast, bring a tide book; some of Alaska's coastal areas have tidal swings of 30 feet–40 feet. If hiking or backpacking overland, know in advance whether you'll have to cross large glacial rivers. Always pay close attention to the weather.

When you're hiking in a national park, national forest, wildlife refuge, state park, or any other kind of protected, administered land, plan to check in and out with a ranger. Leave an itinerary and the names of people to call in case of an emergency with at least one trustworthy person before you go.

Use maps (preferably 1 inch:1 mi maps published by the U.S. Geological Survey) and a compass at the very minimum. Cell phones usually don't work in remote wilderness areas. Other options for emergency use are electronic locator devices and handheld aviation radios.

Weather

The rugged terrain in Alaska brings constantly changing weather. Always be prepared for storms and winterlike conditions, particularly when traveling through the state's mountain ranges or along its jagged coastline.

Be prepared for unexpected delays. One of the most common phrases used by wilderness explorers in Alaska is "weather permitting." Never "push" the weather; over the years, many people have died in aviation, boating, and overland accidents because they wanted to get home on schedule despite dangerously stormy conditions.

Hypothermia

Hypothermia—the lowering of the body's core temperature—is an ever-present threat in Alaska's wilderness. Wear warm clothing (in layers) when the weather is cool and/or wet; this includes a good wind- and waterproof parka or shell, warm head- and hand gear, and waterproof or water-resistant boots. Eat regularly and drink enough liquids to stay properly hydrated.

The onset of hypothermia can be recognized by the following symptoms: shivering, accelerated heartbeat, and goose bumps; this may be followed by clumsiness, slurred speech, disorientation, and unconsciousness and, in the extreme, can result in death. If you notice any of these symptoms in yourself or your traveling companion, stop, add layers of clothing, light a fire or camp stove, and warm yourself; a cup of hot tea also helps. If your clothes are wet, change immediately. Be sure to put on a warm hat (most of the body's heat is lost through the head) and gloves. If there are only two of you, stay together: a person with hypothermia should never be left alone.

Water Safety

Alaska's waters, even its wild rivers, often carry Giardia, a parasite that can cause diarrhea and sap your strength. Boil your drinking water in the backcountry or treat it with iodine tablets.

Glacier Bay national parks. The prime time for nearly all wilderness sports, except for skiing and mushing, is from June through early September. Even the winter sports are generally done at the end of the season, in March and April, when longer hours of daylight have returned and temperatures have started to rise. However you choose to explore Alaska's wilderness, it is always helpful to hire a backcountry guide to provide the necessary expertise. Certain rules apply when picking guides and outfitters, whether for kayaking, hiking, fishing, river rafting, or any other wilderness trip.

The first step is to **obtain a list of outfitters and guides who are permitted to operate on the land.** Such a list is available from the staff of the refuge, forest, or park you plan to visit. It would also help to contact the Alaska Wilderness Recreation and Tourism Association, or AWRTA (🌐 www.awrta.org). When contacting businesses, learn as much as you can about the guides, the nature of the activities they offer, and the area you plan to explore. Also be sure to **determine how well the guides know the area you plan to visit.** How long have they been working in the area? What type of trips do they specialize in? Don't be afraid to **ask for references.**

To reserve a spot, most operators require you to put down a deposit by a particular day and then pay the rest sometime before the starting date. In most cases, if you cancel your reservation, you get at least a partial refund, but policies vary widely. **Find out how far in advance you must cancel to get a full refund,** and ask whether any allowances are made for cancellations due to medical emergencies. If cancellation insurance is available, you may want to take it. You'll receive a full refund regardless of the reason for your cancellation.

Taxes are generally not included in the quoted price, and they can add substantially to the cost of your trip. Depending on the program, you should also **ask about gratuities**—inquire about which members of the tour personnel customarily get tipped and what the average rate is.

In choosing an outfitter, your primary concern should be safety. An outfitter should be equipped with proper technical and first-aid gear and should know how to use it.

If you have no experience in the activity, **ask what sort of training you'll receive.** Clearly explain your own goals and abilities, and be sure to **ask about the difficulty of the terrain** to be covered; 1 mi across hilly, trailless tundra may demand the same energy as 2 or 3 mi on a flat, maintained trail. Most guides plan trips so that you'll have time to relax and enjoy the landscape or look for wildlife, but it's a good idea to **ask about the travel schedule and number of miles to be covered daily.** As a general rule, hikers in good physical condition should be able to travel 2 mi an hour on maintained trails and about 1 mi per hour or less across trailless terrain. Traveling 5 to 6 mi per day, even on trails, is likely to be tiring for a novice. Be honest with the guide when he or she asks about your level of expertise and physical condition.

The amount of weight you'll be carrying on your back will also influence your traveling ability, especially if you haven't carried a heavy pack before, so **determine the amount of gear you'll be required to carry,** particularly if you'll be hiking, backpacking, or glacier trekking. Also be sure to **ask what gear the company will provide.** Guides normally provide group gear, such as tents and tarps, and expect you to provide your own personal equipment, such as boots, a pack, and a sleeping bag. (In some cases, guides can rent you gear such as sleeping bags or packs.)

Ask about the weather you're likely to encounter. The weather varies greatly throughout the state, but hikers and backpackers should always be prepared for cool, wet weather, even in midsummer. The best time to visit also varies greatly. In most parts of the state, June through August are considered the prime months for summer backcountry trips. July is usually the warmest month but also the buggiest. Finally, it's best to **go with a small group to minimize impact on the landscape and wildlife;** fewer than 10 people is ideal.

Ecotourism

Ecotourists aim to travel responsibly, taking care to conserve natural environments and show respect for local, indigenous populations. Ecotourism typically is smaller scale and involves more education than traditional tourism; often, you are led by guides who know the local natural history of plants, animals, and landscape and are familiar with local cultures. Itineraries are slower paced and therefore allow you to have a closer connection to the areas explored. Ecotourists are encouraged to give the landscape and its wildlife its due and not rush from one destination to another. As one Alaskan guide says, "Slow down, take a deep breath, feel where you are."

If you want to enjoy the wilderness while limiting your impact on it, The International Ecotourism Society, a nonprofit group based in Washington, D.C. (🌐 www.ecotourism.org), gives these tips: choose a local guide or a well-trained naturalist as your guided-tour operator; learn about local customs and pertinent facts about the nature of your destination before starting your trip; get clear instructions on how to approach wildlife and how to dispose of wastes; choose low-impact transportation and guided outfits that place limits on group size.

A large and still-growing number of ecotour companies operate in all regions of the state. A state-produced *Alaska Vacation Planner* containing information on ecotourism can be obtained from the **Alaska Travel Industry Association** (✉ 2600 Cordova St., Suite 201, Anchorage 99503 ☎ 907/929–2200, 800/862–5275 to order vacation planners 🌐 www.travelalaska.com). The **Alaska Wilderness Recreation and Tourism Association** (✉ 2207 Spenard Rd., Suite 201, Anchorage 99503 ☎ 907/258–3171 🌐 www.awrta.org) can provide information on many eco-friendly businesses and activities across the state. **Recreational Equipment Inc.** (✉ 1200 W. Northern Lights Blvd., Anchorage 99503 ☎ 907/272–4565 🌐 www.rei.com) has a helpful brochure titled "Minimum Impact Camping" as well as a useful handout on backpacking equipment needs.

Lodging

Wilderness Lodges

To really get away from it all, book a remote lodge in the middle of breathtaking Alaskan wilderness. Some of the most popular are in the river drainages of Bristol Bay, in Southeast Alaska, along the western edge of Cook Inlet, near Katmai and Lake Clark national parks, and along the Susitna River north of Anchorage. Most of these lodges place a heavy emphasis on fishing and/or bear viewing; a stay generally includes daily guided trips as well as all meals. They can be astronomically expensive (daily rates of $250–$600 per person), so if you're not interested in fishing or bear watching, you won't want to seek these out. Lodges in and near Denali National Park emphasize opportunities to explore the wilderness as well as natural history programs; some even include wintertime dogsledding. Activities include hiking, rafting, flightseeing, horseback riding, and gold panning. For getting deep into the wilderness, these lodges are an excellent alternative to the hotels and cabins outside the park entrance.

Camping

Hundreds of campgrounds—both public and private—exist along Alaska's road system. They typically include sites for both tent and RV camping, with fire pits, latrines, running potable water, picnic benches, and other camping amenities.

Most campsites are available on a first-come, first-served basis, so it pays to conduct research in advance when planning road trips. But if you wish to explore Alaska's vast backcountry, you will almost certainly have to establish your own campsites (though some park units do have remote tent sites). Before heading into the backcountry, contact the appropriate management agency, such as the state or national park, wildlife refuge, or national forest unit that you'll be visiting for any advice or restrictions.

Several variables must be considered whenever camping in the backcountry, including water sources, good drainage (you don't want to end up swamped in heavy rains), protection from high winds, and the presence of any game trails (which should be avoided, particularly if bears are known to inhabit the area). Campers are also advised to practice "low-impact" camping techniques to minimize damage to the environment. For example: carry out *all* garbage; avoid camping on fragile vegetation, which can be easily trampled; if possible, camp on already established sites; never cut standing trees; wash yourself, your clothes, and your dishes at least 100 feet from water sources; bring a trowel and dig "cat-hole" latrines for human waste at least 100 feet from your camp, water sources, and trails; burn or carry out toilet paper. When traveling in trail-less areas (particularly tundra), fan out instead of walking single file, again to avoid trampling vegetation. Alaska's weather is unpredictable: anticipate delays, especially when traveling to backcountry areas by plane, and bring more food and fuel than you think you'll need.

Information on roadside camping can be obtained at **Alaska Public Land Information Centers** (🌐 www.nps.gov/aplic/center/) in Tok, Fairbanks, and Anchorage, and at park, refuge, and national forest headquarters scattered across the state. ***The Milepost*** (🌐 www.themilepost.com) includes mile-by-mile information on all of Alaska's main highways.

Equipment

Get the best equipment you can afford; it's a must in Alaska. Not only will it prove to be a good investment, but it just may make your trip to Alaska that much more amazing.

Backpacks

First decide whether to get a pack with an internal or external frame. If you choose the latter, pick one that balances the pack upright when you set it on the ground; this is a great help in the many areas of Alaska that don't have trees. Internal frames are an advantage when going through brush, which is common in Alaska. A rainproof cover for your pack is a good idea, even if it's just a heavy plastic garbage bag (bring along extras).

Tents

Because winterlike storms can occur at almost any time of year, a four-season tent is highly recommended—one that can withstand strong winds and persistent rainfall (or even snow squalls). There are few things worse than being stuck in a battered, leaky tent with a storm raging outside. Tie-down ropes and tent flies are essential items, and mosquito netting is another must.

Sleeping Gear

For sleeping comfort, bring a sleeping pad to add cushioning and insulation beneath your sleeping bag. Be sure your bag is warm enough for the changing conditions; even in midsummer, nighttime temperatures may fall to the freezing mark, especially in the mountains.

Cooking Gear

You should carry a lightweight camping stove with fuel. Firewood is often a scarce item in Alaska, and what there is may be wet. The burning of wood in many parklands is now frowned upon or prohibited in order to protect the surroundings.

Besides a stove, fuel, and matches, necessary cooking items include light but sturdy utensils (for instance, a spoon and fork made of hard plastic); a bowl and mug (drinking plenty of hot beverages is a great way to stay both warm and hydrated); a pot or two for heating water and cooking; a potholder; and a dependable pocketknife. As with other equipment, you'll need to balance quality gear with weight considerations.

Essentials

When setting out for a day hike from a base camp, it's wise to carry a pack stocked with a few essentials. These include a first-aid kit, including bandages and moleskin; a cup and spoon, which you may wish to bang together to alert bears; a plastic bottle of drinking water; extra candy bars or gorp (nuts, chocolate, and raisins); a warm sweater or jacket and windproof rain gear, in case the weather suddenly changes (be sure to avoid cotton clothing as cotton does not retain body warmth when wet); waterproof matches (you can make these by coating kitchen matches with wax) and other fire starters, such as a candle or heat tab; a flare or flashlight; a knife (preferably a multifunctional pocketknife); a topographical map; toilet paper; sunglasses and sunblock; bug repellent; duct tape, for all kinds of emergencies; and a compass.

A note about compasses: the farther north you travel, the more the compass needle will be skewed upward and to the east of north by several degrees. U.S. Geological Survey maps show this difference between magnetic and true north—called magnetic declination—at the bottom of the map. With these maps, you can use your compass accordingly; otherwise, allow for this deviation as you do your compass reading.

2 Anchorage

WORD OF MOUTH

"I spent a week in Anchorage and it wasn't long enough! I enjoyed biking along the Tony Knowles Coastal Trail and hiking north of Anchorage. The beer-battered fried halibut at the Anchorage Saturday Market was fantastic."

—Postal

"From Anchorage you can easily drive south to the Kenai Peninsula (a stunning drive), then from Seward take a day cruise and see some wildlife and glaciers."

—sluggo

"Alaska is a wonderful place for kids. It's all about scenery, mountains, animals, outdoors, hiking, walking, bird watching, flowers, and blooming tundra."

—Wildflower

www.fodors.com/forums

By Robin Mackey Hill and Howard C. Weaver

Updated by Don Pitcher

AMID THE WILD COUNTRYSIDE that crowds around it on all sides, Anchorage has grown into a vigorous, spirited, cosmopolitan city—by far Alaska's largest and most sophisticated. The relative affluence of this white-collar city—with a sprinkling of olive drab from nearby military bases—attracts fine restaurants and pricey shops, first-rate entertainment, and world-class sporting events. Flashy modern towers stab the skyline, and colorful flowers spill from hundreds of baskets on downtown lampposts. Traffic from the city's busy international airport, served by more than 15 international and domestic airlines, lends Anchorage more diversity than you might expect from a city with a population of roughly 261,000, nearly half the people in the state. You'll also discover some development you may not have come to Alaska to see—14 McDonald's, 2 Wal-Marts, a 16-plex movie theater, and dozens of espresso bars. Those who live in the Bush joke about "being able to see Alaska" by visiting Anchorage, but the city has not entirely lost touch with its frontier spirit. Sled-dog races are still among the most revered events held here, moose often roam along city bike trails, and spectacular country is just a short drive away.

First incorporated in 1920, Anchorage is still a young city. Nearly everything was built in the last few decades—an Anchorage home dating from the 1950s almost merits historic status. In addition to acting as the center for oil development in the state, Anchorage hustles its living as a government, banking, transportation, and communications hub. The median age of 32.4 years and an aggressive style make it—not the capital city of Juneau—the state's power center.

Anchorage residents are primarily from elsewhere in America—including oil workers from such conservative oil-patch states as Oklahoma and Texas—and the attitudes they bring have added fuel to the fire of the pro-development mentality that characterizes the city, and Alaska, as a whole. Although representing less than 8% of the population, Alaskan Native peoples add an important cultural dimension, along with rapidly growing Asian and Hispanic populations.

Anchorage got its start with the construction of the federally built Alaska Railroad, completed in 1917, and traces of the railroad heritage remain today. Once the tracks were laid, the town grew because its pioneer forerunners actively sought growth by hook and—not infrequently—by crook. City officials used to delight in telling how they tricked a visiting member of Congress into dedicating a site for a not-yet-approved federal hospital.

Boom and bust periods followed major events: an influx of military bases during World War II; a massive buildup of Arctic missile-warning stations during the cold war; reconstruction following the devastating Good Friday earthquake of 1964; and in the late 1960s the biggest jackpot of all—the discovery of oil at Prudhoe Bay and the construction of the trans-Alaska pipeline. Not surprisingly, Anchorage positioned itself as the perfect home for the Trans-Alaska pipeline administrators and support industries, and it continues to attract a large share of the state's oil-tax dollars.

In the last decade, Anchorage has become an increasingly important focus of travelers to Alaska. The central location, relatively mild climate, and excellent transportation system make it a natural place to begin or end a trip.

EXPLORING ANCHORAGE

Navigating downtown Anchorage's flower-lined streets is simple. The grid plan was laid out with military precision by the Army Corps of Engineers, and streets and avenues run exactly east–west and north–south, with numbers in the first direction and letters of the alphabet or Alaska place-names (Barrow, Cordova, Denali, etc.) in the other. The only aberration is the absence of a J Street—a concession, some say, to the city's early Swedish settlers, who had difficulty pronouncing the letter.

Outside of downtown, Anchorage is considerably less pedestrian friendly, with widely scattered neighborhoods and large shopping malls clustered along busy thoroughfares. Fortunately, the city has a decent local bus system.

You'll find plenty to do year-round in Anchorage, though most visitors, particularly first-timers, might be happiest in June, July, or August, when the days are longer and the temperatures warmer. Locals embrace the 18-plus hours of daylight. Dog walkers, bikers, golfers, and softball players are out until it gets dark, which in late June can be nearly midnight. Spring comes late and fall early to Anchorage. These are less desirable times to visit, because weather can be cool and rainy and some attractions might be closed. But you'll also encounter fewer fellow travelers during the shoulder seasons.

Numbers in the text correspond to numbers in the margin and on the Anchorage map.

Downtown Anchorage

a good walk

Downtown Anchorage is nearly flat, making for a delightful stroll. Throughout the summer, hanging floral baskets line the streets. Start at the **Log Cabin Visitor Information Center** ❶ ⚑, where friendly volunteers answer questions and racks of brochures line the walls. The marble statue in front of **Old City Hall** ❷ next door honors William Seward. Along 4th Avenue are some of Anchorage's original buildings. They date from 1920, when Anchorage was incorporated. Catercorner from the Old City Hall is the **Alaska Public Lands Information Center** ❸, one of four in the state that provide information on all of Alaska's public lands.

Take F Street north downhill to 2nd Avenue, the site of original townsite homes built by the Alaska Engineering Commission, which also built the Alaska Railroad in the early 1900s. A neighborhood marker at the intersection of F Street and 2nd Avenue tells of Anchorage's first mayor, Leopold David, and the start of the Anchorage Women's Club.

Walk east along 2nd Avenue past the Eisenhower Memorial to a set of stairs leading down to the **Alaska Railroad depot** ❹. Salmon run up **Ship**

Before you put on your comfortable shoes and grab your camera, take a few minutes to figure out what you're most interested in—seeing wildlife, shopping, taking a hike in the surrounding Chugach Mountains, or soaking up some of Alaska's rich Native culture.

If you have 1 day

Take a stroll through downtown Anchorage to acquaint yourself with the fine shops and galleries, historic sites, museums, and parks. Walk along the **Tony Knowles Coastal Trail** 6 if the weather's cooperating. If you have a car, explore the city highlights, including the **Alaska Aviation Heritage Museum** 12 and the **Alaska Native Heritage Center** 16. End the day with some window-shopping downtown or dinner and a walk along the Delaney Park Strip. Several places are open late if coffee and dessert—or beer and nachos, for that matter—sound like the perfect nightcap.

If you have 3 days

Follow the one-day itinerary; then head south along the Seward Highway for views of **Potter Marsh** 14 and Turnagain Arm. Drive 40 mi to the community of Girdwood, with its several good restaurants, scenic hiking trails, and inviting shops. Continue farther down the highway to Alyeska Resort at Girdwood, where you can ride the tram to the 2,300-foot level for lunch with a view. Head south of Girdwood to Portage Glacier and the Begich-Boggs Visitor Center, all the while looking for Dall sheep and beluga whales. Back in Anchorage on Day 3, consider visiting some of the special-interest museums or, if it's the season, taking in a baseball game at Mulcahy Stadium. A hike along one of the city's many bike trails or in the neighboring Chugach Mountains lets you see the role nature plays in the lives of those who make Anchorage their home. Bears and moose roam the park, which has trails from 2 mi to 30 mi in length.

Creek 5, north of the depot, all summer, attracting anglers and gawkers alike. It's easy to watch the action from the banks of the creek, where you'll also find photographs from the city's early days.

Ask Anchorage residents what the best thing about living in the city is, and many will say that it's the **Tony Knowles Coastal Trail** 6, a recreational trail that begins west of 2nd Avenue and curls along Cook Inlet. Follow 2nd Avenue to K Street, go south a block to 3rd Avenue, and follow 3rd Avenue westward to **Resolution Park** 7, with its statue of Captain Cook. From here you can admire the grand vistas over Cook Inlet to Mt. McKinley and other peaks in the Alaska Range. The **Oscar Anderson House Museum** 8, off the coastal trail at the north end of Elderberry Park, was Anchorage's first permanent frame house, built in 1915 by city butcher Oscar Anderson. Elderberry Park, just in front of the house, is a good place for children to run off steam, watch passing trains, and look for whales off the coastline. If young travelers are getting restless, head back up the 5th Avenue hill to the **Imaginarium** 9, an experiential science museum with a great gift shop.

Walk down 5th Avenue past the **Egan Convention Center** (✉ *555 W. 5th Ave.* ☎ *907/263–2800*), whose lobby has several modern Native Alaskan sculptures and a beaded curtain that evokes the northern lights. Across the street is a park (Town Square) that's packed with flowers in the summer, and just southwest of it is the **Alaska Center for the Performing Arts** ⑩. Continue on to A Street and 7th Avenue for the entrance to the **Anchorage Museum of History and Art** ⑪, which occupies the whole block between 6th and 7th avenues. The red metal sculpture out front is a favorite hide-and-seek site for children.

TIMING This walking tour should take two to three hours, or longer if you get caught up in shopping and museum-hopping. Volunteers from **Anchorage Historic Properties** (☎ 907/274–3600 ⊕ www.anchoragehistoricproperties.org) lead historic walking tours on weekdays in the summer. These depart from Old City Hall at 524 West 4th Avenue and cost $5.

What to See

⑩ **Alaska Center for the Performing Arts.** The distinctive stone-and-glass building fronts on an expansive park filled with brilliant flowers all summer. Take a look inside for upcoming events, or just relax amid the blossoms on a sunny afternoon. You can watch IMAX films or slide shows on the northern lights. Hour-long tours are available. ✉ *621 W. 6th Ave., at G St., Downtown* ☎ *907/263–2900, 800/478–7328 tickets* ⊕ *www.alaskapac.org* ⏲ *Daily 8–5. Free tours Wed. at 1 PM.*

★ ③ **Alaska Public Lands Information Center.** Stop here for information on all of Alaska's public lands, including national and state parks, national forests, and wildlife refuges. You can make reservations for a state ferry; watch nature videos; plan a hiking, sea-kayaking, bear-viewing, or fishing trip; find out about public-use cabins; learn about Alaska's plants and animals; or head to the theater for films highlighting different parts of the state. The bookstore sells maps and nature books. Guided walks to historic downtown sights depart daily. ✉ *605 W. 4th Ave., #105, at F St., Downtown* ☎ *907/271–2737* ⊕ *www.nps.gov/aplic* ⏲ *Memorial Day–Labor Day, daily 9–5:30; Labor Day–Memorial Day, weekdays 10–5:30.*

④ **Alaska Railroad depot.** Totem poles and a locomotive built in 1907 are outside the station, the headquarters of the Alaska Railroad since 1915. A monument in front of the depot relates the history of the railroad, which brought an influx of people into the city during the early 1900s. During February's Fur Rendezvous festival, model-train buffs set up their displays here. ✉ *411 W. 1st Ave., Downtown* ☎ *907/265–2494* ⊕ *www.akrr.com* ⏲ *Daily, depending on train schedules.*

⑪ Fodor's Choice ★ **Anchorage Museum of History and Art.** An impressive collection of historic and contemporary Alaskan art is exhibited along with dioramas and displays on Alaskan history and village life. The first-floor atrium is often the site of free daily presentations, which occur in July, by local artists and authors. You can join an informative 45-minute tour (given several times daily) or step into the theater to watch a film on Alaska. A café spills out into the atrium, serving delicious lunches from the Marx Brothers' Cafe, and the gift shop sells classy souvenirs. ✉ *121*

Dining Fishing in Alaska is a multimillion-dollar industry employing thousands of people. For those eager to sample the fruits of those labors, dining out in Anchorage is a pleasure. Several restaurants—from formal dining rooms to casual pubs—serve such favorites as halibut, salmon, Alaskan king crab legs, scallops, oysters, and mussels.

Ethnic restaurants, especially Thai and other Asian styles, and a growing number of places with extensive vegetarian menus, veer off from traditional seafood fare. In the last few years, half a dozen microbreweries with adjoining restaurants have opened, two of them downtown, giving the area a convivial spirit. Espresso bars have also taken root all over town. For a quick lunch downtown, track down one of the 4th Avenue vendors for a reindeer sausage with grilled onions.

Hiking & Walking Anchorage is a hiker's paradise, laced with rugged dirt paths through the Chugach Mountains and more than 120 mi of paved urban trails that meander through wooded greenbelts and quiet neighborhoods. Easiest of these is the Tony Knowles Coastal Trail, an 11-mi ribbon of asphalt beginning downtown and stretching west to Kincaid Park. Pick up a guide to local hiking trails at the Alaska Public Lands Information Center or at area bookstores. A note of caution: when hiking in the hills, be sure to wear hiking boots and to take plenty of water, rain gear, and a light jacket—the weather can change with little warning. And although bear encounters are rare, be alert and make noise when walking in thick brush.

Shopping Anchorage's shopping matches any taste and price range. Souvenir shops selling everything from painted gold pans to plastic totem poles can be found on nearly every downtown block. Native Alaskan handicrafts of all kinds are sold at many of the gift shops downtown—the best selection is at the downtown outdoor Saturday Market in the parking lot at 3rd Avenue and E Street. Check for the official polar bear symbol, which means the item was made in Alaska; a hand symbol indicates an article was made locally by Native artisans. Tlingit and Haida traditional arts and crafts include button blankets, wood carvings, and silver jewelry. Athabascan craftspeople are known for their beadwork, which adorns slippers, headbands, and jewelry. Eskimo handicrafts include ivory and soapstone carvings and baleen baskets. Aleut grass baskets are so fine and tightly woven that some can hold water.

W. 7th Ave., at C St., Downtown ☎ 907/343–4326, 907/343–6173 recorded information 🌐 www.anchoragemuseum.org 🎫 $6.50; free for children ⏲ Mid-May–mid-Sept., Fri.–Wed. 9–6, Thurs. 9–9; mid-Sept.–mid-May, Tues.–Sat. 10–6, Sun. 1–5.

❾ **Imaginarium.** Children can stand inside a giant soap bubble at the bubble lab, visit a starfish in the intertidal marine exhibit, check out the creepy insects, learn about the northern lights, take a galaxy tour in the plan-

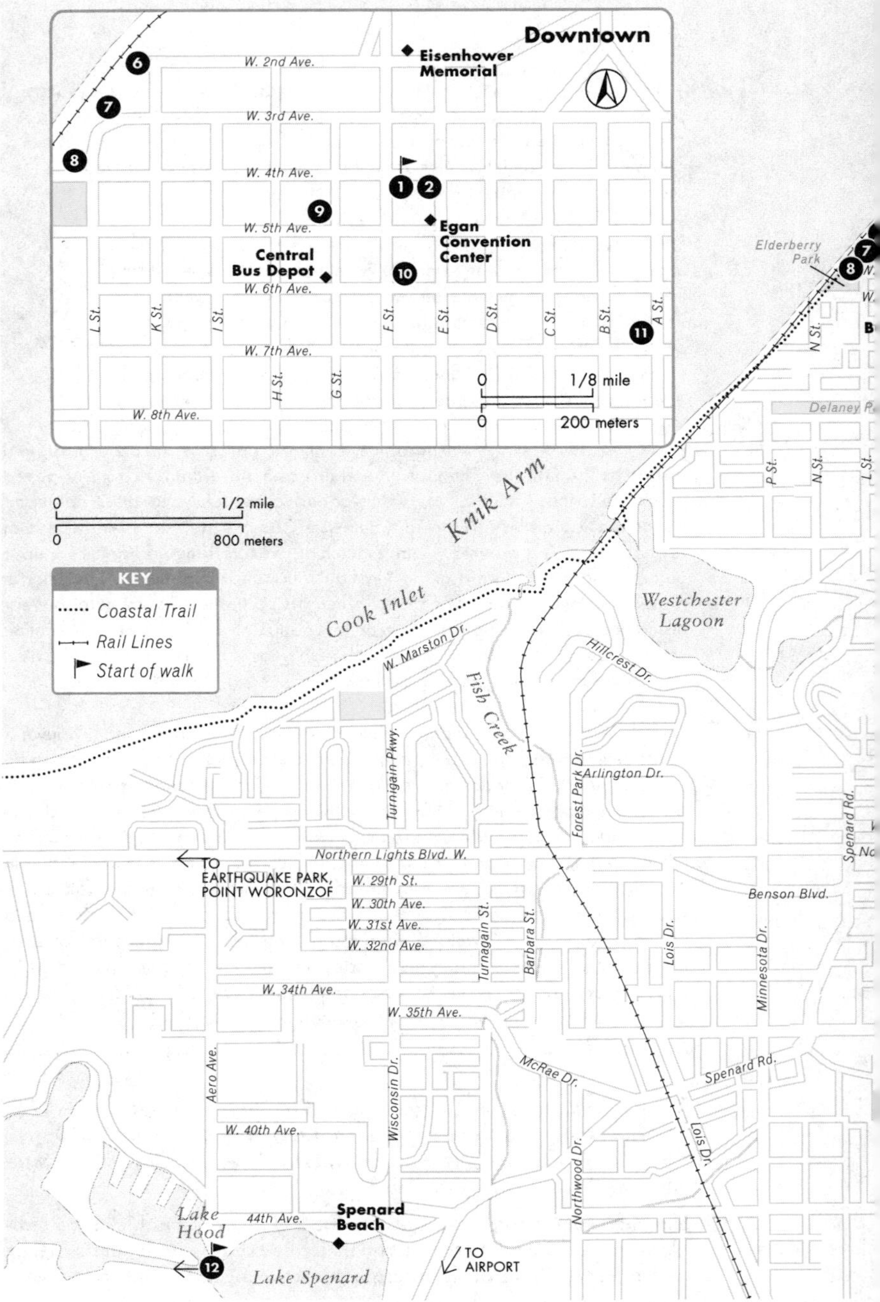
Downtown
W. 2nd Ave.
Eisenhower Memorial
W. 3rd Ave.
W. 4th Ave.
W. 5th Ave.
Egan Convention Center
Central Bus Depot
W. 6th Ave.
L St.
K St.
I St.
F St.
E St.
D St.
C St.
B St.
A St.
W. 7th Ave.
H St.
G St.
W. 8th Ave.
0 1/8 mile
0 200 meters
Elderberry Park
Delaney Park
P St.
N St.
L St.
0 1/2 mile
0 800 meters
Knik Arm
KEY
Coastal Trail
Rail Lines
Start of walk
Cook Inlet
Westchester Lagoon
W. Marston Dr.
Hillcrest Dr.
Fish Creek
Turnigain Pkwy.
Forest Park Dr.
Arlington Dr.
Spenard Rd.
Northern Lights Blvd. W.
TO EARTHQUAKE PARK, POINT WORONZOF
W. 29th St.
W. 30th Ave.
W. 31st Ave.
W. 32nd Ave.
Turnagain St.
Barbara St.
Lois Dr.
Benson Blvd.
Minnesota Dr.
W. 34th Ave.
W. 35th Ave.
McRae Dr.
Spenard Rd.
Aero Ave.
Wisconsin Dr.
W. 40th Ave.
Northwood Dr.
Lois Dr.
Lake Hood
44th Ave.
Spenard Beach
Lake Spenard
TO AIRPORT

Anchorage
Ship Creek
Port Access
Viking Dr.
Christensen Dr.
W. 1st Ave.
E. 1st Ave.
W. 2nd Ave.
Eisenhower Memorial
W. 3rd Ave.
E. 3rd Ave.
Egan Convention Center
4th Ave.
E. 4th Ave.
5th Ave.
E. 5th Ave.
Central Bus Depot
E. 6th Ave.
Post Rd.
Glenn Hwy.
K St.
I St.
H St.
G St.
F St.
E St.
D St.
C St.
B St.
A St.
Barrow St.
City Cemetary
Gambell St.
Hyder St.
Ingra St.
Juneau St.
E. 7th Ave.
E. 8th Ave.
W. 9th Ave.
E. 9th Ave.
W. 10th Ave.
E. 10th Ave.
W. 11th Ave.
E. 11th Ave.
W. 12th Ave.
E. 12th Ave.
W. 13th Ave.
E. 13th Ave.
W. 14th Ave.
E. 14th Ave.
W. 15th Ave.
E. 15th Ave.
Cordova St.
Denali St.
Eagle St.
Fairbanks St.
Karluk St.
Latouche St.
Medfra St.
Nelchina
Orca St.
E. 16th Ave.
Sullivan Sports Arena
E. 17th Ave.
Chester Creek Park
Chester Creek
Arctic Blvd.
C St.
A St.
Eagle St.
W. Fireweed La.
W. 27th Ave.
Northern Lights Blvd.
Redwood St.
Eureka St.
Benson Blvd.
Bering St.
32nd Ave.
Denali St.
E. 33rd Ave.
TO CHUGACH STATE PARK
W. 36th Ave.
E. 36th Ave.
Old Seward Hwy.
1
Seward Hwy.
W. 40th Ave.
Credit Union Dr.
Tudor Rd.

etarium, or learn how planes fly at this experiential science museum. Other attractions include such "radical reptiles" as an iguana, an alligator, and even a 19-foot python. It's an educational fun house for children and adults alike. The upstairs gift shop features all sorts of unusual science toys. ✉ *737 W. 5th Ave., in Glacier Brewhouse Mall, Downtown* ☎ *907/276–3179* 🌐 *www.imaginarium.org* 🎟 *$5.50, children 2 and under free* ⏲ *Mon.–Sat. 10–6, Sun. noon–5.*

❶ **Log Cabin Visitor Information Center.** A giant jade boulder stands outside this Bush-style log cabin, whose sod roof is festooned with huge hanging baskets of flowers. Anchorage calls itself the "Air Crossroads of the World" (it's a major stopping point for cargo jets en route to Asia), and a signpost out front marks the mileage to many international destinations. After a stop in the visitor-center cabin, step out the back door to a more spacious visitor center stocked with brochures. ✉ *4th Ave. and F St., Downtown* ☎ *907/274–3531* 🌐 *www.anchorage.net* ⏲ *June–Aug., daily 7:30–7; May and Sept., daily 8–6; Oct.–Apr., daily 9–4.*

❷ **Old City Hall.** Offices of the Anchorage Convention and Visitors Bureau now occupy this 1936 building. A few exhibits and historic photos are right inside the lobby. Out front, take a look at the marble sculpture of William Seward, the secretary of state who engineered the purchase of Alaska from Russia. ✉ *524 W. 4th Ave., Downtown.*

❽ **Oscar Anderson House Museum.** City butcher Oscar Anderson built Anchorage's first permanent frame house in 1915 at a time when most of Anchorage consisted of tents. A Swedish Christmas open house is held the first two weekends of December. Guided 45-minute tours are available whenever the museum is open. ✉ *420 M St., Downtown* ☎ *907/274–2336* 🎟 *$3* ⏲ *June–mid-Sept., Mon.–Sat. noon–5; mid-Sept.–May, by appointment.*

❼ **Resolution Park.** This tiny park has a cantilevered viewing platform dominated by a monument to Captain Cook (whose explorations in 1778 led to the naming of Cook Inlet and many other geographic features in Alaska). Mt. Susitna, known as the Sleeping Lady, is the prominent low mountain to the northwest. Mt. McKinley—referred to by most Alaskans by its traditional name, Denali—is often visible 125 mi away. ✉ *3rd Ave. at L St., Downtown.*

❺ **Ship Creek.** The creek is dammed here, with a footbridge across the dam. You'll see a waterfall; salmon running upstream; anglers; and, above it all, the tall buildings of downtown. ✉ *Whitney Rd., Downtown.*

❻ **Tony Knowles Coastal Trail.** Strollers, runners, bikers, dog walkers, and in-line skaters cram this recreation trail on sunny summer evenings, particularly around Westchester Lagoon. In winter, cross-country skiers take to it by storm. The trail begins off 2nd Avenue, west of Christensen Drive, and curls along Cook Inlet for approximately 11 mi to Kincaid Park, beyond the airport. In summer, you might spot beluga whales offshore in Cook Inlet. Access points are on the waterfront at the ends of 2nd, 5th, and 9th avenues and at Westchester Lagoon.

Fodor's Choice ★

Midtown & Beyond

a good drive

Head west on Northern Lights Boulevard past Earthquake Park, 2 mi after Minnesota Drive. Signs describe the devastating power of the 1964 earthquake, the largest ever recorded in Alaska, with a magnitude of 9.2 on the Richter scale. Another 1¾ mi west on Northern Lights Boulevard is Point Woronzof, great for scenic views of Cook Inlet, Mt. Susitna (Sleeping Lady), the Alaska Range, and Mt. McKinley.

Turn left out of the parking lot at Point Woronzof and go back east along Northern Lights Boulevard 1½ mi to Aircraft Drive. Turn right and continue south and east along roads skirting the edge of two large lakes, Lakes Spenard and Hood. Lake Spenard has a beach where hardy souls may take a dip. Along Lake Hood—the world's largest and busiest seaplane base—you'll see planes (and geese) take off and land. The **Alaska Aviation Heritage Museum** 12, overlooking the south end of the lake and 1½ mi from the intersection with Aircraft Drive, has more than two dozen vintage aircraft.

Take the first left out of the parking lot at the aviation museum and head 2 mi east on International Airport Boulevard to Minnesota Drive. Take Minnesota south about 9 mi (it becomes O'Malley Road and crosses Seward Highway) and continue uphill to the **Alaska Zoo** 13. From the zoo, take a right on O'Malley and head back 2 mi to Seward Highway. Three miles south on the highway is the turnoff to **Potter Marsh** 14, where Canada geese, arctic terns, and other migratory birds make their home in summer.

From Potter Marsh, head north on Old Seward Highway for 8 mi and turn left (west) on Northern Lights Boulevard to C Street, where you will find the **Alaska Heritage Library and Museum** 15. This outstanding small museum displays Native artifacts and photos. From here, take Benson Boulevard (a one-way street just south of Northern Lights) back to Old Seward Highway. Go left (north) and make a right (east) on 15th Avenue, which becomes DeBarr Road, and a left (north) on Muldoon Road to the Glenn Highway. The entrance to the **Alaska Native Heritage Center** 16 is on the north side of this intersection. The center is a must-see for anyone interested in Native peoples. End your Anchorage tour at the **Alaska Botanical Garden** 17, off Tudor Road. Head south from the base on Boniface Parkway, and turn left onto Tudor Road. Follow it ½ mi, turn right on Campbell Airstrip Road, and continue a block to the floral gardens.

TIMING Driving the route without stopping will take about two hours. You should allow from a half day to a full day, depending on the amount of time you'd like to spend at the sights.

What to See

12 **Alaska Aviation Heritage Museum.** The state's unique aviation history is presented here with 25 vintage aircraft—7 of which have been completely restored—a theater, an observation deck along **Lake Hood,** and a gift shop. Highlights include a historic Fairchild American Pilgrim and a Stearman C2B, the first plane to land on Mt. McKinley, back in the early 1930s. Volunteers are working to restore many of the planes and are

eager to talk shop. ✉ *4721 Aircraft Dr.* ☎ *907/248–5325* 🌐 *www.alaskaairmuseum.com* 🎫 *$5* ⏲ *June–Sept., Wed.–Mon. 10–6; Oct.–May, Fri. and Sat. 10–4, Sun. noon–4.*

17 **Alaska Botanical Garden.** A pleasant 1-mi nature trail leads through the 110-acre garden, where you'll find some 480 varieties of plants. Other trails crisscross the grounds, which include perennial, rock, and herb gardens. An information kiosk is at the entrance. ✉ *4601 Campbell Airstrip Rd., off Tudor Rd. (park at Benny Benson School), East Anchorage* ☎ *907/770–3692* 🌐 *www.alaskabg.org* 🎫 *$5 individual, $10 families, $3 seniors* ⏲ *Daily 9–9.*

★ 15 **Alaska Heritage Library and Museum.** Alaskan Native artifacts are the main draw in the quiet, unassuming lobby of a large midtown bank. You'll also find paintings by Alaskan artists and a library of rare books. ✉ *Wells Fargo Bank, 301 W. Northern Lights Blvd., at C St., Midtown* ☎ *907/265–2834* 🌐 *www.wellsfargohistory.com/museums* 🎫 *Free* ⏲ *Late May–early Sept., weekdays noon–5; early Sept.–late May, weekdays noon–4.*

16 Fodor'sChoice ★ **Alaska Native Heritage Center.** On a 26-acre site facing the Chugach Mountains, this facility provides an introduction to Alaska's Native peoples. The spacious Welcome House has interpretive displays, artifacts, photographs, demonstrations, performances, and films, along with a café and gift shop. Step outside for a stroll around the adjacent lake, where you will pass five village exhibits representing Native cultural groups through traditional structures and exhibitions. The Heritage Center provides a free shuttle from the downtown Log Cabin Visitor Information Center several times a day in summer. You can also hop a bus at the downtown transit center; Route 4 will take you to the Heritage Center front door. ✉ *8800 Heritage Center Dr. (Glenn Hwy. at Muldoon Rd.), East Anchorage* ☎ *907/330–8000 or 800/315–6608* 🌐 *www.alaskanative.net* 🎫 *$21 adults, $19 seniors, Alaska residents $9, $16 children, free for children 6 and under* ⏲ *Mid-May–Sept., daily 9–6; Oct.–mid-May, Sat. 10–5.*

13 **Alaska Zoo.** Caribou, Dall sheep, reindeer, Siberian tigers, musk ox, seals, moose, and various Alaskan birds call this home—you'll even find the state's only elephant. The star attractions are Oreo, a brown bear, and Ahpun, a polar bear; the two were orphaned as cubs and grew up together at the zoo. During the summer, the zoo operates a shuttle from downtown ($10 round-trip). ✉ *4731 O'Malley Rd., South Anchorage, 2 mi east of New Seward Hwy.* ☎ *907/346–3242* 🌐 *www.alaskazoo.org* 🎫 *$9 adults, $8 seniors, $5 children* ⏲ *May–Labor Day, daily 9–6; Labor Day–Apr., daily 10–5. Closed Thanksgiving and Christmas.*

14 **Potter Marsh.** Canada geese and other migratory birds as well as the occasional moose or beaver frequent this marsh about 10 mi south of downtown on the Seward Highway. An elevated boardwalk makes viewing easy. The **Potter Section House,** an old railroad service building just south of the marsh, operates as a state-park office. Out front is an old engine with a rotary snowplow that was used to clear avalanches. ✉ *Seward Hwy., South Anchorage* ☎ *907/345–5014* 🌐 *www.dnr.state.ak.us/parks* ⏲ *Weekdays 8–noon, 1–4:30.*

Self-propelled exploration in the waters of Prince William Sound, South Central Alaska.

(above) Hiking next to astounding blue glaciers in Glacier Bay National Park & Preserve, Southeast Alaska. (opposite page, top) Colorful autumn tundra in Denali National Park & Preserve, Interior Alaska. (opposite page, bottom) A bull moose enjoying Alaskan waters.

(top) The Alaska Raptor Center in Sitka and the yearly winter gathering of bald eagles at the Alaska Chilkat Bald Eagle Preserve near Haines are good bets for seeing eagles in Southeast Alaska. (bottom) Alaskans call Mt. McKinley by its original name, Denali, which means "the high one." (opposite page) A grizzly bear on the move.

(top) Awe-inspiring views across the waters of Prince William Sound, South Central Alaska. (bottom) Prince William Sound's roaring Steller's sea lions, considered an endangered species west of Cape St. Elias.

(top) A humpback whale breaches in the cold Alaskan waters. (bottom) A hiker's fantasy: gorgeous backdrops and miles of coastline right outside Anchorage in Chugach State Park, South Central Alaska.

(top) Herds of magnificent caribou migrate across Alaska's Arctic every year. (bottom left) A colorful totem pole at the Alaska Native Heritage Center in Anchorage. (bottom right) A bald eagle keeps watch.

UNIQUELY ALASKA

ALASKA HAS MORE THAN ITS SHARE *of odd and unexpected attractions, including the handful of offbeat destinations described below. This is just a sampling; see elsewhere in this book for infamous bars (such as the Red Dog Saloon in Juneau and the Salty Dawg Saloon in Homer) and Alaskan thrills, including the Iditarod Trail Sled Dog Race, Alaska's biggest annual event. For a real taste of the weird and wacky, be sure to also take in a show at Mr. Whitekey's Fly by Night Club in Anchorage, where Spam is considered a gourmet food and Alaskan politicians are fair game.*

Chilkoot Charlie's, Anchorage

Van Halen and Aerosmith have played concerts here, and Playboy named it the best bar in America in 2000: ***Chilkoot Charlie's*** *(✉ 2435 Spenard Rd. Anchorage ☎ 907/272–1010), known as Koot's among locals, is not to be missed if you're in the mood for a uniquely Alaskan party. This rockin' and at times very crowded club in Anchorage has stages for rock, swing, DJs, and local Alaskan bands. Get a drink at one of the 11 bars, make your way past the three dance floors, and find a tree stump or an empty beer keg to sit on and enjoy the show.*

Hammers in Haines

Alaska's most peculiar museum is owned by Dave Pahl, whose collection of more than 1,400 hammers is on display in the crowded little ***Hammer Museum*** *(✉ 108 Main St., Haines ☎ 907/766–2374) in downtown Haines. The collection encompasses everything from the bankers' hammers for canceling checks to hammers with 6-foot extensions for hammering posters on barn walls.*

Last Train to Nowhere, Nome

Among Alaska's most interesting Bush settlements, Nome was founded following a major gold discovery in 1898, and is still home to summertime gold dredging operations. During the gold rush, the Council City and Solomon River Railroad envisioned a rail system connecting Nome with the Lower 48—thousands of miles away. Construction only reached 35 miles before storms destroyed the tracks along the Bering Sea in 1907, and the project was abandoned. The company went under, but visitors still marvel at the engines and several railcars rusting away on the tundra south of Nome.

North Pole, Alaska

The world's tallest St. Nick (40 feet in all his wooden splendor) welcomes you to ***Santa Claus House*** *(✉ 101 St. Nicholas Dr., North Pole ☎ 907/488–2200), in the town of North Pole just southeast of Fairbanks. Inside this large red and white store, kids can sit on Santa's lap any time of the year, while parents shop for all sorts of Christmas paraphernalia, from ornaments and musical CDs to certificates that grant you one square inch of land in the Santa Claus subdivision of North Pole. The town was started by Con Miller, who built a trading post here in the 1950s. He and his neighbors incorporated the new town as North Pole.*

Surfing in Southeast

The remote town of Yakutat lies along the Gulf of Alaska halfway between Juneau and Cordova. It isn't a major tourist destination, but it does have the state's longest beach, a 70-mi stretch that starts just outside town. It's never crowded, but local surfers and beach bums ride the swells that roll off the Gulf of Alaska throughout the year. The water is cold most of the time, but by mid-summer it can reach 60 degrees. There's even a small surf shop, aptly named Icy Waves.

—Don Pitcher

off the beaten path

EKLUTNA NATIVE VILLAGE – A small indigenous community in a tiny cluster of homes 26 mi north of Anchorage on the Glenn Highway is the oldest continually inhabited Athabascan Indian site in the area. At the village cemetery, note the hand-built Siberian-style prayer chapel, traditional Russian Orthodox crosses, and 80 colorful Native spirit houses. Admission includes an informative 30-minute tour. A gift shop sells Native crafts. ☎ *907/688–6026* ⊕ *www.eklutna.com* *Tours $6* ⊙ *Mid-May–mid-Sept., daily 8–6.*

GIRDWOOD – A ski resort, summer vacation spot, and home to an eclectic collection of locals, the town of Girdwood, 40 mi southeast of Anchorage near the head of Turnagain Arm, sits in the trees within a deep valley and is backdropped by tall mountains on three sides. The main attraction is the Mt. Alyeska Ski Resort, the largest ski area in Alaska. Besides enjoying the obvious winter attractions, you can mountain hike, rent a bike, or visit several restaurants and gift shops open all year. Girdwood is wetter than Anchorage; it often rains (or snows) here while the sun shines 40 mi to the north. ⊕ *www.girdwoodalaska.com.*

WHERE TO EAT

Smoking has been banned in all Anchorage restaurants, except for bars that also serve meals. Most local restaurants are open daily in summer, with reduced hours in winter. Only a few places require reservations, but it's always best to call ahead, especially for dinner.

WHAT IT COSTS	$$$$	$$$	$$	$	¢
AT DINNER	over $25	$20–$25	$15–$20	$10–$15	under $10

Prices are for a main course at dinner.

Downtown

American/Casual

$–$$$$ ✕ **Glacier BrewHouse.** The scent of hops permeates the air in the cavernous, wood-beam BrewHouse where a dozen or so ales, stouts, lagers, and pilsners are brewed on the premises. Locals mingle with visitors in this always-busy heart-of-town restaurant where dinner selections range from thin-crust, 10-inch pizzas to seafood chowder and from whiskey barbecue pork ribs to jambalaya fettuccine. For dessert, don't miss the wood-oven roasted apple and currant bread pudding. You can watch the hardworking chefs in the open kitchen. The brewery sits behind a glass wall, and the same owners operate the equally popular Ristorante Orso, next door. ✉ *737 W. 5th Ave., Downtown* ☎ *907/274–2739* ⊕ *www.glacierbrewhouse.com* ▭ *AE, D, MC, V.*

$–$$$$ ✕ **Snow Goose Restaurant and Sleeping Lady Brewing Company.** Although you can dine indoors at this comfortable edge-of-downtown eatery, the real attraction at Snow Goose is alfresco dining on the back deck and rooftop. On clear days you can see Mt. McKinley on the northern horizon and the Chugach Mountains to the east side of the city. The menu emphasizes Alaskan fare (including Kachemak Bay seafood pasta with halibut, mussels, scallops, tiger prawns, and clams), but also strays to buffalo burgers, fish-and-chips, and pork tenderloins marinated in the brewery's pale ale and Caribbean jerk seasoning. To sample the specialty beers, gather around oak tables in the upstairs bar for a brewed-on-the-premises ale, India Pale Ale, stout, barley wine, or porter. ✉ *717 W. 3rd Ave., Downtown* ☎ *907/277–7727* 🌐 *www.alaskabeers.com* ▭ *AE, D, DC, MC, V.*

$–$$ ✕ **F Street Station.** Space is at a premium in this minuscule downtown bar where the downtown business crowd heads for a light meal. It isn't for kids, and the bar sometimes gets smoky, but the food is always delicious. The steak sandwich and cheeseburgers are good bets, but also look over the board for today's seafood specials. A giant block of cheese occupies one corner of the bar, and the TVs are usually tuned to sports in this Cheers-type gathering place. ✉ *325 F St., Downtown* ☎ *907/272–5196* ▭ *AE, DC, MC, V.*

¢–$ ✕ **Downtown Deli.** A longtime favorite, this popular café is right across the street from the log cabin visitor center. Although you can choose from familiar sandwiches, like the French dip or the chicken teriyaki, this deli also has Alaskan favorites, like grilled halibut and reindeer stew. The dark, rich chicken soup comes with either noodles or homemade matzo balls, and breakfasts range from omelets and homemade granola to cheese blintzes. You can sit in one of the wooden booths for some privacy or out front at the sidewalk tables for some summertime people-watching. ✉ *525 W. 4th Ave., Downtown* ☎ *907/276–7116* ✍ *Reservations not accepted* ▭ *AE, D, DC, MC, V.*

¢ ✕ **Arctic Roadrunner.** Every year when locals vote for Anchorage's best burger joint, Arctic Roadrunner comes out on top. Forget McDonald's—these cheeseburgers are the real thing. Eat in or drive through and head to nearby Valley of the Moon Park for a sack lunch with the kids. Ultrathick milk shakes and crunchy onion rings are also on everybody's list of favorites. ✉ *2477 Arctic Blvd., Downtown* ☎ *907/279–7311* ▭ *No credit cards* ⏲ *Closed Sundays and most holidays.*

¢ ✕ **Sweet Basil Cafe.** Lunchtime sandwiches (hot or cold) on freshly baked sweet basil bread are a hit at this small and earthy juice bar accented by lavender walls and a big map of the planet. Fresh pastas, salads, wraps, fish tacos, smoothies, pastries, and light breakfasts fill out the menu, but the daily specials are often your best bet. The juice bar is one of a handful in Anchorage, and the lattes may be the best downtown. ✉ *335 E St., Downtown* ☎ *907/274–0070* ▭ *AE, D, MC, V* ⏲ *Closed Sat. and Sun. No dinner.*

Contemporary

$$$$ ✕ **Crow's Nest Restaurant.** In the Hotel Captain Cook, American and French cuisine is the order of the day, along with the best view in Anchorage—the Chugach Mountains to the east, the Alaska Range to the north, and the sprawling city of Anchorage 20 stories below. Equally impressive are the 10,000-bottle wine cellar and hefty portions. The ex-

Downtown
W. 2nd Ave.
W. 3rd Ave.
W. 4th Ave.
W. 5th Ave.
W. 6th Ave.
W. 7th Ave.
W. 8th Ave.
L St.
K St.
I St.
H St.
G St.
F St.
E St.
D St.
0 1/8 mile
0 200 meters
0 1/2 mile
0 800 meters
SEE INSET
Elderberry Park
Delaney Park
W. 9th Ave.
W. 10th Ave.
W. 11th Ave.
W. 12th Ave.
W. 13th Ave.
W. 14th Ave.
W. 15th Ave.
P St.
N St.
KEY
Coastal Trail
Hotels
Rail Lines
Restaurants
Knik Arm
Cook Inlet
Westchester Lagoon
W. Marston Dr.
Fish Creek
Hillcrest Dr.
Turnigain Pkwy.
Arlington Dr.
Forest Park Dr.
Arctic Blvd.
W. Fireweed La.
Spenard Rd.
W. 27th Ave.
Northern Lights Blvd. W.
TO EARTHQUAKE PARK, POINT WORONZOF
W. 29th St.
W. 30th Ave.
W. 31st Ave.
W. 32nd Ave.
Turnagain St.
Barbara St.
Lois Dr.
Minnesota Dr.
Benson Blvd.
Bering St.
32nd Ave.
Eureka St.
W. 34th Ave.
W. 35th Ave.
W. 36th Ave.
McRae Dr.
Spenard Rd.
Aero Ave.
Wisconsin St.
W. 40th Ave.
Northwood Dr.
Lois Dr.
Tudor Rd.
Lake Hood
44th Ave.
Spenard Beach
TO AIRPORT
Lake Spenard

Where to Stay & Eat in Anchorage

Restaurants ▼

Arctic Roadrunner **13**
The Bake Shop **56**
Bombay Deluxe
Restaurant **12**
CampoBello Bistro **8**
Chiang Mai **46**
Club Paris **37**
Crow's Nest **22**
Double Musky Inn **54**
Downtown Deli **35**
F Street Station **31**
Fu Du **52**
Glacier BrewHouse **26**
Gwennie's
Old Alaskan Restaurant . . . **4**
Jens' **9**
Kincaid Grill **5**
Kumagoro **34**
Marx Brothers' Cafe **30**
Mexico in Alaska **50**
Middle Way Cafe &
Coffee House **10**
Moose's Tooth
Pub & Pizzeria **45**
New Sagaya's
City Market **15, 48**
Organic Oasis **11**
Ristorante Orso **27**
Sacks Café **28**
Seven Glaciers **55**
Simon & Seafort's
Saloon & Grill **19**
Snow City Cafe **21**
Snow Goose Restaurant
and Sleeping Lady
Brewing Co. **29**
Sweet Basil Cafe **36**
Twin Dragon
Mongolian Bar-B-Q **44**

Hotels ▼

Alyeska Prince Hotel **53**
Anchorage
Guesthouse **14**
Anchorage Hilton **33**
Anchorage Hotel **32**
Anchorage Marriott
Downtown **38**
Anchorage Westmark
Hotel **25**
Aspen Hotel **42**
Camai Bed &
Breakfast **58**
Comfort Inn
Ship Creek **39**
Copper Whale Inn **20**
Courtyard by Marriott **2**
Dimond Center Hotel **49**
15 Chandeliers
Bed & Breakfast **57**
Hampton Inn **6**
Hotel Captain Cook **23**
Inlet Tower
Hotel and Suites **16**
Long House
Alaskan Hotel **3**
Mahogany Manor **43**
Merrill Field Inn **41**
Millennium Anchorage
Hotel **1**
Oscar Gill House **17**
Parkwood Inn **51**
Qupqugiaq Inn **7**
Sheraton Anchorage **40**
Sleeping Lady B&B **18**
SpringHill Suites
by Marriott **47**
Voyager Hotel **24**

pert waitstaff presents a menu of seafood, along with game and other meats, served in an elegant setting with plenty of starched linen, brass, and teak. It's best known for a leisurely five-course set Chef's Tasting menu: $70 per person or $110 with wine pairings. ✉ *Hotel Captain Cook, 20th floor, 5th Ave. and K St., Downtown* ☎ *907/343–2217* ✍ *Reservations essential* ▭ *AE, D, DC, MC, V* ⏲ *Closed Sun. and Mon. in the winter. No lunch.*

$$$$ Fodor's Choice ★ ✕ **Marx Brothers' Cafe.** Inside a little frame house built in 1916, this nationally recognized 46-seat café opened in 1979 and is still going strong. Elegance is the operative term at this spot where the menu changes every week, and the wine list encompasses more than 400 international choices. For an appetizer, try the king crab–stuffed squash blossoms or fresh Kachemak Bay oysters. The outstanding made-at-your-table Caesar salad is a superb opener for the baked halibut with a macadamia crust served with coconut curry sauce and fresh mango chutney. A second Marx Brothers' Cafe, housed in the Anchorage Museum of History and Arts, provides casual dining for lunch and dinner. ✉ *627 W. 3rd Ave., Downtown* ☎ *907/278–2133* ✍ *Reservations essential* ▭ *AE, DC, MC, V* ⏲ *Closed Sun. and Mon. year-round. No lunch.*

★ $$–$$$$ ✕ **Sacks Café.** This bright and colorful restaurant serves light American cuisine such as homemade butternut squash ravioli; chicken and scallops over udon noodles; and free-range chicken stuffed with prosciutto, spinach, caramelized onion, and sharp cheddar cheese. Be sure to ask about the daily specials, particularly the fresh king salmon. Flowers adorn the tables, and singles congregate along a small bar, sampling wines from California, Australia, and France. The café is especially crowded during lunch, served 11–2:30. The Saturday and Sunday brunch menu includes eggs Benedict, a Mexican scrambled egg dish called *migas,* and various salads and sandwiches. ✉ *328 G St., Downtown* ☎ *907/276–3546 or 907/274–4022* 🌐 *www.sackscafe.com* ✍ *Reservations essential* ▭ *AE, MC, V.*

$$–$$$$ ✕ **Simon & Seafort's Saloon & Grill.** Big windows overlooking Cook Inlet vistas, high ceilings, and a classy brass-and-wood interior have made this an Anchorage favorite since 1978. The diverse menu includes prime rib (aged 28 days), pasta, and sesame chicken salads, but the main attraction here is seafood—fish is blackened, grilled, fried, or prepared any other way you like it. Try the king crab legs or the grilled ahi tuna with ginger and mango salsa. The Brandy Ice—vanilla ice cream whipped with brandy, Kahlúa, and crème de cacao—is always a deliciously decadent affair here. The bar is a great spot for microbrews and martinis; the best tables are adjacent to tall windows facing the water. Validated parking is available at the nearby Hotel Captain Cook garage. ✉ *420 L St., Downtown* ☎ *907/274–3502* 🌐 *www.r-u-i.com/sim* ✍ *Reservations essential* ▭ *AE, DC, MC, V* ⏲ *No lunch weekends.*

Eclectic

¢–$ ✕ **Snow City Cafe.** At this unassuming café along "lawyer row" you'll find dependably good and reasonably priced breakfasts and lunches. Service is fast and the setting is a funky mix of mismatched chairs, Formica tables, and families and singles enjoying some of Anchorage's best breakfasts. Breakfast is served all day, but arrive early on the weekend or be prepared to wait. Snow City's lunch menu consists of hot or cold sandwiches, fresh soups, and salads. The café closes at 4 most afternoons but stays open (with limited food service) until 11 on Wednesday night, when Irish musicians invade the space. ✉ *4th Ave. at L St., Downtown* ☎ *907/272–2489* 📠 *907/272–6338* 🌐 *www.snowcitycafe.com* ⏲ *No dinner* 💳 *AE, D, DC, MC, V.*

Indian

$–$$ ✕ **Bombay Deluxe Restaurant.** Anchorage's only Indian restaurant is a find for travelers searching for something more exotic. The eatery is housed in a collection of international shops at the Valhalla Center strip mall, flanked by a Korean restaurant on one side and an Asian market on the other. Indian music spills from the speakers, and the walls are decorated with Indian posters. Dinners include such spicy standards as lamb korma, chicken vindaloo, *palak paneer* (spinach and cheese), and 10 different types of Indian breads—from tandoori roti to garlic naan. The restaurant is especially popular for weekday lunch, when the big buffet ($10) provides a sampling of Indian favorites, including several vegetarian offerings. ✉ *555 W. Northern Lights Blvd., Midtown* ☎ *907/277–1200* 💳 *AE, D, DC, MC, V.*

Italian

★ $$–$$$$ ✕ **Ristorante Orso.** One of Anchorage's culinary stars, Ristorante Orso ("bear" in Italian), evokes the earthiness of a Tuscany villa. Alaskan touches flavor rustic Mediterranean dishes, including traditional pastas, fresh seafood, wood-grilled meats, and locally famous desserts—most notably a delicious molten chocolate cake. Be sure to ask about the daily specials. If you can't get a table at dinner (reservations are advised), you can select from the same menu at the large, open bar. Upstairs you'll find a cozier, quieter space. ✉ *737 W. 5th Ave., at G St., Downtown* ☎ *907/222–3232* 🌐 *www.orsoalaska.com* 💳 *AE, D, MC, V* ⏲ *Lunch only Mon.–Fri.*

Japanese

$$–$$$$ ✕ **Kumagoro.** A favorite of the suit-and-tie lunch crowd, Kumagoro has traditional Japanese lunches and a take-out deli with such specialties as herring roe on kelp, and a sleek sushi bar (open evenings only). The best items on the dinner menu are the sizzling salmon or beef teriyaki, both served with miso (soybean) soup and salad. With the *shabu-shabu* dinner ($39 for two people), you cook your own meats and vegetables in a stockpot of boiling broth. Inexpensive homemade ramen (deep-fried Japanese-style noodles) soups are also available. All entrée prices include a 10% gratuity. ✉ *533 W. 4th Ave., Downtown* ☎ *907/272–9905* 💳 *AE, D, DC, MC, V.*

Steak

$$$–$$$$ ✕ **Club Paris.** Alaska's oldest steak house has barely changed since opening in 1957, and many of the friendly staff members have been here since the 1980s. The restaurant has dark woods and an old-fashioned feel and serves tender, flavorful steaks of all kinds, including a 4-inch-thick filet mignon. If you have to wait for a table, have a martini at the bar and order the hors d'oeuvres platter ($26)—a sampler of top sirloin steak, cheese, and prawns that could be a meal for two. For dessert, try a tart

key lime pie or triple-chocolate cheesecake. Dinner reservations are advised. ✉ *417 W. 5th Ave., Downtown* ☎ *907/277–6332* 🌐 *www.clubparisrestaurant.com* 💳 *AE, D, DC, MC, V* ⏲ *No lunch Sun.*

Greater Anchorage

American

$–$$$$ ✕ **Gwennie's Old Alaskan Restaurant.** Historic Alaskan photos, stuffed animals, and memorabilia adorn this old family favorite, just south of city center toward the airport. Lunch and dinners are available—including an all-you-can-eat beef barbecue for $17—but the restaurant is best known for its old-fashioned breakfasts, available all day. Try the sourdough pancakes, reindeer sausage and eggs, or crab omelets. Start the morning the right way with Anchorage's best Bloody Mary. ✉ *4333 Spenard Rd., Midtown* ☎ *907/243–2090* 💳 *AE, D, DC, MC, V.*

¢–$ ✕ **The Bake Shop.** The atmosphere is vintage 1975 at this old-time Girdwood favorite where you order at the counter and wait for servers to bring your meal. Breakfasts are filling, with piles of sourdough pancakes, fluffy omelets, and homemade pastries. Skiers and snowboarders drop by for a fast lunch or dinner of homemade soups, sandwiches, or garden-fresh pizzas. Get a loaf of their hearty sourdough or rye bread to go. Dine out front in the summer, surrounded by hanging baskets filled with begonias, lobelias, and impatiens. ✉ *Alyeska Boardwalk, Girdwood* ☎ *907/783–2831* 🌐 *www.thebakeshop.com* 💳 *No credit cards.*

Cajun/Creole

$$$–$$$$ ✕ **Double Musky Inn.** Anchorage residents say eating here is worth the one-hour drive south to Girdwood and the inevitable wait for dinner. It's very noisy, and the interior is completely covered with tacky art and Mardi Gras souvenirs of all types, but the windows frame views of huge Sitka spruce trees. The diverse menu mixes hearty Cajun-style meals with such favorites as garlic seafood pasta, rack of lamb, French pepper steak, and lobster kebabs. For dessert lovers, the biggest attraction here is the gooey, chocolate-rich Double Musky pie. The restaurant and lounge are both smoke-free. ✉ *Crow Creek Rd., Girdwood* ☎ *907/783–2822* 🌐 *www.doublemuskyinn.com* ✍ *Reservations not accepted* 💳 *D, DC, MC, V* ⏲ *Closed Mon. and Nov. No lunch.*

Chinese

¢–$ ✕ **Fu Du.** This is one of the oldest and best Chinese restaurants in Alaska. Although it's surrounded by fast-food spots and gas stations, when you step inside Fu Du, the flame-red Chinese wallpaper and lanterns, ultrafriendly staff (a bit over the top at times), and Asian music take you to another continent. All the standards are available, including beef with oyster sauce, kung pao chicken, sweet-and-sour pork, and various vegetable entrées. Portions are enormous and always include soup, kimchee, rice, egg roll, and tea. Lunch specials are an even better deal, and free delivery is offered if you don't want to leave your hotel. ✉ *2600 E. Tudor Rd., Midtown* ☎ *907/561–6610* 💳 *AE, MC, V.*

¢–$ ✕ **Twin Dragon Mongolian Bar-B-Q.** If you haven't eaten Mongolian barbecue before, you're in for a treat. Choose your stir-fry ingredients and sauces, then watch as the chefs cook your meal with a flourish on the giant wok. The restaurant also has an impressive Chinese buffet with a multitude of choices; it's $8 for lunch or $12 for dinner. ✉ *612 E. 15th Ave., Midtown* ☎ *907/276–7535* ▭ *D, MC, V.*

Contemporary

★ $$$$ ✕ **Seven Glaciers.** A 60-passenger aerial tram (free with dinner reservations, otherwise $16 round-trip) carries you to this refined yet relaxing mountainside restaurant, perched at the 2,300-foot level of Mt. Alyeska. The comfortable dining room overlooks seven glaciers. Try the artfully presented smoked and grilled salmon or mesquite-grilled strip loin of buffalo. Appetizers—particularly the peppered crab cakes—are extraordinary. A la carte prices are high, but a four-course menu ($70 per person, including a matched wine) is available nightly in summer. Both tram and restaurant are wheelchair accessible. Dinner seatings are from 5:30 to 9:30 PM. ✉ *Alyeska Prince Hotel, 1000 Arlberg Rd., Girdwood* ☎ *907/754–2237* 🌐 *www.alyeskaresort.com* ✍ *Reservations essential* ▭ *AE, D, MC, V* ⏲ *Closed Sun.–Thurs. Nov.–May. No lunch.*

★ $$$–$$$$ ✕ **Kincaid Grill.** This out-of-the-way restaurant provides a respite after a summertime hike or wintertime ski in nearby Kincaid Park. Chef and owner Al Levinsohn worked his way up through some of Alaska's finest restaurants, and the experience shines through in the diverse and creative menu. The upscale setting is lively, with old-time jazz spilling from the speakers, the buzz of conversations, and artistically presented meals. Low-backed metal stools line the wine bar, where you can sample a microbrew or vintages from around the globe. The menu changes every few weeks, but always includes filet mignon, grilled Hawaiian game fish, Alaskan salmon or halibut, and a rich seafood gumbo. Try to save room for the pineapple upside-down cake. ✉ *6700 Jewel Lake Rd., South Anchorage* ☎ *907/243–0507* 🌐 *www.kincaidgrill.com* ✍ *Reservations essential* ▭ *AE, MC, V* ⏲ *Closed Sun. and Mon. No lunch.*

★ $$–$$$$ ✕ **Jens'.** Despite its location in a midtown strip mall, Jens' is a surprisingly classy and playful restaurant where the menu changes daily and everyone feels at home. Colorful paintings grace white walls, and friendly gray-haired waiters greet new arrivals. The dinner menu almost always includes Alaskan salmon, halibut, and rockfish, along with such specialties as rack of lamb, tenderloin of veal, and an "almost world-famous" pepper steak. Head chef Jens Haagen Hansen's heritage reveals itself at lunch when the Danish specials appear, along with soups, salads, pastas, and vegetarian meals. For a lighter evening meal, sample the appetizers in the wine bar, where Jens holds court. Reservations are highly recommended. ✉ *701 W. 36th Ave., at Arctic Blvd., Midtown* ☎ *907/561–5367* 🌐 *www.jensrestaurant.com* ▭ *AE, D, DC, MC, V* ⏲ *Closed Sun. and Jan. No lunch Sat., no dinner Mon.*

Eclectic

★ ¢–$ ✕ **New Sagaya's City Market.** Stop here for quick lunches and Kaladi Brothers espresso. The in-house bakery (L'Aroma) cranks out specialty breads and pastries of all types, and the international deli and grocery serves California-style pizzas, Chinese food, lasagna, rotisserie chicken, salads, and even stuffed cabbage. You can eat inside on the sheltered patio or grab an outside table on a summer afternoon. New Sagaya's has one of the best seafood counters in town and will even box and ship your fish. ✉ *900 W. 13th Ave., Downtown* ☎ *907/274–6173, 907/274–9797, or 800/764–1001* ✉ *3700 Old Seward Hwy., Midtown* ☎ *907/562–9797* 🖷 *907/274–2042* 🌐 *www.newsagaya.com* 💳 *AE, D, DC, MC, V.*

Italian

$$–$$$ ✕ **CampoBello Bistro.** Tucked into a midtown mall, CampoBello has surprisingly sophisticated Italian entrées and sinful desserts. Step inside for a romantic lunch or dinner surrounded by splashes of modern art on the walls and candles on the tables. Specialties include ample servings of seafood crepes, wild mushroom cannelloni, veal saltimbocca, housemade four-cheese ravioli, and shrimp and scallops Florentine. Service is attentive, and the wine list—particularly the Italian choices—is impressive. Dinner reservations are advised. ✉ *601 W. 36th Ave., Midtown* ☎ *907/563–2040* 💳 *DC, MC, V* ⏲ *Closed Sun. No lunch Sat.*

Mexican

$$ ✕ **Mexico in Alaska.** Since 1972 the most authentic Mexican food in town, and maybe even in Alaska, has been served here. Owner Maria Elena Ball befriends everyone, particularly young children. Favorite dishes—all are subtle and not greasy—include lime-marinated fried chicken, *chilaquiles* (tortilla casserole with mole sauce), and *entremesa de queso* (melted cheese, jalapeños, and onions with homemade tortillas). Weekday lunch buffets ($10) and Sunday dinner buffets ($12) are popular, and a vegetarian menu is available. The restaurant is several miles south of downtown, so you'll need to drive or catch the city bus. ✉ *7305 Old Seward Hwy., South Anchorage* ☎ *907/349–1528* 💳 *AE, D, MC, V* ⏲ *No lunch Sun.*

Pizza

★ $–$$$ ✕ **Moose's Tooth Pub & Pizzeria.** Always a top pick when local newspapers rate Anchorage pizzerias, Moose's Tooth is packed any night of the week. The reason is obvious at this down-home spot: creative pizzas and handcrafted beers from their own brewery. More than a dozen ales, ambers, porters, and stouts are the order of the day, and the homemade root beers, cream sodas, and ginger ales are also available. You can match these brews with one of the 40 different pizzas with such varied toppings as roasted red peppers, jalapeños, cream cheese, halibut, and capers. Weekday lunches start at $5 for a slice of pizza and a salad. You can do dinner and a movie in one move at the Moose's Tooth Theatre Pub (⇨ *See* Nightlife & the Arts). ✉ *3300 Old Seward Hwy., Midtown* ☎ *907/258–2537* 🌐 *www.moosestooth.net* 💳 *D, DC, MC, V.*

Thai

★ ¢–$ ✕ **Chiang Mai.** Among the Thai restaurants scattered around Anchorage, this is one of the best, with authentic Thai cooking and quick and friendly service—and a new name (its former name was Thai House Restaurant). You will find fare such as fresh rolls (a house specialty), pad thai (spicy cooked noodles with shrimp, chicken, and eggs), and *tom khar gai* (a flavorful soup of coconut milk, chicken, lemongrass, and ginger). Vegetarians have a number of choices, and unique Thai desserts are always on the menu board. The restaurant closes at 9 PM. ✉ *3637 Old Seward Hwy., Midtown* ☎ *907/563–8900* 💳 *AE, MC, V.*

Vegetarian

¢–$$ **Organic Oasis.** Next to a yoga studio and just up the street from Chilkoot Charlie's, this popular café has a dark and airy interior accented by potted plants. Fresh-squeezed juices, smoothies, organic sandwiches, and tofu burgers dominate, but the menu spreads beyond to include buffalo burgers, chicken, fresh mussels, and other food for carnivores. There's live guitar music Tuesday–Saturday nights and free wireless Internet access anytime. Service can be slow at times. ✉ *2610 Spenard Rd., Midtown* ☎ *907/277–7882* 🌐 *www.organicoasis.com* ▭ *AE, D, MC, V.*

¢ **Middle Way Cafe & Coffee House.** Vegetarian and nonvegetarian dishes are served at this cramped little lunchtime niche, including gussied-up grain-and-soy burgers, turkey cranberry sandwiches, avocado melts, vegan baked goods, and jumbo whole-grain tortillas wrapped around combinations of organic veggies, falafel, brown rice, and beans. You can get a fruit smoothie at the juice bar, choose from 35 different teas, or enjoy an espresso. Be sure to check out the daily specials. A kids' menu has smaller portions. ✉ *1200 W. Northern Lights Blvd., Midtown* ☎ *907/272–6433* *Reservations not accepted* ▭ *MC, V* ⏲ *Kitchen closed Sun.*

WHERE TO STAY

Several hotels in Anchorage have top-drawer amenities, with summertime rates to match. Smaller inns and 175 or so bed-and-breakfasts offer character and quaint amenities at more modest prices. Most hotels in Anchorage are downtown, in midtown, or along Spenard Avenue. In the last decade many of the large hotel chains have built modern hotels in Anchorage, most of which include such amenities as indoor pools, Jacuzzis, free Continental breakfasts, large televisions, and in-room refrigerators and microwaves.

Girdwood, 40 mi south of downtown along the Seward and Alyeska highways, has ski-resort amenities and a mountain setting. For a listing of hotels, inns, and B&Bs, contact the Anchorage Convention and Visitors Bureau. For campgrounds in and around town, contact the Alaska Public Lands Information Center (⇨ What to See *in* Exploring Anchorage). In summer, reservations are a must for the major hotels; many fill up months in advance. A good option for budget travelers is Priceline.com, where you can often find rooms in Anchorage hotels for half of the going rate.

WHAT IT COSTS

	$$$$	$$$	$$	$	¢
FOR 2 PEOPLE	over $250	$200–$250	$150–$200	$100–$150	under $100

Prices are for two people in a standard double room in high season, excluding tax and service.

Downtown

$$$$ **Anchorage Hilton.** Alaska's largest hotel is just a block from city center and fills with cruise-ship tourists all summer long. An inviting and

ample lobby includes Alaskan touches and is flanked by a café and a classy sports bar. The hotel's premier restaurant, **Top of the World,** occupies the 15th floor of the west tower. An outdoor deck provides the highest outdoor eating experience in town. Well-maintained rooms, decorated in a contemporary style with oak and maple furnishings, are in two towers, one of which is 22 floors. Request a corner north-facing suite on the upper levels for Mt. McKinley vistas. ✉ *500 W. 3rd Ave., Downtown, 99501* ☎ *907/272–7411 or 800/245–2527* 🖷 *907/265–7044* 🌐 *www.anchoragehilton.com* *572 rooms, 23 suites* *2 restaurants, cable TV with movies and video games, indoor pool, health club, 2 lounges, Internet, meeting rooms* 💳 *AE, D, DC, MC, V.*

$$$$ **Anchorage Marriott Downtown.** One of Anchorage's biggest lodgings, the brightly decorated Marriott appeals to business travelers, tourists, and corporate clients. The hotel's Cafe Promenade serves American cuisine with an Alaskan flair. All guest rooms have huge windows; views are breathtaking from the top floors. Well-designed furnishings include workstation desks with two-line phones and voice mail. If you stay on one of the top three levels of this 20-story hotel, you have access to a concierge lounge and are served a light breakfast as well as evening hors d'oeuvres and desserts. ✉ *820 W. 7th Ave., Downtown, 99501* ☎ *907/279–8000 or 800/228–9290* 🖷 *907/279–8005* 🌐 *www.marriott.com* *392 rooms, 3 suites* *Restaurant, room service, some microwaves, cable TV with movies, indoor pool, gym, hot tub, bar, shops, concierge, Internet, business services, meeting rooms* 💳 *AE, D, DC, MC, V.*

★ **$$$$** **Hotel Captain Cook.** This classy Anchorage hotel recalls Captain Cook's voyages to Alaska and the South Pacific, with dark teak paneling lining the interior and a nautical theme that continues into the recently remodeled guest rooms. All rooms have ceiling fans, and guests can use the full gym, business center, and other facilities, including three restaurants and a coffee bar. The hotel occupies an entire city block with three towers, the tallest of which is capped by the **Crow's Nest Restaurant.** The most luxurious accommodation is found on the 19th floor of Tower III—a sprawling, 1,600-square-foot two-bedroom suite, which costs a mere $1,500 per night. ✉ *4th Ave. and K St., Downtown, 99501* ☎ *907/276–6000 or 800/843–1950* 🖷 *907/343–2298* 🌐 *www.captaincook.com* *451 rooms, 96 suites* *3 restaurants, room service, cable TV with movies and video games, pool, health club, hair salon, hot tub, sauna, racquetball, shop, concierge, Internet, business center, meeting rooms; no a/c* 💳 *AE, D, DC, MC, V.*

$$$$ **Sheraton Anchorage.** A glass-canopy lobby with a jade-tile staircase, acres of cream-color marble, and guest rooms where you can pick up voice mail, iron a suit, and brew your own coffee make this 16-story hotel one of the city's best, despite its marginal neighborhood. Get a room high up on the north side to watch F-16s and other jets flying tight patterns over nearby Elmendorf Air Force Base. A downstairs restaurant (Ptarmigan Bar & Grill) serves three meals a day, and a 15th-floor restaurant (Josephine's) serves a daily seafood buffet and Sunday brunch-with-a-view all summer. ✉ *401 E. 6th Ave., Downtown, 99501* ☎ *907/276–8700 or 800/325–3535* 🖷 *907/276–7561* 🌐 *www.sheraton.com*

◁ *375 rooms, 5 suites △ Restaurant, room service, cable TV with movies and video games, health club, hot tub, sauna, bar, Internet, meeting rooms* ▭ *AE, D, DC, MC, V.*

$$$–$$$$ ▦ **Anchorage Westmark Hotel.** Each comfortable room in this 13-story hotel has a small private balcony and modern furnishings. Reserve a room or suite on the higher floors for the best mountain views. The downstairs restaurant, Solstice Bar & Grill, serves three meals a day, and several notable eateries are nearby, including Ristorante Orso and Glacier Brewhouse. (Do not confuse the Westmark Hotel with the reasonably priced but far more basic Westmark Inn.) Eleven rooms here are handicap accessible. ✉ *720 W. 5th Ave., Downtown, 99501* ☎ *907/276–7676 or 800/544–0970* 🖷 *907/276–3615* ⊕ *www.westmarkhotels.com* ◁ *188 rooms, 12 suites △ Restaurant, coffee shop, room service, cable TV with movies, Internet, meeting room* ▭ *AE, D, DC, MC, V.*

★ **$$$** ▦ **Anchorage Hotel.** The little Anchorage Hotel building has been around since 1916. Experienced travelers call it the only hotel in Anchorage with charm: the original sinks and tubs have been restored, and upstairs hallways are lined with old Anchorage photos. The rooms are nicely updated with dark cherrywood furnishings and stocked minibars. The small lobby, its fireplace crackling in chilly weather, has a quaint European feel, and the staff is adept at meeting your needs. Request a corner room if possible; rooms facing the street may have some traffic noise. The junior suites include comfortable sitting areas. ✉ *330 E St., Downtown, 99501* ☎ *907/272–4553 or 800/544–0988* 🖷 *907/277–4483* ⊕ *www.historicanchoragehotel.com* ◁ *16 rooms, 10 junior suites △ Some kitchenettes, refrigerators, cable TV, Internet, meeting rooms; no a/c, no smoking* ▭ *AE, D, DC, MC, V* ⦿❘ *CP.*

$$–$$$ ▦ **Comfort Inn Ship Creek.** Ship Creek gurgles past this popular family hotel, a short walk northeast of the Alaska Railroad depot. Rooms, which can be a bit noisy at times, come in a variety of configurations. A substantial Continental breakfast is served each morning, and the lobby features an enormous brown bear. The hotel stocks a limited number of fishing poles for those who want to try their luck catching salmon in Ship Creek, just a few steps away. ✉ *111 Ship Creek Ave., Downtown, 99501* ☎ *907/277–6887 or 800/424–6423* 🖷 *907/274–9830* ⊕ *www.comfortinn.com* ◁ *88 rooms, 12 suites △ Some kitchens, microwaves, refrigerators, cable TV with movies and video games, pool, gym, hot tub, Internet, business services, some pets allowed (fee)* ▭ *AE, D, DC, MC, V* ⦿❘ *CP.*

★ **$$–$$$** ▦ **Inlet Tower Hotel and Suites.** Windows overlook either the Chugach Mountains, the Cook Inlet, or downtown Anchorage in the Inlet Tower. Built in 1952 in a residential area a few blocks south of downtown, this 14-story building was Alaska's first high-rise. A major remodeling in 2003 brought spacious rooms and suites, uniquely Alaskan wallpaper, high-end linens, large televisions, high-speed Internet lines (wireless Internet in the lobby), kitchenettes, and blackout curtains for summer mornings when the sun comes up at 3 AM. Corner rooms, particularly those on the northeast side, provide expansive views. Downstairs, Mick's at the Inlet serves three meals a day, with a dinner menu that encompasses roasted duck, blackened wild salmon, elk ribs, and chicken cacciatore. In the winter months, a full breakfast is included. ✉ *1200 L St., Down-*

town, 99501 ☎ 907/276–0110 or 800/544–0786 📠 907/258–4914 🌐 www.inlettower.com 154 rooms, 26 suites Restaurant, some kitchens, microwaves, refrigerators, cable TV, laundry facilities, meeting room, business center, gym, Internet, free airport and railroad shuttle, free parking; no a/c ▭ AE, D, DC, MC, V.

$$ **Aspen Hotel.** Part of a small Alaskan-owned chain, the Aspen opened in 2003 and is Anchorage's newest downtown hotel. Rooms are large and comfortably furnished with a single king or two queen beds, a writing table, 27-inch TV, DVD player, mini-fridge, and microwave. Two-room suites include a larger refrigerator, stovetop, and pull-out sofa; some also feature in-room Jacuzzis. The hotel is just a block from the museum and Delaney Park Strip, and has limited off-street parking plus a pool and Jacuzzi downstairs. ✉ *108 E. 8th Ave., Downtown, 99501* ☎ *907/868–1605 or 888/506–7848* 📠 *907/868–3520* 🌐 *www.aspenhotelsak.com* *75 rooms, 14 suites* *Cable TV with movies, refrigerators, indoor pool, hot tub, exercise room, laundry service, Internet, business services, free airport and railroad shuttle* ▭ *AE, D, DC, MC, V* *CP.*

$$ **Sleeping Lady Bed & Breakfast.** The Tony Knowles Coastal Trail is steps away from this attractive B&B. Unwind on the large back deck and take in the lengthy summer sunsets over Cook Inlet. Four spacious and private guest rooms are attractively furnished, with three facing the water. The largest contains high arched windows and a fireplace. Downtown restaurants and shopping are within easy walking distance. ✉ *545 M St., Downtown, 99501* ☎ *907/258–4455* 📠 *907/258–4955* 🌐 *www.anchsleepingladybnb.com* *4 rooms* *Cable TV; no a/c, no smoking* ▭ *AE, MC, V* *BP.*

$$ **Voyager Hotel.** Both business and leisure travelers stay here for the complete kitchens, sofa beds, coffeemakers, irons and ironing boards, quality linens, voice mail, and cable modems in the rooms. ✉ *501 K St., Downtown, 99501* ☎ *907/277–9501 or 800/247–9070* 📠 *907/274–0333* 🌐 *www.voyagerhotel.com* *40 rooms* *In-room data ports, kitchens, microwaves, refrigerators, cable TV; no smoking* ▭ *AE, D, DC, MC, V* *CP.*

$–$$ **Copper Whale Inn.** A view across Cook Inlet to Sleeping Lady and other mountains, rooms furnished with cherrywood beds, and a little backyard graced with a pleasant flower garden make this small inn on the edge of downtown cozy. Great food is available just a few steps away at Simon & Seafort's or Snow City Cafe. Owner Tony Carter, a marine biologist, leads an excellent all-day wildlife ecotour for $75. ✉ *440 L St., Downtown, 99501* ☎ *907/258–7999* 📠 *907/258–6213 or 888/942–5346* 🌐 *www.copperwhale.com* *15 rooms* *Dining room, Internet; no a/c, no room TVs, no smoking* ▭ *AE, D, DC, MC, V* *CP.*

$ **Merrill Field Inn.** Reasonable prices and surprisingly large rooms make this well-maintained motel, 1 mi east of downtown and across from Anchorage's small-plane airfield, a favorite with families. A light breakfast is available in the lobby in the morning. ✉ *420 Sitka St., East Anchorage, 99501* ☎ *907/276–4547 or 800/898–4547* 📠 *907/276–5064* 🌐 *www.merrillfieldinn.com* *39 rooms, 1 suite* *Microwaves, refrigerators, cable TV, Internet, airport shuttle, some pets allowed (fee); no a/c* ▭ *AE, D, DC, MC, V* *CP.*

¢–$ **Oscar Gill House.** Gill originally built his home in the settlement of Knik (north of Anchorage) in 1913. Three years later, he floated it by boat to Anchorage, where he later served as the mayor for three terms and then Speaker of the Territorial House. The home has been transformed into a comfortable B&B in a quiet neighborhood along Delaney Park Strip, with downtown attractions a short walk away. Two rooms share a bath with a classic claw-foot tub, and the third contains a private bath and Jacuzzi tub. Little touches include down comforters, bicycles, and a delicious breakfast. *1344 W. 10th Ave., Downtown, 99501 907/279–1344 www.oscargill.com 3 rooms Cable TV, Internet; no a/c, no smoking AE, MC, V BP.*

¢ **Anchorage Guesthouse.** Popular with young outdoorsy travelers, this home hostel in a residential neighborhood near downtown has both private rooms and dorm-style accommodations with bunks. All rooms share three bathrooms. You can rent bikes here, then head out for the Tony Knowles Coastal Trail, or store your gear in the garage before taking off for extended trips into the wilderness. The glassed-in sunroom has a computer to check your e-mail or to sip coffee on a chilly morning. Owner Andy Baker is a former engineer turned professional musician. Make-it-yourself breakfast that includes cereal, eggs, milk, bread, and fruit is included with price of room. Book well ahead for the busy summer season. *2001 Hillcrest Dr., Midtown, 99517 907/274–0408 www.akhouse.com 1 dorm room, 2 private rooms Kitchen, bicycles, library, laundry facilities, Internet; no a/c, no room phones, no room TVs, no smoking AE, MC, V CP.*

Greater Anchorage

$$$$ Fodor'sChoice ★ **Alyeska Prince Hotel.** Lush forests surround this large and luxurious hotel at the base of Alyeska Ski Resort, an hour south of Anchorage. Some rooms have views of the Chugach Mountains. Rooms are on the small side, but all have heated towel racks, ski-boot storage lockers, bathrobes, and slippers, plus phones in both the bathrooms and bedrooms. Guests relax in front of the big lobby fireplace, with tall windows facing the mountains. The large heated saltwater pool is a major attraction for families, and the hot tub is a hit after a day on the slopes. Dining choices include a family-style restaurant and a gourmet Japanese grill, Katsura Teppanyaki. A spectacular aerial tram (free if you have dinner reservations) transports diners to the Seven Glaciers Restaurant at the 2,300-foot level of the mountain. *1000 Arlberg Rd. Box 249, Girdwood 99587 907/754–1111 or 800/880–3880 907/754–2200 www.alyeskaresort.com 296 rooms, 12 suites 3 restaurants, room service, in-room safes, refrigerators, cable TV with movies, indoor pool, gym, hot tub, massage, sauna, cross-country skiing, downhill skiing, ice-skating, bar, shop, Internet, concierge, business services, meeting room, no-smoking rooms; no a/c AE, D, DC, MC, V.*

$$$$ **Dimond Center Hotel.** Owned by the Seldovia Native Association, this bright and modern hotel is popular with Alaskans from the Bush who appreciate nearby shopping (along with ice-skating and bowling) at Dimond Center Mall, Wal-Mart, Costco, and other big stores. Non-Alaskans discover a surprisingly plush facility with custom-designed

furnishings and a huge lobby lit by tall windows. Spacious high-ceilinged rooms include 36-inch TVs, relaxing soaking tubs, goose-down comforters on the queen or king beds, and Wi-Fi Web access. Stuff yourself at the breakfast bar, which includes Belgian waffles, fresh fruit, yogurt, and pastries. Guests also receive a pass to an adjacent fitness center that includes two pools, Nautilus, steam rooms, hot tubs, and more. There's even a big freezer if you're bringing home fish from your trip. Check their Web site for frequent special rates. ✉ *700 E. Dimond Blvd., South Anchorage, 99515* ☎ *907/770–5000 or 866/770–5002* 🖷 *907/770–5001* 🌐 *www.dimondcenterhotel.com* *108 rooms* *Microwaves, refrigerators, cable TV with movies, Internet, airport and downtown shuttle; no smoking* *AE, D, DC, MC, V* *CP.*

★ **$$$$** **Millennium Anchorage Hotel.** Perched on the shore of Lake Spenard, the extensively renovated Millennium Anchorage Hotel is one of the city's best spots to watch planes come and go. The lobby resembles a hunting lodge with its stone fireplace, trophy heads, and mounted fish on every wall. The luxuriously appointed guest rooms continue the inviting Alaskan theme. Most have colorful Native Alaskan–style bedding. All rooms have coffeemakers and hair dryers. The **Flying Machine Restaurant** here is locally famous for its enormous Sunday brunch buffets ($29). ✉ *4800 Spenard Rd., Midtown, 99517* ☎ *907/243–2300 or 800/544–0553* 🖷 *907/243–8815* 🌐 *www.millennium-hotels.com* *243 rooms, 5 suites* *Restaurant, room service, refrigerators, cable TV with movies and video games, gym, hot tub, sauna, steam room, lobby lounge, laundry service, Internet, airport shuttle, business center, some pets allowed* *AE, D, DC, MC, V.*

$$$ **Hampton Inn.** Midway between the airport and downtown, the Hampton has all the now-standard features: refrigerators, microwaves, Continental breakfast, designer furnishings, coffeemakers, hair dryers, and voice mail. The same management also runs two nearby places just up A Street, Hilton Garden Inn and Homewood Suites. ✉ *4301 Credit Union Dr., Midtown, 99503* ☎ *907/550–7000 or 800/426–7866* 🖷 *907/561–7330* 🌐 *www.stonebridgecompanies.com* *101 rooms* *In-room data ports, microwaves, refrigerators, cable TV with movies and video games, indoor pool, exercise equipment, hot tub, laundry service, Internet, business services, meeting room* *AE, D, DC, MC, V* *CP.*

$$$ **Mahogany Manor.** Escape from city life at this rambling B&B, hidden behind a tall fence along busy 15th Avenue and decorated with Native Alaskan art throughout. Unwind with the expansive decks, large picture windows, indoor waterfall, fireplaces, and big-screen television. An unusual 19-foot hot tub and jetted lap pool occupies a lower deck, with a solarium to hold in the heat. The spacious three-room suite is perfect for families and small groups. A hearty Continental breakfast is served anytime, and guests have access to a separate kitchen and a computer with high-speed Internet. ✉ *204 E. 15th Ave., Midtown, 99501* ☎ *907/278–1111 or 888/777–0346* 🖷 *907/258–7877* 🌐 *www.mahoganymanor.com* *3 rooms, 1 suite* *Dining room, cable TV, pool, hot tub, Internet; no a/c, no smoking* *AE, D, MC, V* *CP.*

$$–$$$ **Courtyard by Marriott.** Business travelers pack this modern hotel near the airport. The restaurant serves breakfast and dinner and offers limited room service in the evening. Some rooms have a whirlpool bath and king-size bed; all have two phones, coffeemakers, and hair dryers. ✉ *4901 Spenard Rd., Midtown, 99517* ☎ *907/245–0322 or 800/314–0782* 🖷 *907/248–1886* 🌐 *www.marriott.com* *148 rooms, 6 suites* *Restaurant, room service, some in-room hot tubs, cable TV with movies, pool, exercise equipment, hot tub, sauna, laundry service, meeting room, airport shuttle, no-smoking rooms* ▭ *AE, D, DC, MC, V.*

$$ **Long House Alaskan Hotel.** Just five minutes from the airport, this hotel consists of three log-covered two-story buildings. Rooms are large, modern, and comfortable, with two televisions in the suites (where no door separates the rooms). Anglers appreciate the big walk-in freezer to store their catch. ✉ *4335 Wisconsin St., Midtown, 99517* ☎ *907/243–2133 or 888/243–2133* 🖷 *907/243–6060* 🌐 *www.longhousehotel.com* *54 rooms, 3 suites* *Microwaves, refrigerators, cable TV, airport shuttle; no a/c* ▭ *AE, D, DC, MC, V* *CP.*

$$ **SpringHill Suites by Marriott.** The city's main public library and a 16-plex movie theater are near this midtown Anchorage hotel. Spacious one-room suites have separate living and sleeping areas and either a king bed or two double beds with a pull-out sofa, plus two televisions. With no extra charge, up to five people can stay in these suites, and breakfast is included. ✉ *3401 A St., Downtown, 99503* ☎ *907/562–3247 or 888/287–9400* 🖷 *907/562–3250* 🌐 *www.springhillsuites.com* *102 suites* *Microwaves, refrigerators, cable TV with movies, indoor pool, gym, hot tub, meeting rooms, airport shuttle* ▭ *AE, D, DC, MC, V* *CP.*

$–$$ **15 Chandeliers Bed & Breakfast.** One of Alaska's premier B&Bs, 15 Chandeliers is a 7,000-square-foot mansion with a spacious front lawn and a big patio with floral gardens in the rear. Owners James and Audrey Schefers make guests comfortable in five theme rooms, all with private baths, antique furnishings, high ceilings and chandeliers, queen beds, phones, and televisions, plus access to the common areas. A filling breakfast is served buffet style. ✉ *14020 Sabine St., Hillside, 99511* ☎ *907/345–3032* 🖷 *907/345–3990* 🌐 *www.15chandeliers.com* *5 rooms* *Cable TV; no a/c, no kids under age 12, no smoking* ▭ *AE, MC, V* *BP.*

$ **Parkwood Inn.** Originally built as an apartment complex, this hotel provides reasonably priced family accommodations near the intersection of New Seward Highway and Tudor Road. Rooms are large and include full kitchens with dishes, a walk-in closet, and balcony. The two-bedroom suites can sleep six. ✉ *4455 Juneau St., South Anchorage, 99503* ☎ *907/563–3590 or 800/478–3590* 🖷 *907/563–5560* 🌐 *www.parkwoodinn.net* *49 rooms, 2 suites* *Microwaves, refrigerators, cable TV with movies, Internet, airport shuttle, some pets allowed, no-smoking rooms; no a/c* ▭ *AE, D, DC, MC, V.*

¢–$ **Camai Bed & Breakfast.** Open since 1981, this elegant B&B is Anchorage's oldest. Two of the suites have private entries and plenty of space for families. All rooms have private baths and in-room TV and phones. Moose are frequent visitors to the yard, and the B&B is adjacent to Chester Creek Trail, a paved bike path that leads to downtown Anchorage. Breakfast is a high point, with such specials as French toast stuffed with peaches and cream or artichoke frittata. ✉ *3838 Westminster*

Way, 99508 ☎ 907/333–2219 or 800/659–8763 🌐 www.camaibnb.com ⇨ 3 suites ♨ Dining room, cable TV, in-room VCRs, Internet; no a/c, no smoking ▭ No credit cards 🍴 BP.

¢ **Qupqugiaq Inn.** A bland, boxy exterior disguises this cross between a motel and a hostel with an unpronounceable name. The interior architecture of "Q Inn" is distinctive, with curved walls and bright pine accents. This is a good option for budget travelers who tolerate small quarters and the lack of in-room phones but appreciate clean and well-maintained facilities, including antique English beds. You have access to a communal kitchen and sitting room. A pleasant café is downstairs, and Europa Bakery is right across the street. ✉ *640 W. 36th Ave., Midtown, 99503* ☎ *907/563–5633* 🌐 *www.qupq.com* ⇨ *26 rooms, 4 with shared bath* ♨ *Café, kitchens, Internet, meeting rooms; no a/c, no smoking* ▭ *AE, MC, V.*

NIGHTLIFE & THE ARTS

Nightlife

Anchorage does not shut down when it gets dark. Bars here—and throughout Alaska—open early (in the morning) and close as late as 3 AM on weekends. The listings in the *Anchorage Daily News* entertainment section, published on Friday, range from concerts and theater to movies and a roundup of nightspots featuring live music.

Bars & Nightclubs

Fodor'sChoice ★ **Chilkoot Charlie's** (✉ 2435 Spenard Rd., Midtown ☎ 907/272–1010 🌐 www.koots.com), a rambling timber building with sawdust floors, 11 bars (including one bar made of ice), three dance floors, loud music (rock or swing bands and DJs) nightly, and rowdy customers, is where young Alaskans go to get crazy. This legendary bar has all sorts of unusual nooks and crannies, including a room filled with Russian artifacts and serving the finest vodka drinks, plus a reconstructed version of Alaska's infamous Birdhouse Bar. "Koots" even made *Playboy*'s list as the number one bar in America in 2000. If you haven't been to Koots, you haven't seen Anchorage nightlife at its wildest.

F Street Station (✉ 325 F St., Downtown ☎ 907/272–5196), a crowded little downtown bar, is a delightful spot for a perfectly prepared and reasonably priced lunch or dinner. Check the board for the day's specials, or just enjoy a beer and appetizers with the suit-and-tie crowd. A half-dozen small tables are available, or you can eat at the bar and chat with the chefs as they work.

Rumrunners (✉ 501 W. 4th Ave., Downtown ☎ 907/278–4493) is right across from old City Hall in the center of town. A pub-grub menu brings the lunch crowd, but when evening comes the big dance floor gets packed as DJs spin the tunes. Anchorage's favorite martini bar, **Bernie's Bungalow Lounge** (✉ 626 D St., Downtown ☎ 907/276–8808 🌐 www.berniesbungalowlounge.com), is a hip spot, with retro furnishings, splashy art, and a DJ most weekends. The cocktail to order here is a cosmopolitan.

Lots of old-timers favor the dark bar of **Club Paris** (✉ 417 W. 5th Ave., Downtown ☎ 907/277–6332 🌐 www.clubparisrestaurant.com). Once the classiest place in downtown Anchorage, with its Paris mural and French street lamps hanging behind the bar, it has lost the glamour but not the faithful clientele. There's mostly swing on the jukebox.

A trendy place for the dressy "in" crowd, the bar at **Simon & Seafort's Saloon & Grill** (✉ 420 L St., Downtown ☎ 907/274–3502 🌐 www.r-u-i.com/sim) has stunning views of Cook Inlet, a special single-malt Scotch menu, and a wide selection of imported beers.

Snow Goose Restaurant (✉ 717 W. 3rd Ave., Downtown ☎ 907/277–7727 🌐 www.alaskabeers.com) is a good place to unwind with beer inside or on the airy outside deck overlooking Cook Inlet. There's excellent food, too.

Anchorage's gay nightlife centers on a pair of bars, both of which attract a mixed crowd that includes straights, gays, and lesbians. **Mad Myrna's** (✉ 530 E. 5th Ave., Downtown ☎ 907/276–9762 🌐 www.alaska.net/~madmyrna) has karaoke on Wednesday, country dancing (with lessons) on Thursday, and drag shows every Friday. The **Raven** (✉ 708 E. 4th Ave., Downtown ☎ 907/276–9672) is a smoky neighborhood hangout where you'll meet regulars over a game of billiards or darts. In addition to the bars, Anchorage also has a popular alcohol-free **Gay and Lesbian Community Center** (✉ 2110 E. Northern Lights Blvd., Midtown ☎ 907/929–4528). It's open daily.

Comedy

★ Mr. Whitekeys is the proprietor of **Fly by Night Club** (✉ 3300 Spenard Rd., Midtown ☎ 907/279–7726 🌐 www.flybynightclub.com), a self-proclaimed "sleazy Spenard nightclub." Every summer, the "Whale Fat Follies" revue has tacky Alaska jokes, a witty skewering of the state's politicians, accomplished singing, and the boogie-woogie piano of Mr. Whitekeys himself. Go with a local to really appreciate all the inside jokes. Shows start at 8; reserving several days in advance is a good idea. The club is smoke-free Tuesday, Wednesday, and Thursday night; it's closed Sunday–Monday and January–March.

Live Music

See the "8" section in Friday editions of the *Anchorage Daily News* for complete listings of upcoming concerts and other musical performances, or get the same entertainment info online at 🌐 www.adn.com. On most summertime Fridays, open-air concerts are performed at noon on the stage in front of the **Old City Hall** (✉ 524 W. 4th Ave., Downtown). A range of performers play at the **Saturday Market** (✉ 3rd Ave. and E St., Downtown ☎ 907/272–5634 🌐 www.anchoragemarkets.com) every Saturday from late May to mid-September. The music includes everything from family bands (with daughter on violin and dad on guitar and vocals) to Peruvian pan-pipe musicians.

Chilkoot Charlie's (⇨ Bars & Nightclubs) is an exceptionally popular party place, with live music every night of the week. One of Anchorage's favorite singles bars, **Humpy's Great Alaskan Alehouse** (✉ 610 W.

6th Ave., Downtown ☎ 907/276–2337 🌐 www.humpys.com), serves up rock, blues, and folk five nights a week, including open mic on Mondays, along with dozens of microbrews (including more than 40 beers on tap) and surprisingly tasty pub grub. It's noisy, smoky, and always packed.

Blues Central/Chef's Inn (✉ 825 W. Northern Lights Blvd., Midtown ☎ 907/272–1341 🌐 www.bluescentral.net), a modest and smoky eatery, is also a blues mecca that stages bands seven nights a week. Fans of salsa, merengue, and other music crowd the dance floor at the downtown **Club Soraya** (✉ 333 W. 4th Ave., Downtown ☎ 907/276–0670). There are free Latin dance classes at 8 PM on Saturday, followed by live bands. **Latitude 61** (✉ 4848 Old Seward Hwy., Midtown ☎ 907/562–5701) has country music Wednesdays and poker tournaments Monday–Thursday; Friday and Saturday are dance nights. Downstairs, 16 antique billiards tables attract pool sharks. Downtown's **Snow City Cafe** (✉ 4th Ave. at L St., Downtown ☎ 907/272–2489 🌐 www.snowcitycafe.com) has open mic sessions on Sunday evenings along with Irish music jam sessions on Wednesday evening.

The Arts

Anchorage often surprises visitors with its variety—and high quality—of cultural activities. In addition to top-name touring groups and performers, a sampling of local productions, including provocative theater, children's shows, improvisational troupes, Buddhist lectures, photography exhibits, poetry readings, and Native Alaskan dance performances, are always going on around town. The Friday entertainment section of the *Anchorage Daily News* is packed with events and activities. Tickets for many cultural events can be purchased at any Carrs grocery store. **Carrs Tix** (☎ 800/478–7328 🌐 www.tickets.com) has recorded information on cultural events of the week and the option to buy tickets by phone or from the Web site.

The **Alaska Center for the Performing Arts** (✉ 621 W. 6th Ave., Downtown ☎ 907/263–2900 🌐 www.alaskapac.org) has three theaters and hosts local performing groups as well as traveling production companies that in the last few years have brought *Rent, Les Misérables,* and *Lord of the Dance* to the Anchorage stage. The lobby box office, open Monday–Saturday 10–6, sells tickets to the productions and is a good all-around source of cultural information. During the summer, you can watch IMAX movies at the Center for the Performing Arts, along with a special northern lights show.

Film

The popular **Bear Tooth Theatre Pub** (✉ 1220 W. 27th Ave., Midtown ☎ 907/276–4200) screens second-run and art films for only $3 and also serves tasty pizzas, sandwiches, burritos, salads, and beer while you watch. See 🌐 www.beartooththeatre.net for schedule.

Opera & Classical Music

The **Anchorage Opera** (☎ 907/279–2557 🌐 www.anchorageopera.org) produces three operas during its November–March season. The **Anchorage**

Symphony Orchestra (☎ 907/274–8668 🌐 www.anchoragesymphony.org) performs classical concerts October through April. The box office of the Alaska Center for the Performing Arts sells tickets for both.

Theater

The **Alaska Center for the Performing Arts** hosts the Anchorage Opera and the Anchorage Symphony Orchestra, among other major performances. **Cyrano's Off-Center Playhouse** (✉ 4th Ave. and D St., Downtown ☎ 907/274–2599 🌐 www.cyranos.org) mounts innovative productions in a cozy theater connected to a namesake café and bookstore. **Out North Contemporary Art House** (✉ 1325 Primrose St., just west of Bragaw Rd. off DeBarr Rd., East Anchorage ☎ 907/279–3800 🌐 www.outnorth.org), whose productions are thought-provoking and, at times, controversial, often earns critical acclaim from local reviewers. Student productions from the **University of Alaska Anchorage Theater** (✉ 3211 Providence Dr., East Anchorage ☎ 907/786–4849) are timely and well done. The theater is intimate, with seating on three sides.

SPORTS & THE OUTDOORS

Anchorage is an active city, with a blend of spectator and do-it-yourself fun. Wintertime brings hockey, dog mushing, and ski races, and the long summer days provide the chance to watch a semipro baseball game, bike the Coastal Trail, and still have time to watch the sun go down at midnight. **Sullivan Arena** (✉ 334 E. 16th Ave., Midtown ☎ 907/566–1596) is Anchorage's primary venue for large events, from ice hockey to boat shows. **Mulcahy Stadium** (✉ E. 16th Ave. at Cordova St., Midtown) is the center for semi-pro baseball in Anchorage.

Baseball

Two semiprofessional baseball teams, made up of college players, play at Mulcahy Stadium next to the Sullivan Arena. The games played here are intense—many players have gone on to star in the major leagues. The **Anchorage Bucs** (☎ 907/561–2827 🌐 www.anchoragebucs.com) have a dozen or so former players who went on to the majors, including standouts Wally Joyner, Jeff Kent, and Bobby Jones. The most famous player on the **Glacier Pilots** (☎ 907/274–3627 🌐 www.glacierpilots.com) was Mark McGwire, but many other pre–major leaguers have played for them over the years, including Dave Winfield, Randy Johnson, and Reggie Jackson.

Basketball

The University of Alaska Anchorage hosts the **Great Alaska Shootout** (🌐 www.shootout.net) at the Sullivan Arena over Thanksgiving weekend. In addition, the UAA Seawolves men's and women's basketball teams play on campus during the winter months.

Bicycling, Running & Walking

Anchorage has more than 120 mi of paved bicycle trails, and many streets have marked bike lanes. Although busy during the day, downtown streets are uncrowded and safe for cyclists in the evening. The **Tony Knowles Coastal Trail** (🌐 www.trailsofanchorage.com) and other bike trails in Anchorage are used by runners, cyclists, in-line skaters, and walkers. It begins downtown off 2nd Avenue and is also easily accessible from Westchester Lagoon near the west end of 15th Avenue. The trail runs from the lagoon 2 mi to Earthquake Park and then continues an additional 7 mi to Kincaid Park, where a series of unpaved trails provides for more adventurous biking and hiking.

A number of popular running events are held annually in Anchorage, including the **Alaska Run for Women** (🌐 www.akrfw.org) in early June, which raises money for the fight against breast cancer. The late-April **Heart Run** is a fund-raiser for the American Heart Association's work to prevent heart disease. It's been taking place for more than 25 years. Alaska's biggest and most famous running event is the **Mayor's Midnight Sun Marathon** (🌐 www.mayorsmarathon.com), held on summer solstice in late June.

Downtown Bicycle Rental (✉ 333 W. 4th Ave., Downtown ☎ 907/279–5293 🌐 www.alaska-bike-rentals.com) rents mountain bikes and provides trail recommendations. The **Arctic Bicycle Club** (☎ 907/566–0177 🌐 www.arcticbike.org) organizes races and tours.

Bird-Watching

Popular bird-watching places include the Tony Knowles Coastal Trail, which provides access to Westchester Lagoon and nearby tide flats, along with Potter Marsh on the south end of Anchorage. The local chapter of the **Anchorage Audubon Society** (🌐 www.anchorageaudubon.org) refers you to local birders who will advise you on the best bird-watching spots. You can also sign up for bird-watching classes and field trips. The society's **bird hot line** (☎ 907/338–2473) tracks the latest sightings in town. Naturalists Lisa Moorehead and Bob Dittrick of **Wilderness Birding Adventures** (☎ 907/694–7442 🌐 www.wildernessbirding.com) guide backcountry birding trips to remote parts of Alaska.

Canoeing & Kayaking

Local lakes and lagoons, such as Westchester Lagoon, Goose Lake, and Jewel Lake, have favorable conditions for boating. More adventurous paddlers will want to head to Whittier or Seward for sea kayaking. Rent sea kayaks from **Kayak and Custom Adventures Worldwide** (✉ 328 3rd Ave., Seward ☎ 907/224–3960 or 800/288–3134 🌐 www.kayakak.com), which also leads day trips in the Seward area. Better known as REI, **Recreational Equipment Inc.** (✉ 1200 W. Northern Lights Blvd., Midtown ☎ 907/272–4565 🌐 www.rei.com) sells and rents all sorts of outdoor gear, including canoes and sea kayaks.

Dogsled Races

World-championship races are run in mid-February, with three consecutive 25-mi heats through downtown Anchorage, out into the foothills, and back. People line the route with cups of coffee in hand to cheer on their favorite mushers. The three-day races are part of the annual **Fur Rendezvous,** one of the largest winter festivals in the United States; other attractions include a snow-sculpture competition, car races, Eskimo blanket toss, dog weight pulling contests, a carnival, and even snowshoe softball. Fur Rondy events take place from late February to the start of the Iditarod in early March. The **Fur Rondy office** (✉ 400 D St., No.

200, Downtown, 99501 ☎ 907/274–1270 🌐 www.furrondy.net) has a guide to the events.

In March, mushers and their dogs compete in the 1,049-mi **Iditarod Trail Sled Dog Race** (☎ 907/376–5155, 800/545–6874 Iditarod Trail Headquarters 🌐 www.iditarod.com). The race commemorates the delivery of serum to Nome by dog mushers during the diphtheria epidemic of 1925. The serum run was the inspiration for the animated family film *Balto*. Dog teams leave downtown Anchorage and wind through the Alaska Range, across the Interior, out to the Bering Sea coast, and on to Nome. Depending on weather and trail conditions, winners can complete the race in nine days (⇨ The Last Great Race on Earth box).

2

Fishing

Nearly 30 local lakes are stocked with trout. You must have a valid Alaska sportfishing license. Jewel Lake in South Anchorage and Mirror and Fire lakes near Eagle River all hold fish. Coho salmon return to Ship Creek (downtown) in August, and king salmon are caught between late May and early July. Campbell Creek and Bird Creek just south of town are also good spots. Fishing licenses may be purchased at any Carrs grocery or local sporting goods store. Contact the **Alaska Department of Fish and Game** (☎ 907/267–2218 🌐 www.state.ak.us/adfg) for licensing information.

Golf

Anchorage is Alaska's golfing capital, with several public courses. They won't compare to offerings in Phoenix or San Diego, but courses are open until 10 PM on long summer days.

Anchorage Golf Course (✉ O'Malley Rd., South Anchorage ☎ 907/522–3363) has 18 holes with greens. Golf carts and clubs are available for rent. The city-run **Russian Jack Springs** (✉ 5200 DeBar Rd., South Anchorage ☎ 907/343–6992) is generally open May–September. It has 9 holes, synthetic greens, and clubs for rent. **Tanglewood Lakes Golf Club** (✉ 11701 Brayton Dr., South Anchorage ☎ 907/345–4600) is a 9-hole course in South Anchorage.

Hockey

Hockey is in the blood of any true Alaskan, and kids as young as four years crowd local ice rinks in hopes of becoming the next Scott Gomez (who still lives in Anchorage when he's not playing for the New Jersey Devils).

The East Coast Hockey League's **Alaska Aces** (☎ 907/258–2237 🌐 www.alaskaaces.com) play minor-league professional hockey in the Sullivan Arena. The **University of Alaska Anchorage** (☎ 907/786–1293 🌐 www.goseawolves.com) has a Division I NCAA hockey team that draws several thousand loyal fans to home games at the Sullivan Arena.

Ice-Skating

Ice-skating is a favorite wintertime activity in Anchorage, with several indoor ice arenas, outdoor hockey rinks, and local ponds opening when temperatures drop.

Ben Boeke Ice Arena (✉ 334 E. 16th Ave., Midtown ☎ 907/274–5715 🌐 www.benboeke.com) is a city-run indoor ice arena with open skating and skate rentals year-round. The **Dimond Ice Chalet** (✉ 800 E. Dimond Blvd., South Anchorage ☎ 907/344–1212 🌐 www.dimondcenter.com) has an indoor ice rink at Dimond Mall that is open to the public daily, with lessons and skate rentals. In winter, **Westchester Lagoon,** 1 mi south of downtown, is a favorite outdoor family (and competitive) skating area, with smooth ice and piles of firewood next to the warming barrels.

Racquet Sports & Fitness Club

The park strip at 9th Avenue and C Street has several tennis courts. On the south side of Anchorage, the **Dimond Athletic Club** (✉ 800 E. Dimond Blvd., at Old Seward, South Anchorage ☎ 907/344–7788) has a lap pool, Nautilus equipment, free weights, saunas, hot tubs, steam rooms, and racquetball courts, plus various exercise classes. You can buy a daily guest pass for $15.

Rafting

Based in Girdwood, **Class V Whitewater** (📫 Box 591, Girdwood 99587 ☎ 907/783–2004 🌐 www.alaskanrafting.com) leads scenic floats on the Twenty Mile and Portage rivers, along with white-water trips on the Talkeetna and Sixmile rivers. Alaska's oldest adventure and wilderness guiding company (in business since 1975), **Nova** (📫 Box 1129, Chickaloon 99674 ☎ 907/745–5753 or 800/746–5753 📠 907/745–5754 🌐 www.novalaska.com), provides both scenic and white-water wilderness rafting trips statewide.

Skiing

Cross-country skiing is extremely popular in Anchorage. Locals ski on trails in town at Kincaid Park or Hillside and farther away at Girdwood Valley, Turnagain Pass, and Chugach State Park. Downhill skiing is convenient to downtown. A number of cross-country ski events are held annually in Anchorage. The **Alaska Ski for Women** (🌐 www.alaskaskiforwomen.org), held on Super Bowl Sunday in early February, is the biggest women's ski race in North America, attracting more than 1,500 skiers. The **Nordic Skiing Association of Anchorage** (🌐 www.anchoragenordicski.com) sponsors many other ski races and events throughout the winter, from wooden ski classics to the highly competitive Besh Cup series. Biggest of all is the **Tour of Anchorage** (🌐 www.tourofanchorage.com), a grueling 50-km marathon in early March.

Alyeska Ski Resort (☎ 907/754–1111, 800/880–3880, 907/754–7669 recorded information and snow conditions, 907/754–2275 for ticket office 🌐 www.alyeskaresort.com), at Girdwood, 40 mi south of the city, is Alaska's premier destination resort, where snowfall averages 782 inches annually! Owned by a large Japanese corporation, Alyeska features a day lodge, hotel, restaurants, six chairlifts, a tram, a vertical drop of 2,500 feet, and runs for all abilities. Lift tickets cost $48 for adults; $21 for night skiing. The tram ($16) is open during the summer, providing access to the Seven Glaciers restaurant and hiking trails. **Alyeska Accommodations** (☎ 907/783–2000 or 888/783–2001 📠 907/783–2425 🌐 www.alyeskaaccommodations.com) can set you up in a privately owned cabin or condo. **Alpenglow at Arctic Valley** (☎907/428–1208 🌐www.skialpenglow.com) is a small ski area just north of Anchorage. On the eastern edge of town, **Hilltop Ski Area** (✉ Abbott Rd. near Hillside Dr., East Anchorage ☎ 907/346–1446 🌐 www.hilltopskiarea.org) is a favorite ski area with families.

The locally owned **Alaska Mountaineering and Hiking** (✉ 2633 Spenard Rd., Midtown ☎ 907/272–1811 🌐 www.alaskamountaineering.com) outdoors shop has a highly experienced staff and plenty of cross-country skis for sale or rent. Ski sales and rentals are available from **Recreational Equipment Inc.** (REI; ✉ 1200 W. Northern Lights Blvd., Midtown ☎ 907/272–4565 🌐 www.rei.com).

Water Sports

★ **H2Oasis Water Park** (✉ 11030 Chelea St., South Anchorage ☎ 907/522–4420 or 888/426–2747 🌐 www.h2oasiswaterpark.com) is Alaska's first—and only—water park. Housed within a medieval castle–shaped structure, this large indoor facility opened in 2003. Attractions include a pool that generates 3-foot bodysurfing waves, a 475-foot-long water-powered roller coaster, a 350-foot open flume slide, plus a pirate ship with water cannons and slides. A children's lagoon and lazy river, a splash pool, and two hot tubs are some of the calmer soaks. All told, the park has pools filled with more than 350,000 gallons of water. H2Oasis is open daily year-round and costs adults $20 for all day; kids pay $15.

For something simple, head to the **West High School Pool** (✉ 2508 Blueberry Rd., Midtown ☎ 907/343–4506), where a spiral waterslide is available, along with diving boards and lap lanes. The large pool and high ceilings at the **University of Alaska Anchorage** (✉ 2801 Spirit Way, off Providence Dr. ☎ 907/786–1231 🌐 www.uaa.alaska.edu) are geared toward fitness swimmers. Your $5 admission to the UAA pool also provides access to the ice rink, weight room, saunas, racquetball courts, and gym.

SHOPPING

Stock up for your travels around Alaska in Anchorage, where prices are reasonable and there's no sales tax. It's a good choice for souvenirs as well; downtown gift shops sell trinkets and artwork. The Saturday market is packed with Alaskan-made products of all types, and you're likely to meet local artisans.

Malls & Department Stores

Anchorage's **5th Avenue Mall** occupies a city block at 5th Avenue and A Street and contains dozens of stores spread over several levels, including a JCPenney. The top level houses a food court for quick, inexpensive meals. Just across 6th Avenue, and connected by a skywalk to the 5th Avenue Mall, is Alaska's only **Nordstrom.** The city's largest shopping mall, **Dimond Center,** is on the south end of town at Dimond Boulevard and Old Seward Highway. In addition to dozens of shops, Dimond Center houses a movie theater. Nearby are several big-box discount stores, including Costco, Best Buy, and Wal-Mart.

ALASKA'S WELL-WORN TRAIL

SINCE 1973 MUSHERS AND THEIR SLED-DOG TEAMS *have raced over 1,000 mi across Alaska in a marathon vision quest unlike any other: the Iditarod Trail Sled Dog Race, the longest sled-dog race in the world. After a ceremonial start in downtown Anchorage on the first Saturday in March, dog teams wind through Alaska, battling almost every imaginable winter challenge. Ten days later, the "Last Great Race on Earth" ends with spectacular fanfare in Nome, on the Bering Sea coast.*

The Iditarod's origins can be traced to two events: an early 1900s long-distance race called the All-Alaska Sweepstakes and the delivery of a lifesaving serum to Nome by dog mushers during a diphtheria outbreak in 1925. Fascinated with the trail's history, Alaskan sled-dog enthusiasts Dorothy Page and Joe Redington Sr. staged the first race in 1967 to celebrate the role of mushing in Alaska's history. Only 50 mi long and with a purse of $25,000—no small amount at that time—it attracted the best of Alaska's competitive mushers. Enthusiasm waned in 1969, however, when the available winnings fell to $1,000. Instead of giving up, Redington enlarged it.

In 1973, after three years without a race, he organized a 1,000-mi race from Anchorage to Nome, with a then-outrageous purse of $50,000. Critics scoffed, but 34 racers entered. First place went to a little-known musher named Dick Wilmarth, who finished in 20 days. Redington then billed the Iditarod as a 1,049-mi race to symbolize Alaska, the 49th state (still the official distance, even though the race really covers 1,100 mi).

The race actually begins in Wasilla, home of the Iditarod headquarters, a few miles from Anchorage. The first few hundred miles take mushers and dogs through wooded lowlands and flat hills, including a stretch known as Moose Alley. Teams then cross the Alaska Range. Then they enter Interior Alaska, with Athabascan villages and gold-rush ghost towns, including Iditarod. Next, the trail follows the frozen Yukon River, then cuts over to the Bering Sea coast for the final 270-mi "sprint" to Nome. It was here, in 1985, that Libby Riddles drove her team into a blinding blizzard, en route to a victory that made her the first woman to win the race. After that, Susan Butcher won the race four times, but the all-time record holder is Rick Swenson, with five victories. The fastest time was recorded in 2002, when Swiss-born musher Martin Buser finished in just under nine days.

Iditarod mushers and dogs may have to endure extreme cold, deep snow, gale-force winds, whiteouts, river overflow, and moose attacks, not to mention fraying tempers. The race has sparked harsh criticism from animal rights supporters, and Iditarod policy continues to enforce humane care and treatment of dogs. Fodor's discusses the sport with the expectation and hope that all of the participating individuals are treating the animals with care and respect.

More than three decades after its establishment, the Iditarod race purse tops $600,000, with more than $60,000 to the champion. International journalists report from the trail, and entrants have come from more than a dozen countries. Though racers such as Swenson, Dee Dee Jonrowe, Martin Buser, and Jeff King draw the most media attention, all mushers—and dogs—who reach Nome are appropriately treated like champions after surviving their run across Alaska's wilderness.

Markets

Fodor's Choice ★ During the summer, Anchorage's **Saturday Market** (☎ 907/272–5634 🌐 www.anchoragemarkets.com) is open in the parking lot at 3rd Avenue and E Street. Browse here for Alaskan-made crafts, ethnic imports, and deliciously fattening food. It's open from mid-May to mid-September, Saturday and Sunday 10–6. A smaller market sells local produce and crafts July–August, Wednesday 11–5, at Northway Mall in East Anchorage.

Specialty Shops

Art

Anchorage's **First Friday** art openings have become a popular monthly event, with 15 or so galleries offering a chance to sample hors d'oeuvres while looking over the latest works by regional artists. Alaska's oldest gallery, **Artique** (✉ 314 G St., Downtown ☎ 907/277–1663 🌐 www.artiqueltd.com), sells paintings, prints, and jewelry by prominent Alaskan artists. **Arctic Rose Gallery** (✉ 420 L St., Downtown ☎ 907/279–3911) is in the same building as Simon and Seafort's restaurant. The **International Gallery of Contemporary Art** (✉ 427 D St., Downtown ☎ 907/279–1116 🌐 www.igcaalaska.org) is Anchorage's premier fine arts gallery, with changing exhibits monthly. **One People** (✉ 425 D St., Downtown ☎ 907/274–4063) offers the works of Alaskan artists and crafts workers, including an excellent selection of Native pieces.

Books & Music

Barnes & Noble Booksellers (✉ 200 E. Northern Lights Blvd., at A St., Midtown ☎ 907/279–7323 🌐 www.bn.com) is one of Anchorage's most popular bookstores, with books, CDs, and magazines plus a Starbucks. The store stays open late, with literary events some nights. **Borders Books & Music** (✉ 1100 E. Dimond Blvd., west of Seward Hwy., South Anchorage ☎ 907/344–4099 🌐 www.borders.com) stocks a diverse selection of titles and has a café. **Cook Inlet Book Company** (✉ 415 W. 5th Ave., Downtown ☎ 907/258–4544 or 800/240–4148 🌐 www.cookinlet.com) has the largest collection of Alaskan titles in the state and a substantial newspaper and magazine section. **Metro Music & Book Store** (✉ 530 E. Benson Blvd., Midtown ☎ 907/279–8622) carries a well-thought-out inventory of fiction and nonfiction, but the main draw is the impressive collection of CDs; use their players to listen to any of them before buying. Also here is Felix Cafe, serving crepes, espresso, and house-made yogurt.

Easily the largest independent bookstore in Alaska, **Title Wave Books** (✉ 1360 W. Northern Lights Blvd., Midtown ☎ 907/278–9283 or 888/598–9283 🌐 www.wavebooks.com) fills a sprawling store next to REI. The shelves are filled with new and used titles, and the staff is very knowledgeable. Also here is a **Kaladi Brothers Coffee Shop** with Wi-Fi access for Web surfers.

Gift Ideas

Several downtown shops sell quality Native Alaskan artwork, but the best buys can be found in the gift shop at the **Alaska Native Medical Center** (✉ 4315 Diplomacy Dr., at Tudor and Bragaw Rds., East Anchorage

☎ 907/729–1122), which is open weekdays 10–2 and 11–2 on the first and third Saturday of the month. The gift shop at **Alaska Native Heritage Center** (✉ 8800 Heritage Center Dr. [Glenn Hwy. at Muldoon Rd.], East Anchorage ☎ 907/330–8000 or 800/315–6608 🌐 www.alaskanative.net) sells Native crafts.

Laura Wright Alaskan Parkys sells distinctive Eskimo-style "parkys" (parkas) and will custom-sew one for you. They're available at **Heritage Gifts** (✉ 333 W. 4th Ave., #227, at D St. ☎ 907/274–4215 🌐 www.alaskan.com/parkys). **Oomingmak** (✉ 6th Ave. and H St., Downtown ☎ 907/272–9225 or 888/360–9665 🌐 www.qiviut.com), a Native-owned co-operative, sells items made of qiviut, the warm undercoat of the musk ox. Scarves, shawls, and tunics are knitted in traditional patterns.

Frozen seafood and smoked fish are available from **10th and M Seafoods** (✉ 1020 M St., Downtown ☎ 907/272–3474 or 800/770–2722 🌐 www.10thandmseafoods.com ✉ 301 Muldoon Rd. ☎ 907/337–8831). **New Sagaya's City Market** sells an excellent selection of fresh seafood. If you don't want to carry the fish with you, the market will pack and ship it home. Get smoked reindeer meat and salmon products at **Alaska Sausage Company** (✉ 2914 Arctic Blvd., Midtown ☎ 907/562–3636 or 800/798–3636 🌐 www.alaskasausage.com).

Although furs may not be to everyone's taste or ethics, a number of Alaska fur companies have stores and factories in Anchorage. One of the city's largest and best-known furriers is **David Green Master Furrier** (✉ 130 W. 4th Ave., Downtown ☎ 907/277–9595). **Alaska Fur Exchange** (✉ 4417 Old Seward Hwy., Midtown ☎ 907/563–3877 🌐 www.alaskafurexchange.com) has a large midtown store that sells both furs and Native artwork.

Jewelry

The **Kobuk Valley Jade Co.** (✉ Olympic Cir., Girdwood ☎ 907/783–2764), at the base of Mt. Alyeska, sells hand-polished jade pieces as well as Native masks, baskets, and jewelry.

ANCHORAGE A TO Z

To research prices, get advice from other travelers, and book travel arrangements, visit www.fodors.com.

AIRPORTS & TRANSFERS

Ted Stevens Anchorage International Airport is 6 mi from downtown Anchorage on International Airport Road. It is served by Alaska, American, Continental, Delta, Northwest, and United airlines, along with a number of international carriers. Several carriers, including ERA and PenAir, connect Anchorage with smaller Alaskan communities. Floatplane operators and helicopters serve the area from Lake Hood, which is adjacent to and part of Anchorage International Airport. There are also a number of smaller air taxis and air-charter operations at Merrill Field, 2 mi east of downtown on 5th Avenue.

A major redevelopment project at Ted Stevens Anchorage International Airport has brought a new air terminal and Alaska Railroad station with direct service to downtown.

Ted Stevens Anchorage International Airport ☎ 907/266-2529 ⊕ www.anchorageairport.com.

AIRPORT TRANSFERS

Taxis queue up at the lower level of the airport terminal outside the baggage-claim area. Alaska Cab, Borealis Shuttle, Checker Cab, Yellow Cab, and Anchorage Taxi Cab (⇨ Taxis) all operate here; you'll get whichever cab is next in line. All are on a meter system, and you'll pay about $17, not including tip, for the ride to downtown hotels.

BOAT & FERRY TRAVEL

Cruise ships sailing the Gulf of Alaska and the Alaska Marine ferries call in Seward, two hours by train or bus south of Anchorage. The South Central route of the Alaska Marine Highway connects Kodiak, Port Lions, Homer, Seldovia, Seward, Valdez, Cordova, and Whittier.

Alaska Marine Highway System ✉ 605 W. 4th Ave., inside Alaska Public Lands Information Center, Downtown ☎ 907/272-4482 or 800/642-0066 ℻ 907/277-4829 ⊕ www.ferryalaska.com.

BUS TRAVEL

The municipal People Mover covers the whole Anchorage bowl. Get schedules and information from the central bus depot at 6th Avenue and G Street. The one-way fare is $1.25 for rides outside the downtown area; rides within downtown are free.

People Mover ☎ 907/343-6543 ⊕ www.peoplemover.org.

CAR TRAVEL

The Glenn Highway enters Anchorage from the north and becomes 5th Avenue near Merrill Field; this route will lead you directly into downtown. Gambell Street leads out of town to the south, becoming New Seward Highway at about 20th Avenue. South of town, it becomes the Seward Highway.

EMERGENCIES

Doctors & Dentists **Physician-referral service** ☎ 888/254-7884 Alaska Regional Hospital, 907/261-4900 Providence Alaska Medical Center.

Emergency Services **Police, fire, and ambulance** ☎ 911. **Poison Control Center** ☎ 800/222-1222.

Hospitals **Alaska Regional Hospital** ✉ 2801 DeBarr Rd., East Anchorage ☎ 907/276-1131 ⊕ www.alaskaregional.com. **First Care** ✉ 3710 Woodland Dr., East Anchorage ☎ 907/248-1122 ✉ 1301 Huffman Rd. ☎ 907/345-1199. **Providence Alaska Medical Center** ✉ 3200 Providence Dr., East Anchorage ☎ 907/562-2211 ⊕ www.providence.org.

WHERE TO STAY

BED & BREAKFASTS

Local Agents **Alaska Sourdough Bed & Breakfast Association** ✉ 889 Cardigan Cir., Anchorage 99503 ☎ 907/563-6244 ℻ 907/563-6073. **Anchorage Alaska Bed & Breakfast Association** Box 242623, Anchorage 99524-2623 ☎ 907/272-5909 or 888/584-5147 ⊕ www.anchorage-bnb.com.

TAXIS

Prices for taxis are $2 for pickup, plus an additional $2 for each mile. Most people in Anchorage telephone for a cab; it is not common to hail one. Allow 20 minutes for arrival of the cab during morning and evening rush hours. Alaska Cab has taxis with wheelchair lifts. Borealis Shuttle has lower rates if you are willing to share the ride.

Taxi Companies **Alaska Cab** ☎ 907/563-5353 www.alaskacabs.com. **Checker Cab** ☎ 907/276-1234. **Yellow Cab** ☎ 907/272-2422.

TOURS

FLIGHTSEEING Any air-taxi company (check the Anchorage Yellow Pages) can arrange for a flightseeing trip over Anchorage and environs. The fee will be determined by the length of time you are airborne and the size of the plane. Tours of about an hour and a half generally cost around $200 per person. Three-hour flights over Mt. McKinley, including a landing on a remote backcountry lake, run about $250 per person.

ERA Helicopters offers a 50-minute trip over Anchorage and the Chugach Mountains as well as a two-hour glacier expedition that includes a landing on the ice. ERA Classic Airlines offers travelers a nostalgic air cruise aboard elegantly restored DC-3s from the 1940s. These 90-minute flights vary in destination, depending upon the weather, flying over Mt. McKinley or the mountains of South Central Alaska. Ketchum Air Service on Lake Hood has a number of flightseeing tours, including one to Mt. McKinley, as well as fly-in service to remote lake cabins for hunting and fishing, and houseboat rentals. Also at Lake Hood, Rust's Flying Service flies ski-planes over Mt. McKinley that include a landing on Ruth Glacier—a spectacular alpine amphitheater high on the mountain.

ERA Classic Airlines ☎ 907/266-8394 or 800/866-8394 907/266-8483. **ERA Helicopters** ☎ 907/266-8351 or 800/843-1947 907/266-8349 www.eraaviation.com. **Regal Air** ☎ 907/243-8535 www.alaska.net/~regalair. **Rust's Flying Service** ☎ 907/243-1595 or 800/544-2299 www.flyrusts.com.

ORIENTATION TOURS A number of companies offer bus tours of the Anchorage area; the visitor center has their brochures. For a quick one-hour overview, hop on the City Trolley Tour ($10), which takes you from downtown to Earthquake Park, along Cook Inlet, and to older neighborhoods. Gray Line's city tour ($46) lasts three hours and includes an hour or more at the Alaska Native Heritage Center. Another highlight for many of these tours is a stop at the Alaska Wild Berry Chocolate factory.

Anchorage City Trolley Tours ✉ 612 W. 4th Ave., Downtown, 99501 ☎ 907/276-5603. **Gray Line of Alaska** ✉ 745 W. 4th Ave., No. 200, Downtown, 99501 ☎ 907/277-5581 or 888/312-5581 www.graylineofalaska.com.

WILDLIFE VIEWING Kenai Fjords Tours has day packages to Kenai Fjords National Park April through November.

Kenai Fjords Tours ✉ 509 W. 4th Ave., Downtown ☎ 907/276-6249 or 800/468-8068 907/777-2888 www.kenaifjords.com.

TRAIN TRAVEL

The Alaska Railroad runs between Anchorage and Fairbanks via Denali National Park and Preserve daily, mid-May–September, and also south between Anchorage and Seward during the same period. Year-round passenger service is available from Anchorage north to Talkeetna. Call for schedule and fare information.

Alaska Railroad ☎ 907/265-2494 or 800/544-0552 📠 907/265-2323 🌐 www.akrr.com.

TRANSPORTATION AROUND ANCHORAGE

If, like many visitors to Alaska, you bring your RV or rent one on arrival, you should note that parking an RV downtown on weekdays is challenging. The big parking lot on 3rd Avenue between C and E streets is a good place to park and walk. Parking usually is not a problem in other parts of town, and most of the big discount stores allow free parking in their lots.

VISITOR INFORMATION

Alaska Public Lands Information Center ✉ 4th Ave. and F St., Downtown ☎ 907/271-2737 📠 907/271-2744 🌐 www.nps.gov/aplic. **Anchorage Convention and Visitors Bureau** (ACVB) ✉ 524 W. 4th Ave., Downtown, 99501-2212 ☎ 907/276-4118, 800/478-1255 to order visitor guides 📠 907/278-5559 🌐 www.anchorage.net. **Daily events** ☎ 907/276-3200. **Log Cabin Visitor Information Center** ✉ 4th Ave. and F St., Downtown ☎ 907/274-3531 🌐 www.anchorage.net.

3

South Central Alaska

Including Prince William Sound, Homer & the Kenai Peninsula

WORD OF MOUTH

"We loved the Kenai Peninsula. We drove from Seward to Homer and saw wildlife, had some wonderful hikes and picnics, went clamming, visited art galleries and museums, and ate great food."

—lcuy

"There is no way to predict what kind of weather you will have; it's so variable from place to place. South Central is huge, and at any given time the weather may change. Dress in layers and be prepared for wet, cold weather. Don't forget warm gloves!"

—dwooddon

"Exit Glacier is wonderful. It's a 1/2-mile hike to get up close and personal with a spectacular glacier. Early June is a wonderful time to go."

—tcapp

www.fodors.com/forums

By Robin Mackey Hill and Kent Sturgis

Updated by Tom Reale

ANCHORAGE MAY DOMINATE THE REGION IN SIZE, recognition, and political clout, but don't let that mislead you into thinking Anchorage *is* South Central Alaska. The city is actually an anomaly—a modern, urban environment amid historic ports, wilderness outposts, and fishing towns. It also functions as the gateway to some of Alaska's most spectacular parks and wilderness areas, most of which are accessible by floatplane, the Alaska Railroad, or car.

The city lies near the convergence of two of Alaska's most magnificent mountain systems. To the east of the city and sweeping on to the southwest are the Chugach Mountains, a young, active, and impressively rugged range notable for its high coastal relief. Near-mile-high valley walls and peaks rise almost directly from the sea. Across Cook Inlet to the southwest march the high volcanic peaks of the Alaska Range, part of the Pacific Ocean's great Ring of Fire, but snowcapped nonetheless. Farther north in the Alaska Range, and visible from Anchorage on clear days, shimmers Mt. McKinley, with Mt. Foraker at its shoulder—the towering granite giants of the North American continent. Also visible from town are the Talkeetna Range, to the northeast, and the Kenai Range, just across Turnagain Arm and forming the spine of Anchorage's playground, the Kenai Peninsula.

South Central starts with the port towns on the Gulf of Alaska, Prince William Sound, and Cook Inlet—Cordova, Valdez, Whittier, Seward, Seldovia, Kodiak, Homer, Kenai—with their harbors, ferries, glaciers, and ocean life. Unlike the towns and cities of Interior Alaska, where the common theme of gold-rush history links most of the communities, South Central towns and cities have very different personalities. Kodiak, for example, is a busy commercial-fishing port, whereas Homer is a funky tourist town and artists' colony on beautiful Kachemak Bay. Then come those mountains, curled like an arm embracing the region. Talkeetna, at the western limits of South Central, is where mountaineers gather to launch their assaults on towering Mt. McKinley. On the eastern border, the defunct copper mine outside McCarthy lies at the foot of the Wrangell Mountains.

Nature lovers can rejoice at the meeting of these mountain ranges, for they bring together a wide sampling of Alaska's flora and fauna. Dall sheep and mountain goats dance their way around the heights of the Chugach and Kenai mountains. Tree species mingle here, too, including three different varieties of spruce—Sitka, black, and white. You'll see larch, birch, cottonwood, and aspen turn golden in the crisp days of late summer and early autumn. South Central is also Alaska's farm country. In the Matanuska-Susitna Valley, under an ever-present summertime sun, 75-pound cabbages are common.

Exploring South Central

South Central Alaska can be broken down into three general subregions—the towns and bays of Prince William Sound, communities south of Anchorage on the Kenai Peninsula, and communities north of Anchorage in the Matanuska-Susitna (Mat-Su) Valley and beyond. The region is ideal for exploring by boat, train, car, RV, or plane. All but a couple of the coastal communities are on the road system. For the most part, roads have two lanes and are paved. Traffic, especially on the Kenai Peninsula, can be bumper to bumper on summer weekends, so give yourself plenty of time; better yet, try to travel midweek. Long summer days give you plenty of daylight for exploring.

About the Restaurants

When you leave Anchorage, your menu options in South Central Alaska tend to contract. There are bright spots to be found along the road and in the smaller towns, but exotic cuisines aren't among them. However, the prospects for finding good food prepared well have increased in recent years. Fresh salmon, halibut, crab, and shellfish are readily available even in places far from the seashore. And it's easy to find items like pasta dishes, fresh-baked pastries, and even the occasional vegetarian main course in places where, in past years, you could have your food however you liked it, as long as you liked it fried.

Among the things that haven't changed are the lack of formality in the eating establishments—the folks at the next table just might be wearing hip waders and fishing vests—and the friendliness of the locals. The need for reservations is minimal even during the busy summer season, but you may have the occasional short wait for a table. It's also taking a while for restaurants and cafés to catch up to Anchorage in the smoking department. Alaska's largest city bans all smoking in restaurants while still allowing it in bars. No such restrictions exist across the state, so there are quite a few places where smoking sections still prevail.

About the Hotels

The hotel scene is undergoing the same kind of changes as the restaurants. More properties are being built or remodeled to meet the demands of the growing tourist trade, and the upgrades in facilities and service are a welcome trend. You can find everything from budget-price hostels to remote deluxe accommodations guaranteed to satisfy even the most jaded sybarite. There's a lot in between, including some national chains, some local and regional chains, and more than a few mom-and-pop operations. Reservations are not always required during the summer but are usually a good idea between Memorial Day and Labor Day. The growing numbers of bed-and-breakfasts means that you can always find someplace to stay, even late at night at the height of the tourist season.

WHAT IT COSTS

	$$$$	$$$	$$	$	¢
RESTAURANTS	over $25	$20–$25	$15–$20	$10–$15	under $10
HOTELS	over $225	$175–$225	$125–$175	$75–$125	under $75

Restaurant prices are for a main course at dinner. Hotel prices are for two people in a standard double room in high season, excluding service charges and tax.

Numbers in the text correspond to numbers in the margin and on the South Central Alaska map.

If you have 3 days

Spend them on the Kenai Peninsula. Head south out of Anchorage on the Seward Highway alongside Turnagain Arm and stop in the ski town of Girdwood for a light lunch and a stroll before continuing southeast to **Portage Glacier** 3 and the Begich-Boggs Visitor Center in the **Chugach National Forest** 2. Take a day hike out of **Hope** 7 or a boat trip into **Kenai Fjords National Park** 9 out of **Seward** 8. After spending the night in Seward, work your way down to **Homer** 13. There's plenty to see and do along Kachemak Bay, including taking a dinner cruise over to Halibut Cove or trying your luck at landing a huge halibut. On your way back up to Anchorage, stop for a bite to eat in **Soldotna** 12 and make any other stops you missed during the trip down.

If you have 5 days

Follow the three-day itinerary above, return to Anchorage, and head north out of town the next day along the Glenn Highway. Wander the back roads between **Palmer** 18 and **Wasilla** 19, continuing up to Hatcher Pass and the Independence Mine. Visit a couple of area attractions, such as the Musk Ox Farm or the Iditarod Trail Headquarters, before working your way up to **Talkeetna** 20 for the night. The other option for Day and Night 3 is a backpacking trip into **Denali State Park** 21. On your way back to Anchorage, stop along the roadside for a short hike or a picnic.

If you have 7 days

Follow the five-day itinerary before cutting over to **Valdez** 5, which you should use as a base. Take a day trip past Columbia Glacier; see the sights, including the Valdez Museum; or take a hike in the surrounding Chugach Mountains. Consider flying or taking the ferry across the sound to **Cordova** 6, or drive or fly into McCarthy and the nearby Kennicott Mine in **Wrangell–St. Elias National Park & Preserve** 23. Adventurers may consider an excursion to **Kodiak Island** 16 to watch for Kodiak brown bears and to explore the island's Russian origins. If hiking is your passion, you can spend the entire seven days on a guided backcountry trip through the park or venture farther afield to the pristine **Lake Clark National Park & Preserve** 17. If exploring Prince William Sound is more to your liking, arrange for a kayak trip out of Valdez or Cordova.

Timing

The region is most alive with visitors and recreational activities between Memorial Day and Labor Day, which is also when it is the most crowded with people enjoying the spectacular fishing and boating, hiking and backpacking, and wildlife spotting and flightseeing. Fall comes early—in mid- to late August—to South Central but can be a gorgeous time to travel. Trees are painted gold and orange, and mountaintops are dusted with snow. Dining and lodging options outside Anchorage may be limited in winter, as many businesses close during the off-season.

PRINCE WILLIAM SOUND

The sound covers some 15,000 square mi—15 times the size of San Francisco Bay. It receives an average of 150 inches of rain a year and is home to more than 150 glaciers, 20 of them reaching tidewater. Along its shoreline are quiet bays, trickling waterfalls, and hidden coves perfect for camping. In addition to hosting brown bears, gray wolves, and marten, the sound thrives with a variety of birds and all manner of marine life, including salmon, halibut, humpback and killer whales, sea otters, sea lions, and porpoises. Bald eagles often soar overhead or perch in tall trees. The sound was heavily damaged by the *Exxon Valdez* oil spill in 1989. The oil has sunk into the beaches below the surface and is sometimes uncovered after storms and high tides. What lasting effect this lurking oil will have on the area is still being studied and remains the topic of much debate.

Chugach State Park

❶ *Bordering Anchorage to the east.*

Chugach State Park is Alaska's most accessible wilderness. Nearly half a million acres in size, the park rises from the coast to more than 8,000 feet, with mountains bearing such colorful names as Williwaw Peak, Temptation Peak, Mt. Magnificent, and Mt. Rumble. The park has nearly 30 trails—from 2 mi to 30 mi long—totaling more than 150 mi, suitable for shorter hikes, weeklong backpacking, and mountain biking. Easy-to-follow cross-country routes extend from one park entrance to another, allowing multiday excursions and a variety of loop trips. This is not your typical urban park—it's real wilderness, home to Dall sheep, mountain goats, brown bears, and several packs of wolves who reside on the edge of Anchorage. Many of the trails were blazed by early miners who usually sought the easiest passes. There are also some comfortable roadside campgrounds for people traveling by car or bicycle. Trailheads are scattered around the park's perimeter from Eklutna Lake, 30 mi north of Anchorage, to the trailhead for the Crow Pass Trail near Girdwood, 37 mi to the south. Some of the more popular trailheads charge a daily parking fee of $5. The Eagle River Nature Center or the park headquarters near Potter Marsh 12 mi south of town has park information. ✉ *Headquarters, Mile 115, Seward Hwy.* 📫 *HC 52, Box 8999, Indian 99540* ☎ *907/345–5014.*

The views from high perches in this park are heady. You can look down on the city of Anchorage, observe the great tides in Cook Inlet, gaze north toward Mt. McKinley, or delineate the grand procession of snowy peaks across the inlet, marching down the Alaska Peninsula. The most frequently climbed alpine perch in Alaska is **Flattop Mountain**, on Chugach Park's western edge, ascended by hikers of all abilities. The trailhead is at the Glen Alps parking lot on the hillside above town.

Eagle River Road leads 12 mi into the mountains from the bedroom community of Eagle River. The **Eagle River Nature Center**, at the end of Eagle River Road, has wildlife displays, telescopes for wildlife spotting, hik-

3

Boating You'll find abundant opportunities for boating on lakes, rivers, and the ocean in South Central. Canoe and kayak parties in the South Central utilize Prince William Sound, Kachemak Bay, and the Tangle Lakes region. Access to the Tangle Lakes system is off the Denali Highway, 20 mi west of Paxson. This mountainous country on the southern flank of the Alaska Range forms the headwaters of the Delta River. You can spend a few lazy hours paddling near the road or take an extended trip requiring overnight camping and portages.

Boaters should exercise caution, however, because local waters are icy cold and can be deadly. Even a life jacket will not save you if hypothermia sets in. Ask locals about conditions before setting out on any but the smallest, most placid lakes. Also, beware of the exposed land on the mudflats of Turnagain Arm between Anchorage and Portage—the huge expanse of seemingly dry ground can quickly turn into a muddy morass when the tide comes roaring in. Keep off, no matter how safe it appears to be.

Fishing South Central has Alaska's most accessible fishing. Thousands of tourists flock to the Kenai River and its tributaries for trophy king salmon, which can reach nearly 100 pounds. Saltwater fishing yields huge halibut, cod, and shellfish. Drift boats are a good means of access to the rivers. Boat rentals and guide services are available all along the South Central coastline. Fishing licenses are required for all fresh- and saltwater fishing, including gathering clams and shellfish. Licenses are available at sporting-goods, grocery, and drug stores statewide. Nonresident licenses can be purchased for 1-, 3-, 7-, or 14-day periods or for an entire calendar year. King salmon stamps are also required if you intend to pursue kings. Call the **Alaska Department of Fish and Game** (☎ 907/267–2218) for information.

---

ing trails, and volunteers to answer questions, lead hikes, and host naturalist programs throughout the year. A cabin that sleeps eight and a pair of yurts (insulated tents) that sleep four and six are available for rental. Cost is $65 per night for nonmembers of the nature center, and a walk-in of about 1½ mi is required. Amenities include woodstoves, firewood, and outdoor latrines. ✉ *Eagle River Rd.* ☎ *907/694–2108* 🌐 *www.ernc.org* *Parking $5* ⏲ *May, Tues.–Sun. 10–5; June–Aug., Sun.–Thurs. 10–5, Fri. and Sat. 10–7; Sept., Tues.–Sun. 10–5; Oct.–Apr., Fri.–Sun. 10–5.*

Where to Stay

¢ **Alaska State Park Campgrounds.** You'll find three road-accessible campgrounds in Chugach Park: at Eklutna Lake, Bird Creek, and Eagle River. All are within a short drive from Anchorage. The sites have pit toilets, drinking water, fire grates, and picnic tables, and are available on a first-come, first-served basis. In addition, the Eklutna Lake site has

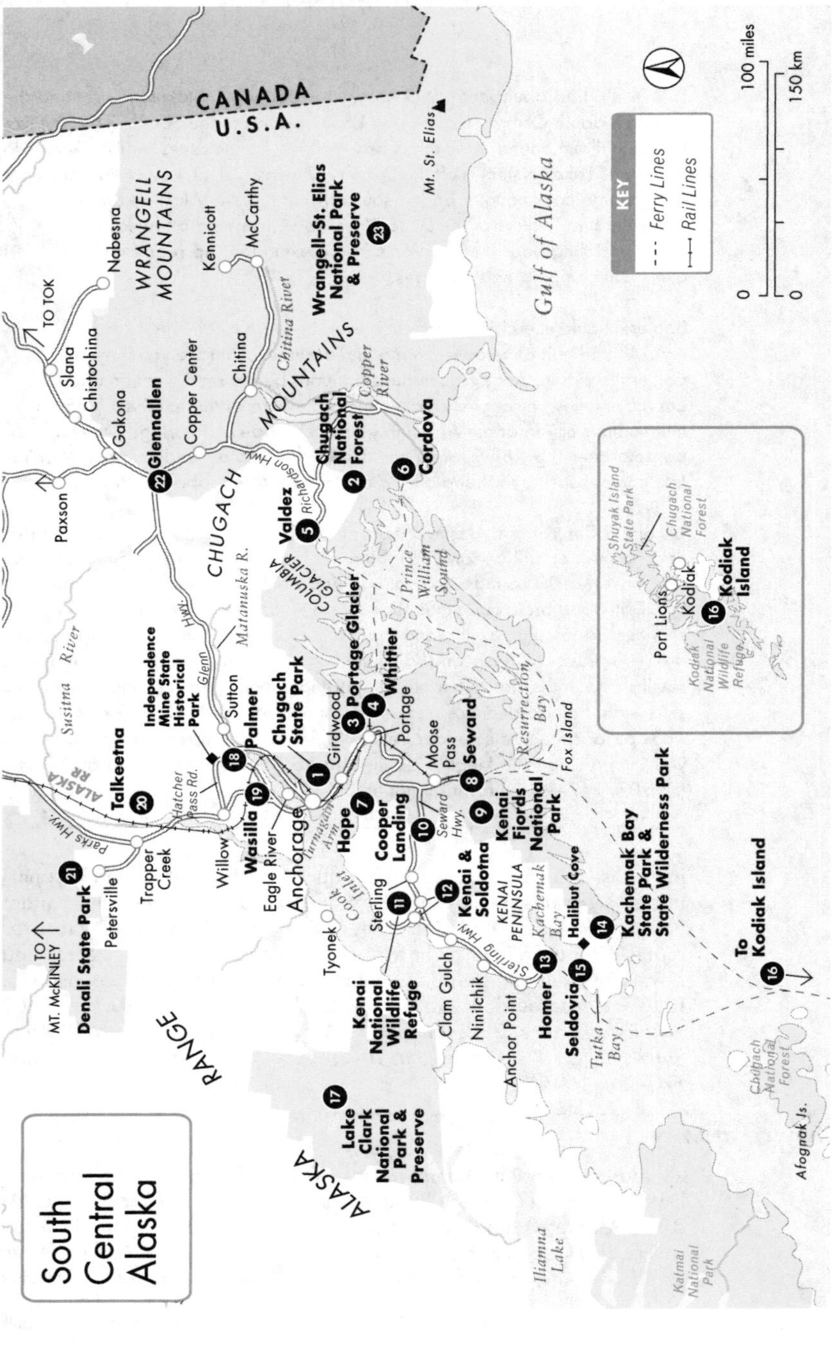
South Central Alaska
CANADA
U.S.A.
WRANGELL MOUNTAINS
CHUGACH MOUNTAINS
ALASKA RANGE
Gulf of Alaska
KEY
Ferry Lines
Rail Lines
0 100 miles
0 150 km
TO MT. McKINLEY
21 Denali State Park
Petersville
Trapper Creek
Parks Hwy.
ALASKA RR
20 Talkeetna
Hatcher Pass Rd.
Willow
19 Wasilla
18 Palmer
Independence Mine State Historical Park
Sutton
Susitna River
Glenn Hwy.
Matanuska R.
Eagle River
Anchorage
Turnagain Arm
1 Chugach State Park
Girdwood
3 Portage Glacier
4 Whittier
Portage
7 Hope
Cooper Landing
10
Seward Hwy.
Moose Pass
8 Seward
9 Kenai Fjords National Park
Resurrection Bay
Fox Island
Cook Inlet
Tyonek
Sterling
11
12 Kenai & Soldotna
KENAI PENINSULA
Sterling Hwy.
Kenai National Wildlife Refuge
Clam Gulch
Ninilchik
Anchor Point
13 Homer
Kachemak Bay
Halibut Cove
14 Kachemak Bay State Park & State Wilderness Park
15 Seldovia
Tutka Bay
16 To Kodiak Island
17 Lake Clark National Park & Preserve
Iliamna Lake
Katmai National Park
Afognak Is.
Chugach National Forest
Paxson
22 Glennallen
Gakona
Chistochina
Slana
TO TOK
Nabesna
Copper Center
Chitina
Chitina River
Kennicott
McCarthy
Wrangell-St. Elias National Park & Preserve 23
Mt. St. Elias
COLUMBIA GLACIER
5 Valdez
Richardson Hwy.
2 Chugach National Forest
6 Cordova
Copper River
Prince William Sound
Shuyak Island State Park
Chugach National Forest
Port Lions
Kodiak
16 Kodiak Island
Kodiak National Wildlife Refuge

a ranger station, and Eagle River has running water and a dump station. Fishing is best at Bird Creek during the annual silver salmon run, and there are several hiking trails of varying degrees of difficulty at Eklutna. *Alaska State Parks, HC 52, Box 8999, Indian 99540 907/345–5014 www.dnr.state.ak.us/parks/units/chugach/facility.htm 3 campgrounds, 135 campsites No credit cards Closed roughly Oct.–Apr.*

Sports & the Outdoors

Main trailheads in the park are at the top of O'Malley, Huffman, and DeArmoun roads; south of Anchorage at Potter Valley, McHugh Creek, and Bird Ridge on the Seward Highway; and to the north of town at Arctic Valley Road (6 mi out) and Eagle River Road (13 mi out). The **Little Rodak Trail** is less than 1 mi long and has a viewing platform that overlooks the Eagle River valley. **Albert Loop Trail** behind the nature center has markers that coordinate with a self-guided hike along its 3-mi route; pick up a brochure at the Eagle River Nature Center.

Chugach National Forest

❷ *40 mi east of Anchorage.*

Sprawling east of Chugach State Park, Chugach National Forest encompasses nearly 6 million acres to embrace a major part of the Kenai Peninsula as well as parts of Prince William Sound. It's the second-largest national forest in the United States, exceeded in size only by the Tongass in Southeast Alaska.

Recreational opportunities here include hiking; camping; backpacking; fishing; boating; mountain biking; horseback riding; hunting; rock climbing; flightseeing; and, in the winter, snowshoeing, cross-country skiing, ice climbing, snowmobiling, and dog mushing. Hiking trails offer easy access into the heart of the forest. You can go for a short walk in the woods, pack a lunch and go for a hike looking for birds and wildlife, or embark on a multiday backpacking excursion. You can also take the opportunity to fish a backcountry lake or just indulge yourself in a part of Alaska that's seldom seen by visitors. At all but the most popular trailheads, a five-minute stroll down a wooded trail leads you to the sights, smells, and tranquillity of backcountry Alaska.

The Seward Highway between Anchorage and Seward has a number of trail access points. (Check the highway for mile markers, with the distance measured from Seward.) At Mile 63.7 south of Turnagain Pass is the turnoff to the Johnson Pass Trail, a relatively flat trail to walk. Seven miles farther south, take the Hope Highway 18 mi to its end and find the Porcupine Campground. From there, the Gull Rock Trail follows the shore of Turnagain Arm for 5 mi, offering scenic views across the Arm and the chance to spot beluga whales as they forage for salmon. Farther south on the Seward Highway at Mile 23.1, the Ptarmigan Creek trail starts at the campground and climbs into the mountains, ending next to a placid lake surrounded by snowy peaks.

Be prepared to be self-sufficient when entering Chugach Forest. Trailheads typically offer nothing more than a place to park and perhaps an outhouse. Running water, trail maps, and other amenities that you may have come to expect when visiting national forests in the Lower 48 are not available here. Also, be "bear aware" whenever you travel in bear country—and all of Alaska is bear country (⇨ Bear Facts box *in* Chapter 1). Be aware of your surroundings, and make noise when traveling, especially in areas of reduced visibility. Bears will most likely make themselves scarce as long as they've got some advance warning of your arrival.

For information on recreational opportunities in the forest, call **forest headquarters** (☎ 907/743–9500 Anchorage) or the **Alaska Public Lands Information Center** (☎ 907/271–2737 🌐 www.nps.gov/aplic).

Sports & the Outdoors

★ **Resurrection Pass Trail,** a 38-mi-long backpacking trail through the Chugach National Forest, draws hikers and backpackers from around the world for its colorful wildflowers in spring and summer and the chance to spot wildlife. Moose, caribou, Dall sheep, mountain goats, black and brown bears, wolves, coyotes, and lynx all traverse the forest. Carry binoculars for the best viewing opportunities. Scan every place for movement or anything that doesn't look like a rock, a bush, or a tree, especially whenever you see an open area.

The northern end of the trail starts south of the town of Hope, following an old mining trail through the Kenai Mountains to its end near the town of Cooper Landing. Side trails lead to trailheads along the Seward Highway at Summit Creek and Devil's Pass Creek. The well-maintained trail offers easy access to open country above the tree line. Besides U.S. Forest Service cabins, the Forest Service has provided several "official" campsites along the trail where you'll find a cleared patch of ground and a fire ring; however, you're free to pitch your tent wherever you like.

Where to Stay

¢ **U.S. Forest Service Cabins.** Along trails, near wilderness alpine lakes, in coastal forests, and on saltwater beaches, these rustic cabins offer retreats for the solo hiker or a group of friends. Some cabins are built of logs, and some are A-frames. Most have tables, chairs, wood-burning stoves, and bunks but no electricity, running water, or bedding. Many require a fly-in or boat ride, although some can be reached by car and then foot. ☎ *877/444–6777 reservations* 🌐 *www.reserveusa.com* *41 cabins* *D, MC, V.*

¢ **U.S. Forest Service Campgrounds.** The Forest Service maintains 18 campgrounds, 14 of them road-accessible, within Chugach National Forest. All of the road-accessible campgrounds have toilet facilities—usually outhouses—picnic tables, fire grates, and drinking water available from hand pumps, but no hookups for RVs. The Russian River Campground has a three-day limit during salmon-fishing season in June and July. Most have sites suitable for RVs as well as tents. Reservations (for a fee) are accepted at only five campgrounds—Cooper Creek South, Ptarmigan Creek, Russian River, Trail River, and Williwaw. ☎ *877/444–6777 reservations* 🌐 *www.reserveusa.com* *18 campgrounds* *D, MC, V.*

AFFORDABLE WILDERNESS & SOLITUDE

IF YOU'RE LOOKING FOR A REAL ALASKA BACKCOUNTRY EXPERIENCE, *but don't feel like shelling out a couple grand (or more) for the privilege, there is an alternative. And it doesn't involve squeezing into a leaky tent while waiting for the neighborhood bears to come by and inspect you at close range.*

Alaska has a system of remote public-use cabins rented out by five land-management agencies. Locations include tidewater spots in Southeast Alaska and Prince William Sound; lake-, stream-, and seaside cabins in Kenai Fjords National Park, Kodiak Island, and South Central; and tundra and mountain venues in the Interior. With well over 200 cabins to choose from, and at a reasonable price by any calculation (from $25 to $50 per cabin, per night), there's something for everyone.

The cabins offer little in the way of creature comforts other than a roof, four solid walls, wooden bunks and benches, counters, and a heating stove. Water must be hauled from nearby streams or lakes, and the facilities consist of an outhouse. If you don't mind roughing it for a few nights, the advantages are many—after all, a trip to Alaska is the time to forgo usual amenities in favor of a memorable wilderness experience.

Solitude is the main advantage to staying at a public-use cabin. Quite often you won't see anyone who hasn't hiked, boated, or flown in with you. Some cabins are near busy trails, although what passes for busy in Alaska is likely to be much less human contact than you're used to. Recreational possibilities include hiking, fishing, wildlife viewing, boating, climbing, or simply enjoying the peace and quiet of the wilderness.

One slight downside of these remote venues is the access cost. You'll either pay with sweat equity by hiking in with all of your gear on your back, or you'll have to charter a boat or airplane to get you in and back out. With that comes the pressure of making sure you've got absolutely everything on hand—including food, sleeping and cooking gear, and fuel—before your boat or airplane motors away. Running down to the store to pick up snacks, matches, toilet paper, or some other essential won't be an option, so make a list and check it twice. Then check it once more.

Arranging for boat or air access to the cabins means contacting a charter boat company in the nearest town for tidewater cabins, or arranging a fly-in trip with an air taxi. Since both modes of transport are weather dependent, always allow an extra day or two on either end of the trip, and bring extra food and supplies.

If you're willing to do the necessary planning and forgo the conveniences that large lodges and hotels can offer, you'll find that public-use cabins provide an outstanding opportunity to get away from the crowds. You'll experience true Alaskan wilderness as few other visitors do.

Links to all five agencies renting cabins: 🌐 www.nps.gov/aplic/cabins/

List of Alaska air taxis: 🌐 www.flyalaska.com/directoryp.html

U.S. Forest Service reservation system concessionaire: 🌐 www.reserveusa.com or call 877/444–6777.

—Tom Reale

Portage Glacier

❸ *54 mi southeast of Anchorage.*

Portage Glacier is one of Alaska's most frequently visited tourist destinations. A 6-mi side road off the Seward Highway leads to the **Begich-Boggs Visitor Center** (☎ 907/783–2326 🌐 www.fs.fed.us/r10/chugach/chugach_pages/bbvc), on the shore of Portage Lake and named after two U.S. congressmen who disappeared on a small-plane journey out of Anchorage in 1972. The center is staffed by Forest Service personnel, who can help plan your trip and explain the natural history of the area. A film on glaciers is shown hourly, and icebergs frequently drift down to the center from Portage Glacier.

The glacier has receded from view in recent years, as have most of the glaciers in Alaska. Whether or not it's attributable to global warming is a question for environmental scientists, but the fact of Portage Glacier's disappearance from view at the visitor center is undeniable. If you want to see the glacier close-up, the Gray Line tour on the ***Ptarmigan*** is the way to go. The view of Portage Lake and the surrounding peaks and hanging glaciers (the ones high up that terminate at the tops of cliffs), is spectacular, especially on a sunny day when the icy blue hues of the glaciers shine through.

The mountains surrounding Portage Glacier are covered with smaller glaciers. A 1-mi hike west brings you to the **Byron Glacier** overlook. The glacier is notable for its accessibility—it's one of the few places where you can hike onto a glacier from the road system. In summer, naturalists lead free weekly treks in search of microscopic ice worms. Several hiking trails are accessible from the Seward Highway, including the Old Johnson Trail and the path up Bird Ridge. Both offer spectacular views of **Turnagain Arm,** where explorer Captain Cook searched for the Northwest Passage. Local lore has it that the Arm is so named because Cook entered it repeatedly, only to be forced to turn back by the huge tide. The tide is so powerful it sometimes rushes up the arm as a tidal bore—a wall of water that goes up an inlet. During the summer months, beluga whales are frequent visitors to the Arm as they patrol the muddy waters in search of salmon and hooligan, a variety of smelt. The whales travel in pods of adult and juvenile animals, the adults distinguishable by their bright white color. They're smaller than other whales that frequent Alaska's coastal waters, reaching "only" 15 feet in length and weighing up to a ton. When the tide is high and the surface of the water is calm, belugas are often spotted from the highway, frequently causing traffic jams as tourists and residents alike pull off the road for a chance to view the whales as they travel up and down the shoreline. Also, keep an eye out for black bears in all the Portage side valleys in the summer.

Alaska Wildlife Conservation Center is a 144-acre drive-through wildlife center just before the Portage Glacier turnoff. Moose, bison, elk, caribou, Sitka black-tailed deer, musk ox, great horned owls, a brown bear, and a bald eagle, many of them orphaned in the wild, now live in the park. There are also snack and gift shops. ✉ *Mile 79, Seward Hwy.*

☎ *907/783–2025* 📠 *907/783–2370* 🌐 *www.alaskawildlife.org* 🎫 *$5* ⏲ *May–Sept., daily 8–8; Oct.–Apr., daily 10–dusk.*

Little remains of the community of **Portage** as a result of the 1964 earthquake. The ghost forest of dead spruce in the area was created when the land subsided by 6 feet–10 feet after the quake, and salt water penetrated inland from Turnagain Arm, killing the trees. A tumbledown building or two still stand along the highway, and there's a café at the turnoff to Portage Glacier.

Guided Tours

Gray Line of Alaska (☎ 907/277–5581 or 800/544–2206 🌐 www.graylinealaska.com) leads summer boat tours (from mid-May to mid-September) along the face of Portage Glacier aboard the 200-passenger *Ptarmigan* for $29.

Shopping

On your way to Portage, look for **Indian Valley Meats** (✉ Huot Cir., 23 mi south of Anchorage on Seward Hwy. at Mile 103.9 ☎ 907/653–7511 🌐 www.indianvalleymeats.com), where workers sell the smoked salmon and musk ox, reindeer, and buffalo sausage made on the premises. They'll also smoke, can, and package the fish you've caught and arrange for shipping anywhere in the world.

Whittier

❹ *60 mi south of Anchorage.*

Whittier serves as an access point for those who want to visit Prince William Sound, and as a cruise-ship port. In years past, the only way to get to the town was by boat or through a pair of railroad tunnels through the surrounding mountains. Things have changed quite a bit in the last few years, however, and now the tunnel into town is a combination rail and highway road. Travel hours are restricted, so it's not always possible to just breeze into and back out of Whittier. Tolls through the tunnel are $12 for passenger vehicles and $20–$35 for RVs and trailers; waits of up to an hour, however, are possible, and summer hours are from 6 AM until 11 PM. Along with the return of cruise ships to the port after a long respite, the town is looking forward to increased visitor traffic. There's a small-boat harbor, a ferry terminal for trips to Valdez, Seward, and Cordova, fishing and sightseeing charter companies, and sea-kayak rentals and tours. A few small restaurants and shops surround the harbor, but lodging facilities are limited. New in 2004 is a cruise-ship terminal and dock.

The most charitable description of the town is that it's unlovely. The dominant structure in town and home to almost all of the local inhabitants is a large World War II–era apartment building known as Begich Towers. Due to its recent paint job it no longer resembles a structure from the Russian gulag, but the rest of the buildings in town are a hodgepodge of hastily erected and largely unplanned businesses, many surrounding a single parking lot. Weather is also a bit of a problem here. The annual precipitation in nearby Anchorage is a mere 16 inches per year, but once you pass through the tunnel to the sound, that figure jumps more than tenfold to 200 inches.

However, the view looking away from the town on a clear day is jaw-droppingly gorgeous. The surrounding mountain peaks cradle alpine glaciers, and when the summer weather melts off the huge winter snow load, you can catch glimpses of the brilliant blue ice underneath. Sheer cliffs drop into Passage Canal and provide nesting places for flocks of black-legged kittiwakes, sea otters and harbor seals cavort in the small-boat harbor, and salmon return to spawn in nearby streams. A short boat ride out into the sound reveals tidewater glaciers, and an alert wildlife watcher can catch sight of mountain goats clinging to the mountain-sides and black bears patrolling the beaches and hillsides in their constant search for food. Waterborne traffic includes commercial fishing boats, charter boats, cruise ships, tugboats, and the Alaska state ferry. It can be an amazingly memorable place.

Where to Eat

¢–$$$ ✕ **Varly's Swiftwater Seafood.** Place your order at the window and then grab a seat at the counter and wait for your food. There's outdoor seating that overlooks the small-boat harbor. Menu items include homemade chowders, hand-battered seafood, peel-and-eat shrimp, burgers, and chicken, with a smoked prime rib dinner served on Friday and Saturday nights. ✉ *Harbor Loop* ☎ *907/472–2550* ▭ *MC, V* ⊙ *Closed mid–Sept.–May.*

¢–$$ ✕ **Tunnel's End Café.** The café is primarily a breakfast and lunch joint, but owner and waitress Jo Anne also serves up a diner-style dinner, with meat loaf, seafood, burgers and sandwiches. Breakfast and lunch items take up a couple of pages of the menu, with breakfast burritos, omelets, and pancakes, and lunches consisting of Philly cheese steaks, burgers, hot dogs, and deli sandwiches. A cute little dining room has American farm house–style furnishings and a fireplace, and you can receive take-out and espresso from the order window. ✉ *12 Harbor Loop Dr.* ☎ *907/472–3000* ▭ *MC, V.*

Where to Stay

$$$–$$$$ **The Inn At Whittier.** In anticipation of Whittier's Renaissance as a cruise port and tourist destination, the Inn opened its doors in 2005. The four-story timber-frame structure is built around a 70-foot-tall lighthouse, and guests are free to climb to the top and take in the views. The lobby features a great room and fireplace, and expansive windows framing panoramic views of the sound. ✉ *Box 609, 99693* ☎ *907/472–7000, or 866/472–5757* 🖷 *800/858–7549* 🌐 *www.innatwhittier.com* *23 rooms, 2 suites* *Restaurant, in-room data ports, in-room hot tubs, cable TV, lounge, meeting room; no a/c* ▭ *AE, D, MC, V.*

$–$$$$ **June's Whittier Condo Suites.** June's rents out 10 condominiums in the Begich Towers building, half with bay views, half with mountain views. With the large room selection, they can accommodate large groups and families. June's also operates Bread-n-Butter Charters, and can arrange fishing or sightseeing tours and even overnight trips into the sound. *Box 715, 99693* ☎ *888/472–2396* 🖷 *907/472–2503* 🌐 *www.breadnbuttercharters.com* *10 rooms* *Kitchens, micro-*

waves, refrigerators, cable TV, in-room VCRs, no-smoking rooms; no a/c ▭ *AE, MC, V* 🍽 *CP.*

$–$$ **Soundview Getaway.** When the Begich Towers building was used by the military during the war, the Bachelor Officer's Quarters were home to soldiers stationed in Whittier. Today these rooms have been refurbished as B&B condos with full kitchens and full baths. The larger rooms sleep four, and two smaller rooms can be joined as a suite sleeping up to six. *5800 E. 142nd Ave., Anchorage 99516* ☎ *800/515–2358, 907/472–2358, 907/440–9114* 🖷 *907/260–4657* 🌐 *www.soundviewalaska.com* *5 rooms* *Microwaves, cable TV, in-room VCRs; no a/c, no smoking* ▭ *AE, MC, V* 🍽 *CP.*

3

Sports & the Outdoors

Alaska Sea Kayakers. This outfit can supply sea kayaks and gear for exploring Prince William Sound and also conducts guided day trips, multiday tours, instruction, and boat-assisted and boat live-aboard kayaking trips. They practice a leave-no-trace camping ethos, and are very conscientious about avoiding bear problems by using preventive measures. ☎ *877/472–2534 or 907/440–4155* 🌐 *www.alaskaseakayakers.com* ⏲ *May–Sept. 15.*

Honey Charters. This small fleet of boats is available for charter, sightseeing, and sea kayak drop-offs. They can take groups of up to 30 people on trips through Prince William Sound, and will transport people and cargo to Cordova and Valdez. Standard sightseeing trips run from three to six hours, and custom tours are available on request. ✉ *Box 708, 99693* ☎ *907/472–2493* 🖷 *907/472–2491* 🌐 *www.honeycharters.com.*

Major Marine Tours. This cruise from Whittier visits two tidewater glaciers during a five-hour trip. The waters of Prince William Sound are well protected and relatively calm, making this a good option if you're inclined toward queasiness. Seals, sea lions, and sea otters are frequently sighted, and several species of whale and porpoise inhabit the area as well. Seabirds, waterfowl, and bald eagles are always present, and the chance to get close to the enormous walls of ice of the glaciers is not to be missed. You can opt for an onboard meal for $15. ☎ *800/764–7300 or 907/274–7300* 🌐 *www.majormarine.com* *$109* ⏲ *Mid-May–mid-Sept.*

Prince William Sound Cruises and Tours. From Whittier, tours travel through the sheltered bays, fjords, and canals of Prince William Sound, viewing glaciers, sea birds, and wildlife such as seals, sea lions, sea otters, whales, bears, and mountain goats. Transportation options include traveling from Anchorage by motor coach or rail, or meeting the tour in Whittier in your own vehicle. Prices vary according to length of trip and travel options. ✉ *2525 C St., Anchorage* ☎ *877/777–2805* 🖷 *877/777–2888* 🌐 *www.alaskaheritagetours.com/475.cfm* ⏲ *Mid-May–mid-Sept.*

Sound Eco Adventures. Retired marine biologist Gerry Sanger runs a number of tours in his six-passenger, 30-foot boat. He'll take you whale watching, glacier viewing, or on a general wildlife-viewing trip for anywhere from 5 to 10 hours. He can also transport sea kayakers, cabin renters, and anyone else needing a charter boat out of Whittier. Group discounts are available, and longer trips include lunch and a beach stop. ☎ *888/471–2312 or 907/472–2312* 🌐 *www.SoundEcoAdventure.com* ⏲ *Mar.–mid-Nov.*

26 Glacier Cruise. Phillips' Cruises and Tours has been running this tour through Prince William Sound for many years. Their high-speed catamaran covers 135 mi of territory in four-and-a-half hours, leaving Whittier and visiting Port Wells, Barry Arm, and College and Harriman Fjords. The boat is a very stable platform, and even visitors who might be prone to seasickness can take this cruise with no ill effects. The heated cabin has large windows, upholstered booths, and wide aisles for passenger comfort. There's a snack bar and a saloon on board, and wildlife encounters are commonplace. You can drive to Whittier and catch the boat there, or you can arrange with the company to travel from Anchorage by rail or by motor coach. *519 West 4th Ave., Anchorage 99501* ☎ *800/544–0529, 907/276–8023* 🌐 *www.26glaciers.com* *$129* ⏲ *May–Sept.*

Valdez

❺ *6 hrs northeast of Whittier by water, 304 mi east of Anchorage.*

Valdez (pronounced val-*deez*) is the largest of the Prince William Sound communities. This year-round ice-free port was originally the entry point for people and goods going to the Interior during the gold rush. Today that flow has been reversed, with Valdez harbor being the southern terminus of the trans-Alaska pipeline, which carries crude oil from Prudhoe Bay and surrounding oil fields nearly 800 mi to the north. This region, with its dependence on commercial fishing, is still feeling the aftereffects of 1989's massive oil spill. Much of Valdez looks modern because the business area was relocated and rebuilt after its destruction by the 1964 Good Friday earthquake. Even though the town is younger than the rest of "civilized" Alaska, it's gradually acquiring a lived-in look.

Many Alaskan communities have summer fishing derbies, but Valdez may hold the record for the number of such contests, stretching from late May into September for halibut and various runs of salmon. If you go fishing, by all means enter the appropriate derby. Every summer the newspapers run sob stories about tourists who landed possible prizewinners but couldn't share in the glory because they hadn't forked over the five bucks to officially enter the contest. The **Valdez Silver Salmon Derby** is held the entire month of August. Fishing charters abound in this area of Prince William Sound, and for good reason: these fertile waters provide some of the best saltwater sportfishing in all of Alaska.

A pleasant attraction on a rainy day, if you ever tire of gazing at the 5,000-foot mountain peaks surrounding Valdez, is the **Valdez Museum.** It explores the lives, livelihoods, and events significant to Valdez and surrounding regions. Exhibits include a restored 1880s Gleason & Baily hand-pumped fire engine, a 1907 Ahrens steam fire engine, a 19th-century saloon, information on the local Native peoples, and an exhibit on the 1989 oil spill. Every summer the museum hosts an exhibit of quilts and fiber arts made by local and regional artisans. At a separate site, a 35-by-40-foot model of **Historical Old Town Valdez** (✉ 436 Hazlet Ave.) depicts the original town, which was devastated by the 1964 earthquake. There's also an operating seismograph and an exhibit on local seismic activity. A Valdez History Exhibits Pass includes admission to both the museum and the annex. ✉ *217 Egan Dr.* ☎ *907/835–2764* 🌐 *www.valdezmuseum.org* *$5* ⏲ *June–Aug., daily 9–6; Sept.–May, weekdays 1–5, Sat. noon–4.*

★ A visit to **Columbia Glacier,** which flows from the surrounding Chugach Mountains, certainly should be on the agenda. Its deep aquamarine face is 5 mi across, and it calves icebergs with resounding cannonades. This glacier is one of the largest and most readily accessible of Alaska's coastal glaciers. The state ferry travels past the face of the glacier, and scheduled tours of the glaciers and the rest of the sound are available by boat and aircraft from Valdez and Whittier.

3

Where to Stay & Eat

If you roll into town without reservations, especially if it's after hours, stop at the **Valdez Visitor's Center** (✉ 200 Chenega St. ☎ 907/835–2984) on the corner of Fairbanks. They post vacancies in bed-and-breakfasts on the window when they close for the day, and there's a pay phone there so you can start making calls.

$$–$$$$ ✕ **Alaska's Bistro.** The view of the small-boat harbor is complemented inside by the nautical theme and color scheme. Local art adorns the walls, and the two-tier dining room guarantees a view for all. The house specialty is paella for two (or more), and fresh local seafood dominates the menu. There's also a large selection of appetizers, salads, and poultry, pork, steaks, and pizza. The wine cellar includes more than 250 selections. ✉ *100 Fidalgo Dr.* ☎ *907/835–5688* ▭ *AE, MC, V.*

$–$$$ ✕ **Mike's Palace.** On the harbor, this convivial restaurant with Italian-diner decor is a local favorite. The menu includes veal, terrific pizza, beer-batter halibut, steaks, and Greek gyros. ✉ *201 N. Harbor Dr.* ☎ *907/835–2365* ▭ *MC, V.*

¢–$$ ✕ **Alaska Halibut House.** A very casual place: order at the counter, sit at the Formica-covered tables, and check out the photos of local fishing boats. The battered halibut is excellent—light and not a bit greasy. There are other items on the menu, including homemade clam chowder, but if you're eating at the Halibut House, why try anything else? ✉ *208 Meals Ave.* ☎ *907/835–2788* ▭ *MC, V.*

$$$$ **Prince William Sound Lodge.** This fly-in lodge on a remote shore of Prince William Sound offers opportunities for a wide range of vacation activities, including hiking, bird-watching, exploring nearby Alaska Native villages, and the chance for some of the best silver salmon fishing in the state. There's also halibut fishing, and there are seaplane rides, and boat trips on a converted commercial fishing boat. Gourmet meals add to the list of attractions, and one of the local bears just might amble past during your stay. Lodging price does not include the $150 per person floatplane flight to the lodge. ✉ *Ellamar* 📫 *3900 Clay Products Dr., Anchorage 99517* ☎ *907/248–0909 or 907/440–0909* 🌐 *www.princewilliamsound.us/~pwslodge* *5* *Dining room, beach, boat-*

ing, fishing; no a/c, no room phones, no room TVs, no smoking ▭ *No credit cards* ⊙ *Closed late Sept.–May* 🍽 *FAP.*

$$ **Aspen Hotel Valdez.** The Aspen hotels are part of a small, local chain with hotels in Anchorage, Fairbanks, Juneau, and Soldotna, all with modern and up-to-date facilities. The owners pride themselves on hiring service-oriented and compassionate personnel. The Valdez hotel is within easy walking distance of shops, restaurants, and the small-boat harbor, the center of summertime activity. The business center and pool are especially noteworthy in small-town Alaska. ✉ *100 Meals Ave., 99686* ☎ *907/835–4445* 🖷 *907/835–2437* 🌐 *www.aspenhotelsak.com/valdez.htm* ⇨ *102 rooms* ♁ *In-room data ports, microwaves, refrigerators, cable TV, in-room VCRs, pool, exercise room, hot tub, spa, laundry facilities, Internet, business services, meeting room no-smoking rooms; no a/c* ▭ *AE, D, DC, MC, V* 🍽 *CP.*

$ **Best Western Valdez Harbor Inn.** Near the small-boat harbor, this hotel has a canal right outside the lobby windows. Rooms are decorated with Alaska artwork, and wooden crown moldings complement the furnishings. Colorful floral bedspreads add color to the rooms. ✉ *100 Harbor Dr., Box 468, 99686* ☎ *907/835–3434 or 888/222–3440* 🖷 *907/835–2308* 🌐 *www.bestwestern.com* ⇨ *88 rooms* ♁ *Restaurant, room service, in-room data ports, microwaves, refrigerators, cable TV, exercise equipment, spa, laundry facilities, Internet, meeting room, some pets allowed, no-smoking rooms* ▭ *AE, D, DC, MC, V.*

Bayside RV Park. This full-service RV park with a few tent site areas has a panoramic view of the mountains, and wide, crushed-stone parking spots. The folks here can also help you book fishing and sightseeing trips with local charter outfits. ♁ *Flush toilets, full hookups, dump station, drinking water, guest laundry, showers, grills, picnic tables, electricity, public telephone* ⇨ *110 spaces* ✉ *230 E. Egan Dr., 99686* ☎ *888/835–4425, 907/835-4425* 🖷 *907/835–8544* 🌐 *http://baysiderv.homestead.com/index.html* ▭ *MC, V* ⊙ *May–Oct. 10.*

Sports & the Outdoors

Guided Tours

Alpine Aviation Adventures (☎ 907/835–4304, 800/478–4304 in Alaska 🖷 907/835–2523), based in Valdez, gives aerial tours of Columbia Glacier, Prince William Sound, and the Wrangell Mountains.

Valdez-based **Columbia Glacier Wildlife Cruises/*Lu-Lu Belle*** (☎ 907/835–5141 or 800/411–0090 🖷 907/835–5899 in summer ☎🖷 800/411–0090 off-season 🌐 www.lulubelletours.com) leads small-group whale-watching, wildlife-viewing, and Columbia Glacier cruises.

Keystone Raft & Kayak Adventures (☎ 907/835–2606 or 800/328–8460 🖷 907/835–4638 🌐 www.alaskawhitewater.com) provides all gear for guided raft and kayak tours on rivers rated up to Class V in the Valdez and Copper River valley areas.

Stan Stephens Glacier & Wildlife Cruises (☎ 907/835–4731 or 866/867–1297 🖷 907/835–3765 🌐 www.stanstephenscruises.com), based in Valdez, leads Prince William Sound glacier and wildlife-viewing cruises to Columbia and Meares glaciers from mid-May through mid-September. The company is Alaskan owned and they bill themselves as "the local experts since 1971."

Anadyr Adventures (☎ 907/835–2814 or 800/865–2925 🌐 www.anadyradventures.com) offers sea kayak trips into Prince William Sound. Guides will escort you on day trips, multiday camping trips, "mothership" adventures based in a remote anchorage, or lodge-based trips for the ultimate combination of adventure by day and comfort by night. If you're already an experienced kayaker, they'll outfit you and you can travel on your own. They can also arrange water-taxi service to transport you to or from anyplace in the sound.

Cordova

❻ *6 hrs southeast of Valdez by water, 150 mi east of Anchorage by air.*

A small town with the spectacular backdrop of snowy Mt. Eccles, Cordova is the gateway to the Copper River Delta—one of the great birding areas of North America. Perched on Orca Inlet in eastern Prince William Sound, Cordova began life early in the 20th century as the port city for the Copper River–Northwestern Railway, which was built to serve the Kennicott copper mines 191 mi away in the Wrangell Mountains. Since the mines and the railroad shut down in 1938, Cordova's economy has since depended heavily on fishing. Attempts to develop a road along the abandoned railroad line connecting to the state highway system were dashed by the 1964 earthquake, so Cordova remains isolated. Access to the community is limited to airplane or ferry.

The **Cordova Museum** emphasizes Native artifacts as well as pioneer, mining, and fishing history. Displays include an 1840s handcrafted lighthouse lens and a stuffed 800-pound leatherback turtle. Afternoon video programs and an informative brochure outline a self-guided walking tour of the town's historical buildings. The gift shop sells masks, pottery, and children's and local history books. ✉ *622 1st St.* ☎ *907/424–6665* 🌐 *www.cordovamuseum.org* 🎟 *$1* ⏲ *Memorial Day–Labor Day, Mon.–Sat. 10–6, Sun. 2–4; Labor Day–Memorial Day, Tues.–Fri. 1–5, Sat. 2–4.*

Drive out of town along the Copper River Highway and visit the **Copper River Delta.** This 700,000-acre wetland is one of North America's most spectacular vistas. The two-lane highway crosses marshes, forests, streams, lakes, and ponds that are home to countless shorebirds, waterfowl, and other bird species. Numerous terrestrial mammals including moose, wolves, lynx, mink, and beavers live here as well, and the Copper River salmon runs are world famous. When the red and king salmon hit the river in the spring, there's a frantic rush to net the tasty fish and rush them off to waiting markets and restaurants all over the country.

At Mile 17 there's a turn-off to **Alaganik Slough.** This 5-mi road leads to a wheelchair-accessible boardwalk as well as covered viewing shelters, restrooms, and picnic areas. A dedicated bird-watcher can spend hours poking along the waterways and peering into the vegetation, seeking out rare and interesting avian species at every turn.

The **Million Dollar Bridge,** at Mile 48, was a railroad project completed in 1910 for the Copper River and Northwestern Railway to carry copper ore to market from the mines at Kennicott. Soon after construction was completed, the nearby Childs and Miles glaciers threatened to overrun the railroad and bridge. Although the glaciers stopped short of the railroad, the copper market collapsed in 1938, making the route economically obsolete. The far span of the bridge was toppled by the Good Friday earthquake in 1964 and has not been rebuilt. There's still occasional talk about restoring the bridge and punching a road through from Cordova to connect with the road system, but the money required has not been forthcoming.

From the end of the road you can view the **Childs Glacier.** Although there is no visitor center, a covered viewing area next to the bridge enables you to watch the face of the glacier and read the informational plaques while you wait for a huge chunk of ice to topple into the river. The waves produced by falling ice frequently wash migrating salmon onto the riverbank, and the local brown bears have been known to patrol the river's edge looking for an easy meal, so keep your eyes wide open.

Where to Stay & Eat

$–$$$ ✕ **Powder House Bar & Restaurant.** On clear summer evenings you can relax on the deck overlooking Eyak Lake at this roadside bar and enjoy whatever the cook's in the mood to fix: homemade soups, sandwiches, sushi, and seasonal seafood are all possibilities. If you're lucky or skillful in your fishing endeavors, the kitchen staff will cook your catch. On Friday and Saturday, shrimp and steak are added to the menu. ✉ *Mile 2.1, Copper River Hwy.* ☎ *907/424–3529* ▭ *AE, D, MC, V.*

¢–$$ ✕ **Ambrosia.** Pastas, hamburgers, and steaks are served behind the storefront, but it's the hearty pizzas that have earned this place its reputation among locals. ✉ *410 1st St.* ☎ *907/424–7175* ▭ *AE, MC, V.*

¢ ✕ **Killer Whale Café.** Have a breakfast of espresso and baked goods or an omelet at this café. For lunch you can choose from a deli menu of soups, salads, and sandwiches, followed by a fresh, homemade dessert. On the back balcony, tables overlook the harbor. ✉ *Main St.* ☎ *907/424–7733* ▭ *MC, V* ⊗ *Closed Sun.*

$$ ✕ **Cordova Lighthouse Inn.** If you've ever dreamed of living in a bakery, here's your chance. This four-room inn is home to an artisan bakery and restaurant where everything is made from scratch. The restaurant serves breakfast and lunch only, along with a very creative and extensive menu of wood-fired pizzas. Two of the rooms have mountain views, but if at all possible, get one of the two with harbor views for the full Alaskan fishing-village ambience. ✉ *112 Nicholoff Way* *Box 1495, 99574* ☎ *907/424–7080* 🌐 *www.cordovalighthouseinn.com* *6 rooms* *Restaurant, in-room data ports, cable TV; no a/c, no room phones, no smoking* ▭ *MC, V.*

$–$$ **Reluctant Fisherman Inn.** At this waterfront hotel and restaurant you can watch the commercial-fishing fleet and other maritime traffic sail by. Comfortable, nautical-theme rooms overlook the harbor, and Native art and artifacts decorate the public spaces. The restaurant serves local seafood, including a king salmon chili, as well as pastas and espresso. ✉ *407 Railroad Ave., 99574* ☎ *907/424–3272 or 800/770–3272* 📠 *907/424–7465* 🌐 *www.cordovaak.com* *41 rooms* *Restaurant, in-room data ports, cable TV, bar, laundry facilities, meeting rooms, airport shuttle, car rental, travel services, some pets allowed; no a/c* *AE, D, DC, MC, V.*

¢–$ **Northern Nights Inn B&B.** Commanding a dramatic view of Orca Inlet just a couple of blocks above downtown Cordova, this bed-and-breakfast has rooms furnished with turn-of-the-20th-century antiques. If owner Becky Chapek doesn't have room for you, she'll serve as a valuable source of information on other B&Bs in town. She operates bus tours around town and to the Million Dollar Bridge, and she can transport you to and from the airport as well. She also operates Chinook Auto Rentals at the airport. ✉ *500 3rd St.* *Box 1564, 99574* ☎ *907/424–5356* *3 rooms, 1 suite* *Some kitchens, some microwaves, cable TV, some in-room VCRs, laundry facilities, car rental; no a/c* *AE, D, MC, V.*

$$ **Orca Adventure Lodge.** The list of activities at the lodge goes on and on: fishing, kayaking, river rafting, hiking, bear viewing, flightseeing. There's also the opportunity to fly out to one of Orca's remote wilderness camps for fishing or just relaxing. The lodge is a converted cannery and it oozes old Alaska charm. *Box 2105, 99574* ☎ *907/424–7249, 866/424–6722* 📠 *907/424–3579* 🌐 *www.orcaadventurelodge.com* *23 rooms, 4 suites* *Restaurant, airport shuttle; no a/c, no room phones, no room TVs, no smoking* *AE, MC, V* *Restaurant closed Oct.–May.*

$–$$ **Cordova Rose Lodge.** A truly unique lodge, the Cordova Rose sits on a barge on the Prince William Sound breakwater. There's a working lighthouse on the site, used by boats transiting the channel. The accommodations range from cabins to semi-private to private rooms, and families and groups are especially welcomed. A large, hot breakfast is the order of the day, and dinner can be arranged if enough guests request it. Vacation packages including hiking, fishing, bird-watching, and wildlife viewing are also available. ✉ *1315 Whitshed* *Box 1494, 99574* ☎ *907/424–7673* 🌐 *www.cordovarose.com* *11 rooms, 2 cabins* *Dining room, kitchens, sauna, Internet, airport shuttle; no a/c, no room phones or TVs except in cabins, no smoking* *MC, V* *BP.*

¢ **U.S. Forest Service Cabins.** The Cordova Ranger District of the Chugach National Forest maintains a series of 18 backcountry cabins for rent. These cabins are very basic: four walls, roof, floor, wooden bunks, usually a woodstove, table, benches, counter space for preparing meals, and a pit toilet out back. There's no bedding, cooking utensils, electricity, or running water. Bring everything you need to be self-sufficient for your stay. Most of the cabins are accessible only by boat or floatplane, although the McKinley Trail cabin is accessible by motor vehicle on the Copper River Highway. Two others can be reached by hiking from the road. A map of the district and the cabin locations is available at 🌐 www.fs.fed.us/r10/chugach/cordova/pages/cabins/cabmap.html. Rentals are arranged through a Forest Service concessionaire, Reserve USA. ☎ *877/444–6777* 🌐 *www.reserveusa.com* *18 cabins* *AE, D, MC, V.*

Guided Tours

Cordova Air Service (☎ 907/424–3289, 800/424–7608 in Alaska) leads aerial tours of Prince William Sound on planes with wheels or floats. **Alaskan Wilder-**

ness Outfitting Co. (☎ 907/424–5552 🖷 907/424–5564 🌐 www.alaskawilderness.com) operates an air-taxi service out of Cordova and arranges fresh- and saltwater fly-out fishing experiences, from drop-offs to guided tours with lodge accommodations. **Cordova Coastal Outfitters** (☎ 800/357–5145 🌐 www.cdvcoastal.com) conducts half-day and full-day sea kayak tours. They rent kayaks for overnight trips, and can arrange custom tours to fit your desired level of activity. They also run half- and full-day tours in their 31-foot jet boat tours, observing local wildlife and the commercial-fishing fleet at work. If you rent a kayak or bring your own, they'll provide pickup and drop-off service anywhere on the road system.

Sports & the Outdoors

BIRD-WATCHING Spring migration to the **Copper River delta** provides some of the finest avian spectacles in the world. Species include the Western sandpiper, American dipper, orange-crowned warbler, and short-billed dowitcher. Trumpeter swans and dusky Canada geese can also be seen. The **Copper River Delta Shorebird Festival** (☎ 907/424–7260 🌐 www.cordovachamber.com), held the first week of May, includes five days of workshops and guided field trips. As many as 5 million birds, mostly western sandpipers and dunlins, descend on the Copper River Delta, feeding and resting on their long migration to their northern nesting grounds. This migration respite is critical for these birds, and the food they gather from the rich mudflats of the delta keeps them alive and healthy.

Shopping

Orca Book & Sound Co. (✉ 507 1st St. ☎ 907/424–5305) is much more than a bookstore. In addition to books, it sells music, art supplies, children's toys, and locally produced art. The walls often double as a gallery for local works or traveling exhibits, and the store specializes in old, rare, out-of-print, and first-edition books, especially Alaskana. In the back is an espresso/smoothie bar; upstairs is Internet/wireless access for a small fee. Closed Sunday.

KENAI PENINSULA

The Kenai Peninsula, thrusting into the Gulf of Alaska south of Anchorage, is South Central's playground, offering salmon and halibut fishing, spectacular scenery, and wildlife viewing. Commercial fishing is important to the area's economy; five species of Pacific salmon run up the aqua-color Kenai River every summer. Campgrounds and trailheads for backwoods hiking are strung along the roads. Along the way, you can explore three major federal holdings on the peninsula—the western end of the sprawling Chugach National Forest, Kenai National Wildlife Refuge, and Kenai Fjords National Park.

Hope

7 *39 mi west of Portage, 87 mi south of Anchorage.*

The little gold-mining community of Hope is 87 mi south of Anchorage by road but just across Turnagain Arm. To visit, however, you must drive all the way around, as no ferry service exists. It's at the end of a 16-mi-long spur road, so it's not on the way to anywhere—you really have to go there on purpose. However, your reward is a quiet little community, accessible but not overrun with tourists, where the pace of life slows just a little. Hope was founded by miners in 1896 but now consists mainly of retirement homes for former Anchorage residents. The old log cabins and weathered frame buildings in the town center are favorite photography subjects. You'll find lots of gold panning, fishing, and hiking opportunities here, and the northern trailhead for the 38-mi-long Resurrection Pass Trail is nearby. Contact the U.S. Forest Service for information on campgrounds, cabin rentals, and hikes in this area.

Where to Eat & Stay

¢–$$$ ✕ **Summit Lake Lodge.** One of the Kenai peninsula's most popular roadside restaurants, the lodge has been satisfying the appetites of residents and visitors for more than 50 years. The building is made of local, handhewn spruce timbers, and the dining room has expansive windows to take in the view of Summit Lake and the mountains. Main courses include fresh seafood, pasta, and a nice selection of steaks. Desserts are worth stopping for even if you've already had dinner. ✉ *Mile 45.5, Seward Hwy., Moose Pass* ☎ *907/244–2031* 🌐 *www.summitlakelodge.com* 💳 *MC, V* ⏲ *Closed Oct.–mid-Apr.*

¢–$ ✕ **Tito's Discovery Cafe.** When the "Original Tito's" restaurant burned down, uninsured, in 1999, the owner was faced with financial ruin. However, this tiny community got together and put Tito back on his feet and rebuilt the restaurant. Today Tito's serves basic American road house food, along with seafood pasta, the ubiquitous halibut, and fresh-baked pies. ✉ *Mile 16.5, Hope Hwy.* ☎ *907/782–3274* 💳 *MC, V.*

$ ✕🏨 **Bowman's Bear Creek Lodge.** Of the five cabins here, four are around a pond and one is down by the creek. Each is carpeted and has both a woodstove and an electric heater. Interior walls are chinked logs, beds are covered with colorful quilts, and the lighting fixtures are modeled after gold rush–era styles. The cabins vary in size, with the largest sleeping up to six. A central bathhouse has hot showers and toilets. The lodge café serves breakfast, lunch, and dinner, with nightly dinner and pasta specials, local seafood, and smoked salmon chowder every day (the specialty of the house). Bowman's runs guided fishing and rafting trips, rents mountain bikes, and sets up a nightly campfire around the pond. ✉ *Mile 15.9, Hope Hwy.* 📪 *Box 4, Hope 99605* ☎ *907/782–3141* 🌐 *www.bowmansbearcreeklodge.com* 🛏 *5 cabins without bath* 👍 *Café, some pets allowed; no a/c, no room phones, no room TVs, no smoking* 💳 *MC, V.*

$ ✕🏨 **Seaview Cafe & Bar.** The Seaview is a rustic little establishment situated where Resurrection Creek flows into Turnagain Arm. There are a café with outdoor seating, a bar, a campground and RV park on the property, and two cabins to rent as well. The room is very basic, but you've got a great view of the Arm and the Chugach Mountains, you can pan for gold or fish for trout and salmon in the creek, or you can just relax in the unhurried atmosphere of small-town Alaska. ✉ *Main St.* 📪 *Box 110, 99605* ☎ *907/782–3300* 📠 *907/782–3344* 🌐 *home.gci.net/~hopeak* 🛏 *50 tent sites, 16 RV sites with hookups, 1 cabin* 👍 *Restaurant, bar, some kitchens, fishing; no a/c, no room phones, no room TVs* 💳 *MC, V* ⏲ *Closed mid-Sept.–mid-May.*

¢ **Porcupine Campground.** This campground really is at the end of the road: the highway dead-ends into the campsites. You're right on the shore of Turnagain Arm, with access to the Gull Rock trail along the shoreline. The trail is relatively flat as it traces the shore for 5 mi. Occasionally you can spot beluga whales as they prowl for salmon up and down the coast. Under no circumstances should you venture onto the mudflats at low tide—it's very dangerous out there, and chances for rescue if you're stranded are nil. Be careful! Some of the campsites overlook the Arm, but you'll have to be quick or lucky to snag one of these. *Pit toilets, drinking water, fire pits, picnic tables* *24 sites* *Mile 17.8, Hope Highway,* *www.fs.fed.us* *$10* *Closed mid-Sept.–mid-May.*

¢ **Coeur d'Alene Campground.** If you really want to get away from the civilized camping spots you'll find elsewhere, this place is for you. It sits high above the Resurrection Creek valley, quite literally in mountain goat country. It's a great place for spotting goats on the nearby peaks, and numerous black bears frequent the area as well. The road up is a twisty 6-mi drive over areas not recommended for RVs or trailers. There's no water at the site, but the views of the Kenai Mountains are world class. No reservations are taken for the site, and there's no charge for camping. From Hope take the Resurrection Creek road for 1.6 mi to the Palmer Creek Road, and head up the mountain. The road is frequently closed due to avalanches until mid- to late May. *Pit toilets, fire pits, picnic tables* *6 sites* *Free* *Closed Oct.–Apr.*

Seward

8 *74 mi south of Hope, 127 mi south of Anchorage.*

Seward, at the head of Resurrection Bay, was founded in 1903 when survey crews arrived at this ice-free port to begin planning for a railroad to the Interior. Since then the town has relied heavily on tourism and commercial fishing, and its harbor is important for loading coal bound for Asia. One of the peninsula's major communities, it lies at the south end of the Seward Highway, which connects with Anchorage and is the southern terminus of the Alaska Railroad. Seward also is the launching point for excursions into Kenai Fjords National Park, where you can spy calving glaciers, sea lions, whales, and otters.

Seward, like Valdez, was badly damaged by the 1964 earthquake. A movie illustrating the upheaval caused by the disaster is shown from Memorial Day until Labor Day, Monday through Saturday at 2 PM in the **Seward Community Library.** Russian icons and paintings by prominent Alaskan artists are on exhibit. *5th Ave. and Adams St.* *907/224–4082* *Movie $3* *Weekdays 10–9, Sat. 10–7.*

The **Seward Museum** displays photographs of the quake's damage, model rooms and artifacts from the early pioneers, and historical and current information on the Seward area. *336 3rd Ave., at Jefferson St.* *907/224–3902* *$3* *Mid-May–Sept., daily 9–5; Oct.–mid-May, weekends noon–4. Hrs may vary seasonally; call for recorded information.*

The first mile of the historic original **Iditarod Trail** runs along the beach and makes for a nice, easy stroll, as does the city's printed walking tour—available at the visitor's bureau, the converted railcar at the corner of 3rd Avenue and Jefferson Street, or the Seward Chamber of Commerce Visitor Center at Mile 2 on the Seward Highway. For a different view of the town, drive out **Nash Road,** around Resurrection Bay, and see Seward as it appears nestled at the base of the surrounding mountains.

Fodor'sChoice ★ The **Alaska SeaLife Center** is a world-class research and visitor facility complete with massive cold-water tanks and outdoor viewing decks. The center performs cold-water research on fish, seabirds, and marine mammals, including harbor seals and sea lions. It also rehabilitates injured marine wildlife and provides educational experiences for the general public and school groups. The center was partially funded with reparations money from the *Exxon Valdez* oil spill. Films, hands-on activities, a gift shop, and behind-the-scenes tours ($6) complete the offerings. ✉ *301 Railway Ave.* ☎ *907/224–6300 or 800/224–2525* 🌐 *www.alaskasealife.org* *$14* ⏲ *Apr. 15–Sept. 15 8–7; Sept. 16–Apr. 14, daily 10–5.*

★ A short walk from the parking lot along a paved path will bring you face to face with **Exit Glacier** (⇨ Kenai Fjords National Park), just outside Seward. Look for the marked turnoff at Mile 3.7 as you enter town or ask locals for directions. There's a small walk-in campground here, a ranger station, and access to the glacier. This enormous mass of ice caps the Kenai Mountains, covering more than 1,100 square mi, and it oozes more than 40 glaciers from its edges and down the mountainsides. From Mile 3.7 you can also access **Harding Icefield.** The hike to the icefield from the parking lot is a 9-mi round trip that gains 3,000 feet in elevation, so it's not for the timid or out of shape. But if you're game and feeling up to the task, the hike and views are, literally, breathtaking. Local wildlife of note includes mountain goats and bears both black and brown, so keep a sharp eye out for them. Once you reach the ice, don't travel across it unless you have the gear and experience for glacier travel. Glacier ice is notoriously deceptive—the surface can look solid and unbroken, while underneath a thin crust of snow, crevasses lie in wait for the unwary.

Where to Stay & Eat

$–$$$$ ✕ **Chinooks Waterfront Restaurant.** On the waterfront in the small-boat harbor, Chinooks has a dazzling selection of fresh seafood items, an extensive wine list, and a great view from the upstairs window seats. The theme is marine, with fish photos and carvings, antique fishing tackle, and mounted fish on the walls. Pasta dishes and a few beef specialties round out the menu. ✉ *1404 4th Ave.* ☎ *907/224–2207* ⏲ *Closed mid-Sept.–May.*

$–$$$$ ✕ **Christo's Palace.** Serving a menu of Greek, Italian, Mexican, and seafood meals, this ornately furnished downtown restaurant is a surprisingly elegant hidden treasure. The nondescript facade belies the high, beamed ceilings, dark-wood accents, ornate chandeliers, and large, gorgeous mahogany bar reputed to have been built in the mid-1800s and imported from San Francisco. There's an extensive wine list to complement the menu, a decent selection of wines by the glass, and salads for those looking for lighter fare. For those less concerned with counting calories, meal portions are very generous, desserts are tempting, and there is a small selection of after-dinner cognacs. ✉ *133 4th Ave.* ☎ *907/224–5255* 💳 *MC, V.*

$–$$$$ ✕ **Harbor Dinner Club.** Don't let the name deter you—it's not a private club. The dining room is broken up into small sections, and lots of green plants contribute to the intimate feel. Alaskan artwork, mostly with a nautical theme, adorns the walls. The large menu, complete with multipage wine list, features local seafood, fresh whenever possible (it's frozen during the off-season), as well as steaks. ✉ *220 5th Ave.* ☎ *907/224–3012* 💳 *AE, D, DC, MC, V.*

★ $$–$$$ ✕ **Ray's Waterfront.** True to its name, this dining spot has views of the bay and a small-boat harbor. Sea otters and sea lions have occasionally been known to swim right past the large picture windows. Seafood is the specialty here; the seafood chowder is a must-try. The walls are lined with stuffed and mounted fish so you can point to the kind you'd like to eat. ✉ *Small-boat harbor* ☎ *907/224–5606* 💳 *AE, D, MC, V* ⏲ *Closed Nov.–mid-Mar.*

¢ ✕ **Railway Cantina.** This little hole-in-the-wall near the small-boat harbor is a local favorite. A wide selection of burritos, quesadillas, and tacos incorporates local seafood and is supplemented by an array of hot sauces, many contributed by customers who bring back exotic items from their travels. Feel free to add to the collection. ✉ *1401 4th Ave.* ☎ *907/224–8226* 💳 *MC, V.*

¢–$$ ✕🏨 **Salmon Bake Cabins.** Hidden from the main flow of tourist traffic along Exit Glacier Road, the Salmon Bake Restaurant is a local favorite. The rough-hewn decor of the restaurant and the cabins fits in well with the forest environment. There's outdoor seating in the summer, dinner specials featuring local seafood, and Alaskan beers served in Mason jars. The cabins rent for a straight $100 per night, with room for two to four adults. Each room has a microwave and refrigerator, and there's freezer storage available if you get lucky on your fishing trip. ✉ *Mile 0.5, Exit Glacier Rd.* 📫 *Box 3151, 99664* ☎ *907/224–4752 cabin rentals, 907/224–2204 restaurant* 🌐 *www.sewardalaskacabins.com* 🛏 *4 cabins* 👍 *Restaurant, microwaves, refrigerators, cable TV, some pets allowed; no a/c, no room phones, no smoking* 💳 *MC, V* ⏲ *Oct.–May, restaurant closed Sun.–Wed.*

$$$$ 🏨 **Kenai Fjords Wilderness Lodge.** An hour's boat ride from Seward, this wilderness lodge sits within a quiet, forest-lined cove on Fox Island in Resurrection Bay. Built of local wood with natural finish on interior walls, each cabin has two beds, private baths with shower, propane stoves, and expansive views of the bay and mountains. Lodging rates include meals, boat transportation to the island, and a cruise of Kenai Fjords National Park. Meals are served family style in the main lodge. Hiking trails make it possible to explore the island. Guided kayak trips and coastal wildlife tours can also be arranged. 📫 *Box 1889, 99664* ☎ *907/224–8068 or 800/478–8068* 📠 *907/777–2888* 🌐 *www.kenaifjords.com* 🛏 *8 cabins* 👍 *Dining room, hiking, travel services; no a/c, no room phones, no room TVs, no smoking* 💳 *AE, D, MC, V* 🍽 *FAP* ⏲ *Closed Sept.–May.*

$$–$$$$ 🏨 **Hotel Edgewater.** The rooms at Seward's newest and snazziest hotel overlook Resurrection Bay, and on days of bluebird weather, the panorama of mountains, glaciers, and the bay is breathtaking. Continental breakfast is served in the lobby, a three-story atrium complete with a small waterfall, lots of plants, plus plush seating. A side room has a fireplace and a selection of work by local artists. Rooms are decorated with warm colors, artwork, and wooden crown moldings that complement the cabinetwork. The downtown location is convenient to the SeaLife center, restaurants, and shops. ✉ *200 5th Ave., 99664* ☎ *888/793–6800 or 907/224–2700* 📠 *907/224–2701* 🌐 *www.hoteledgewater.com* *76 rooms* *Coffee shop, in-room data ports, some microwaves, some refrigerators, cable TV, in-room VCRs, exercise equipment, hot tub, sauna, shop, laundry service, concierge, Internet, meeting room, airstrip, railroad, and cruise-ship shuttle, travel services, no-smoking rooms* 💳 *AE, D, MC, V* 🍴 *CP.*

$$–$$$$ **Hotel Seward.** Decorated in resplendent gold-rush style, this downtown hotel is convenient to restaurants, shopping, and the Alaska SeaLife Center. In each of its rooms, you'll find a king- or queen-size pillow-top bed, and a phone in the bathroom as well as the bedroom; some rooms have bay views. The hotel is close to the ferry. ✉ *221 5th Ave.* *Box 670, 99664* ☎ *907/224–2378 or 800/655–8785* 📠 *907/224–3112* 🌐 *www.hotelsewardalaska.com* *38 rooms* *In-room data ports, refrigerators, cable TV, outdoor hot tub, no-smoking rooms; no a/c* 💳 *AE, D, DC, MC, V.*

¢–$$$$ **Miller's Landing.** This one-stop-shopping choice for lodging and services offers cabins, B&Bs, campsites for tents and RVs, water-taxi service to remote sites, sea kayak rentals, and a booking service for fishing trips, dogsled rides, and wildlife cruises. The range of available lodgings runs the gamut from one-room cabins with no running water and a woodstove for heat, to a full-service cottage with full kitchen, TV, and VCR that sleeps eight. The campground has wooded sites and full hookups for motor homes. To reach Miller's, take the road to Lowell Point from the SeaLife Center and follow the shoreline for 3½ mi until you hit its parking lot on the beach. ✉ *Lowell Point Rd.* *Box 81 99664* ☎ *907/224–5739, 866/541–5739* 📠 *907/224–9197* 🌐 *www.millerslandingak.com* *7 cabins, 17 tent sites, 29 RV sites with hookups, 13 B&B rooms, 1 cottage* 💳 *D, MC, V.*

$$$ **Seward Windsong Lodge.** The Seward Windsong rests in a forested setting near the banks of the Resurrection River. Rooms are decorated in warm plaids, pine furniture, and Alaskan prints and include coffeemakers. The lodge is just down the road from Exit Glacier. A full-service restaurant is on the premises. ✉ *Mile 0.5, Exit Glacier Rd., about 2 mi north of Seward* *2525 C St., Anchorage 99503* ☎ *907/265–4501 or 888/959–9590* 📠 *907/777–2888* 🌐 *www.sewardwindsong.com* *98 rooms, 10 suites* *Restaurant, in-room data ports, cable TV, in-room VCRs, bar, shop, meeting rooms, travel services; no a/c, no smoking* 💳 *AE, D, MC, V.*

$–$$$ **Van Gilder Hotel.** Built in 1916 and listed on the National Register of Historic Places, the Van Gilder is an elegant building steeped in local history. Photos of Seward from the early 20th century adorn the walls, beds are brass or carved wood, and the common rooms foster a cozy, B&B feel. This is definitely not a mass-market, chain hotel, and the staff gives tours of the property, pointing out interesting historical information. There's a common kitchen area for guests' use, a sitting room with books of local interest, and a player piano in the lobby. ✉ *308 Adams St., 99664* ☎ *907/224–3079 or 800/204–6835* 📠 *907/224–3689* 🌐 *www.vangilderhotel.com* *20 rooms, 4 suites* *Kitchen, cable TV, shuttle; no a/c, no smoking* *AE, D, DC, MC, V.*

$$ **Spruce Moose B&B.** The Spruce Moose provides guests with maximum privacy in a spectacular setting with views of the Kenai Mountains and Trail Lake. Two fully equipped chalets sleep up to eight people each. A breakfast of fresh baked goods is delivered to your door every morning, and if your fishing trips are successful, there's a gas grill available. You can bask in the hot tub while your salmon sizzles on the grill. ✉ *Box 7, Moose Pass, 99631* ☎ *907/288–3667* 📠 *907/288–3667* 🌐 *http://seward.net/sprucemoose* *2 chalets* *Kitchens, microwaves, refrigerators, cable TV, VCR, outdoor hot tub; no a/c, no smoking* *AE, D, MC, V* *CP.*

★ $ **Alaska's Treehouse B&B.** Enjoy spectacular views of the Chugach Mountains from the solarium and from the hot tub on the tiered deck at this quiet, rustic retreat. The house has vaulted cedar ceilings and skylights, and the suite has a skylight, too. Custom floral tilework complements the view of the national forest right outside the window. The hand-built wood-fired sauna is perfect for relaxing in after a hike or ski along nearby trails. Breakfast includes sourdough pancakes with homemade wild-berry sauces. A two-bedroom suite sleeps five comfortably, and occupants of the three-person room can also rent the adjoining Loft Room for the kids. ✉ *Mile 7, ½ mi off Seward Hwy.* *Box 861, 99664* ☎📠 *907/224–3867* 🌐 *www.virtualcities.com/ak/treehouse.htm* *2 suites* *Dining room, cable TV, outdoor hot tub, sauna; no a/c* *No credit cards* *BP.*

$ **Breeze Inn.** A mile or so from downtown and across the street from the small-boat harbor, this modern hotel is convenient—very convenient if you're planning an early morning fishing or sightseeing trip. Shops and restaurants are all within easy strolling distance. The rooms are bright and airy, with custom-made wooden furnishings and Alaskan wildlife photos on the walls. Some rooms in the annex building overlook the harbor. *Box 2147, 99664* ☎ *907/224–5237 or 888/224–5237* 📠 *907/224–7024* 🌐 *www.breezeinn.com* *86 rooms* *Restaurant, coffee shop, refrigerators, cable TV, lounge, shop, Internet, some pets allowed, no-smoking rooms; no a/c in some rooms* *AE, D, MC, V.*

$ **Teddy's Inn the Woods.** Fodor's Choice ★ Set back from the road in a forest of spruce trees in parklike surroundings, this B&B has room for up to six in an outbuilding. The furnishings are impeccable, with lots of natural wood accents, comfortable seating, local artwork, and flower arrangements. Two cubbyhole bunks are especially child friendly, and the two decks are prime sun-lounging spots. The breakfast of fresh homemade pastries just might be complemented by freshly smoked salmon. ✉ *Mile 23, Seward Hwy. in Moose Pass* *29792 Seward Hwy., 99664* ☎ *907/288–3126* 🌐 *www.seward.net/teddys* *1 room* *MC, V* *BP.*

¢ **Waterfront Park.** The city of Seward operates Waterfront Park, a sprawling facility that occupies some of the town's premier real estate.

Campsites are all first-come, first served except for "caravans" of 10 units or more. The payoff is camping on the shore of Resurrection Bay with an unparalleled view of the waterfront and the mountains across the way. Fishing boats, cruise ships, ferries, pleasure craft, and work boats parade past the park day and night, seals, sea lions, and sea otters cruise past, seabirds, waterfowl, and bald eagles glide overhead, and the fishing from the beach is very good during the silver salmon run that peaks in July. Expect crowds and a limited selection of sites on holiday and salmon derby weekends and anytime the fishing is especially hot. ✉ *Ballaine Blvd.* *Pit toilets, full hookups, drinking water, fire pits, picnic tables* *500 spaces, 99 with hookups* *City of Seward, SPRD / Parks & Campgrounds, Box 167, 99664-0167* ☎ *907/224–4055* *www.cityofseward.net* *$8 tent, $12 RV, $25 utility site* *No credit cards* *Open year-round.*

Guided Tours

Alaska Native–owned and operated, **Alaska Heritage Tours** (☎ 907/265–4500 or 877/258–6877 907/777–2888 www.ahtours.com) offers booking for lodges, day cruises, and custom packages to Talkeetna, Denali, Prince William Sound, and Kenai Fjords National Park. **Alaska Wildland Adventures** (☎ 907/783–2928 or 800/334–8730 www.alaskawildland.com), in Cooper Landing, operates a tidy, pleasant resort and outdoor adventure center on the Kenai River at Mile 50.1 of the Sterling Highway. It arranges a large variety of adventure travel packages all over the state, from 2-day fishing trips and 12-day exploration safaris to small-ship cruising trips, bear-viewing adventures, and trips to backcountry lodges in several locations. **Major Marine Tours** (☎ 907/274–7300 or 800/764–7300 www.majormarine.com) conducts half-day and full-day cruises of Resurrection Bay and Kenai Fjords National Park. Park cruises are narrated by a National Park Ranger, and meals of salmon and prime rib are an option. They can also arrange transportation between Anchorage and Seward. **Renown Charters and Tours** (☎ 907/272–1961 or 800/655–3806 www.renowncharters.com) is the only outfit that operates tours into Resurrection Bay all year round. Summer cruises include a four-hour whale-watching tour and a seven-hour Kenai Fjords trip, and in the winter (October through March), they conduct a two-and-a-half-hour bay cruise for hardy souls who want to brave the Alaska winter weather. **Fish House** (✉ Small-boat harbor ☎ 907/224–3674 or 800/257–7760 www.thefishhouse.net) is Seward's oldest booking agency for deep-sea fishing.

Sports & the Outdoors

RUNNING The footrace best known among Alaskans is Seward's annual **Mt. Marathon Race,** run on July 4 since 1915. Its tenure in the United States is second only to the Boston Marathon. It doesn't take the winners very long—44 minutes or so—but the route is straight up the mountain (3,022 feet) and back down to the center of town. The field is limited, past participants have priority, and early registration is required—applications go out February 1. For more information, contact the **Seward Chamber of Commerce** (Box 749, Seward 99664 ☎ 907/224–8051 907/224–5353 www.sewardak.org).

Nightlife

The **New Seward Saloon** (✉ 209 5th Ave. ☎ 907/224–3095) is the best bet for Seward nightlife. They've got a carved-wood bar, a great bar menu of oysters, seafood, appetizers, and soups, and a large beer selection. You can check your e-mail here or play a game of pool. Weekends during the summer they have a DJ and outdoor seating (with heaters—this is Alaska, after all).

Shopping

Bardarson Studio (✉ Across from small-boat harbor ☎ 907/224–5448 🌐 www.bardarsonstudio.com), selling everything from prints and watercolors to sculpture and beaded earrings, is a browser's dream. There's a kiddie cave for children and a video-viewing area with Alaska programs for nonshoppers. At **I.R.B.I. Custom Alaska Knives** (✉ Mile 20, Seward Hwy. ☎ 907/288–3616) father-and-son craftsmen Irvin and Virgil Campbell handcraft beautiful, functional knives and *ulus* (Alaska Native "women's knives"), with local and exotic antler ivory and horn for handles. The **Ranting Raven** (✉ 224 4th Ave. ☎ 907/224–2228) is a combination gift shop, bakery, and lunch spot, adorned with raven murals on the side of the building. You can indulge in fresh baked goods, espresso drinks, and daily lunch specials such as quiche, focaccia, and homemade soups while perusing the packed shelves of Russian handicrafts and artwork, Native crafts, and jewelry.

Kenai Fjords National Park

★ ❾ *125 mi south of Anchorage.*

Photogenic Seward is the gateway to the 670,000-acre Kenai Fjords National Park. This is spectacular coastal parkland incised with sheer, dark slate cliffs rising from the sea, ribboned with white waterfalls, and tufted with deep-green spruce. Kenai Fjords presents a rare opportunity for an up-close view of blue tidewater glaciers as well as some remarkable ocean wildlife, but access is quite limited unless you charter a boat or airplane, or arrange for a tour with one of the local companies. If you take a day trip on a tour boat out of Seward, you can be pretty sure of seeing sea otters, crowds of Steller's sea lions lazing on the rocky shelves along the shore, a porpoise or two, bald eagles soaring overhead, and tens of thousands of seabirds. Humpback whales and orcas are also sighted occasionally, and mountain goats frequent the seaside cliffs. Tours range in length from 4 hours to 10 hours. The park's coastal fjords are also a favorite of sea kayakers, who can camp or stay in public-use cabins reserved through headquarters.

Before venturing out into the far reaches of the park, you should gather as much data as possible from the locals concerning the weather, tides, dangerous beaches, etc. Once you leave Seward, you're a long way from help, and it's not uncommon for unwary kayakers to fall victim to the harsh conditions. Backcountry travelers should also be aware that some of the park's coastline has been claimed by local Native organizations and is now private property. Be sure to check with park headquarters to avoid trespassing. Access by land is also sketchy, with the Exit Glacier area being the best way to walk into the park's fringes.

One of the park's chief attractions is **Exit Glacier,** which can be reached only by the one road that passes into Kenai Fjords. Trails inside the park lead to an overlook of the vast **Harding Icefield.** *Box 1727, Seward 99664 907/224–7500 www.nps.gov/kefj.*

Guided Tours

Kenai Coastal Tours (907/277–2131 or 800/478–8068) leads day trips into Kenai Fjords National Park. It also conducts combination train–cruise–motor-coach trips from Anchorage. **Kenai Fjords Tours** (907/276–6249, 800/478–8068, 907/224–8068 in Seward 907/777–2888 www.kenaifjords.com) is the oldest and largest company running tours through the park. From March through November, it leads 3- to 10-hour cruises, which include lunch. Transportation and overnight options are also available. **Mariah Tours** (907/224–8068 or 800/270–1238 907/777–2888 www.kenaifjords.com) operates smaller boats through the park and into the Chiswell Islands, with a maximum of 16 passengers per boat mid-May through mid-September. This is a great option for birders or groups. **Major Marine Tours** (907/274–7300 or 800/764–7300 www.majormarine.com) runs ranger-led boat tours through the park, with both half- and full-day excursions available.

Where to Stay

¢ **National Park Service Cabins.** The Kenai Fjords National Park manages four cabins, including three along the coast, favored by sea kayakers and for summer use only. Accessible only by boat or floatplane, they must be reserved in advance. The cabins cost $50 per night: three have a three-night limit, and the North Arm cabin can be reserved for up to nine nights, since it's considerably farther out than the others. The park's lone winter cabin is at Exit Glacier and is a stopping place for many skiers, mushers, and snow machiners (the local name for snowmobilers). Cabins have wooden bunks, heating stoves, and tables. There's no electricity, running water, indoor plumbing, or bedding. *1212 4th Ave. Box 1727, Seward 99664 907/224–7500 to reserve winter cabin, 907/271–2737 in Anchorage for summer rentals www.nps.gov/kefj/PUC.htm 4 cabins MC, V.*

Cooper Landing

10 *100 mi south of Anchorage.*

Centrally located on the Kenai Peninsula, Cooper Landing is within striking distance of some of Alaska's most popular fishing locations. The **Russian River** flows into the **Kenai River** here, and spectacular fishing opportunities abound. Solid lines of traffic head south from Anchorage every summer weekend, and the confluence of the two rivers can get very crowded with enthusiastic anglers, to the point where the pursuit of salmon is often referred to as "combat fishing." However, a short walk upstream will separate you from the crowds and afford a chance to enjoy this gorgeous little river.

The Russian River supports two runs of red (sockeye) salmon every summer, and it's known as the most popular fishery in the state. The Kenai River is famous for its runs of king, red, and silver (coho) salmon, as well as the resident populations of large rainbow trout and Dolly Varden char. Several guide services operate out of Cooper Landing, and the travel services at Gwin's Lodge and the Kenai Princess can recommend competent and trustworthy fishing guides. A number of nearby freshwater lakes, accessible only by hiking trail, also provide excellent fishing for rainbow trout and Dolly Varden.

Cooper Landing serves as a trailhead for the 38-mi-long Resurrection Pass trail, which connects to the village of Hope, and the Russian Lakes/ Resurrection River trails, which run south to Exit Glacier near Seward. The town's central location also affords easy access to saltwater recreation in Seward and Homer.

Where to Stay & Eat

$–$$ ✕ **Sunrise Inn.** On the shore of Kenai Lake, this restaurant serves breakfast, lunch, and dinner, dishing up homemade soups, chowders, and salsas. The eclectic and very reasonably priced menu includes wraps and vegetarian items. Fish feature prominently in what the owners describe as a "backwoods bistro" environment. There's even a spotting scope in the parking lot for spying on the Dall sheep and mountain goats in the surrounding peaks. The bar hosts live music on Saturday in summer. ✉ *Mile 45, Sterling Hwy., 99572* ☎ *907/595–1222* 🌐 *www.alaskasunriseinn.com* 💳 *D, MC, V.*

$–$$ ✕🏨 **Gwin's Lodge.** Gwin's is surely the epicenter of much of the activity on the peninsula. This roadside establishment is a one-stop shop for visitors and locals alike, providing food, lodging, shopping, and fishing tackle around the clock in the summer. The lodge is the fishing headquarters of prospective anglers during the annual salmon runs on the nearby Russian and Kenai rivers. Cabins vary in configuration from standard log cabin with beds and private baths to deluxe chalets with lofts, vaulted ceilings, and full kitchens. The restaurant serves a full menu, including fresh fish when available, as well as sandwiches, steaks, and very hearty breakfasts. The travel agency can book fishing, hiking, rafting, and other adventure travel anywhere on the peninsula. ✉ *Mile 52, Sterling Hwy., 99572* ☎ *907/595–1266* 📠 *907/595–1681* 🌐 *www.gwinslodge.com* *13 rooms* *Restaurant, bar, shop, travel services, no-smoking rooms; no a/c, no room phones, no room TVs* 💳 *D, MC, V* ⏲ *Restaurant closed Oct.–Mar.*

★ **$$$$** 🏨 **Great Alaska Adventure Lodge.** Midway between Seward and Homer, this lodge lives up to its name. Activities include natural history, soft-adventure options, and a remote bear-viewing camp. If you're here to fish, you've come to the right place: the guides are top-notch, and seven world records have been set along the camp's riverbanks. They offer 2- to 10-day trips with any-day arrivals and free Anchorage pick up. Rates include lodging, meals, and most activities, and the basic fishing package—two days and one night, all expenses covered, including a fishing guide—runs $995 per person. Rooms, which are in the main lodge or in riverside cabins, have fireplaces, painted walls, artwork, and comfortable seating. Some of the cabins are two-story, complete with spiral staircases. ✉ *Mile 82.5, 33881 Sterling Hwy., Sterling 99672* 📫 *Box 2670, Poulsbo, WA 98370* ☎ *907/262–4515, 800/544–2261, 360/*

697–6454 in winter 907/262–8797, 360/697–7850 in winter www.greatalaska.com 25 rooms Dining room, boating, fishing, hiking, bear-viewing trips, airport shuttle; no a/c, no room phones, no room TVs AE, MC, V FAP Closed Oct.–mid-May.*

$$$$ Fodor'sChoice ★ **Kenai Princess Wilderness Lodge.** "Elegantly rustic" might best describe this sprawling complex approximately 45 mi from Seward, on a bluff overlooking the Kenai River. Paths lead from the main lodge to charming bungalows, each containing four spacious units. Buildings higher on the bluff house eight units. Each has a king or two double beds, a wood-burning fireplace, a comfortable sitting area, and a porch. Vaulted ceilings of natural-finish wood complement the Alaskan art prints on the walls. Staff can arrange for fishing, flightseeing, horseback riding, and river rafting. There's also a nature trail. The Eagle's Crest Restaurant serves a variety of Alaska fare, including seafood. *Mile 47.7, Sterling Hwy. Box 676, Cooper Landing 99572 907/595–1425 or 800/426–0500 907/595–1424 www.princessalaskalodges.com 86 rooms Restaurant, cable TV, exercise equipment, 2 outdoor hot tubs, bar, shop, travel services; no a/c AE, DC, MC, V Closed Oct.–May.*

$–$$$ **Ingram's Base Camp.** Cabins come in three variations—regular, deluxe, and riverfront, all with private baths and heat, some with kitchens. Ingram's serves as an overnight base for fishing, sightseeing, or bear viewing anywhere on the peninsula. You can arrange for a remote guided or unguided fishing trip, a backpacking drop-off, or for air transportation to one of the Forest Service cabins in the area. They also offer guided drift boat fishing from the camp, boat rentals, and fly-in trips for bear watching, and can transport you and your mountain bikes to a remote mountain trail for an exhilarating ride back to civilization. One of their floatplanes, the Norseman, was filmed for a History Channel feature, and represents a chapter in Alaska's aviation history. *Milepost 48.1, Sterling Hwy. Box 748, 99572 907/595–1213 or 866/595–1213 www.ingramsbasecamp.com 10 cabins Picnic area, BBQs, boating, fishing, some pets allowed; no a/c, no room phones, no room TVs, no smoking AE, D, MC, V.*

$$ **The Inn at Tern Lake.** The owners of the Spruce Moose B&B in nearby Moose Pass completed their dream house and B&B here in June 2003. The house sits in a valley of spruce trees between the jagged peaks of the Kenai mountain range. The location is within a short drive of Seward and Cooper Landing, providing easy access to the myriad recreational opportunities of those communities. Or you can stay at the inn and walk (or in the winter, cross-country ski) through the woods to the shore of Tern Lake, soak in the hot tub, practice your tennis or putting, or just scan the mountainsides for Dall sheep, mountain goats, or bears. As many as seven black bears at a time have been spotted during the evening bear watch. The rooms and common areas are decorated with antiques and Alaskan artifacts, and the Hetricks will help you book any other adventures. There's also a barbecue, and a sitting area with TV and fireplace. *Mile 36, Seward Hwy. Box 7, Moose Pass 99631 907/288–3667 907/288–3667 www.ternlakeinn.com 4 rooms In-room data ports, kitchen, microwave, refrigerator, cable TV, putting green, tennis court,*

gym, outdoor hot tub, cross-country skiing, Internet, business services, airstrip; no a/c, no smoking. ▭ *AE, D, MC, V* 🍽 *CP.*

$$ **Kenai River Sportfishing Lodge.** This lodge is actually a collection of buildings on the bank of the Kenai River. Guests stay in clean, comfortable cabins and share a bathhouse. Cabins, with two double beds or a double and single, have heat and electricity but no running water. Meals are served family style in the log-cabin dining room. Fishing expeditions ranging from two to five days can be arranged, along with transportation to and from Anchorage, Kenai Fjords sightseeing trips, and Alaska Railroad travel options. The lodge can also arrange half- and full-day rafting trips on the Kenai River, as well as trips to its Kenai Backcountry Lodge downstream on Skilak Lake. ✉ *Milepost 50.1, Sterling Hwy.* ⓓ *Box 389, Girdwood 99587* ☎ *907/783–2928 or 800/478–4100* 🖷 *907/783–2130* 🌐 *www.alaskarivertrips.com or www.alaskasportfish.com* *16 cabins* *Dining room, sauna; no a/c, no room phones, no room TVs, no smoking* ▭ *D, MC, V* ⊙ *Closed Oct.–mid-May* 🍽 *CP.*

Kenai National Wildlife Refuge

⓫ *95 mi northwest of Kenai Fjords National Park, 150 mi southwest of Anchorage.*

The U.S. Fish and Wildlife Service administers nearly 2 million acres on the Kenai Peninsula in one of its prime wildlife refuges. The **Kenai National Wildlife Refuge** takes in a portion of the Harding Icefield as well as two large and scenic lakes, Skilak and Tustumena. The refuge is not only the finest moose habitat in the region, but its waterways are great for canoeing and kayaking. The refuge maintains two **visitor centers.** The main one, open all year, is in Soldotna on Ski Hill Road. Turn south on Funny River Road just west of the Kenai River bridge and follow the signs. The center has wildlife dioramas, free films and information, and a bookstore and gift shop. There's also a seasonal visitor center at Mile 57.8 of the Sterling Highway, open from Memorial Day to Labor Day.

Access to the refuge's interior regions is limited. The Sterling Highway skirts the edges, and the Funny River Road from Soldotna takes you into a small section of the refuge's nonwilderness area. The Skilak Lake Loop intersects the highway at mileposts 58 and 75 and provides the best way for car-bound visitors to reach camping, fishing, and hiking opportunities.

Wildlife is plentiful by Alaska standards. That doesn't mean you're going to find herds of animals standing around looking photogenic. To consistently spot wild animals, you have to make an effort to always actively look for them. Learn to scan every opening in the woods, every meadow you come across, every cliff and mountainside you see when you're hiking or even riding in the car. Every member of your party should carry binoculars at all times. Once something interesting shows up, having to share field glasses can provoke even the most even-tempered soul.

Moose are the most commonly seen large animal on the refuge—it was originally named the Kenai National Moose Range for good reason. There are caribou here, but they seldom appear near the road. Dall sheep and mountain goats live on the peaks near Cooper Landing, and black and brown bears, wolves, coyotes, lynx, beavers, and lots of birds abide here as well. Mornings and evenings are the prime hours for spotting game, but don't be lulled into complacency during midday. The best time to spot animals is when you see them, so keep watching, always.

Other than canoeing, the only other way to get into the far reaches of the refuge is by airplane. Floatplane services in Soldotna can fly you into the backcountry, and the Fish and Wildlife Service maintains a series of shelter cabins on a first-come, first-served basis.

Where to Stay

$$$$ **Kenai Backcountry Lodge.** A trip to the Kenai Backcountry lodge involves much more than driving up to the door and booking a room—in fact, that's not even an option. Access is by boat across Skilak Lake to reach the lodge. There you can stay in a traditional Alaskan tent cabin or a log cabin, taking all your meals, included in the price, at the main lodge. Hot water and showers are available at the shared bathhouse, and the company stresses a low-impact, environmentally friendly facility. Trip cost also includes all guided activities, such as hiking, kayaking, motorboat tours, and wildlife viewing. Local wildlife is plentiful and includes moose, caribou, wolves, bears, eagles, and spawning salmon—chances are you'll see more animals than people during your stay (two-night minimum). *Box 389, Girdwood 99587 800/334–8730 or 907/783–2928 907/783–2130 www.alaskawildland.com/kenai-national-wildlife-refuge.htm 2 log cabins, 6 tent cabins Dining room, lake, boating, fishing, hiking, airport shuttle; no a/c, no room phones, no room TVs, no smoking D, MC, V Closed Sept.–May FAP.*

¢ **Kenai National Wildlife Refuge Campgrounds.** The U.S. Fish and Wildlife Service maintains 14 road-accessible campgrounds in the Kenai refuge, with a total of 130 sites, 110 of which are suitable for RVs, though there are no hookups. Only two of the campgrounds (Hidden Lake and Upper Skilak Lake) charge fees for camping. All have toilet facilities, and all but three have drinking water. The campgrounds also have picnic tables, fire pits, nearby hiking trails, and fishing. The maximum length of stay is 14 consecutive days, with a few exceptions—Russian River ferry site limit is three days, and Hidden Lake and Upper Skilak limit is seven. *Kenai National Wildlife Refuge, Box 2139, Soldotna 99669-2139 907/262–7021 http://kenai.fws.gov 130 sites Reservations not accepted No credit cards.*

Sports & the Outdoors

CANOEING If you have the time and inclination, the best way to experience the refuge's backcountry is by canoe. The **Swan Lake Canoe System** and the **Swanson River Canoe System** are accessed from the road system at the turnoff at milepost 83.4 of the Sterling Highway. These systems link a large number of lakes with two rivers in the wilderness area. There are several loop trips that enable visitors to fish, hike, and camp away from the road system and motorized boat traffic. Fishing for trout, salmon, and Dolly Varden is excellent, and the series of lakes and portages offer access to more than 100 mi of waterways. Canoe rentals are available in Sterling and Soldotna. The visitor center has a list of outfitters.

HIKING Hiking trails branch off from the Sterling Highway and the Skilak Lake Loop. Degree of difficulty ranges from easy half-mile walks to strenuous climbs to mountain lakes. These trails are all "primitive" when compared with what you may be used to in the Lower 48. There's usually a sign and parking lot at the trailhead, and not much else in the way of amenities. Be prepared with topographic maps, water, food, insect repellent, and bear awareness before you set out. You won't find toilets, water fountains, or signposts. Once you leave the parking lot, you're on your own, and you're responsible for your party's safety. Brown and black bears are numerous on the Kenai Peninsula, and if you have any questions about how best to avoid them, consult with refuge staff, the Alaska Department of Fish and Game, or any of the bear behavior books available nearly everywhere in South Central Alaska (⇨ Bear Facts box *in* Chapter 1).

Kenai & Soldotna

⓬ *116 mi northwest of Seward, 148 mi southwest of Anchorage.*

The towns of Kenai and Soldotna are often mentioned almost interchangeably due to their physical proximity. Soldotna, with its strategic location on the peninsula's northwest coast, takes its name from a nearby stream; it's a corruption of the Russian word for "soldier," although some say the name came from a Native American word meaning "stream fork." Today this city of 3,900 residents is the commercial and sportfishing hub of the Kenai Peninsula. Along with its sister city, Kenai, whose onion-dome Holy Assumption Russian Orthodox Church highlights the city's old town, it is home to Cook Inlet oil-field workers and their families. Soldotna's commercial center stretches along the Sterling Highway, making this a stopping point for those traveling up and down the peninsula. The town of Kenai lies near the end of the road that branches off the Sterling Highway in Soldotna. Near Kenai is Captain Cook State Recreation Area, one of the least-visited state parks on the road system. This portion of the peninsula is level and forested, with numerous lakes and streams pocking and crisscrossing the area. Trumpeter swans return here in the spring, and sightings of moose are common.

In addition to fishing, clam digging is also popular at **Clam Gulch,** 24 mi south of Soldotna on the Sterling Highway. This is a favorite of local children, who love any excuse to dig in the muddy, sloppy goo. Ask locals on the beach how to find the giant razor clams (recognized by their dimples in the sand). The clam digging is best when tides are minus 4 or 5 feet. A sportfishing license, available at grocery, sporting-goods, and drug stores, is required.

Where to Stay & Eat

★ $–$$$ ✕ **The Duck Inn.** The variety of items on the menu—pizzas, burgers, chicken, steaks, and seafood—guarantees something for everyone. Portions are generous and the pricing is reasonable. Locally caught halibut is a specialty, prepared in enough different ways to stave off feelings of halibut overload. Muted lighting, soft background music, hanging plants, and lots of artwork featuring ducks create an enjoyable dining experience. ⊠ *43187 Kalifornsky Beach Rd., Soldotna* ☎ *907/262–1849* ▭ *AE, D, MC, V.*

¢–$$ ✕ **Suzie's Cafe.** This roadside café is a cut above most roadside cafés in Alaska. There's a deck for outside dining, the interior has antiques, and fresh flowers adorn the tables. Food is homemade and portions are very generous. Main courses include burgers, seafood, pot roast, real mashed potatoes with a choice of gravies, and homemade soups and desserts. The coffee is excellent, another rarity on the road system. ✉ *Mile 82.7, Sterling Hwy., Sterling* ☎ *907/260–5751* ▭ *MC, V.*

$ ✕ **Sal's Klondike Diner.** A true diner-type atmosphere, Sal's is open 24 hours and the menu tends toward breakfast and lunch items rather than dinner main courses. Portions are very generous; there's even a sign on the wall that says, "If you're still hungry, tell us." Burgers, sandwiches, fish-and-chips, halibut, salmon, and some steaks are available, and they bake their own bread and pies every day. You can buy loaves of sourdough, white, or wheat bread. The decor is busy, to say the least, and it's a favorite spot for locals as well as visitors. ✉ *44619 Sterling Hwy., Soldotna* ☎ *907/262–2220* ▭ *AE, D, MC, V.*

$–$$ ✕ **Timber Wolf Lodge & The Cabin Restaurant.** The lodge sits on the bank of the Kenai River and has a small fleet of fishing boats and guides. Four species of salmon run up the Kenai from May through September, and if that's not enough for you, the lodge also has a floatplane and access to remote fishing spots on the far side of Cook Inlet. They also offer bear-viewing trips, sightseeing, and rafting adventures. Patios overlook the river, and three barbecue grills are available for fortunate fishermen. The restaurant is an intimate, elegant room (eight tables) with a fireplace, soft background music, table linens, fresh flowers, and candles. The varied menu of beef, fish, lamb, and local seafood is exquisitely prepared and presented. ✉ *44485 Sterling Hwy., Soldotna 99669* ☎ *907/260–5752 or 888/352–3888* 🖷 *907/260–7787* 🌐 *www.timberwolflodgeak.com* *9 rooms* *Restaurant, picnic area, kitchens, microwaves, refrigerators, cable TV, dock, fishing, pool table, Ping-Pong, travel services; no a/c* ▭ *AE, D, DC, MC, V.*

$$ **Aspen Hotel Soldotna.** You'll find Aspen Hotels in five Alaska cities; the Soldotna facility opened in spring of 2002. It sits on a bluff overlooking the Kenai River, a world-famous fishing destination drawing hopeful anglers from all over the world. Rooms that face away from the street overlook the river, and during the very popular salmon runs, you'll have a front-row seat to the fishing action. The contemporary decor is open and airy, with bright wood accents throughout. ✉ *326 Binkley Cir., Soldotna 99669* ☎ *907/260–7736 or 888/308–7848* 🖷 *907/260–7786* 🌐 *www.aspenhotelsak.com* *63 rooms* *In-room data ports, microwaves, refrigerators, cable TV, in-room DVD players, pool, exercise equipment, spa, laundry facilities, Internet, business services, meeting room; no a/c* *CP* ▭ *AE, D, DC, MC, V.*

$–$$ **Best Western King Salmon Motel.** This member of the reliable Best Western franchise has large, airy rooms, including some with kitchenettes. If you're traveling by RV, you'll find a park complete with full hookups available for $20 per night. ✉ *35546-A Kenai Spur Hwy., Soldotna 99669* ☎ *907/262–5857 or 888/262–5857* 🖷 *907/262–9441* 🌐 *www.bestwestern.com* *49 rooms* *Restaurant, in-room data ports, some kitchenettes, some microwaves, cable TV, laundry facilities, meeting room* ▭ *AE, D, DC, MC, V.*

Sports & the Outdoors

FISHING Anglers from around the world come for the salmon-choked streams and rivers, most notably the **Kenai River** and its companion, the **Russian River.** The Kenai is home to the largest king salmon in the world. In 1985 a local resident, Les Anderson, caught a 97-pound, 4-ounce fish. That record still stands, but knowledgeable fisheries professionals figure it's only a matter of time before someone with sport-fishing gear catches a 100-pounder. There are two runs of kings up the Kenai every summer. The first run starts in mid-May and tapers off in early July, and the second run is from early July until the season closure on July 31. Generally speaking, the first run has more fish, but they tend to be a bit smaller than second-run fish. Smaller, of course, has a whole different meaning when it comes to these fish. Fifty- and sixty-pounders are unremarkable here, and 40-pound fish are routinely tossed back as being "too small." The limit is one king kept per day, five per season, no more than two of which can be from the Kenai. The river also supports two runs of red (sockeye) salmon every year, as well as runs of silver (coho) and pink (humpback) salmon. Rainbow trout of near mythic proportions inhabit the river, as do Dolly Varden char. Fishing pressure is heavy, so don't expect a wilderness experience, especially in the lower river near Soldotna.

Farther up the river, between Kenai Lake in Cooper Landing and Skilak Lake, motorboats are banned, so a more idyllic experience can be had. Scores of guide services ply the river, and if you're inexperienced at the game, hiring a guide for a half-day or full-day trip can more than pay for itself. Fishing techniques are quite specialized and unlike anything you're likely to be used to in the Lower 48. Deep-sea fishing for salmon and halibut out of **Deep Creek** is challenging Homer's position as the preeminent fishing destination on the southern Kenai Peninsula. This fishery is unusual in that tractors launch boats off the beach and into the Cook Inlet surf. The local campground and RV lot is packed on summer weekends.

Area phone books list some 300 fishing charters and guides, all of whom stay busy during the hectic summer fishing season. **Hi Lo Charters** (☎ 907/283–9691 or 800/757–9333 🌐 www.hilofishing.com) runs salmon-fishing trips on the world-famous Kenai River. The **Sports Den** (☎ 907/262–7491 🌐 www.alaskasportsden.com) arranges fishing trips on the river, on the salt water, or to a remote fly-in location for salmon, trout, or halibut.

HOMER

⓭ *77 mi south of Soldotna, 226 mi south of Anchorage.*

At the southern end of the Sterling Highway lies the city of Homer, at the base of a narrow spit that juts 4 mi into beautiful Kachemak Bay. Glaciers and snowcapped mountains form a dramatic backdrop across the bay. Founded just before the turn of the 20th century as a gold-prospecting camp, this community was later used as a coal-mining headquarters. (Chunks of coal are still common along local beaches; they wash into the bay from nearby slopes where the coal seams are exposed.) Today the town of Homer is an eclectic community filled with tacky tourist paraphernalia, commercial-fishing facilities—including boats, canneries, and repair yards—and a thriving group of local artists, sculptors, actors, and writers. Much of the commercial fishing centers on halibut, and the popular Homer Jackpot Halibut Derby is often won by enormous fish weighing more than 300 pounds. The local architecture includes everything from homes that are little more than assemblages of driftwood, flotsam, and jetsam to featureless steel commercial buildings and magnificent homes on the hillside overlooking the surrounding bay, mountains, forests, and glaciers. In addition to highway and air access, Homer also has regular ferry service to Seldovia and Kodiak Island.

Exploring Homer

What to See

Start your visit with a stop at the Homer Chamber of Commerce's **Visitor Information Center,** where racks are filled with brochures from local businesses and attractions. ✉ *Homer Bypass at Main St.* ☎ *907/235–7740* 🌐 *www.homeralaska.org* ⏲ *Memorial Day–Labor Day, weekdays 9–7, weekends 10–6; early Sept.–late May, weekdays 9–5.*

Fodor's Choice ★ Protruding into Kachemak Bay, the **Homer Spit** provides a sandy focal point for visitors and locals. A paved path stretches most of the 4 mi, providing a delightful biking or walking option, and at the end are a boat harbor filled with commercial-fishing boats, restaurants and lodging places, charter fishing businesses, sea kayaking outfitters, art galleries, and on-the-beach camping spots. Fly a kite, walk the beaches, drop a line in the Fishing Hole, or just wander through the shops looking for something interesting; this is one of Alaska's favorite summertime destinations.

★ The **Pratt Museum** has a saltwater aquarium; an exhibit on the 1989 Prince William Sound oil spill; a wildflower garden; a gift shop; and pioneer, Russian, and Alaska Native displays. You can spy on wildlife with a robotic video camera set up on a seabird rookery. There's also a refurbished homestead cabin and outdoor summer exhibits along the trail out back. ✉ *Bartlett St. off Pioneer Ave.* ☎ *907/235–8635* 🌐 *www.prattmuseum.org* *$6* ⏲ *May–Sept., daily 10–6; Oct.–Dec. and Feb.–Apr., Tues.–Sun. noon–5.*

★ **Islands and Oceans Center** provides a wonderful introduction to the **Alaska Maritime National Wildlife Refuge.** The refuge covers some 3.5 million acres spread across some 2,500 Alaskan islands, from Prince of Wales Island in the south to Barrow in the north. Newly opened in 2003, this 37,000-square-foot facility is a must-see for anyone interested in wild places. The lobby features towering windows facing Kachemak Bay, and first stop is the theater, where a film takes visitors along on a voyage of the Fish and Wildlife Service's research ship, the M/V *Tiglax*. Interactive exhibits detail the birds and marine mammals of the refuge (the largest seabird refuge in America), and one room even re-creates the noisy sounds and pungent smells of a bird rookery. During the summer, guided bird-watching treks and beach walks are offered. ✉ *95 Sterling Hwy.* ☎ *907/235–6961* 🌐 *www.islandsandocean.org* *Free* ⏲ *Memorial Day–Labor Day, daily 9–6; Labor Day–Memorial Day, Mon.–Sat. 9–5.*

Kachemak Bay abounds in wildlife, including a large population of puffins and eagles. Tour operators take you past bird rookeries or across the bay to gravel beaches for clam digging. Most fishing charters include an opportunity to view whales, seals, porpoises, and birds close up. At the end of the day, walk along the docks on Homer Spit and watch commercial-fishing boats and charter boats unload their catch.

Directly across from the end of the Homer Spit is **Halibut Cove,** a small community of people who make their living on the bay or by selling handicrafts. Spend a relaxing afternoon or evening meandering along the boardwalk and visiting galleries. The cove itself is lovely, especially during salmon runs, when fish leap and splash in the clear water. You'll find several lodges on this side of the bay, on pristine coves away from summer crowds. The *Danny J* ferries people across from Homer Spit, with a stop at the rookery at Gull Island and two or three hours to walk around Halibut Cove, for $47 adults; $25 children. The ferry makes two trips daily: the first leaves Homer at noon and returns at 5 PM, and the second leaves at 5 PM and returns at 10 PM. **Central Charters** (☎ 907/235–7847 or 800/478–7847) handles all bookings.

The town of **Seldovia** is another off-the-road-system settlement on the south side of Kachemak Bay. For many years this was the primary fishing town on the bay, but today the focus is on tourism. The town was heavily damaged in the 1964 earthquake, but a few stretches of old boardwalk still exist and houses stand on stilts along Seldovia Slough. Access is via the Alaska Marine Highway ferry (twice weekly from Homer), aboard a water taxi ($35–$45), or by air from Homer ($50). Seldovia has several restaurants (Mad Fish Restaurant is particularly notable) and lodging places, plus a small museum and a hilltop Russian Orthodox church. The area abounds with hiking, mountain biking, and sea kayaking options.

Across Kachemak Bay from the Homer Spit lies one of the largest coastal parks in America, the 400,000-acre **Kachemak Bay State Park** (☎ 907/235–7024 🌐 www.alaskastateparks.org). The park encompasses a line of snowcapped mountains and several large glaciers; the prominent one visible from the Spit is called Grewingk Glacier. Several state park cabins can be rented for $50–$65 a night, and a number of luxurious private lodges occupy remote coves. Park access is primarily by water taxi from the Spit, and one of the most popular trails leads 2 mi, ending at the lake in front of Grewingk Glacier. For access, contact **Mako's Water Taxi** (☎ 907/235–9055 🌐 www.makoswatertaxi.com).

Where to Stay & Eat

$$–$$$$ Fodor's Choice ★ ✕ **Homestead Restaurant.** This former log roadhouse 8 mi from town is a favorite of locals who appreciate artfully presented food served amid contemporary art. The Homestead specializes in seasonal fish and shellfish prepared with garlic, citrus fruits, or spicy ethnic sauces, as well as steak, rack of lamb, and prime rib. Epic views of the bay, mountains, and hanging glaciers are yours for the looking. An extensive wine list and locally brewed beer on tap are available. ✉ *Mile 8.2, East End Rd.* ☎ *907/235–8723* 💳 *AE, MC, V* ⊗ *Closed Jan.–Mar.*

★ $–$$$$ ✕ **Café Cups.** It's hard to miss this place as you drive down Pioneer Avenue—look for the huge namesake cups on the building's facade. A longtime Homer favorite, this café serves lunches and dinners that make the most of the locally abundant seafood, complemented by a terrific wine list. The menu includes a mix of fare, from Reubens to a better-than-it-sounds "twisted fettuccine" that blends seafood, raspberries, and chipotle in an Alfredo cream sauce. But locals know to ignore the menu and just ask the waitress for the day's specials; there's always a big variety of meats and fresh seafood dishes that never fails to please. Vegetarian options are also offered, and singles enjoy dining at the wine bar. ✉ *162 W. Pioneer Ave.* ☎ *907/235–8330* ▭ *MC, V* ⊙ *Closed Sun.*

$–$$$ ✕ **Saltry Restaurant.** On a hill overlooking Halibut Cove, this is a wonderful place to soak up a summer afternoon. Local seafood, naturally, is the main attraction, prepared in everything from curries and pastas to sushi. For libations, you can choose from a wide selection of imported beers. The restaurant is small, and although the tables aren't exactly crowded together, it's definitely intimate. When weather permits, get a table on the deck. Dinner seatings are at 6 and 7:30; before or after dinner, you can stroll around the boardwalks at Halibut Cove and visit the art galleries or just relax on the dock. Sea otters often play just offshore. Reservations are essential for the ferry (at a reduced $25 round-trip), which leaves Homer Spit at 5 PM. A noon ferry ($47; $25 children) will take you to Halibut Cove for lunch ($5–$17), stopping along the way for wildlife viewing. ✉ *Halibut Cove* ☎ *907/235–7847, 800/478–7847 Central Charters* ✍ *Reservations essential* ▭ *D, MC, V* ⊙ *Closed Labor Day–Memorial Day.*

Fodor'sChoice ★

★ $$ ✕ **Fat Olives Restaurant.** Pumpkin-colored walls, light streaming through tall front windows, and a playful collection of Italian posters add to the appeal of this fine Tuscany-inspired bistro. The atmosphere is noisy and fun, and the menu encompasses enticing appetizers, salads, sandwiches, calzones, and pizzas throughout the day, along with oven-roasted chicken, fresh seafood, pork loin, and other fare in the evening. If you're in a hurry, just get a giant slice of the thin-crust pizza to go for $3. Singles can order meals at the bar, and there's always something decadent for dessert. Fat Olives is just off the Homer Bypass near the Chamber of Commerce office. ✉ *276 Olson La.* ☎ *907/235–8488* ▭ *D, MC, V.*

★ ¢ ✕ **Fritz Creek Store.** Directly across the road from Homestead Restaurant is this old-fashion country store, gas station, liquor store, post office, video rental shop, and deli. The last of these is the main reason for a visit, and the food is amazingly good, from the hot and fattening turkey sandwiches to freshly baked breads and pastries, pizza by the slice, veggie burritos, tamales, and ribs to go. Pull up a chair at a table crafted from an old cable spool and join the back-to-the-land crowd as they drink espresso, talk Alaskan politics, and pet the cats. ✉ *Mile 8.2, East End Rd.* ☎ *907/235–6521* ▭ *AE, D, MC, V.*

$$–$$$ ✕▣ **Land's End Resort.** This sprawling blue-and-white complex at the end of the spit has wide-open views of the bay. Most of the rooms face the bay; some have nautical decor, and others are more floral. Some are perfect for a couple, some are big enough for a family—five rooms have lofts.

Its restaurant ($$–$$$$) specializes in seafood, including salmon, halibut, scallops, and oysters; burgers and steak are also served. Call ahead to reserve a window table facing Kachemak Bay and the Kenai Mountains. During the winter, chefs craft a special once-a-month "Uncorked" themed dinner with paired wines for $60 per person. ✉ *4786 Homer Spit Rd., 99603* ☎ *907/235–0400 or 800/478–0400* 📠 *907/235–0420* 🌐 *www.lands-end-resort.com* *96 rooms* *Restaurant, cable TV, pool, hot tub, spa, bar, meeting rooms, travel services; no a/c* 💳 *AE, D, DC, MC, V.*

$ ✕ **Two Sisters Bakery.** This very popular café has an ideal location just a short walk from both Bishops Beach and the Islands and Ocean Center. In addition to fresh breads and pastries, Two Sisters specializes in deliciously healthful lunches, such as vegetarian focaccia sandwiches, homemade soups (including a ginger carrot almond soup), quiche, and salads. Sit on the wraparound porch on a summer afternoon, or take your espresso and pastry down to the beach to watch the waves roll in. Upstairs are three comfortable guest rooms, all with private baths. Your latte and Danish pastry breakfast is served in the café. ✉ *233 E. Bunnell Ave.* ☎ *907/235–2280* 🌐 *www.twosistersbakery.net* *3 rooms* *No a/c, no smoking* 💳 *MC, V.*

$$$$ **Land's End Lodges.** Adjacent to the Land's End Resort and owned by the same people, this group of fully furnished luxury condos sits at the end of the Homer Spit, with decks and windows fronting on Kachemak Bay. Commercial and charter fishing boats, Alaska Marine Highway ferries, and pleasure boats parade past your front door day and night, against a stunning view of snowcapped mountains, spruce forest, and glaciers. Units sleep six comfortably, and with a mere additional $10 per-person charge per night above two people, these places can be surprisingly economical for a small group. ✉ *4786 Homer Spit Rd., 99603* ☎ *907/235–0400 or 800/478–0400* 📠 *907/235–0420* 🌐 *www.landsendlodges.com* *5 condos* *Kitchens, microwaves, refrigerators, cable TV, laundry facilities; no a/c* 💳 *AE, D, DC, MC, V.*

$$$$ **Tutka Bay Wilderness Lodge.** On a small cove 9 mi from the Homer Spit, this luxurious small resort is surrounded by Kachemak Bay State Park. The deluxe modern cabins have private baths and comfortable beds. Other facilities include a cozy main lodge, sauna, hot tub, and three filling meals a day. Hikers can head into the park from the lodge for a guided day trip, watch eagles and otters just offshore, or pay extra for guided sea kayaking, charter fishing trips, and other activities. Access is by water taxi ($70 extra) from Homer. *Box 960, 99603* ☎ *907/235–3905 or 800/606–3909* 📠 *907/235–3909* 🌐 *www.tutkabaylodge.com* *4 cabins, 2 suites* *Hot tub, sauna; no a/c* 💳 *MC, V* *FAP.*

$$$–$$$$ **Alaskan Suites.** These modern log cabins offer million-dollar views from a hilltop on the west side of Homer. Each contains two queen beds and a kitchenette, plus a BBQ grill on the deck. Guests can soak in a large hot tub with a backdrop of Kachemak Bay, snowcapped mountains, glaciers, and three volcanoes. In addition to the cabins, there's a private two-level cottage that sleeps eight. ✉ *3255 Sterling Hwy., 99603* ☎ *907/235–1972 or 888/239–1972* 📠 *907/235–7641* 🌐 *www.alaskansuites.com* *5 cabins, 1 cottage* *Kitchenettes, cable TV, hot tub; no a/c, no smoking* 💳 *AE, D, MC, V.*

¢–$$ Driftwood Inn. Rooms here are bright, with large windows, expansive views of the bay, and light pastel walls and bedspreads. Room configurations include standard hotel-type bedrooms and a "ship's quarters," with cedar walls and a pull-down bed. The suite is family friendly, with queen-size beds, dining room table, microwave, refrigerator, full private bath, and private outside entrance. Downstairs has a comfortable sitting room with fireplace, TV, books, and videos. A small eating area has serve-yourself coffee, tea, pastries, and hot and cold cereal. A microwave, refrigerator, barbecue, and fish-cooking and -cleaning area are also available. An on-site camping area and full-hookup RV park have full access to the inn's facilities. ✉ *135 W. Bunnell St., 99603* ☎ *907/235–8019 or 800/478–8019* 🖷 *907/235–8019* 🌐 *www.thedriftwoodinn.com* *20 rooms, 11 with bath, lodge for up to 12 guests, cottage for up to 8 guests* *Dining room, cable TV, laundry facilities, some pets allowed; no a/c, no phones in some rooms, no smoking* 💳 *D, MC, V.*

$ **Old Town Bed & Breakfast.** Housed in a restored trading post, the Old Town B&B is on the second floor, above the Bunnell Street Art Gallery and Panarelli's Deli. Rooms are elegantly appointed with period furnishings and fixtures, and the second-story setting provides sweeping views of the bay and mountains. The art gallery hosts evening programs, and breakfast is served in the deli downstairs. ✉ *106 W. Bunnell St., 99603* ☎ *907/235–7558* 🌐 *www.oldtownbedandbreakfast.com* *3 rooms, 1 with bath* *No a/c, no room phones, no room TVs, no smoking* 💳 *MC, V* *BP.*

¢ **Homer Spit Campground.** Homer's 4-mi-long Spit is popular not just as a jumping-off point for fishing, kayaking, and other adventures, but also because it provides great camping with a view. Find a spot on the sand between the other tents and RVs and pay your fee at the city's camping office. The beach is often windy, and it's not far from the road, but it's hard to beat the spectacular setting. A few campsites are open year-round. Two private RV parks on the Spit provide amenities such as showers, water and sewer hookups, and laundry. ☎ *907/235–8206* 🌐 *www.homeralaska.org* 💳 *No credit cards.*

Guided Tours

Central Charters (✉ 4241 Homer Spit Rd., 99603 ☎ 907/235–7847 or 800/478–7847 🌐 www.centralcharter.com) arranges fishing and ferry trips to Halibut Cove, around Kachemak Bay, and across to Seldovia. **Homer Ocean Charters** (☎ 907/235–6212 or 800/426–6212 🌐 www.homerocean.com) on the Spit sets up fishing and sightseeing trips, as well as sea kayaking and water-taxi services and remote cabin rentals. Some of their most popular cruises go to the **Rookery Restaurant** at Otter Cove Resort. The narrated lunch cruise leaves at noon ($55), and dinner trips to the restaurant leave at 4:30 and 7; the ferry trip is $20, and dinner main courses run $18–$24.

Nightlife

Dance to lively bands on weekends at **Alice's Champagne Palace** (✉ 195 E. Pioneer Ave.). The bar attracts nationally known singer-songwriters on ★ a regular basis. The Spit's infamous **Salty Dawg Saloon** (☎ 907/235–6718) is a tumbledown lighthouse of sorts, sure to be frequented by a carousing fisherman or two, along with half the tourists in town. The ceilings are low and the pool table is usually busy, woodchips cover the floors, and the Dawg's walls are covered with business cards, signed dollar bills, and bras. The members of **Pier One Theater** (☎ 907/235–7333 🌐 www.pieronetheatre.org) perform plays on weekends throughout the summer. Find them in the old barn-like building on the Spit.

Festivals

Early-summer visitors to Homer join thousands of migrating shorebirds for the **Kachemak Bay Shorebird Festival** on the first weekend of May. Experts offer bird-watching trips and photography demonstrations, and a simultaneous **Wooden Boat Festival** provides a fun chance to meet some of Alaska's finest boatbuilders. Various kid events add to the fun. In late July the **KBBI Concerts on the Lawn** (☎ 907/235–7721 🌐 www.kbbi.org) brings a weekend of folk and rock music to Karen Hornaday Park.

Sports & the Outdoors

Bear Watching

Homer is a favorite departure point to view Alaska's famous brown bears in coastal Katmai National Park. **Emerald Air Service** (☎ 907/235–6993 🌐 www.emeraldairservice.com) is one of several companies offering all-day trips for around $525 per person. **Hallo Bay Wilderness** (☎ 907/235–2237 🌐 www.hallobay.com) is popular for day trips, but the comfortable camp is primarily used by visitors on guided multinight bear-viewing trips.

Fishing

Homer is both a major commercial fishing port (especially for halibut) and a very popular destination for sport anglers in search of giant halibut or feisty king and silver salmon. Quite a few companies offer charter fishing in the summer, for around $175 per person per day (including bait and tackle). Several booking agencies set up fishing charters, including **Central Charters** and **Homer Ocean Charters** (both ⇨ Guided Tours). Also try **Inlet Charters** (☎ 907/235–6126 or 800/770–6126 🌐 www.halibutcharters.com). Anyone heading out on a halibut charter is advised to buy a $10 ticket for the **Homer Jackpot Halibut Derby** (☎ 907/235–7740 🌐 www.homerhalibutderby.com); first prize for the largest halibut is more than $40,000.

Near the end of the Spit, Homer's famous **Fishing Hole** is a small bight that is stocked with king and silver salmon smolt (baby fish) by the Alaska Department of Fish and Game. The salmon then head out to sea, returning several years later to the Fishing Hole, where they are easy targets for wall-to-wall bankside anglers throughout the summer. The Fishing Hole isn't anything like casting for salmon along a remote Kodiak Island stream, but your chances are good and you don't need to drop $800 for a flight into the wilderness. Fishing licenses and rental poles are available from fishing supply stores on the Spit.

Sea Kayaking

Several local companies offer guided sea kayaking trips to protected coves within Kachemak Bay State Park and nearby islands. **True North Kayak Adventures** (☎ 907/235–0708 🌐 www.truenorthkayak.com) has a range of such adventures, including a six-hour paddle to Elephant Rock for $115 and an all-day boat and kayak trip to Yukon Island for $135 (both trips include lunch). For something more unique, book an overnight trip to Kasitsna Bay through **Across the Bay Tent & Breakfast** (☎ 907/235–3633 🌐 www.tentandbreakfastalaska.com). Facilities are basic, but guests can take kayak tours, rent a mountain bike, or just hang out on the shore.

Shopping

Art & Gifts

A variety of art by the town's residents can be found in the galleries on and around Pioneer Avenue. The gift shop at the **Pratt Museum** stocks natural-history books, locally crafted or inspired jewelry, note cards, and gifts for children. The **Bunnell Street Gallery** (✉ Corner of Main St. and Bunnell Ave. ☎ 907/235–2662 🌐 www.bunnellstreetgallery.org) displays innovative contemporary art primarily produced in Alaska. The gallery, which occupies the first floor of a historic trading post, also hosts workshops, lectures, musical performances, and other community events. **Ptarmigan Arts** (✉ 471 E. Pioneer Ave. ☎ 907/235–5345 🌐 www.homerart.org) is one of just three cooperative galleries in Alaska, with photographs, paintings, pottery, jewelry, woodworking, and other pieces by local artisans.

Clothing

Nomar (✉ 104 E. Pioneer Ave. ☎ 907/235–8363 or 800/478–8364 🌐 www.nomaralaska.com) creates Polarfleece garments and other rugged Alaskan outerwear, plus duffel bags, purses, raingear, and children's clothing. The company also manufactures equipment and clothing for commercial fishermen, so you know their gear will hold up to years of use. You'll find a good choice of outdoor supplies and home accessories next door at **Main Street Mercantile** (✉ 102 E. Pioneer Ave., Suite 2 ☎ 907/235–9102), housed in a 1936 building.

Foodstuffs

Alaska Wild Berry Products (✉ 528 E. Pioneer Ave. ☎ 907/235–8858 🌐 www.alaskawildberryproducts.com) sells chocolate-covered candies, jams, jellies, sauces, and syrups made from wild berries handpicked on the Kenai Peninsula, as well as Alaskan-theme gifts and clothing. Drop by for free samples of the chocolates. **Two Sisters Bakery** (✉ 235 E. Bunnell Ave. ☎ 907/235–2280) serves fresh bread baked on the premises as well as coffee, muffins, soup, and pizza. **Fritz Creek Store** (✉ Mile 8.2, East End Rd. ☎ 907/235–6521) sells fresh, homemade food in an old log building. Homer is famous for its halibut, salmon, and Kachemak Bay oysters. For fresh fish, head to **Coal Point Trading Company** on the Spit (☎ 907/235–3877 🌐 www.welovefish.com). In addition to selling salmon and halibut, Coal Point will package and ship fish that you caught.

Kachemak Bay State Park & State Wilderness Park

14 *10 mi southeast of Homer.*

Kachemak Bay State Park & State Wilderness Park, accessible by boat or Bush plane, protects more than 350,000 acres of coast, mountains, glaciers, forests, and wildlife on the lower Kenai Peninsula. Recreational opportunities include boating, sea kayaking, fishing, hiking, and beachcombing. Facilities are minimal but include 20 primitive campsites, five public-use cabins, and a system of trails accessible from Kachemak Bay. *Kenai State Parks Office, Box 1247, Soldotna 99669 907/262–5581 or 907/235–7024 www.dnr.state.ak.us/parks/units/kbay/kbay.htm.*

Where to Stay

★ $$$$ **Kachemak Bay Wilderness Lodge.** Across Kachemak Bay from Homer, this luxurious lodge provides wildlife-viewing opportunities and panoramic mountain and bay vistas in an intimate setting for up to 12 guests. The main log building has a piano and a big stone fireplace to warm you after a day of hiking, fishing, kayaking, or touring in one of the lodge's five guided boats (some of the guided fly-out trips may cost extra). Scattered throughout the woods, the rustic cabins, all with electricity, full baths, and decks, are decorated with antiques, original artworks, and homemade quilts. Cabin layouts differ slightly; some are suited for couples, some for groups or families. Dinners spotlight seafood—clams, mussels, and fish—caught in the bay. The price is per person for a five-day, four-night all-inclusive package. *Box 956, Homer 99603 907/235–8910 907/235–8911 www.alaskawildernesslodge.com 4 cabins, 1 room in lodge Dining room, hot tub, sauna, boating, fishing, hiking; no room phones, no room TVs, no smoking FAP No credit cards Closed Oct.–Apr.*

¢ **Alaska State Parks Cabins.** Three public-use cabins are within Kachemak Bay's Halibut Cove Lagoon area, another is near Tutka Bay Lagoon, and a fifth is at China Poot Lake. All but the lakeside cabin are accessible by boat; China Poot can be reached only by foot from the boat landing on the beach or by floatplane to the lake. The Spartan cabin furnishings consist of wooden bunks and sleeping platforms, table, and chairs but no running water or electricity. Four of the five cabins sleep up to six people (the other, the Overlook cabin at Halibut Cove, sleeps eight), and all must be reserved up to six months in advance. *Alaska State Parks Information Center, 550 W. 7th Ave., Suite 1260, Anchorage 99501-3557 907/269–8400 nutmeg.state.ak.us/ixpress/dnr/parks/kenai.dml 5 cabins No credit cards.*

¢ **Alaska State Parks Campsites.** Twenty primitive, free campsites with pit toilets and fire rings are scattered along the shores of Kachemak Bay across from Homer and are accessible by boat (water taxis operate here daily in summer). The sites are available on a first-come, first-served basis, and camping is allowed nearly everywhere in the park, not restricted to developed sites. *Alaska State Parks, Kenai Area Office, Box 1247, Soldotna 99669 907/235–7024 or 907/262–5581 www.dnr.state.ak.us/parks/units/kbay/kbay.htm 6 campgrounds Free Reservations not accepted No credit cards.*

Seldovia

15 *16 mi south of Homer.*

Seldovia, isolated across the bay from Homer, retains the charm of an earlier Alaska. The town's Russian bloodline shows in its onion-dome church and its name, meaning "herring bay." Those who fish use plenty of herring for bait, catching record-size salmon, halibut, and king or Dungeness crab. You'll find excellent fishing whether you drop your line into the deep waters of Kachemak Bay or cast into the surf for silver salmon on the shore of Outside Beach, near town. Stroll through town and along the slough, where frame houses rest on pilings.

Where to Stay

$$–$$$ **Across the Bay Tent & Breakfast Adventure Co.** A step up the comfort ladder from camping, this beachfront compound is reachable via water taxi from Homer. You stay in sturdy canvas-wall tents with carpeted floors and twin beds, and a large common room has hardwood floors and a piano. Prices vary depending on whether you do your own cooking or eat meals prepared by the staff. A propane stove and grill, as well as pots, pans, and picnic tables, are provided. Otherwise, host-prepared meals are hearty and served family style. A beach is great for walking and beachcombing; escorted kayak trips and mountain bikes are available for an extra charge. It's open Memorial Day through Labor Day. ✉ *Mile 8, Jakalof Bay Rd., 8 mi from Seldovia* *Box 81, Seldovia 99663* ☎ *907/235–3633 in summer, 907/345–2571 in winter* *www.tentandbreakfastalaska.com* *5 tents* *Dining room, sauna, beach, bicycles; no a/c, no room phones, no room TVs* *MC, V* *Closed early Sept.–late May.*

$ **Seldovia Boardwalk Hotel.** This hotel with a fabulous view of the harbor has immaculate modern rooms, half of which face the water. The rooms are bright, with white walls and ceilings, lots of plants, and old photos of local interest. A large, sunlit parlor downstairs has a woodstove and coffee service. The proprietors can also arrange charter-fishing or sea kayaking trips. *Box 72, 99663* ☎ *907/234–7816 or 800/238–7862* *www.alaskaone.com/boardwalkhotel* *14 rooms* *Travel services; no room TVs, no smoking* *MC, V.*

Kodiak Island

16 *248 mi southwest of Anchorage by air.*

Alaska's largest island is accessible only by air from Anchorage and by ferry from Homer and Seward. Russian explorers discovered the island in 1763, and Kodiak served as Alaska's first capital until 1804, when the government was moved to Sitka. Situated as it is in the northwestern Gulf of Alaska, Kodiak has been subjected to several natural disasters. In 1912 a volcanic eruption on the nearby Alaska Peninsula covered the town site in knee-deep drifts of ash and pumice. A tidal wave resulting from the 1964 earthquake destroyed the island's large fishing fleet and smashed Kodiak's low-lying downtown area.

Today, commercial fishing is king in Kodiak. Despite its small population—about 15,000 people scattered among the several islands in the Kodiak group—the city is among the busiest fishing ports in the United States. The harbor is also an important supply point for small communities on the Aleutian Islands and the Alaska Peninsula.

Floatplane and boat charters are available from Kodiak to numerous remote attractions not served by roads. Chief among these areas is the 1.6-million-acre **Kodiak National Wildlife Refuge,** lying partly on Kodiak Island and partly on Afognak Island to the north, where spotting the enormous Kodiak brown bears is the main goal of a trip. Seeing the Kodiak brown bears, which weigh a pound at birth but up to 1,500 pounds when fully grown, is worth the trip to this rugged country. The bears are spotted easily in July and August, feeding along salmon-spawning streams. Charter flightseeing trips are available to the area, and exaggerated tales of encounters with these impressive beasts are frequently heard. ✉ *1390 Buskin River Rd., Kodiak* ☎ *907/487–2600* 🌐 *www.r7.fws.gov/nwr/kodiak.*

As part of America's North Pacific defense in World War II, Kodiak was the site of an important naval station, now occupied by the Coast Guard fleet that patrols the surrounding fishing grounds. Part of the old military installation has been incorporated into **Fort Abercrombie State Historical Park,** 3½ mi north of Kodiak on Rezanof Drive. Self-guided tours take you past concrete bunkers and gun emplacements. There's a spectacular scenic overlook, great for bird and whale watching and there are 13 campsites with pit toilets, drinking water, fire grates, and picnic tables. ✉ *Rezanof Dr.* 📫 *Alaska State Parks, Kodiak District Office, 1400 Abercrombie Dr., Kodiak 99615* ☎ *907/486–6339* 📠 *907/486–3320* 🌐 *www.dnr.state.ak.us/parks/units/kodiak* 🎫 *$10 for campsite* 💳 *No credit cards.*

The **Baranov Museum** presents artifacts from the area's Russian origins. On the National Register of Historic Places, the building was built in 1808 by Alexander Baranov to warehouse precious sea-otter pelts. W. J. Erskine made it his home in 1911. On display are samovars, Russian Easter eggs, Native baskets, and other relics from the early Native Koniags and the later Russian settlers. A collection of 40 albums of archival photography portrays various aspects of the island's history. ✉ *101 Marine Way* ☎ *907/486–5920* 🌐 *www.ptialaska.net/~baranov* 🎫 *$2* ⏲ *May–Sept., daily 10–4; Oct.–Apr., Mon.–Wed., Fri., and Sat. 10–3.*

The ornate **Holy Resurrection Russian Orthodox Church** is a visual feast, both inside and out. The cross-shape building is topped by two onion-shape blue domes, and the interior contains brass candle stands, distinctive chandeliers, and numerous icons representing Orthodox saints. Three different churches have stood on this site since 1794. Built in 1945, the present structure is on the National Register of Historic Places. ✉ *Corner of Mission and Kashevaroff Rds.* ☎ *907/486–3854 (parish priest)* ⏲ *By appointment* 🎫 *Donations accepted.*

★ The **Alutiiq Museum and Archaeological Repository** is home to one of the largest collections of Eskimo materials in the world and contains archaeological and ethnographic items dating back 7,500 years. The museum displays only a fraction of its more than 100,000 artifacts, including harpoons, masks, dolls, stone tools, seal-gut parkas, grass baskets, and pottery fragments. The museum store sells Native arts and educational materials. ✉ *215 Mission Rd., Suite 101* ☎ *907/486–7004* 🌐 *www.alutiiqmuseum.com* 🎟 *$3 donation requested* ⏲ *Memorial Day–Labor Day, weekdays 9–5, Sat. 10–5, Sun. by appointment; Labor Day–Memorial Day, Tues.–Fri. 9–5, Sat. 10:30–4:30.*

3

Where to Stay & Eat

¢–$$$$ ✕ **Henry's Great Alaskan Restaurant.** Henry's is a big, boisterous, friendly place at the mall near the small-boat harbor. The menu is equally big, ranging from fresh local seafood and barbecue to pastas and even some Cajun dishes. Dinner specials, a long list of appetizers, salads, rack of lamb, and a tasty dessert list round out the choices. ✉ *512 Marine Way* ☎ *907/486–8844* 💳 *AE, MC, V.*

¢ ✕ **Mill Bay Coffee & Pastries.** Serving soups, sandwiches, and fabulous pastries, this charming little shop is well worth the trip. The coffee is fresh roasted on-site every other day. Inside, elegant antique furnishings are complemented by local artwork and handicrafts. ✉ *3833 Rezanof Dr. E* ☎ *907/486–4411* 🌐 *www.millbaycoffee.com* 💳 *MC, V* ⏲ *No dinner.*

★ $$ ✕🏨 **Kodiak Buskin River Inn.** This modern lodge is a five-minute walk from the main terminal at the airport, about 4½ mi from downtown. Dark woods and bedspreads offset the light-colored walls in the large, well-kept rooms. You can fish for salmon in the river out back. The Eagle's Nest ($$–$$$$) serves local seafood, including king crab, scallops, and a chilled seafood sampler. It also serves Cajun prawns, tempura vegetables, pasta, and steaks. The atmosphere is semiformal (in Alaska that means hip waders would be a bit out of place), with candlelike lamps on each table. ✉ *1395 Airport Way, 99615* ☎ *907/487–2700 or 800/544–2202* 📠 *907/487–4447* 🌐 *www.kodiakadventure.com* 🛏 *50 rooms* 👍 *Restaurant, some in-room data ports, cable TV, fishing, bar, Internet, meeting room, airport shuttle, some pets allowed (fee), no-smoking rooms; no a/c* 💳 *AE, D, DC, MC, V.*

$$ 🏨 **Best Western Kodiak Inn.** Rooms here have soothing floral decor, and some overlook the harbor. However, the rooms with harbor views are on the street, so if a quiet room is a priority, take one in the back. The Chartroom Restaurant has harbor views and serves local seafood and American fare, including steak and pasta. ✉ *236 W. Rezanof Dr., 99615* ☎ *907/486–5712 or 888/563–4254* 📠 *907/486–3430* 🌐 *www.kodiakinn.com* 🛏 *81 rooms* 👍 *Restaurant, in-room data ports, microwaves, refrigerators, cable TV, hot tub, bar, some pets allowed (fee); no a/c* 💳 *AE, D, DC, MC, V.*

$ 🏨 **Kodiak B&B.** Kodiak's first B&B commands a view of the St. Paul harbor and the waterways beyond. It's within a short walk of downtown and easily accessible to most of the town's businesses. Owner Mary Monroe is a gracious and knowledgeable host and can help you make the most of your Kodiak stay with plenty of helpful local information. The guest rooms share a bath and common sitting area, and bookshelves contain loads of local history. Internet available. ✉ *308 Cope St., 99615* ☎ *907/486–5367* *2 rooms share 1 bath* ⏲ *Closed Dec. and Jan.* *BP.*

Guided Tours

Dig Afognak (📫 Box 968, Kodiak 99615 🌐 www.afognak.org/dig.php) gives would-be archaeologists a chance to work alongside professionals during a seven-day dig and to learn about the island's natural history. **Kodiak Island Charters** (☎📠 907/486–5380 or 800/575–5380 🌐 www.ptialaska.net/~urascal) operates boat tours for fishing, hunting, and sightseeing aboard the 43-foot *U-Rascal*. They'll take you on a combined halibut and salmon trip, with sightseeing and whale watching thrown in as well.

MAT-SU VALLEY & BEYOND

Giant homegrown vegetables and the headquarters of the best-known dogsled race in the world are among the most prominent attractions of the Matanuska-Susitna (Mat-Su) Valley. The valley, lying an hour north of Anchorage by road, draws its name from its two largest rivers, the Matanuska and the Susitna, and is bisected by the Parks and Glenn highways. Major cities are Wasilla on the Parks Highway and Palmer on the Glenn Highway. To the east, the Glenn Highway connects to the Richardson Highway by way of several high mountain passes sandwiched between the Chugach Mountains to the south and the Talkeetnas to the north. At Mile 103 of the Glenn Highway, the massive Matanuska Glacier comes almost to the road.

Lake Clark National Park & Preserve

17 *100 mi west of Anchorage by air.*

When the weather is good, an idyllic choice beyond the Mat-Su Valley is the 3.4-million-acre Lake Clark National Park & Preserve, on the Alaska Peninsula and a short flight from Anchorage. There's no road access to the park, so all visits are via small plane. The parklands stretch from the coast to the heights of two grand volcanoes: **Mt. Iliamna** and **Mt. Redoubt,** both topping out above 10,000 feet. The country in between holds glaciers, waterfalls, and turquoise-tinted lakes. The 50-mi-long **Lake Clark,** filled by runoff waters from the mountains that surround it, is an important spawning ground for thousands of red (sockeye) salmon.

The river running is superb in this park. You can make your way through dark forests of spruce and balsam poplars or you can hike over the high, easy-to-travel tundra. The animal life is profuse: look for bears, moose, Dall sheep, wolves, wolverines, foxes, beavers, and minks on land; seals, sea otters, and white (or beluga) whales offshore. Wildflowers embroider the meadows and tundra in spring, and wild roses bloom in the shadows of the forests. Plan your trip to Lake Clark for the end of June or early July, when the insects may be less plentiful. Or consider late August or early September, when the tundra glows with fall colors. ✉ *Administrative Headquarters: 4230 University Dr., Suite*

311, Anchorage 99508 ☎ 907/271–3751 ✉ Park visitor center: 1 Park Pl., Port Alsworth ☎ 907/781–2218 🌐 www.nps.gov/lacl/index.htm.

Where to Stay

$$$$ **Farm Lodge.** Near park headquarters in Port Alsworth, the farm was built as a homestead back in the 1940s and has been a lodge since 1977. Five modern duplexes house as many as 40 guests in private rooms that have either bunk or double beds. A large, manicured, and fenced lawn with flower and vegetable gardens surrounds the main lodge, where home-cooked meals including fresh vegetables, salmon, wild game, and domestic meats are served. The lodge also provides flight services and guided trips. *Box 1, Port Alsworth 99653 ☎ 907/781–2208 or 888/440–2281 907/781–2215 🌐 www.lakeclarkair.com/lodge.htm 10 rooms FAP Dining room, some microwaves, fishing, meeting room, travel services; no a/c, no room TVs, no smoking AE, D, MC, V.*

3

Palmer

18 *40 mi north of Anchorage.*

In 1935 the federal government relocated about 200 farm families from the Depression-ridden Midwest to the Mat-Su Valley, and some elements of these early farms remain around Palmer. The valley has developed into the state's major agricultural region. Good growing conditions of rich soil combined with long hours of summer sunlight result in some outsize vegetables—such as 100-pound cabbages.

You'll find a variety of outsize vegetables, such as a record cabbage in excess of 105 pounds and a 300-plus-pound summer squash that took four people to carry. There are also excellent shopping opportunities for Alaskan-made gifts and crafts at various vendor booths at the **Alaska State Fair,** which runs 12 days, ending on Labor Day (it will be held August 25–September 5 in 2005). Locals whoop it up with midway rides, livestock and 4-H shows, bake-offs, home-preserved produce contests, food, and live music. *✉ Alaska State Fairgrounds, Mile 40.2, Glenn Hwy. 2075 Glenn Hwy., Palmer 99645 ☎ 907/745–4827 or 800/850–3247 907/746–2699 🌐 www.alaskastatefair.org $8.*

On a sunny day the town of Palmer looks like a Swiss calendar photo, with its old barns and log houses silhouetted against craggy Pioneer Peak. On nearby farms (on the Bodenburg Loop off the old Palmer Highway) you can pay to pick your own raspberries and other fruits and vegetables. At **Pyrah's Pioneer Peak Farm** (✉ Mile 2.8, Bodenburg Loop ☎ 907/745–4511), which cultivates 35 kinds of fruits and vegetables and begins harvesting in mid-June, the peak picking time occurs around mid-July.

Forty-some animals roam at the **Musk Ox Farm,** which conducts 30-minute guided tours from May to September. There's a hands-on museum and a gift shop featuring hand-knitted items made from the cashmere-like underfur (qiviut) combed from the musk ox. The scarves and caps and more are made by Oomingmak, an Alaskan Native collective. *✉ Mile 50.1, Glenn Hwy. ☎ 907/745–4151 🌐 www.muskoxfarm.org $8.50 May–Sept., daily 10–6; Oct.–Apr., by appointment.*

Gold mining was an early mainstay of the Mat-Su Valley's economy. ★ You can tour the long-dormant **Independence Mine** on the Hatcher Pass Road, a loop that in summer connects the Parks Highway just north of Willow to the Glenn Highway near Palmer. The road to Independence Mine from the Palmer side was paved in the summer of 2003. The remainder of the roadway to Willow is gravel. In the 1940s as many as 200 workers were employed by the mine. Today it is a 271-acre state park and a cross-country ski area in winter. Only the wooden buildings remain; one of them, the red-roof manager's house, is now used as a visitor center. Guided tours are given on weekdays at 1:30 and 3:30 PM. ✉ *Independence Mine State Historical Park, 19 mi from Glenn Hwy. on Hatcher Pass Rd.* ☎ *907/745–3975* 🌐 *www.dnr.state.ak.us/parks/units/indmine.htm* 🎫 *$5 per vehicle, tours $3* ⏲ *Visitor center early June–Labor Day, daily 11–7; grounds year-round.*

Where to Stay & Eat

$ **Colony Inn.** All guest rooms in this lovingly restored historic building are tastefully decorated with antiques and quilts. The building was used as a women's dormitory during the farm colonization of the 1930s. The small café ($–$$) serves light breakfasts, lunches, and Friday- and Saturday-night dinners. Be sure to try one of the homemade pies; the recipes have won blue ribbons at the Alaska State Fair. Inn reservations and check-in are handled at the Valley Hotel at 606 S. Alaska Street. ✉ *325 E. Elmwood Ave., 99645* ☎ *907/745–3330, 800/478–7666 in Alaska* 📠 *907/746–3330* *12 rooms* *Restaurant, in-room data ports, cable TV; no smoking* 💳 *AE, D, MC, V.*

$ **Hatcher Pass Lodge.** This lodge has spectacular views and can serve as base camp for hiking, berry picking, and—in fall and winter—skiing. Most rooms and cabins have queen-size beds. Three dormer-style rooms provide cozy accommodations for one or two guests. The cabins, some with lofts, are carpeted and have large picture windows with views of Hatcher Pass Valley. The cabins' half baths have chemical toilets and water coolers; showers are in the lodge. The restaurant's Continental menu ($$–$$$) includes fondues, halibut, and pizzas. The bar serves cappuccinos and hot buttered rum for chilly nights. ✉ *Mile 17, Hatcher Pass Rd.* *Box 763, 99645* ☎ *907/745–5897 or 907/745–1200* 🌐 *www.hatcherpasslodge.com* *3 rooms, 9 cabins without shower* *Restaurant, sauna, bar, some pets allowed (fee); no a/c, no room phones, no room TVs, no smoking* 💳 *AE, D, MC, V.*

$ **Valley Hotel.** Built in 1948, this three-story budget hotel was remodeled in 2003. Small, well-kept rooms have quilts and carpets. The hotel is close to shopping, the library, and the local tourist information center. All desserts in the restaurant, the only 24-hour operation in the area, are homemade. ✉ *606 S. Alaska St., 99645* ☎ *907/745–3330, 800/478–7666 in Alaska* 📠 *907/746–3330* *43 rooms* *Restaurant, in-room data ports, cable TV, bar, no-smoking rooms; no a/c* 💳 *AE, D, MC, V.*

Wasilla

19 *42 mi north of Anchorage, 10 mi west of Palmer.*

Wasilla is one of the valley's original pioneer communities and over time has served as a supply center for farmers, gold miners, and mushers. Today, fast-food restaurants and strip malls line the Parks Highway. Rolling hills and more scenic vistas can be found by wandering the area's back roads.

The **Museum of Alaska Transportation and Industry,** on a 20-acre site, exhibits some of the machines that helped develop Alaska, from dogsleds to jet aircraft, and everything in between. The Don Sheldon Building houses aviation artifacts as well as antique autos and photographic displays. A snow-machine exhibit also is on display. ✉ *Take Parks Hwy., turn south onto Neuser Rd. at Mile 47, follow road ¾ mi to end* ☎ *907/376–1211* 🌐 *www.museumofalaska.org* 🎫 *$8* ⏲ *May–Sept., daily 10–6.*

Wasilla is the headquarters and official starting point for the Iditarod Trail Sled Dog Race, run each March from here to Nome, more than 1,000 mi to the northwest. A ceremonial start is held on Anchorage's 4th Avenue the first Saturday in March, then continues from Wasilla the following day. The **Iditarod Trail Headquarters** displays dogsleds, mushers' clothing, and trail gear, and you can catch video highlights of past races. The gift shop sells Iditarod items. During the summer, dogsled rides on wheels are available for $5. ✉ *Mile 2.2, Knik Rd.* ☎ *907/376–5155* 🌐 *www.iditarod.com* 🎫 *Free* ⏲ *Memorial Day–mid-Sept., daily 8–7; mid-Sept.–Memorial Day, weekdays 8–5.*

Where to Stay & Eat

$–$$$ ✕ **Evangelo's Trattoria.** The food is good and the servings are ample at this spacious local favorite on the Parks Highway. Try the garlic-sautéed shrimp in a white-wine butter sauce or a mammoth calzone. The pizzas are loaded with goodies, and a salad bar provides a fresh selection. ✉ *Mile 40, Parks Hwy.* ☎ *907/376–1212* 💳 *AE, MC, V.*

$–$$ ✕ **Cadillac Café.** Hearty fare fills the menu at this diner-style café, including homemade pies; big, hand-pressed burgers; exotic pizzas turned out of a stone, wood-fired oven; and southwestern-style Mexican food. The decor is described by the owner as "Alaska minimalist," but the booths are plush and comfortable, and hand-rubbed wood is much in evidence. Breakfast is served only on weekends. ✉ *Mile 49, Parks Hwy., at Pittman St.* ☎ *907/357–5533* 💳 *AE, D, MC, V.*

$$ 🏨 **Best Western Lake Lucille Inn.** This well-maintained resort on Lake Lucille provides easy access to several recreational activities, including boating in summer and ice-skating and snowmobiling in winter. Half of the inn's bright and cheery rooms have private balconies overlooking the lake. Room decor includes art prints and quilts. ✉ *1300 W. Lake Lucille Dr., 99654, Mile 43.5 on the Parks Highway* ☎ *907/373–1776 or 800/528–1234* 📠 *907/376–6199* 🌐 *www.bestwestern.com/lakelucilleinn* 🛏 *50 rooms, 4 suites* 🛎 *Restaurant, in-room data ports, cable TV, health club, hot tub, sauna, boating, lobby lounge, meeting room, some pets allowed; no a/c* 💳 *AE, D, DC, MC, V.*

A PRIVILEGED COMMUNION

BETWEEN 1903 AND 1912, *eight expeditions walked the slopes of 20,320-foot Mt. McKinley. But none had reached the absolute top of North America's highest peak (also commonly known by the Native name Denali, meaning "the high one"). Among those who failed were some of North America's premier explorers and climbers. Thus the stage was set for Hudson Stuck, a self-described American amateur mountaineer who had previously climbed in Great Britain, the western United States, and Canada.*

Stuck came to Alaska in 1904, drawn not by mountains but by a missionary calling. As the Episcopal Church's archdeacon for the Yukon River region, he visited Native villages year-round. His passion for climbing was unexpectedly rekindled in 1906, when he saw from afar the "glorious, broad, massive uplift" of McKinley, the "father of mountains." Five years after that wondrous view, Stuck pledged to reach McKinley's summit—or at least try. For his climbing party he picked three Alaskans experienced in snow and ice travel, though not in mountaineering: Harry Karstens, a well-known explorer and backcountry guide who would later become the first superintendent of Mt. McKinley National Park; Robert Tatum, Stuck's missionary assistant; and Walter Harper, part Native, who served as Stuck's interpreter and dog-team driver.

Assisted by two sled-dog teams, the group began its expedition on St. Patrick's Day, 1913, at Nenana, a village 90 mi northeast of McKinley. A month later, they began their actual ascent of the great peak's northern side, via the Muldrow Glacier. The glacier's surface proved to be a maze of crevasses, some of them wide chasms with no apparent bottom. Carefully working their way up-glacier, the climbers established a camp at 11,500 feet. From there they had to ascend a steep and jumbled ridgeline. Moving slowly, the team chopped a staircase up several miles—and 3,000 vertical feet—of rock, snow, and ice. Their progress was delayed several times by high winds, heavy snow, and near-zero visibility.

By May 30 the climbers had reached the top of the ridge (later named in Karstens's honor) and moved into a high glacial basin. Despite temperatures ranging from subzero to 21°F, they kept warm at night by sleeping on sheep and caribou skins and covering themselves with down quilts, camel's-hair blankets, and a wolf robe.

On June 6 the team established its high camp at 18,000 feet. The following morning was bright, cloudless, and windy. Three of the climbers suffered headaches and stomach pains, but given the clear weather everyone agreed to make an attempt. They left camp at 5 AM and by 1:30 PM stood within a few yards of McKinley's summit. Harper, who had been leading all day, was the first to reach the top, soon followed by the others. After catching their breath, the teammates shook hands, said a prayer of thanks, made some scientific measurements, and reveled in their magnificent surroundings. In his classic book The Ascent of Denali, *Hudson Stuck later reflected, "There was no pride of conquest, no trace of that exultation of victory some enjoy upon the first ascent of a lofty peak, no gloating over good fortune that had hoisted us a few hundred feet higher than others who had struggled and been discomfited. Rather, was the feeling that a privileged communion with the high places of the earth had been granted."*

★ $–$$ **Pioneer Ridge Bed and Breakfast Inn.** Each of the spacious, log-partitioned rooms in this converted barn is decorated according to a theme. The Denali Room has posters of the mountain, snowshoes, crampons, and other climbing gear. A dogsled and other race paraphernalia mark the Iditarod Room. A rooftop common room has a spectacular 360° panorama of the mountains and river valleys. ✉ *2221 Yukon Cir.* *HC31, Box 5083K, 99654* ☎ *907/376-7472 or 800/478-7472* *907/376-7470* 🌐 *www.pioneerridge.net* *1 suite, 1 cabin, 4 rooms with private baths, 1 room with separate, unshared bath* *Exercise equipment, sauna; no a/c, no room TVs* *BP* *AE, D, MC, V.*

Talkeetna

20 *56 mi north of Wasilla, 112 mi north of Anchorage.*

Talkeetna lies at the end of a spur road near Mile 99 of the Parks Highway. Mountaineers congregate here to begin their assaults on Mt. McKinley in Denali National Park. The Denali mountain rangers have their climbing headquarters here, as do most glacier pilots who fly climbing parties to the mountain. A carved pole at the town cemetery honors deceased mountaineers. The **Talkeetna Historical Society Museum,** across from the Fairview Inn, explores the history of Mt. McKinley climbs. The museum has a scale model of Mt. McKinley and features information on the history of climbing attempts on the continent's highest peak. A Talkeetna walking tour map points out sites of historical interest. ✉ *1st Alley and D St.* ☎ *907/733-2487* 🌐 *www.talkeetnahistory.org* *$3* *May 15–Sept. 15, daily 10–6.*

Where to Stay & Eat

$ **Swiss-Alaska Inn.** Family-run since 1976, this rustic-style property is well known among those who come to fish in the Talkeetna, Susitna, and Chulitna rivers. Floral decor embellishes the bright rooms. Menu selections at the restaurant ($$) include halibut, salmon, buffalo burgers, and the owner's secret-recipe Swiss-style French toast. ✉ *East Talkeetna, by boat launch* *Box 565, 99676* ☎ *907/733-2424* *907/733-2425* 🌐 *www.swissalaska.com* *20 rooms* *Restaurant, in-room VCRs, Internet; no a/c, no room phones, no room TVs, no smoking* *AE, D, MC, V.*

¢–$ **Talkeetna Roadhouse.** This circa 1917 log roadhouse has a common sitting area and rooms in a variety of sizes, including a bunk room with four beds ($21). Rooms are very basic—bed, table, window, period. Sizable breakfasts are the order of the day at the restaurant (¢–$), along with soup, sandwiches, desserts, and pies, all made from scratch. It's a popular place with locals and with climbers who use Talkeetna's air taxis to reach Mt. McKinley. In the winter, the café is open only on weekends and evenings, but rooms are available year-round. ✉ *Main St.* *Box 604, 99676* ☎ *907/733-1351* *907/733-1353* 🌐 *www.talkeetnaroadhouse.com* *8 rooms share 4 baths* *Restaurant, Internet, some pets allowed; no a/c, no room phones, no room TVs, no smoking* *MC, V.*

★ $$$$ **Talkeetna Alaskan Lodge.** This luxury hotel has excellent views of Mt. McKinley as well as access to nature trails. Rooms are modern, in the style of an Alaska lodge, and mountainside upgrades are available. The Great Room has comfortable seating, a 45-foot river-rock fireplace in the center of the room, and an espresso bar. The tour desk can arrange flightseeing, river trips, or any other Alaska adventure you can imagine. *2525 C St., Suite 405, Anchorage 99503 907/265–4501 or 888/959–9590 907/263–5559 www.talkeetnalodge.com 201 rooms, 3 suites Restaurant, in-room data ports, some microwaves, cable TV, hiking, bar, meeting room, travel services; no a/c, no smoking AE, D, MC, V.*

¢ **Fairview Inn.** Built in 1923, the Fairview is listed on the National Register of Historic Places. It oozes local color, from the bear rug nailed to the ceiling over the bar to photographs of local characters and former owners on the wall. You're likely to meet members of Mt. McKinley climbing expeditions during the early-summer climbing season. You'll also hear lots of good, local music, but be forewarned: you'll hear it even if you don't want to, so if a good night's sleep is important, check first to see if the band will be playing. The inn is open year-round, but food is served only from Memorial Day to Labor Day in the outdoor beer garden. *101 Main St. Box 1109, 99676 907/733–2423 907/733–1067 www.denali-fairview.com 5 rooms, shared baths Restaurant, bar; no a/c, no room phones, no room TVs AE, MC, V.*

Guided Tours

Hudson Air Service (907/733–2321 or 800/478–2321 907/733–2333 www.hudsonair.com) has a fleet of four airplanes to take you on flightseeing trips, glacier landings, and remote drop-offs. **K2 Aviation** (907/733–2291 or 800/764–2291 907/733–1221 www.flyk2.com) specializes in flightseeing and glacier landings in the Alaska Range, as well as in charter flights throughout the state of Alaska. **Talkeetna Air Taxi** (907/733–2218 or 800/533–2219 907/733–1434 www.talkeetnaair.com) conducts a breathtaking exploration flight close to massive Mt. McKinley, as well as fly-in hiking trips and glacier landings.

Mahay's Riverboat Service (907/733–2223 or 800/736–2210 www.mahaysriverboat.com) conducts guided jet-boat tours, scenic cruises, and fishing on the Susitna and Talkeetna rivers. **Denali Floats** (907/733–2384 or 800/651–5221) leads scenic raft trips on the Susitna River, complete with shore lunch and occasional musical accompaniment, and can arrange wilderness expeditions to suit your schedule. **Tri-River Charters** (Box 312, 99676 907/733–2400 www.tririvercharters.com) operates fishing trips out of Talkeetna and on the nearby Deshka River and can provide all the necessary tackle and gear.

Denali State Park

21 *34 mi north of Talkeetna, 132 mi north of Anchorage.*

Overshadowed by the larger and more charismatic Denali National Park & Preserve in the Interior, "Little Denali" offers excellent access (it's bisected by the Parks Highway), beautiful views of Mt. McKinley, scenic campgrounds, and prime wilderness hiking and backpacking opportunities within a few miles of the road system. Between the Talkeetna

Mountains and the Alaska Range, Denali State Park combines wooded lowlands and forested foothills topped by alpine tundra. ✉ *From Parks Highway Milepost 131.7 to Mile 169.2* *Alaska State Parks, Mat-Su Area Office, HC 32, Box 6706, Wasilla 99687* ☎ *907/745–3975.*

The park's chief attraction, other than McKinley views, is the 35-mi-long **Curry-Kesugi Ridge,** which forms a rugged spine through the heart of the park that is ideal backpacking terrain. The trail runs from the Troublesome Creek trailhead at Mile 137.3 to the Little Coal Creek trailhead at Mile 163.9. The Byers Lake campground at Mile 147 has a trailhead for a spur trail that intersects the Kesugi Ridge trail, offering an alternative to hiking the entire 35 mi of the main trail. Views of Mt. McKinley and the Alaska Range from the ridge trail are stunning, but be advised that this is a very bear-intensive area, especially the Troublesome Creek area in late summer when the salmon runs are in full force—be bear aware!

Another destination favored by backcountry travelers is the **Peters Hills,** accessible from Petersville Road in Trapper Creek.

Where to Stay

$$$ **McKinley Princess Wilderness Lodge.** When the sky is clear and Mt. McKinley is visible, this lodge has excellent views of North America's highest peak, especially from the lobby, with its large stone fireplace. On private land inside Denali State Park, this hillside lodge is surrounded by forest and overlooks the Chulitna River. You stay in bungalow-style guest rooms with separate sitting rooms. The tour desk can arrange horseback rides, river-rafting trips, naturalist walks, flightseeing excursions, fishing trips, mountain-bike rentals, and alpine hikes. ✉ *Mile 133, Parks Hwy.* ☎ *907/733–2900 or 800/426–0500* *907/733–2922* *www.princessalaskalodges.com* *238 rooms, 4 suites* *Restaurant, café, some in-room hot tubs, cable TV, gym, hiking, shop, meeting rooms, travel services; no a/c* *AE, D, DC, MC, V* *Closed mid-Sept.–mid-May.*

¢ **Alaska State Parks Cabins.** Two public-use cabins are in Denali State Park, along the shores of Byers Lake. One cabin is on a gravel road, 1 mi from the highway, and the other is accessible by canoe or by a ½-mi walk-in trail. Both are equipped with bunks to sleep six, wood-burning stove, table, and benches, but they have no running water or electricity. ✉ *Alaska State Parks Information Center, 550 W. 7th Ave., Suite 1260, Anchorage 99501-3557, Mile 43.5 on the Parks Hwy.* ☎ *907/269–8400* *www.dnr.state.ak.us/parks/cabins/matsu.cfm* *2 cabins without bath* *No credit cards.*

¢ **Alaska State Parks Campgrounds.** Three roadside campgrounds are within Denali State Park—Byers Lake, Lower Troublesome Creek, and Denali View North. All are easily accessible from the Parks Highway and have picnic tables, fire pits, drinking water, and latrines. The Byers Lake campground also has a boat launch and nearby hiking trails. Sites are available on a first-come, first-served basis. *Alaska State Parks, HC 32, Box 6706, Wasilla 99654* ☎ *907/745–3975* *www.dnr.state.ak.us/parks/units/denali2.htm* *No credit cards* *Closed Oct.–May.*

Glennallen

22 *187 mi northeast of Anchorage.*

This community of 900 residents is the gateway to Wrangell–St. Elias National Park and Preserve. It's 124 mi from Glennallen to McCarthy, the last 58 mi on unpaved gravel. This town is also the service center for the Copper River basin and is a fly-in base for several wilderness outfitters.

Where to Stay & Eat

¢–$$ ✕ **Caribou Restaurant.** This convivial place serves such typical roadside fare as burgers, hot sandwiches, meat loaf, pancakes, and charbroiled steak. Sweet rolls, pies, and other treats are baked fresh daily. If you haven't managed to spy any of the local wildlife on your trip, just check out the walls here for numerous taxidermied examples. ✉ *Mile 186.5, Glenn Hwy.* ☎ *907/822–4222* ▭ *AE, D, MC, V.*

$$ **Caribou Hotel.** Rooms decorated in mauve and sea green fill this modern hotel. Unless you're on a strict budget, ask for a room in the main building and not in the trailer-like annex out front, where rooms are Spartan and share a bath. There are also a pair of rustic cabins available for those who want to get a taste of living in "Bush Alaska." Several rooms in the main building have hot tubs. The owners operate a nearby B&B and a property with three two-bedroom apartments and a one-bedroom apartment. *Box 329, 99588* ☎ *907/822–3302 or 800/478–3302* *907/822–3711* *www.caribouhotel.com* *83 rooms, 63 with bath; 3 suites, 2 cabins.* *In-room data ports, some in-room hot tubs, some kitchens, some microwaves, some refrigerators, cable TV, meeting room, some pets allowed; no a/c* ▭ *AE, D, DC, MC, V.*

Wrangell–St. Elias National Park & Preserve

23 *77 mi southeast of Glennallen, 264 mi east of Anchorage.*

In a land of many grand and spectacularly beautiful mountains, those in the 9.2-million-acre Wrangell–St. Elias National Park and Preserve have been singled out by many Alaskans as the finest of them all. This extraordinarily compact cluster of immense peaks toward the southeastern part of Alaska belongs to four different mountain ranges. ✉ *Mile 106.8, Richardson Hwy.* *Box 439, Copper Center 99573* ☎ *907/822–5234* *www.nps.gov/wrst/index.htm.*

Covering an area some 100 mi by 70 mi, the **Wrangells** tower above the 2,500-foot-high Copper River Plateau, and the peaks of Mts. Jarvis, Drum, Blackburn, Sanford, and Wrangell rise 15,000 feet–16,000 feet from sea level. The white-iced spire of **Mt. St. Elias,** in the St. Elias Range, reaches more than 18,000 feet. It's the fourth-tallest mountain on the North American continent and the crown of the planet's highest coastal range.

The park's coastal mountains are frequently wreathed in snow-filled clouds, their massive height making a giant wall that contains the great storms brewed in the Gulf of Alaska. As a consequence, they bear some of the continent's largest ice fields, with more than 100 glaciers radiating from them. One of these, the **Malaspina Glacier,** is 1,500 square mi—

larger than the state of Rhode Island. This tidewater glacier has an incredible pattern of black-and-white stripes made by the other glaciers that coalesced to form it. Look for it on the coast north of Yakutat if you fly between Juneau and Anchorage.

Rising through many life zones, the Wrangell–St. Elias Park and Preserve is largely undeveloped wilderness parkland on a grand scale. The area is perfect mountain-biking and hiking terrain, and the rivers invite rafting for those with expedition experience. The mountains attract climbers from around the world; most of them fly in from Glennallen or Yakutat. The nearby abandoned **Kennicott Mine** is one of the park's main visitor attractions. Limited services are available in the end-of-the-road town of **McCarthy.** Facilities include guest lodges, a B&B, and a restaurant. There's no gas station or post office.

The park is accessible from Alaska's highway system, via one of two gravel roads. The unpaved **Nabesna Road** leaves the Glenn Highway–Tok Cutoff at the village of Slana and takes you 45 mi into the park's northern foothills. The better-known route is the **McCarthy Road,** which stretches 60 mi as it follows an old railroad bed from Chitina to the Kennicott River. At the end of the road you must park and cross the river via a footbridge.

Before setting out make sure both you and your car are prepared. Your car should be equipped with a working jack and a properly inflated spare tire, or else potholes, old railroad ties, and occasional railroad spikes may leave you stranded.

Where to Stay

$$$$ ☒ **Ultima Thule Outfitters.** This remote fly-in-only lodge on the Chitina River in Wrangell–St. Elias National Park and Preserve provides a wonderful chance to experience an "air-safari adventure." The cost is $990 per person per day, with a four-day minimum. Included in your stay are breathtaking flightseeing, rafting, climbing, hiking, fishing, mushing, and skiing excursions, among others. Any adventure you can dream up, the Claus family will make it happen. Three generations of the family make their home here, and their knowledge of the area is unsurpassed. At the age of 18, daughter Ellie was the youngest person to ever finish the Iditarod Trail sled dog race as a rookie in 2004. The family-style meals include local foods such as fish, game, and vegetables from the garden as well as homemade bread, pies, and cakes. Oak floors, wallpaper, wood-burning stoves, and brass beds provide the comforts of home Bavarian style. ✉ *Box 109, Chitina 99566* ✉ *Box 770361, Eagle River 99577* ☎ *907/688–1200* ⊕ *www.ultimathulelodge.com* ⇄ *6 cabins* ♨ *Dining room, sauna, boating, fishing, hiking, cross-country skiing, Internet; no a/c, no room phones, no room TVs, no smoking* ▭ *No credit cards* ⦿l *FAP.*

$$$ ☒ **Copper River Princess Wilderness Lodge.** At the gateway to the park, this lodge has views of the Wrangell–St. Elias mountain range and the Copper and Klutina rivers. A wall of windows two stories high provides dramatic views of towering peaks and the Copper River. Dark-wood accents and Alaska wildlife and scenery prints, conveying the ambience

of a well-appointed hunting lodge, adorn each room. ✉ *Brenwick Craig Rd., Mile 102, Richardson Hwy., Copper Center 99573* ☎ *907/822–4000, 800/426–0500 reservations* 🖷 *907/822–4480* 🌐 *www.princesslodges.com* *85 rooms* *Restaurant, coffee shop, cable TV, bar, shop, meeting room, airport shuttle; no smoking* 💳 *AE, DC, MC, V* ⏲ *Closed mi-Sept.–mid-May.*

★ $$$ **Kennicott Glacier Lodge.** Artifacts and photos of the era when mining was the main order of business in the ghost town of Kennicott adorn the small rooms in this modern, wooden lodge. Rooms have cold-water sinks and share bath and shower facilities. Dinner is a "wilderness gourmet" of breads and desserts served family style. Breakfast and lunch are served restaurant style, with the same exceptional attention to detail and freshness. Afterward, you can relax in the spacious living room or on the front porch. The front desk can arrange glacier trekking, flightseeing, rafting, and alpine hiking for additional fees, and an evening tour of Kennicott is included in the room rate. A vacation package that includes room and all meals is available. *Box 103940, Anchorage 99510* ☎ *907/258–2350 or 800/582–5128* 🖷 *907/248–7975* 🌐 *www.kennicottlodge.com* *35 rooms, 10 with private bath* *Dining room, hiking, meeting room; no a/c, no room phones, no room TVs, no smoking* 💳 *AE, D, MC, V* ⏲ *Closed mid-Sept.–mid-May.*

¢ **Alaska State Parks Campgrounds.** The state maintains 23 road-accessible campgrounds in the Matanuska-Susitna–Copper River region. Most can accommodate RVs up to 35 feet long, though electrical hookups are not available. Length of stay varies from 4 to 15 days. All have toilet facilities, and most have drinking water, picnic sites, fire pits, fishing, and nearby hiking trails. *Alaska State Parks, Mat-Su Area Office, HC 32, Box 6706, Wasilla 99654* ☎ *907/745–3975* *Reservations not accepted* *23 campgrounds* 💳 *No credit cards* ⏲ *Closed Oct.–May.*

Sports & the Outdoors

St. Elias Alpine Guides (☎ 888/933–5427, 907/554–4445 mid-May–mid-Sept. 🌐 www.steliasguides.com) gives introductory mountaineering lessons, leads excursions ranging from half-day glacier walks to month-long backpacking trips, and is the only company contracted by the Park Service to conduct guided tours of historic Kennicott buildings. They also offer day raft trips from Kennicott. This service, which is owned by experienced mountaineer Bob Jacobs, has been in business more than 25 years.

SOUTH CENTRAL ALASKA A TO Z

To research prices, get advice from other travelers, and book travel arrangements, visit www.fodors.com.

AIR TRAVEL

Anchorage is the air hub of the South Central region, served by major national and international airlines and well stocked with smaller carriers and local air-taxi operators. ERA Aviation flies to Homer, Kenai, Valdez, Cordova, and Kodiak. Reservations are handled by Alaska Airlines. For flights to the Alaska Peninsula, the Aleutians, and western Alaska Bush villages, call PenAir. Frontier Flying Service flies to Fairbanks, Deadhorse, Barrow, and several western Alaska Bush villages.

ERA Aviation ☎ 907/243-3300 or 800/866-8394 🌐 www.flyera.com. **Frontier Flying Service** (800/478-6779 in Alaska; 907/474-0014 reservations). **PenAir** ☎ 907/243-2323 or 800/448-4226.

BOAT & FERRY TRAVEL

Ferries are a great way to explore the South Central coast, with its glaciers, mountains, fjords, and sea mammals. The ferries between Valdez and Whittier run by way of Columbia Glacier in summer, where it is not unusual to witness giant fragments of ice calving from the face of the glacier into Prince William Sound.

The Alaska Marine Highway, the state-run ferry operator, has scheduled service to Valdez, Cordova, Whittier, Seward, Homer, and Seldovia on the mainland; to Kodiak and Port Lions on Kodiak Island; and to the port of Dutch Harbor in the Aleutian Islands. The same agency runs the ferries that operate in Southeast Alaska, but the two systems connect only on once-a-month sailings. The system operates on two schedules; summer (May–September) sailings are considerably more frequent than fall and winter service. Check your schedules carefully: ferries do not stop at all ports every day. Reservations are required on all routes; they should be made as far in advance as possible, particularly in summer.

Alaska Marine Highway ✉ 6858 Glacier Hwy., Juneau 99801 ☎ 907/465-3941 or 800/642-0066 📠 907/277-4829 🌐 www.ferryalaska.com.

BUS TRAVEL

Year-round service runs between Fairbanks and Anchorage by way of Denali National Park and also down to Homer, at the very tip of the Kenai Peninsula. Alaska Direct Bus Lines provides service between Anchorage and Fairbanks and also to Whitehorse and Skagway. The Park Connection has regularly scheduled shuttle service between Seward, Anchorage, and Denali National Park mid-May to mid-September. Seward Bus Line serves Anchorage, Portage, and Seward. A subsidiary offers service between Anchorage and Homer.

Alaska Direct Bus Lines ☎ 907/277-6652 or 800/770-6652 📠 907/338-1951. **Park Connection** ☎ 800/208-0200, 907/224-7116 for Seward same-day bookings, 907/683-1240 for Denali same-day bookings. **Seward Bus Line** ☎ 907/563-0800 or 907/224-3608 📠 907/224-7237.

CAR TRAVEL

Keep in mind that all but a few miles of the road system consist of two-lane highways, not all of which are paved. Two highway routes offer a choice for travel by car between Fairbanks and Anchorage. Heading north from Anchorage, the Parks Highway (turn left off Glenn Highway near Palmer) passes through Wasilla, up the Susitna River drainage area and through a low pass in the Alaska Range, then down into the Tanana Valley and Fairbanks. This route passes the entrance to Denali National Park and roughly parallels the Alaska Railroad. A longer route (436 mi) follows the Glenn Highway to the Richardson Highway, then heads north to Fairbanks through the Copper River valley. This route makes possible a side trip to Valdez, and it's the most direct connection to the Alaska Highway, joining it at Tok.

You can also link the two routes by using the Denali Highway, which, despite its name, doesn't run through Denali National Park. Rather, it connects the Richardson Highway with the Parks Highway between the towns of Paxson and Cantwell. You can make a huge figure eight by using the Denali, but be advised that this 135-mi-long road isn't paved except for relatively short sections at either end, and services are limited. Don't start the trip without a full tank of gas and at least one real spare tire, just to be on the safe side.

Chinook Auto Rentals ✉ Cordova Airport ☎ 877/424-5279. **State Department of Transportation** ☎ 907/835-4242 in Anchorage for hot-line reports on highways during snow season.

EMERGENCIES

Police, ambulance, emergency ☎ 911. **Alaska State Troopers** ☎ 907/269-5722 in Anchorage, 907/822-3263 in Glennallen, 907/235-8239 in Homer, 907/486-4121 in Kodiak, 907/745-2131 in Palmer, 907/224-3346 in Seward, 907/262-4052 in Soldotna, 907/835-4359 in Valdez.

Hospitals Cordova: **Cordova Medical Center** ✉ 602 Chase Ave. ☎ 907/424-8000. Glennallen: **Crossroads Medical Center** ✉ Mile 187.5, Glenn Hwy. ☎ 907/822-3203. Homer: **South Peninsula Hospital** ✉ 4300 Bartlett St. ☎ 907/235-8101. Kodiak: **Providence Kodiak Island Medical Center** ✉ 1915 E. Rezanof Dr. ☎ 907/486-3281. Palmer: **Valley Hospital** ✉ 515 E. Dahlia St. ☎ 907/746-8600. Seldovia: **Seldovia Medical Clinic** ✉ 252 Seldovia St. ☎ 907/234-7825. Seward: **Providence Seward Medical Center** ✉ 417 1st Ave. ☎ 907/224-5205. Soldotna: **Central Peninsula General Hospital** ✉ 250 Hospital Pl. ☎ 907/262-4404. Valdez: **Community Hospital** ✉ 911 Meals Ave. ☎ 907/835-2249.

WHERE TO STAY

BED & BREAKFASTS

Local Agents **Accommodations on the Kenai** Box 2956-F, Soldotna 99669 ☎ 907/262-2139. **Alaska Private Lodgings/Stay with a Friend** ✉ 704 W. 2nd Ave., Anchorage 99501 ☎ 907/258-1717 📠 907/258-6613 www.alaskabandb.com. **Alaska Sourdough Bed and Breakfast Association** ✉ 889 Cardigan Cir., Anchorage 99501 ☎ 907/563-6244 📠 907/563-6073 www.alaskan.com/aksourdoughbba.

TOURS

BOATING & GLACIERS

Tour Operators **Alaskan Wilderness Sailing & Kayaking** Box 1313, Valdez 99686 ☎ 907/835-5175 📠 907/835-3765. **Columbia Glacier Wildlife Cruises/*Lu-Lu Belle*** ☎ 907/835-5141 or 800/411-0090 📠 907/835-5899 in summer ☎📠 800/411-0090 off-season. **Homer Ocean Charters** ☎ 907/235-6212 or 800/426-6212. **Kenai Coastal Tours** ☎ 907/277-2131 or 800/770-9119. **Kenai Fjords Tours** ☎ 907/224-8068 in Seward, 907/276-6249, 800/478-8068 📠 907/777-2888. **Keystone Raft & Kayak Adventures, Inc.** ☎ 907/835-2606 or 800/328-8460 📠 907/835-4638. **Kodiak Island Charters** ☎📠 907/486-5380 or 800/575-5380. **Mariah Tours** ☎ 907/224-8623 or 800/270-1238 📠 907/777-2888. **Prince William Sound Cruises and Tours** ☎ 907/835-4731 or 800/992-1297 📠 907/835-3765. **26 Glacier Cruise** ✉ Phillips' Cruises & Tours, 519 W. 4th Ave., Suite 100, Anchorage 99510 ☎ 800/544-0529 or 907/276-8023 📠 907/265-5890 www.26glaciers.com.

FISHING **Tour Operators** **Central Charters** ✉ 4241 Homer Spit Rd., Homer 99603 ☎ 907/235-7847 or 800/478-7847. **Fish House** ✉ Small-boat harbor, Seward ☎ 907/224-3674 or 800/257-7760. ***U-Rascal*** ☎ 907/486-5380.

FLIGHTSEEING **Tour Operators** **Alpine Aviation Adventures** ✉ Valdez ☎ 907/835-4304, 800/478-4304 in Alaska 📠 907/835-2523. **Cordova Air Service** ☎ 907/424-3289, 800/424-7608 in Alaska 📠 907/424-3495. **Prince William Sound Adventures** ☎ 907/424-3350.

GENERAL INTEREST **Tour Operators** **Alaska Heritage Tours** ☎ 907/265-4500 or 877/258-6877 📠 907/263-5559. **Alaska Wildland Adventures** ☎ 907/783-2928 or 800/334-8730. **Gray Line of Alaska** ☎ 206/281-3535 or 800/544-2206.

HIKING Information on locations and difficulty of trails is available at the Alaska Public Lands Information Center at 4th and F streets in Anchorage. Another good resource is *55 Ways to the Wilderness in South Central Alaska,* published by the Mountaineers and available at most local bookstores.

TRAIN TRAVEL

The Alaska Railroad Corporation operates the Alaska Railroad, which is said to be the last railroad in North America that still makes flag stops to accommodate the homesteaders, hikers, fishing parties, and other travelers who get on and off in remote places. The 470-mi main line runs up Alaska's rail belt between Seward and Fairbanks via Anchorage. There's daily service between Anchorage and Fairbanks in summer, and in winter there's one round-trip per week (Anchorage to Fairbanks on Saturday, Fairbanks to Anchorage on Sunday). Service to Seward from Anchorage runs mid-May to September 1 only. Adults are allowed two pieces of luggage to a maximum of 50 pounds. There's a $20 charge for bicycles; camping equipment is allowed on a space-available basis.

For information on the luxury-class Ultradome service between Anchorage and Fairbanks, contact Princess Tours about its *Midnight Sun Express.* Westours/Gray Line of Alaska operates the *McKinley Explorer* on Alaska Railroad trains as well.

Alaska Railroad Corporation Box 107500, Anchorage 99510 ☎ 907/265-2494 or 800/544-0552 📠 907/265-2323 🌐 www.akrr.com. **Princess Tours** ☎ 206/728-4202 or 800/835-8907. **Westours/Gray Line of Alaska** ☎ 907/277-5581 or 800/478-6388.

TRANSPORTATION AROUND SOUTH CENTRAL ALASKA

Anchorage is the central hub, connected by rail and road to Seward and Whittier. Valdez can be reached by a rather indirect but interesting road route (the Glenn Highway to the Richardson Highway) out of Anchorage. The Seward and Sterling highways connect to most of the places you'll want to see on the Kenai Peninsula, including the small towns of Hope, Soldotna, and Homer. South Central's other "highway," the ferry-driven Alaska Marine Highway, connects with Kodiak, Whittier, Seward, Valdez, Dutch Harbor, Homer, Seldovia, and Cordova via the gulf. Air taxis are also a viable means of transportation around South Central.

VISITOR INFORMATION

Alaska Public Lands Information Center ✉ 605 W. 4th Ave., Anchorage 99501 ☎ 907/271-2737 📠 907/271-2744 🌐 www.nps.gov/aplic. **Bureau of Land Management** Box

147, Glennallen 99588 907/822-3217 www.glennallen.ak.blm.gov. **Cordova Chamber of Commerce** Box 99, Cordova 99574 907/424-7260 907/424-7259 www.cordovachamber.com. **Homer Chamber of Commerce** 135 Sterling Hwy. Box 541, Homer 99603 907/235-5300 907/235-8766 www.homeralaska.org. **Kenai Peninsula Visitor Information Center** 44790 Sterling Hwy., Soldotna 99669 907/262-1337. **Kodiak Island Convention and Visitors Bureau** 100 Marine Way, Kodiak 99615 907/486-4782 907/486-6545 www.kodiak.org/cvb.html. **Palmer Chamber of Commerce** Box 45, Palmer 99645 907/745-2880 907/746-4164 www.palmerchamber.org. **Seward Visitors Bureau** Mile 2, Seward Hwy. Box 749, Seward 99664 907/224-8051 907/224-5353 www.sewardak.org. **U.S. Fish and Wildlife Service** Alaska Regional Office, 1011 E. Tudor Rd., Anchorage 99503 907/786-3487 http://alaska.fws.gov. **U.S. Forest Service** 3301 C St., Room 300, Anchorage 99503 907/271-2500 907/743-9476 www.fs.fed.us/r10/chugach. **Valdez Convention and Visitors Bureau** 200 Chenega St. Box 1603, Valdez 99686 907/835-2984 907/835-4845 www.valdezalaska.org. **Wasilla Chamber of Commerce** 1830 E. Parks Hwy., A-116, Wasilla 99654 907/376-1299 907/373-2560 www.wasillachamber.org.

Southeast Alaska

4

Including Ketchikan, Juneau, Haines, Sitka & Skagway

WORD OF MOUTH

"Juneau! With that gorgeous harbor and the way the mountains rise up behind town, it has to be the prettiest capital in the country. It's just big enough to have all the comforts of home, but just small enough to be charming and cozy."

—Julie304

"Glacier Bay National Park is amazing. I took my son on an overnight trip and we saw breaching humpbacks, a bear on the beach with cubs, puffins, eagles, sea otters, and sea lions."

—wolfie11

"We took the Alaska State ferry up the Inside Passage. We were lucky to see a couple of orcas and also stopped, with the engines turned off, to watch a glacier calve."

—dfrostnh

www.fodors.com/forums

By Mike Miller
Updated by
Don Pitcher

SOUTHEAST ALASKA STRETCHES BELOW THE STATE like the tail of a kite. It is a world of massive glaciers, cliff-rimmed fjords, and snowcapped peaks. The largest concentration of coastal glaciers on Earth can be viewed at spectacular Glacier Bay National Park and Preserve, one of the region's most prized attractions. Lush stands of spruce, hemlock, and cedar blanket thousands of islands. Bays, coves, lakes of all sizes, and swift, icy rivers provide some of the continent's best fishing grounds—and scenery as majestic and unspoiled as any in North America. Many of Southeast Alaska's wildest and most pristine landscapes are within Tongass National Forest, which encompasses nearly 17 million acres—or almost three-quarters of the Panhandle's land.

Like anywhere else, the Southeast has its drawbacks. For one thing, it rains a lot. If you plan to spend a week or more here, you can count on showers during at least a few of those days. Die-hard southeasterners simply throw on a slicker and rubber boots and shrug off the rain. Their attitude is philosophical: without the rain, there would be no forests; no lakes; no streams running with world-class salmon and trout; and no healthy populations of brown and black bears, moose, deer, mountain goats, and wolves. Locals also know that the rain keeps people from moving in; without it in such profusion, Southeast Alaska would probably be as densely populated as Seattle.

Another disadvantage—or advantage, depending on your point of view—is an almost total lack of connecting roads between the area's communities. To fill this void, Alaskans created the Marine Highway System of passenger and vehicle ferries, which have staterooms; observation decks; cafeterias; cocktail lounges; and heated, glass-enclosed solariums.

The Southeast's natural beauty and abundance of wildlife have made it one of the world's fastest-growing cruise destinations. About 20 big cruise ships ply the Inside Passage—once the traditional route to the Klondike goldfields and today the centerpiece of many Alaskan cruises—during the height of the summer. Regular air service to the Southeast is available from the Lower 48 states and other parts of Alaska.

The Native peoples you'll meet in the Southeast coastal region are Tlingit, Haida, and Tsimshian. These peoples, like their coastal neighbors in British Columbia, preserve a culture rich in totemic art forms, including deeply carved poles, masks, baskets, and ceremonial objects. Many live among non-Natives in modern towns and continue their own traditions.

A pioneer spirit dominates the towns of Southeast Alaska. Residents—some from other states, some who can trace their ancestors back to the gold-rush days, and some whose ancestors came over the Bering Land Bridge from Asia thousands of years ago—are an adventurous lot. The rough-and-tumble spirit of the Southeast often combines with a worldly sophistication: those who fish are also artists, Forest Service workers may run a bed-and-breakfast on the side, and homemakers may be Native-dance performers.

Like all of Alaska's regions, the Southeast covers a vast area (even though it represents a thin slice of the state), and most of its communities, as well as its parks, national forest lands, and other wildlands, are accessible only by boat or plane. You should therefore allow yourself at least a week here. If you have only a few days, it might be best to fly into one of Southeast Alaska's larger communities—such as Juneau, Sitka, or Ketchikan—and then take a state ferry to one or two nearby Panhandle communities. Or fly to a remote destination. Most visitors explore the Inside Passage on cruise ships, which generate their own schedules. But plenty of adventures await ambitious independent travelers who plan ahead and ride state ferries instead of cruise ships.

If you have 5 days

Spend two or three days in **Juneau** 45–56. Go south via the state ferry to **Sitka** 35–44, ancestral home of the Tlingits and once the capital of Russian America. Spend the next two days exploring this town and nearby sights, possibly taking in a performance by Russian-style dancers at Centennial Hall. Active travelers can go sea kayaking, hiking, fishing, and wildlife cruising. Instead of going south from Juneau, another option is to travel northwest to **Gustavus** 59 and nearby **Glacier Bay National Park & Preserve** 58, one of America's premier parklands, where tidewater glaciers, rugged mountain scenery, and abundant marine wildlife await.

If you have 7 days

Many cruises to Southeast Alaska last seven days, and a week is also sufficient time for independent travelers to see at least a cross section of the region by traveling aboard state ferries and aircraft. Starting at **Ketchikan** 1–17, known for its totem poles, the Alaska Marine Highway regularly makes stops at all of the region's larger communities: **Wrangell** 22–29, with its ancient petroglyphs; **Petersburg** 30–34, which has a strong Norwegian influence; **Sitka** 35–44, former capital of Russian America; **Juneau** 45–56, the state capital; **Haines** 60–65, known for its bald eagles and Native dance troupe; and **Skagway** 66–71, a gold-rush-era throwback. It also serves several smaller communities such as **Kake, Angoon, Tenakee Springs,** and **Hoonah.** Give yourself time to see local sights and visit one or more out-of-town destinations, such as **Admiralty Island** 57, **Glacier Bay National Park & Preserve** 58, **Misty Fiords National Monument** 18, **Hyder** 20, or **Prince of Wales Island** 21.

Exploring Southeast Alaska

The Southeast Panhandle stretches some 500 mi from Yakutat at its northernmost point to Ketchikan and Metlakatla at its southern end. At its widest the region measures only 140 mi, and in the upper Panhandle just south of Yakutat, it's a skinny 30 mi across. Most of the Panhandle consists of a sliver of mainland buffered by islands.

More than 1,000 islands line the Inside Passage—most of them mountainous with lush covers of timber (though large clear-cuts are also common). Collectively they constitute the Alexander Archipelago. Most communities are on islands rather than on the mainland. The principal exceptions are Juneau, Haines, and Skagway, plus the hamlets of Gustavus and Hyder. Island outposts include Ketchikan, Wrangell, Petersburg, Sitka, and the villages of Craig, Pelican, Metlakatla, Kake, Angoon, and Hoonah. Bordering Alaska just east of the Panhandle lies the Canadian province of British Columbia.

You can get to and around Southeast Alaska by ship or by plane, but forget arriving by car or RV unless your destination is Haines, Skagway, or Hyder, which are connected by road to the Alaska Highway. Elsewhere in the Southeast, the roadways typically run just a few miles out from towns and villages; then they dead-end. (If you wish to drive up the Alaska Highway and then visit road-isolated communities, you can reserve vehicle space on Alaska's state ferries.)

Numbers in the text correspond to numbers in the margin and on the Ketchikan, Wrangell, Petersburg, Sitka, Juneau, Glacier Bay Park & Preserve, Haines, and Skagway maps.

About the Restaurants

The people of Southeast Alaska are closely connected to the sea, not just in their proximity to the water, but also in the food that graces local restaurants. Fresh seafood often dominates the menus, from scallops to king salmon. You'll find simple but tasty fish-and-chips most anywhere, but grilled fish is always a favorite. Many restaurants will cook fish that you caught, but call ahead to be sure. American standards such as burgers, steaks, chicken, and pizza can be found in any settlement, and the larger towns of Juneau, Sitka, and Ketchikan all have a variety of ethnic eateries, along with notable gourmet restaurants. You'll also discover fine dining in some unexpected places, including Gustavus, Haines, and Skagway. Dinner entrée prices at midrange restaurants are typically around $12–$18.

The restaurants we list are the cream of the crop in each price category. Restaurants are indicated in the text by a knife-and-fork icon, ✕, and establishments denoted by ✕🏨 stand out equally for their restaurants and rooms.

WHAT IT COSTS

	$$$$	$$$	$$	$	¢
AT DINNER	over $25	$20–$25	$15–$20	$10–$15	under $10

Prices are per person for a main course at dinner.

About the Hotels

Lodging choices along the Inside Passage range from remote Forest Service cabins to top-end hotels. In general, these accommodations are pricey, with midrange rooms costing $125–$175 in the peak summer season. Rates drop substantially in the off-season (mid-September to mid-May), sometimes by 50% or more. Budget travelers will find hostels in Ketchikan, Wrangell, Petersburg, Sitka, Juneau, Skagway, and Haines, and adventure travelers should be sure to investigate the remote cabins that dot Tongass National Forest; most of the latter require an expen-

Ferry-Hopping The Alaska Marine Highway is the primary means of transportation along the Inside Passage, with service to most towns on a daily basis. Most northbound travelers hop aboard the ferry in Bellingham, Washington, or Prince Rupert, British Columbia. Ferries can transport vehicles of all sizes, but reservations are necessary, especially out of Bellingham. A fast catamaran car-and-passenger ferry began service connecting Juneau, Sitka, Haines, and Skagway in 2004. The Inter-Island Ferry Authority operates daily car-and-passenger ferry service between Ketchikan and Hollis on Prince of Wales Island. It expects to add service from Coffman Cove (also on Prince of Wales) to Wrangell and Petersburg in 2006.

Fishing Southeast Alaska is an angler's paradise. You'll find salmon and halibut charter boats, fishing lodges (some near the larger communities, others remote and accessible only by floatplane), fly-in mountain-lake lodges where the fishing is for trout and char, and—bargain hunters, take special note—more than 150 remote but weather-tight cabins operated by the U.S. Forest Service.

Hiking & Backpacking Trekking woods, mountains, and beaches is Southeast Alaska's unofficial regional sport. Some of the trails are abandoned mining and logging roads. Others are natural routes—in some sections, even game trails—meandering over ridges, through forests, and alongside streams and glaciers. A few—most notably the Chilkoot Trail out of Skagway—offer historical significance along with grand scenery. The Alaska Division of Parks Southeast regional office in Juneau will send you a list of state-maintained trails and parks in the Panhandle; local visitor bureaus and recreation departments can also help.

Shopping Southeast Alaska has an abundance of fine artists and artisans, and most towns have galleries exhibiting their works. Tlingit and Haida handicrafts include totem poles of all sizes—from miniature versions for your coffee table to life-size replicas that must be shipped by barge—wooden masks, paddles, bentwood boxes, and button blankets (blankets with traditional Native designs accented by patterns produced from buttons sewn on the fabric). You'll find these items at gift shops up and down the coast. If you want to be sure of authenticity, buy items tagged with the state-approved AUTHENTIC NATIVE HANDICRAFT FROM ALASKA label. Virtually every community has at least one canning and/or smoking operation that packs and ships local seafood, smoked and canned salmon included.

Tongass National Forest America's largest national forest, the **Tongass** (✉ 648 Mission St., Ketchikan 99901 ☎ 907/225–3101 🌐 www.fs.fed.us/r10/tongass), stretches the length of Alaska's Panhandle and encompasses nearly 17 million acres, or three-fourths of the Southeast region. Old-growth, temperate rain forest covers much of the area, which includes rugged mountains, steep fjords, glaciers, and ice fields within its boundaries. Its lands and waters teem with animals: black and brown bears, bald eagles, Sitka black-tailed deer, mountain goats, wolves, marine mammals, and dozens of sea- and shorebird species. Two national monuments, Admiralty Island near Juneau and Misty Fiords near Ketchikan, are within its borders.

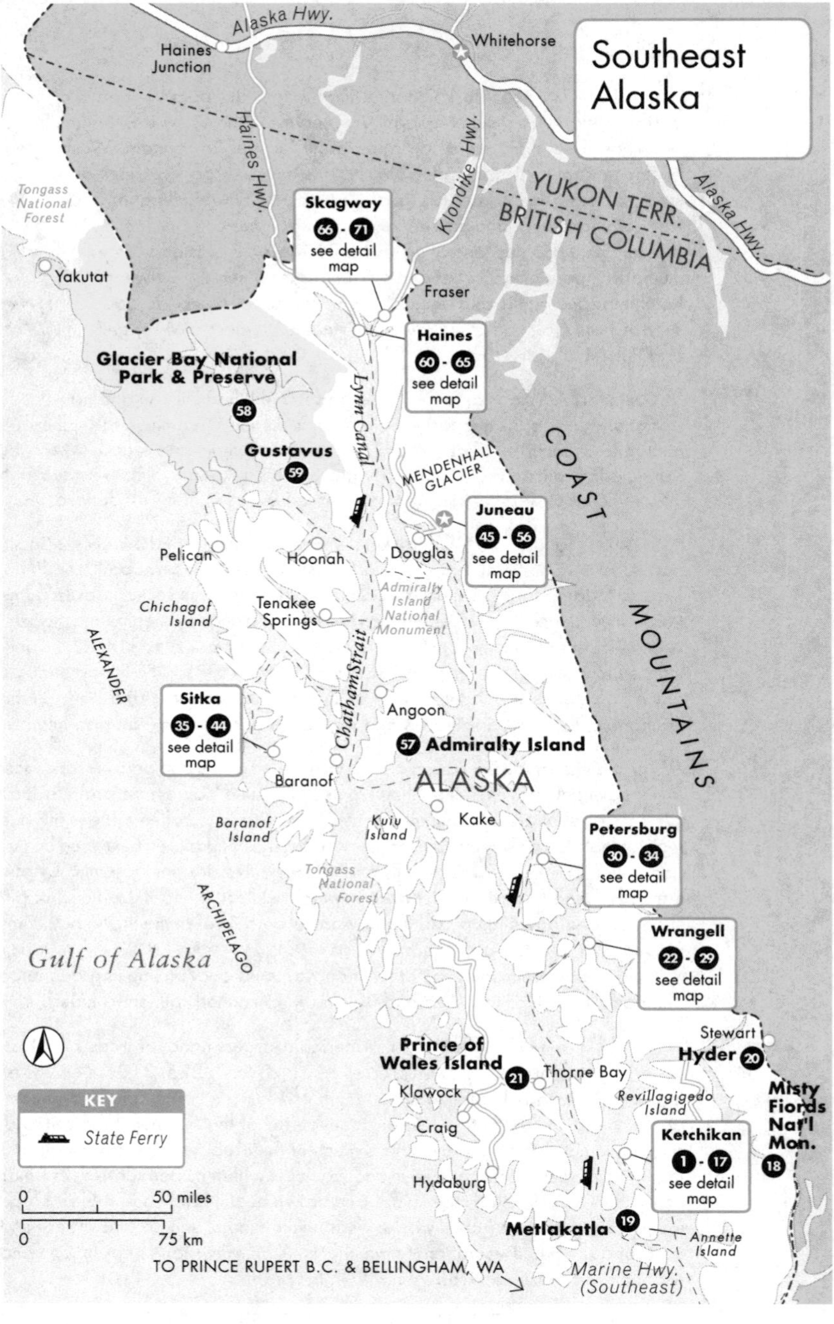
Southeast Alaska
Alaska Hwy.
Haines Junction
Whitehorse
Haines Hwy.
Klondike Hwy.
YUKON TERR.
BRITISH COLUMBIA
Alaska Hwy.
Tongass National Forest
Yakutat
Skagway
66 - 71
see detail map
Fraser
Haines
60 - 65
see detail map
Glacier Bay National Park & Preserve
58
Lynn Canal
Gustavus
59
MENDENHALL GLACIER
COAST MOUNTAINS
Juneau
45 - 56
see detail map
Pelican
Hoonah
Douglas
Admiralty Island National Monument
Chichagof Island
Tenakee Springs
ALEXANDER
Chatham Strait
Sitka
35 - 44
see detail map
Angoon
57 Admiralty Island
Baranof
ALASKA
Kake
Baranof Island
Kuiu Island
Tongass National Forest
Petersburg
30 - 34
see detail map
ARCHIPELAGO
Wrangell
22 - 29
see detail map
Gulf of Alaska
Stewart
Hyder 20
Prince of Wales Island
21
Thorne Bay
Klawock
Revillagigedo Island
Misty Fiords Nat'l Mon.
18
Craig
Ketchikan
1 - 17
see detail map
Hydaburg
KEY
State Ferry
0
50 miles
0
75 km
Metlakatla
19
Annette Island
TO PRINCE RUPERT B.C. & BELLINGHAM, WA
Marine Hwy. (Southeast)

sive floatplane flight from town. Several fine hotels are found in Ketchikan and Juneau, and luxurious fishing lodges attract anglers on Prince of Wales Island and other places in the Southeast. Dozens of regional B&Bs provide an excellent alternative to hotels, particularly for couples in search of a romantic getaway. B&Bs also provide the opportunity to meet fellow travelers, dig into a homemade breakfast (sometimes with smoked salmon omelets or authentic sourdough pancakes), and learn about the area from a local.

The lodgings we list are the cream of the crop in each price category. We always list the facilities that are available—but we don't specify whether they cost extra: when pricing accommodations, always ask what's included and what costs extra.

WHAT IT COSTS					
	$$$$	**$$$**	**$$**	**$**	**¢**
FOR 2 PEOPLE	over $225	$175–$225	$125–$175	$75–$125	under $75

Prices are for two people in a standard double room in high season.

Timing

The best time to visit is from May through September, when the weather is mildest, rain is less frequent, daylight hours are longest, wildlife is most abundant, the fishing is best, and festivals and tourist-oriented activities are in full swing.

KETCHIKAN

Famous for its colorful totem poles, rainy skies, steep-as–San Francisco streets, and lush island setting, Ketchikan is a favorite stop for travelers. Some 8,000 people call the town home, and during the summer, cruise ships crowd the shoreline, floatplanes depart noisily for Misty Fiords, and commercial fishing boats head home to Tongass Narrows laden down with salmon. Ketchikan has a rowdy, blue-collar heritage of logging and fishing, somewhat softened by the loss of many timber industry jobs and the dramatic rise of cruise-ship tourism in the last decade.

The town perches at the foot of 3,000-foot Deer Mountain, near the southeast corner of Revillagigedo (locals shorten it to Revilla) Island. The site at the mouth of Ketchikan Creek was a summer fish camp of the Tlingit until white miners and fishermen came to settle the town in 1885. Gold discoveries just before the turn of the 20th century brought more immigrants, and valuable timber and commercial fishing resources spurred new industries. By the 1930s the town bragged it was the "salmon-canning capital of the world." You will still find some of the Southeast's best salmon fishing here.

Exploring Ketchikan

This town is the first bite of Alaska that many travelers taste, and they're usually not disappointed. Ketchikan is easy to walk through, yet

ALASKA'S WILD SALMON & THE AQUACULTURE DEBATE

FIVE SPECIES OF WILD PACIFIC SALMON ARE FOUND IN ALASKAN WATERS. *All are anadromous, and all five species have at least two common names, making them confusing to newcomers: pink (humpback) salmon, chum (dog) salmon, coho (silver) salmon, sockeye (red) salmon, and king (Chinook) salmon. The smallest of these five, the pink salmon, has an average weight of only about 3 or 4 pounds, while king salmon can often tip the scales at more than 25 pounds (the largest weighed 126 pounds). King salmon is generally considered the most flavorful, but sockeye and coho are also very highly regarded. Pinks and chum salmon are the mainstay of canneries, and have a poor reputation with Alaskans.*

After spending a year or more in the ocean (the length of time varies among the species), Pacific salmon return to their native streams to spawn and die. The annual summertime return of adult salmon is a major event in Alaska, both for the animals (including bears) that depend upon this bounty, and also for thousands of commercial fishers and sport anglers who crowd local waters.

Alaska has long been famous for its seafood, and one of the first acts following statehood in 1959 was to protect fisheries from over-harvesting. Today the stocks of salmon and other fish remain healthy, and careful management ensures that they will be there in the future. In the 1980s and 1990s, aquaculture, or fish-farming, grew into an enormous international business, particularly in Norway, Chile, the United Kingdom, and British Columbia. Leery of the consequences to wild salmon, Alaska has never allowed any salmon aquaculture.

Pen-raised fish are affordable, available year-round, and of a consistent quality, but controversy surrounds the practice of fish-farming. Many people believe it has a disastrous impact on the environment, citing such examples as disease spreading to wild fish from farmed salmon, which are more susceptible to diseases; pollution from the waste of huge concentrations of fish; and fish farms harvesting non-native species, such as Atlantic salmon.

On the other side of the debate, there are those who believe that fish-farming is helping to protect the earth's valuable—and decreasing—populations of salmon. Proponents of fish farms point out that the practice also offers revenue and more jobs. Offshore fish-farming in the United States is a hugely incendiary topic of current debate; those supporting it believe that if the farms are placed in deep ocean pockets, the pollution from and medication given to the pen-raised fish will be scattered better by strong currents. Many environmentalists beg to differ, hoping to establish stringent guidelines before opening the ocean to fish-farming corporations.

As scientific studies report more benefits from eating wild salmon, consumers have come to appreciate wild Alaskan salmon; not surprisingly, its value has appreciated dramatically. One Alaskan bumper sticker says: "Friends don't let friends eat farmed salmon." Just across the border, in British Columbia, many people find employment as fish-farm workers. No matter which side you agree with in the aquaculture debate, be sure to enjoy a plate of delicious barbecued wild salmon during your visit to Alaska—with luck and timing, it could even be a fish you've hooked yourself!

— Don Pitcher

rises steeply from the busy fishing docks, with staircases climbing to hillside homes. Downtown's favorite stops include the Spruce Mill Development shops and Creek Street. A bit farther away you'll find the Totem Heritage Center and Deer Mountain Hatchery. Out of town (but included on most bus tours) are two longtime favorites: Totem Bight State Historical Park and Saxman Native Village.

If you're traveling on the highway in either direction, you won't go far before you run out of road. The North Tongass Highway ends about 18 mi from downtown, at Settler's Cove Campground. The South Tongass Highway terminates at a power plant about 8 mi from town. Side roads soon end at campgrounds and at trailheads, viewing points, lakes, boat-launching ramps, and private property.

a good walk

The best place to begin a walking tour of Ketchikan is from the helpful **Ketchikan Visitors Bureau** 1. Just a few steps up Mill Street is the **Spruce Mill Development** 2, filled with shops and restaurants. Next door learn about Southeast Alaska's wild places at the **Southeast Alaska Discovery Center** 3. Continue up Mill Street past minuscule **Whale Park** 4, with its Chief Kyan totem pole, and turn right on Stedman Street. Cross the bridge to **Thomas Street** 5, overlooking a busy boat harbor. Continue walking along Stedman to the ***Return of the Eagle*** 6 mural before turning left on Deermont Street. Follow it uphill several blocks to the **Totem Heritage Center** 7 and its collection of ancient totem poles. Just across the footbridge are **Deer Mountain Hatchery and Eagle Center** 8, where you can see young salmon and rehabilitated bald eagles and **City Park** 9. From here, Park Avenue runs parallel to Ketchikan Creek, heading downhill to the fish ladder and the Salmon Carving next to **Salmon Falls** 10. Look uphill from the falls to see historic **Grant Street Trestle** 11, where the road becomes a steep plank bridge supported on pilings. It's about a 20-minute walk down Park Avenue from the hatchery, or you can call a cab if your legs are getting tired.

From the fish ladder, a boardwalk path parallels Ketchikan Creek and leads to trendy **Creek Street** 12. For a side trip, take the short funicular ($2) to **WestCoast Cape Fox Lodge** 13 to get a great view of the harbor, and then take it back before continuing down Creek Street boardwalk to **Dolly's House** 14, once a brothel and now a house museum. Retrace your steps up the boardwalk and cross the **Creek Street Footbridge** 15, where you can watch salmon heading upstream in the summer. In front of you is the Chief Johnson Totem Pole, and just to your right is the **Tongass Historical Museum** 16, with interesting relics from the early days of mining and fishing. Turn left on Bawden Street to pass historic **St. John's Church** 17.

TIMING This walking tour should take around two or three hours, stops included. If you are looking for an easier and shorter version (approximately one hour), omit the leg of the walk that leads to Totem Heritage Center, Deer Mountain Hatchery, and City Park. (Local bus tours typically include these sights as well as Totem Bight State Historical Park and Saxman Native Village.)

City Park 9
Creek Street . . .12
Creek Street Footbridge 15
Deer Mountain Hatchery and Eagle Center 8
Dolly's House 14
Grant Street Trestle 11
Ketchikan Visitors Bureau 1
Return of the Eagle 6
St. John's Church 17
Salmon Falls . .10
Southeast Alaska Discovery Center 3
Spruce Mill Development . . .2
Thomas Street 5
Tongass Historical Museum 16
Totem Heritage Center 7
WestCoast Cape Fox Lodge 13
Whale Park 4

What to See

9 City Park. The Deer Mountain Hatchery and Eagle Center lead into this small park, which has picnic tables and paved paths and is bisected by Ketchikan Creek. ✉ *Park and Fair Sts.*

★ **12 Creek Street.** Ketchikan's infamous red-light district once existed here. During Prohibition, this was the only local place to buy alcohol, and at its peak, more than 30 houses of prostitution operated here. Today the small, colorful houses, built on stilts over the creek waters, have been restored as trendy shops. Sea kayakers often paddle up the creek at high tide.

15 Creek Street Footbridge. Stand over Ketchikan Creek for good salmon viewing when the fish are running. During the summer, you can see coho, king, pink, and chum salmon, along with smaller numbers of steelhead and rainbow trout heading upstream to spawn.

8 Deer Mountain Hatchery and Eagle Center. Tens of thousands of king and coho (silver) salmon are raised at this hatchery on Ketchikan Creek. Midsummer visitors can observe both natural spawning in the creek by pink and chum salmon and workers collecting and fertilizing the salmon eggs for the hatchery. Tanks hold young salmon and those old enough to head out to the ocean, and a video details the fascinating life cycle of salmon. Owned by the Ketchikan Indian Corporation, the hatchery has exhibits on traditional Native fishing. Also here is a nesting pair of injured bald eagles. Although both are unable to fly, you may see them catching salmon that swim into their enclosure. ✉ *1158 Salmon Rd.* ☎ *907/225–6760 or 800/252–5158* 🌐 *www.kictribe.org/Hatchery.htm* 🎫 *$9* ⏲ *Early May–Sept., daily 8–4:30.*

14 **Dolly's House.** Once Creek Street's most famous brothel, the house has been preserved as a museum, complete with furnishings, beds, and a short history of the life and times of Ketchikan's best-known madam. ✉ *Creek St.* ☎ *907/225–6329* 🎫 *$4* ⏲ *Daily whenever cruise ships are in port (typically May to mid-Sept.).*

11 **Grant Street Trestle.** At one time virtually all of Ketchikan's walkways and streets were made from wooden trestles, but now only one of these wooden streets remains, constructed in 1908.

1 **Ketchikan Visitors Bureau.** The helpful visitor's bureau is right next to the cruise-ship docks. Half the space is occupied by day-tour, flightseeing, and boat-tour operators. ✉ *131 Front St., 99901* ☎ *907/225–6166 or 800/770–3300* 🌐 *www.visit-ketchikan.com* ⏲ *May–Sept., daily 7–5 (until 6 PM when cruise ships are docked); Oct.–Apr., weekdays 8–5.*

6 ***Return of the Eagle.*** Twenty-one Native students created this colorful mural on a wall of the Robertson Building on the Ketchikan campus of the University of Alaska–Southeast. ✉ *Stedman St.*

17 **St. John's Church.** Built in 1903, this church is the oldest remaining house of worship in Ketchikan. Its interior is formed from red cedar cut in the Native-operated sawmill in nearby Saxman. ✉ *Bawden St.*

10 **Salmon Falls.** Get out your camera and set it for fast speed at the fish ladder, a series of pools arranged like steps that allow fish to travel upstream over a dam or falls. When the salmon start running in midsummer, from June onward, thousands leap the falls (or take the easier fish-ladder route) to spawn in Ketchikan Creek's waters farther upstream. Many can also be seen in the creek below the falls. The falls, fish ladder, and a large carving of a jumping salmon are just off Park Avenue on Married Man's Trail. (The trail was once used by married men for discrete access to the red-light district on Creek Street.) ✉ *Married Man's Trail, off Park Ave.*

3 **Southeast Alaska Discovery Center.** Museum-quality exhibits, including one on the rain forest, focus on the resources, Native cultures, and ecosystems of Southeast Alaska at this impressive visitor center. The U.S. Forest Service and other federal agencies provide information on Alaska's public lands, and a large gift shop sells natural history books, maps, and videos about the sights in Ketchikan and the Southeast. The multimedia show "Mystical Southeast Alaska" is shown every half hour during the summer in the center's theater. ✉ *50 Main St.* ☎ *907/228–6220* 🌐 *www.nps.gov/aplic* 🎫 *$5 May–Sept., free Oct.–Apr.* ⏲ *May–Sept., daily 8:30–5; Oct.–Apr., Tues.–Sat. 10–4:30.*

2 **Spruce Mill Development.** The attractive Mill Street complex is modeled after 1920s-style cannery architecture. Spread over 6½ acres along the waterfront, five buildings contain a mix of retail stores, souvenir shops, gal-

leries, and restaurants. Cruise ships moor just a few steps away, filling the shops with tourists all summer long. ✉ *Spruce Mill and Front Sts.*

5 **Thomas Street.** From this street you can see Thomas Basin, one of four harbors in Ketchikan and home port to pleasure and commercial fishing boats. Old buildings, including the Potlatch Bar, sit atop pilings, and you can walk out to the breakwater for a better view of busy Tongass Narrows.

16 **Tongass Historical Museum.** Native artifacts and pioneer relics revisit the mining and fishing eras at this small museum in the same building as the library. Exhibits include a big, brilliantly polished lens from Tree Point Lighthouse and the bullet-riddled skull of a notorious brown bear called Old Groaner. Other exhibits change periodically but always include Tlingit Native items. ✉ *629 Dock St.* ☎ *907/225–5600* 🎫 *$2* ⏲ *May–Sept., daily 8–5; Oct.–Apr., Wed.–Fri. 1–5, Sat. 10–4, Sun. 1–4.*

★ **7** **Totem Heritage Center.** Many of the authentic Native totems in this rare collection are well over a century old. The totems were brought here from abandoned village sites on nearby islands, where they were in danger of being lost to gradual decay. You can also watch a video about the preservation efforts and take a guided tour. Outside are several more poles carved in the three decades since this center opened. ✉ *Deermount St.* ☎ *907/225–5900* 🎫 *$5* ⏲ *May–Sept., daily 8–5; Oct.–Apr., weekdays 1–5.*

13 **WestCoast Cape Fox Lodge.** For a stunning view of the harbor and fine dining, walk to the top of steep Venetia Avenue or take the funicular ($2) up from Creek Street. ✉ *800 Venetia Way* ☎ *907/225–8001 or 800/426–0670* 🌐 *www.westcoasthotels.com.*

4 **Whale Park.** This park, catercorner from St. John's Church, is the site of the **Chief Kyan Totem Pole,** now in its third incarnation. The original was carved in the 1890s, but over the decades it deteriorated and was replaced in the 1960s. The current replica was erected in 1993 with the 1960s version now housed in the Totem Heritage Center.

Where to Stay & Eat

$$$$ ✕🏨 **Salmon Falls Resort.** Perched along Clover Passage next to a beautiful waterfall, this resort is near the end of the road, 17 mi north of Ketchikan. Guests focus on the variety of deals, starting with a three-night package that includes two days of fishing, guide, cabin cruiser, and all meals for $1,350 per person. The huge, octagonal restaurant is worth the half-hour drive from town even for nonguests. Specialties include steaks and Alaskan seafood, including blackened salmon or halibut. The restaurant is built of pine logs and in the center, a 40-foot section of 48-inch pipe manufactured to be part of the Alaska pipeline rises to support the roof. Big windows overlook the waters of Clover Passage, with islands and verdant forests as a backdrop. ✉ *Mile 17, N. Tongass Hwy.* ☎ *907/225–2752, 800/247–9059 outside Alaska* 📠 *907/225–2710* 🌐 *www.salmonfallsresort.net* 🛏 *52 rooms* 👍 *Restaurant, lounge, airport shuttle; no a/c, no room TVs* 💳 *AE, MC, V* ⏲ *Closed mid-Sept.–May.*

TOTEM POLE PARKS

THERE ARE 14 POLES at Ketchikan's two most famous totem-pole parks. For the most part, they're 60-year-old replicas of older totem poles brought in from outlying villages as part of a federal works–cultural project during the late 1930s.

***Totem Bight** (✉ N. Tongass Hwy., 10 mi north of town ☎ 907/247–8574 🎫 Free ⏲ Dawn–dusk 🌐 www.alaskastateparks.org) has many totem poles and a hand-hewn Native tribal house and sits on a scenic spit of land facing the waters of Tongass Narrows. The clan house here is open daily in the summer. Most bus tours of Ketchikan include Totem Bight in their itinerary, but there is no public transportation to the site.*

*A 2½-mi paved walking path–bike trail parallels the road from Ketchikan to **Saxman Native Village** (✉ S. Tongass Hwy., 2 mi south of town ☎ 907/225–4846 🌐 www.capefoxtours.com), named for a missionary who helped Native Alaskans settle here before 1900. A totem park dominates the center of Saxman, with poles moved here in the 1930s from abandoned village sites. The poles represent a wide range of human and animal-inspired figures, including bears, ravens, whales, and eagles.*

Saxman's Beaver Clan tribal house is said to be the largest in the world. Carvers create totem poles and totemic art objects in the adjacent carver's shed (free and open whenever the carvers are working). You can get to the park on foot, by taxi, or by city bus, and you can visit the totem park on your own, but to visit the tribal house and theater you must take a tour. Tickets are sold at the gift shop across from the totems. Call ahead for tour schedules.

4

$$–$$$$ ✕ **Annabelle's Keg and Chowder House.** Within the historic Gilmore Hotel, this Victorian-style restaurant serves a tempting choice of seafood and pastas, including five kinds of chowder and steamer clams. Prime rib on Friday and Saturday evenings is a favorite, and an espresso bar and lounge with a jukebox add a friendly vibe. ✉ *326 Front St.* ☎ *907/225–6009* 📠 *907/225–7442* 🌐 *www.gilmorehotel.com* 💳 *AE, D, DC, MC, V.*

$$–$$$$ ✕ **Steamers.** Anchoring Ketchikan's Spruce Mill Mall, this lively, noisy, and spacious restaurant has an extensive menu of fresh seafood (including king crab and steamer clams), pasta, and steaks. Vegetarian choices are also available, and the servings are certain to fill you up. The bar pours 125 draft beers, including a number of Alaskan brews, along with a substantial wine list and 300 different liquors. Tall windows face Ketchikan's busy waterfront, where cruise ships and floatplanes vie for your attention. ✉ *76 Front St.* ☎ *907/225–1600* 💳 *AE, D, MC, V* ⏲ *Closed Oct.–Mar.*

$–$$ ✕ **Ocean View Restaurant.** This locals' favorite eatery has a wide range of food, from burgers and steaks to pasta, pizzas, and seafood. They're all fine, but the main draw is authentic and very filling south-of-the-border dishes prepared under the direction of the Mexican-American owners. Service is fast and the atmosphere is nice enough for a date night. The restaurant is open until 11 PM nightly all year, and the TV always has Spanish-language sports. ✉ *1831 Tongass Ave.* ☎ *907/225–7566* ▭ *MC, V.*

$$$ **The Landing.** This Best Western property is named for the state ferry landing directly across the road. Rooms are modern with Mission-style furniture; a two-bedroom apartment is available for families. No need for a car; the free shuttle provides transport around town. The Landing Restaurant is always packed with a hungry breakfast clientele and with families. Upstairs, Jeremiah's Fine Food and Spirits offers upscale dining in cozy digs and a relaxing no-smoking lounge built around a stone fireplace. ✉ *3434 Tongass Ave., 99901* ☎ *907/225–5166 or 800/428–8304* 🖷 *907/225–6900* 🌐 *www.thelandinghotel.com* *107 rooms, 1 apartment* *2 restaurants, microwaves, refrigerators, cable TV, exercise equipment, meeting rooms, airport shuttle, some pets allowed (fee); no a/c* ▭ *AE, D, DC, MC, V.*

$$ **WestCoast Cape Fox Lodge.** One of Ketchikan's nicest properties offers scenic views of the town and harbor from 135 feet above the village. The setting is cozy and luxurious, with an open lobby accented by Tlingit and Haida artwork, an interesting collection of museum-quality artifacts, and a roaring fire. The spacious rooms are attractively decorated with traditional tribal colors and watercolors of Alaskan birds. All rooms have views of either Tongass Narrows or Deer Mountain. Heen Kahidi Dining Room serves seafood, pasta, chicken, and steaks. Be sure to reserve one of the window tables that overlook Ketchikan. ✉ *800 Venetia Way, 99901* ☎ *907/225–8001, 866/225–8001 reservations* 🖷 *907/225–8286* 🌐 *www.westcoasthotels.com* *70 rooms, 2 suites* *Restaurant, room service, cable TV with movies and video games, lounge, meeting room; no a/c* ▭ *AE, D, DC, MC, V.*

★ **$–$$** **New York Hotel and Cafe.** Now more than a century old, this quaint little hotel has delightful rooms and one of the nicest eateries in Ketchikan. The menu includes breakfasts and lunches, plus dinners on Friday and Saturday nights that always include steak and fresh seafood. Hotel rooms are not large, but are comfortably furnished in antiques and queen beds. Three luxury suites along Creek Street are the real attraction here. Each of these includes a full kitchen, jetted tub, loft bedroom (with spiral staircase), and deck overlooking the water. ✉ *207 Stedman St., 99901* ☎ *907/225–0246 or 866/225–0246* 🌐 *www.thenewyorkhotel.com* *11 12 rooms* *Restaurant, some in-room hot tubs, some kitchens, cable TV; no a/c, no smoking* ▭ *AE, D, MC, V* ⏲ *Restaurant closed mid-Sept. to May.*

$ **Gilmore Hotel.** Think of the Gilmore as a boutique hotel without boutique prices. The 1930s-era lobby has a European feel, and rooms, though not large, blend old-fashioned comfort with modern furnishings. The lack of elevator may be a problem for some travelers, but all the other amenities are here, including a courtesy van to shuttle you around town. A light breakfast is included each morning. Downstairs, Annabelle's Keg and Chowder House serves seafood, pasta, and prime rib. ✉ *326 Front St., 99901* ☎ *907/225–9423 or 800/275–9423* 🖷 *907/225–7442* 🌐 *www.gilmorehotel.com* *38 rooms, 2 suites* *Restaurant, cable*

TV, bar, lounge, wireless Internet, some pets allowed; no a/c ▤ AE, D, DC, MC, V |O| CP.

$$–$$$ ▦ **The Narrows Inn.** Four miles from town and a mile north of the airport ferry terminal, the Narrows is a modern lodge where rustic wood trim and themed prints on the walls brighten the small hotel rooms. Waterside rooms, including three spacious suites, have balconies overlooking Tongass Narrows—a good place to watch seals, otters, and eagles. There is a van with scheduled runs into Ketchikan for dining and shopping and a delicious on-the-premises steak-and-seafood restaurant with a waterfront bar. ⌖ *Box 8296, 99901* ☎ *907/247–2600 or 888/686–2600* 🖷 *907/247–2602* ⊕ *www.narrowsinn.com* ⇝ *44 rooms, 3 suites* ⌂ *Restaurant, microwaves, refrigerators, cable TV, bar, Internet, airport shuttle; no a/c* ▤ *AE, D, MC, V.*

$–$$$ ▦ **Cedars Lodge.** This small lodge has motel-style accommodations on the street side and deluxe suites whose large windows face Tongass Narrows. The latter are great for a front-row view of the floatplanes, boats, and cruise ships that parade past all summer. All rooms have Jacuzzi baths, and suites also include full kitchens. Various fishing and lodging packages are available, including four nights' lodging and three days of meals and guided fishing for $1,646–$1,875 per person. Lodging-only rates apply if space is available. ⊠ *1471 Tongass Ave., Box 8331, 99901* ☎ *907/225–1900 or 800/813–4363* 🖷 *907/225–8604* ⊕ *www.cedarslodge.com* ⇝ *8 rooms, 5 suites* ⌂ *Restaurant, in-room hot tubs, some kitchens, cable TV; no a/c* ▤ *AE, D, DC, MC, V* ⊘ *Closed Oct.–mid-May.*

$$ ▦ **Madame's Manor Bed & Breakfast.** This luxurious B&B provides the full Victorian treatment, with three extravagantly decorated suites. You'll find rose wallpaper, queen-size canopy beds, antique furnishings, kitchenettes, dramatic harbor views, and exquisite private baths. The nicest suite includes a hot tub and solarium. Enjoy a gourmet breakfast on the deck overlooking bustling Tongass Narrows. A two-night minimum stay is required for the B&B. Two hillside apartments (Country Manor Vacation Rentals) are also available, starting for $110 a night plus $15 for extra guests. These are perfect for families. ⊠ *324 Cedar St., 99901* ☎ *907/247–2774 or 877/531–8159 Ext. 2484* ⊕ *www.madamesmanor.com* ⇝ *3 suites* ⌂ *Cable TV; no a/c, no smoking* ▤ *MC, V* |O| *BP.*

$–$$ ▦ **Blueberry Hill Bed & Breakfast.** On a downtown hillside near the tunnel, this charming historic home features four bright and spacious second-floor guest rooms with handmade quilts, down comforters, private baths, and friendly owners. The parlor and dining room are on the main level, and a filling home-cooked breakfast is served each morning. Alaskan art and collectibles provide a homey touch, and guests can picnic in the flower-filled yard. Kids are welcome, and one room is set up for families. ⊠ *500 Front St., 99901* ☎ *907/247–2583 or 877/449–2583* 🖷 *907/247–2583* ⊕ *www.blueberryhillbb.com* ⇝ *4 rooms* ⌂ *Cable TV, parking; no a/c, no smoking* ▤ *D, MC, V* |O| *BP.*

¢ △ **Ward Lake Campgrounds.** Two rain-forest campgrounds are located 8 mi north of Ketchikan; turn right onto Revilla Road and follow it to the exceptionally scenic Ward Lake area. Both are managed by the Forest Service, with sites reservable ($9 extra) through **Reserve USA** (☎ 518/885–3639 or 877/444–6777 🌐 www.reserveusa.com). Signal Creek Campground has 24 campsites adjacent to Ward Lake, a popular fishing, hiking, and picnicking area. Last Chance Campground is a mile farther up Revilla Road, and has 19 creekside sites. Running water and restrooms (no showers) are provided. ☎ *907/225–2148* 🌐 *www.fs.fed.us/r10/tongass* 🎫 *$10* 💳 *AE, D, MC, V.*

Guided Tours

Owned by Goldbelt Native corporation, **Alaska Cruises** (☎ 907/225–6044 or 800/228–1905 📠 907/225–8636 🌐 www.mistyfjord.net) runs harbor tours of the Ketchikan waterfront during which you'll learn local history and get a sea-level view of this bustling town. The company also provides speedy catamaran excursions from downtown Ketchikan to Misty Fiords National Monument. A Native-owned company, **Cape Fox Tours** (☎ 907/225–4846 📠 907/225–3137 🌐 www.capefoxtours.com) leads tours of Saxman Native Village and the historic George Inlet Cannery. You can book most of these tours aboard the cruise ships or at Ketchikan Visitors Bureau.

Nightlife & the Arts

Bars

Ketchikan has quieted down in recent years as the economy shifted away from logging into tourism, but remains something of a party town, especially when crews stumble off fishing boats with cash in hand. You won't have any trouble finding something going on at several downtown bars. **First City Saloon** (✉ 830 Water St. ☎ 907/225–1494) is the main dance spot, with live rock, blues, or jazz Tuesday–Saturday. The **Potlatch Bar** (✉ Thomas Basin ☎ 907/225–4855) delivers up music most weekends.

Sports & the Outdoors

Fishing

Sportfishing for salmon and trout is excellent in the Ketchikan area, in either saltwater or freshwater lakes and streams. Contact the **Ketchikan Visitors Bureau** for information on guide services and locations.

Spectator Sports

The **Great Alaskan Lumberjack Show** is a 90-minute lumberjack contest providing a Disneyesque taste of old-time woodsman skills, including ax throwing, bucksawing, springboard chopping, log-rolling duels, and a 50-foot tree climb that ends in a free fall. Shows take place in a covered grandstand directly behind the Spruce Mill Development and go on rain or shine all summer. ✉ *50 Main St.* ☎ *907/225–9050 or 888/320–9049* 🌐 *www.lumberjackshows.com* 🎫 *$31* ⏲ *May–Sept., 3 times daily; hrs vary.*

Hiking

Get details on hiking opportunities around Ketchikan from the Southeast Alaska Discovery Center (⇨ What to See, *above*). If you're an avid hiker, the 3-mi trail from downtown to the 3,000-foot summit of **Deer Mountain** will repay your efforts with a spectacular panorama of the city below and the wilderness behind. The trail begins at the corner of Fair and Deermount streets, and passes through dense forests before emerging into the alpine. A shelter cabin near the summit provides a place to warm up.

Ward Lake Recreation Area, about 6 mi north of town, has hikes next to lakes and streams and beneath towering spruce and hemlock trees; it also has several covered picnic spots and a pleasant campground. An easy 1.3-mi nature trail circles the lake, which is popular for steelhead and salmon fishing. **Ward Creek Trail** begins from the lake and follows the creek 2.5 mi, with shoreside paths to creekside platforms. The trail is hard-packed gravel, but wide and gentle enough for wheelchairs. More ambitious hikers head up the 2-mi **Perseverance Trail,** a challenging set of steps and boardwalk that take hikers through the open muskeg (peat bog) to a small lake.

Scuba Diving

Alaska Diving Service (✉ 5194 Shoreline Dr. ☎ 907/225–3667) rents tanks and equipment and guides you to the best places to dive in these pristine waters. You'll see colorful fish, sea cucumbers, starfish, soft corals, and other creatures.

Sea Kayaking

Popular with cruise-ship travelers, **Southeast Exposure** (☎ 907/225–8829 🌐 www.southeastexposure.com) offers waterfront paddles on Clover Pass. **Southeast Sea Kayaks** (☎ 907/225–1258 or 800/287–1607 🌐 www.kayakketchikan.com) leads kayak tours of Ketchikan's historic waterfront and offers kayak lessons and rentals. They specialize in guided multinight trips to Misty Fiords.

Shopping

Art Galleries

AlaskaMade Gallery (✉ 123 Stedman St. ☎ 907/225–5404 or 888/877–9706 🌐 www.alaskamade.com) is a small creekside gallery with art, *ulus* (a curved Eskimo knife), cards, gifts, and even Alaskan-roasted coffees.

In business since 1972, **Scanlon Gallery** (✉ 318 Mission St. ☎ 907/247–4730 or 888/228–4730 🌐 www.scanlongallery.com) carries prints from a number of well-known Alaska artists, including Byron Birdsall, Rie Muñoz, John Fehringer, Barbara Lavallee, and Jon Van Zyle.

Design, art, and clothing converge in the stylish **Soho Coho Contemporary Art and Craft Gallery** (✉ 5 Creek St. ☎ 907/225–5954 or 800/888–4070 🌐 www.trollart.com), where you'll find an eclectic collection of art and T-shirts featuring the work of owner Ray Troll—best known for his wacky fish art—as well as that of other Southeast Alaskan artists.

Books

Upstairs from the Soho Coho Gallery, **Parnassus** (✉ 5 Creek St. ☎ 907/225–7690) is a book lover's bookstore, with many Alaskan titles and a knowledgeable staff.

Seafood

For some of the Southeast's best canned, smoked, or frozen salmon and halibut, along with crab, clams, and all kinds of other seafood, try either of the two locations of **Salmon Etc.** (✉ 10 Creek St. ☎ 907/225–6008 or 800/354–7256 ✉ 322 Mission St. ☎ 907/225–6008 🌐 www.salmonetc.com).

AROUND KETCHIKAN

Misty Fiords National Monument

18 *40 mi east of Ketchikan by air.*

Misty Fiords National Monument is a wilderness of cliff-faced fjords (or fiords, if you follow the monument's spelling), mountains, and islands with an abundance of spectacular coastal scenery, wildlife, and recreation. Small boats enable close-up views of breathtaking vistas. Travel on these waters can be an almost mystical experience, with the greens of the forest reflected in waters as still as black mirrors. You may find yourself in the company of a whale, see a bear fishing for salmon along the shore, or even pull in your own salmon for an evening meal. Note, however, that the name Misty refers to the weather you're likely to encounter in this rainy part of Alaska.

Fodor'sChoice ★ Most visitors to Misty Fiords arrive on day trips via floatplane from Ketchikan or on board a catamaran run by **Alaska Cruises** (☎ 907/225–6044 or 800/228–1905 🌐 www.mistyfjord.net). ✉ *3031 Tongass Ave., Ketchikan 99901* ☎ *907/225–2148* 🌐 *www.fs.fed.us/r10/tongass.*

Metlakatla

19 *12 mi south of Ketchikan.*

The village of Metlakatla is on Annette Island, just a dozen miles from busy Ketchikan but a world away culturally. A visit to this quiet and conservative place offers the chance to learn about life in a small Inside Passage native community. Local taxis can take you to other sights around the island, including Yellow Hill and the old air force base.

In most Southeast Native villages, the people are Tlingit or Haida in heritage. Metlakatla is the exception, as most folks are Tsimshian (*sim*-shee-ann). They moved to the island from British Columbia in 1887, led by William Duncan, an Anglican missionary from England. The town grew rapidly and soon included dozens of buildings laid out on a grid of streets—a cannery, a sawmill, and a church that could seat a thousand people. Congress declared Annette Island a federal Indian reservation in 1891, and it remains the only reservation in Alaska today. Father Duncan continued to control life in Metlakatla for decades, until the government finally stepped in shortly before his death in 1918.

During World War II the U.S. Army built a major air base 7 mi from Metlakatla that included observation towers for Japanese subs, airplane hangars, gun emplacements, and housing for 10,000 soldiers.

After the war, it served as Ketchikan's airport for many years, but today the long runways are virtually abandoned save for a few private flights.

Metlakatla's religious heritage still shows through today. The clapboard **William Duncan Memorial Church,** topped with two steeples, burned in 1948 but was rebuilt several years later. It is one of nine churches in tiny Metlakatla. **Father Duncan's Cottage** is maintained as it was when he was alive and includes numerous artifacts, personal items, and historic photographs. ✉ *Corner of 4th Ave. and Church St.* ☎ *907/886–8687* 🌐 *www.metlakatlatours.com* 🎟 *$2* ⏲ *Weekdays 8:30–12:30 or when cruise ships are in port.*

Father Duncan worked hard to eliminate traditional Tsimshian beliefs and dances, but today the people of Metlakatla have resurrected their past for tourists, and perform some of these old dances and stories in traditional regalia. The best place to see this is at the traditional **longhouse,** which faces Metlakatla's boat harbor. Three totem poles stand on the back side of the building, and the front is covered with a Tsimshian design. Inside are displays of Native crafts and a model of the fish traps that were once common throughout the Inside Passage. Native dance groups perform here on Wednesday and Friday in summer. Just next to the longhouse is an **Artists' Village** where booths display locally made arts and crafts. The village and longhouse open when groups and tours are present.

Two miles from town is a boardwalk path that leads up the 540-foot **Yellow Hill.** Distinctive yellow sandstone rocks and panoramic vistas make this a worthwhile detour on clear days.

Where to Stay & Eat

$ **Metlakatla Inn and Café.** This two-story building offers standard motel accommodations with private decks off the upstairs rooms. The restaurant has the usual American favorites such as burgers and steak, but the fresh halibut and shrimp are the real attractions. Breakfast is available only for hotel guests. ✉ *3rd Ave. and Lower Milton St., 99926* ☎ *907/886–3456* 📠 *907/886–3455* *7 rooms, 2 apartments* *Restaurant, microwaves, refrigerators, cable TV, in-room VCRs; no a/c, no smoking* 💳 *AE, D, MC, V.*

$ **Tuck'em Inn Bed & Breakfast.** This family-run lodging is located in two downtown houses. Rooms are functional, with down comforters, quilts, and access to a kitchen and sitting room. Ingredients for a make-yourself Continental breakfast are included. ✉ *Hillcrest and Calvin Sts., 99926* ☎ *907/886–6611* 📠 *907/886–7855* *6 rooms* *Cable TV; no a/c, no smoking* 🌐 *www.alaskanow.com/tuckem-inn* 💳 *MC, V* *CP.*

Guided Tours

You can catch a ferry operated by the **Alaska Marine Highway System** to Metlakatla from Ketchikan. Run by the Metlakatla community, **Metlakatla Tours** (☎ 907/886–4441 📠 907/886–4346 🌐 www.metlakatlatours.com) leads local tours that include visits to Duncan Cottage, the cannery, and the longhouse, along with a Tsimshian dance performance. **ProMech Air** (☎ 907/886–3845 or 800/860–3845 🌐 www.promechair.com) has scheduled floatplane flights between Ketchikan and Metlakatla.

Hyder

20 *90 mi northeast of Ketchikan.*

The tiny town of Hyder sits at the head of narrow Portland Canal, a 70-mi-long fjord northeast of Ketchikan. The fjord marks the border between Canada and the United States, and Hyder sits just 2 mi from the larger town of Stewart, British Columbia. Highway 37A continues over spectacular Bear Pass from Stewart, connecting these towns with the rest of Canada.

The 1898 discovery of gold and silver in the surrounding mountains brought a flood of miners to the Hyder area, and the town eventually became a major shipping port. Mining remained important for decades, but a devastating 1948 fire destroyed much of the town, which had been built on pilings over the water. A small amount of mining still takes place here, but the beauty of the area now attracts increasing numbers of tourists. Today, quiet Hyder calls itself "the friendliest ghost town in Alaska."

The town of Hyder is small and has only a handful of tourist-oriented businesses, a post office, and library. Nearby Stewart has more to offer, including a bank, museum, hotels, restaurants, and camping. You will need to check in at Canadian customs (open 24 hours) before crossing the border from Hyder into Stewart. Canadian money is primarily used in Hyder, but greenbacks are certainly accepted.

The **Stewart Historical Society Museum** contains wildlife displays and exhibits on the region's mining history. ✉ *6th and Columbia Sts.* ☎ *250/636–2568* 🌐 *www.stewartmuseum.homestead.com* 🎟 *$2* ⏲ *May, June, and Sept., weekends 1–4; July and Aug., daily 1–4.*

A small, empty **stone storehouse** stands along the road as you enter Hyder. Built in 1896, this is the oldest masonry building in Alaska.

Six miles north of Hyder on Salmon River Road is the **Fish Creek Wildlife Observation Site.** From late July to early September, a large run of salmon attracts black and brown bears here, which, in turn, attract more than a few photographers. The creek produces some of the largest chum salmon anywhere. Twenty-five miles east of Stewart on Highway 37A is the imposing **Bear Glacier.** The glacier sits across a small lake that is often crowded with icebergs. A dirt road from Hyder leads 17 mi to remote **Salmon Glacier,** one of few glaciers accessible by road in Southeast Alaska.

Getting "Hyderized" (which involves drinking and drinking-related silliness) is a term that you will hear upon arrival in the area. You can get Hyderized at **Glacier Inn** (✉ Main St. ☎ 250/636–9243), where the walls are papered with thousands of signed bills. The tradition supposedly began when prospectors would tack a dollar bill on the wall in case they were broke when they returned.

Where to Stay & Eat

$–$$$ ✕ **Bitter Creek Cafe.** This bustling Stewart café serves a variety of cuisine, including gourmet steaks, pizzas, lasagna, burgers, seafood, and even Mexican dishes. It's all homemade, including the freshly baked breads. The quirky interior is adorned with a fun collection of antiques as well as a 1930 Pontiac. Relax on the outside deck on a summer afternoon. *5th Ave., Stewart* *250/636–2166* *AE, MC, V* *Closed Oct.–Apr.*

¢–$ **Ripley Creek Inn.** Stewart's best lodging option covers three historic downtown buildings. All rooms are bright, with Mission-style furnishings; some also include sofa beds, decks, and glacier views. The main building also houses Toastworks Museum, a repository of antique toasters and other kitchen items. Fittingly enough, this is where Continental breakfasts are served for inn guests. *Box 625, Stewart* *250/636–2344* *250/636–2623* *www.ripleycreekinn.homestead.com* *34 rooms* *Cable TV, sauna, some pets allowed; no a/c* *AE, DC, MC, V* *CP.*

Guided Tours

Seaport Limousine (250/636–2622 www.tkp-biz.com/seaportlimousine) leads guided tours of the Hyder area, including Fish Creek and Salmon Glacier. **Taquan Air** (907/225–8800, 800/770–8800, or 250/636–9150 www.taquanair.com) has year-round service between Ketchikan and Hyder every Monday and Thursday ($165 one-way).

Prince of Wales Island

21 *15 mi northwest of Ketchikan.*

Prince of Wales Island stretches more than 130 mi from north to south, making it the largest island in Southeast Alaska. Only two American islands—Kodiak in Alaska and Hawaii in the Hawaiian chain—are larger. Prince of Wales (or "P.O.W." as locals call it) has a diversity of landforms, a plethora of wildlife, and exceptional sportfishing. The island has long been a major source of timber, both on Tongass National Forest lands and those owned by Native corporations. Much of the Native land has been cut over, and environmental restrictions on public lands have greatly reduced logging activity. The island's economy is now supported by small-scale logging operations, tourism, sportfishing, and commercial fishing.

Approximately 7,000 people live on Prince of Wales Island, scattered in small villages and towns around the island. A network of 1,500 mi of roads—nearly all built to access clear-cuts—crisscrosses the island, providing connections to even the smallest settlement. Paved roads now link Craig, Hollis, Thorne Bay, and Hydaburg, and the road will be completed to Coffman Cove by 2005. The prevalence of roads, combined with ferry and air access from Ketchikan, makes it easy to explore this island.

The primary commercial center for Prince of Wales is **Craig,** on the island's western shore. This town of 2,000 retains a hard-edged aura fast disappearing in Inside Passage towns, where tourism now holds sway. Commercial fishing, sportfishing, and logging and government jobs support this community. Although sightseeing attractions are slim, the town exudes a frontier spirit, and its small-boat harbors buzz with activity. *Prince of Wales Chamber of Commerce, Box 490, Klawock 99925* *907/755–2626* *www.princeofwalescoc.org.*

The **Inter-Island Ferry Authority** (☎ 907/826–4848 or 866/308–4848 🌐 www.interislandferry.com) operates a daily vehicle and passenger ferry between Ketchikan and Prince of Wales Island. The ferry terminal is in the tiny settlement of Hollis, 31 mi from Craig on a paved road. In 2006 a separate ferry service connecting Coffman Cove on the north end of Prince of Wales with the towns of Wrangell and Petersburg is scheduled to begin.

A half-dozen miles from Craig is the Tlingit village of **Klawock,** with a sawmill, cannery, hatchery, and the island's only airport. The town is best known for its striking 21 totem poles in **Totem Park.** Several of these colorful poles were moved here in the 1930s when an old village site was abandoned; others are more recent carvings. You can watch carvers restoring old totems at the carving shed, across the road from the grocery store. Klawock is also home to **Prince of Wales Hatchery** (☎ 907/755–2231 🌐 www.powhasalmon.org ⏲ Tours June–Aug., Mon.–Sat. 1–5), where salmon are raised in a canal adjacent to Klawock Lake. It's open for free summertime tours, and it also has a small visitor center with an aquarium full of young coho salmon. Along the bay, you'll find **St. John's by the Sea Catholic Church,** with stained-glass windows picturing Alaskan Natives.

The Haida village of **Hydaburg,** approximately 40 mi south of Klawock (via chip-sealed road), lies along scenic Sukkwan Strait. A small collection of **totem poles** occupies the center of this Haida settlement, the only one in Alaska. Originally from British Columbia's Queen Charlotte Islands, the Haida settled here around 1700.

A number of large natural caverns pockmark northern Prince of Wales Island. The best-known of these, **El Capitan Cave,** has one of the deepest pits in the United States and is open to the public. Paleontologists have found a wealth of black bear, brown bear, and other mammal fossils in the cave, including some that date back more than 12,000 years. The Forest Service leads free two-hour El Capitan tours several times a week in the summer. Reservations are required, and no children under age seven are permitted. Rubber boots and a light jacket are a good idea for spelunkers. ✉ *Mile 51 along North Prince of Wales Rd.* ☎ *907/828–3304 (Forest Service).*

Where to Stay & Eat

$$$$ ✕🏨 **Shelter Cove Lodge.** Tall windows front the water at this modern restaurant and lodge along the South Boat Harbor in Craig. Fresh seafood tops the menu, along with steaks, delectable desserts, and nightly specials. Prime rib attracts the locals on Friday and Saturday nights. The lodge here runs all-inclusive fishing packages, starting at $1,750 per person for a three days and four nights. Rooms are modern and each contains a queen and twin bed. Six of them face the harbor. ✉ *703 Hamilton Dr., Craig 99921* ☎ *907/826–2939 or 888/826–3474* 📠 *907/826–2941* 🌐 *www.sheltercovelodge.com* *10 rooms* *Microwaves, refrigerators, cable TV, boating, fishing; no a/c* 💳 *AE, MC, V* ⏲ *Restaurant closed Oct.–May.*

$$$$ 🏨 **McFarland's Floatel.** You'll need a boat or floatplane to access this quiet resort across the bay from the logging town of Thorne Bay on the eastern side of Prince of Wales. Each of the four beachfront log cabins sleeps up to six people and includes a loft, woodstove, full kitchen, and private bath. A 200-foot walkway leads to the floating main lodge, which serves hearty home-cooked seafood dinners for $25 (reservations required). Co-owner Jeannie McFarland teaches basketry workshops and sells her pine-needle raffia baskets here. Charter-fishing trips are available, or you can rent a skiff and fishing gear and head out on your own. *Box 19149, Thorne Bay 99919 907/828–3335 or 888/828–3335 www.mcfarlandsfloatel.com 4 cabins Boating, fishing, car rental; no a/c, no room phones, no room TVs, no smoking MC, V.*

$$$$ Fodor's Choice ★ **Waterfall Resort.** At this upscale fishing lodge, you sleep in Cape Cod–style cottages from the 1930s, eat bountiful meals with all the trimmings, and fish from custom-built 25-foot cabin cruisers under the care of a fishing guide. You can also have the fish you catch processed, packaged, and shipped. A three-night minimum stay with all meals, including floatplane fare from Ketchikan, comes to around $3,265 per person. This former commercial salmon cannery is a popular retreat for business groups. *Box 6440, Ketchikan 99901 907/225–9461 or 800/544–5125 907/225–8530 www.waterfallresort.com 10 lodge rooms, 4 suites, 26 cabins Restaurant, boating, fishing, meeting rooms; no a/c, no room phones, no room TVs, no kids under 10 AE, D, MC, V FAP Closed Sept.–late May.*

$ **Ruth Ann's Motel.** Victorian-style furnishings and details flavor this classy motel. The honeymoon suite includes a large hot tub and kitchenette. Across the street, the popular Ruth Ann's Restaurant serves home-style food with seafood and steaks at dinner, and burgers, sandwiches, and fish-and-chips at lunch. Ask for a table in the back room, where picture windows face the harbor; a tiny bar at the front of the restaurant fills up most nights. *300 Water St., Craig 99921 907/826–3378 907/826–3293 14 rooms, 1 suite Restaurant, some microwaves, refrigerators, cable TV; no a/c AE, D, DC, MC, V.*

WRANGELL

22–29 *50 mi northwest of Thorne Bay on Prince of Wales Island.*

A small, unassuming timber and fishing community, Wrangell is on an island near the mouth of the fast-flowing Stikine River and like much of the Southeast, has suffered in recent years from a poor economy. Wrangell has flown three different national flags in its time. Russia established Redoubt St. Dionysius here in 1834. Five years later, Great Britain's Hudson's Bay Company leased the southern Alaska coastline, renaming the settlement Fort Stikine. It became Wrangell when the Americans took over in 1867; the name came from Baron Ferdinand Petrovich von Wrangel, governor of the Russian-American Company.

Exploring Wrangell

The rough-around-the-edges town of Wrangell is off the track of the larger cruise ships, so it does not suffer from tourist invasions to the degree that Ketchikan and Juneau do. The town is fairly compact, and most sights are within walking distance of the city dock or ferry terminal.

a good walk

A good place to start your tour is the surprisingly impressive **Nolan Museum and Civic Center** 22 which also houses a helpful visitor center. Head through town along Front Street, stopping at **Kiksetti Totem Park** 23 before turning onto Shakes Street to see Wrangell's most interesting sight, **Chief Shakes Island** 24. You will probably want to spend time here just soaking in the harbor view and examining the old totem poles. **Chief Shakes's grave site** 25 is on the hill overlooking Wrangell Harbor. Get there from Chief Shakes Island by turning right on Case Avenue. From the grave site, head up Church Street to the **Irene Ingle Public Library** 26 by continuing up Church Street and turning right on 2nd Street. Head ⅔ mi north of the ferry terminal along Evergreen Avenue to **Petroglyph Beach** 27, where ancient etchings are visible along the shore. For a woodsy hike, climb **Mount Dewey** 28, the hill right behind town. Farther afield (5 mi south of town) is the fun hike to **Rainbow Falls** 29.

TIMING It is a 1½-mi walk between Petroglyph Beach and Chief Shakes Island, so you should plan at least three hours to complete the walk and sightseeing around town.

What to See

off the beaten path

ANAN CREEK WILDLIFE OBSERVATORY – About 30 mi southeast of Wrangell in the Tongass National Forest, Anan is one of Alaska's premier black- and brown-bear viewing areas. Each summer, from early July to mid-August, as many as 30 to 40 black bears gather at this Southeast stream to feed on pink salmon. On an average visit of about two hours you might spot two to four bears. Forest Service interpreters are on hand to answer questions. The site is accessible only by boat or floatplane. **Alaska Waters** (☎ 907/874–2378 or 800/347–4462 🌐 www.alaskawaters.com) is one of several local companies that offer day trips to Anan Creek. For additional details, contact the **Tongass National Forest Wrangell Ranger District** (☎ 907/874–2323 🌐 www.fs.fed.us/r10/tongass).

★ 24 **Chief Shakes Island.** This small island sits in the center of Wrangell's protected harbor, and is accessible by a footbridge from the bottom of Front Street. Seven totem poles surround a traditional-style tribal house, built in the 1930s as a replica of one that was home to many of the various Shakes and their peoples. ✉ *Off Shakes St.* ☎ *907/874–3747* 🎫 *$2* ⏲ *Daily when cruise ships are in port (ask at Wrangell Visitor Center) or by appointment.*

25 **Chief Shakes's grave site.** Buried here is Shakes V, who led the local Tlingit during the first half of the 19th century. A white picket fence surrounds the grave, and two killer-whale totem poles mark his resting spot overlooking the harbor. Find the grave on Case Avenue. ✉ *Case Ave.*

26 **Irene Ingle Public Library.** The library, behind the post office, has two ancient petroglyphs out front, and is home to a large collection of Alaskana books along with computers to check your e-mail. ✉ *124 2nd St.* ☎ *907/874–3535.*

23 **Kiksetti Totem Park.** You'll find a couple of recently carved totem poles at this pocket-size park of Alaska greenery. ✉ *Front St.*

Chief Shakes Island 24
Chief Shakes's grave site 25
Irene Ingle Public Library 26
Kiksetti Totem Park 23
Mount Dewey 28
Nolan Museum and Civic Center . . .22
Petroglyph Beach 27
Rainbow Falls 29

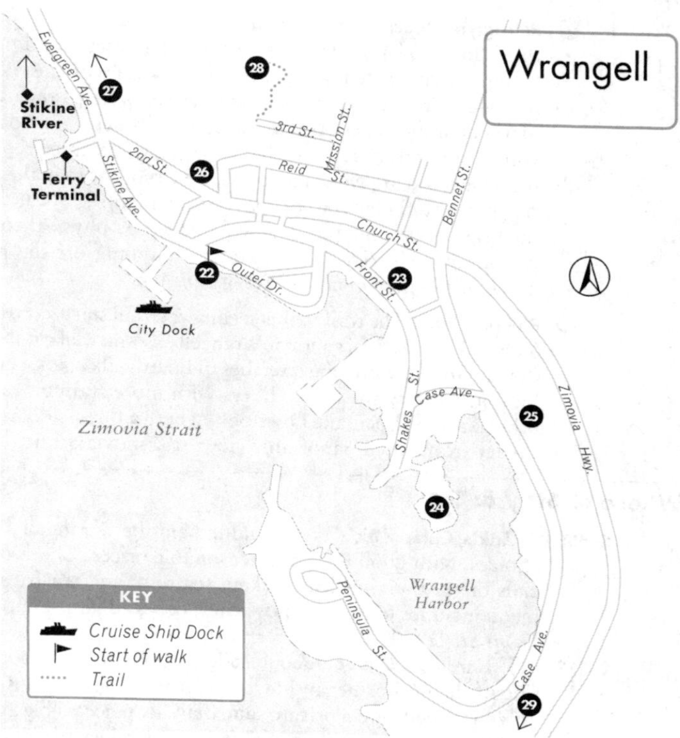

28 **Mount Dewey.** Despite the name, this is actually just a small hill right behind Wrangell. It's a steep 15-minute climb to the top through a second-growth forest. The trail begins from 3rd Street behind the high school, and a viewpoint on top provides an obscured vista across protected waterways and forested islands.

22 **Nolan Museum and Civic Center.** Wrangell's museum moved into spacious new quarters in 2004, a building that acts as a centerpiece for cultural life in Wrangell. Professionally produced exhibits provide a window on the region's rich history. Featured pieces include decorative posts from Chief Shakes's clan house (carved in the late 1700s), petroglyphs, century-old spruce-root and cedar-bark baskets, masks, items from Russian and English settlers, gold-rush memorabilia, and a fascinating photo collection. The building also houses a 200-seat movie theater/performance space and the **Wrangell Visitor Center** (☎ 907/874–3901 or 800/367–9745 🖷 907/874–3905 🌐 www.wrangellchamber.org). The latter is staffed when the museum is open and has details on local adventure options; stop by to watch videos on the Stikine River and the town of Wrangell. ✉ *296 Outer Dr.* ☎ *907/874–3770* 🎟 *$5* ⏲ *May–Sept., Tues.–Sat. 10–5, and when ferry or cruise ships are in port; Oct.–Apr., Tues.–Sat. 1–5.*

27 **Petroglyph Beach.** Scattered among other rocks at this public beach are three dozen or more large stones bearing designs and pictures chiseled by unknown, ancient artists. No one knows why the rocks at this curious site were etched the way they were; perhaps they were boundary markers or messages. You can access the beach via a boardwalk, where you'll find signs describing the site along with carved replicas of the petroglyphs. You are welcome to use these replicas to make a rubbing from rice paper and charcoal or crayons (available in local stores). Because the original petroglyphs can be damaged by physical contact, the state discourages visitors from creating a rubbing off the rocks. ✉ *⅔ mi north of ferry terminal off Evergreen Ave.*

29 **Rainbow Falls.** The trail to this scenic waterfall starts across the road from Shoemaker Bay, 5 mi south of Wrangell. A ¾-mi trail climbs uphill through the rain forest, with long stretches of boardwalk steps, ending at an overlook just below the falls. Hikers with more stamina can continue another 3 mi to Shoemake Overlook, where a three-side Adirondack-style shelter fronts on a panoramic view of Zimovia Strait.

Where to Stay & Eat

$–$$$ ✕ **Zak's Cafe.** Zak's is a standout among Wrangell's limited dining choices, with good food and reasonable prices. Check out today's specials or try their steaks, chicken, seafood, and stir-fries. At lunch, the menu includes burgers, sandwiches, fish-and-chips, and wraps. ✉ *314 Front St.* ☎ *907/874–3355* ▭ *MC, V.*

$–$$$ ✕🏨 **Harding's Old Sourdough Lodge.** This rambling lodge on the south side of the harbor began life as a construction camp. Rooms are modestly furnished, and a private suite (handicap-accessible and large enough for six people) has a large bathroom with a heated floor and a hot tub. Home-style meals ($16–20 for dinner), including fresh sourdough breads and fresh seafood, are also available for those not staying here (advance reservations required). ✉ *1104 Peninsula St., Box 1062, 99929* ☎ *907/874–3613 or 800/874–3613* 📠 *907/874–3455* 🌐 *www.akgetaway.com* 🛏 *16 rooms* 👍 *Dining room, sauna, steam room, boating, Internet, meeting room, airport shuttle, some pets allowed; no a/c, no TV in some rooms, no smoking* ▭ *AE, D, DC, MC, V* 🍽 *BP.*

★ $$$$ 🏨 **Rain Haven Lodge.** This one-room lodge is actually a surprisingly cozy houseboat and a wonderful way to enjoy the wilderness in comfort. During the summer, the houseboat is anchored in a remote cove south of Wrangell, with a canoe for access to nearby hiking trails and spectacular scenery. It's perfect for couples and small families, with a double bed and pull-out couch. The galley (stocked with staples) is equipped with a stove, sink, and cooler. There's a sunny atrium at the stern and a covered deck on the bow. Three-day stays cost $700, including transportation from Wrangell and a Stikine River jet-boat trip. Owner Marie Oboczky leads local tours, and is very knowledgeable about the area. 📫 *Box 2074, 99929* ☎ *907/874–2549* 📠 *907/874–2548* 🌐 *www.rainwalkerexpeditions.com* 🛏 *1 room* 👍 *Kitchen; no a/c, no room TVs, no smoking* ▭ *No credit cards.*

$ 🏨 **Grand View Bed & Breakfast.** Two miles from town, this contemporary hillside home provides spectacular views across Zimovia Strait.

Rooms, some with antiques and some decorated Alaskan style, have private baths and entrances, plus access to a large common area. Friendly owners John and Judy Baker have lived in Alaska for more than 50 years, and prepare delectable breakfasts, including freshly baked rolls. *Box 927, 99929 907/874–3225 www.grandviewbnb.com 3 rooms Cable TV; no a/c No credit cards BP.*

$ **Rooney's Roost Bed & Breakfast.** This century-old home just a block from downtown has been lovingly remodeled and decorated with a country theme that includes an amusing collection of rooster art (hence the name). Friendly owners, a large-screen television, and a filling breakfast add to its homey appeal. *206 McKinnon St., 99929 907/874–2026 www.rooneysroost.com 6 rooms, 3 with bath Airport shuttle; no TV in some rooms MC, V BP.*

¢ **Shakes Slough Cabins.** If you're a hot-springs or hot-tub enthusiast, these Forest Service cabins on the Stikine River, accessible from Wrangell, are worth checking out. Shakes Slough Hot Springs are a short boat ride away from the cabins. Here you can soak in both an open-air hot tub and an enclosed version. These remote and very rustic cabins sleep six on plywood bunks, and feature basic facilities, including outhouses and woodstoves, but no water or electricity. Bring your own sleeping bag, food, and cooking utensils. Reservations are required for the cabins; request details from the Forest Service office in Wrangell or make reservations by calling **ReserveUSA** (877/444–6777). *Forest Service, 525 Bennett St., Wrangell 99929 907/874–2323 907/874–7595 www.reserveusa.com 2 cabins Hot tub AE, D, MC, V.*

Guided Tours

Alaska Vistas (907/874–3006 or 866/874–3006 www.alaskavistas.com) has jet-boat trips to Anan Creek Wildlife Observatory that depart from Wrangell, plus a variety of guided sea-kayak adventures. **Breakaway Adventures** (907/874–2488 or 888/385–2488 www.breakawayadventures.com) leads day trips up the majestic Stikine River by jet boat, including a visit to Chief Shakes Glacier, along with time to take a dip at Chief Shakes Hot Springs. Mark Galla of **Alaska Peak Adventures** (907/874–2454 www.wedoalaska.com) guides wildlife trips, Stikine jet-boat tours, and boat trips to surrounding areas. **Rain Walker Expeditions** (907/874–2549) leads excellent natural-history tours of the Wrangell area. **Sunrise Aviation** (907/874–2319 or 800/874–2311 907/874–2546 www.sunriseflights.com) is a charter-only air carrier that offers trips to the Anan Creek Wildlife Observatory, LeConte Glacier, or Forest Service cabins.

Sports & the Outdoors

Fishing

Numerous companies schedule salmon- and trout-fishing excursions ranging in length from an afternoon to a week. Contact the **Wrangell Visitor Center** for information on guide services and locations.

Golf

Muskeg Meadows Golf Course (☎ 907/874–4653 🖷 907/874–4654 🌐 www.wrangellalaskagolf.com), in a wooded area ½ mi from town, is a well-maintained 9-hole course with a driving range. Golf clubs and pull carts can be rented.

Hiking & Biking

Rain Walker Expeditions (☎ 907/874–2549 🌐 www.rainwalkerexpeditions.com) leads two-hour, half-day, and full-day guided natural-history, botany, wildlife, and bird-watching tours of wild places near Wrangell. The company also rents mountain bikes, canoes, and sea kayaks if you want to head out on your own.

Shopping

A rocky ledge near the Stikine River is the source for **garnets** sold by local children for 25¢ to $10. The site was deeded to the Boy Scouts in 1962, so only children can collect these colorful but imperfect stones, the largest of which are an inch across. At several covered shelters near the city dock, you can buy locally crafted items or book an adventure. Local artist **Brenda Schwartz** (✉ 463 Shakes Ave. ☎ 907/874–3508 🌐 www.marineartist.com) has created a unique style that combines marine paintings with navigational charts. Find her studio at the base of Chief Shakes Island.

PETERSBURG

30–34 *22 mi north of Wrangell.*

Getting to Petersburg is an experience, whether you take the "high road" by air or the "low road" by sea. Alaska Airlines claims the shortest jet flight in the world, from takeoff at Wrangell to landing at Petersburg. The schedule calls for 20 minutes of flying, but it's usually more like 15. At sea level only ferries and smaller cruisers can squeak through Wrangell Narrows with the aid of more than 50 buoys and range markers along the 22-mi crossing, which takes almost four hours. The inaccessibility of Petersburg is part of its charm. Unlike in several other Southeast communities, you'll never be overwhelmed here by hordes of cruise passengers; only the smaller ships can reach the town.

At first sight Petersburg invokes the spirit of Norway: tidy white homes and storefronts line the streets, bright-color swirls of leaf and flower designs (called rosemaling) decorate a few older homes, and row upon row of sturdy fishing vessels pack the harbor. No wonder—this prosperous fishing community was founded by Norwegian Peter Buschmann in 1897.

The Scandinavian heritage is gradually being submerged by the larger American culture, but you may still occasionally hear Norwegian spoken, especially during the Little Norway Festival, held here each year on the weekend closest to May 17. If you're in town during the festival, be sure to partake in one of the fish feeds that highlight the Norwegian Independence Day celebration. You won't find better folk dancing and beer-batter halibut outside Norway.

One of the most pleasant things to do in Petersburg is to roam among the fishing vessels tied up at dockside in the town's expanding harbor. This is one of Alaska's busiest, most prosperous fishing communities, and the variety of seacraft is enormous. You'll see small trollers, big halibut vessels, and sleek pleasure craft. Wander, too, around the fish-processing structures (though be prepared for the pungent aroma). By watching shrimp, salmon, or halibut catches being brought ashore, you can get a real appreciation for this industry and the people who engage in it. The fresh fish gets flown out on the Alaska Airlines jet; the frozen or canned fish goes out on boats or barges.

Petersburg's biggest draw, LeConte Glacier, lies about 25 mi east of town and is accessible only by water or air. It's the continent's southernmost tidewater glacier and one of its most active, often calving off so many icebergs that the tidewater bay at its face is carpeted shore to shore with floating bergs. Ferries and cruise ships pass it at a distance.

Exploring Petersburg

Although Petersburg is a pretty enough town to explore, here commercial fishing is more important than tourism. The main attractions are the town's Norwegian heritage and its magnificent mountain-backed setting. The country around Petersburg provides a wide array of outdoor fun, from whale watching and glacier gazing to brown-bear viewing, hiking, and fishing.

a good walk

The **Petersburg Visitor Information Center** 30 at 1st and Fram streets is a logical spot to begin any walking (or biking) tour of Petersburg. Just a block up the hill, the **Clausen Memorial Museum** 31 is a testimony to life in Petersburg. From here, head back downhill to Nordic Drive (Main Street), turning left and then right onto historic Sing Lee Alley. Follow it to the **Sons of Norway Hall** 32 along scenic **Hammer Slough** 33. Walk back through the center of town on Nordic Drive. On the north side of downtown, steps lead down to the water at scenic **Eagle's Roost Park** 34.

TIMING Petersburg is small enough to walk around in an hour, but you may want to spend more time biking around the back roads farther from town.

What to See

31 **Clausen Memorial Museum.** The museum has exhibits exploring commercial fishing and the cannery industry, the era of fish traps, the social life of Petersburg, and Tlingit culture. Don't miss the 126½-pound king salmon, the largest ever caught commercially, as well as the Tlingit dugout canoe; two fish-trap anchors; the Cape Decision lighthouse station lens; and *Earth, Sea and Sky,* a 3-D sculptured wall mural outside. *203 Fram St. 907/772–3598 www.clausenmuseum.alaska.net $2 May–early Sept., Mon.–Sat. 10:30–4:30; mid-Sept.–Apr. by appointment.*

34 **Eagle's Roost Park.** Just north of the Petersburg Fisheries cannery, this small roadside park is a great place to spot eagles, especially at low tide. On a clear day you will also discover dramatic views of the sharp-edged Coast Range, including the 9,077-foot summit of Devils Thumb.

Clausen Memorial Museum 31
Eagle's Roost Park 34
Hammer Slough 33
Petersburg Visitor Information Center 30
Sons of Norway Hall 32

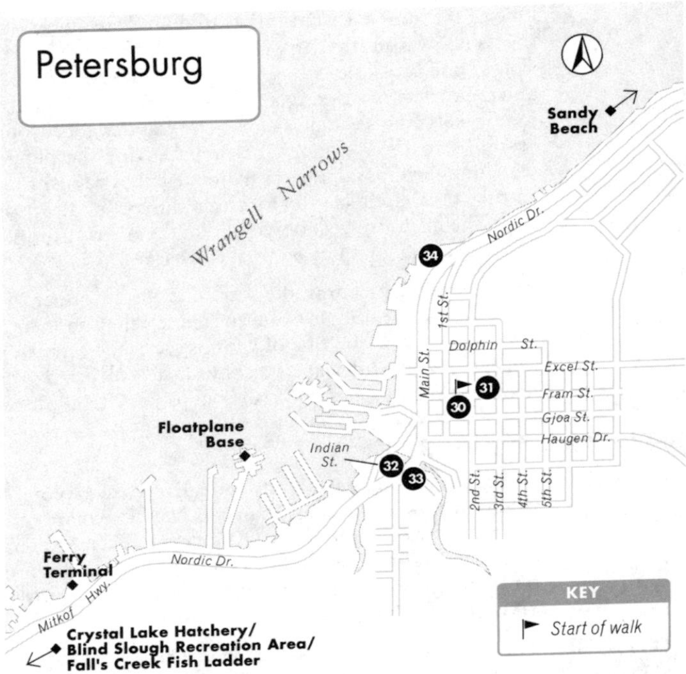

33 **Hammer Slough.** Houses on high stilts and the historic Sons of Norway Hall border this creek that floods with each high tide, creating a photogenic reflecting pool in the still waters.

30 **Petersburg Visitor Information Center.** This small office is a good source for local information, including details on nearby Forest Service recreation opportunities. ✉ *1st and Fram Sts.* ☎ *907/772–4636* 🌐 *www.petersburg.org* ⏲ *May–Sept., Mon.–Sat. 9–5, Sun. noon–4; Oct.–Apr., weekdays 10–2.*

32 **Sons of Norway Hall.** The large, white barnlike structure that stands just south of the Hammer Slough is the headquarters of an organization devoted to keeping alive the traditions and culture of Norway. The window shutters are decorated with colorful Norwegian rosemaling designs. Outside sits a replica of a Viking ship that is a featured attraction in the annual Little Norway Festival each May. On the south of the building is **Fisherman's Memorial Park,** where local fishermen lost at sea are memorialized with a bronze statue of a working fisherman. ✉ *Sing Lee Alley* ☎ *907/772–4575.*

off the beaten path

FALLS CREEK FISH LADDER – Coho and pink salmon migrate upstream in late summer and early fall at this fish ladder south of town. The ladder consists of a water channel with a series of small steps. Fish head up the ladder to get around a small falls. ✉ *Mile 10.8, Mitkof Hwy.*

BLIND SLOUGH RECREATION AREA (☎ 907/772–4772) – This recreation area includes a number of sites scattered along the Mitkof Highway 15–20 mi south of Petersburg. **Blind River Rapids Trail** is a wheelchair-accessible 1-mi path that leads to a three-sided shelter overlooking the river before looping back through the muskeg. Not far away is a bird-viewing area where several dozen trumpeter swans spend the winter. In the summer you're likely to see many ducks and other waterfowl here. At Mile 18, the state-run **Crystal Lake Hatchery** releases thousands of king and coho salmon each year. The kings return in June and July, the coho in August and September. Nearby is a popular picnic area. Four miles south of the hatchery is a Forest Service campground.

4

Where to Stay & Eat

$–$$$ ✕ **Northern Lights Restaurant.** Big windows face the harbor from this restaurant along Sing Lee Alley across from the Sons of Norway Hall. Family dining includes everything from a simple spaghetti with meat sauce to cranberry pecan chicken, rib steaks, and fresh-off-the-boat salmon and halibut. Kids will want to get an ice cream cone to go. Boxed lunches are available if you're heading out to explore the country around Petersburg. The restaurant is open for breakfast, lunch, and dinner from 6 AM to 10 PM. ✉ *203 Sing Lee Alley* ☎ *907/772–2900* ▭ *D, DC, MC, V.*

$$ ✕ **Alaskafe.** This comfortable lunch spot in downtown Petersburg, above Coastal Cold Storage, serves fresh-baked pastries, along with panini sandwiches, pasta, salads, and espresso. The café is open weekdays for breakfast and lunch and Saturday for brunch, with seafood dinners on Friday and Saturday evenings. ✉ *306-B Nordic Dr.* ☎ *907/772–5282* ▭ *No credit cards* ⏲ *No dinner Mon.–Thur.*

$ ✕ **Papa Bear's Pizza.** Although it has a few tables, this oft-crowded pizza joint primarily specializes in take-out pizzas, pizza by the slice, wraps, and giant calzones. It also serves ice cream and espresso. Upstairs is a bar with pool tables. ✉ *1105 S. Nordic Dr., across from ferry terminal* ☎ *907/772–3727* ▭ *MC, V.*

¢ ✕ **Coastal Cold Storage.** This busy little shop in the heart of Petersburg serves daily lunch seafood specials, including fish chowders and halibut beer bits, along with grilled chicken wraps, steak sandwiches, and breakfast omelets and waffles. Live or cooked crab is available for takeout, and the shop can process your sport-caught fish. ✉ *306 N. Nordic Dr.* ☎ *907/772–4171* ▭ *AE, D, MC, V.*

$–$$$ 🏨 **Scandia House.** Exuding an old Norwegian flavor, this hotel on Petersburg's main street, a fixture since 1910, was rebuilt following a 1995 fire. Rosemaling designs adorn the exterior. The interior is squeaky clean, with contemporary oak furniture; some rooms have kitchenettes, king-size beds, or in-room hot tubs and a view of the harbor. Homemade muffins and coffee warm the small but relaxing lobby in the morning. ✉ *110 Nordic Dr., Box 689, 99833* ☎ *907/772–4281 or 800/722–5006* 🖷 *907/772–4301* 🌐 *www.scandiahousehotel.com* *30 rooms, 3 suites* *Some kitchenettes, cable TV; no a/c* *AE, D, DC, MC, V* *CP.*

$ **Tides Inn.** This is the largest hotel in town, a block uphill from Petersburg's main thoroughfare. Rooms have comfortable, but older furnishings; some have kitchenettes. Rooms in the newer wing have views of the boat harbor. The coffee is always on in the small lobby, and in the morning there are complimentary juices, muffins, and pastries. ✉ *307 N. 1st St., Box 1048, 99833* ☎ *907/772–4288 or 800/665–8433* 🖷 *907/772–4286* 🌐 *www.tidesinnalaska.com* *48 rooms* *Some kitchenettes, cable TV, Internet, car rental; no a/c* *AE, D, DC, MC, V* *CP.*

$ **Water's Edge Bed & Breakfast.** Along the shore of Frederick Sound 1½ mi north of Petersburg, this family-run B&B offers either creekside or waterside rooms. Seals, eagles, and whales are often seen just outside the door. A substantial Continental breakfast is served, and the library is stocked with books on Alaska and natural history. Take advantage of the owners' Kaleidoscope Cruises or borrow the bikes or canoe to explore on your own. Lodging-cruise packages are offered. ✉ *705 Sandy Beach Rd., Box 1201, 99833* ☎ *907/772–3736 or 800/868–4373* 🌐 *www.petersburglodgingandtours.com* *2 rooms* *Bicycles, library, airport and ferry shuttle; no a/c, no room phones, no room TVs, no smoking* *No credit cards* *CP.*

¢ **Petersburg Bunk & Breakfast Hostel.** This friendly home hostel with no curfew offers separate male and female dorms, plus a family room. The second-floor kitchen and living room overlook the mountains and muskegs of Mitkof Island, and there's a big library of Alaskan books to thumb through in the evening. A guest phone and high-speed Internet access are available, along with luggage storage and a laundry. The owners provide ingredients for a self-serve breakfast, including freshly baked breads. Advance reservations are required in the winter. ✉ *805 Gjoa St., Box 892, 99833* ☎ *907/772–3632* 🌐 *www.bunkandbreakfast.com* *3 dorm rooms* *Laundry facilities, Internet; no a/c, no kids under 12* *MC, V* *CP.*

Guided Tours

Stop by the visitor center for a complete listing of local tour companies. **Kaleidoscope Cruises** (☎ 907/772–3736 or 800/868–4373 🌐 www.alaska.net/~bbsea) conducts whale-watching and glacier-ecology boat tours led by professional biologists and naturalists. **Pacific Wing** (✉ 1500 Haugen Dr. ☎ 907/772–9258 🌐 www.pacificwing.com) is an air-taxi operator that gets high marks from locals for its flightseeing tours over the Stikine River and LeConte Glacier. **Tongass Kayak Adventures** (☎ 907/772–4600 🖷 907/772–4646 🌐 www.tongasskayak.com) leads multiday sea-kayak trips to the Stikine River, LeConte Glacier, and elsewhere in the area. Their half-day trip up Petersburg Creek is especially popular. **Viking Travel** (✉ 101 Nordic Dr. ☎ 907/772–3818 or 800/327–2571 🖷 907/772–3940 🌐 www.alaska-ala-carte.com) books whale-watching, glacier, sea-kayaking, and other charters with local and regional operators.

Nightlife

The **Harbor Bar** (✉ Nordic Dr. ☎ 907/772–4526), with ships' wheels, ship pictures, and a mounted red snapper, is true to the town's seafaring spirit. Sample the brew and blastingly loud music at the smoky **Kito's Kave** (✉ Sing Lee Alley ☎ 907/772–3207). The odd collection of wall hangings include a Mexican painting on black velvet, a mounted Alaska king salmon, and two stuffed sailfish from a tropical fishing expedition.

Sports & the Outdoors

Hiking

For an enjoyable loop hike from town, follow Dolphin Street uphill from the center of town. At the intersection with 5th Street a boardwalk path leads 900 feet through forested wetlands to a baseball field, where a second boardwalk takes you to 12th Street and Haugen Drive. Turn left on Haugen and follow it past the airport to **Sandy Beach Park,** where low tide reveals a number of ancient petroglyphs. The park has covered picnic tables and a playground. From here, you can return to town via Sandy Beach Road., or hike the beach when the tide is out. Along the way is a covered **whale observatory** with binoculars to scan for humpback whales, orcas, or other marine mammals. A pullout at Hungry Point provides fine views to the Coast Range and Frederick Sound. Across the road, the half-mile **Hungry Point Trail** takes you back to the baseball field, where you can return downtown on the nature boardwalk. Plan on an hour and a half for this interesting walk.

For something more strenuous, a 4-mi trail begins at the airport and climbs 1,600 feet in elevation to **Raven's Roost Cabin.** Along the way you can pause to take in a panorama that reaches from the permanently icy mountain ranges to the protected waters and forested islands of the Inside Passage far below. The two-story Forest Service cabin is available for rent ($35 per night); contact **ReserveUSA** (☎ 518/885–3639 or 877/444–6777 🌐 www.reserveusa.com). Get details on these and other hikes from the Petersburg Visitor Information Center, or from the **Forest Service office** (✉ Nordic and Haugen Sts. ☎ 907/772–3871 🌐 www.fs.fed.us/r10/tongass).

Shopping

Seafood

At **Tonka Seafoods,** across the street from the Sons of Norway Hall, you can tour the small custom seafood plant and sample smoked or canned halibut and salmon. It will also ship. *✉ Sing Lee Alley ☎ 907/772–3662 or 888/560–3662 🎟 Free ⏲ Mon.–Sat. 8–5; tours at 1 PM (minimum 6 people).*

Bookstore

Off an alley in a beautiful big white house that served as a boardinghouse to fishermen and schoolteachers, **Sing Lee Alley Books** stocks books on Alaska, best sellers, cards, and gifts. ✉ *11 Sing Lee Alley* ☎ *907/772–4440.*

Norwegian Crafts

The appropriately named **CubbyHole** sells items decorated by Norwegian-style rosemaling, including plates, trays, key chains, and other items. The museum gift shop also sells distinctive locally made crafts with Nordic designs. It's two blocks south of the Clausen museum. ✉ *14 Sing Lee Alley* ☎ *907/772–2717.*

SITKA

35–44 *110 mi west of Petersburg.*

Sitka was the home to the Tlingit people for centuries prior to the 18th-century arrival of the Russians. In canoes up to 60 feet long, the Tlingits fished and traded throughout the Alaskan Panhandle and even as far south as California. Unfortunately for them, Russian territorial governor Alexander Baranof coveted the Sitka site for its beauty, mild climate, and economic potential. In the island's massive timber forests he saw raw materials for shipbuilding. Its location offered trading routes as far west as Asia and as far south as California and Hawaii. In 1799 Baranof negotiated with the local chief to build a wooden fort and trading post some 6 mi north of the present town. He called the outpost St. Michael Archangel and moved a large number of his Russian and Aleut fur hunters there from their former base on Kodiak Island.

The Tlingits soon took exception to the ambitions of their new neighbors. Reluctant to pledge allegiance to the czar and provide free labor, they attacked the settlers and burned their buildings in 1802. Baranof, however, was away on Kodiak at the time. He returned in 1804 with a formidable force, including shipboard cannons. He attacked the Tlingits at their fort near Indian River, site of the present-day 105-acre Sitka National Historical Park, and forced them to flee north to Chichagof Island.

In 1821 the Tlingits returned to Sitka to trade with the Russians, who were happy to benefit from the tribe's hunting skills. Under Baranof and succeeding managers, the Russian-American Company and the town prospered, becoming known as the Paris of the Pacific. Besides engaging in the fur trade, the community built a major shipbuilding and repair facility, sawmills, and forges and even initiated an ice industry. The Russians shipped blocks of ice from nearby Swan Lake to the booming San Francisco market.

The town declined after its 1867 transfer from Russia to the United States but became prosperous again during World War II, when it served as a base for the U.S. effort to drive the Japanese from the Aleutian Islands. Today its most important industries are fishing, government, and tourism.

Exploring Sitka

It is hard not to like Sitka, with its eclectic blending of Native, Russian, and American history and its dramatic and beautiful setting. This is one of the best Inside Passage towns to explore on foot, with such sights as St. Michael's Cathedral, Sheldon Jackson Museum, Sitka National Historical Park, and the Alaska Raptor Center topping the town's must-see list.

a good walk

A good place to begin a tour of Sitka is the distinctive onion-dome **St. Michael's Cathedral** 35, right in town center. A block behind the cathedral along Harbor Drive is **Harrigan Centennial Hall** 36. Inside are the worthwhile Isabel Miller Museum and an information desk that opens when cruise ships are in port. From here, turn right on Lincoln Street and continue a block to the **Russian Bishop's House** 37, one of the symbols of Russian rule, dating from 1842. Continue out on Lincoln Street along the harbor to Sheldon Jackson College, where the **Sheldon Jackson Museum** 38 is packed with Native cultural artifacts. Another ½ mi out is the **Sitka National Historical Park** 39, where you can watch Native artisans craft carvings and silver jewelry. Behind the main building, paths take you through the rain forest past tall totem poles and to the site of a Tlingit fort from the battle of 1804. A signed trail crosses the Indian River (watch for spawning salmon in late summer) and heads to the **Alaska Raptor Center** 40, for an up-close look at bald eagles.

Return to town along Sawmill Creek Road to the small Sitka National Cemetery, where you turn left on Jeff Davis Street. Continue downhill to Lincoln Street and turn right, following it back to Harrigan Centennial Hall. From here, walk along Harbor Drive for two blocks and take the path to the summit of **Castle Hill** 41, where Russia transferred Alaska to American hands. Follow the path down the other side of the hill to view the impressive **Sitka State Pioneers' Home** 42, with the statue of pioneer "Skagway Bill" Fonda. Across the street is **Totem Square** 43, with its tall totem pole and three ancient anchors. Adjacent to the Pioneers' Home is the **Sheet'ka Kwaan Naa Kahidi Community House** cultural center. Native dances take place here in the summer. Turn right at the center and pass the reconstructed Russian blockhouse that tops a nearby hill. End your walk at the **Russian and Lutheran cemeteries** 44, along Marine Street a block from the blockhouse. The grave of Princess Maksoutoff, a member of the Russian royal family, is here.

TIMING Sitka has many attractions, and you can easily spend a full day exploring this culturally rich area. You can accomplish the walk in two to three hours if you do not spend much time at each stop.

What to See

★ 40 **Alaska Raptor Center.** View two dozen American bald eagles and other wild Alaskan raptors up close at this beautifully wooded tract of land just a 20-minute walk from downtown. There's a short video, and guides provide an introduction to the rehabilitation center, including a visit with one of these majestic birds. The Raptor Center's primary attraction is a 20,000-square-foot flight training center, built to replicate

Alaska Raptor Center **40**
Castle Hill **41**
Harrigan Centennial Hall **36**
Russian and Lutheran cemeteries **44**
Russian Bishop's House **37**
St. Michael's Cathedral **35**
Sheldon Jackson Museum **38**
Sitka National Historical Park **39**
Sitka State Pioneers' Home **42**
Totem Square **43**

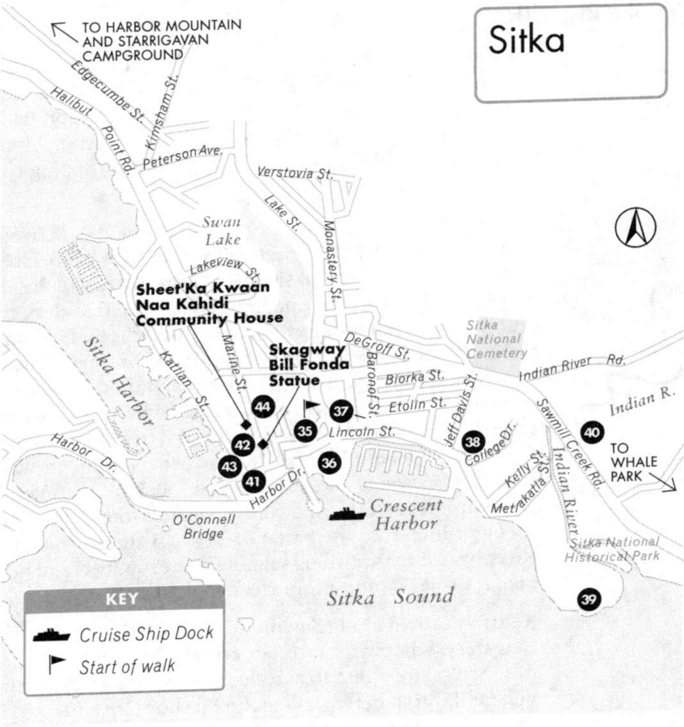

the rain forest. In this enormous enclosed space, injured eagles relearn survival skills, including flying and catching salmon. Visitors watch through one-way glass windows. A large deck out back faces an open-air enclosure for eagles and other raptors whose injuries prevent them from returning to the wild. Additional mews with hawks, owls, and other birds are along a rain-forest path. The gift shop sells all sorts of eagle paraphernalia. ✉ *1000 Raptor Way (off Sawmill Creek Rd.)* ☎ *907/747–8662 or 800/643–9425* 🌐 *www.alaskaraptor.org* 🎫 *$12* ⏲ *Mid-May–Sept., Sun.–Fri. 8–4.*

41 **Castle Hill.** On this hill Alaska was formally handed over to the United States on October 18, 1867, and the first 49-star U.S. flag was flown on January 3, 1959, signifying Alaska's statehood. To reach the hill and get one of Sitka's best views, take the first right off Harbor Drive just before the O'Connell Bridge; then go into the **Baranof Castle Hill State Historic Site** entrance. A paved path takes you to the top, overlooking Crescent Harbor and downtown Sitka. Several Russian residences on the hill, including Baranof's castle, burned down in 1894.

Harbor Mountain. During World War II the U.S. Army constructed a road to the 2,000-foot level of Harbor Mountain, providing the perfect vantage point to watch for invading Japanese subs or ships (none were seen).

This road has been improved over the years, and those with vehicles can drive 5 mi to a spectacular summit viewpoint across Sitka Sound. A trail climbs uphill from the parking lot, and then follows the ridge 2.5 mi to a Forest Service shelter. From there, ambitious hikers could continue downhill another 3.5 mi to Sitka via the **Gavan Hill Trail.**

36 **Harrigan Centennial Hall.** A Tlingit war canoe sits in front of this contemporary brick building. Inside you'll find a volunteer-staffed information desk provided by the Sitka Convention and Visitors Bureau; the **Isabel Miller Museum,** with its collection of Russian and American historical artifacts; and an auditorium for New Archangel Dancers performances, which take place when cruise ships are in port. ✉ *Harbor Dr.* ☎ *907/747–6455 museum, 907/747–5940 Visitors Bureau* 🌐 *www.sitkahistory.org* 🎫 *Free* ⏲ *Museum May–Sept., daily 8–5; Oct.–Apr., Tues.–Sat. 10–4. Information desk May–Sept., daily 8–5.*

44 **Russian and Lutheran cemeteries.** Most of Sitka's Russian dignitaries are buried in these sites off Marine Street. The most distinctive grave belongs to Princess Maksoutoff (died 1862), wife of the last Russian governor and one of the most illustrious members of the Russian royal family to be buried on Alaskan soil.

37 **Russian Bishop's House.** A registered historic landmark, this house facing the harbor was constructed by the Russian-American Company for Bishop Innocent Veniaminov in 1842. Inside the house, one of the few remaining Russian-built log structures in Alaska, are exhibits on the history of Russian America, including a room where a portion of the house's structure is peeled away to expose Russian building techniques. Guided tours are given of the second floor. ✉ *501 Lincoln St.* ☎ *907/747–6281* 🌐 *www.nps.gov/sitk* 🎫 *$3* ⏲ *May–Sept., daily 9–5; Oct.–Apr. by appointment.*

★ 35 **St. Michael's Cathedral.** One of Southeast Alaska's best-known national landmarks had its origins in a log structure erected between 1844 and 1848. In 1966 the church was destroyed in a fire that swept through the downtown business district. As the fire engulfed the building, townspeople risked their lives and rushed inside to rescue the cathedral's precious icons, religious objects, vestments, and other treasures brought to the church from Russia. Using original measurements and blueprints, an almost exact replica of onion-dome St. Michael's was built and dedicated in 1976. Today you can see what could possibly be the largest collection of Russian icons in the United States, among them the much-prized *Our Lady of Sitka* (also known as the *Sitka Madonna*) and the *Christ Pantocrator* (*Christ the Judge*) on either side of the doors of the interior altar screen. Other objects include ornate Gospel books, chalices, crucifixes, much-used silver-gilt wedding crowns dating to 1866, and an altar cloth made by Princess Maksoutoff. ✉ *Lincoln St.* ☎ *907/747–8120* 🎫 *$2* ⏲ *May–Sept., when large cruise ships are in port; Oct.–Apr., hrs vary.*

★ 38 **Sheldon Jackson Museum.** At **Sheldon Jackson College,** this octagonal museum, which dates from 1895, contains priceless Aleut and Eskimo items collected by Dr. Sheldon Jackson (1834–1909), who traveled the remote regions of Alaska as an educator and missionary. Carved masks, Chilkat blankets, dog sleds, kayaks—even the impressive helmet worn by Chief Katlean during the 1804 battle against the Russians—are displayed. Native artisans are here all summer, creating baskets, carvings, or masks. ✉ *104 College Dr.* ☎ *907/747–8981* 🌐 *www.museums.state.ak.us* 🎫 *$4* ⏲ *Mid-May–mid-Sept., daily 9–5; mid-Sept.–mid-May, Tues.–Sat. 10–4.*

★ 39 **Sitka National Historical Park.** The main building at this park houses a small museum with fascinating historical exhibits and photos of Tlingit Native culture. Highlights include a brass peace hat given to the Sitka Kiksadi by Russian traders in the 1830s and a Chilkat robe. Head to the theater to watch a video about 19th-century conflicts between Tlingits and Russians. Also here is the **Southeast Alaska Indian Cultural Center,** where Native artists and artisans demonstrate silversmithing, weaving, wood carving, and basketry. The artisans are happy to talk about their work and Tlingit cultural traditions. At the far end of the building are seven totems (some more than a century old) that have been brought indoors to protect them from decay. Behind the center, a wide 1-mi path takes you through the forest and along the shore of Sitka Sound. Scattered along the way are some of the most skillfully carved Native totem poles in Alaska, including several from the 1904 St. Louis World's Fair. The trail passes a grassy meadow that once contained a sturdy Tlingit fort; the 1804 battle between the Russians and Tlingits was fought here. Keep going on the trail to see spawning salmon from the footbridge over Indian River. Park Service rangers lead historical walks in the summer. ✉ *106 Metlakatla St.* ☎ *907/747–6281* 🌐 *www.nps.gov/sitk* 🎫 *$3* ⏲ *Mid-May–Sept., daily 8–5; Oct.–mid-May, Mon.–Sat. 8–5.*

42 **Sitka State Pioneers' Home.** The large, four-level, red-roof structure with the imposing 14-foot statue in front is the first of several state-run retirement homes for Alaska's senior citizens. The statue, symbolizing Alaska's frontier sourdough spirit (a "sourdough" generally refers to Alaska's American pioneers), was modeled by an authentic pioneer, William "Skagway Bill" Fonda. It portrays a determined prospector heading for the gold country with pack, pick, rifle, and supplies on his back. Adjacent to the Pioneers' Home is **Sheet'ka Kwaan Naa Kahidi Community House,** where you can watch Native dance performances throughout the summer. A re-created Russian blockhouse caps the small hill directly behind the community center. ✉ *Lincoln and Katlian Sts.* ☎ *907/747–3213.*

43 **Totem Square.** On this square directly across the street from the Pioneers' Home are three anchors discovered in local waters believed to be of 19th-century British origin. Look for the double-headed eagle of czarist Russia carved into the cedar of the totem pole in the park.

Whale Park. This small waterside park sits in the trees 4 mi east of Sitka out by Sawmill Creek Road. Boardwalk paths lead to five viewing platforms and steps take you down to the rocky shoreline. A gazebo next to the parking area contains signs describing the whales that visit Silver Bay, and you can listen to their sounds from recordings and an offshore hydrophone here. Tune your radio to FM 88.1 anywhere in Sitka to hear a broadcast of humpback whale (and other) sounds picked up by the hydrophone.

Where to Stay & Eat

$$–$$$$ ✕ **Channel Club.** Once you've surveyed the dozens of salads arrayed on the salad bar, you might not even make it to the steak and seafood for which this restaurant, festooned with fishnet, floats, and whalebone carvings, is known. A courtesy van provides door-to-door service if you're without transportation. ✉ *Mile 3.5, 2906 Halibut Point Rd.* ☎ *907/747–9916* ▭ *AE, DC, MC, V.*

$$–$$$$ FodorśChoice ★ ✕ **Ludvig's Bistro.** This convivial and remarkably creative eatery escapes detection by most tourists. And that's just fine with the Sitkans who pack Ludvig's for lunch and dinner. The interior evokes an Italian bistro, with rich yellow walls, copper-topped tables, Italian and Spanish wines filling one wall, and a three-seat bar. The menu changes often, and the blackboard lists the specials. Seafood (particularly king salmon and scallops) is a centerpiece, but you'll also find Caesar salads, vegetarian specials, and prime rib. From 3 to 5 each evening, the café serves Spanish-style tapas with house wine for $8–$10. Lunch includes fish-and-chips with locally caught rockfish; pita sandwiches; and house-made seafood chowders. Buen Provecho! ✉ *256 Katlian Ave.* ☎☎ *907/966–3663* ▭ *AE, MC, V* ⊙ *Closed mid-Feb.–mid-Mar.*

$–$$$ ✕ **Little Tokyo.** Sitka is probably the last place you might expect to find Japanese food, but Little Tokyo hits the sushi spot. Dining is nothing fancy, but this small restaurant does have a sushi bar where you can watch the chef preparing all the standards, plus Alaska rolls (with smoked salmon and cream cheese). Udon noodle soups are popular on rainy afternoons, and Bento box dinners—complete with sushi, pot stickers, miso soup, teriyaki chicken wings, and salad—are a real bargain at $11. No alcohol is served. ✉ *315 Lincoln St.* ☎ *907/747–5699* ▭ *MC, V.*

$–$$ ✕ **Nugget Restaurant.** Travelers flying out from Sitka head here while hoping their jet will make it through the pea-soup fog outside. The setting is standard, and the menu encompasses burgers (15 kinds), sandwiches, tuna melts, salads, steaks, stir-fries, pasta, seafood, and Friday-night prime rib. There's a big breakfast menu, too, but the real attraction is their justly famous pies, with several types available daily. Get a slice á la mode, or buy a whole pie to take home. ✉ *Sitka Airport Terminal* ☎ *907/966–2480* ▭ *MC, V.*

¢ ✕ **Mojo Cafe.** Just a few steps from the Russian Orthodox church in the heart of town, this is a relaxing brunch spot; it closes at 2 PM. Sample the pastries, sip an espresso while reading the *Sitka Sentinel,* or just take in the rock music, mismatched chairs and tables, ceiling draped with Christmas lights, and rubber-booted locals. Lunch specials include soups, sandwiches, burritos, pirogies, and calzones. If you aren't counting calories, try one of the earthquake brownies. The same owners also run a popular espresso hangout called Backdoor Cafe, just up the street and behind Old Harbor Books. ✉ *203 Lincoln St.* ☎ *907/747–0667* ▭ *No credit cards* ⊙ *No dinner.*

$$$$ **Baranof Wilderness Lodge.** This cozy fishing lodge is nestled in Warm Springs Bay, 20 air miles from Sitka on the wild east side of Baranof Island. Guest cabins have pine paneling, private baths, and electricity from a small hydroelectric plant. Packages range from two-night stays ($1,185 per person) to seven-night fishing adventures ($4,350 per person). All include floatplane transport from Sitka, boats and guide service, lodging in cabins with private baths, plus gourmet meals and wines served at communal meals. Special wildlife photography seminars, Elderhostel programs, and fly-fishing schools are offered throughout the summer. The lodge has two wood-fired hot tubs, and nearby is a natural hot springs that pours 110° water into a series of pools overlooking a waterfall. Most of the surrounding land is within Tongass National Forest, but a small settlement exists along the bay a half-mile from the lodge. *Box 2187, 99835 907/738–3597 or 800/613–6551 530/222–3572 www.flyfishalaska.com 2 rooms, 6 cabins Hot tubs, Internet; no a/c No credit cards FAP Closed Oct.–Apr.*

$$–$$$$ **Westmark Shee Atika.** Sitka's nicest hotel has large rooms and a lobby dominated by a beautifully carved Tlingit screen. Many rooms overlook Crescent Harbor; the best rooms are the corner suites. Downstairs, the Raven Dining Room is open for three meals a day, with seafood (including beer-batter halibut), pasta, chicken, pork, and steak. Top dinner off with a slice of ultrarich Mississippi mud pie. *330 Seward St., 99835 907/747–6241, 800/544–0970 in U.S., 800/999–2570 in Canada 907/747–5486 www.westmarkhotels.com 97 rooms, 4 suites Restaurant, room service, cable TV, bar; no a/c AE, D, DC, MC, V.*

★ $$ **Rockwell Lighthouse.** On an island ¾ mi from town, Burgess Bauder (a local veterinarian) rents out his 1,600-square-foot four-story lighthouse, which was hand-built in the 1980s with coastal woods and brass lights. The light at the top is built to Coast Guard specifications. The lighthouse can accommodate eight people in four rooms ($200 for four, plus $35 per person for extra guests)—you must rent the whole property. A curving staircase wraps up the inside of the lighthouse. The price includes transportation to and from the lighthouse; it's $35 per day extra for use of the hot tub. In summer, you can use a small motorboat to reach the island, but when it's stormy the owner runs a shuttle service. Call up to a year ahead for midsummer reservations. *Box 277, 99835 907/747–3056 Dining room, kitchen, hot tub; no a/c, no room TVs No credit cards.*

$–$$ **Cascade Inn.** Two miles northwest of town, this modern but unpretentious three-story motel is conveniently attached to a small grocery, video, and liquor store. The large rooms have simple furnishings and balconies facing the water and Mt. Edgecumbe volcano. Some include kitchenettes. Out back and right on the water is a deck with a glass-enclosed cedar sauna and a barbecue grill. *2035 Halibut Point Rd., 99835 907/747–6804 or 800/532–0908 907/747–6572 www.cascadeinnsitka.com 10 rooms Grocery, some kitchenettes, cable TV, in-room VCRs, sauna, boating; no a/c, no smoking AE, MC, V.*

$ **Alaska Swan Lake Bed & Breakfast.** Sitka has more than 20 B&Bs, and this is one of the best, with a lakeside setting, attractively appointed rooms with private baths, and friendly owners. Two downstairs rooms share a comfortable sitting room, while the two rooms upstairs adjoin a glassed-in porch. Private entrances provide access. Children have fun with the play equipment on the lawn that drops down to Swan Lake. The B&B is just six blocks from the center of town. ✉ *206½ Lakeview Dr., 99835* ☎ *907/747–5746* 🌐 *www.sitka.org/swanlake* *4 rooms* *Cable TV; no a/c* *MC, V* *CP.*

¢–$ **Sitka Hotel.** Right in downtown, this comfortable, old-fashioned hotel was built in 1939. The lobby and hallways emphasize a Victorian charm, with floral wallpaper and plush carpets. Some rooms feature contemporary furnishings, whereas others are small and not yet remodeled. Guests can use the computer workstation, and those with laptops can access the hotel's free wireless system. An adjacent lounge (Victoria's Pourhouse) provides a comfy place to relax, and Victoria's Restaurant opens early for filling breakfasts. Convenient off-street parking is available. ✉ *118 Lincoln St., 99835* ☎ *907/747–3288* *907/747–8499* 🌐 *www.sitkahotel.com* *55 rooms, 43 with bath* *Some refrigerators, cable TV; no a/c, no smoking* *AE, MC, V.*

¢ **Starrigavan Campground.** Seven miles north of town, and just a mile from the ferry terminal, this popular Tongass National Forest campground has a mix of sites for car campers, backpackers, and RV travelers. All sites have tree cover, and facilities include tables, grills, potable water, and vault restrooms. Everything is fully ADA accessible, and group sites include a covered cooking shelter. Campsites are open year-round. ☎ *907/747–6671 information, 877/444–6777 reservations* 🌐 *www.reserveusa.com* *AE, D, MC, V.*

¢ **White Sulphur Springs Cabin.** This Tongass National Forest public-use cabin is 65 mi outside Sitka. Like many other Forest Service cabins, this cabin sleeps four (bring your own sleeping bags) and has bunk beds, woodstove, table, and an outhouse. No mattresses, cooking utensils, or any services are provided, so you must bring all of your own supplies. The cabin faces the Pacific Ocean and has a nearby hot-springs bathhouse. Access is by boat (you'll need to walk in from a nearby cove) or helicopter. ☎ *907/747–6671 information, 877/444–6777 reservations* 🌐 *www.reserveusa.com* *1 cabin* *AE, D, MC, V.*

Guided Tours

Sitka Tours (☎ 907/747–8443 907/747–7510) meets ferries and cruise ships and leads both bus tours and historical walks. In addition, it transports ferry passengers into Sitka. **Tribal Tours** (☎ 907/747–7290 or 888/270–8687 907/747–3770 🌐 www.sitkatribal.com) emphasizes Sitka's rich Native culture, with bus or walking tours and with dance performances at the Tribal Community House.

Allen Marine Tours (☎ 907/747–8100 or 888/747–8101 🌐 www.allenmarinetours.com) leads boat-based Sitka Sound tours four times a week in the summer. These "Wildlife Quest" tours are a fine opportunity to view humpback whales, sea otters, puffins, eagles, and other birds and mammals in a spectacular setting. When seas are calm enough, these trips include a visit to the bird sanctuary at **St. Lazaria Islands National**

Wildlife Refuge. The company also offers challenging all-day Saturday trips that combine a boat ride with a guided 6-mi rain-forest hike across the northern end of Kruzoff Island. Brown bears are sometimes seen on these hikes, and participants must be relatively fit.

Sea Life Discovery Tours (☎ 907/966–2301 or 877/966–2301 🌐 www.sealifediscoverytours.com) operates the only semi-submersible tour vessel in Alaska. Large underwater windows provide views of kelp forests, fish, crab, sea urchins, anemones, starfish, and other creatures, and an underwater camera zooms in for close-up views via the video monitor.

Nightlife & the Arts

Bars

As far as the locals are concerned, a spot in one of the green-and-white-vinyl booths at **Pioneer Bar** (✉ 212 Katlian St. ☎ 907/747–3456), across from the harbor, is a destination unto itself. It's vintage Alaska, with hundreds of pictures of local fishing boats, occasional live music, and pickup pool games.

Dance

★ The **New Archangel Dancers of Sitka** perform authentic Russian Cossack–type dances whenever cruise ships are in port. This all-female troupe tours extensively, with a mix of traditional dance styles. Tickets are sold a half hour before performances. A **recorded message** (☎ 907/747–5516 🌐 www.newarchangeldancers.com) gives the schedule a week in advance. Performances take place in Harrigan Centennial Hall. **Sheet'ka Kwaan Naa Kahidi Dancers** (☎ 907/747–7290 or 888/270–8687 🌐 www.sitkatribal.com) performs Tlingit dances in full Native regalia at the Sheet'ka Kwaan Naa Kahidi Community House on Katlian Street. The dance schedule is listed on the board at Harrigan Centennial Hall.

Festivals

Southeast Alaska's major classical chamber-music festival is the annual **Sitka Summer Music Festival** (📫 Box 3333, 99835 ☎ 907/747–6774 🌐 www.sitkamusicfestival.org), a three-week June celebration of concerts and special events held in Harrigan Centennial Hall. The **Sitka WhaleFest** (☎ 907/747–7964 🌐 www.sitkawhalefest.org) is held around town the first weekend of November when the whales are plentiful (as many as 80) and tourists are not.

Sports & the Outdoors

Bicycling

If it isn't raining, rent a high-quality mountain bike from **Yellow Jersey Cycle Shop** (✉ 329 Harbor Dr. ☎ 907/747–6317) and head out on the nearby dirt roads and trails.

Fishing

Sitka is a well-known commercial-fishing port, but the town is also home to an ever-growing fleet of charter boats. The Sitka Convention and Visitors Bureau Web site (🌐 www.sitka.org) has descriptions of and Web links to several dozen sport-fishing operators. A good one is **Sitka's Secrets** (✉ 500

Lincoln St., No. 641 ☎ 907/747–5089 🌐 www.sitkasecret.com), operated by naturalists who combine wildlife viewing with fishing.

Hiking & Bird-Watching

Seven miles north of Sitka, **Starrigavan Recreation Area** is a peaceful, end-of-the-road place to explore the rain forest. The state ferry terminal is less than a mile from Starrigavan, and a popular Forest Service campground is also here. Several easy trails lead hikers through the area, including the ¼-mi boardwalk (wheelchair accessible) **Estuary Life Trail.** It circles a small estuary and includes a bird-viewing shelter and access to a nearby artesian well. The ¾-mile **Forest and Muskeg Trail** winds through a spruce-hemlock forest and traverses a muskeg, with interpretive signs along the way. Across the road is the delightful 1¼-mi loop **Mosquito Cove Trail,** which skirts the rocky shoreline to Mosquito Cove before returning through thickly forested hills. Get a map of local trails from **Sitka Trail Works** (✉ 801 Halibut Point Rd. ☎ 907/747–7244).

Kayaking

Alaska Travel Adventures (☎ 907/789–0052 or 800/478–0052 🌐 www.alaskaadventures.com) leads a three-hour kayaking tour in protected waters south of Sitka and has a remote cabin on the water.

Shopping

Art Galleries

Fairweather Prints (✉ 209 Lincoln St. ☎ 907/747–8677 🌐 www.fairweatherprints.com) consists of "wearable art," with hand-printed Alaskan designs on shirts, dresses, and other clothing. In addition to boutique clothing, the shop also has two back rooms packed with works by local artisans. **Fishermen's Eye Fine Art Gallery** (✉ 239 Lincoln St. ☎ 907/747–5502 or 877/650–6080 🌐 www.fishermenseye.com) is a fine downtown gallery with art prints and limited editions from Southeast Alaskan artists, including Evon Zerbetz and Rie Muñoz. Housed within a Victorian-style 1895 home next to the Bishop's House, **Sitka Rose Gallery** (✉ 419 Lincoln St. ☎ 907/747–3030 or 888/236–1536 🌐 www.sitkarosegallery.com) has two small galleries with Alaskan paintings, sculptures, Native art, and jewelry.

Bookstore

Old Harbor Books (✉ 201 Lincoln St. ☎ 907/747–8808 🌐 litsite.alaska.edu/akbooksellers/oldharbor.html) has an impressive collection of Alaskan titles, along with a knowledgeable staff. It's a book lovers' bookstore. Directly behind the bookstore is the ever-popular **Backdoor Cafe** (☎ 907/747–8856), with espresso and pastries.

Gifts

Fresh Fish Company (✉ Katlian St. ☎ 907/747–5565, 888/747–5565 outside Alaska) sells fresh locally caught salmon, halibut, and shrimp. Located in the old pulp mill building 5 mi east of Sitka, **Theobroma Chocolate Company** (☎ 907/966–2345 or 888/985–2345 🌐 www.theobromachocolate.com) produces a range of rich treats, including chocolates shaped like halibut and salmon. Tours of this gourmet chocolate factory are available daily. **WinterSong Soap Company** (✉ 419 Lincoln St. ☎ 907/747–8949 or 888/819–8949 🌐 www.wintersongsoap.com) sells colorful and scented soaps handcrafted on the premises.

JUNEAU

45–56 *100 mi northeast of Sitka.*

Juneau, Alaska's capital and third-largest city, is on the North American mainland but can't be reached by road. The city owes its origins to two colorful sourdoughs (Alaskan pioneers), Joe Juneau and Dick Harris, and to a Tlingit chief named Kowee. The chief led the two men to rich reserves of gold in the outwash of the stream that now runs through the middle of town and in quartz formations back in the gulches and valleys. That was in 1880, and shortly after the discovery a modest stampede resulted in the formation of first a camp, then a town, then finally the Alaska district government capital in 1906.

For 60 years or so after Juneau's founding, gold was the mainstay of the economy. In its heyday the AJ (for Alaska Juneau) Gold Mine was the biggest low-grade ore mine in the world. It was not until World War II, when the government decided it needed Juneau's manpower for the war effort, that the AJ and other mines in the area ceased operations. After the war, mining failed to start up again, and government became the city's principal employer.

Juneau is full of contrasts. Its dramatic hillside position and historic downtown buildings provide a frontier feeling, but the city's cosmopolitan nature comes through in fine museums, noteworthy restaurants, and a literate and outdoorsy populace. In addition to enjoying the city itself, you will discover a tramway to alpine trails atop Mt. Roberts, densely forested wilderness areas, quiet bays for sea kayaking, and even a famous drive-up glacier. Surrounded by beautiful wilderness and glaciers in its backyard, Juneau is the cultural center of Alaska.

Exploring Juneau

Juneau is an obligatory stop on the Inside Passage cruise and ferry circuit and enjoys an overabundance of visitors in midsummer. Downtown Juneau is compact enough so that most of its main attractions are within walking distance of one another. Note, however, that the city is very hilly, so your legs will get a real workout. Look for the 20 signs around downtown that detail Juneau's fascinating history. Along with the Alaska State Museum and Mt. Roberts Tramway, be sure to make time for a tour to Mendenhall Glacier and the Macaulay Salmon Hatchery.

a good walk

A good starting point is **Marine Park** 45 ⚑, right along the cruise-ship dock. For an introduction to public lands in the area, walk up Marine Way and turn right on Whittier Street to reach the engaging **Alaska State Museum** 46, filled with artifacts and art from around the state. From here, circle back along Willoughby Avenue to the **State Office Building** 47. Catch the elevator to the eighth-floor atrium and head out onto the observation deck for vistas across Gastineau Channel. Then continue out the east side of the building onto 4th Street. The small but informative **Juneau-Douglas City Museum** 48 sits a short distance away at 4th and Calhoun streets. The unimpressive banklike building across the street is the **Alaska State Capitol** 49. Next stop is the **Governor's Mansion** 50, a few minutes uphill on Calhoun Street. If you have the time and energy, you may want to continue along Calhoun, across the Gold Creek Bridge, and then down along 12th Street to the quiet **Evergreen Cemetery** 51, where town fathers Joe Juneau and Dick Harris are buried.

Backtrack to the Governor's Mansion and retrace your steps down Calhoun Street to the overpass. Climb the steps and cross the footbridge to 5th Street. The **St. Nicholas Russian Orthodox Church** 52 occupies the corner of 5th and Gold streets, and the **Centennial Hall Visitor Center** 53 is just a couple of blocks away, at the intersection of Egan Drive and Willoughby Avenue. By now you probably have a good taste of Juneau; step inside for the complete details.

Now it's time to explore the historic buildings and busy shops of downtown Juneau, particularly those along **South Franklin Street** 54. Check out the Alaskan Hotel, the Alaska Steam Laundry Building, and the Senate Building before dipping inside the always crowded **Red Dog Saloon** 55 at the intersection of South Franklin Street and Admiral Way. A few more minutes' walking will take you to the **Mt. Roberts Tramway** 56, a great way to reach alpine country for a hike overlooking Juneau and Gastineau Channel.

TIMING To cover downtown Juneau's many interesting sights, you should allow at least three or four hours for exploring. Add more time to ride the Mt. Roberts Tramway or for the side trip to Evergreen Cemetery.

What to See

49 **Alaska State Capitol.** Built in 1930, this rather unassuming building with southeastern Alaskan marble pillars houses the governor's office and hosts state legislature meetings during the winter months. Historic photos line the upstairs walls. You can pick up a self-guided tour brochure as you enter. ✉ *Corner of Seward and 4th Sts.* ☎ *907/465–4648* ⏲ *Weekdays 8–5.*

★ 46 **Alaska State Museum.** Alaska's finest museum appeals to all tastes. Native Alaskan buffs will enjoy examining the 38-foot walrus-hide *umiak* (an open, skin-covered Eskimo boat) built by Eskimos and a re-created interior of a Tlingit tribal house. Natural-history exhibits include stuffed brown bears and a two-story-high eagle nesting tree. Russian-American and gold rush displays, a kids' room, and contemporary art complete the collection. Be sure to visit the cramped gift shop with its

Alaska State Capitol 49
Alaska State Museum 46
Centennial Hall Visitor Center 53
Evergreen Cemetery 51
Governor's Mansion 50
Juneau-Douglas City Museum 48
Marine Park . . .45
Mt. Roberts Tramway 56
Red Dog Saloon 55
St. Nicholas Russian Orthodox Church 52
South Franklin Street 54
State Office Building 47

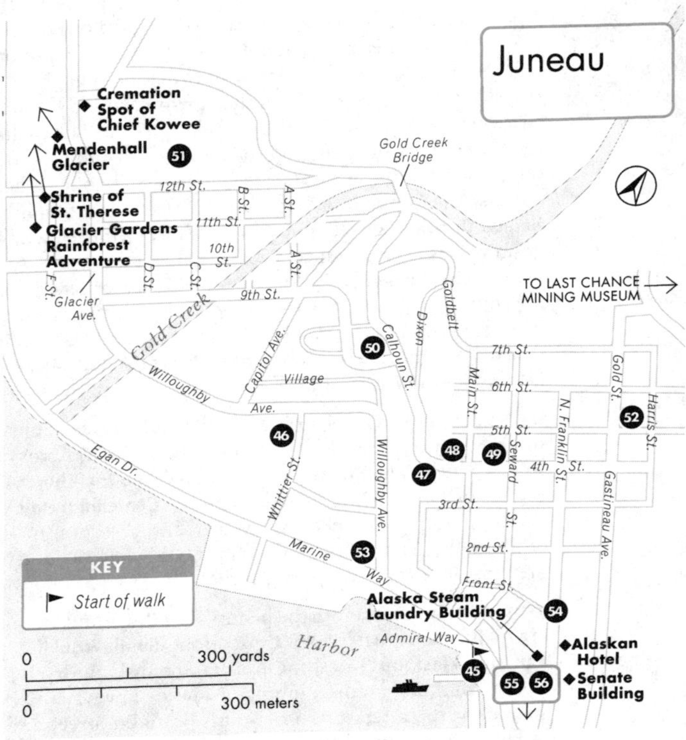

extraordinary selection of Native art from around the state, including baskets, carvings, and masks. ✉ *395 Whittier St.* ☎ *907/465–2901* 🌐 *www.museums.state.ak.us* *$5* ⏲ *Mid-May–mid-Sept., daily 8:30–5:30; mid-Sept.–mid-May, Tues.–Sat. 10–4.*

53 **Centennial Hall Visitor Center.** Here you can get complete details on Juneau sights and activities, plus walking-tour maps. You can also make ferry reservations and find out about hiking trails and other activities on nearby Tongass National Forest lands. If it's raining outside, you may want to select one of their Alaskan videos and watch it in the little theater here. ✉ *101 Egan Dr.* ☎ *907/586–2201 or 888/581–2201* 🌐 *www.traveljuneau.com* ⏲ *May–Sept., weekdays 8:30–5, weekends 9–5; Oct.–Apr., weekdays 9–4.*

51 **Evergreen Cemetery.** Many Juneau pioneers, including Joe Juneau and Dick Harris, are buried here. A meandering gravel path leads through the graveyard, and at the end of it is the monument commemorating the cremation spot of Chief Kowee.

50 **Governor's Mansion.** Completed in 1912, this white three-level colonial-style home overlooks downtown Juneau. Out front is a totem pole that tells the tale of a giant that turned into Alaska's ubiquitous mosquitoes.

Tours of the residence are, unfortunately, not permitted. ✉ *716 Calhoun Ave.*

48 **Juneau-Douglas City Museum.** Among the exhibits interpreting local mining and Tlingit history are old mining equipment (from gold scales to pack saddles), a three-dimensional model of the AJ Mine, many historic photos, exhibits on ice-field research, and pioneer artifacts, including a century-old store and kitchen. Youngsters will appreciate the hands-on room where they can try on clothes similar to ones worn by the miners or look at stereoscopes from the gold rush. Also of interest is the half-hour video of Juneau's history. ✉ *114 4th St.* ☎ *907/586–3572* 🌐 *www.juneau.org/parksrec/museum* *$3* ⏲ *Mid-May–Sept., weekdays 9–5, weekends 10–5; Oct.–mid-May, Tues.–Sat. noon–4.*

45 **Marine Park.** On the dock where the cruise ships tie up is a little urban oasis with benches, shade trees, and shelter. It's a great place to enjoy an outdoor meal purchased from one of Juneau's many street vendors. A visitor kiosk is staffed according to cruise-ship schedules.

★ 56 **Mt. Roberts Tramway.** The tram whisks you from the cruise terminal 1,800 feet up the side of Mt. Roberts. After the six-minute ride, you can take in a film on the history and legends of the Tlingits, visit the nature center, go for an alpine walk on hiking trails, purchase Native crafts, meet an eagle from the Juneau Raptor Center, or experience fine mountain-view dining from the decks. A local company leads guided wilderness hikes from the summit, and the smoke-free bar serves locally brewed beers. ☎ *907/463–3412 or 888/461–8726* 🌐 *www.goldbelttours.com* *$22* ⏲ *May–Sept., daily 9–9.*

55 **Red Dog Saloon.** The frontierish quarters of the Red Dog have housed an infamous Juneau watering hole since 1890. Every conceivable surface in this two-story bar is cluttered with life preservers, business cards, and college banners, and when tourist season hits, a little atmospheric sawdust covers the floor as well. Bands pump out dance tunes when cruise ships are docked. ✉ *278 S. Franklin St.* ☎ *907/463–9954.*

52 **St. Nicholas Russian Orthodox Church.** Quaint, onion-domed, and built in 1894 by Tlingit Natives and Slavic immigrants, St. Nicholas is the oldest Russian church building in Southeast Alaska. The tiny white-and-blue church is used for services (sung in Slavonic, English, and Tlingit) on Saturdays and Sundays, and a small gift shop is adjacent. ✉ *326 5th St.* ☎ *907/845–2288* *$2 requested donation* ⏲ *Tours mid-May–Sept., Mon.–Sat. 9–5.*

54 **South Franklin Street.** The buildings on South Franklin Street (and Front Street as well), among the oldest and most interesting structures in the city, house curio and crafts shops, snack shops, and two salmon shops. Many reflect the architecture of the 1920s and '30s, and some are even older. The small **Alaskan Hotel** opened in 1913 and retains its period trappings. The barroom's massive, mirrored oak back bar is accented by Tiffany lights and panels. The 1901 **Alaska Steam Laundry Building,** with a windowed turret, now houses a coffeehouse and other stores. The **Senate Building** is across the street.

47 **State Office Building.** At this government building you can have a picnic lunch with the state workers on the eighth-floor patio facing Gastineau Channel and Douglas Island. On most Fridays at noon, concerts inside the four-story atrium feature a grand old theater pipe organ, a veteran of the silent-movie era. Also here is the historic old witch totem pole, the Alaska State Library, with a fine collection of historical photos, plus computers with public Internet access. ✉ *4th and Calhoun Sts.*

off the beaten path

LAST CHANCE MINING MUSEUM – A 1½-mi hike or taxi ride behind town, this small museum is housed in one of the buildings from Juneau's historic AJ Gold Mine. The collection includes old mining tools and equipment, minerals, and a 3-D map of the ore body. The surrounding country is steep and wooded, with trails leading in all directions, including one to the summit of Mt. Juneau. ✉ *1001 Basin Rd.* ☎ *907/586–5338* *$4* ⏲ *Mid-May–mid-Sept., daily 9:30–12:30 and 3:30–6:30.*

Where to Eat

$$$$ ✕ **Gold Creek Salmon Bake.** Trees, mountains, and the rushing water of Salmon Creek surround the comfortable, canopy-covered benches and tables at this authentic salmon bake. Fresh-caught salmon is cooked over an alder fire and served with a succulent sauce of brown sugar, margarine, and lemon juice. For $29 there are all-you-can-eat salmon, pork spareribs, and chicken along with baked beans, rice pilaf, salad, corn bread, and blueberry cake. Wine and beer are extra. After dinner you can pan for gold in the stream or wander up the hill to explore the remains of the Wagner gold mine. A round-trip bus ride from downtown is included. ✉ *1061 Salmon Lane Rd.* ☎ *907/789–0052 or 800/323–5757* 🌐 *www.alaskaadventures.com* 💳 *MC, V* ⏲ *Closed Oct.–Apr.*

$$–$$$$ ✕ **The Fiddlehead.** Juneau's favorite restaurant is actually two dining spots in one, both smoke-free. Downstairs you can get a casual breakfast, lunch, or dinner in a bright room accented by stained glass and modern art. The menu includes plenty of vegetarian items and an eclectic assortment of entrées ranging from halibut tacos to Black Angus meat loaf. Homemade bread and cookies from the restaurant's bakery are always a hit. Di Sopra, upstairs, is more formal, with a full bar, tall windows facing the mountains, music on summer weekends, and a heartier menu that includes Sicilian fisherman's stew, pasta, and vegetarian specialties. Or you can just graze on the substantial appetizers and salads. ✉ *429 Willoughby Ave.* ☎ *907/586–3150* 💳 *AE, D, DC, MC, V.*

Fodor'sChoice ★

$$$ ✕ **Thane Ore House Salmon Bake.** Four miles south of town is this all-you-can-eat-for-$22.95 restaurant with a waterside setting and indoor dining; it's one of the oldest and most authentic salmon bakes in the state. Your meal includes salmon, halibut, barbecued beef ribs, salad, baked beans, and corn bread. A free round-trip bus ride from downtown hotels is included. ✉ *4400 Thane Rd., 4 mi south of Juneau* ☎ *907/586–3442* 💳 *MC, V* ⏲ *Closed Oct.–Apr.*

$–$$$ ✕ **Hangar on the Wharf.** Crowded with both locals and travelers, the Hangar is in the building where Alaska Airlines started business. The comfortably worn wood, stainless-steel accents, and vintage airplane photos create a casual dining experience. There are expansive views of Gastineau Channel and Douglas Island from every seat. A wide selection of entrées, including locally caught halibut and salmon, filet mignon, great burgers, and daily specials makes this a Juneau hot spot. You'll also find two dozen draft beers available. On Friday and Saturday nights, jazz or rock bands take over the Hangar's stage, and prime rib arrives on the menu. ✉ *2 Marine Way, Merchants Wharf Mall* ☎ *907/586–5018* ▭ *AE, D, MC, V.*

¢–$ ✕ **BaCar's.** This is the spot for hearty, inexpensive breakfasts and satisfying lunches. Fluffy omelets are $9 and come with home fries and a big side pancake. Lunches, including the halibut fish-and-chips, prime rib, and French dips, are simple and good. There are also a few interesting variations on diner standards, such as a salmon melt and tempura Spam strips. ✉ *230 Seward St.* ☎ *907/463–4202* ▭ *AE, MC, V* ⊙ *No dinner.*

¢–$ ✕ **Douglas Cafe.** Many locals call this out-of-the-way café the best fast-food stop in the Juneau area, with 15 types of burgers available, including jalapeño burgers and Hawaiian burgers. Located in the heart of Douglas, across the bridge and a couple of miles from downtown Juneau, this comfortable family eatery has Formica tables and a three-meals-a-day menu that includes omelets, blueberry pancakes, sandwiches, kids' favorites, and chicken adobo cooked by the Philipine-American chefs. ✉ *916 3rd St., Douglas* ☎ *907/364–3307* ▭ *MC, V.*

¢ ✕ **Heritage Coffee Company.** Juneau's favorite coffee shop, this is a downtown instutition, with locally roasted coffees, fresh pastries, and all sorts of specialty drinks. The windowfront bar is especially popular for people-watching while you read the newspaper and sip a chai latte. The same folks also operate the **Glacier Cafe** in Mendenhall Valley, with a bigger menu that includes breakfast burritos and omelets, along with lunchtime paninis, wraps, soups, salads, and burgers, plus various vegetarian items. ✉ *174 S. Franklin St.* ☎ *907/586–1087* ▭ *No credit cards* ✉ *Mendenhall Mall Rd.* ☎ *907/789–0692* 🌐 *www.glaciercafe.com* ▭ *MC, V* ⊙ *No dinner.*

¢ ✕ **Rainbow Foods.** Housed in a building that began life as an Assembly of God church, this crunchy natural foods market is a popular lunch-break spot for downtown workers. Organic groceries, soy ice cream, vitamin supplements, and other items fill the shelves, but the real attraction is the weekday buffet, with various hot entrées, salads, soups, and deep-dish pizzas. Get there before 11 AM for the best choices. Rotating ethnic menus every Thursday 5–7. Espresso and freshly baked breads are available, along with a few inside tables. ✉ *224 4th St.* ☎ *907/586–6476* ▭ *MC, V.*

Where to Stay

$$–$$$ ✕🏨 **Goldbelt Hotel Juneau.** A high-rise by local standards, the seven-story Goldbelt is one of Juneau's better lodging places, with well-appointed rooms that include amenities such as speaker phones, hair dryers, and irons. Waterside rooms on the upper level have views across Gastineau

Channel, and some rooms have king-size beds. A Chilkat blanket and other artifacts are displayed in the lobby, and the adjacent Chinook's restaurant serves three meals a day. ✉ *51 W. Egan Dr., 99801* ☎ *907/586–6900 or 888/478–6909* 🖷 *907/463–3567* 🌐 *www.goldbelt.com* *104 rooms, 1 suite* *Restaurant, room service, cable TV with movies, lounge, meeting room, airport shuttle; no a/c* *AE, D, DC, MC, V.*

$–$$ **Frontier Suites Airport Hotel.** Near the airport in Mendenhall Valley, 9 mi from Juneau, this rambling hotel is a great option for families. All rooms have modern, functional furniture and full kitchens with a stove, refrigerator, microwave, dishes, silverware, and pans. Suites have separate bedrooms and living rooms (with sleeper sofas) and two televisions. Two bunk rooms include a mini-loft for older children. **Pasta Garden,** downstairs, serves American, Asian, Mexican, and Mediterranean fare three meals a day. ✉ *9400 Glacier Hwy., 99801* ☎ *907/790–6600 or 800/544–2250* 🖷 *907/790–6612* 🌐 *www.frontiersuites.com* *104 rooms, 32 suites* *Restaurant, café, kitchens, microwaves, refrigerators, cable TV, bar; no a/c* *AE, D, DC, MC, V.*

$$$$ Fodor'sChoice ★ **Pearson's Pond Luxury Inn and Adventure Spa.** On a small pond near Mendenhall Glacier, this large home may be Alaska's finest B&B. Owners Diane and Steven Pearson pull out all the stops for guests, with two outdoor hot tubs, an indoor fountain, gas fireplaces, whirlpool tubs with rain showers, Wi-Fi computer network, a big library of videotapes, four-poster beds, private balconies, and a well-stocked breakfast nook. Diane Pearson helps with itinerary planning, and is even licensed to perform weddings (which are common at the B&B). Guests can paddle around the pond in a waterbike, or borrow a fishing pole. There's yoga on the deck each morning and fine wine and cheese in the evening. The Pearsons also have two condos ($179) closer to town, which sleep four people each. A two-night minimum stay is required for the B&B; five nights for the condos. ✉ *4541 Sawa Cir., 99801* ☎ *907/789–3772 or 888/658–6328* 🖷 *907/789–6722* 🌐 *www.pearsonspond.com* *5 suites* *Cable TV, in-room VCRs, gym, massage, bicycles, Internet, meeting room, travel services; no a/c, no smoking* *AE, D, DC, MC, V* *BP.*

$$–$$$$ Fodor'sChoice ★ **Alaska's Capital Inn.** Gold-rush pioneer John Olds built this American foursquare home in 1906, and a major restoration in 2003 transformed it into Juneau's most elegant B&B. Rooms are furnished in Arts and Crafts pieces, blending a nostalgic charm with such modern conveniences as an outdoor hot tub, in-room phones, TVs and VCRs, and high-speed Internet access. The Governor's Suite covers the entire fourth floor and includes a king-size sleigh bed, gas fireplace, and hot tub. Two small rooms on the bottom level have private entrances. Breakfast is a highlight, with a variety of Alaskan seafood dishes. This B&B fills quickly for the summer season. ✉ *113 W. 5th St., 99801* ☎ *907/586–6507 or 888/588–6507* 🖷 *907/586–6508* 🌐 *www.alaskacapitalinn.com* *4 rooms, 3 suites* *Cable TV, in-room VCRs, hot tub, Internet; no a/c, no kids under 12* *AE, D, MC, V* *BP.*

$$–$$$$ **Baranof Hotel.** The Baranof has long been Juneau's most prestigious address. Tasteful woods and period lamps in the dark art-deco lobby create an old-money atmosphere reminiscent of 1939, when the hotel first opened. Downstairs dining is available in a casual restaurant as well as in the Gold Room with its embroidered chairs. Rooms on the front side have the best views, but street noise may keep you awake at the lower levels. The best are spacious corner suites on the upper floors, which overlook Juneau's busy harbor to the forested mountains of Douglas Island. Some of the other rooms are fairly small. Alaska Airlines and Grayline have offices downstairs. ✉ *127 N. Franklin St., 99801* ☎ *907/586–2660 or 800/544–0970* 📠 *907/586–8315* 🌐 *www.westmarkhotels.com* *179 rooms, 17 suites* *Restaurant, coffee shop, some kitchenettes, cable TV, hair salon, lobby lounge, meeting room, travel services; no a/c* 💳 *AE, D, DC, MC, V.*

$$ **Aspen Hotel.** This corporate-style inn, within walking distance of the airport and 9 mi from downtown, is perfect for business travelers and families. Rooms are large and clean, with in-room refrigerators, microwaves, and big TVs. This is also one of the few Juneau lodging options with an indoor pool, fitness center, hot tub, and hot breakfast. ✉ *1800 Shell Simmons Dr., 99801* ☎ *907/790–6435 or 866/483–7848* 📠 *907/790–6621* 🌐 *www.aspenhotelsak.com* *86 rooms, 8 suites* *Kitchenettes, microwaves, refrigerators, cable TV, indoor pool, exercise equipment, hot tub, Internet, business services, meeting rooms, airport shuttle; no a/c* 💳 *AE, D, MC, V* *BP.*

$$ **Grandma's Feather Bed.** This small Victorian-style hotel is part of the Best Western chain and is less than a mile from the airport in Mendenhall Valley. Cheerful colors brighten each of the spacious and homey rooms, which come with jetted bathtubs and feather comforters. Two of the rooms have gas fireplaces. Guests especially appreciate the big breakfast buffet that includes omelets and hot cereals. Dinners are also available. The hotel is not really set up for children. ✉ *2348 Mendenhall Loop Rd., 99801* ☎ *907/789–5566 or 888/781–5005* 📠 *907/789–2818* *14 rooms* *Restaurant, microwaves, refrigerators, cable TV, Internet, business services, airport shuttle; no a/c, no smoking* 💳 *AE, D, DC, MC, V* *BP.*

$$ **Silverbow Inn.** Conveniently located in Juneau's historic downtown, the Silverbow combines a downstairs bakery and café with a half-dozen rustic hotel rooms on the two upper levels. Four of the rooms are tiny, but all are tastefully furnished and guests stroll downstairs each morning for a filling breakfast along with evening wine and cheese. Owned by former New Yorkers, the bakery crafts Alaska's most authentic bagels, and also serves deli sandwiches on homemade bread, salads, soups, and pastries. The back room is used for live music, films, and a dinner theater throughout the year. ✉ *120 2nd St.* ☎ *907/586–4146 or 800/586–4146* 📠 *907/586–4242* 🌐 *www.silverbowinn.com* *6 rooms* *Cable TV; no a/c* 💳 *AE, D, MC, V* *CP.*

$–$$ **Glacier Trail Bed & Breakfast.** Owned by backcountry guides, this comfortable Victorian-style home is right on Mendenhall Lake across from Mendenhall Glacier. Guests can stay in two guest rooms with whirlpool baths or a private apartment with a full kitchen. Kayaks are available to explore Mendenhall Lake ($30 extra). ✉ *1081 Arctic Circle, 99801* ☎ *907/789–5646* 📠 *907/789–5697* 🌐 *www.juneaulodging.com* *2 rooms, 1 apartment* *Some in-room hot tubs, boating; no a/c, no smoking* 💳 *MC, V* *BP.*

$–$$ **The Prospector Hotel.** A short walk west of downtown and next door to the Alaska State Museum, this nicely appointed hotel is frequented by business travelers and legislators (during the winter session). Rooms are spacious and have cherrywood furnishings, leather chairs, and ottomans. T. K. McGuire's dining room and lounge serves prime rib, steaks, and seafood, along with a popular Sunday brunch. ✉ *375 Whittier St., 99801* ☎ *907/586–3737, 800/331–2711 outside Alaska, 800/478–5866 in Alaska* 📠 *907/586–1204* 🌐 *www.prospectorhotel.com* *55 rooms, 7 suites* *Restaurant, kitchenettes, microwaves, refrigerators, cable TV, lobby lounge, meeting rooms, some pets allowed (fee); no a/c* *AE, D, DC, MC, V.*

$ **Driftwood Lodge.** This downtown motel is one of Juneau's best values for the money, with well-maintained rooms, all of which include kitchenettes stocked with dishes, silverware, pots, and pans. The one- and two-bedroom units have twice the space of standard rooms, but cost just a few extra dollars. The acclaimed Fiddlehead Restaurant is right next door. The shuttle to the airport and ferry is free. ✉ *435 Willoughby Ave., 99801* ☎ *907/586–2280 or 800/544–2239* 📠 *907/586–1034* 🌐 *www.driftwoodalaska.com* *31 rooms, 31 suites* *Kitchenettes, airport and ferry shuttle; no a/c* *AE, D, DC, MC, V.*

$ **Sentinel Island Lighthouse.** A few miles north of Juneau and adjacent to a rock where Steller's sea lions haul out, this operating lighthouse provides a spectacular spot to watch whales and eagles. You have the entire 6-acre island to roam around on. Simple accommodations include bunks in the lighthouse and in an adjacent building; you can also pitch a tent on a platform facing the water. Water and cooking facilities are provided for all accommodations. The lighthouse is managed by Gastineau Channel Historical Society, and access is by charter boat, sea kayak, or helicopter. *Box 21264, 99802* ☎ *907/586–5338* *6 bunks in 2 buildings* *Kitchenettes* *No credit cards.*

★ ¢–$ **Alaskan Hotel.** This historic 1913 hotel in the heart of downtown Juneau sits over the popular bar of the same name; be prepared for noise Thursday through Saturday nights when bands are playing. The older but well-maintained guest rooms ramble across three floors and include pedestal sinks, old-fashioned radiators, and a smattering of antiques. The flocked wallpaper, red floral carpets, and Tiffany windows are reminiscent of the hotel's original gold rush–era opulence. The least-expensive rooms share a bath down the hall. ✉ *167 S. Franklin St., 99801* ☎ *907/586–1000 or 800/327–9347* 📠 *907/463–3775* 🌐 *www.ptialaska.net/~akhotel* *42 rooms, 22 with bath* *Bar; no a/c, no phones in some rooms, no TV in some rooms* *D, DC, MC, V.*

¢ **U.S. Forest Service Cabins.** Scattered throughout Tongass National Forest, these rustic cabins offer a charming and cheap escape for just $25–$45 per cabin. Most are fly-in units, accessible by floatplanes from virtually any community in the Southeast. These public-use cabins have bunks for six to eight occupants, tables, stoves, and outdoor privies but no electricity or running water. You provide your own sleeping bag, food, and cooking utensils. Bedside reading in most cabins includes a diary kept by visitors—add your own adventure. ✉ *Juneau Ranger District, 8465 Old Dairy Rd., 99801* ☎ *907/586–8800, 877/*

Fodor's Choice ★

444–6777 reservations ⊕ *www.reserveusa.com* *150 cabins* ▭ *AE, D, MC, V.*

¢ **U.S. Forest Service Campgrounds.** Eight Forest Service–maintained campgrounds are scattered around Tongass National Forest and are accessible from the communities of Juneau, Sitka, Ketchikan, Petersburg, and Thorne Bay. All have pit toilets and sites for RVs and tents, but not all provide drinking water. Reservations are possible for some of these campgrounds, but space is generally available without a reservation. ✉ *Juneau Ranger District, 8465 Old Dairy Rd., 99801* ☎ *907/586–8800, 877/444–6777 reservations* ⊕ *www.reserveusa.com* *$8* ▭ *D, MC, V.*

Guided Tours

4

Boating & Kayaking

Alaska Travel Adventures (☎ 907/789–0052 or 800/478–0052 ⊕ www.alaskaadventures.com) leads Mendenhall River floats. The Native-owned **Auk Ta Shaa Discovery** (☎ 907/586–8687 or 800/820–2628 ⊕ www.goldbelttours.com) also guides rafting trips down the Mendenhall River. **Above and Beyond Alaska** (☎ 907/364–2333 ☎ 907/364–2553 ⊕ www.beyondak.com.com) guides overnight camping and kayaking trips in the Juneau area.

Alaska Fjordlines (☎ 907/766–3395 or 800/320–0146 ⊕ www.alaskafjordlines.com) provides roundtrips connecting Skagway and Haines with Juneau on a daily basis in the summer. The boat leaves Skagway at 8 AM, Haines at 9 AM, and reaches Juneau at 11:45 AM, where a bus transports visitors into town, returning to the boat at 4:45 PM for the ride back to Haines.

Auk Nu Tours (☎ 907/586–8687 or 800/820–2628 ⊕ www.auknutours.com) has all-day catamaran tours to the beautiful glaciers of Tracy Arm Fjord. **Adventure Bound** (☎ 907/463—2509 or 800/228–3875 ⊕ www.adventureboundalaska.com) offers all-day trips to Sawyer Glacier within Tracy Arm during the summer.

Helicopter Flightseeing

Several local companies operate helicopter flightseeing trips that take you to the spectacular glaciers flowing from Juneau Icefield. Most have booths along the downtown cruise-ship dock. All include a touchdown on a glacier, with a chance to romp on these rivers of ice. Some also lead trips that include a dogsled ride on the glacier. Note that though we recommend the best companies, even some of the most experienced pilots have been killed in helicopter accidents; always ask a carrier about their recent safety record before booking a trip. Flightseeing is quite controversial in Juneau, where locals are concerned about the almost constant din of helicopter activity throughout the summer. **Coastal Helicopters** (☎ 907/789–5600 or 800/789–5610 ⊕ www.coastalhelicopters.com) lands on several glaciers within the Juneau Icefield. **ERA Helicopters** (☎ 907/586–2030 or 800/843–1947 ⊕ www.eraaviation.com) has a one-hour trip that includes landing on Norris Glacier. **NorthStar Trekking** (☎ 907/790–4530 ⊕ www.glaciertrekking.com) leads a variety of excellent glacier hikes, starting with a one-hour interpretive walk, up to a four-hour hike that includes the chance to practice basic climbing and rope techniques. No experience is necessary. **Temsco Helicopters** (☎ 907/789–9501 or 877/789–9501 ⊕ www.temscoair.com) lands on Mendenhall Glacier.

Sightseeing

Juneau Trolley Car Company (☎ 907/586–7433 ⊕ www.juneautrolley.com) conducts narrated tours, stopping at a dozen or so of Juneau's historic and shopping attractions for $12. **Mighty Great Trips** (☎ 907/789–5460 ⊕ www.mightygreattrips.com) leads guided bus tours that include a visit to Mendenhall Glacier. The **Juneau Convention and Visitors Bureau** (☎ 907/586–2201 or 888/581–2201 ⊕ www.traveljuneau.com) has a list of other companies that provide tours to Mendenhall Glacier.

Former miners lead three-hour tours of the historic **AJ Gold Mine** (☎ 907/463–5017) south of Juneau. A gold-panning demonstration is included, and approximately 45 minutes of the tour take place inside the old tunnels that lace the mountains. Mine tours depart from downtown by bus.

★ **Taku Glacier Lodge** (☎ 907/586–8258 🖷 907/789–6970 ⊕ www.takuglacierlodge.com) is a remote, historic lodge south of Juneau along Taku Inlet. Hole-in-the-Wall Glacier is directly across the inlet from the lodge, and nature trails wind through the surrounding country, where black bears and bald eagles are frequently sighted. Floatplanes fly from Juneau on a scenic trip to the lodge, where you are served a delicious lunch or dinner and then flown back three hours later. No overnight stays are available.

Several companies lead whale-watching trips from Juneau. **Juneau Sportfishing & Sightseeing** (☎ 907/586–1887 ⊕ www.juneausportfishing.com) has been around for many years, and its boats carry a maximum of six passengers, providing a personalized trip. **Four Seasons Marine** (☎ 907/790-6671 or 877/774–8687 ⊕ www.4seasonmarine.com) combines whale watching with an hour at Orca Point Lodge on Colt Island where guests are served a grilled salmon lunch. The boat departs from Auke Bay with a free shuttle from Juneau.

Nightlife & the Arts

Bars

The **Alaskan Hotel bar** (✉ 167 S. Franklin St. ☎ 907/586–1000) is about as funky a place as you'll find in Juneau: flocked-velvet walls, antique chandeliers above the bar, and vintage Alaskan frontier-brothel decor. Sit back and enjoy the live music or take turns with the locals at the open mike. When the ships are in, the music at **Red Dog Saloon** (✉ 278 S. Franklin St. ☎ 907/463–9954) is live and the crowd gets livelier. Past visitors to Juneau may recall **Imperial Saloon** (✉ 241 Front St. ☎ 907/586–1960) as one of the downtown dives, but a major remodeling transformed it into a favorite place to dance (live bands most weekends), drink, shoot pool, and meet singles.

If you're a beer fan, look for **Alaskan Brewing Company** (✉ 5429 Shaune Dr. ☎ 907/780–5866 ⊕ www.alaskanbeer.com) Alaskan Amber, Pale

Ale, Stout, and Smoked Porter beers, brewed and bottled in Juneau. You can also visit the microbrewery and sample various brews after touring the bottling operation May–September, Monday–Saturday 11–5, with 20-minute tours every half hour. Between October and April, tours take place Thursday–Saturday 11–4. The gift shop sells classy T-shirts and beer paraphernalia.

Music Festivals

The annual weeklong **Alaska Folk Festival** (Box 21748, 99802 907/463–3316 www.juneau.com/aff) is staged each April in Juneau, drawing singers, banjo masters, fiddlers, and even cloggers from all over the state. During the last week of May, Juneau is the scene of **Juneau Jazz 'n Classics** (Box 22152, 99802 907/463–3378 www.jazzandclassics.org), which celebrates music from Bach to Brubeck.

Symphony

The **Juneau Symphony** (Box 21236 907/586–4676 www.juneau.com/symphony) performs classical works November through April in the high school auditorium.

Theater

Southeast Alaska's only professional theater company, **Perseverance Theatre** (914 3rd St., Douglas 907/364–2421 www.perseverancetheatre.org), presents everything from Broadway and Shakespeare to locally written plays year-round.

Sports & the Outdoors

Mountain Biking

Drop by the Centennial Hall Visitor Center for details on local trails open to bikes. Nearby is **Driftwood Lodge** (435 Willoughby Ave. 907/586–2280 www.driftwoodalaska.com), which has mountain bikes for rent, along with trailers for toddlers.

Climbing Gym

South of Juneau off Thane Road, the **Rock Dump** (1310 Eastaugh Way 907/586–4982 www.rockdump.com) is a large indoor climbing facility with something for all abilities. Day passes are $10, and rental equipment is available.

Cross-Country Skiing

During the winter, the **Parks and Recreation Department** (907/586–5226, 907/586–0428 24-hr info www.juneau.lib.ak.us/parksrec) sponsors a group ski and snowshoe outing each Wednesday and Saturday when there's sufficient snow. Find groomed cross-country ski trails near the Eaglecrest Ski Area and at Mendenhall Campground in the winter. You can rent skis and get advice about touring the trails and ridges around town from **Foggy Mountain Shop** (134 N. Franklin St. 907/586–6780 www.foggymountainshop.com).

Downhill Skiing

The only downhill area in Southeast Alaska, **Eaglecrest** (155 S. Seward St., Juneau 99801 907/790–2000, 907/586–5330 recorded ski information www.juneau.org/eaglecrest), on Douglas Island, just 30 minutes from downtown Juneau, offers late-November to mid-April skiing and snowboarding on a well-groomed mountain with two double chairlifts, cross-country trails, a beginner's platter pull, ski school, ski-rental shop, cafeteria, and trilevel day lodge. Enjoy the northern lights while you night-ski from January through mid-March.

Fishing

Sportfishing is a popular activity in the Juneau area, and many charter boats depart local harbors. The **Juneau Convention and Visitors Bureau** (☎ 907/586–1887 🌐 www.traveljuneau.com) Web site has a complete listing.

Fitness Clubs

The **Juneau Racquet Club/Alaska Club** (✉ 2841 Riverside Dr. ☎ 907/789–2181 🌐 www.thealaskaclub.com), about 10 mi north of downtown, adjacent to Mendenhall Mall, houses first-class indoor tennis and racquetball courts. There's a $9 daily fee for nonmembers. Other facilities include a sauna, a hot tub, exercise equipment, massage tables, a sports shop, and a snack bar. **JRC/Alaska Club Downtown** (✉ W. Willoughby Ave. ☎ 907/586–5773) is a smaller version of the JRC on Riverside Drive. There's a $10.50 charge per day for nonmembers.

Gold Panning

Gold panning is fun, especially for children, and Juneau is one of the Southeast's best-known gold-panning towns. Sometimes you actually uncover a few flecks of the precious metal in the bottom of your pan. You can buy a pan at almost any Alaska hardware or sporting-goods store. **Alaska Travel Adventures** (☎ 907/789–0052 or 800/478–0052 🌐 www.alaskaadventures.com) has gold-panning tours near the famous Alaska-Juneau Mine.

Golf

Juneau's par-three, 9-hole **Mendenhall Golf Course** (✉ 2101 Industrial Blvd. ☎ 907/789–1221) is pretty modest but does rent clubs and has spectacular views.

Hiking

The **Parks and Recreation Department** (☎ 907/586–5226, 907/586–0428 24-hr info 🌐 www.juneau.lib.ak.us/parksrec) in Juneau sponsors a group hike each Wednesday morning and on Saturday in summer. Hikers can contact the **U.S. Forest Service** (☎ 907/586–8790) for trail books and maps. A private company, **Gastineau Guiding** (☎ 907/586–2666 🌐 www.stepintoalaska.com), leads hikes from the top of the tram on Mt. Roberts, including an early bird version that departs at 8 AM to avoid the crowds.

Sea Kayaking & Canoeing

Experienced kayakers can rent boats and equipment from **Alaska Boat and Kayak Rental** (☎ 907/586–8220 🌐 www.juneaukayak.com) at the Auke Bay boat harbor 12 mi north of Juneau. **Alaska Travel Adventures** (☎ 907/789–0052 🌐 www.alaskaadventures.com) conducts sea-kayaking trips to Mendenhall Glacier. **Auk Ta Shaa Discovery** (☎ 907/586–8687 or 800/820–2628 🌐 www.goldbelttours.com) operates sea-kayaking trips in the Juneau area.

Shopping

Art Galleries

Annie Kaill's Gallery (✉ 244 Front St. ☎ 907/586–2880 🌐 www.annieandcojuneau.com).displays a mix of playful and whimsical original prints, pottery, jewelry, and other arts and crafts from Alaskan artists. The cooperatively run **Juneau Artists Gallery** (✉ 175 S. Franklin St. ☎ 907/586–9891 🌐 www.juneauartistsgallery.com), on the first floor of the old Senate Building, sells a nice mix of watercolors, jewelry, etchings, photographs, art glass, ceramics, Ukranian-style decorated eggs, and pottery from more than 20 artists. Head upstairs above Heritage Coffee for **Wm. Spear Designs** (✉ 174 S. Franklin St. ☎ 907/586–2209 🌐 www.wmspear.com), where this lawyer-turned-artist produces a fun and colorful collection of enameled pins and zipper pulls. Across from the tram, the **Raven's Journey** (✉ 439 S. Franklin St. ☎ 907/463–4686) specializes in high-quality Native Alaskan masks, grass baskets, carvings, dolls, ivory and silver jewelry, and more.

Juneau's airport gift shop, **Hummingbird Hollow** (☎ 907/789–4672 🌐 www.hummingbirdhollow.net), is another fine place for authentic Native art, including a surprisingly diverse selection of jewelry, baskets, and Eskimo dolls.

Rie Muñoz, of the **Rie Muñoz Gallery** (✉ 2101 Jordan Ave. ☎ 907/789–7411, 800/247–3151 🌐 www.riemunoz.com) in Mendenhall Valley, is one of Alaska's best-known artists. She's the creator of a stylized, simple, and colorful design technique that is much copied but rarely equaled. Other artists' work is also on sale at the Muñoz Gallery, including wood-block prints by nationally recognized artist Dale DeArmond. Various books illustrated by Rie Muñoz and written by Alaskan children's author Jean Rogers are for sale. In downtown Juneau, see Rie Muñoz's paintings and tapestries at **Decker Gallery** (✉ 233 S. Franklin St. ☎ 907/463–5536 or 800/463–5536).

Clothing

Kodiak Coat (✉ 255 Marine Way ☎ 907/463–2625 🌐 www.kodiakcoats.com) occupies a small shop inside the Emporium Mall. Owner Bridget Milligan designs and sews waterproof and breathable coats, hats, and mittens, all made to withstand Alaska's rugged climate. Her kids' coats are especially worth a look. Custom-made coats are the same price, making this a great place to purchase a durable one-of-a-kind gift.

Seafood

Taku Smokeries (✉ 550 S. Franklin St. ☎ 907/463–5033 or 800/582–5122 🌐 www.takusmokeries.com), at the south end of town near the cruise-ship docks, processes nearly 6 million pounds of fish, mostly salmon, a year. You can view the smoking procedure through large windows and then purchase the packaged fish in the deli-style gift shop or have some shipped back home.

AROUND JUNEAU

Just a few miles outside of the city are some great day trips, including a salmon hatchery and an unusual set of gardens. Juneau's most popular attraction is Mendenhall Glacier. Admiralty Island is also very popular—it has hikes through rainforest and great wildlife viewing and sea-kayaking.

If you're interested in knowing how the Native Alaskan village peoples of Southeast Alaska live today, you can fly or take the state ferry *LeConte* to **Kake, Angoon,** or **Hoonah.** Hoonah's historic cannery building has been beautifully restored, and now serves as a center for cruise-ship visitors. Independent travelers won't find much organized touring in any of these communities, but you will find hotels (advance reservations are strongly suggested), and guided fishing, natural-history, and wildlife-watching trips can be arranged by asking around. In Kake, contact the **Keex' Kwaan Lodge** (☎ 907/785–3434 ⊕ www.kakealaska.com). In Angoon, try the **Favorite Bay Sportfishing Lodge** (☎ 907/788–3344 or 866/788–3344 ⊕ www.favoritebay.com). In Hoonah, **Icy Strait Lodge** (☎ 907/945–3434 ⊕ www.icystraitlodge.com) provides very comfortable on-the-water accommodations.

Macaulay Salmon Hatchery

3 mi northwest of downtown Juneau.

Watch through an underwater window as salmon fight their way up a fish ladder, from mid-June to mid-October. Inside the busy hatchery—it produces almost 125 million young salmon annually—you will learn about commercial fishing and the lives of salmon. A retail shop sells gifts and salmon products, and you can fish off the adjacent dock in midsummer. Fishing poles are available for rent. ✉ *2697 Channel Dr.* ☎ *907/463–4810 or 877/463–2486* ⊕ *www.dipac.net* 🎫 *$3 including short tour* ⏲ *Mid-May–mid-Sept., weekdays 10–6, weekends 10–5; Oct.–Apr. by appointment.*

Glacier Gardens Rainforest Adventure

6½ mi northwest of Juneau.

Spread over 50 acres of rain forest 8 mi north of Juneau are ponds, waterfalls, hiking paths, a large atrium, and gardens. The roots of fallen trees, turned upside down and buried in the ground, act as bowls to hold planters that overflow with begonias, fuchsias, and petunias. Guided tours (on covered golf carts) lead you along the 4 mi of paved paths, and a 580-foot-high overlook provides dramatic views across Mendenhall Glacier. A café and gift shop are here, and the conservatory is a popular wedding spot. The city bus stops right in front of Glacier Gardens. ✉ *7600 Glacier Hwy.* ☎ *907/790–3377* ⊕ *www.glaciergardens.com* 🎫 *$15 including guided tour* ⏲ *May–Sept., daily 9–6.*

Mendenhall Glacier

★ *13 mi north of Juneau.*

Juneau's famous drive-up glacier spans 12 mi and is fed by the massive Juneau Icefield. Like many other Alaskan glaciers, it is slowly retreating up the valley, losing 100 feet a year as massive chunks of ice calve into the small lake separating Mendenhall from the **Mendenhall Visitor Center.** The center has exhibits on the glacier, a theater and bookstore, educational exhibits, and panoramic views. Nature trails lead along Mendenhall Lake and into the mountains overlooking Mendenhall Glacier. Look for spawning sockeye and coho salmon in Steep Creek, ½ mi south of the visitor center along the Moraine Ecology Trail. Several companies lead bus tours to the glacier. ✉ *End of Glacier Spur Rd., off Mendenhall Loop Rd.* ☎ *907/789–0097* 🌐 *www.fs.fed.us/r10/tongass* 🎫 *Visitor center $3* ⏲ *May–Sept., daily 8–6:30; Oct.–Apr., Thurs.–Sun. 10–4.*

Shrine of St. Therese

23 mi northwest of downtown Juneau.

A self-guided pilgrimage to the shrine is well worth the 23-mi journey from downtown Juneau (a taxi costs at least $45 round-trip). Built in the 1930s, this stone church and its 14 stations of the cross are the only inhabitants of a serene tiny island that is accessible via a 400-foot-long pedestrian causeway. Sunday services are held at 1 PM from June through August. Rustic log cabin lodging is also available on the nearby shore, but guests are asked to follow the spirit of this contemplative place. ✉ *5933 Lund St.* ☎ *907/780–6112* 🌐 *www.shrineofsainttherese.org* ⏲ *Daily.*

Admiralty Island

57 *10 mi west of Juneau.*

The island is famous for its lush rain forests and abundant wildlife, including one of the largest concentrations of brown bears anywhere on the planet. The island's Tlingit inhabitants called it Kootznoowoo, meaning "fortress of the bears." Ninety-six miles long, with 678 mi of coastline, Admiralty—the second-largest island in Southeast Alaska—is home to an estimated 1,500 bears, almost one per square mile. The Forest Service's **Admiralty Island National Monument** has a system of public-use cabins, a canoe route that crosses the island via a chain of lakes and trails, the world's highest density of nesting bald eagles, large concentrations of humpback whales, and some of the region's best sea kayaking and sportfishing. ✉ *8461 Old Dairy Rd., Juneau* ☎ *907/586–8790.*

★ More than 90% of Admiralty Island is preserved within the Kootznoowoo Wilderness. Its chief attraction is **Pack Creek,** where you can watch brown bears feeding on salmon. One of Alaska's premier bear-viewing sites, Pack Creek is co-managed by the U.S. Forest Service and the Alaska Department of Fish and Game. Permits are required during the main viewing season, from June 1 through September 10, and only 24 people per day are allowed to visit Pack Creek from July 5 through August 25. Reservations can be mailed to the Forest Service beginning February 20. ✉ *8461 Old Dairy Rd., Juneau 99801* ☎ *907/586–8800* 🌐 *www.fs.fed.us/r10/tongass* 🎫 *$50.*

Where to Stay

★ $$$$ **Thayer Lake Lodge.** One of the Southeast's oldest lodges, Thayer Lake is on the sandy shores of a 9-mi lake within the Admiralty Island National Monument. Built in 1952 by Bob and Edith Nelson and now run by their grandkids, this wonderful rustic lodge with cabins houses up to 10 people (5 in each cabin). Borrow a canoe or motorboat for unsurpassed cutthroat and Dolly Varden trout fishing. Simple family-style meals are served. Packages are available, but rates are $700 per person per night for lodging, all meals, bear excursions, fishing, other activities, and guides. You'll be deep in nature, without any neighbors for at least 25 mi around. *Box 8897, Ketchikan 99901 907/247–8897 907/247–7053 www.thayerlakelodge.com 2 cabins Dining room, kitchenettes, boating, fishing, hiking; no a/c, no room TVs MC, V Closed mid-Sept.–late May.*

Guided Tours

Alaska Discovery (5310 Glacier Hwy., Juneau 907/780–6226 or 800/586–1911 www.akdiscovery.com) leads single- and multiday trips to Pack Creek that include a floatplane trip, sea kayaking, and guided bear viewing. **Ward Air** (907/789–9150 www.wardair.com) conducts flightseeing trips to Glacier Bay and the Juneau Icefield. **Wings of Alaska** (907/789–0790 www.wingsofalaska.com) leads flightseeing trips to many areas around Juneau.

GLACIER BAY NATIONAL PARK & PRESERVE

58 *60 mi northwest of Juneau.*

Fodor's Choice ★

Near the northern end of the Inside Passage, Glacier Bay National Park and Preserve is one of the jewels of the entire national park system. Visiting Glacier Bay is like stepping back into the Little Ice Age—it's one of the few places in the world where you can approach massive tidewater glaciers. With a noise that sounds like cannons firing, bergs the size of 10-story office buildings sometimes come crashing from the "snout" of a glacier. The crash sends tons of water and spray skyward, and it propels mini–tidal waves outward from the point of impact. **Johns Hopkins Glacier** calves so often and with such volume that large cruise ships can seldom come within 2 mi of its face.

Glacier Bay is a still-forming body of water fed by the runoff of the ice fields, glaciers, and mountains that surround it. Captain James Cook and then Captain George Vancouver sailed by Glacier Bay and didn't even know it. At the time of Vancouver's sailing in 1794, the bay was hidden behind and beneath a vast glacial wall of ice. The glacier face was more than 20 mi across and in places more than 4,000 feet in depth. It extended more than 100 mi to its origins in the St. Elias Mountain Range. Since then, due to warming weather and other factors not fully understood, the face of the glacial ice has melted and retreated with amazing speed, exposing 65 mi of fjords, islands, and inlets.

It was Vancouver who named the magnificent snow-clad **Mt. Fairweather,** which towers over the head of the bay. Legend has it that Vancouver named Fairweather on one of the Southeast's most beautiful blue days—and the mountain was not seen again during the following century. That's an exaggeration, to be sure, but overcast, rainy weather is certainly the norm here.

In 1879, about a century after Vancouver's sail-by, one of the earliest white visitors to what is now Glacier Bay National Park and Preserve came calling. Naturalist John Muir was drawn by the flora and fauna that had followed in the wake of glacial withdrawals and fascinated by the vast ice rivers that descended from the mountains to tidewater. Today the naturalist's namesake glacier, like others in the park, continues to retreat dramatically. Its terminus is now scores of miles farther up the bay from the small cabin he built at its face during his time there.

Glacier Bay is a marvelous laboratory for naturalists of all persuasions. Glaciologists, of course, can have a field day. Animal lovers can hope to see the rare glacial "blue" bears of the area, a variation of the black bear, which is here along with the brown bear; whales feasting on krill; mountain goats in late spring and early summer; and seals on floating icebergs. Birders can look for the more than 200 species that have already been spotted in the park, and if you're lucky, you may witness two bald eagles engaging in aerobatics.

A remarkable panorama of plants unfolds from the head of the bay, which is just emerging from the ice, to the mouth, which has been ice-free for more than 200 years. In between, the primitive plants—algae, lichens, and mosses—that are the first to take hold of the bare, wet ground give way to more complex species: flowering plants such as the magenta dwarf fireweed and the creamy dryas, which in turn merge with willows, alders, and cottonwood. As the living plants mature and die, they enrich the soil and prepare it for new species to follow. The climax of the plant community is the lush spruce-and-hemlock rain forest, rich in life and blanketing the land around **Bartlett Cove.** *Box 140, Gustavus 99826* *907/697–2230* *www.nps.gov/glba.*

Gustavus

59 *50 mi west of Juneau, 75 mi south of Skagway.*

For airborne visitors, Gustavus is the gateway to Glacier Bay National Park. The long, paved jet airport, built as a refueling strip during World War II, is one of the best and longest in Southeast Alaska, all the more impressive because of its limited facilities at the field. Alaska Airlines, which serves Gustavus daily in the summer, has a large, rustic terminal at the site, and from a free telephone on the front porch of the terminal you can call any of the local hostelries for a courtesy pickup. Smaller, light-aircraft companies that serve the community out of Juneau also have on-site shelters. In addition a daily passenger ferry provides service between Juneau and Gustavus throughout the summer.

Gustavus has no downtown. In fact, Gustavus is not a town at all. The 150 or so year-round residents are most emphatic on this point; they regularly vote down incorporation. Instead, Gustavus is a scattering of homes, farmsteads, arts-and-crafts studios, fishing and guiding charters,

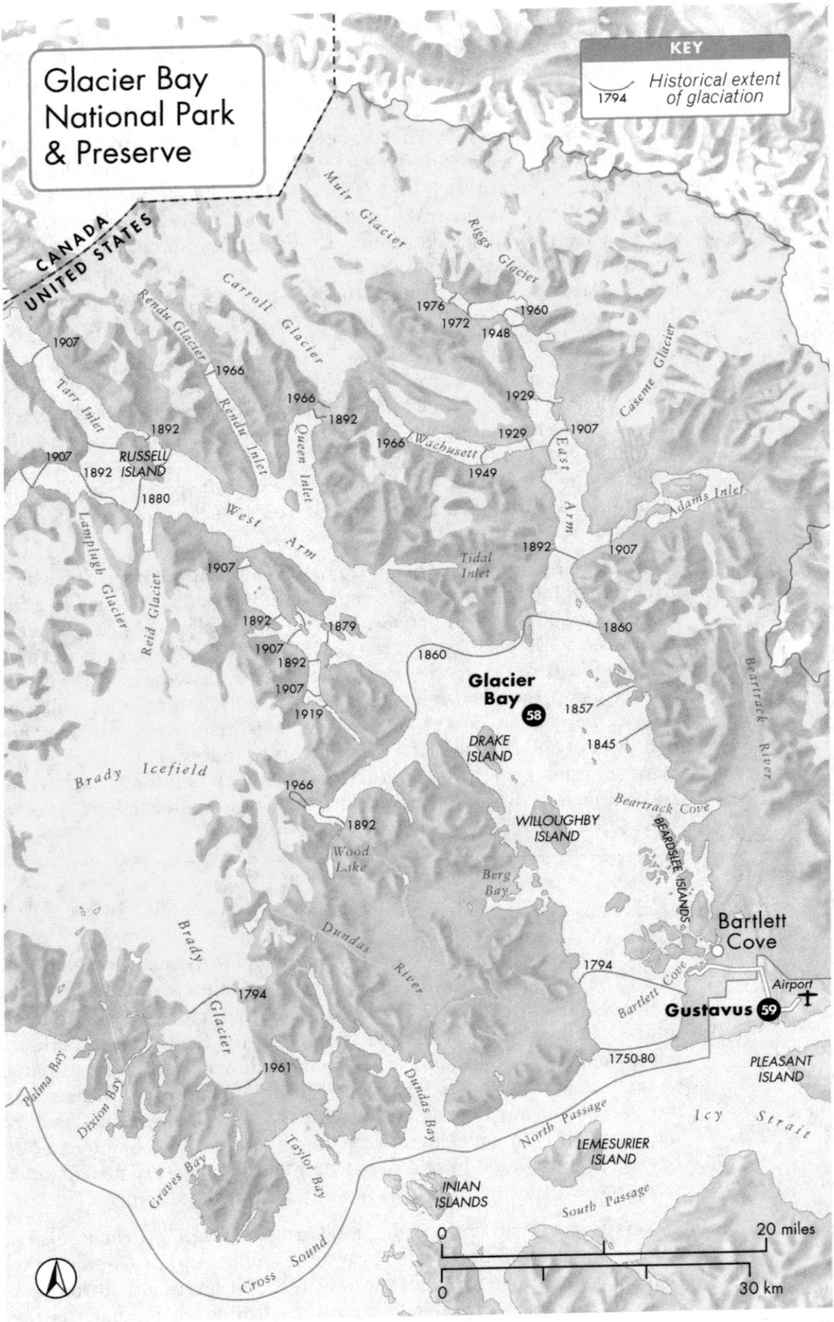
Glacier Bay
National Park
& Preserve
KEY
Historical extent of glaciation
1794
CANADA
UNITED STATES
Muir Glacier
Riggs Glacier
Carroll Glacier
Rendu Glacier
Caseme Glacier
Tarr Inlet
Rendu Inlet
Queen Inlet
Wachusett
East Arm
Adams Inlet
RUSSELL ISLAND
West Arm
Lamplugh Glacier
Reid Glacier
Tidal Inlet
Glacier Bay
58
DRAKE ISLAND
Beartrack River
Brady Icefield
Beartrack Cove
WILLOUGHBY ISLAND
BEARDSLEE ISLANDS
Wood Lake
Berg Bay
Bartlett Cove
Dundas River
Brady Glacier
Bartlett Cove
Airport
Gustavus
59
PLEASANT ISLAND
Palma Bay
Dixon Bay
Dundas Bay
North Passage
Icy Strait
LEMESURIER ISLAND
Graves Bay
Taylor Bay
INIAN ISLANDS
South Passage
Cross Sound
1976
1972
1960
1948
1907
1966
1966
1892
1929
1929
1907
1966
1892
1907
1892
RUSSELL
1949
1880
1907
1892
1907
1892
1879
1907
1892
1860
1860
1907
1919
1857
1845
1966
1892
1794
1794
1961
1750-80
0
20 miles
0
30 km

and other tiny enterprises peopled by hospitable individualists. It is, in many ways, a contemporary example of the frontier spirit in Alaska.

Where to Stay & Eat

$$$$ **Bear Track Inn.** Built of handcrafted spruce logs, this inn sits on a 57-acre property facing Icy Strait. Soaring ceilings open up the lobby, where a central fireplace, overstuffed couches, rustic wooden tables, and moose-antler chandeliers invite relaxation. Spacious guest rooms are luxuriously furnished, and a full-service restaurant (open to the public for dinner; $32) specializes in seafood but also serves steak, pork chops, and even wild game. Room rates start at $454 per person per night (there are better prices for multiple-night packages), including air transport from Juneau and meals. *255 Rink Creek Rd., 99826 907/697–3017 or 888/697–2284 907/697–2284 www.beartrackinn.com 14 rooms Restaurant, boating, fishing, glacier tours, Internet, airport shuttle, some pets allowed; no a/c, no room phones, no room TVs, no smoking D, MC, V FAP Closed Oct.–Apr.*

$$$$ Fodor'sChoice ★ **Gustavus Inn.** Built in 1928 and established as a hotel in 1965, this inn continues a tradition of gracious Alaska rural living. In the remodeled original homestead building, rooms are decorated in New England–farmhouse style. Here you can indulge in Glacier Bay sightseeing trips, fishing expeditions, bicycle rides around the community, and berry picking in season. Hosts David and Jo Ann Lesh heap bountiful servings of seafood and fresh vegetables on the plates of overnight guests (all meals are included in the price) and others who reserve for family-style meals in the cozy farmhouse-style dining room in advance ($30). Dinnertime is 6:30 sharp. *Mile 1, Gustavus Rd., Box 60, 99826 907/697–2254 or 800/649–5220 907/697–2255 www.gustavusinn.com 13 rooms, 11 with bath Restaurant, fishing, Internet, airport shuttle; no a/c, no room phones, no room TVs, no smoking AE, MC, V Closed mid-Sept.–mid-May FAP.*

$$$ **Glacier Bay Lodge.** Within the national park, this lodge is constructed of massive timbers and blends well into the thick rain forest surrounding it on three sides. The modern yet rustic rooms are accessible by boardwalks. If it swims or crawls in the sea hereabouts, you'll find it on the menu in the rustic dining room, which is open to nonlodge guests as well. One favorite is the halibut baked *aleyeska*, a fillet baked in a rich sauce of sour cream, cheese, and onions. Activities include whale watching, kayaking, and naturalist-led hikes. *199 Bartlett Cove Rd., Gustavus 99826 907/264–4600 or 888/229–8687 206/258–3668 www.visitglacierbay.com 56 rooms Restaurant, boating, bicycles; no a/c, no room phones, no room TVs AE, D, DC, MC, V Closed mid-Sept.–mid-May.*

$$$$ **Annie Mae Lodge.** This quiet two-story lodge, one of the few Gustavus places open year-round, faces the Goode River and is a five-minute walk from the beach. Seven guest rooms have doors that open to a wraparound veranda; one room is entirely wheelchair accessible. Lodging includes three meals a day plus ground transportation. Kayaking, flightseeing, Glacier Bay cruises, and other activities are arranged by the owner. *Box 55, 99826 907/697–2346 or 800/478–2346 www.anniemae.*

com ⟿ *11 rooms, 9 with bath* ᗌ *Internet; no a/c, no room phones, no room TVs, no smoking* ⊟ *AE, D, DC, MC, V* †◯† *FAP.*

★ $$$$ ▦ **Glacier Bay Country Inn.** Bears and moose might peek into this rambling log structure with its marvelous cupolas, dormers, gables, and porches. Some cabins include antiques and open log-beam ceilings. Innkeepers Ponch and Sandi Marchbanks offer charter-fishing trips (extra charge) and a variety of sightseeing options. Meals are included in the room rate. Among the guests' favorites are steamed Dungeness crab, ale-marinated alder-grilled salmon, and crème brûlée. ⊠ *Halfway between airport and Bartlett Cove* ⌖ *Box 5, 99826* ☎ *907/697–2288 or 800/628–0912* 🖶 *907/697–2289* ⊕ *www.glacierbayalaska.com* ⟿ *5 rooms, 5 cabins* ᗌ *Restaurant, boating, fishing, Internet; no a/c, no room phones, no room TVs, no smoking* ⊟ *AE, D, MC, V* †◯† *FAP* ⊙ *Closed mid-Sept.–mid-May.*

Guided Tours

Glacier Bay is best experienced from the water, whether from the deck of a cruise ship, on a tour boat, or from the level of a sea kayak. National Park Service naturalists come aboard to explain the great glaciers; to point out features of the forests, islands, and mountains; and to help spot black bears, brown bears, mountain goats, whales, porpoises, and birds.

Air Excursions (☎ 907/697–2375, 800/354–2479 in Alaska ⊕ www. airexcursions.com) operates Glacier Bay flightseeing tours from Gustavus, plus flights to Juneau several times a day in the summer. **Huna Totem Corporation/Aramark** (☎ 907/264–4600 or 888/229–8687 ⊕ www. visitglacierbay.com) provides daily summertime boat tours from the dock at Bartlett Cove, near Glacier Bay Lodge. These eight-hour trips into Glacier Bay have a Park Service naturalist and Native guide aboard a 155-passenger catamaran. A light lunch is included. Campers and sea kayakers heading up the bay ride the same boat. **Allen Marine** (☎ 888/ 289–0081 ⊕ www.allenmarine.com) provides daily passenger ferry service between Juneau and Gustavus in the summer.

Sports & the Outdoors

SEA KAYAKING The most adventurous way to explore Glacier Bay is by paddling your own kayak through the bay's icy waters and inlets. But unless you're an expert, you're better off signing on with the guided tours. You can book a five- or eight-day guided expedition through **Alaska Discovery** (☎ 907/780–6226 or 800/586–1911 ⊕ www.akdiscovery.com). Alaska Discovery provides safe, seaworthy kayaks and tents, gear, and food. Its guides are tough, knowledgeable Alaskans, and they've spent enough time in Glacier Bay's wild country to know what's safe and what's not. You can also take a guided one-day kayak trip from Bartlett Cove if you're just looking for a chance to explore the area. **Spirit Walker Expeditions** (☎ 907/697–2266 or 800/529–2537 🖶 907/697–2701 ⊕ www. seakayakalaska.com) leads 1- to 10-day sea-kayaking trips to various parts of Icy Strait (but not within Glacier Bay itself).

Kayak rentals for unescorted Glacier Bay exploring and camping can be arranged through **Glacier Bay Sea Kayaks** (⊠ Bartlett Cove ☎ 907/ 697–2257 ⊕ www.glacierbayseakayaks.com). Prior to going out, you will be given instructions on handling the craft plus camping and routing suggestions. **Sea Otter Kayak** (☎ 907/697–3007 in summer, 907/226–2338 in winter 🌐 www.he.net/~seaotter) rents kayaks, gives instructions on their use, and supplies the essentials.

HAINES

60–65 *75 mi north of Gustavus.*

The town of Haines encompasses an area that has been occupied by Tlingit peoples for centuries. Missionary S. Hall Young and famed naturalist John Muir were intent on establishing a Presbyterian mission in the area, and with the blessing of local chiefs, they chose the site that later became Haines. It's hard to imagine a more beautiful setting—a heavily wooded peninsula with magnificent views of Portage Cove and the snowy Coast Range. Unlike most other cities in Southeast Alaska, Haines, 80 mi northwest of Juneau, can be reached by the 152-mi Haines Highway, which connects at Haines Junction with the Alaska Highway. It's also accessible by the state ferry and by scheduled plane service from Juneau. The Haines ferry terminal is 4½ mi northwest of downtown, and the airport is 4 mi west.

The town has two distinct personalities. On the northern side of the Haines Highway is the portion of Haines that grew up around the Presbyterian mission. In the 1890s, Jack Dalton maintained a toll route from the settlement of Haines into the Yukon, charging $1 for foot passengers and $2.50 per horse. His Dalton Trail later provided access for miners during the 1897 gold rush to the Klondike. The following year, when gold was discovered on the nearby Porcupine River, Haines became a supply center and jumping-off place for those goldfields as well.

South of the highway the town looks like a military post, which is what it was for nearly half a century. In 1903 the U.S. Army established a post—Ft. William Henry Seward—at Portage Cove just south of town. For 17 years (1923–39) the post, renamed Chilkoot Barracks in commemoration of the gold-rush route, was the only military base in the territory. That changed with World War II. Following the war, the post closed down and the buildings were sold to private individuals. They are now part of a National Historic Landmark.

The Haines–Fort Seward community today is recognized for the Native dance and art center at Fort Seward, as well as for the superb fishing, camping, and outdoor recreation to be found at Chilkoot Lake, Portage Cove, Mosquito Lake, and Chilkat State Park on the shores of Chilkat Inlet. Northwest of the city is the Alaska Chilkat Bald Eagle Preserve. Thousands of eagles come here each winter to feed on a late run of chum salmon, making it one of Alaska's premier bird-watching sites.

Exploring Haines

Haines is a delightful place to explore on foot. Local weather is drier than in much of Southeast Alaska, and the town exudes a down-home friendliness. Perhaps this is because Haines sees fewer cruise ships, or maybe it's the grand landscape and ease of access to the mountains and sea.

a good walk

Start your walking tour of Haines downtown at the helpful **Haines Convention and Visitors Bureau** 60 on 2nd and Willard streets, where you can pick up a walking-tour brochure. Walk two blocks up 2nd Avenue and turn right on Main Street; the **Sheldon Museum and Cultural Center** 61 is just a block away. Step inside for an introduction to the area and its history. From here, head a block downhill to the busy small-boat harbor, filled with commercial fishing boats and pleasure craft. Turn right on Front Street and follow the shoreline ¼ mi to Lookout Park, a fine place to take in the view on a sunny day. Turn uphill here on steps next to a small cemetery with graves dating from the 1880s. The steps emerge on Mission Street; follow it to 2nd Avenue and turn left for one block to the **American Bald Eagle Foundation** 62, a museum and research center for these majestic birds. Continue out 2nd Avenue another ⅓ mi to the most interesting sight in Haines, **Fort William H. Seward National Historic Landmark** 63. Turn right as you enter the grounds past **Hotel Halsingland Hotel** 64, originally the commanding officers' quarters. Circle the parade ground, passing the line of officers' homes along the top, and then proceed back down to **Alaska Indian Arts** 65, housed within the old fort hospital. The Chilkat Center for the Arts is just behind, and the central parade ground contains a tribal house and trapper's cabin.

TIMING Plan to take two hours for this ramble around Haines and longer if you want to explore the various sights in depth. Local companies offer bus tours that include all these sights plus the "Dalton City" buildings at the fairgrounds and the Alaska Chilkat Bald Eagle Preserve (get information at the visitors bureau).

What to See

65 **Alaska Indian Arts.** Dedicated to the revival of Tlingit art, this nonprofit organization is housed in the former fort hospital, between the parade ground and the Chilkat Center for the Arts. You can watch Tlingits carving totem poles, metalsmiths working in silver, and other artists doing blanket weaving. *Fort Seward 907/766–2160 www.alaskaindianarts.com Free Weekdays 9–5, and evenings when cruise ships are in port.*

62 **American Bald Eagle Foundation.** The main focuses here are bald eagles and the Chilkat Preserve, explored in lectures, displays, and videos. A diorama also shows examples of local animals. The gift shop sells natural-history items. The foundation also sponsors bald-eagle research cooperatively with the University of Alaska. *2nd Ave. at Haines Hwy., Box 49, 99827 907/766–3094 907/766–3095 www.baldeagles.org $3 May–Nov., daily 8–6 or whenever cruise ships are in port.*

★ 63 **Fort William H. Seward National Historic Landmark.** Circle the sloping parade ground of Alaska's first U.S. army post, where clapboard structures stand against a mountain backdrop. The Haines Convention and Visitors Bureau provides a walking-tour brochure of the fort.

60 **Haines Convention and Visitors Bureau.** At this helpful tourist office you can pick up walking tours of both Haines and Fort Seward, learn about

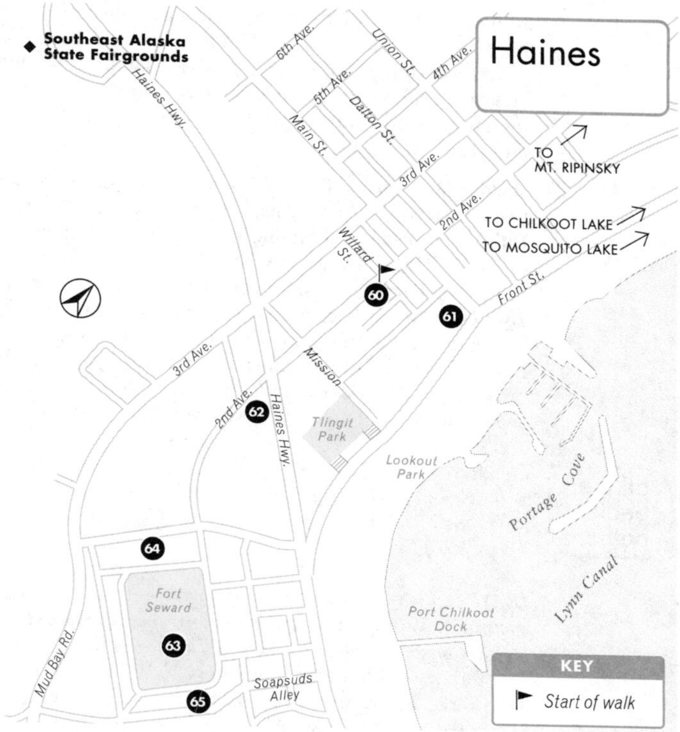

lodging and attractions, check out menus from local restaurants, or pick up a hiking brochure. ✉ *2nd Ave. near Willard St., Box 530, 99827* ☎ *907/766–2234 or 800/458–3579* 🌐 *www.haines.ak.us* ⏲ *Mid-May–mid-Sept., weekdays 8–7, weekends 10–5; mid-Sept.–mid-May, weekdays 8–5; and when cruise ships are in port.*

64 **Halsingland Hotel.** In Fort Seward wander past the huge, stately, white-column former commanding officers' home, now a part of the hotel on Officers' Row.

Haines Highway. Whether you plan to travel its full length or not, you should spend at least a bit of time on this scenic highway, which is paved on both sides of the border. It starts at Mile 0 in Haines and continues 152 mi to Haines Junction, where it joins the Alaska Highway in the Canadian Yukon. At about Mile 6 there's a delightful picnic spot near the Chilkat River. At Mile 9.5 the view of Cathedral Peaks, part of the Chilkat Range, is magnificent. From Mile 19 to Mile 21 you can see the Alaska Chilkat Bald Eagle Preserve. At Mile 33 is a roadside restaurant called, aptly, **Mile 33 Roadhouse,** where you can refill your gas tank and coffee mug, grab a burger, and stock up on home-baked goods. The United States–Canada border lies at Mile 42; stop at Canadian customs and be sure to set your clock ahead one hour.

In winter, the **Alaska Chilkat Bald Eagle Preserve** (☎ 907/766–2292), on Mile 19–Mile 21 of the Haines Highway, harbors the largest concentration of bald eagles in the world. Thousands come to feast on the late run of salmon in the clear, ice-free waters of the Chilkat River, heated by underground warm springs. November and December are the best months for viewing.

61 **Sheldon Museum and Cultural Center.** Steve Sheldon began assembling Native artifacts, Russian items, and gold-rush memorabilia, such as Jack Dalton's sawed-off shotgun, in the 1880s and started an exhibit of his finds in 1925. The core of what's here is this Alaskan family's personal collection. Particularly noteworthy are the Chilkat artifacts, including an 18th-century carved ceremonial hat from the Murrelet Clan, Chilkat blankets, and a model of a Tlingit tribal house. The impressive lens came from Eldred Rock Lighthouse, just south along Lynn Canal. ✉ *11 Main St.* ☎ *907/766–2366* 🌐 *www.sheldonmuseum.org* *$3* ⏲ *Mid-May–mid-Sept., Mon.–Fri. 10–5, weekends 2–5; Winter hours, Mon.–Fri. 1–4.*

off the beaten path

CHILKAT STATE PARK – This park on the Chilkat Inlet has beautiful and accessible viewing of both the Davidson and Rainbow glaciers along with public campgrounds. ☎ *907/766–2292* 🌐 *www.dnr.state.ak.us/parks.*

DALTON CITY – An 1890s gold-rush town was re-created as a set for the movie *White Fang* and moved to the **Southeast Alaska State Fairgrounds** (☎ 907/766–2476), less than a mile from downtown. The movie-set buildings now house local businesses, including the **Klondike Restaurant and Saloon,** with good Tex-Mex, an old-fashioned bar, a microbrewery, and live music on Friday night. The five-day-long **Southeast Alaska State Fair,** held the second week of August, is one of several official regional blowouts, and in its homegrown, homespun way it's a real winner. In addition to the usual collection of barnyard animals, the fair has live music, rides on a vintage 1920 Herschal-Spillman carousel, local culinary arts, and Native dances, totemic crafts, and fine art and photography. ☎ *907/766–2476* 🌐 *www.seakfair.org* *$7.*

Where to Stay & Eat

$–$$$ ✕ **Bamboo Room.** Pop culture meets greasy spoon in this unassuming coffee shop with red vinyl booths. The menu includes sandwiches, burgers, fried chicken, chili, and halibut fish-and-chips, but the place really is at its best for an all-American breakfast (available until 3 PM). The bar has pool, darts, a big-screen TV, and a jukebox. ✉ *2nd Ave. near Main St.* ☎ *907/766–2800* *AE, D, DC, MC, V.*

$–$$$ ✕ **The Wild Strawberry.** Just a few doors down from the visitor center, this café provides a bright escape from a rainy day. Owned by a family of commercial fishermen, the restaurant specializes in fresh salmon and halibut caught on its own boats. Popular lunchtime menu items include smoked-salmon chowder, crab-and-artichoke three-cheese melt (with fresh Dungeness crab), and panini sandwiches. For dinner try the fresh king salmon, shrimp, or halibut. Everything is homemade, and some of the produce is locally grown. The outside deck is a delight on sunny afternoons. ✉ *138 2nd Ave.* ☎ *907/766–3608* ▭ *MC, V* ⊗ *Closed Oct.–Apr.*

¢ ✕ **Mountain Market.** Meet the locals over coffee (including espresso in all its variations) and a fresh-baked pastry at this busy corner natural-foods store and deli. Mountain Market is also great for lunchtime sandwiches, wraps, soups, and salads. Friday is pizza day, but get there early since it's often gone by dinnertime. ✉ *3rd Ave. and Haines Hwy.* ☎ *907/766–3340* ▭ *MC, V.*

$$$$ ✕ **Weeping Trout Sports Resort.** Enjoy wilderness with style at this small resort on Chilkat Lake—reachable only by boat or plane—where you can golf on a 9-hole course, fish, relax, and refresh and *not* be bothered by telephones (the lodge has one for emergencies). All-inclusive package trips are available starting at $270 per person for one night and two days, and you stay in clean but simple cabins; showers are in the main lodge. Day trips are available for $135, including transport from Haines, a day of golf, and a meal. The restaurant is open to the public Saturday nights with a set four-course, family-style meal ($48 with transportation from Haines). *Box 129, 99827* ☎ *907/766–2827 or 877/948–7688* *907/766–2824* *www.weepingtrout.com* *4 cabins* *Restaurant, 9-hole golf course, fishing; no a/c, no room phones, no room TVs* ▭ *MC, V* *FAP* ⊗ *Closed Oct.–mid-May.*

¢–$ ✕ **Ft. Seward Lodge.** This lodge, restaurant, and saloon has, over time, served as the fort's PX, soda fountain, bowling alley, and gymnasium. The raw-wood decor and sparse interior bring the pioneering spirit of Alaska to life. The dining room even comes with a mechanical red-velvet swing left over from wilder times. All-you-can-eat Dungeness crab dinners are $23, or choose beef, chicken, or pasta from the menu. Save room for the "ice screaming" pie. The lodge's rooms are clean but not at all fancy; the least expensive share a bath and lack televisions, and two have well-equipped kitchenettes and ocean views. ✉ *39 Mud Bay Rd.* ☎ *907/766–2009 or 800/478–7772* *907/766–2006* *www.ftsewardlodge.com* *10 rooms, 6 with bath* *Restaurant, some kitchenettes, cable TV, bar, airport shuttle; no a/c, no room phones, no smoking* ▭ *D, MC, V.*

¢–$ ✕ **Hotel Halsingland.** Fort Seward's commanding officers once lived in the big white Victorian building that today houses this gracious hotel. On the National Register of Historic Places, the hotel has original claw-foot bathtubs and nonworking fireplaces decorated with Belgian tiles. Rooms are charming and nicely maintained, but not large. A few inexpensive ones share a hall bath. The **Commander's Room Restaurant and Lounge** is one of the finest in the area, with a menu that includes locally caught crab and salmon, Caesar salads, filet mignon, and delicious desserts. ✉ *Fort Seward, Box 1649, 99827* ☎ *907/766–2000 or 800/542–6363* *907/766–2060* *www.hotelhalsingland.com* *58 rooms, 52 with bath* *Restaurant, cable TV, bar, Internet, meeting rooms, some pets allowed; no a/c* ▭ *AE, D, DC, MC, V.*

$ **Captain's Choice Motel.** In the summer overflowing flower boxes surround the perimeter of this contemporary motel in downtown Haines. Rooms are standard, but those on the 2nd floor open onto a deck with tables and chairs. A patio down below serves as a nightly meeting place where you can enjoy libations and conversation, and a Continental breakfast is available in the morning. The honeymoon suite has a hot tub. ✉ *108 2nd Ave. N, Box 392, 99827* ☎ *907/766–3111 or 800/478–2345* 📠 *907/766–3332* 🌐 *www.capchoice.com* *39 rooms, 4 suites* *Microwaves, refrigerators, cable TV, car rental, laundry, some pets allowed; no a/c* 💳 *AE, D, DC, MC, V* 🍽 *CP.*

Guided Tours

Adventure

Alaska Nature Tours (☎ 907/766–2876 📠 907/766–2844 🌐 www.alaskanaturetours.net) conducts bird-watching and natural-history tours through the Alaska Chilkat Bald Eagle Preserve and leads hiking treks in summer and ski tours in winter. A full-service kayak outfitter in Haines, **Deishu Expeditions** (☎ 907/766–2427 or 800/552–9257 🌐 www.seakayaks.com) leads guided trips for a day or a week. It also rents kayaks for do-it-yourselfers.

Boating & Fishing

Alaska Fjordlines (☎ 907/766–3395 or 800/320–0146 🌐 www.alaskafjordlines.com) operates a high-speed catamaran between Skagway, Haines, and Juneau throughout the summer, stopping along the way to watch sea lions and other marine mammals. **Chilkat Cruises** (☎ 907/766–2100 or 888/766–2103 🌐 www.chilkatcruises.com) provides a passenger catamaran ferry between Skagway and Haines, with service several times a day in the summer. **Glacier Valley Wilderness Adventures** (☎📠 907/767–5522 🌐 www.glaciervalleyadventures.com) conducts fly-in trips to a remote gold-mine base camp, with a variety of rafting, jet boat, or helicopter options. Overnight accommodations are available in tents at a working gold mine.

For information on numerous sportfishing charter boats in Haines, contact the **Haines Convention and Visitors Bureau** (☎ 907/766–2234 or 800/458–3579 🌐 www.haines.ak.us).

Flightseeing

Housed a few doors up the street from the visitor center, **Mountain Flying Service** (☎ 907/766–3007 or 800/954–8747 🌐 www.flyglacierbay.com) leads flightseeing trips to nearby Glacier Bay National Park. **Wings of Alaska** (☎ 907/789–0790 🌐 www.wingsofalaska.com) has scheduled service to Juneau and Skagway.

Nightlife & the Arts

Bars

Locals might rule the pool tables at **Fogcutter Bar** (✉ 122 Main St. ☎ 907/766–2555), but the jukebox is often up for grabs at this lively spot. **Haines Brewing Company** (✉ 108 Whitefang Way ☎ 907/766–3823) is a microbrewery in the Dalton City buildings at the fairgrounds. Commercial fisherfolk gather nightly at **Harbor Bar** (✉ Front St. at the Harbor ☎ 907/766–2444), a bar and restaurant dating from 1907. You might catch some live music here in summer. Inside one of the oldest buildings in town (it was once a brothel), the **Pioneer Bar** (✉ 2nd Ave. near Main St. ☎ 907/766–3443) has historical photographs on the walls, a large-screen television for sports, and occasional bands.

Dance

The **Chilkat Dancers' Storytelling Theater** (☎ 907/766–2540 🌐 www.tresham.com/show) performs at the Tribal House on the fort's parade grounds during the summer. This unique theatrical production includes elaborate carved masks and impressive costumes as dancers tell ancient Tlingit legends. Performances cost $12 and are held most weekdays at 4:30 PM.

The **Hammer Museum** (☎ 907/766–2374 ✉ 108 Main St.) is Haines at its most peculiar; check out this shrine to hammers on Main Street. The owner started his collection decades ago; among his impressive collection of 1,400 hammers are ones once used by bankers to cancel checks and 6-foot-long farming hammers used to secure posts into the sides of barns.

Sports & the Outdoors

Bicycling

Sockeye Cycle Company (✉ 24 Portage St., Box 829, 99827 ☎ 907/766–2869 🌐 www.cyclealaska.com) specializes in guided mountain tours in and around the backcountry of Haines; the outfit also rents, services, and sells bikes.

Hiking

Battery Point Trail is a fairly level path that hugs the shoreline for 2 mi, providing fine views across Lynn Canal. The trail begins a mile east of town, and a campsite can be found at Kelgaya Point near the end. For other hikes, pick up a copy of "Haines Is for Hikers" at the Haines Convention and Visitors Bureau.

Shopping

Galleries & Gifts

A surprising number of artists live in the Haines area, and you will find their works in several local galleries. Tresham Gregg's **Sea Wolf Gallery** (✉ Fort Seward ☎ 907/766–2540 🌐 www.tresham.com) sells wood carvings, prints, and T-shirts with his Native-inspired designs. One of the nicest galleries in Haines, **Wild Iris Gallery** (✉ Portage St. ☎ 907/766–2300) displays attractive jewelry, prints, and fashion wear created by owners Madeleine and Fred Shields. It's just up from the cruise-ship dock.

Birch Boy Products (☎ 907/766–5660 or 877/769–5660 🌐 www.birchboy.com) produces tart and tasty birch syrup; it's sold in local gift shops.

SKAGWAY

61–71 *14 mi northeast of Haines.*

Skagway is a short ride from Haines on the Alaska Marine Highway ferry. If you go by road, the distance is 359 mi, as you have to take the

Haines Highway up to Haines Junction, Yukon, then take the Alaska Highway 100 mi south to Whitehorse, and then drive a final 100 mi south on the Klondike Highway to Skagway. North-country folk call this well-traveled sightseeing route the Golden Horseshoe or Golden Circle tour, because it takes in a lot of gold-rush country in addition to lake, forest, and mountain scenery.

However you get to Skagway, you'll find the town an amazingly preserved artifact from one of North America's biggest, most storied gold rushes. Most of the downtown district forms part of the Klondike Gold Rush National Historical Park, a unit of the national park system dedicated to commemorating and interpreting the frenzied stampede that extended to Dawson City in Canada's Yukon. Old false-front stores, saloons, and brothels—built to separate gold-rush prospectors from their grubstakes going north or their gold pokes heading south—have been restored, repainted, and refurnished by the federal government and Skagway's citizens. Although the town feels a little like a Disney theme park in spots, when you walk down Broadway today, the scene is not appreciably different from what the prospectors saw in the days of 1898, except the street is now paved to make your exploring easier.

Skagway had only a single cabin still standing when the Yukon gold rush began. At first, the argonauts, as they liked to be called, swarmed to Dyea and the Chilkoot Trail, 9 mi west of Skagway. Skagway and its White Pass Trail didn't seem as attractive until a dock was built in town. Then it mushroomed overnight into the major gateway to the Klondike, supporting a wild mixture of legitimate businesspeople, con artists (among the most cunning was Jefferson "Soapy" Smith), stampeders, and curiosity seekers.

Three months after the first boat landed in July 1897, Skagway numbered perhaps 20,000 people and had well-laid-out streets, hotels, stores, saloons, gambling houses, and dance halls. By the spring of 1898, the superintendent of the Northwest Royal Mounted Police in neighboring Canada would label the town "little better than a hell on earth."

A lot of the "hell" ended with a shoot-out one pleasant July evening in 1898. Good guy Frank Reid (the surveyor who laid out Skagway's streets so wide and well) faced down bad guy Soapy Smith on a dock downtown near the present ferry terminal. After a classic exchange of gunfire, Smith lay dead and Reid lay dying. The town built a substantial monument at Reid's grave. You can see it in Gold Rush Cemetery and read the inscription on it: HE GAVE HIS LIFE FOR THE HONOR OF SKAGWAY. For Smith, whose tombstone was continually chiseled and stolen by vandals and souvenir seekers, today's grave marker is a simple wooden plank.

When the gold rush played out after a few years, the town of 20,000 dwindled to 700. The White Pass & Yukon Railroad kept the town alive until 1982, when it began to run in summers only. By this time, however, tourism revenue was sufficient to compensate for any economic loss suffered as a result of the railroad's more limited schedule.

Exploring Skagway

Skagway's compact downtown makes it ideal to explore by foot. Nearly all the historic sights are within a few blocks of the cruise-ship and ferry dock, so you can take all the time you want. Skagway runs on tourism, as you will discover the minute you step from a ferry or cruise ship. Unless you're willing to hike into the backcountry on the Chilkoot Trail, you aren't likely to find a quiet Alaskan experience around Skagway.

a good walk

A good starting point is the corner of 1st Avenue and Main Street, where a marker notes the infamous 1898 gun battle between Soapy Smith and Frank Reid. Head two blocks east along 1st Avenue and turn left on Broadway Street into the heart of the town. Be sure to stop by the old White Pass & Yukon Railroad Depot at 2nd Avenue and Broadway, which now houses the **Klondike Gold Rush National Historical Park** 66 visitor center. Check out the exhibits and films, or join a ranger-led tour to learn more about Skagway's fascinating history. Next door is the White Pass & Yukon Route Depot, a modern structure that blends well with the town's many Victorian-era buildings.

The next block up Broadway contains several of the town's best-known buildings. The two-centuries-old Red Onion Saloon remains a favorite place to imbibe under the watchful eyes of "working girl" mannequins. Next door is the **Arctic Brotherhood Hall** 67, with its driftwood-stick false front. Inside you'll find the helpful **Skagway Convention and Visitors Bureau** for local information. Next up the street is the **Golden North Hotel** 68, with its distinctive golden dome. Across the street sits the old Mascot Saloon, which now houses Park Service historical exhibits and public restrooms. Back on Broadway, continue two more blocks until you reach **Corrington's Museum of Alaskan History** 69, with its large collection of scrimshaw. Turn right on 5th Avenue to the Park Service's **Moore Cabin** 70, Skagway's oldest structure. The beautifully restored Skagway City Hall is housed in the same building as the **Skagway Museum** 71. Return to Broadway and follow it to 6th Avenue, where you can see *The Days of '98 with Soapy Smith* show inside historic Eagles Hall.

If you are up for a longer walk continue 2 mi out of town along Alaska Street to the **Gold Rush Cemetery,** where you'll find the graves of combatants Soapy Smith and Frank Reid. (A city bus takes you most of the way to the cemetery for $2 each direction.) No tour of Skagway is complete without a train ride on the famed **White Pass & Yukon Route.** Trains depart from the corner of 1st Avenue and Broadway several times a day in the summer.

TIMING The six blocks that compose the heart of downtown Skagway can be explored in a half hour, but you will almost certainly want to spend more time learning about the gold rush in the Park Service's historical buildings and the Skagway Museum. (If you include the 4-mi round-trip walk to the Gold Rush Cemetery, plan on three to four hours.) Also, leave time to explore Skagway's many shops, restaurants, and other attractions.

What to See

★ 67 **Arctic Brotherhood Hall.** The Arctic Brotherhood was a fraternal organization of Alaskan and Yukon pioneers. To decorate the exterior false

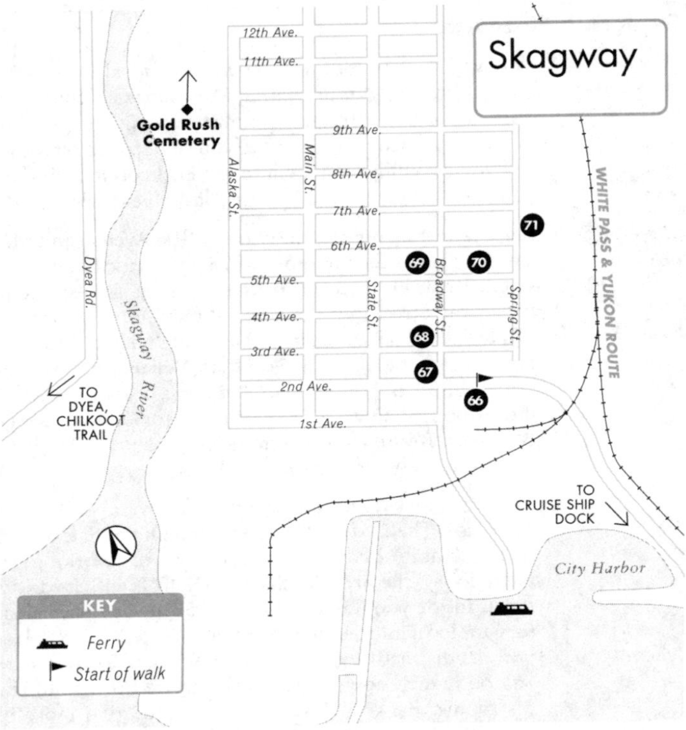

front of their Skagway lodge building, local members created a mosaic out of 20,000 pieces of driftwood and flotsam gathered from local beaches. The AB Hall now houses the **Skagway Convention and Visitors Bureau,** along with public restrooms. ✉ *Broadway, between 2nd and 3rd Aves., Box 1029, 99840* ☎ *907/983–2854, 888/762–1898 message only* 🌐 *www.skagway.org* ⏲ *May–Sept., daily 8–6; Oct.–Apr., weekdays 8–noon and 1–5.*

69 **Corrington's Museum of Alaskan History.** Inside a gift shop, this impressive and free scrimshaw museum highlights more than 40 exquisitely carved walrus tusks and other exhibits that detail Alaska's history. A bright flower garden decorates the exterior. ✉ *5th Ave. and Broadway* ☎ *907/983–2579* 🎫 *Free* ⏲ *Open when cruise ships are in port (mid-May–mid-Sept.).*

68 **Golden North Hotel.** Built during the 1898 gold rush, the Golden North Hotel was—until closing in 2002—Alaska's oldest hotel. It retains its gold rush–era appearance; a golden dome tops the corner cupola. Today, the downstairs houses shops, with employee housing upstairs. ✉ *3rd Ave. and Broadway.*

★ ⚑ 66 **Klondike Gold Rush National Historical Park.** In what was once the White Pass & Yukon Route Depot, this park contains exhibits, photos, and artifacts from the White Pass and Chilkoot trails and is of special interest if you plan to take a White Pass train ride, drive the nearby Klondike Highway, or hike the Chilkoot "Trail of '98." Films, ranger talks, and walking tours are offered. Special free Robert Service poetry performances by Buckwheat Donahue—a beloved local character and head of the chamber of commerce—take place two evenings a week at the visitor center. ✉ *2nd Ave. at Broadway* ☎ *907/983–2921 or 907/983–9224* 🌐 *www.nps.gov/klgo* 🎫 *Free* ⏲ *June–Aug., daily 8–8; May and Sept., daily 8–6; Oct.–Apr., weekdays 8–5.*

off the beaten path

KLONDIKE HIGHWAY – The highway, which starts at the foot of State Street, often parallels the older White Pass railway route as it travels northwest to Carcross and Whitehorse in the Canadian Yukon. It meets the Alaska Highway, which you follow northwest into Whitehorse, and then heads on its own again to terminate at Dawson City, on the shores of the Klondike River. From start to finish, it covers 435 mi. Along the way the road climbs steeply through forested coastal mountains with jagged, snow-covered peaks. It passes by deep, fish-filled lakes and streams in the Canadian high country, where you might spot a mountain goat, moose, black bear, or grizzly. If you're driving the Klondike Highway north from Skagway, you must stop at Canadian customs, Mile 22. If you're traveling south to Skagway, check in at U.S. customs, Mile 6. And remember that when it's 1 PM in Canada at the border, it's noon in Skagway.

70 **Moore Cabin.** Built in 1887 by Captain William Moore, the tiny cabin marks the birthplace of Skagway. An early homesteader, Moore prospered from the flood of miners, constructing a dock, warehouse, and sawmill to supply them, and selling land for other ventures. Its interior walls are covered with turn-of-the-20th-century newspapers. Next door, the larger **Moore House** (1897–98) contains interesting exhibits on the Moore family. Both structures are maintained by the Park Service, and the main house is open daily in the summer. ✉ *Off 5th Ave.* 🎫 *Free* ⏲ *Memorial Day–Labor Day, hrs vary.*

71 **Skagway Museum.** This nicely designed museum occupies the ground floor of a historic building that also houses Skagway City Hall. Inside, you'll find gambling paraphernalia from the old Board of Trade Saloon on display along with a 19th-century Tlingit canoe (one of the only two like it on the West Coast), historic photos, gold scales, a red-and-black sleigh, and other gold rush–era artifacts, along with Native baskets, beadwork, and carvings. ✉ *7th and Spring Sts.* ☎ *907/983–2420* 🌐 *www.skagwaymuseum.org* 🎫 *$2* ⏲ *Mid-May–Sept., weekdays 9–5, weekends 1–4; Oct.–mid-May., hrs vary.*

Fodor's Choice ★ **White Pass & Yukon Route.** Visitors to Skagway can travel at least part of the way along the gold-rush route aboard the White Pass & Yukon Route (WP & YR) narrow-gauge railroad. The historic (started in 1898)

CloseUp

THE CHILKOOT TRAIL

*I**F YOU'RE A STRONG AND EXPERIENCED BACKPACKER** who likes a challenge, you might want to hike the highly scenic, historic Chilkoot Trail, route of the 1897–98 gold-rush sourdoughs, from Skagway into Canada. Most hikers will need four to five days for the 33-mi hike. Expect steep slopes and wet weather, along with exhilarating vistas at the summit across the much drier Canadian landscape. Deep snow often covers the pass until late summer. The trail stretches from Dyea (9 mi out a dirt road from Skagway) to Lake Bennett and includes a climb up Chilkoot Pass at the United States–Canada border. The National Park Service maintains the American side of the pass as part of **Klondike Gold Rush National Historical Park**; the Canadian side is part of the **Chilkoot Trail National Historic Park.** A backcountry permit is required.*

The trail is generally in good condition (particularly in the lower stretches); the forest, mountain, and lake country is both scenic and richly historic, and primitive campsites are strategically located along the way. The Chilkoot is not, however, an easy walk: you'll encounter lots of ups and downs before you cross the pass and reach the Canadian high country, and rain is likely. To return to Skagway, hikers usually catch the White Pass & Yukon Route train from Lake Bennett. The fare is $65, and these trains run daily (except Sundays) in the summer, departing at 1 PM.

*For details, maps, and backcountry permits (C$50), contact the Park Service's summer-only **Chilkoot Trail Center** (✉ 1st Ave. and Broadway ☎ 907/983–9234 🌐 www.nps.gov/klgo) in the historic Martin Itgen House. Trail permits are also available through **Parks Canada** (☎ 907/983–2921, 867/667–3910, or 800/661–0486 🌐 parkscan.harbour.com/ct).*

gold-rush railroad's diesel locomotives tow vintage viewing cars up the steep inclines of the route, hugging the walls of precipitous cliff sides and providing views of craggy peaks, plummeting waterfalls, lakes, and forests. It's open mid-May to late September only, and reservations are highly recommended.

Several options are available. Twice daily during the season (three times on Tuesday and Wednesday) the WP & YR leaves Skagway for a three-hour round-trip excursion to the White Pass summit. Sights along the way include Bridal Veil Falls, Inspiration Point, and Dead Horse Gulch. The fare is $89. Through service to Whitehorse, Yukon, is offered daily as well—in the form of a train trip to Fraser, where bus connections are possible on to Whitehorse. The one-way fare to Whitehorse is $95. Also offered are special steam excursions (Saturday for $160) and a Chilkoot Trail hikers' service ($65 to Skagway from Lake Bennett), as well as a 4-hour Sunday Fraser Meadows tour ($135). ☎ *907/983–2217 or 800/343–7373* 🌐 *www.whitepassrailroad.com* ⏲ *Mid-May–late Sept., daily.*

Where to Stay & Eat

★ **$$–$$$$** **Stowaway Cafe.** Always crowded, this noisy little harborside café is just a few steps from the cruise-ship dock. Not surprisingly, seafood is the attraction—including prawns with Gorgonzola, seafood lasagna, and a hot scallop-and-bacon salad—but you also can choose tasty steaks, chicken, or smoked ribs. The café is open daily for lunch and dinner. *Congress Way 907/983–3463 Reservations essential AE, MC, V Closed Oct.–Apr.*

$$ **Skagway Fish Company.** This small, seasonal eatery serves fresh seafood including salmon, oysters, clams, halibut, and prawns. Most popular are the halibut fish-and-chips, served with a side of homemade coleslaw. Tables overlooking the harbor surround the central bar. Baby-back ribs, pork chops, and steaks, along with a New York–style cheesecake topped with strawberries, fill out the menu. *On waterfront 907/983–3474 MC, V Closed Oct.–Apr.*

$–$$ **Skagway Inn Bed & Breakfast.** Each room in this downtown Victorian inn (once a bordello) is named after a different gold-rush gal. The building, one of Skagway's oldest, was built in 1897 and has been lovingly restored. Rooms share a Victorian motif, with period antiques and cast-iron beds; some have mountain views. A big homemade breakfast is served downstairs each morning in Olivia's Restaurant, and the restaurant is open to everyone for light lunches and dinners of fresh Alaskan seafood. Outdoor seating is available next to the colorful gardens. Chilkoot Trail hikers who spend two nights at the hotel get free transport to the trailhead and storage of their gear while hiking. *655 Broadway, Box 500, 99840 907/983–2289 or 888/752–4929 907/983–2713 www.skagwayinn.com 10 rooms, 6 with private bath Restaurant, Internet, airport shuttle; no a/c, no room TVs, no smoking AE, D, MC, V Closed Oct.–Apr. BP.*

$$ **Mile Zero Bed & Breakfast.** In a quiet residential area a few blocks from downtown, this modern and comfortable B&B contains spacious and well-insulated guest rooms, all with private entrances, phones, and baths. Most have two queen beds and one room is entirely handicap-accessible. A buffet-style breakfast is served each morning. Children are welcome, and those with laptops will appreciate the Wi-Fi throughout the B&B. *9th Ave. and Main St., 99840 907/983–3045 907/983–3046 www.mile-zero.com 6 rooms Internet; no a/c, no smoking MC, V BP.*

$–$$ **The White House.** This B&B is about two blocks from downtown Skagway. Built in 1902 by Lee Guthrie, a gambler and owner of one of the town's most profitable gold-rush saloons, the white clapboard two-story house is furnished with original Skagway antiques and handmade quilts. The warm dining room and sitting room invite conversation while the light breakfasts are served, and children are welcome. *8th Ave. and Main St., Box 41, 99840 907/983–9000 907/983–9010 www.atthewhitehouse.com 10 rooms Cable TV; no a/c, no smoking AE, D, MC, V CP.*

Guided Tours

Alaska Excursions and Sled Dog Adventures (☎ 907/983–4444 🖷 907/983–3392 🌐 www.alaskasleddog.com) leads a 2½-hour wheeled (no snow) sled-dog tour on a dirt road that ends at historic Dyea. For an on-the-snow version, **Temsco Helicopters** (☎ 907/789–9501 or 877/789–9501 🌐 www.temscoair.com) will fly you to Denver Glacier for an hour of learning about mushing and riding on a dogsled.

Alaska Fjordlines (☎ 907/766–3395 or 800/320–0146 🌐 www.alaskafjordlines.com) operates a high-speed catamaran connecting Skagway with Juneau throughout the summer, stopping along the way to watch sea lions and other marine mammals. The boat leaves at 8 AM, and gets to Juneau at 11:45 AM, where a bus transports visitors into town, returning to the boat at 4:45 PM for the ride back to Skagway. **Chilkat Cruises** (☎ 907/766–2100 or 888/766–2103 🌐 www.chilkatcruises.com) provides a fast passenger catamaran ferry between Skagway and Haines, with service several times a day in the summer.

Packer Expeditions (☎ 907/983–2544 🌐 www.packerexpeditions.com) guides day trips that include a helicopter flight from Skagway, a 5-mi hike to Laughton Glacier, and a train ride back to town.

Skagway Street Car Co. (☎ 907/983–2908 🖷 907/983–3908 🌐 www.skagwaystreetcar.com) revisits the gold-rush days in lovingly renovated, bright yellow 1920s sightseeing buses. Costumed conductors lead these popular two-hour tours, but advance reservations are recommended for independent travelers, since most seats are sold aboard the cruise ships. Call a week ahead in peak season to reserve a space.

Nightlife & the Arts

Bars

Imbibe with the locals at **Moe's Frontier Bar** (✉ Broadway between 4th and 5th Aves. ☎ 907/983–2238), a longtime fixture on the Skagway scene. At **Red Onion Saloon** (✉ Broadway at 2nd Ave. ☎ 907/983–2222), where upstairs was once a gold-rush brothel, you'll find a convivial crowd of Skagway locals and visitors. An impromptu jam with cruise-ship musicians gets under way almost every afternoon. Thursday night is when local musicians strut their stuff. The saloon closes up shop for winter.

Theater

★ Since 1927 locals have performed a show called ***The Days of '98 with Soapy Smith*** at Eagles Hall. You'll see cancan dancers, learn a little local history, and watch desperado Soapy Smith being sent to his reward. If you stop in for the evening show, you can enjoy a few warm-up rounds of mock gambling with Soapy's money. Buckwheat Donahue's performances of Robert Service poetry start a half hour before each show time. *✉ Broadway and 6th Ave. ☎ 907/983–2545 May–mid-Sept., 808/328–9132 mid-Sept.–Apr. 🌐 www.alaskan.com/daysof98 🎫 $14 ⏲ Mid-May–mid-Sept., daily at 10:30, 12:30, 2:30, and 8.*

SOUTHEAST ALASKA A TO Z

To research prices, get advice from other travelers, and book travel arrangements, visit www.fodors.com.

AIR TRAVEL

Alaska Airlines operates several flights daily from Seattle and other Pacific Coast and southwestern cities to Ketchikan, Wrangell, Petersburg, Sitka, Glacier Bay, and Juneau (⇨ Smart Travel Tips for airline numbers). The carrier connects Juneau to the northern Alaskan cities of Yakutat, Cordova, Anchorage, Fairbanks, Nome, Kotzebue, and Prudhoe Bay. Wings of Alaska can connect you from Juneau to several towns, including Haines and Skagway.

Every large community in Southeast Alaska, and many smaller ones, has air-taxi services that fly you from town to town and, if you're seeking backcountry adventures, into remote wilderness cabins. Local chambers of commerce can provide lists of Bush-plane services.

Wings of Alaska ☎ 907/789-0790 🌐 www.wingsofalaska.com.

BOAT & FERRY TRAVEL

From the south, the Alaska Marine Highway operates stateroom-equipped vehicle and passenger ferries from Bellingham, Washington, and from Prince Rupert, British Columbia. The vessels call at Ketchikan, Wrangell, Petersburg, Sitka, Juneau, Haines, and Skagway, and they connect with smaller vessels serving Bush communities; in all, 11 Southeast towns are served by state ferries. B.C. Ferries operates similar passenger and vehicle ferries from Vancouver Island, British Columbia, to Prince Rupert. From here, travelers can connect with the Alaska Marine Highway System. A separate ferry, operated by the Inter-Island Ferry Authority, runs between Ketchikan and Prince of Wales Island, with additional service to Wrangell and Petersburg to start in 2006.

In the summer, staterooms on the ferries are always sold out before sailing time; reserve months in advance. If you are planning to take a car on the ferry, early reservations for vehicle space are also highly recommended. This is particularly true for recreational vehicles.

Alaska Marine Highway ✉ 6858 Glacier Hwy., Juneau 99801-7909 ☎ 907/465-3941 or 800/642-0066 🖷 907/277-4829 🌐 www.ferryalaska.com. **B.C. Ferries** ✉ 1112 Fort St., Victoria, BC V8V 4V2 Canada ☎ 250/386-3431, 888/223-3779 in B.C. 🌐 www.bcferries.com. **Inter-Island Ferry Authority** 📫 Box 495, Craig 99921 ☎ 907/826-4848 or 866/308-4848 🖷 907/826-2829 🌐 www.interislandferry.com.

BUS TRAVEL

Alaska Direct Bus Lines has year-round service connecting Anchorage, Fairbanks, and Skagway. Though it's nearly a 29-hour ride, you can travel Greyhound Lines of Canada from Edmonton to Whitehorse (a $207 one-way fare; huge discounts for 7-day and 14-day advance purchase) and make a connection (nondaily) there with Alaska Direct buses to Skagway (a three-hour trip).

Alaska Direct Bus Lines 📫 Box 100501, Anchorage 99510 ☎ 907/277-6652, 800/770-6652, 403/668-4833 in Whitehorse, Canada. **Greyhound Lines of Canada** ☎ 604/482-8747 or 800/661-8747 🌐 www.greyhound.ca.

CAR TRAVEL

Only Skagway and Haines, in the northern Panhandle, and tiny Hyder, just across the border from Stewart, British Columbia, are accessible by conventional highway. To reach Skagway or Haines, take the Alaska Highway to the Canadian Yukon's Whitehorse or Haines Junction, respectively, and then drive the Klondike Highway or Haines Highway southwest to the Alaska Panhandle. You can reach Hyder on British Columbia's Cassiar Highway, which can be reached, in turn, from Highway 16 just north of Prince Rupert.

EMERGENCIES

Police, fire, ambulance ☎ 911.

HOSPITALS **Bartlett Memorial Hospital** ✉ 3260 Hospital Dr., Juneau ☎ 907/586-2611 🌐 www.bartletthospital.org. **Haines Medical Clinic** ✉ Next to Convention and Visitors Bureau ☎ 907/766-6300. **Ketchikan General Hospital** ✉ 3100 Tongass Ave. ☎ 907/225-5171. **Petersburg Medical Center** ✉ 103 Fram St. ☎ 907/772-4291 🌐 www.hisea.org/psg.html. **Sitka Community Hospital** ✉ 209 Moller Ave. ☎ 907/747-3241 🌐 www.sitkahospital.org. **Dahl Memorial Clinic** ✉ 310 11th Ave., between State St. and Broadway ☎ 907/983-2255. **Wrangell General Hospital** ✉ 310 Bennett St. ☎ 907/874-7000 🌐 www.wrangellmedicalcenter.com.

PHARMACIES Juneau **Juneau Drug Co.** ✉ 202 Front St. ☎ 907/586-1233. **Ron's Apothecary Shoppe** ✉ 9101 Mendenhall Mall Rd., about 10 mi north of downtown in Mendenhall Valley, next to Super Bear market ☎ 907/789-0458, 907/789-9522 after hours for prescription emergencies.

Ketchikan **Downtown Drugstore** ✉ 300 Front St. ☎ 907/225-3144. **Race Avenue Drugs** ✉ 2300 Tongass Ave., across from Plaza shopping mall ☎ 907/225-4151. After hours, call **Ketchikan General Hospital** ☎ 907/225-5171.

Petersburg **Rexall Drugs** ✉ 215 N. Nordic Dr. ☎ 907/772-3265. After hours, call **Petersburg Medical Center** ☎ 907/772-4291.

Sitka **Harry Race Pharmacy** ✉ 106 Lincoln St. ☎ 907/747-8006. **Sitka Community Hospital** ✉ 209 Moller Dr. ☎ 907/747-3241 after hours. **White's Pharmacy** ✉ 705 Halibut Point Rd. ☎ 907/747-8233.

Wrangell **Stikine Drugs** ✉ 202 Front St. ☎ 907/874-3422. **Wrangell General Hospital** ✉ 310 Bennett St. ☎ 907/874-7000 after hours.

LODGING

B&B RESERVATION SERVICE The Alaska Bed & Breakfast Association Innside Passage Chapter books B&B accommodations in most Southeast communities.

Local Agents **Bed & Breakfast Association of Alaska Innside Passage Chapter** ☎ 907/789-8822 🖷 907/780-4673 🌐 www.accommodations-alaska.com.

TOURS

ADVENTURE **Alaska Discovery** ✉ 5310 Glacier Hwy., Juneau ☎ 907/780-6226 or 800/586-1911 🖷 907/780-4220 🌐 www.akdiscovery.com. **Cape Fox Tours** ☎ 907/225-4846 🖷 907/225-3137 🌐 www.capefoxtours.com. **Tongass Kayak Adventures** ☎ 907/772-4600 🌐 www.tongasskayak.com.

AIR CHARTERS & FLIGHTSEEING **Air Excursions** ☎ 907/697-2375, 800/354-2479 in Alaska 🌐 www.airexcursions.com, in Gustavus. **Mountain Flying Service** ☎ 907/766-3007 or 800/954-8747 🌐 www.flyglacierbay.com, in Haines. **Pacific Airways** ☎ 907/225-3500 or 877/360-3500 🌐 www.flypacificairways.com, in Ketchikan. **Pacific Wing** ☎ 907/772-9258 🌐 www.

pacificwing.com, in Petersburg. **ProMech Air** ☎ 907/886-3845 or 800/860-3845 🌐 www.promechair.com, in Ketchikan. **Sunrise Aviation** ☎ 907/874-2319 or 800/874-2311 🖷 907/874-2546 🌐 www.sunriseflights.com, in Wrangell. **Wings of Alaska** ☎ 907/789-0790 🌐 www.wingsofalaska.com, in Juneau.

BICYCLING **Sockeye Cycle Company** ✉ 24 Portage St. (Ft. Seward) 📫 Box 829, Haines 99827 ☎ 907/766-2869 🌐 www.cyclealaska.com.

BOATING **Alaska Travel Adventures** ☎ 907/789-0052 or 800/478-0052 🌐 www.alaskaadventures.com. **Auk Nu Tours** ☎ 907/586-8687 or 800/820-2628 🌐 www.auknutours.com. **Auk Ta Shaa Discovery** ☎ 907/586-8687 or 800/820-2628 🌐 www.goldbelttours.com. **Glacier Valley Wilderness Adventures** ☎🖷 907/767-5522 🌐 www.glaciervalleyadventures.com. **Spirit Walker Expeditions, Inc.** 📫 Box 240, Gustavus 99826 ☎ 907/697-2266 or 800/529-2537 🖷 907/697-2701 🌐 www.seakayakalaska.com.

HELICOPTER FLIGHTSEEING A one-hour flight costs approximately $180; variations like a 1½-hour flight combined with a dogsled tour can cost around $365. All of the following operators fly from Juneau.

Coastal Helicopters ☎ 907/789-5600 🌐 www.coastalhelicopters.com. **ERA Helicopters** ☎ 907/586-2030 or 800/843-1947 🌐 www.eraaviation.com. **Northstar Trekking** ☎ 907/790-4530 🌐 www.glaciertrekking.com. **Temsco Helicopters** ☎ 907/789-9501 or 877/789-9501 🌐 www.temscoair.com.

NATURE Alaska Nature Tours runs bird-watching and nature trips, plus hiking and skiing trips, from Haines. Kaleidoscope Cruises runs whale-watching and glacier-ecology boat tours from Petersburg.

Alaska Nature Tours ☎ 907/766-2876 🖷 907/766-2844 🌐 www.alaskanaturetours.net. **Kaleidoscope Cruises** ☎ 907/772-3736 or 800/868-4373 🌐 www.alaska.net/~bbsea.

SIGHTSEEING Alaska Cruises has catamaran cruises from Ketchikan to Misty Fiords National Monument. Juneau Trolley Car Company makes stops at a dozen or so of Juneau's sights. Metlakatla Tours conducts tours from Metlakatla. Seaport Limousine leads guided tours of the Hyder area. Sitka Tours runs sightseeing, historical, and raptor tours in Sitka. Skagway Street Car Co. lets you revisit Skagway's gold-rush days in the original 1937 White Motor Company streetcars while showing you the sights.

Alaska Cruises ☎ 907/225-6044 or 800/228-1905 🖷 907/225-8636 🌐 www.mistyfjord.net. **Juneau Trolley Car Company** ☎ 907/586-7433 🌐 www.juneautrolley.com. **Metlakatla Tours** ☎ 907/886-4441 or 877/886-8687 🌐 tours.metlakatla.net. **Seaport Limousine** ☎ 250/636-2622 🌐 www.tkp-biz.com/seaportlimousine. **Sitka Tours** ☎ 907/747-8443 🖷 907/747-7510. **Skagway Street Car Co.** ☎ 907/983-2908 🖷 907/983-3908 🌐 www.skagwaystreetcar.com. **Tribal Tours** ☎ 907/747-7290 or 888/270-8687 🖷 907/747-3770 🌐 www.sitkatribal.com.

TRAIN TRAVEL

Southeast Alaska's only railroad, the White Pass & Yukon Route, operates between Skagway and Fraser, British Columbia. The tracks follow the historic path over the White Pass summit—a mountain-climbing, cliff-hanging route of 28 mi each way. Bus connections are available at Fraser to Whitehorse, Yukon.

White Pass & Yukon Route (WP & YR) ☎ 907/983-2217 or 800/343-7373 🌐 www.whitepassrailroad.com.

VISITOR INFORMATION

Hours of operation of the following visitor information centers are generally mid-May–August, daily 8–5, and additional hours when cruise ships are in port; September–mid-May, weekdays 8–5.

Tourist Information **Alaska Department of Fish & Game** Box 25526, Juneau 99802-5526 907/465-4112, 907/465-4180 sportfishing seasons and regulations, 907/465-2376 license information www.state.ak.us/adfg. **Alaska Division of Parks** 400 Willoughby Ave., Suite 400, Juneau 99801 907/465-4563 www.alaskastateparks.org. **Haines Convention and Visitors Bureau** 2nd Ave. near Willard St. Box 530, Haines 99827 907/766-2234 or 800/458-3579 www.haines.ak.us. **Juneau Convention and Visitors Bureau** 1 Sealaska Plaza, Suite 305, Juneau 907/586-2201 or 888/581-2201 www.traveljuneau.com. **Ketchikan Visitors Bureau** 131 Front St., Ketchikan 99901 907/225-6166 or 800/770-3300 www.visit-ketchikan.com. **Klondike Gold Rush National Historical Park** visitor center 2nd Ave. and Broadway Box 517, Skagway 99840 907/983-2921 or 907/983-9224 www.nps.gov/klgo. **Petersburg Visitor Information Center** 1st and Fram Sts. Box 649, Petersburg 99833 907/772-4636 907/772-3646 www.petersburg.org. **Prince of Wales Chamber of Commerce** Box 497, Craig 99921 907/826-3870 www.princeofwalescoc.org. **Sitka Convention and Visitors Bureau** 303 Lincoln St. Box 1226, Sitka 99835 907/747-5940 www.sitka.org. **Skagway Convention and Visitors Bureau** Box 1029, Skagway 99840 907/983-2854 or 888/762-1898 www.skagway.org. **Stewart-Hyder Chamber of Commerce** Box 306, Stewart, BC VOT 1WO 250/636-9224 250/636-2199 www.stewartbchyderak.homestead.com. **U.S. Forest Service** 648 Mission St., Ketchikan 99901 907/225-3101 www.fs.fed.us/r10/tongass. **Wrangell Visitor Center** 107 Stikine Ave. Box 49, Wrangell 99929 907/874-3901 or 800/367-9745 www.wrangellchamber.org.

The Interior and Denali National Park & Preserve

With Fairbanks & The Yukon

5

WORD OF MOUTH

"Backcountry hiking is wonderful in Denali. With the tundra, there's little need for bushwhacking. For those trying backcountry camping, the rewards are tremendous."

—repete

"The Denali shuttle was great. We saw moose, caribou, bears, and Dall sheep. On the return, it was warmer and fewer animals were out. Definitely take the earliest shuttle."

—Julie304

"Dawson City is a stunning, eye-opening glimpse of history, and the Yukon River is grand to behold."

—John

www.fodors.com/forums

By Kent Sturgis
Updated by
Tom Reale

THE IMAGE OF 1890 ALASKA, with its heady gold rushes set to the harsh pitches of countless honky-tonk saloons and the clanging of pans, has its roots in the Interior. Gold fever struck in Circle and Eagle in the 1890s, spread into Canada's Yukon Territory in the big Klondike gold rush of 1898, then came back to Alaska's Interior when Fairbanks hit pay dirt in the 1900s. The broad, swift Yukon River was the rush's main highway. Flowing almost 2,300 mi from Canada to the Bering Sea, just below the Arctic Circle, it carried prospectors across the border in search of instant fortune.

Although Fairbanks has grown up into a small city, many towns and communities in the Interior seem little changed. While soaking in the water of the Chena Hot Springs Resort, you can almost hear the whispers of gold seekers exaggerating their finds and claims, ever alert for the newest strike. When early missionaries set up schools in the Bush, the nomadic Native Alaskan peoples were herded to these regional centers for schooling and "salvation," but Interior Alaska is still flecked with Native villages. Fort Yukon, on the Arctic Circle, is the largest Athabascan village in the state.

Alaska's current gold rush—the pipeline carrying black gold from the oil fields in Prudhoe Bay south to the port of Valdez—snakes its way through the heart of the Interior. The pipeline itself is something of an enigma: it's a symbol of commercial interests against the environment yet also a monumental construction that hugs the land like a giant necklace. The Richardson Highway, which started as a gold stampeders' trail, parallels the trans-Alaska pipeline on its route south of Fairbanks.

Gold glitters anew in the Interior. Fairbanks, the site of the largest gold production in Alaska in pre–World War II days, is home to the Fort Knox Gold Mine, which is expected to double Alaska's gold production. The mine started up in 1996, nearly a century after the discovery of gold in the Klondike in 1896 and the massive stampede of prospectors to Dawson City in 1898.

The Alaska Range—the "great wall" dividing the Interior from the South Central region—rises more than 20,000 feet. Its grandest member, Mt. McKinley (known among Athabascan-speaking Native people as *Denali,* or "the high one"), rises 18,000 sky-filling feet from base to peak (one of the highest uplifts in the world); and at 20,320 feet above sea level, it is the highest peak in North America. (Although Mt. Everest reaches more than 29,000 feet above sea level, it rises only 11,000 feet above the Tibetan Plateau.)

This tumultuous landscape was formed by the head-on collision of two tectonic plates. Between them, in the Denali fault system, lies the largest crack in the Earth's crust on the North American continent. This barrier between South Central and the Interior Plateau gathers colder weather and bears a fine glacial system because of its high altitude. These ice-capped mountains resemble the way a large part of the continent looked during the Ice Age. Flying in a small plane over the black-striped glaciers of the Alaska Range can be a dazzling experience.

Numbers in the text correspond to numbers in the margin and on the Interior and the Yukon, Fairbanks, Denali National Park & Preserve, and Dawson City maps.

If you have 3 days

Spend a day in **Fairbanks** 1–7, taking in the trans-Alaska pipeline, University of Alaska Museum, and the Riverboat Discovery tour. Try to end your day at Pioneer Park so that you can have dinner at the Alaska Salmon Bake. The next day head to **Denali National Park & Preserve** 14 and do some hiking or take a whitewater rafting trip down the nearby Nenana River. Spend the night in the park area, but be sure to call ahead for room or campsite reservations and for seats on the bus—the park area is very crowded in the summer. The next morning get up early to take a shuttle bus to Eielson Visitor Center at the park entrance, and start the third day exploring the national park. Stay in Fairbanks the last night, catching dinner and a show at the Ester Gold Camp.

If you have 5 days

Follow the three-day itinerary; then spend the fourth day in **Fairbanks** 1–7, taking the tour of El Dorado Gold Mine, where you can pan for gold, and visiting the **Fairbanks Ice Museum** 2 if you missed it earlier. That afternoon head out to the scenic Chena Hot Springs Road for a relaxing soak at Chena Hot Springs Resort in **Chena Hot Springs** 8. Spend the night at the resort or head back to town and consider stopping for dinner at Two Rivers Lodge.

If you have 10 days

Follow the five-day itinerary; then head east to the Fortymile and Klondike gold-rush areas, visiting some of the unique attractions along the Richardson and Alaska highways, such as the Santa Claus House in **North Pole** 15, the Knotty Shop just south of North Pole, and Rika's Roadhouse in **Delta Junction** 16. Spend the night in **Tok** 17. The next day take the gravel Taylor Highway up to **Eagle** 19 and the Yukon River. Take the walking tour of Eagle in the morning, and then drive to **Dawson City** 20–23, spending a day or two there. From Dawson you can go back to Fairbanks the way you came, or—if you're up for the 337-mi drive—you can continue on to **Whitehorse** 24, on the Alaska Highway. If a long drive doesn't suit you, on Day 6 hop a flight to Dawson, spend a couple of days there, and then return for more Fairbanks attractions.

Exploring the Interior

Interior Alaska is neatly sandwiched between two monumental mountain ranges—the Brooks Range to the north and the Alaska Range to the south. Important cities and towns are spread along two major transportation routes. The Yukon River flows east–west in the northern half of the region. Interior Alaskans often define their area by the road system. A few highways cut through this great land, and only one connects Alaska to the rest of the world. The Alaska Highway, still often referred to as the Alcan (Alaska-Canada Highway), enters Alaska by way of Yukon Territory, Canada.

On the eastern edge of the state lies Fortymile Country and, just across the border, the Yukon Territory. In Alaska the Taylor Highway cuts through Fortymile Country, connecting Eagle, a gold-rush town, to the Alaska Highway. A cutoff connects the Taylor to the Top of the World Highway, which runs through Dawson City, a town that's a celebration of mining history. Both highways are gravel. The Alaska Highway officially ends in Delta Junction, where the Richardson Highway leads to Fairbanks. The highways run through fairly flat land, by Alaska standards, though they do get close to some mountains. The George Parks Highway connects Fairbanks to Anchorage, passing right by Denali National Park. If you're fortunate enough to make the drive on a clear day, Mt. McKinley seems to loom over the highway as you approach Talkeetna. There are a couple of marked viewpoints along the road so you don't have to risk your life in traffic to get some good photos. Then as you near the town of Cantwell, the road passes through high taiga forest and is flanked by the Talkeetna Mountains to the east and the Alaska Range to the west.

North of Fairbanks are three highways, one of which stretches into the Arctic. All three wind through wild, wooded country. The Steese Highway heads northeast through alpine landscapes and dead-ends in Circle at the Yukon River. The Elliott Highway takes you northwest to the beginning of the Dalton Highway and then turns south to a dead-end at Manley Hot Springs on the Tanana River. The final main highway in the Interior, the Dalton, splits from the Elliott Highway at Livengood. It cuts through the Brooks Range, an imposing collection of rocky Arctic peaks, and spills out onto the tundra coast of the North Slope.

The Denali Highway, oddly enough, isn't in Denali National Park. It connects the towns of Paxson and Cantwell, running for 135 mi through tundra and spruce forests. Most of the road is unpaved, and services are few and far between, so make sure you've got a full tank of gas and at least one real spare tire.

About the Restaurants

Travelers and locals expect fresh seafood, and even though the salmon streams and salt water are hundreds of miles away, most restaurants oblige by flying in salmon and halibut regularly. Meat-and-potatoes main courses and the occasional pasta dish fill out the menus. Vegetarians might have a tough time, but there's usually something on the bill of fare that will suffice. Most restaurants stay open late during the summer, and attire is definitely casual—wear a coat and tie to most places and you'll draw puzzled stares. National chains are almost nonexistent, so local ownership and knowledge prevail.

About the Hotels

Lodging choices range from hostels and intimate bed-and-breakfasts to national chain hotels and stop just short of ultraluxury spots. However, options exist to please even the most discriminating travelers. Swimming pools are a rarity, but most other amenities that you've come to expect

Dogsledding Alaska is to dog mushing what Kentucky is to horse racing, and the Interior is arguably the prime mushing spot in Alaska. A number of dog-mushing races are held here, ranging from short sprint races with small teams to the Yukon Quest International, the second-longest sled-dog race in the world next to the Iditarod. But this isn't a sport solely for racers. Many people live in the Interior just so they can spend their free time in winter mushing their dogs. Skijoring—being pulled on skis by dogs—is also a pastime. A web of trails surrounds many communities. Dog-mushing outfits tend to be now-you-see-them, now-you-don't, so your best up-to-date source for information on outfitters is the Alaska Public Lands Information Center.

Flora & Fauna This part of Alaska has, through many millennia, escaped the onset of glaciers and thus formed a refuge for the Ice Age flora and fauna that were crowded out of other areas by ice and intense cold. Many species of plants and animals survived only in this refugium. Certain species of birds notably follow age-old patterns of migration and spend summers in the Interior's vast, prodigiously rich wetlands.

Below the tundra of the Alaska Range, the trees of the taiga take over: dark, spiky spruce; paper birch; aspen; and, in the wetter places, cottonwood. The soft green leaves of the deciduous trees shine golden in autumn. Among and around the trees, fireweed paints the landscape soft magenta. Spring paints the meadows blue with lupine, summer brings succulent berries, and fall splashes the berry leaves with crimson. Winter turns the region frigid, white, and crisp with ice.

As it stretches farther to the north, the Interior's near-vertical terrain near the Alaska Range flattens out into low, rounded hills. Tundra and taiga persist, with soft greens spiked by dark spruce trees, and deep green-gold mossy muskegs squish like soggy trampolines underfoot. Lakes gleam like black mirrors.

Hiking Below the high, snowy reaches of the Alaska Range, the lower foothills are often stained with color, evidence of their ancient, restless past. Polychrome Pass in Denali National Park is aptly named: it commands a vista of rose-, orange-, gray-, and soft brown–shaded slopes fingered by swards of green alpine tundra. This high tundra is fine hiking country, but in other areas, the ground is tufted with slippery tussocks, and even the most nimble-footed will be forced into balancing acts.

Several developed trails offer hikers everything from an afternoon outing to an expedition of several days. Water is often scarce along the trails, so make sure you pack enough. Those adventurous souls interested in forging their own paths off the developed trails will find lots of space to explore. Alaska's beauty, however, is still mostly wild and can be dangerous if you're not well informed, and trespassing on private property is illegal. The Alaska Public Lands Information Center in Fairbanks is a crucial stop for all hikers. The staff is helpful and knowledgeable, and in many cases, they can tell you about areas from personal experience.

Hot-Springs Retreats Forty below zero isn't a temperature that inspires thoughts of swimming, but that's what visitors have done for many years at the three hot-springs resorts in the Interior. Early miners discovered natural hot springs in the frozen wilderness just north of Fairbanks and scrambled to build communities around this heaven-sent phenomenon. The areas around the hot springs also make excellent bases for fishing, hiking, snowshoeing, or cross-country skiing. Each of the resorts is accessible by road and air from Fairbanks.

Wild & Scenic Rivers Great rivers travel through this landscape: the Tanana, the Nenana, the Kuskokwim, and one of the world's most powerful—the mighty Yukon. (Only four rivers in the Americas have a greater capacity of water than the Yukon: the Amazon, the St. Lawrence, the Mississippi, and the Missouri.) Twenty miles wide in places, the Yukon travels for 2,300 mi, from Canada to the Bering Sea, and runs through some of the most beautiful country of the Interior Plateau. Countless people traversed this pathway as they moved through the North American continent, and many people still travel the river by boat in the summer and by snowmobile across its frozen surface in the winter.

The Bureau of Land Management is in charge of three Wild and Scenic Rivers, each of which has a special draw. Beaver Creek threads through the White Mountain National Recreation Area north to the Yukon and offers good fishing—arctic grayling, northern pike, and burbot—and spectacular vistas. Along the rapid-ripped Birch Creek, moose, caribou, and birds are easily spotted. The beautiful Fortymile River provides a range of canoeing terrain, from Class I to IV rapids.

---

in the Lower 48 are available. Reservations for summer dates at the more popular hotels and destinations, including campsites near Denali, need to be made months in advance, but even at the last minute comfortable choices can usually be found.

WHAT IT COSTS

	$$$$	$$$	$$	$	¢
RESTAURANTS	over $25	$20–$25	$15–$20	$10–$15	under $10
HOTELS	over $225	$175–$225	$125–$175	$75–$125	under $75

Restaurant prices are per person for a main course at dinner. Hotel prices are for two people in a standard double room in high season.

Timing

Among the warmest in Alaska, Interior summers have a few days each month with temperatures in the high 80s or 90s. From the first week of May to the middle of August, it's bright enough at midnight to read a newspaper outdoors. Sunny days or partly cloudy ones, sometimes

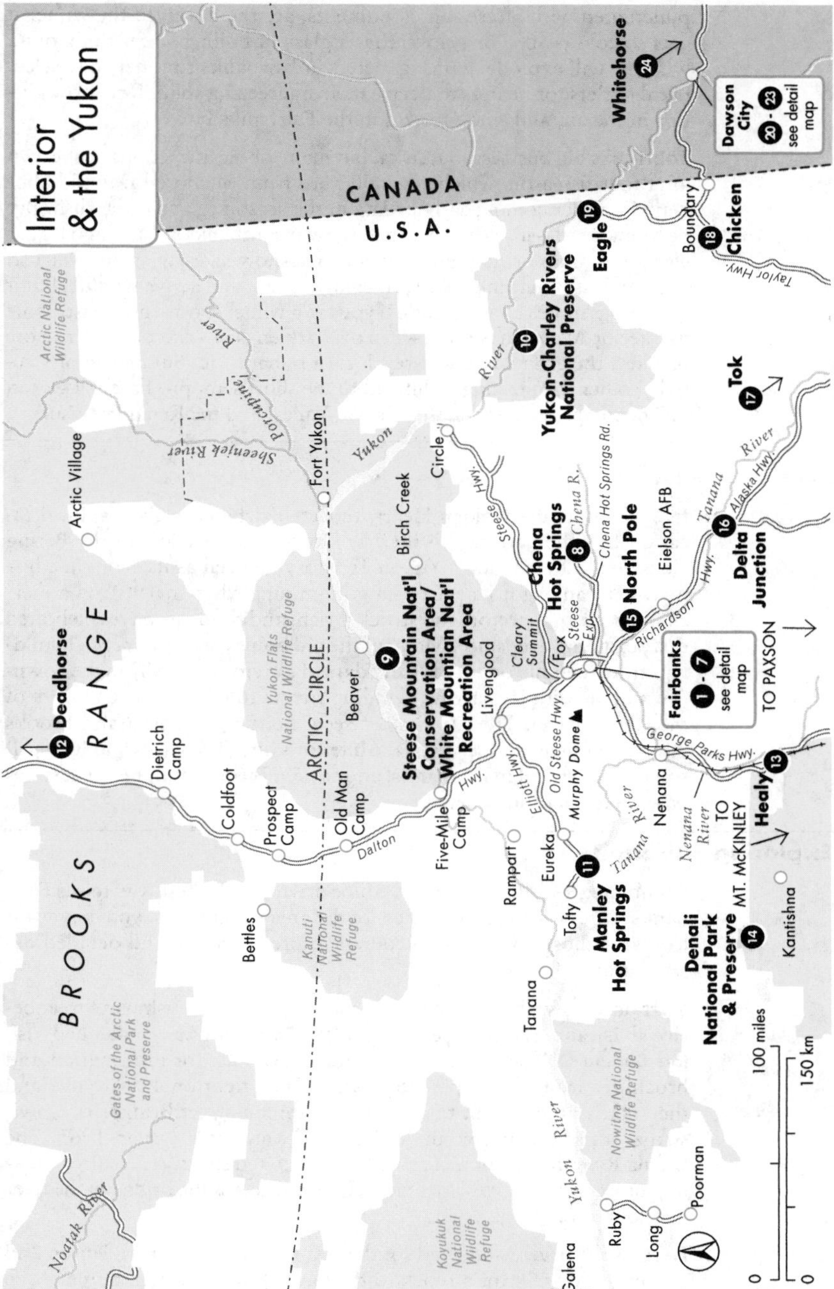
Interior & the Yukon
CANADA
U.S.A.
24 Whitehorse
Dawson City 20 - 23 see detail map
19 Eagle
Boundary
18 Chicken
Taylor Hwy.
10 Yukon-Charley Rivers National Preserve
17 Tok
Tanana River
Alaska Hwy.
16 Delta Junction
Eielson AFB
15 North Pole
8 Chena Hot Springs
Chena R.
Chena Hot Springs Rd.
Steese Hwy.
Circle
Birch Creek
Fort Yukon
Yukon River
Porcupine River
Sheenjek River
Arctic Village
Arctic National Wildlife Refuge
12 Deadhorse
BROOKS RANGE
Yukon Flats National Wildlife Refuge
ARCTIC CIRCLE
Beaver
9 Steese Mountain Nat'l Conservation Area/ White Mountain Nat'l Recreation Area
Cleary Summit
Fox
Steese Exp.
Richardson Hwy.
Fairbanks 1 - 7 see detail map
TO PAXSON
Livengood
Old Steese Hwy.
Murphy Dome
Elliott Hwy.
George Parks Hwy.
Nenana
Nenana River
TO MT. McKINLEY
13 Healy
Dietrich Camp
Coldfoot
Prospect Camp
Old Man Camp
Dalton Hwy.
Five-Mile Camp
Rampart
Eureka
11 Manley Hot Springs
Tanana River
Tofty
Tanana
Bettles
Kanuti National Wildlife Refuge
14 Denali National Park & Preserve
Kantishna
Gates of the Arctic National Park and Preserve
Nowitna National Wildlife Refuge
Yukon River
Koyukuk National Wildlife Refuge
Noatak River
Galena
Ruby
Long
Poorman
0 100 miles
0 150 km

punctuated with afternoon cloudbursts, are the norm. In the winter it gets so cold (–50°F or below) that a glass of boiling water flung out a window will explode. Parking meters in Fairbanks routinely have electrical outlets for heaters to keep cars from freezing solid. Dry snow glitters in the air, and smog freezes in the Fairbanks bowl.

Tourism is big business in Alaska, but many of the attractions shut down after tourist season, which generally runs from Memorial Day to Labor Day. Consider coming early or late in the season to avoid the rush. But be forewarned—it's been known to snow in Fairbanks in May, and higher elevations and northern areas could have snow as early as mid-August. Late August brings fall colors, ripening berries, and active wildlife, but it also brings more chance of rain. If you are a winter sports enthusiast, come to Interior Alaska in March, when the dark days of winter are over, snow blankets the ground, and there's lots of radiant sun. Summer sports activity, other than fishing, is limited to the short semi-pro baseball season in Anchorage, Fairbanks, the Mat-Su Valley, and the Kenai Peninsula.

FAIRBANKS

Its nickname, the Golden Heart, reflects Fairbanks's geographical location (it's the gateway to the Far North—the Arctic and the Bering Coast—and to Canada's Yukon Territory) as well as its economic history. Fairbanks got its start as a gold-mining town in 1901 by a merchant and a prospector who struck it rich, and residents have celebrated this beginning ever since. Many of the old homes and commercial buildings trace their history to the early days of the city, especially in the downtown area, with its narrow, winding streets following the contours of the Chena River. The city lies between the rugged Alaska and Brooks mountain ranges and serves as the Interior's hub. The Parks and Richardson highways end in Fairbanks, and several Bush commuter air services base their operations here.

Exploring Fairbanks

Combining a walking tour with some driving is the best way to see Fairbanks. After getting an overview of the area's highlights, you may want to revisit those spots that encourage more extensive and detailed examination.

a good tour

Start downtown by parking in the two-hour lot on Cushman Street between 1st and 2nd avenues. Stop at the **Fairbanks Convention and Visitors Bureau** ① ⚑, in the log cabin on 1st Avenue, for information and brochures from the helpful local staff. Turn right on 1st Avenue, and then take another right to cross the Cushman Street Bridge. Try to visualize all of downtown under 8 feet of water as it was in 1967. The Chena River flood-control project was initiated shortly thereafter, making future recurrences highly unlikely. Stroll across the bridge to the river overlook on the right.

Recross the bridge and head south on Cushman Street, then left on 2nd Avenue, and walk for a block to the Lacey Street Theater, home of the

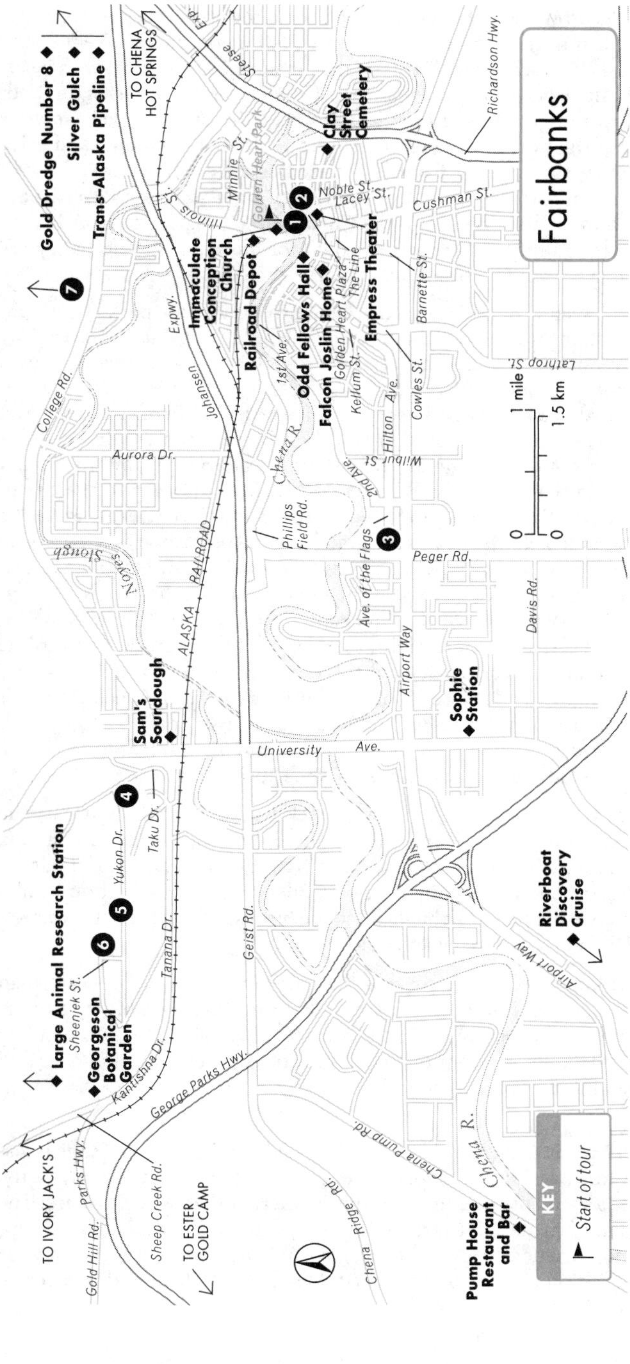
Fairbanks
KEY
Start of tour
Alaska Range Overlook 5
Creamer's Field Migratory Waterfowl Refuge 7
Fairbanks Convention and Visitors Bureau 1
Fairbanks Ice Museum 2
Pioneer Park 3
University of Alaska Fairbanks 4
University of Alaska Museum of the North 6
Gold Dredge Number 8
Silver Gulch
Trans-Alaska Pipeline
TO CHENA HOT SPRINGS
Clay Street Cemetery
Immaculate Conception Church
Railroad Depot
Odd Fellows Hall
Falcon Joslin Home
Empress Theater
Golden Heart Plaza
The Line
Noble St.
Lacey St.
Cushman St.
Barnette St.
Cowles St.
Lathrop St.
Richardson Hwy.
Steese Exp.
Illinois St.
Minnie St.
Golden Heart Park
1st Ave.
2nd Ave.
Kellum St.
Hilton Ave.
Wilbur St.
Johansen Expwy.
College Rd.
Aurora Dr.
Chena R.
Phillips Field Rd.
Ave. of the Flags
Peger Rd.
Davis Rd.
Airport Way
Noyes Slough
ALASKA RAILROAD
Sam's Sourdough
Sophie Station
University Ave.
Geist Rd.
Large Animal Research Station
Georgeson Botanical Garden
Sheenjek St.
Yukon Dr.
Taku Dr.
Tanana Dr.
Kantishna Dr.
George Parks Hwy.
Riverboat Discovery Cruise
TO IVORY JACK'S
Gold Hill Rd.
Parks Hwy.
Sheep Creek Rd.
TO ESTER GOLD CAMP
Pump House Restaurant and Bar
Chena Pump Rd.
Chena Ridge Rd.
0 1 mile
0 1.5 km

Fairbanks Ice Museum 2. Cool off and take in the artfully carved ice sculptures. Turn north (left) on Lacey Street, left again on 1st Avenue, and stop at the Golden Heart Plaza, on the far side of 1st Avenue, with beautiful floral displays in summer and the *Unknown First Family* statue dedicated to Interior Alaska families. Retrace your steps to pick up your car. Turn right on Cushman Street, take a left on 1st Avenue, and drive parallel to the river to Cowles Street, the third left. Follow Cowles Street to Airport Way, and turn right, then right again on Peger Road. Take an immediate right into the **Pioneer Park** 3 parking lot. A Native village and mining artifacts at the outdoor museum Mining Valley are just a couple of the attractions at this 44-acre park.

Take the Avenue of the Flags exit as you drive out of the park. Turn right onto Wilbur Street and right again on Airport Way. Take Airport Way to University Avenue and turn right. Cross the Chena River and stay on University Avenue until you get to Taku Drive. Turn left onto the **University of Alaska Fairbanks** 4 campus. Take the first right on Tanana Drive, and then go left at the stop sign at Yukon Drive. Take Yukon Drive for ½ mi to the **Alaska Range overlook** 5. If it's a clear day, and it usually is, you can see the Alaska Range and Mt. McKinley far to the south. Continue on Yukon Drive to Sheenjek Street and the **University of Alaska Museum of the North** 6 on the right. No trip to Fairbanks is complete without a visit to this museum. A fascinating series of informative displays presents Alaska history, anthropology, natural history, and geography. When you leave the museum, continue on Yukon Drive to Kantishna Drive and turn right, then left on Sheep Creek Road to the Georgeson Botanical Garden, where researchers study the unique growing environment of the Far North. Continue on Sheep Creek Road for 1 mi and turn right on Miller Hill Road, then right again on Yankovich Road for just under ½ mi to the Large Animal Research Station, where scientists study the habits of musk ox, caribou, and reindeer.

Retrace your route back to Sheep Creek Road, and follow it past the intersection with Kantishna Drive, where the road turns into Tanana Drive. After the sharp left curve, turn right on Taku Drive, right again on Farmers Loop Road, then left on College Road. Turn left on Danby and follow the road straight ahead to the bird-watching area at **Creamer's Field Migratory Waterfowl Refuge** 7.

TIMING The walking and driving parts of the tour can be done in an hour to an hour and a half, but you can extend that time considerably by exploring the various spots. Lingering over the University Museum exhibits alone can extend the tour to nearly an entire day. Let your interests and the weather determine your schedule.

What to See

5 **Alaska Range Overlook.** The entire north side of the Alaska Range is visible at this overlook, a favorite spot for time-lapse photography of the midwinter sun just peeking over the southern horizon on a low arc. The three major peaks, called the Three Sisters because of their similar appearance, are nearly always distinguishable on a clear day. From your left are **Mt. Hayes,** 13,832 feet; **Mt. Hess,** 11,940 feet; and **Mt. Debo-**

rah, 12,339 feet. Much farther to the right, toward the southwest, hulks **Mt. McKinley,** the highest peak in North America. On some seemingly clear days it's not visible at all. At other times the base is easy to see but the peak is lost in cloud cover. When Mt. McKinley is entirely visible, **Mt. Foraker** can often be seen just to the right of Mt. McKinley's base—at 75 mi away from Mt. McKinley, it appears as a small pyramid, but it's actually the second-highest peak in the Alaska Range. ✉ *West Ridge, University of Alaska Fairbanks campus, Yukon Dr.; look for parking area just east of University of Alaska Museum.*

❼ **Creamer's Field Migratory Waterfowl Refuge.** Three pleasant nature trails lead through fields, forest, and wetlands. This is a great place to view waterfowl, cranes, songbirds, and moose. The barns and buildings of **Creamer's Dairy** are also still standing here. Now on the National Register of Historic Places, Creamer's Dairy was the farthest-north dairy in North America from 1910 to 1966. The farmhouse is now a nature and visitor center. ✉ *1300 College Rd., Lemeta* ☎ *907/459–7307 or 907/459–7301* 🌐 *www.creamersfield.org.*

⚑ ❶ **Fairbanks Convention and Visitors Bureau.** At this visitor center on the river at the Cushman Street Bridge you can pick up a map for a self-guided 1½-hour walking tour through the historic downtown area. The bureau also has maps for a two-hour do-it-yourself driving tour. Points of interest on the tours include **Golden Heart Park,** home of the *Unknown First Family* statue; the **Clay Street Cemetery,** with its marked and unmarked graves of early pioneers; the **Empress Theater,** the first concrete structure in Interior Alaska; the stately **Falcon Joslin Home,** the oldest frame house in Fairbanks still at its original location; the **Line,** home of the red-light district until the mid-1950s; **Odd Fellows Hall,** a bathhouse for gold miners until the pipes froze in the winter of 1910–11; and the historic **Immaculate Conception Church,** which was raised off its foundation in 1911 and rolled across the frozen Chena River on logs pulled by horses. ✉ *550 1st Ave., Downtown* ☎ *907/456–5774, 800/327–5774 recording* 📠 *907/452–4190* 🌐 *www.explorefairbanks.com.*

★ ❷ **Fairbanks Ice Museum.** You'd think that the last thing that Fairbanksans would want to hang onto through the too-brief summer would be a reminder of the brutal winters. However, the folks at the Ice Museum do just that every year. The ice carvings showcased at the Ice Art competition held in March are on display, along with new creations added for summer visitors. Billed as "the coolest show in town," the Ice Showcase, a large glass-wall display, is kept at 20°F. The chilly environment allows ice sculptors to demonstrate their skills and sculptures throughout the summer. "Freeze Frame" is a large-screen film demonstrating the techniques of ice sculpture. The museum is in the historic Lacey Street Theater, on the corner of 2nd Avenue and Lacey Street. ✉ *500 2nd Ave., Downtown* ☎ *907/451–8222* 🌐 *www.icemuseum.com* 🎟 *$6* ⏲ *June–Sept., daily 10–8.*

★ **Georgeson Botanical Garden of the Agricultural and Forestry Experiment Station Farm.** This is where researchers at the University of Alaska Fairbanks study Interior Alaska's unique, short, but intense midnight-sun growing season. Scientists and students explore the unique challenges of propagating flowers and vegetables in the harsh northern environment, both studying the varieties of berries and ferns that are native to the north, and researching how to grow non-native plants here, like tomatoes. When most people think of Alaska vegetation they tend to conjure up images of flat, treeless tundra, so an unexpected aspect of the garden is the amazing variety of native and cultivated flowers on exhibit. A visit to the garden should be on your must-see list of Fairbanks attractions. Self-guided tours of the facility are possible during the summer. ✉ *117 West Tanana Dr., west end of campus* ☎ *907/474–6921* ⏲ *May–Sept., daily 8–8* 🎟 *$2.*

★ ❸ **Pioneer Park.** The 44-acre park, formerly known as Alaskaland, is set along the Chena River near downtown Fairbanks and has several museums, an art gallery, theater, civic center, Native village, large children's playground, miniature-golf course, antique merry-go-round, restaurants, and a gold-rush town consisting of historic buildings saved from urban renewal. The complex has log-cabin gift shops and **Mining Valley,** an outdoor museum of mining artifacts surrounding an indoor-outdoor Alaska salmon bake restaurant. President Warren Harding traveled in the plush *Denali* railcar when he came north in 1923 to hammer the golden spike on the Alaska Railroad. The 227-foot stern-wheeler *Nenana* is the second-largest wooden vessel in existence and a national historic landmark. The railroad built the *Nenana* in 1933 to serve the rivers of the Interior. A diorama inside the stern-wheeler details the course the riverboat took on the Yukon and Tanana rivers around the turn of the 20th century. The **Crooked Creek and Whiskey Island Railroad,** a small-gauge train, circles the park. No-frills RV camping is available for $10 a night in the west end of the large parking lot on Airport Way. ✉ *Pioneer Park, Airport Way, and Peger Rd.* ☎ *907/459–1087* 🌐 *http://co.fairbanks.ak.us/parks&rec/pioneerpark/* 🎟 *Free* ⏲ *Park is open year-round; Museum and shops open daily 11–9 Memorial Day through Labor Day.*

★ ❹ **University of Alaska Fairbanks.** The university has earned an international reputation for its Arctic research, including a study of the aurora borealis, or northern lights. A free two-hour student-guided campus walking tour is offered weekdays throughout the summer. Tours of some campus facilities are also conducted from June through August (hours and admission fees vary). Out on the fringes of the university campus is the **Large Animal Research Station** (✉ Yankovich Rd. off Ballaine Rd. behind university ☎ 907/474–7207 tour information ⏲ Tour Memorial Day–Labor Day, daily 1:30 and 3:30), a 134-acre home to small herds of musk ox, caribou, and domestic reindeer. Resident and visiting scientists study these large ungulates to better understand their physiologies and the ways that they adapt to arctic conditions. Besides investigating these animals and their nutritional needs, reproductive capacities, and behavioral activities, the station serves as a valuable outreach program. Most people have little chance to see these animals in their natural habitats, especially the musk oxen. Once nearly eradicated from Alaska, these shaggy, prehistoric-looking beasts are marvels of adaptive physiques and behaviors. They are also being studied for potential commercial uses—the soft, delicate underfur called qiviut is combed out and made into scarves, hats, and gloves by Alaska Native women. The clothing has the feel of cashmere and is remarkably warm. The tour presenters emphasize the natural history and environmental adaptations of the animals, and give an outline of the research conducted at the facility and in the field. You'll tour the pens and get close-up looks at the animals and their young.

Researchers at the **Arctic Region Supercomputing Center** (✉ Butrovitch Bldg., Yukon Dr.) use high-performance supercomputers to solve problems in science and engineering for the high latitudes and the Arctic. The **Geophysical Institute** (✉ West Ridge, about 1 mi from campus center ☎ 907/474–7588 tour information) is a center of atmospheric and earthquake research. The university launches rockets at the **Poker Flat Research Range** (✉ Steese Hwy., 33 mi northeast of Fairbanks ☎ 907/474–7558 tour information) to study the aurora borealis. ✉ *Office of University Relations, 202 Eielson Bldg.* ☎ *907/474–7581* 🌐 *www.uaf.edu* ⏲ *Tour schedule varies; call for details or inquire at Fairbanks Convention and Visitors Bureau.*

❻ Fodor's Choice ★ **University of Alaska Museum of the North.** A stuffed grizzly bear—8 feet, 9 inches tall—guards the entrance to the Gallery of Alaska, divided into five Alaska regions: Southeast, Interior, South Central, Southwest, and the western Arctic coast. The collection includes the state's largest display of gold. Alaska Native art and artifacts, and Blue Babe, a mummified steppe bison that lived 36,000 years ago during the Pleistocene. Babe was preserved in permafrost (permanently frozen ground), complete with claw marks indicating attack by an American lion. The bison's remains were found by gold miners in 1979. Besides the usual "don't touch" exhibits, the museum has several "please touch" items, including the molars of a mammoth and a mastodon, a gray-whale skull, and a 5,495-pound copper nugget. The new wing, opened in 2004, doubled the size of the museum with a new Alaska art gallery, a northern lights exhibit, and a two-story viewing window looking out on the Alaska Range and the Tanana Valley. Audio guides are available for an additional $3. ✉ *907 Yukon Dr., West Ridge, University of Alaska Fairbanks campus* ☎ *907/474–7505* 🌐 *www.uaf.edu/museum* 🎟 *$5* ⏲ *Mid-May–mid-Sept., daily 9–7; mid-Sept.–mid-May, weekdays 9–5, weekends noon–5.*

off the beaten path

GOLD DREDGE NUMBER 8. – Imagine a giant gold dredge making its own waterway as it chews through the gold pay dirt, crawling along at a snail's pace and processing tons of rock and gravel. Built by Bethlehem Shipbuilders in 1928, the dredge was operated by the Fairbanks Exploration Company until its retirement in 1959. The five-deck ship is more than 250 feet long and took millions of dollars' worth of gold out of the Goldstream and Engineer creeks north of Fairbanks. *Gold Dredge Number 8* has been declared a National Historic District by the National Park Service, one of the few privately owned districts in the nation. This mining vessel came to rest at Mile 9, Old Steese Highway. The price of admission entitles you to the necessary tools, some gold-panning instructions, and a chance to find "colors" at the sluice or to seek gold independently in old tailings from the mining days. A sit-down, family-style, all-you-can-eat, miner's beef stew is served from 11 AM to 3 PM for an additional $9.50. The dredge (and the miner's stew) is a featured stop on Holland America's tours. ✉ *1755 Old Steese Hwy. N, Fairbanks 99712* ☎ *907/457–6058* 🌐 *www.golddredgeno8.com* 🎫 *$24* ⏲ *Mid-May–mid-Sept., daily 9:30–3:30.*

TRANS-ALASKA PIPELINE – Just north of Fairbanks you can see and touch the famous trans-Alaska pipeline. This 48-inch diameter pipe travels 800 mi from the oil fields on the north slope of the Brooks Range over three mountain ranges and more than 800 rivers and streams to the terminal in Valdez. There the crude oil is pumped onto tanker ships and transported to oil refineries in the lower 48 states. Since the pipeline began operations in 1977, more than 14 billion barrels of North Slope crude have been pumped. Currently the pipe is carrying approximately 1 million 42-gallon barrels of oil per day. The parking lot is right off the Steese Highway and has a sign loaded with information. Informative guides staff a small visitor center, and there's a gift shop with pipeline-company memorabilia. ✉ *Mile 7.5, Steese Hwy.* ☎ *907/457–3344* 🎫 *Free* ⏲ *Visitor center mid-May–Sept., daily 8–5.*

SILVER GULCH BREWING AND BOTTLING CO – You'll find some unique souvenirs and an interesting collection of Fairbanks citizens at North America's farthest-north brewery. Brewing a variety of styles since 1998, Silver Gulch is probably best known for its Pilsner. Fairbanks and Anchorage are the major markets, but a few spots on the Kenai carry Silver Gulch as well. Stop by for free tours and beer tastings every Friday evening from 5 to 7 PM or by appointment. The brewery is in the Fox Roadhouse building (around the right and through the side door) 10 mi from Fairbanks. ✉ *2195 Old Steese Hwy., Fox* ☎ *907/452–2739* 🌐 *www.silvergulch.com* 🎫 *Free* ⏲ *Fri. 5–7 PM.*

Where to Stay & Eat

★ **$$$–$$$$** ✕ **Pike's Landing.** Enjoy lunch on a huge outside deck (it seats 420) overlooking the Chena River, or dine inside in the elegant dining room of an extended log cabin. The meals run in price up to $38 for steak and lobster and rank with the best in the Interior. For a dinner in the $10 range, relax in the sports bar and catch a view of the river. The palate-pleasing Sunday brunch delivers tempting dishes and an irresistible dessert table. ✉ *4438 Airport Way* ☎ *907/479–7113* 💳 *AE, D, DC, MC, V.*

¢–$$$$ ✕ **Ivory Jack's.** Jack "Ivory" O'Brien used to deal in Alaskan ivory and whalebone out of this small restaurant tucked into the gold-rich hills of the Goldstream Valley on the outskirts of Fairbanks. Paraphernalia of the New York Yankees, Elvis, Dartmouth University, and dog-mushing adorns the large, open, and airy bar-restaurant. You can choose from more than 15 appetizers as well as burgers, pizza, and entrées such as halibut Dijon and Alaskan king crab. You'll catch some live local music on some weekends; cover charge depends on the band. ✉ *2581 Goldstream Rd., Goldstream* ☎ *907/455–6666* ▭ *AE, D, DC, MC, V.*

★ $$$ ✕ **Alaska Salmon Bake.** Mouthwatering salmon cooked over an open fire with a special lemon and brown-sugar sauce is a favorite at this indoor-outdoor restaurant in Pioneer Park's Mining Valley. Halibut, cod, a single serving of prime rib, a salad bar, and homemade blueberry cake are also available at the nightly all-you-can-eat dinner. ✉ *Airport Way and Peger Rd., Pioneer Park* ☎ *907/452–7274 or 800/354–7274* 🌐 *http://akvisit.com/salmon.html* ▭ *MC, V* ⊗ *No lunch mid-May–mid-Sept.*

$$–$$$ Fodor's Choice ★ ✕ **Pump House Restaurant.** Alongside the Chena River this mining pump–station-turned-restaurant turns out several variations of salmon and halibut main courses. Alaskan reindeer stew and seafood chowder are house specialties. The furnishings and floor are rich, polished wood, and an Alaskan grizzly bear in a glass case is on sentry next to the hostess station. Wednesday night is karaoke night in the bar. ✉ *Mile 2.0, Chena Pump Rd.* ☎ *907/479–8452* ▭ *AE, D, MC, V* ⊗ *No lunch mid-Sept.–June 1.*

★ $–$$ ✕ **The Cookie Jar.** Tucked away in a nondescript neighborhood on a street not found on most Fairbanks maps, this gorgeous little restaurant is well worth tracking down. The open, airy space predictably features lots of cookie jars, along with plants and artwork to complete the picture. Spanning breakfast, lunch, and dinner, the huge menu includes scads of homemade items, an extensive kids' menu, and vegetarian selections. Entrées range from steak and shrimp to coq au vin. For dessert, try the homemade tortes or a variety of cookies to match anything your grandma ever baked. Weekend breakfasts are especially popular, so allow extra time. Take Danby Street off the Johansen Expressway, and the restaurant is behind Aurora Motors. ✉ *1006 Cadillac Ct.* ☎ *907/479–8319* ▭ *AE, D, MC, V.*

★ $–$$ ✕ **Gambardella's Pasta Bella.** Locals crowd the family-run Italian restaurant at the edge of downtown known simply as Gambardella's. The place is small but cozy, with covered outside seating in the summer. The menu includes salads, pasta, pizza, vegetarian entrées, and submarine sandwiches on homemade bread. Its specialties, however, are lasagna, which the *Seattle Times* described as "the mother of all lasagnas"; the seafood *fra diavolo*; and the tiramisu. ✉ *706 2nd Ave., Downtown* ☎ *907/456–3417* ▭ *AE, MC, V* ⊗ *No lunch Sun.*

★ ¢–$$ ✕ **Sam's Sourdough Cafe.** Although Sam's serves meals all day, Fairbanksans know it as the best breakfast place in town. Sourdough recipes are a kind of minor religion in Alaska, and Sam's serves an extensive menu of sourdough specialties, including hotcakes and French toast, as well as standard meat-and-eggs items, all at very reasonable prices. On weekends get here early or be prepared for a wait. The address is Cameron Street, but it's really fronted on University, just over the railroad tracks. ✉ *3702 Cameron St.* ☎ *907/479–0523* ▭ *MC, V.*

¢–$ ✕ **Cafe Alex.** Part dinner destination, part wine bar, Alex has an eclectic menu that includes dependable salmon and halibut preparations, as well as tapas. Private side rooms off the main dining area are available for groups or couples. ✉ *310 1st Ave.* ☎ *907/452–2539* ▭ *MC, V.*

★ **$$$** **Fairbanks Princess Riverside Lodge.** An expansive wooden deck facing a scenic section of the Chena River draws a crowd at this luxury lodge in summer. Gold, russet, green, and burgundy accents warm the rustic decor. You can stop by the tour desk to book additional excursions around Fairbanks. The Edgewater Restaurant welcomes diners in suits and evening gowns or duct-tape-patched Carhartt's work clothes, and there's a daily breakfast buffet during the high season. You'll find the lodge just off the road to Fairbanks International Airport. ✉ *4477 Pikes Landing Rd., 99709* ☎ *907/455–4477 or 800/426–0500* 🖷 *907/455–4476* 🌐 *www.princesslodges.com/fairbanks_lodge.cfm* *326 rooms* *2 restaurants, cable TV, in-room data ports, health club, steam room, bar, shop, laundry facilities, business services, meeting rooms, airport shuttle, travel services, no-smoking rooms* ▭ *AE, D, DC, MC, V.*

★ **$$$** **Pike's Waterfront Lodge.** Log columns and beams support the high-ceiling lobby of this hotel and conference center on the banks of the Chena River. The grounds are strewn with more than 20,000 flowering plants, and a ½-mi river walk borders the property. There are several warm and cozy common areas, including a piano room and a fireplace lounge, and during the summer there's an ice cream parlor run on the premises. Rooms with a river view are worth the extra $15 per night. If you're looking for real Alaskan ambience, there are also 28 log cabins available for $250 per night. ✉ *1850 Hoselton Rd., 99709* ☎ *877/774–2400 or 907/456–4500* 🖷 *907/456–4515* 🌐 *www.pikeslodge.com* *179 rooms* *Restaurant, cable TV with movies and video games, in-room data ports, gym, sauna, spa, steam room, bar, concierge, Internet, business services, meeting rooms, airport shuttle, no-smoking rooms* ▭ *AE, D, MC, V.*

$$$ **Sophie Station Hotel.** Its quiet location and helpful staff make this spacious hotel near the airport one of Fairbanks's best. It has comfy furniture, rich upholstery, and Alaskan artwork throughout. Rooms are suites with kitchens that include a full-size range and refrigerator. You can try a buffalo burger at Zach's, the hotel restaurant, which serves breakfast, lunch, and dinner. ✉ *1717 University Ave., 99709* ☎ *907/479–3650 or 800/528–4916* 🖷 *907/479–7951* 🌐 *www.fountainheadhotels.com* *148 suites* *Restaurant, kitchenettes, microwaves, refrigerators, cable TV, bar, Internet, meeting room, airport shuttle* ▭ *AE, D, DC, MC, V.*

$–$$$ **Cranberry Ridge B&B.** The proprietors, Mike and Floss Caskey, a fifth-generation Alaskan family, designed and built this small B&B, north of Fairbanks off Farmers Loop Road. The contemporary house's position affords magnificent views of the Alaska Range. The two-bedroom apartment is perfect for families or for couples traveling together. Mike Caskey leads custom Arctic Circle and Mt. McKinley flightseeing tours in his Cessna 185 for up to three passengers. Special room rates are available for extended stays. ✉ *705 Cranberry Ridge Dr., Farmers Loop, 99712* ☎ *907/457–4424 or 888/326–4424* 🌐 *www.alaskaflyingtours.com* *1 apartment* *Cable TV, Internet; no a/c, no smoking* ▭ *D, DC, MC, V* *CP.*

$$ **Bridgewater Hotel.** In the heart of downtown Fairbanks, overlooking the Chena River, this elegant hotel has gone through a number of incarnations. Built when stern-wheelers were plying Alaska's rivers in the early 1900s the Bridgewater is now a thoroughly modern, European-style hotel. Open only in the summer, the downtown location is convenient to shops and restaurants. Rooms have floral accents, and the ambience is a far cry from the sameness and sterility of too many chain motels. ✉ *723 1st Ave., 99701* ☎ *907/452–6661 or 800/528–4916* 🖷 *907/452–6126* 🌐 *www.fountainheadhotels.com/bridgewater/bridgewater.htm* *94 rooms* *Café, cable TV, in-room data ports, dry cleaning, airport shuttle; no smoking* 💳 *AE, D, DC, MC, V* 🕒 *Closed mid-Sept–mid-May.*

$$ **Comfort Inn–Chena River.** Its location on a wooded bank of the Chena River directly across the water from Pioneer Park makes this hotel a popular choice. It also has a full-length, glass-enclosed indoor pool and hot tub. Rooms are done in green and dark wood and punctuated with artwork, and all were renovated in 2002 with new bedding, furniture, and window treatments. The room rate includes Continental breakfast. ✉ *1908 Chena Landings Loop, 99701* ☎ *907/479–8080 or 800/228–5150* 🖷 *907/479–8063* 🌐 *www.choicehotels.com* *74 rooms* *Some microwaves, some refrigerators, cable TV with movies and video games, in-room data ports, indoor pool, hot tub, airport shuttle, some pets allowed, no-smoking rooms* 💳 *AE, D, DC, MC, V* 🍴 *CP.*

$$ Fodor's Choice ★ **Wedgewood Resort.** Both wild and cultivated flowers adorn the landscaped grounds of the Wedgewood Resort, which borders on the Creamer's Field Migratory Waterfowl Refuge. Headquartered on the very resort is the Alaska Bird Observatory, a local nonprofit that researches and promotes the conservation of Alaska's birds. You'll also find a replica of a miner's cabin, a Bush plane, courtyards, and gazebos. All rooms are suites, decorated with local artwork that's available for purchase. The Bear Lodge hotel—also part of the resort—has 157 large rooms available in summer. Shuttles make the run to downtown Fairbanks and local shopping spots. ✉ *212 Wedgewood Dr., 99701* ☎ *800/528–4916 or 907/456–3642* 🖷 *907/451–8184* 🌐 *www.fountainheadhotels.com* *297 rooms* *2 restaurants, kitchens, microwaves, refrigerators, cable TV, in-room data ports, shops, dry cleaning, business services, meeting rooms, airport shuttle* 💳 *AE, D, DC, MC, V.*

$$ **Westmark Fairbanks Hotel and Conference Center.** Built on a courtyard on a quiet street, this full-service, snazzy complex is within easy walking distance of downtown. All rooms, done in rose and burgundy, have a writing desk; some have a StairMaster or stationary bike. A conference center and personal voice mail make it a good choice for business travelers. The Red Lantern serves steaks and seafood. ✉ *813 Noble St., 99701* ☎ *907/456–7722 or 800/544–0970* 🖷 *907/451–7478* 🌐 *www.westmarkhotels.com* *400 rooms* *Restaurant, cable TV with movies, in-room data ports, exercise equipment, bar, shop, laundry service, Internet, meeting room, airport and railroad shuttle, no-smoking floor* 💳 *AE, D, DC, MC, V.*

$ **Crestmont Manor B&B.** Handmade quilts and furnishings and antique fixtures accent this elegant colonial-style B&B. The rooms provide privacy, and comfort is a top priority of the house. You can relax on the deck while contemplating the sweeping view of the Chena River valley and the Alaska Range. Breakfast, with quiche, fresh pastries, juice, and coffee, is a pleasant affair. ✉ *510 Crestmont Dr., 99709* ☎ *907/456–3831* 🖷 *907/456–3841* 🌐 *www.mosquitonet.com/~crestmnt* *5 rooms* *Laundry service, business services; no a/c, no smoking* 💳 *AE, MC, V* 🍽 *BP.*

Guided Tours

Adventure

Northern Alaska Tour Company (📫 Box 82991, Fairbanks 99708 ☎ 907/474–8600 or 800/474–1986 🖷 907/474–4767 🌐 www.northernalaska.com) leads year-round half- and full-day excursions to the Arctic Circle and the Yukon River and two- and three-day fly-drive tours to Prudhoe Bay, Barrow, and the Brooks Range. They also offer aurora-watching trips in the winter.

Cruising & Canoeing

The excitement and color of the city's riverboat history and the Interior's cultural heritage are relived each summer aboard the **Riverboat Discovery** (✉ 1975 Discovery Dr. ☎ 907/479–6673 or 866/479–6673 🌐 www.riverboatdiscovery.com), a 3½-hour narrated trip by sternwheeler along the Chena and Tanana rivers to a rustic Native village on the Tanana River. The cruise provides a glimpse of the lifestyle of the dog mushers, subsistence fishermen, traders, and Native Alaskans who populate the Yukon River drainage. Sights along the way include operating fish wheels, a Bush airfield, floatplanes, a smokehouse and cache, log cabins, and Iditarod champion Susan Butcher's dog kennels. Captain Jim Binkley, his wife, Mary, and their children have operated the Discovery cruises for more than 50 years. Their family, with its four generations of river pilots, has run the great rivers of the north for more than 100 years. The cruise costs $44.95, and two cruises run daily (8:45 and 2) mid-May to mid-September.

Sightseeing

Gray Line of Alaska (☎ 800/478–6388 🌐 www.graylinealaska.com) runs several scenic and informative trips through the Fairbanks area, including a four-hour Discover the Gold sightseeing tour of the city that features the *Gold Dredge Number 8* and a lunch of miner's stew for $60.

Nightlife & the Arts

Fairbanks supports a year-round arts program that rivals that of many larger communities. In summer you will find that the lack of a true "night"—thanks to the midnight sun—doesn't seem to hinder nightlife at all. Check the "Kaleidoscope" section in the Thursday *Fairbanks Daily News–Miner* for current nightspots, plays, concerts, and art shows.

The Arts

FESTIVALS The **Fairbanks Summer Arts Festival** (📫 Box 80845, Fairbanks 99708 ☎ 907/474–8869 🖷 907/479–4329 🌐 www.fsaf.org) has grown from a small jazz festival for adults to a major University of Alaska Fairbanks–affiliated annual event attracting students worldwide. The festival presents music, dance, theater, opera theater, storytelling, creative writing, healing arts, visual arts, and ice-skating instruction. Performances spread over two weeks in late July.

Every July Fairbanks hosts the **World Eskimo-Indian Olympics** (🌐 www.weio.org), when northern peoples from Alaska and Canada gather to compete in traditional athletic games, and dances. The **World Ice Art Championships** (🌐 www.icealaska.com) in March draws ice artists from around the world for an international ice-sculpting competition. The annual **Winter Carnival** (🌐 www.fairbankswintercarnival.com), held in mid-March, hosts dog-mushing and skijoring competitions, basketball tournaments, a crafts fair, fur auctions, and various winter events in Fairbanks and in outlying areas.

5

Nightlife

CABARET THEATER For an evening of varied and high-quality entertainment head to **Ester Gold Camp** (✉ Ester ☎ 907/479–2500 or 800/676–6925 📠 907/474–1780 🌐 www.akvisit.com/ester.html), a former gold-mining town about 5 mi west of Fairbanks on the Parks Highway. Its 11 historical structures date to the early 1900s and include the rustic Malemute Saloon, which is open daily from 2 PM to midnight. The camp, which is on the National Register of Historic Places, comes alive at night with a show in the saloon ($15) featuring gold rush–era songs, stories, and Robert Service poetry; a beautiful northern-lights photography show ($8) in the Firehouse Theatre; and a dinner buffet ($17.95) serving halibut and reindeer stew in yet another building. Plan your evening to catch dinner and all the shows. The camp has a hotel with semiprivate bathrooms, RV parking, a gift shop, and evening bus service to and from Fairbanks. The camp is open late May to early September.

The **Palace Theatre and Saloon** (✉ Airport Way and Peger Rd. ☎ 907/456–5960 or 800/354–7274 🌐 www.akvisit.com/palace.html) at Pioneer Park is one of the livelier summer spots. The Palace's *Golden Heart Revue* ($16), a musical-comedy show about the founding and building of Fairbanks, begins at 8:15 nightly.

SALOONS The **Blue Loon** (✉ Parks Hwy., Mile 353.5 ☎ 907/457–5666), between ★ Ester and Fairbanks, presents year-round rock and roll and folk music, concerts, DJ events, and dance events. Microbrews complement its full-service menu. The head chef formerly worked at the Chena Pump House, and the menu is steps above standard bar fare. There are a volleyball court, a campfire area, RV parking, and movies every evening at 5:30 and 8. After a brief hiatus and change of ownership, the **Howling Dog Saloon** (✉ 2160 Old Steese Hwy. ☎ 907/456–4695) is back, with live music, bar food, a beer, wine, and liquor menu, and huge gobs of atmosphere. The clientele is a mix of college students, airline pilots, tourists, miners, and bikers. Out back there are a volleyball court, horseshoe pit, and 10 very basic cabins for rent. The **Senator's Saloon** (✉ Mile 2.0, Chena Pump Rd. ☎ 907/479–8452) at the Pump House Restaurant is the place to hear easy-listening music alongside the Chena River on a warm summer evening. Don't be alarmed by the exterior ap- ★ pearance of the **Midnight Mine** (✉ 308 Wendell St. ☎ 907/456–5348), within walking distance of downtown. It's a friendly, *Cheers*-like neighborhood bar with darts, Foosball, pool, and a big-screen TV. Sam the dog is likely to greet you as you come in—be sure to ask to see her trick. It'll cost you a buck, but it's well worth it.

SQUARE DANCING There are square-dancing clubs in Fairbanks, North Pole, Delta Junction, and Tok. The groups are affiliated with the **Northern Lights Council of Dancers** (☎ 907/452–5699 🌐 www.fairnet.org/agencies/dance/farnofed.html), which holds frequent dances.

Sports & the Outdoors

BASEBALL Scores of baseball players, including Tom Seaver, Dave Winfield, and Jason Giambi, have passed through Fairbanks on their way to the major leagues. The Interior city is home to the **Alaska Goldpanners** (☎ 907/451–0095 🌐 www.goldpanners.com), a member of the Alaska Baseball League, a string of amateur baseball organizations throughout the state. Players are recruited from college teams nationwide, and the summer season (mid-June–early August) generates top-caliber competition. Home games are played at Growden Field, along Lower 2nd Avenue at Wilbur Street, not far from Pioneer Park. The baseball park hosts the **Midnight Sun Baseball Game,** a Fairbanks tradition in which the Goldpanners play baseball at midnight of the summer solstice without benefit of artificial lights. This is thrilling (and possibly chilly) to watch on a clear, sunny night when the daylight never ends.

BICYCLING Bicyclists in Fairbanks use the paved paths from the University of Alaska campus around Farmers Loop to the Steese Highway. Another path follows Geist and Chena Pump roads into downtown Fairbanks. A shorter, less strenuous route is the bike path between downtown and Pioneer Park along the south side of the Chena River. Maps showing all the bike paths are available at the **Fairbanks Convention and Visitors Bureau** (⇨ Exploring Fairbanks). Mountain bikers can test their skills during the summer on the ski trails of the University of Alaska Fairbanks and the Birch Hill Recreation Area or on many of the trails and dirt roads around Fairbanks. Stop by the **Alaska Public Lands Information Center** (✉ 250 Cushman St. ☎ 907/456–0527) for mountain-biking information.

BOATING For relaxing boating in or near Fairbanks, use Chena River access points at Nordale Road east of the city, the Cushman and Wendell Street bridges near downtown, Pioneer Park above the Peger River Bridge, the state campground, and the University Avenue Bridge.

The Tanana is riverboat country. On this river and others in the Yukon River drainage, Alaskans use long, wide, flat-bottom boats powered by one or two large outboard engines. The boats include a lift to raise the engine a few inches, allowing passage through the shallows, and some of the engines come equipped with a jet unit instead of a propeller to allow more bottom clearance. Arrangements for riverboat charters can be made in almost any river community. Ask at the **Fairbanks Convention and Visitors Bureau** (⇨ Exploring Fairbanks).

CURLING Hundreds of Fairbanksans participate each year in curling, a game in which people with brooms play a giant version of shuffleboard on ice.

Curlers have an almost fanatical devotion to their sport, and they're eager to explain its finer points to the uninitiated. This ancient Scottish game was brought to Alaska and the Yukon during the Klondike gold rush. The **Fairbanks Curling Club** (✉ 1962 2nd Ave., 99701 ☎ 907/452–2875 🌐 www.curlfairbanks.org) hosts an annual international bonspiel (match) on the first weekend of April. The club season runs from early October through the middle of April.

FISHING Although a few fish can be caught right in town from the Chena River, avid fishermen can find outstanding angling by hopping a plane or riverboat. Fishing trips include air charters to **Lake Minchumina** (an hour's flight from Fairbanks), known for good pike fishing and a rare view of the north sides of Mt. McKinley and Mt. Foraker. Another charter trip by riverboat or floatplane will take you pike fishing in the **Minto Flats,** west of Fairbanks off the Tanana River, where the mouth of the Chatanika River spreads through miles of marsh and sloughs.

Salmon run up the **Tanana River** most of the summer, but they're not usually caught on hook-and-line gear. Residents take them from the river with gill nets and fish wheels, using special commercial and subsistence permits. Check the "Outdoors" section in the Friday *Fairbanks Daily News–Miner* for weekly updates on fishing in the Interior.

GOLD PANNING You can pan for gold in several places without fear of jumping a claim. **Alaskan Prospectors** (✉ 504 College Rd., Lemeta ☎ 907/452–7398 🌐 www.mosquitonet.com/~lmadonna) is the oldest mining and prospecting supply store in the state, and is considered the gold information center for Interior Alaska. In addition to maintaining a rocks and minerals museum, it sells gold pans and books and videos on mining. The employees can offer lots of valuable advice for the neophyte gold bug, even though the store's outward appearance may put you off—once you get inside, you'll find enough interesting material to keep you occupied for hours.

El Dorado Gold Mine (✉ 1975 Discovery Dr. ☎ 907/479–6673 or 866/479–6673 🌐 www.eldoradogoldmine.com) conducts two-hour tours of a seasonal mining operation that include a ride on a narrow-gauge railroad. The tours cost $27.95.

Chatanika Gold Camp (✉ Mile 27.9, Steese Hwy. ☎ 907/389–2414 🌐 www.fegoldcamp.com) provides a water trough for panners at an authentic gold camp.

GOLF **Chena Bend** (☎ 907/353–6223), a well-maintained army course open to civilians, is an 18-hole spread on nearby Ft. Wainwright. The 9-hole course at the **Fairbanks Golf and Country Club** (☎ 907/479–6555) straddles Farmers Loop just north of the university. The 18-hole course at the **North Star Golf Club** (✉ 330 Golf Club Dr. ☎ 907/457–4653, 907/455–8362 in winter 📠 907/457–3945) is on the Old Steese Highway, 7/10 mi past Chena Hot Springs Road.

HIKING **Creamer's Field Migratory Waterfowl Refuge** (⇨ Exploring Fairbanks) has three nature trails within its 1,800 acres on the edge of Fairbanks. The longest trail is 2 mi, and one is accessible to people who use wheelchairs.

HOCKEY At the nearby University of Alaska Fairbanks, the **Nanooks** (☎ 907/474–6868) play NCAA Division I hockey.

RIVERBOAT RACING Another summer highlight is riverboat racing sanctioned by the **Fairbanks Outboard Association** (☎ 907/459–2023 🌐 www.yukon800.com). These specially built 24-foot racing boats are powered by 50-horsepower engines and reach speeds of 75 mph. Weekend races throughout the summer and fall begin and end either at the Pump House Restaurant or at Pike's Landing, just off Airport Way near Fairbanks International Airport. The season's big event in late June is the **Yukon 800 Marathon,** a two-day, 800-mi race between Fairbanks and Galena by way of the Chena, Tanana, and Yukon rivers. The **Roland Lord Memorial Race,** from Fairbanks to Nenana and back, is held in early August, and the **Tanana 440** is held in late July.

RUNNING Check with local sporting-goods stores for race schedules. The **Midnight Sun Run** (☎ 907/452–6046 for race director Terry Strle 🌐 www.midnightsunrun.org) is held each June on the weekend nearest the summer solstice. The September **Equinox Marathon** (🌐 www.equinoxmarathon.org) is a tough run up and down the large Ester Dome, northwest of the city.

SKIING The Interior has some of the best weather and terrain in the nation for cross-country skiing, especially during the late fall and early spring. Among the developed trails in the Fairbanks area, the ones at the **Birch Hill Recreation Area,** on the city's north side, and the **University of Alaska Fairbanks** are lighted to extend their use into the winter nights. Cross-country ski racing is a staple at several courses on winter weekends. The season stretches from October to late March or early April. Other developed trails can be found at **Chena Hot Springs Resort, White Mountain National Recreation Area,** the **Chena Lakes Recreation Area,** and the **Two Rivers Recreation Area.** For more information check with the **Alaska Public Lands Information Center.**

For downhill skiing, **Mt. Aurora/Skiland** (☎ 907/456–7669 or 907/389–2314), on the Steese Highway about 20 mi from Fairbanks at Cleary Summit, has a chairlift, 20-plus runs ranked intermediate to expert, and a 1,100-foot vertical drop. There's lodging in an old gold-camp bunkhouse, dog mushing, snowmobile rides, and aurora viewing. It's open weekends from December to mid-April. **Moose Mountain** (☎ 907/479–8362, 907/459–8132 for ski report 🌐 www.shredthemoose.com), off Murphy Dome Road, has 42 runs from two summits for all skiing levels, all accessed by a bus lift system; it's open November–April, Friday–Sunday, plus school and government holidays. **Birch Hill** (☎ 907/353–7053), in Ft. Wainwright, has a chairlift and beginner and intermediate runs; it's open November–April, Thursday–Sunday.

SLED-DOG RACES From November to March, a constant string of sled-dog races is held throughout the region, culminating in the **North American Open Sled-Dog Championship,** which attracts international competition to Fairbanks. Throughout Alaska, sprint races, freight hauling, and long-distance endurance runs are held in late February and March, during the Alaska season when longer days afford enjoyment of the remaining winter

CELESTIAL RAYS OF LIGHT

THE LIGHT SHOW OFTEN BEGINS *simply, as a pale yellow-green luminous band that arches across Alaska's night sky. Sometimes the band will quickly fade and disappear. Other nights, however, it may begin to waver, flicker, and pulsate. Or the quiescent band may suddenly explode and fill the sky with curtains of celestial light that ripple wildly above the northern landscape. Growing more intense, these dancing lights take on other colors: pink, red, blue, or purple. At times they appear to be heavenly flames, leaping across the sky. Or perhaps they're exploding fireworks or cannon fire.*

Known to scientists as the aurora borealis, the dazzling nighttime bands and ribbons that appear in Alaska's skies are also commonly called the northern lights. As you watch them, it is sometimes possible to see a rhythm in their movements—or at least imagine one. It's also easy to imagine why many northern cultures, including Alaska's Native peoples, have created myths to explain auroral displays. What start out as patches, arcs, or bands can be magically transformed into vaporous, humanlike figures. Some of Alaska's Native groups have traditionally believed the lights to be spirits of their ancestors. According to one belief, the spirits are celebrating with dance and drumming; another says they're playing games. Yet another tradition says the lights are torches, carried by spirits who lead the souls of recently deceased people to life in the "afterworld."

During Alaska's gold-rush era some non-native stampeders supposed the aurora to be reflections of ore deposits. Even renowned wilderness explorer John Muir allowed the northern lights to spark his imagination. Once while traveling through Southeast Alaska in 1890, Muir stayed up all night to watch a gigantic, glowing auroral bridge and bands of "restless electric auroral fairies" who danced to music "too fine for mortal ears."

Scientists have a more technical explanation for these heavenly apparitions. The aurora borealis is an atmospheric phenomenon that's tied to explosive events on the sun's surface, known as solar flares. Those flares produce a stream of charged particles, the "solar wind," which shoots off into space. When such a wind intersects Earth's magnetic field, most of the particles are deflected; some, however, are sent into the upper atmosphere, where they collide with gas molecules such as nitrogen and oxygen. The resulting reactions produce glowing colors. The aurora is most commonly a pale yellowish green, but its borders are sometimes tinged with pink, purple, or blue. Especially rare is the all-red aurora, which appears when charged solar particles collide with oxygen molecules up to 150 mi high.

Alaska has some of the world's brightest auroras, with the best light shows occurring in a band that stretches from the Alaska Range into the Arctic. In Fairbanks, northern lights may appear more than 200 nights per year (they're much less common in Anchorage, partly because of urban glare). Alaska's long hours of daylight hide the aurora in summer, so the best viewing is from September through April. ***Chena Hot Springs Resort*** *(✉ Chena Hot Springs ☎ 907/452–7867) has a glassed-in and heated hut set up on a hillside for gazing at the northern lights.* ***North Star Tours*** *(📬 Box 71677, Fairbanks ☎ 907/451–1125) runs aurora tours to Mt. Aurora/ Skiland from December into April. It will arrange pickup and delivery to your hotel and offer an "aurora insurance" plan if you're the gambling type: you can pay an additional fee, and if there's no aurora, your trip is half price.*

snow. Men and women often compete in the same classes in the major races. For children, various racing classes are based on age, starting with the one-dog category for the youngest.

In Fairbanks many of the sprint races are organized by the **Alaska Dog Mushers Association** (☎ 907/457–6874 🌐 www.sleddog.org), one of the oldest organizations of its kind in Alaska, and held at its Jeff Studdert Sled Dog Racegrounds at Mile 4, Farmers Loop. The **Yukon Quest International Sled-Dog Race** (☎ 907/452–7954 🌐 www.yukonquest.org) is an endurance race held in February that covers more than 1,000 mi between Fairbanks and Whitehorse, Yukon Territory, via Dawson and the Yukon River. You can get more details from the visitor center in either city or by calling the Yukon Quest office in Fairbanks.

Shopping

Crafts

The **Arctic Travelers Gift Shop** (✉ 201 Cushman St., Downtown ☎ 907/456–7080) has a wide selection of Athabascan beadwork. **Beads and Things** (✉ 537 2nd Ave., Downtown ☎ 907/456–2323) sells Native handicrafts from around the state. The **Great Alaskan Bowl Company** (✉ 4630 Old Airport Rd. ☎ 907/474–9663 🌐 www.woodbowl.com) sells lathe-turned bowls made out of Alaskan birch.

Jewelry

In her small, eponymous shop, **Judie Gumm Designs** (✉ 3600 Main St., Ester ☎ 907/479–4568 🌐 www.judiegumm.com), Ms. Gumm fashions stunning silver and gold designs best described as sculptural interpretations of northern images. Moderately priced and easy to pack, her jewelry makes a nice memento of your trip north. Ester is 6 mi south of Fairbanks off the George Parks Highway—follow the signs.

Outerwear & Outdoor Gear

Apocalypse Design (✉ 201 Minnie St. ☎ 907/451–7555 or 866/451–7555 🌐 www.akgear.com) makes its own specialized cold-weather clothing for dog mushers and other winter adventurers. Travelers from colder sections of the Lower 48 will appreciate the double-layer fleece mittens, among other items.

AROUND FAIRBANKS

The three roads north of Fairbanks head straight out of civilization. They all dead-end at water—two at rivers and one on the Arctic Ocean. If you want to see untamed Alaska and cross paths with some rugged, independent people, head in this direction.

Chena Hot Springs

❽ *62 mi northeast of Fairbanks.*

The 57-mi paved Chena Hot Springs Road, which starts 5 mi outside Fairbanks, leads to Chena Hot Springs, a favorite playground of many Fairbanks residents. Several attractions lie along the road, including Chena

River State Recreation Area and Chena Hot Springs Resort. If you're heading to the resort, there are ample opportunities along the way to prolong your trip with hiking, fishing, camping, and canoeing. The chances of spotting the occasional moose along the way are excellent if you keep a sharp eye on the roadside.

From Mile 26 to Mile 51, the road passes through the **Chena River State Recreation Area,** a diverse facility of nearly 400 square mi. You can also stop for a picnic, take a hike for an hour or an extended backpacking trip, fish for the beautiful yet gullible arctic grayling, or rent a rustic backcountry cabin and savor a truly wild Alaska adventure. Grayling fishing in the Chena River is catch-and-release, single-hook artificial lure only, but there are several stocked lakes along the road affording catch-and-keep fishing for grayling and rainbow trout. Both species are well suited to the frying pan, but local anglers advise fishing for grayling with "your fishing rod in one hand and a frying pan in the other," a testament to their short-lived taste appeal.

Where to Stay & Eat

★ $–$$$$ ✕ **Two Rivers Lodge.** Fairbanksans are known to make the 40-mi roundtrip for the delicious dinners here, including hand-cut, aged filet mignon; prime rib; and frequent crab specials and other Alaskan seafood dishes. Don't be discouraged by the outward appearance of the building. Rustic logs belie the elegance of the menu. For a study in contrasts, Alaskan style, stop in the Trapline Lounge first for a predinner refreshment. ✉ *Mile 16, Chena Hot Springs Rd.* ☎ *907/488–6815* 📠 *907/488–9761* 🌐 *www.tworiverslodge.com* 💳 *AE, D, MC, V* 🕑 *No lunch.*

$$ Fodor'sChoice ★ **Chena Hot Springs Resort.** Fairbanksans come in droves to this resort to soak in the hot-springs-warmed hot tubs and natural-water rock lake or indoor, chlorinated swimming pool. Summer activities include gold panning, flightseeing, and mountain biking. In winter you can go snowmobiling, dogsledding, and Snow-Cat touring. ATV tours are given year-round. The Aurorarium is a large, glassed-in room for viewing the northern lights in the winter, and there's a snow-coach ride to a hilltop yurt offering a 360-degree panorama. There are sports-equipment rentals, camping sites, and heated cabins without running water. Cabins rent for $65–$200. 📫 *Box 58740, Fairbanks 99711* ☎ *907/451–8104 or 800/478–4681* 📠 *907/456–3122* 🌐 *www.chenahotsprings.com* *80 rooms, 10 cabins* *$135* *Restaurant, cable TV, massage, fishing, mountain bikes, horseback riding, cross-country skiing, sleigh rides, snowmobiling, bar, laundry facilities, Internet, meeting room, some pets allowed (fee); no phones in some rooms* 💳 *AE, D, DC, MC, V.*

¢ **Department of Natural Resources.** Five cabins in the Chena River State Recreation Area are often used by those with more extensive backcountry experience. These cabins provide woodstoves, bunks, and pit toilets, as well as tools for cutting wood. You have to supply everything else—food, bedding, water, cooking utensils. This is basic, Alaskan shelter, but it can't be beat for leaving the "real" world behind. Hiking distance in from the road varies from a few hundred yards (one site) up to 8 mi, and the nightly fee ranges from $25 for the Colorado and Angel Creek cabins to $40 per night for the larger North Fork and Chena River cabins. Wildlife in the area includes moose, porcupines, lynx, fox, pine marten, wolves, coyotes, and black and, occasionally, grizzly bears. ⊠ *3700 Airport Way, Fairbanks 99709–4699* ☎ *907/451–2705* 🖷 *907/451–2706* ⊕ *www.dnr.state.ak.us* ☒ *$25–$40.*

¢ ⚏ **Red Squirrel Campground.** If you want to combine easy fishing access with your camping, the Red Squirrel at Mile Marker 42.8 has a pond stocked with grayling. ♿ *Pit toilets, drinking water, bear boxes, fire pits, picnic tables, swimming* ☒ *$10* 🛏 *12 sites* ⊙ *Year-round.*

¢ ⚏ **Rosehip Campground.** At Mile 27 you'll find these campgrounds are very basic but have the essentials for family camping. There's a nature trail nearby, but access to the river is limited. ♿ *Pit toilets, drinking water, bear boxes, fire pits, picnic tables* ☒ *$10* 🛏 *37 sites* ⊙ *Year-round.*

¢ ⚏ **Tors Trail Campground.** Campers at Mile 39.5 have easy access to the Granite Tors Trail, a 15-mi loop into the high country. ♿ *Pit toilets, drinking water, bear boxes, fire pits, picnic tables* ☒ *$10* 🛏 *24 sites* ⊙ *Year-round.*

Sports & the Outdoors

The **Chena River State Recreation Area** has numerous well-marked river-access points (the Chena Hot Springs Road parallels the Chena River, and canoeists use several put-in points along the way). The lower sections of the river area are placid, but the area above the third bridge, at Mile 44.1, can be hazardous for inexperienced boaters.

The Granite Tors Trail, a 15-mi loop, can be done in a day and offers a view of the upper Chena Valley and an opportunity to see these dramatic "tors" (fingers of rock protruding through grassy meadow) which look very "Easter Island"-ish. The trail is steep and not to be taken lightly, but the views at the top are worthwhile. Although the Interior landscapes lack the impressive mountain views of other parts of the state, the enormous expanse of rolling hills and seemingly endless tracts of forest are every bit as awe inspiring. However, one of the consequences of a lack of high mountains to collect snow and contribute to the water table is that water sources along the way are unreliable. Be sure to carry plenty for your party, and don't underestimate your hydration requirements. Hiking uphill on a hot summer day means carrying a couple of liters per person to be safe. Also, weather is quite fickle here, and a bright, sunny morning can easily turn into an overcast, rainy, and windy afternoon. Be prepared with adequate clothing, including rain gear, no matter how promising the skies look in the morning. A shorter hike is the 3½-mi Angel Rocks Trail, near the eastern boundary of the area.

Steese Highway

From Fairbanks: 128 mi northeast to Central, 162 mi to Circle.

The Steese Highway follows the Chatanika River and several other creeks along the southern part of the White Mountains. It eventually climbs into weatherworn alpine mountains, peaking at Eagle Summit (3,624 feet), about 100 mi from Fairbanks, and drops back down into forested creek beds en route to Central. At Central you can drive the 30-plus mi on a winding gravel road to Circle, a small town on the Yukon River. The highway is paved to Mile 44 and usually in good shape. A possible exception is during winter, when Eagle Summit is sometimes closed due to drifting snow.

Where to Stay

¢–$ **Historic Chatanika Gold Camp.** Miners working the dredges for the F. E. Gold Co. in the early 1900s bunked at this 55-acre site, formerly known as the Old F. E. Gold Camp. The grounds are on the National Register of Historic Places, and the world's largest coal cookstove is still operating in the dining room. The rooms in the hotel share bathrooms. Additionally, there are two four-room log cabins that share four complete baths. The area is a wonderland for local winter-sports enthusiasts, summertime hikers, and aurora viewers. *Mile 27.9, 5550 Steese Hwy., Fairbanks 99712 907/389–2414 907/457–6463 www.fegoldcamp.com $55–$80 26 rooms share 6 baths, 2 four-unit cabins share 4 baths Restaurant, bar, meeting room; no a/c, no room phones, no room TVs MC, V.*

¢ **Chatanika Lodge.** Rocket scientists from the nearby Poker Flat Research Range gather at this cedar lodge, as do mushers (guests can take dogsled rides), snowmobilers, and local families. The eclecticism of the clientele is matched by that of the furnishings: diamond willow lamps and a variety of wild-animal trophy heads and skins, including bear, lynx, and wolf. The rooms generally have a double and single bed, sink, and TV. The bathrooms and showers are down the hall. *Mile 28.6, 5760 Steese Hwy., Fairbanks 99712 907/389–2164 907/389–2166 10 rooms share 2 baths Restaurant, cable TV, snowmobiling, bar, some pets allowed; no a/c, no room phones MC, V.*

Sports & the Outdoors

The **Chatanika River,** a choice spot for canoeists and kayakers, has a wilderness feel to it yet it's still fairly close to Fairbanks. The most northerly access point is at Cripple Creek campground, near Mile 60 of the Steese Highway. Other commonly used access points are at Long Creek (Mile 45, Steese Highway); at the state campground, where the Chatanika River crosses the Steese Highway at Mile 39; and at the state's Whitefish Campground, where the river crosses the Elliott Highway at Mile 11. The stream flows into the Minto Flats below this point, and river access is more difficult.

Water in the Chatanika River may or may not be clear, depending on mining activities along its upper tributaries. In times of very low water, the upper Chatanika River is shallow and difficult to navigate. Avoid the river in times of high water, especially after heavy rains, because of the danger of sweepers, floating debris, and hidden gravel bars. Contact the Alaska Public Lands Information Center to find out the status of the river.

Steese Mountain & White Mountain

9 The **Bureau of Land Management** (✉ BLM Headquarters, 1150 University Ave., Fairbanks 99709 ☎ 907/474–2200) administers the Steese Mountain National Conservation Area and the White Mountain National Recreation Area. Both preserves are accessible by car. The White Mountain Recreation Area has limited camping facilities from June to November. The BLM also has three campsites on the Taylor Highway between Tok and Eagle at Miles 48.5, 82, and 160.

In the Steese National Conservation Area you can take a four- to five-day float trip on the lively, clear-water **Birch Creek,** a challenge with its several rapids along its 126 mi. Moose, caribou, and birds are easily spotted. Access is at Mile 94 of the Steese Highway. This stream winds its way north through the historic mining country of the Circle District. The take-out point is at the Steese Highway Bridge, 15 mi from Circle. From there Birch Creek meanders on to the Yukon River well below the town.

Rising out of the White Mountain National Recreation Area, **Beaver Creek** makes its easy way north. If you have enough time, it's possible to run its entire 268-mi length to the Yukon (if you make a shorter run, you will have to go out by small plane).

Where to Stay

¢ **BLM Public-Use Cabins.** The BLM manages 11 public-use cabins in the White Mountain National Recreation Area, with 300 mi of interconnecting trails. Designed primarily for winter use by dog mushers, snow machiners (snowmobilers), and cross-country skiers, cabins provide shelter for summer backpackers, although summer access is limited by mountainous and boggy terrain. The cabins have bunk beds, woodstoves, tables, pit toilets, and chairs. Permits are required and available up to 30 days in advance. ✉ *BLM Headquarters, 1150 University Ave., Fairbanks 99709* ☎ *907/474–2200 or 800/437–7021* 🌐 *http://aurora.ak.blm.gov/WhiteMtns/html/cabins.html* *11 cabins* *MC, V.*

¢ **BLM Campgrounds.** The BLM manages three road-accessible campgrounds in the Steese Highway area and another along the Dalton Highway. They all have picnic tables, fire pits, latrines, and well water. They're available on a first-come, first-served basis. In addition, you'll find several undeveloped campsites along the Dalton—old gravel pits with no facilities, available free of charge. ✉ *BLM Headquarters, 1150 University Ave., Fairbanks 99709* ☎ *907/474–2200 or 800/437–7021* 🌐 *http://aurora.ak.blm.gov/WhiteMtns/html/nomecr.html* *$6* *4 campsites* *No credit cards.*

Sports & the Outdoors

HIKING The BLM maintains the moderately difficult 20-mi **Summit Trail,** from the Elliott Highway, near Wickersham Dome, north into the White Mountain National Recreation Area. This hiking trail can be done as a day hike or overnight backpacking trip. It quickly rises into alpine country with 360° vistas that include lots of wildland, the trans-Alaska pipeline, and a pipeline pump station. You can see many wildflowers in early summer. Look for the parking lot at Mile 28.

Yukon–Charley Rivers National Preserve

10 *20 mi north of Eagle, 100 mi east of Fairbanks.*

The 126-mi stretch of the Yukon River running between the small towns of Eagle and Circle—former gold-rush metropolises—is protected in the 2.5-million-acre **Yukon–Charley Rivers National Preserve** (✉ National Park Service, 201 1st Ave., Doyon Bldg., Fairbanks 99701 ☎ 907/457–5752 🌐 www.nps.gov/yuch/index.htm). As its name suggests, this parkland also covers the pristine watershed of the Charley River, a crystalline white-water stream flowing out of the Yukon-Tanana uplands that provides fine river running. You can put in a raft or a kayak (with a small plane) at the headwaters of the Charley River and travel 88 mi down this joyful, bouncing waterway.

In great contrast to the Charley River, the Yukon River is an inexorably powerful stream, dark with mud and glacial silt. The only bridge built across it holds the trans-Alaska pipeline, north of Fairbanks. The river surges deep, and to travel on it in a small boat is a humbling, if magnificent, experience. You can drive from Fairbanks to Eagle (via the Taylor Highway off the Alaska Highway) and to Circle (via the Steese Highway) and from either of these arrange for a ground-transportation shuttle back to your starting city at the end of your Yukon River trip. Weeklong float trips down the river from Eagle to Circle, 150 mi away, are possible. For information contact the **National Park Service** (☎ 907/547–2233) in Eagle. Note that no developed campgrounds or other visitor facilities exist within the preserve itself, though low-impact backcountry camping is permitted.

Sports & the Outdoors

HIKING The Alaska Public Lands Information Center (⇨ Interior A to Z, *below*) has detailed information about the trails in the Yukon–Charley Rivers National Preserve.

The BLM maintains the **Pinnell Mountain National Recreation Trail,** connecting Twelve-Mile Summit and Eagle Summit on the Steese Highway. This 27-mi-long trail passes through alpine meadows and along mountain ridges, all above the tree line. It has two emergency shelters. No dependable water supply is available in the immediate vicinity. Most hikers spend three days making the trip.

The **Circle-Fairbanks Historic Trail** stretches 58 mi from the vicinity of Cleary Summit to Twelve-Mile Summit. This route, which is not for novices, follows the old summer trail used by gold miners; in winter they generally used the frozen Chatanika River to make this journey. The trail has been roughly marked and cleared, but there are no facilities and water is scarce along much of it. Most of the trail is on state land, but it does cross valid mining claims, which must be respected. Although you'll find rock cairns and mileposts while hiking, no well-defined tread exists, so it's easy to become disoriented. The State Department of Natural Resources strongly recommends that backpackers on this trail equip themselves with the following USGS topographical maps: Livengood (A-1), Circle (A-6), Circle (A-5), and Circle (B-4).

WINTER SPORTS Once past Mile 20 of the Steese Highway you enter a countryside that seems to have changed little in 100 years, even though you're only an hour from downtown Fairbanks. Mountains loom in the distance, and in winter, a solid snowpack of 4–5 feet makes the area great for snowshoeing, backcountry skiing, and riding snowmobiles—Alaskans refer to them as snowmachines, and calling them snowmobiles automatically brands you as someone from "Outside."

Snow-RV (✉ 5760 Old Steese Hwy., off Steese Hwy. at Mile 28.5, at Chatanika Lodge 📫 Box 10804, Fairbanks 99710 ☎ 907/389–7669 📠 907/389–5665) rents Arctic Cat snowmobiles. Rentals are available by the hour or for several days. Guided rides are required for those from out of state. They'll supply the guides.

Elliott Highway

From Fairbanks: 28 mi north to Wickersham Dome, north 73 mi to Dalton Hwy. junction, 152 mi northwest to Manley.

11 The Elliott Highway, which starts in Fox, takes you to the Tanana River and the small community of **Manley Hot Springs.** A colorful, close-knit "end-of-the-road" place, this town originally was a trading center for placer miners who worked the nearby creeks. Residents maintain a small public campground, across from Manley Roadhouse. Northern pike are caught in the nearby slough, and a dirt road leads to the Tanana River with its summer runs of salmon. The Manley Hot Springs Resort has closed, but the hot springs are only a short walk from the campground. The highway is paved for 28 mi outside Fairbanks.

Where to Stay

¢–$ **Manley Roadhouse.** Built in 1906 in the midst of the gold rush into the Interior, this roadhouse is among the oldest in Alaska. Today it caters to a diverse crowd of vacationers, miners, and road maintenance crews. Not only is the roadhouse known for the food and the rooms, which occupy the original roadhouse and several cabins, but the bar earns bragging rights for its 250 brands of liquor and 20 varieties of beer. The restaurant serves breakfast, lunch, and dinner. ✉ *Mile 152, Elliott Hwy., Box 1, Manley Hot Springs 99756* ☎ *907/672–3161* *13 rooms, 6 with bath; 3 cabins* *Restaurant, bar, some pets allowed; no a/c, no room phones, no TV in some rooms* *AE, MC, V.*

Sports & the Outdoors

HIKING The BLM maintains the 22-mi **Summit Trail** from the Elliott Highway, near Wickersham Dome, north into the White Mountain National Recreation Area. Water is scarce on the trail, so be sure to carry plenty with you.

Dalton Highway

From Fairbanks: 140 mi north to the Yukon River, 199 mi to the Arctic Circle, 259 mi to Coldfoot, 329 mi to Atigun Pass, 499 mi to Deadhorse.

The Dalton Highway is a road of "onlys." It's the only road that goes to the Beaufort Sea, it's the only Alaskan road to cross the Arctic Circle, and it has the state's only bridge across the Yukon River. The 414-mi gravel road starts 84 mi from Fairbanks on the Elliott Highway and runs northwest of Fairbanks to the North Slope oil fields at Prudhoe Bay. It was built in 1974 and 1975 to open a truck route necessary to build the facilities at Prudhoe and the northern half of the trans-Alaska pipeline. For a few months a ferry was used to carry loads across the Yukon River, until the present bridge was completed in late 1975.

The road is named for James Dalton, a pioneer Alaskan engineer who recognized early the potential of oil on the North Slope. If you are planning to drive the Dalton Highway, remember these tips: slow down and move to the side of the road for trucks; leave your headlights on at all times; yield on one-lane bridges; pull to the side of the road when stopping for pictures or the view; carry at least one spare tire; and consider bringing extra gas and purchasing a citizens band radio. Remember there are no services between Coldfoot and Prudhoe Bay, a distance of nearly 250 mi.

The Dalton Highway has two **visitor centers** open in the summer. One is just north of the Yukon River bridge at Mile 56 and has no phone. The other is in **Coldfoot** (☎ 907/678–5209). The centers are operated by the Fish and Wildlife Service, the National Park Service, and the BLM. A picnic area and a large, colorful sign mark the spot where the road crosses the Arctic Circle.

The **Wiseman Trading Co.,** a museum and general store 12 mi north of Coldfoot, is run by Coldfoot Services–Slate Creek Inn.

12 Today the road is still used to carry oil-field supplies and is now open all the way to **Deadhorse,** just shy of the Arctic coast. This town exists mainly to service the oil fields of Prudhoe Bay, so although scenery isn't in great supply, it does have important facilities for travelers, including fuel, vehicle maintenance, a general store, an airport, a post office, hotels, and restaurants.

Oil-field tours (☎ 877/659–2368) and shuttles to the Arctic Ocean leave daily from the two hotels in Deadhorse, Arctic Caribou Inn and Prudhoe Bay Hotel. The tours include a video presentation of the oil field and a tour of the grounds with a stop at the Arctic Ocean for $37 for adults, 12 and under, $17. Due to security considerations, a minimum 24-hour advance reservation is required to go on the tour. When making reservations you will need to have the names of everyone in your group and a valid government ID number for everyone (drivers license, state ID, passport, Social Security card, etc.). All guests will be required to have this ID in their possession at the time of the tour. Children will be required to be with their legal guardian and need only to give their date of birth.

Where to Stay

Five camping areas plus many scenic turnouts are along the road. Only one of the camping areas (Marion Creek, at Mile 180) is developed. Most of the rest are gravel pads, sometimes with outhouses. Call the Alaska Public Lands Information Center for more information.

$$ **Prudhoe Bay Hotel.** Like most of Deadhorse, this hotel was originally built to house mining workers. Spartan but comfortable guest rooms are the result. There is a TV room with a big-screen TV. The restaurant (all meals are included in the room rate) serves pizza and American fare in an all-you-can-eat buffet. *Airport Rd., across from airport Pouch 340004, Prudhoe Bay 99734 907/659–2449 907/659–2752 www.prudhoebayhotel.com 180 rooms, 15 with bath Restaurant, gym; no phones in some rooms, no TV in some rooms MC, V FAP.*

¢–$$ **Coldfoot Camp.** Fuel, tire repairs, and towing are available here in Coldfoot. Basic and clean rooms are built from surplus pipeline-worker housing. The 24-hour restaurant serves generous portions of truck-stop fare. The complex has a 20-space RV hookup and post office. Although the place looks more than a little offbeat, bear in mind that it's the only facility of any sort within 100 mi or more, so you may have to adjust your standards accordingly. Adventure travel options include flightseeing, river rafting, and mountain bike rentals in the summer and aurora safaris and dog mushing trips and school in the winter. *Mile 175, Dalton Hwy. Box 81512, Fairbanks 99708 866/474–3400 907/474–4767 www.coldfootcamp.com $15–$165 81 rooms, 52 with bath Restaurant, shop; no room phones, no room TVs MC, V.*

$ **Arctic Caribou Inn.** This hotel is made up of trailer-type units, with basic rooms. The restaurant serves American fare in an all-you-can-eat buffet. *Airport Rd. Box 340111, Deadhorse 99734 907/659–2368 or 877/659–2368 907/659–2692 www.arcticcaribouinn.com 45 rooms Restaurant, cable TV, airport shuttle; no a/c MC, V Closed Labor Day–Memorial Day.*

$ **Yukon Ventures Alaska.** You'll find a motel, a tire repair shop, and gasoline, diesel fuel, and propane on this property on the Yukon River. The motel is basic and clean, built from surplus pipeline-worker housing. None of the rooms has a private bath, but two (one for men, one for women) have showers and are centrally located. The restaurant serves large portions of diner fare. *Mile 56, Dalton Hwy. Box 60947, Fairbanks 99706 907/655–9001 40 rooms share 3 baths Restaurant; no a/c, no room TVs MC, V.*

Guided Tours

Northern Alaska Tour Company (907/474–8600) conducts van tours and boat tours of the Yukon River with Yukon River Tours. **Princess Tours** (907/479–9660 or 800/426–0442) runs tour buses on the Dalton from Fairbanks all the way to Prudhoe Bay, with a variety of services, including an overnight at Coldfoot, a tour of the oil field, and air service from Prudhoe Bay back to Fairbanks or Anchorage. Tours operate once a week from June through August. **Trans Arctic Circle Treks** (907/479–5451 or 800/336–8735 907/479–8908 www.arctictreks.com) has an extensive menu of guided trips ranging in duration from half or full day up to seven days covering areas from Anchorage and South Central Alaska to Barrow and Prudhoe Bay. They also offer a winter "Adventures to the North Slope" trip, and seven-day trips including Fairbanks, Valdez, Prince William Sound, Seward, Kenai Fjords, Anchorage, Kantishna, Denali National Park, and the Arctic Circle.

Sports & the Outdoors

FISHING Although this is not a prime fishing area, fish, mostly grayling, populate the streams along the Dalton. You'll do better if you are willing to hike more than ¼ mi from the road, where fishing pressure is the heaviest. Lakes along the road have grayling, and some have lake trout and arctic char. The Alaska Department of Fish and Game puts out a pamphlet titled "Sport Fishing Along the Dalton Highway," which is also available at the Alaska Public Lands Information Center.

HIKING No trails have been officially established along the road, but hikers willing to pick their own route can explore much of the area. The road passes near the **Yukon Flats National Wildlife Refuge,** the **Kanuti National Wildlife Refuge,** the **Arctic National Wildlife Refuge,** and just east of **Gates of the Arctic National Park and Preserve.** Check with the Alaska Public Lands Information Center. Chances of seeing wildlife are fairly good, as this is grizzly bear and caribou habitat.

Healy

13 *11 mi north of Denali National Park, 109 mi south of Fairbanks, 251 mi north of Anchorage.*

Each summer overflow crowds from Denali National Park & Preserve stream into this small community of 500 people on the George Parks Highway, north of the entrance, to park. However, more and more frequently, Fairbanks-area residents and travelers are seeking out Healy's year-round lodging and the magnificent views.

Coal mining fuels the economy of Healy, which is home to the **Usibelli Coal Mine,** the largest mine of its kind in the state and Alaska's only commercially viable coal mining operation.

Healy is close to the **Stampede Trail,** which offers those interested in snowmobiling, mushing, cross-country skiing, and mountain biking a way to enter the northern expanse of Denali National Park & Preserve. This wide, well-traveled path begins where Stampede Road ends and leads to the former gold-rush boomtown of Kantishna, 90 mi inside the park. Take the George Parks Highway 2 mi north of Healy to Mile 251.1, where Stampede Road intersects the highway. Eight miles west on Stampede Road is a parking lot and the start of the Stampede Trail.

Where to Stay & Eat

¢–$$ ✕ **Totem Inn.** Travelers from along the George Parks Highway, Healy, and Denali National Park come here for standard American food at reasonable prices. Pizzas, steaks, sandwiches, and a Sunday lunch buffet are served year-round. The kitchen is open daily 7 AM–10 PM. ✉ *Mile 248.7, George Parks Hwy.* ☎ *907/683–2420* ▭ *D, MC, V.*

$–$$ **Motel Nord Haven.** Five wooded acres protect this motel from the road, providing a secluded feeling that other lodgings along the George Parks Highway lack. There's wood trim throughout, and rooms have one or two queen-size beds, a telephone, television, and a private bath. Rooms with two queen beds can accommodate up to five people at no additional charge. A Continental breakfast is served, and for a minimal charge, box lunches can be prepared to carry along on your explorations. No breakfast is served in the winter. ✉ *Mile 249.5, George Parks Hwy.* *Box 458, Healy 99743* ☎ *907/683–4500 or 800/683–4501* 🖷 *907/683–4503* 🌐 *www.motelnordhaven.com* *28 rooms* *Some kitchenettes, cable TV, meeting room; no smoking* ▭ *AE, D, MC, V* 🍴 *CP.*

$ **Denali Dome Home.** A huge, 7,200-square-foot, modified geodesic dome houses this all-year B&B. Each guest room (remodeled in 2004) has a private bath, TV, VCR, and phone; one has a sauna and two rooms have jetted tubs. A common room has a TV, fireplace, and Alaska-related books and videos. The fireplace fits 5-foot-long logs, and the high ceiling is enhanced by tall windows that provide spectacular views of nearby mountains. There's an extensive videotape and DVD collection at your disposal as well as DSL Internet access. ✉ *137 Healy Spur Rd., Box 262, 99743* ☎ *907/683–1239 or 800/683–1239* 🌐 *www.denalidomehome.com* *7 rooms* *In-room hot tubs, in-room VCRs, Internet; no a/c, no smoking* ▭ *AE, D, MC, V.*

$ **Earthsong Lodge.** Above the treeline at the edge of Denali National Park, Earthsong yields views of open tundra backed by peaks of the Alaska Range. Each hand-built cabin has a decor theme (Denali, Sled Dog, Mountaineering) and private bath, a rarity in such small cabins in remote settings. In winter, the lodge is one of two concessionaires permitted to lead multiday dog-mushing tours into Denali National Park. The restaurant, Henry's Coffeehouse, named after a beloved sled dog, serves a surprisingly varied menu of pizza and pasta, Middle Eastern fare including vegetarian entrées, sandwiches, subs, and baked goods along with espresso drinks. Slide shows of Denali are a nightly treat, and tours of the sled-dog kennel are offered as well. ✉ *Box 89, Healy 99743* ☎ *907/683–2863* 🖷 *907/683–2868* 🌐 *www.earthsonglodge.com* *11 cabins* *Restaurant, fans, Internet; no a/c, no room phones, no room TVs, no smoking* ▭ *MC, V* 🍴 *EP.*

DENALI NATIONAL PARK & PRESERVE

14 Fodor's Choice ★

11 mi south of Healy, 120 mi south of Fairbanks, 240 mi north of Anchorage.

The most accessible of Alaska's national parks and one of only three connected to the state's highway system, 6-million-acre Denali National Park & Preserve is one of North America's finest and easiest places to see wildlife in its natural environment. Nowhere in the world is there more spectacular background scenery to these wildlife riches, with 20,320-foot Mt. McKinley looming above forested valleys, tundra-topped hills, and the glacier-covered peaks of the Alaska Range.

Also commonly known by its Athabascan Indian name, *Denali,* meaning "the high one," North America's highest mountain is also the world's tallest when measured from base to top: the great mountain rises more than 18,000 feet above surrounding lowlands. Unfortunately for visitors with little time to spend in the area, McKinley is wreathed in clouds an average of two days of every three during the summer. However, if you plan ahead and venture far enough into the park, you'll have a better chance of seeing the mountain in all its glacier-capped magnificence.

Although most Denali visitors are content to contemplate Mt. McKinley from afar, more than 1,000 adventurers walk the mountain's slopes each summer. About half of them succeed in "summiting" the peak during the May-to-July climbing season. The great majority of McKinley mountaineers fly to the mountain's base camp on the Kahiltna Glacier at 7,200 feet, then follow the West Buttress Route, generally considered the safest and easiest path to the top. Whatever route they take, climbers must deal with avalanches, glacial crevasses, high altitude, and extreme cold. Even in summer, temperatures on McKinley can fall to –30°F or –40°F. The mountain is so large it creates its own weather, and storms frequently batter its upper slopes with winds of 100 mph or more. If you feel you must attempt the peak, talk to the Park Service people about procuring a guide. The hazards of climbing Denali are frequently underestimated, and prospective adventurers must be aware of the dangers. Fatalities are unfortunately an occasional occurrence.

You need not climb Mt. McKinley to appreciate Denali; the park is both a hiker's and wildlife-watcher's paradise. The one 88-mi road into the heart of the park is unpaved after the first 14¾ mi, and in summer you can travel on shuttle buses, from which you can see grizzly bears, wolves, caribou, and moose. The bulk of the parkland, however, is accessible only on foot in summer or by dog team or cross-country skis in winter.

For all the challenges of access and planning, those who explore Denali are certain to reap many rewards: wilderness solitude, a sense of discovery, wildlife encounters, and a greater appreciation of the landscape's immensity and the rigors of the sub-Arctic climate.

Geology & Terrain

Several of Denali's most spectacular landforms are deep in the park. The multicolored volcanic rocks at Cathedral Mountain and Polychrome Pass remind many travelers of the vivid hues of the desert Southwest. The braided channels of glacially fed streams such as the Teklanika, Toklat, and McKinley rivers serve as "highway routes" for both animals and hikers. The debris- and tundra-covered ice of the Muldrow Glacier, one of the largest glaciers to flow out of Denali National Park's high mountains, is visible from Eielson Visitor Center, at Mile 66 of the park road. Wonder Lake, a dark and narrow "kettle pond" that's a remnant from Alaska's Ice Ages, lies at the end of the park road near Kantishna.

The most prominent geological feature of the park is the Alaska Range, a 600-mi-long crescent of summits that separates South Central Alaska from the Interior. These peaks are all immense, but the truly towering ones are Mt. Hunter (14,573 feet), Mt. Foraker (17,400 feet), and Mt. McKinley (20,320 feet). Mt. McKinley's granite heart is covered with glacial ice, which is hundreds of feet thick in places. Glaciers, in fact, are abundant along the entire Alaska Range, and a few are visible from the park road. Muldrow Glacier is only 5 mi from the road, near Mile 67.

Flora

Vegetation in the park consists largely of taiga and tundra. Taiga is coniferous forest that exists in moist areas below a tree line of 2,000 feet and consists mainly of spruce trees. These trees have very shallow root systems due to the layer of permafrost that lies just under the surface of the land, and they are subject to the vagaries of wind and land movements. A turnoff and informational sign on the road near the park entrance points out an area of "drunken forest," where the uppermost layer of soil has shifted on the permafrost, moving the trees around and leaving them in a disheveled state that suggests some sort of arboreal inebriation. Ground cover in the taiga forest includes such shrubs as dwarf birch, blueberry, and willows. From the road the taiga looks open, with wide views and very few trees, but the dense bushes make it difficult for inexperienced travelers.

The rest of the land mass that isn't permanently covered by ice and snow is overlaid by tundra, which consists of a variety of plant types including lichens, berries, and woody plants—all in miniature. This complex carpet of low-lying vegetation generates brilliant color, especially in August, when the subtle variations of green begin to turn into the colors similar to those sought out by "leaf peepers" in the Lower 48. By the time the autumn colors max out in September, the tundra is ablaze with brilliant swaths of deep red among more restrained hues of yellows and greens. Most tundra areas enable easy hiking, but there are exceptions. After a while you may learn to evaluate tundra "walkability" from a distance, distinguishing by color and texture which areas are like a springy carpet and delightful to walk on and which are too moist for comfort and can turn an enjoyable hike into a boot-sucking slog.

Fauna

Nearly every wild creature that walks or flies in South Central and Interior Alaska inhabits the park. Thirty-eight species of mammals reside here, from wolves and bears to little brown bats and pygmy shrews that weigh a fraction of an ounce. The park also has a surprisingly large avian population in the summer, when some 160 species have been identified. Most of the birds migrate in fall, leaving only two dozen year-round resident species, including ravens, boreal chickadees, and hawk owls. Some of the summer birds travel thousands of miles to nest and breed in sub-Arctic valleys, hills, and ponds. The northern wheatear comes here from southern Asia, warblers fly here from Central and South America, and the arctic tern annually travels 24,000 mi while seasonally commuting between Denali and Antarctica.

The most sought-after species among visitors are the large mammals: grizzlies, wolves, Dall sheep, moose, and caribou. All inhabit the forest or tundra landscape that surrounds Denali Park Road. While traveling the park road you can expect to see Dall sheep finding their way across high meadows, grizzlies and caribou frequenting stream bottoms and tundra, moose in the forested areas both near the park entrance and deep in the park, and the occasional wolf or fox that may dart across the road. Keep in mind that, as one park lover put it, "this ain't no zoo." You might hit an off day and have few viewings—enjoy the surroundings anyway. Under no circumstances should you feed the animals or birds (a mew gull or ground squirrel may try to share your lunch).

Exploring Denali

You can have one of North America's premier hiking and wilderness experiences in Denali with the proper planning: know your goals, consult park staff before setting out, carry proper clothing, food, and water, and don't try to cover too much ground in too short a time. With 6 million acres of sub-arctic wilderness, Denali National Park & Preserve has too much area for even the most dedicated vacationer to explore. The prudent visitor must make wise choices.

Park Basics

Admission to Denali is $10 per person and $20 per family. The **visitor center** near the park's entrance (at Milepost 237.3 of the George Parks Highway) can fulfill all your information needs, including campground registration, bus reservations, backcountry permits, daily schedules for naturalist presentations, and sled-dog demonstrations by the park ranger. A video kiosk provides park information about flora, fauna, and bear safety. For more in-depth information about Denali's animals, wildflowers, and geology, check out the bookstore. The Backcountry Reservations desk has hiking information, including current data on animal sightings, river-crossing conditions, weather, and closed areas. Permits are required for overnight backpacking trips, but you won't need one for day hiking. Other than the restricted areas, recognizable by signs posted prominently next to the road, the park is yours to roam.

Box 9, Denali National Park 99755 ☎ *907/683–2294* 🌐 *www.nps.gov/dena.*

Roads & Transportation

You can reach the park by bus or by car along the George Parks Highway. On its route between Anchorage and Fairbanks, the Alaska Railroad line runs through Denali and makes a stop as well. Only one road penetrates Denali's expansive wilderness: the 88-mi Denali Park Road, which winds from the park entrance to Wonder Lake and Kantishna, the historic mining community in the heart of the park. The first 14 mi of the road are open to all vehicles, but beyond the checkpoint at Savage River only tour and shuttle buses and vehicles with permits are allowed to travel. Bicycles are currently allowed on the park road, which is suitable only for mountain bikes.

Beyond Savage

Past the Savage River checkpoint at Mile 15, private vehicle traffic is restricted. Campers with permits for the Teklanika campground can drive into and back out from their campsites at Mile 29. Except for a few professional photographers with special permits and permit holders from the community of Kantishna near Wonder Lake, the only other vehicles are tour buses, shuttle buses, and those driven by Park Service employees.

If you decide to venture past the gatekeepers at Savage, and you won't be camping, you have two choices: either sign up for one of the sight-

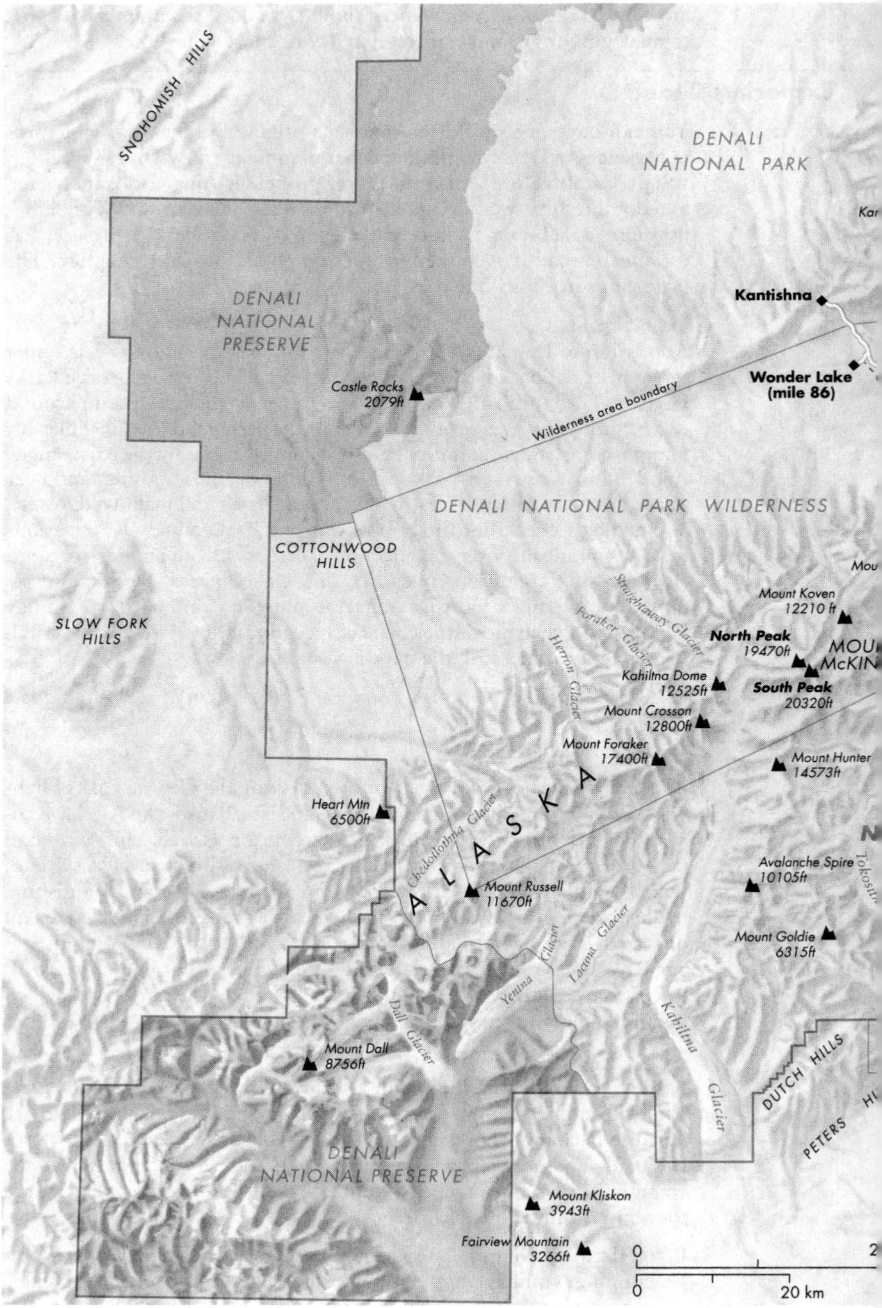
SNOHOMISH HILLS
DENALI NATIONAL PARK
DENALI NATIONAL PRESERVE
Kantishna
Wonder Lake (mile 86)
Castle Rocks 2079ft
Wilderness area boundary
DENALI NATIONAL PARK WILDERNESS
COTTONWOOD HILLS
SLOW FORK HILLS
Straightaway Glacier
Foraker Glacier
Herron Glacier
Mount Koven 12210 ft
North Peak 19470ft
Kahiltna Dome 12525ft
South Peak 20320ft
Mount Crosson 12800ft
Mount Foraker 17400ft
Mount Hunter 14573ft
Heart Mtn 6500ft
ALASKA
Chedotlothna Glacier
Avalanche Spire 10105ft
Mount Russell 11670ft
Yentna Glacier
Lacuna Glacier
Mount Goldie 6315ft
Kahiltna Glacier
Dall Glacier
Mount Dall 8756ft
DUTCH HILLS
PETERS
DENALI NATIONAL PRESERVE
Mount Kliskon 3943ft
Fairview Mountain 3266ft
0
0
20 km

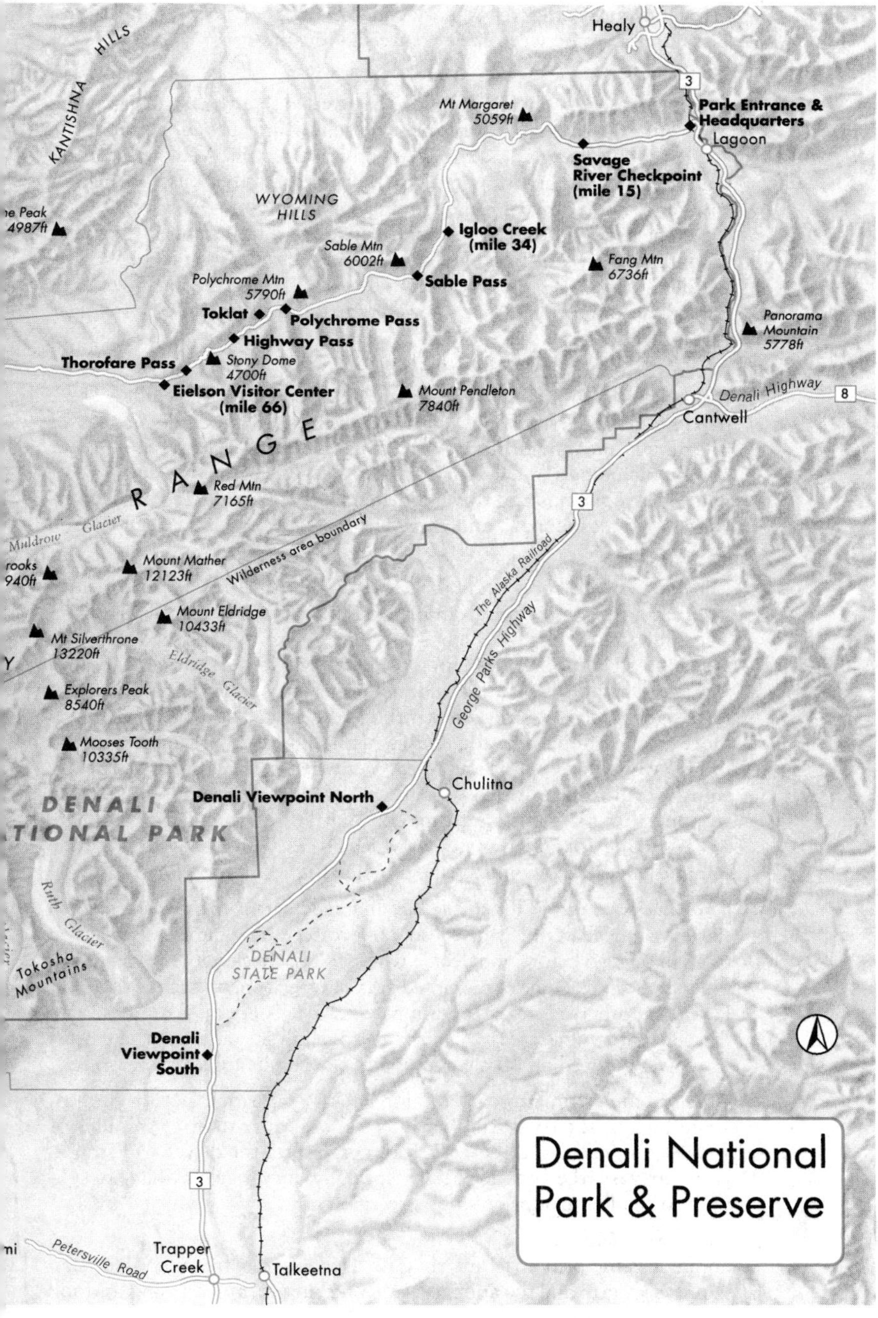
Denali National Park & Preserve
Healy
Park Entrance & Headquarters
Lagoon
Mt Margaret 5059ft
Savage River Checkpoint (mile 15)
KANTISHNA HILLS
WYOMING HILLS
Igloo Creek (mile 34)
Sable Mtn 6002ft
Sable Pass
Fang Mtn 6736ft
Polychrome Mtn 5790ft
Toklat
Polychrome Pass
Highway Pass
Panorama Mountain 5778ft
Thorofare Pass
Stony Dome 4700ft
Eielson Visitor Center (mile 66)
Mount Pendleton 7840ft
Denali Highway
Cantwell
RANGE
Red Mtn 7165ft
Muldrow Glacier
Wilderness area boundary
Mount Mather 12123ft
Mount Eldridge 10433ft
Mt Silverthrone 13220ft
Eldridge Glacier
Explorers Peak 8540ft
Mooses Tooth 10335ft
The Alaska Railroad
George Parks Highway
Chulitna
Denali Viewpoint North
DENALI NATIONAL PARK
Ruth Glacier
Tokosha Mountains
DENALI STATE PARK
Denali Viewpoint South
Petersville Road
Trapper Creek
Talkeetna
3
8

seeing bus tours offered by a park concessionaire or ride the shuttle bus. The differences between the two are significant.

Tour & Shuttle Buses

Before you decide on a destination, be advised that the bus trips in and back out take quite a bit of time. The road is not paved past the Savage River checkpoint, and the speed limit is 35 mph. Add in rest stops, wildlife sightings, and slowing down to let other buses pass on the narrow road, and you've got the makings of a fairly long day if you want to see the park's interior. The round-trip journey to Eielson Visitor Center and Fish Creek is roughly 8 hours, and the extended trip to Wonder Lake is a good 11-hour day. Seeing the best part of the park demands a full-day commitment, but it's well worth the effort.

Tour buses (☎ 907/276–7234) offer varying rides through the park, from a 5-hour Natural History Tour to a Tundra Wilderness Tour, which lasts from 4 to 8 hours depending on season and weather. These trips are fully narrated and led by naturalists, and include a snack or box lunch and hot drinks. Prices range from $67.50 to $94.00 for adults, including the $10 park admission fee. These trips don't allow you to leave the bus and travel independently through the park. Reservations for all bus trips and campsite stays are accepted beginning in late February.

The park's **shuttle buses** (☎ 800/622–7275, 907/272–7275) don't include a formal interpretive program or food and drink. They're less expensive, and you can get off the bus and take a hike or just stop and sightsee, and catch another bus along the road. Most of the drivers are well versed in the park's features and will point out plant, animal, and geologic sights as the bus progresses through the park. The shuttles are much more free form than the tour buses, with all of the passengers enlisted to help watch for wildlife and to call out when animals are spotted. The shuttles will stop to watch wildlife, but there is a schedule to keep, so stopping time is somewhat limited. Shuttle bus round-trip fares are $18.50 to the Toklat River stop at Mile 53; $23.75 to Fish Creek at Mile 63; and $32.50 to Wonder Lake at Mile 86.

If you decide to get off the shuttle bus and head across the tundra, just tell the driver ahead of time where you'd like to get out. Some areas are closed to all hiking, so before you decide where to go, check with the rangers at the visitor center. Some of the closed areas are permanent, such as the Sable Pass area; others close as conditions warrant. There may be a sensitive den site that's vulnerable to disturbance, or a kill site (an area where bears or wolves are feeding off a carcass) that's off limits for safety reasons.

When it comes time to catch a ride back to your point of origin, just stand next to the road and wait; it's seldom more than 15 minutes or so between buses, and if there's room on board, the driver will stop. If your party is large and the park is especially busy, you may have to split up into smaller groups or singles to catch a lift.

When to Go

Summer is the prime visiting time for Denali—the area is loosed from winter's icy grip and the animals are awake, active, and cruising for food and/or companionship. In early summer trails may be muddy and all the trees won't be fully leafed out, but young animals may be more readily visible. Most of the park lies above the tree line and gets 16 to 20 hours of daylight—which means you'll have plenty of time to enjoy the expansive view of unspoiled landscape and catch a few glimpses of Alaskan wildlife in the open spaces.

Late spring and early autumn also provide opportunities to see the area when visitor traffic is lessened, but be advised that the onset of winter and the appearance of spring are far different from those in the Lower 48 and even from the seasonal changes in Anchorage.

The park is open all winter, although services are curtailed and the road into the park is blocked by snow. Intrepid travelers can visit the park on dogsleds, snowshoes, or cross-country skis and get a glimpse of Denali that's seldom enjoyed by outsiders.

Weather conditions can change in a hurry in Alaska, going from bluebird weather to duck or even penguin weather in a short time. Carry a couple of layers of clothing at all times, including decent rain gear, no matter how sunny and clear the day looks. There's little or no shelter available, so pack accordingly.

What to Pack

Whether hiking in the high mountains or cruising the park road, you should always come prepared for the park's highly variable weather. At lower elevations the summer weather can vary from hot and sunny to near freezing and drizzly, and those changes can sometimes occur within a few hours, so you'll want to bring along appropriate clothing and gear. Dress in layers. If you'll be hiking, carry polypropylene long underwear followed by layers of wool or synthetic materials such as fleece.

Even if you're not planning on taking a long hike, you should carry durable rain gear, preferably made of a breathable material. In the Far North, cotton is not your friend—once it gets wet, it stays wet for too long, drawing warmth away from your body. Remember to bring binoculars and a camera, as Denali is one of the country's premier outdoor photography locations. Carry plenty of water and some snack food; water in the park isn't considered safe to drink, and once you pass the park entrance, there's no food available unless you want to compete with the bears for roots and berries.

Making the Most of the Scenery

If you get an early start on a morning bus, you will get far enough into the park to increase your wildlife-viewing opportunities, and maybe catch a glimpse of Mt. McKinley. The animals are most active early in the morning and in the evening.

On the way to the Savage River checkpoint at Mile 15, there are chances of spotting plenty of wildlife: moose, black bears, and red foxes frequent the spruce forest areas near the road. Once you get above treeline, scan the open tundra for caribou and grizzlies. From the parking lot at Savage River, get out your binoculars and glass the ridges to the west of the river for Dall sheep, usually visible as white specks on or near the skyline.

The farther into the park you venture and the longer you stay, the better your chances of seeing the park's charismatic megafauna. Moose and caribou are common sightings; your chances of seeing grizzlies and wolves increase considerably if you persevere to Fish Creek or Eielson. However, getting an early start or making your way deep in the park doesn't guarantee that you'll see wildlife. Keep in mind that wild animals are unpredictable, so there's no guarantee that you'll see wildlife—but the possibility is always present, so stay alert.

Hiking Terrains

Trails are rare in the park interior, but the open tundra is very conducive to cross-country travel, with a few caveats. For starters, not all tundra is created equal. There's wet tundra and dry tundra, and your ability to make good time across the landscape depends on which type you're dealing with.

Dry tundra, composed mostly of ankle-high woody vegetation, makes for fairly easy walking. The wet stuff is more problematic; it's usually composed of tussocks, knobby growths of grassy vegetation surrounded by water and mud. Hiking wet tundra can be slow and inconvenient at best, or it can be a nightmare, depending on local conditions. Stepping between the tussocks demands careful foot placement, and trying to walk on top of them is a fool's errand. They look firm and stable until you try walking on them, which is when they collapse and dump you off. After a while you can identify tundra types from a distance, but it takes some practice.

Another deceptive aspect of tundra hiking is the distortion of distance—that hill over there is a lot farther away than it looks. With no trees to help judge perspective, it's difficult to gauge distances and heights. Hiking times tend to expand considerably over terrain that looks like it's no more challenging than walking across a carpet, so be conservative when making plans.

Nature Trails & Short Walks

Both day hiking and backpacking can be supreme in Denali. The park's entrance area has a system of forest and tundra trails. These range from easy to challenging and are therefore suitable for all ages and hiking abilities. Along these paths you may see beavers working on their lodges in Horseshoe Lake; red squirrels chattering in trees; red foxes hunting squirrels and other rodents; sheep grazing on tundra plants; golden eagles soaring above high alpine ridges; and moose feeding on willow, one of their favorite foods. You should be cautious around moose and enjoy them from a distance; weighing 1,000 pounds or more, they can cause severe injuries despite their harmless appearance. If you encounter a moose at close range acting aggressively, run from it immediately to leave its "personal space." Just the opposite is true for Denali's grizzlies. Most important, **never** run from a bear. You may trigger its predatory chase instincts and have the bear respond to you as prey (⇨ Bear Facts box *in* Chapter 1). A little caution and a large dose of common sense will assure you a safe trip in the park. A summary of bear-safety tips is available at the Denali visitor center.

Longer Hikes

The only relatively long, marked trail for hiking in the park, Mt. Healy Overlook Trail, gains 1,700 feet in 2½ mi and takes about 4 hours round-trip, with outstanding views of the Nenana River below and the Alaska Range above. It's also a great starting point for backcountry hiking. You'll find few trails in the backcountry, however. In tundra areas, you set your own routes, and in forested and brushy areas, you have to bushwhack. The one exception is to find game trails through thick brush, but be advised that these trails were pioneered by bears, moose, and caribou. Whenever you're in an area of restricted visibility, make plenty of noise to announce your presence, and allow the resident creatures to move away ahead of you. Because this is bear country, the Park Service provides backpackers with bearproof food containers. Use of these containers is mandatory. You can plan your itinerary with park rangers and use the shuttle bus for transportation to and from your starting point. No firearms are permitted.

Scenic Drives & Views

You can disembark at any point along the road in the park for hiking and sightseeing, then catch the next bus in either direction to continue your trip. Buses run continuously, and you'll seldom have to wait more than a half hour to catch a ride. Polychrome Pass, at Mile 46 of the park road, is a popular place to disembark, walk around, and take in the wide views of the stream valleys and tundra below. Many visitors turn around at Eielson Visitor Center, at Mile 66 of the park road. But on blue-sky days you might wish to go the distance to Wonder Lake, which has one of the grandest views of Denali. The Eielson–Wonder Lake stretch is particularly beautiful from mid-August to early September, when the tundra is ablaze with autumn's yellows, reds, and oranges. If you can't get a spot on one of the buses into the park, you can drive to the parking lot next to the Savage River at Mile 15. From there you can hike on nearby trails, climb the rock that gives the river its name, or head up onto one of the nearby ridge tops.

Where to Eat

$$–$$$$ ✕ **Tamarack Inn.** Dine on American cuisine by the light of a fireplace at this inn, which houses one of the best-known restaurants on the road from Anchorage to Fairbanks. It serves breakfast, lunch, and dinner in summer and dinner only in winter. ✉ *Mile 298, Parks Hwy., 6 mi south of Nenana* ☎ *907/832–5455* ▭ *AE, MC, V* ⏲ *Closed Mon. and Tues. in Jan. No lunch mid-Sept.–mid-May.*

$–$$$$ ✕ **The Perch.** The bay windows of this fine-dining restaurant atop a forested hillside present a panoramic view of the surrounding Alaska Range foothills. The Perch serves breakfast, lunch, and dinner, offering home-baked breads and desserts along with steak and seafood, and the Panorama Pizza Pub also serves soup and sandwiches. Cabin rentals are available year-round (summer rates are $95 with a private bath, $75 shared, with breakfast included; call for winter rates). ✉ *Mile 224, Parks Hwy., Denali Park* ☎ *907/683–2523 or 888/322–2523* 🌐 *www.denaliperchresort.com/9.html* ▭ *D, MC, V.*

FLIGHTSEEING IN ALASKA

THE MAGNITUDE OF ALASKA *can perhaps best be comprehended from the air. Every major destination from the Southeast to the Arctic has flightseeing services that will show you Alaska from a bird's-eye view. It's a spectacular experience. What follows are several tips you should know about this mode of travel.*

First, if you're an extremely nervous flier, flightseeing may not be for you. In a small plane, you can feel the effects of updrafts, downdrafts, and even breezes, and the pilot can make sharp, steeply banked turns to view wildlife or scenery. It's thrilling and fun, but only if you're in the proper frame of mind.

Once you've decided to take a flight, keep in mind that charter companies can vary in size from one-pilot, one-plane outfits to larger operations flying fleets of aircraft of varying sizes. The smaller companies are often more flexible in their schedules and destinations, while the multi-plane companies can better match plane size to your needs.

When you're arranging a flight, ask for and check references. Also ask about insurance coverage and safety record—any hesitation to completely and fully answer your questions and address your concerns should be a sign to look elsewhere.

Many fleet operations fly to popular destinations on a regular basis and will charge a seat fare, just like buying a ticket on a scheduled airline. Other outfits use charter rates, meaning you pay by the hour for the airplane and divvy up the cost among the passengers. If there's a drop-off and pick-up involved, you pay for all the time the plane is operating, in both directions. So, if your destination is a one-hour flight from the airstrip, you pay for four hours flying time for a drop-off and pick-up package. Generally, a half-hour flightseeing trip will run each person somewhere between $50 and $75, usually with a two- or three-person minimum, depending on aircraft size. Hourly rates, again depending on how big the plane is and on how much competition there is in the area, can run from $75 to over $300.

Any time you fly in a small plane, dress as though you'll be spending some time on the ground and out of the airplane, even if that's not part of your plan. Wear hiking clothes and dress in layers, and always carry rain gear. If traveling by floatplane, you can buy, borrow, or rent hip waders; landing on beaches often requires a bit of wading or walking through shoreline mud.

If you're going to be dropped off at a location, pack your gear in several small, soft-sided bags. Gear gets stashed in all sorts of nooks and crannies of the plane, and your hard-shelled suitcase will not be a welcome sight.

Remember that small-plane travel is extremely weather dependent. Always allow extra time to account for the vagaries of Alaska weather; don't schedule a small-plane pick-up for the same day you're flying out of Alaska on a large airliner.

Flying into remote locations and flightseeing over spectacular terrain is a terrific way to see Alaska and to take in its dramatic scope and scenery. Adding it to your other adventures is well worth the cost.

Helpful Web Sites:

List of Alaska air taxis: www.flyalaska.com/directoryp.html

National Transportation Safety Board database to check air taxi safety records: www.ntsb.gov/NTSB/query.asp

—Tom Reale

¢–$$$ **Lynx Creek Pizza.** Locals hang out here for pizza, sandwiches, salads, ice cream, and some Mexican entrées. You order at the front and grab a seat at picnic-table benches. It's 1 mi north of the park entrance. *Mile 238.5, Parks Hwy. 907/683–2547 AE, D, DC, MC, V Closed mid–Sept.–mid-May.*

$–$$ **McKinley/Denali Salmon Bake.** Baked fresh salmon tops the menu at this rustic building, which looks as if it might blow away in a stiff wind. Steaks, burgers, and chicken are also available, and breakfast, lunch, and dinner are served. It's 1 mi north of the park entrance, and shuttle service is provided to area hotels. *Mile 238.5, Parks Hwy. 907/683–2733 in summer AE, D, DC, MC, V Closed Oct.–Apr.*

Where to Stay

Hotels, motels, RV parks, B&Bs, and campgrounds are clustered along the highway near the park entrance and in the town of Healy, 10 mi north. Camp Denali/North Face and the Denali Backcountry Lodge are in Kantishna, a private inholding at the end of the park road. All other lodging is on the Parks Highway. The park entrance is at Mile 237.3, so you can judge distance from the park by mileage markers.

★ $$$$ **Camp Denali and North Face Lodge.** Camp Denali and North Face are in the heart of the park near the end of the park road, and both properties have views of "the Mountain." At Camp Denali, guests stay in one of 17 cozy and comfortable cabins. North Face Lodge is a north country–style inn with 15 rooms, each with private bath. The knowledgeable naturalist guides on staff take guests on outings during the three-, four- or seven-night stays. Each property has its own kitchen and dining room. Evening programs focus on the natural and cultural history of Alaska and the park. Lodging costs include round-trip transport from the park entrance on custom buses, all meals, guided activities, and use of canoes, mountain bikes, and fishing gear. The rate is based on a three-night minimum stay at $1,275 per person. *Box 67, Denali Park 99755 907/683–2290 907/683–1568 www.campdenali.com 17 cabins (Camp Denali), 15 rooms (North Face Lodge) Dining room, boating, fishing, mountain bikes, hiking; no a/c, no room phones, no room TVs No credit cards Early June–mid-Sept. FAP.*

$$$$ Fodor's Choice ★ **Denali Backcountry Lodge.** These cabins in the community of Kantishna at the end of the park road have private baths and individual climate controls, a rarity in such remote parts. Activities include naturalist programs; hiking; fishing; gold panning; mountain biking; and, for an extra fee, flightseeing when weather permits. Family-style meals emphasizing Alaskan fare are included in the room rate. Access to the lodge by private bus along the park road is the same system used by Camp Denali, and it takes a good part of a day to travel either way. Staying for at least two nights is necessary if you want to participate in any activities. *410 Denali St., Anchorage 99501 907/644–9980 or 800/841–0692 907/644–9981 www.denalilodge.com 38 cabins Restaurant, fishing, mountain bikes, hiking, bar; no a/c, no room phones, no room TVs, no smoking MC, V FAP Closed mid-Sept.–early June.*

$$$ **Denali Princess Wilderness Lodge.** Views from this hotel take in the Nenana River, and rich forest colors in rooms mimic the surroundings. Complimentary shuttle service is provided to the park and railroad station. The large Summit Dining Room offers an estimable view and fine dining. Burgers and more casual fare are available at the Cruiser's Café, which can also supply picnic lunches. ✉ *Mile 238.5, Parks Hwy., 1 mi north of park entrance* *Box 110, Denali Park 99755* ☎ *907/683–2282, 800/426–0500 reservations* *907/683–2545* *www.princesslodges.com/denali_lodge.cfm* *353 rooms* *Restaurant, café, cable TV, outdoor hot tub, bar, meeting room; no a/c, no smoking* *AE, DC, MC, V* *Closed mid-Sept.–mid-May.*

$$–$$$ **Denali Cabins.** Cabins share hot tubs and barbecue grills at this complex near the highway and 8 mi south of the park entrance. All units have private baths. Complimentary shuttle service to the park visitor center is provided, and a four-day, three-night package links the cabins with the Denali Backcountry Lodge in the park. For $995 per person (all inclusive), you spend one night at the cabins, then take a wildlife tour into the park and overnight at the Backcountry Lodge. Drive back out the following day for your third night at the cabins again. ✉ *Mile 229, Parks Hwy.* *410 Denali St., Anchorage 99701* ☎ *907/644–9980 or 888/560–2489* *907/644–9981* *www.denali-cabins.com* *43 cabins* *MC, V* *2 outdoor hot tubs, travel services; no a/c, no smoking* *CP* *Closed mid-Sept.–mid-May.*

$$ **Denali Crow's Nest Log Cabins.** These individually crafted log cabins 1 mi north of the park entrance are on a forested hillside with river and mountain views. Each has two double beds and its own bath, and a 180-degree view of the park entrance area. The Overlook Bar and Grill, a full-service restaurant, claims to have the largest beer selection in the state. ✉ *Mile 238.5, Parks Hwy.* *Box 70, Denali Park 99755* ☎ *907/683–2723 or 888/917–8130* *907/683–2323* *www.denalicrowsnest.com* *39 rooms* *Restaurant, hot tub, bar, courtesy park shuttle from train, travel services; no a/c, no room phones, no room TVs* *MC, V* *Closed Oct.–mid-May.*

$$ **Denali River Cabins and Cedars Lodge.** The cabins, clustered along the Nenana River, are next to McKinley Village Lodge and 6 mi south of the park entrance. A boardwalk connects the cedar-sided cabins, all with double beds, and leads down to the river. Cedars Lodge has standard hotel rooms. The management operates park excursions and a courtesy shuttle service to and from the train depot. ✉ *Mile 231.1, Parks Hwy.* *Box 210, Denali Park 99755* ☎ *907/683–8000 in summer, 907/459–2121 in winter, 800/230–7275 year-round* *907/683–8040 in summer, 907/459–2160 in winter* *www.denalirivercabins.com or www.seedenali.com* *48 rooms, 54 cabins* *Restaurant, cable TV, sauna, bar; no a/c, no smoking* *AE, D, MC, V* *Closed mid-Sept.–mid-May.*

$$ **Denali River View Inn.** This hotel sits atop a bluff overlooking the Nenana River, just north of the park entrance. Modern rooms—with a blue-and-beige color scheme, private baths, and a no-smoking policy—set above the highway rather than along it, offer a quiet experience. ✉ *Mile 238.4, Parks Hwy.* *Box 49, Denali Park 99755* ☎ *907/683–2663 or 866/683–2663* *907/683–7433* *www.denaliriverviewinn.com*

12 rooms Cable TV; no a/c, no room phones, no smoking D, MC, V Closed mid-Sept.–mid-May.

Camping

If you want to camp in the park, either in a tent or an RV, six campgrounds are available with varying levels of access and facilities. Three of the campgrounds—Riley Creek (near the park entrance), Savage River (Mile 15), and Teklanika (Mile 29)—have spaces that accommodate tents, RVs, and campers. Sanctuary River (Mile 22), Igloo Creek (Mile 34), and Wonder Lake (Mile 86) have tent spaces only. Access to these three camping areas is by shuttle bus only. The bus service runs special camper buses with extra storage space for campers with gear.

If you're camping overnight in Denali's wilderness, you must obtain a special permit (free of charge) from rangers at the visitor center. You must also choose an area to camp in. Denali's backcountry is divided into 43 units, and only a limited number of campers are allowed each night in most units. The most desirable units are near the middle of the park, in areas with open tundra and wide-open vistas. These fill up faster than the low-lying areas, many of which are moist and have high mosquito populations. The best strategy for securing good backpacking areas is to arrive a couple of days early, stay at one of the facilities near the park entrance, and check in at the backcountry desk early each morning until you can get the unit you desire.

¢ **McKinley RV Park and Campground.** A variety of RV sites, from "basic" to those with full electricity, water, and sewer, as well as two-person tent sites are available at this campground, about 10 mi outside the park. A dump station, public showers, laundry facilities, deli, espresso bar, ice, and gasoline, diesel, and propane are also available. *Mile 248.5, Parks Hwy., Healy 99743 907/683–2379 or 800/276–7234 www.mtaonline.net/~rvcampak $16–$27.*

¢ **National Park Service Campgrounds.** Six campgrounds are inside the park: three are open to private vehicles for tent and RV camping, three are reached by shuttle bus only and are restricted to tent camping. All have toilet facilities, most have drinking water, and a couple have nearby hiking trails. All are open from late May to September, depending on snow conditions, and one is open year-round. There is a onetime $4 reservation fee, in addition to the nightly rate. You can apply for a site at the visitor center, but it's wise to reserve in advance. *Denali National Park Headquarters, Box 9, Denali Park 99755 907/683–2294 information, 907/272–7275, 800/622–7275 reservations www.nps.gov $9–$18 AE, D, MC, V All but Riley Creek (no visitor facilities) closed Oct.–late May.*

Guided Tours

Privately operated bus trips are available through **Denali Park Resorts** (907/276–7234 or 800/276–7234). The Tundra Wilderness Tour costs $94, lasts 6 to 8 hours, and includes a boxed snack. The Natural History Tour lasts three to four hours and costs $67.50. **Alaska Mountaineering School** (907/733–1016 907/733–1362 www.climbalaska.org) leads backpacking trips in Denali National Park and elsewhere in the state, including the Brooks Range. It also conducts 6- and 12-day mountaineering courses, mountaineering expeditions to Denali and other peaks in the Alaska Range, and climbs for all levels of climbing expertise. **Mountain Trip** (☎ 907/243–0039, 866/886–8747 🌐 www.mountaintrip.com) guides climbing expeditions on Mt. McKinley and other Alaska Range peaks (experience required).

Besides exploring the park on your own, you can take free ranger-guided "discovery hikes" and learn more about the park's natural and human history. Rangers lead daily hikes throughout the summer. Ask about them at the visitor center.

Sports & the Outdoors

Kayaking & Rafting

Several privately owned raft and tour companies operate along the Parks Highway near the entrance to Denali, and they schedule daily rafting, both in the fairly placid areas on the Nenana and through the 10-mi-long Nenana River canyon, which contains some of the roughest white water in North America.

Alaska Raft Adventures books white-water and scenic raft trips along Nenana River through **Denali Park Resorts** (☎ 907/276–7234 or 800/276–7234 🖷 907/258–3668 🌐 www.denaliparkresorts.com/rafting.shtml). **Denali Outdoor Center** (✉ Mile 238.5, Parks Hwy. 📫 Box 170, Denali Park 99755 ☎ 907/683–1925 or 888/303–1925 🌐 www.denalioutdoorcenter.com) takes visitors of all ages and abilities on rafting trips on the Nenana River. It also leads more adventurous trips down the Nenana River rapids in inflatable kayaks. No river experience is necessary. The kayaks, called Duckies, are easy to get out of, stable, and self-bailing. The company also leads a variety of rafting trips and teaches white-water kayaking. All gear is provided, including full dry suits. Mountain-bike tours and rentals are also available, and there's a free local shuttle from hotels, lodges, AKRR depot, the Denali National Park visitor center, and elsewhere.

Denali Raft Adventures (☎ 907/683–2234 or 888/683–2234 🖷 907/683–1281 🌐 www.denaliraft.com) launches its rafts several times daily on 2- or 4-hour, all-day, and overnight scenic and white-water raft trips on the Nenana River. Dry suits are provided. Guests under the age of 19 must have a release waiver signed by a parent or guardian. Contact the company for copies before the trip. Courtesy pickup at hotels and the train depot is available. **Nenana Raft Adventures** (☎ 907/683–7238 or 800/789–7238 🖷 907/683–1618 🌐 www.alaskaraft.com) runs 4- and 6-hour rafting trips along Nenana River and provides dry suits.

Mountain Biking

Mountain biking is allowed on the park's dirt road, and no permit is required for day trips. The first 14 mi of the road is paved. Beyond the Savage River checkpoint the road is dirt and gravel and during the day is traversed by the park buses, which can make for a very dust-intensive experience. It can also be a bit sloppy if it's raining. Late night, when the midnight sun is shining and buses have ceased shuttling passengers for the day, can be a rewarding time to bike and view the park's wildlife. When biking on the road, you need to be very aware of your surroundings and observe park rules if you decide to get off the road. Off-road riding is forbidden, and some sensitive wildlife areas are closed to hiking. The Sable Pass area is always closed to off-road excursions on foot because of the high bear population, and other sites are posted due to denning activity or recent signs of carcass scavenging. **Denali Outdoor Center** (✉ Mile 238.5, Parks Hwy. ☎ 907/683–1925 or 888/303–1925 🌐 www.denalioutdoorcenter.com) rents mountain bikes by the hour or day, and conducts guided tours of the park.

Winter Sports

Snowshoers and skiers generally arrive with their own gear and park or camp at the Riley Creek campground at the park entrance. Dog mushing can also be done with your own team, or you can contact one of the park concessionaires that run day or multiday trips: **Denali West Lodge** (☎ 907/674–3112 🌐 www.denaliwest.com) and **Earthsong Lodge Dog Sled Adventures** (☎ 907/683–2863, 888/607–5566 🌐 www.earthsonglodge.com).

RICHARDSON HIGHWAY

The Richardson Highway stretches 364 mi, from Fairbanks to the all-year, ice-free port of Valdez. The Richardson takes travelers the final 98 mi from the official end of the Alaska Highway in Delta Junction to Fairbanks, but it's more than a mere connecting route. The first road built in Alaska offers fantastic mountain views while also providing excellent river and lake fishing. Named after General Wilds P. Richardson, first president of the Alaska Road Commission, the highway evolved from a pack-train trail and dogsled route that mail carriers and gold seekers followed in the early 1900s to a two-lane asphalt highway in 1957. It's a four-lane, divided highway from Fairbanks to North Pole, home of the Santa Claus House gift shop, with its towering Santa silhouette, and the North Pole Coffee Roasting Company, which provides many Fairbanks-area restaurants with fresh-roasted coffee. The Richardson also links Fairbanks with Delta's farm country and the winter and summer recreation areas near Summit Lake in the Alaska Range. At Paxson, the Richardson takes travelers to the Denali Highway, a gravel road leading west through the Alaska Range to campgrounds and fishing in the Tangle Lakes area and, later, to Denali National Park & Preserve. Fifty-six miles south of the Denali Highway, the Richardson borders Wrangell–St. Elias National Park, the largest U.S. national park.

North Pole

15 *15 mi southeast of Fairbanks, 85 mi northwest of Delta Junction.*

Though it may be a featureless suburb of Fairbanks, it does have a cool name: Christmas lives in North Pole all year long. Many of the street names maintain the theme, including Santa Claus Lane and St. Nicholas Drive. The prime attraction here is the **Santa Claus House Gift Shop** (⇨ Shopping, *below*), a must-see if you have young children.

Off the Richardson Highway just south of North Pole, **Chena Lakes Recreation Area** (✉ Mile 346.8, Richardson Hwy.) offers hiking, swimming, boating, camping, picnicking, dog mushing, and cross-country skiing. Created by the Army Corps of Engineers as part of the Chena River Flood-Control Project, it is now operated by the local government, the **Fairbanks North Star Borough** (☎ 907/488–1655 Parks and Recreation Department).

Sports & the Outdoors

FISHING Rainbow trout are not native to the Interior, but they are stocked in some lakes. **Birch Lake** (Mile 303.5), **Harding Lake** (Mile 321.4), and **Quartz Lake** (Mile 277.8), easily accessible from the Richardson Highway between Fairbanks and Delta Junction, are good trout-fishing spots. All have campgrounds and boat-launching areas. To catch migrating salmon in the fall, head to **Salcha River,** 40 mi below Fairbanks on the Richardson Highway.

Shopping

The **Knotty Shop** (✉ Mile 332, 6565 Richardson Hwy., 32 mi south of Fairbanks ☎ 907/488–3014 🌐 www.alaskangifts.com ⏲ Closed Jan.–Feb. 15) has a large selection of Alaskan handicrafts as well as a mounted wildlife display and a yard full of spruce burl sculptures, including a 6-foot mosquito. It also serves soft drinks and ice cream over a counter carved from spruce burl.

The **Santa Claus House Gift Shop** (✉ Mile 349, 101 St. Nicholas Dr., 14 mi south of Fairbanks ☎ 907/488–2200 or 800/588–4078 🌐 www.santaclaushouse.com) is hard to miss. Look for the giant Santa statue and the Christmas mural on the side of the building. The store has a variety of toys, gifts, and Alaskan handicrafts. Santa is often on duty to talk to children, and two reindeer are kept in a pen outside the store.

Delta Junction

⓰ *100 mi southeast of Fairbanks, 106 mi northwest of Tok, 266 mi north of Valdez.*

As the hub of the state Delta Agricultural Project, Delta Junction has the manner of a small farming town. Although the project has had many difficulties, grain and dairy farms still define the area. In summer Delta becomes a bustling rest stop for road-weary tourists traveling the Alaska and Richardson highways. Delta is also known for its access to good fishing and its proximity to the Delta Bison Range. However, don't expect to see the elusive bison, as they roam free and generally avoid people.

Where to Stay & Eat

$–$$$$ ✕ **Pizza Bella.** Delicious pizzas and other Italian and American entrées compose the menu here. Italian scenic paintings and maps bring a slice of Italy to Alaska. ✉ *Mile 265, Richardson Hwy.* ☎ *907/895–4841 or 907/895–4524* 💳 *MC, V.*

★ ¢–$ ✕ **Rika's Roadhouse.** This historic landmark, part of Big Delta State Historical Park, is well worth a detour if you're nearby. There are free tours of the beautifully restored and meticulously maintained grounds, gardens, and historic buildings. The restaurant serves breakfast and lunch. The home-baked goods, including pies, muffins, cookies, sweet rolls, and breads, are delectable. ✉ *Mile 275, Richardson Hwy.* ☎ *907/895–4201* 🌐 *www.rikas.com* 💳 *AE, D, MC, V* ⏲ *Closed mid-Sept.–mid-May. No dinner.*

$ **Alaska 7 Motel.** Cheap and clean accommodations right off the highway are what you get here. Some units have kitchenettes, and all have phones and microwaves. ✉ *Mile 270.3, Richardson Hwy., Box 1115, 99737* ☎ *907/895–4848* 📠 *907/895–4193* 🌐 *www.alaska7motel.com* *16 rooms* *Some kitchenettes, refrigerators, cable TV; no a/c* 💳 *AE, D, DC, MC, V.*

$ **Kelly's Country Inn Motel.** Delta residents most often put visitors up at this downtown motel. It has clean, modern rooms, including some with kitchenettes, decorated in neutral colors. ✉ *Mile 266.5, Richardson Hwy., Box 849, 99737* ☎ *907/895–4667* 📠 *907/895–4481* 🌐 *www.kellysalaskacountryinn.com* *20 rooms* *Some kitchenettes, some microwaves, cable TV; no a/c* 💳 *AE, D, MC, V.*

FORTYMILE COUNTRY

A trip through the Fortymile Country up the Taylor Highway will take you back in time more than a century—when gold was the lure that drew hardy travelers to Interior Alaska. It's still one of the few places to see active mining without leaving the road system.

The 160-mi Taylor Highway runs north from the Alaska Highway at Tetlin Junction, 12½ mi south of Delta Junction. It's a narrow rough-gravel road that winds along mountain ridges and through valleys of the Fortymile River. The road passes the tiny community of Chicken and ends in Eagle at the Yukon River. This is one of only three places in Alaska where the river can be reached by road. A cutoff just south of Eagle connects to the Canadian Top of the World Highway leading to Dawson City in the Yukon Territory. This is the route many Alaskans take to Dawson City. The highway is not plowed in winter, so it is snowed shut from fall to spring. Watch for road reconstruction.

Tok

17 *12 mi west of Tetlin Junction, 175 mi southwest of Dawson City.*

Loggers, miners, and hunting guides who live and work along Tok's surrounding streams or in the millions of acres of spruce forest nearby come here for supplies, at the junction of the Glenn Highway and the Alaska Highway. Each summer the city, with a resident population of fewer than 1,500, becomes temporary home to thousands of travelers, including those journeying up the Alaska Highway from the Lower 48.

It's hard to overestimate the importance of the Alaska Highway in the state's development history. Before World War II, there was no road connection between the Alaskan Interior and the rest of North America. Alaska's population center was in the coastal towns of the Southeast panhandle region, and most of the state's commerce was conducted along its waterways. Access to the Interior was via riverboat, until 1923 when the railroad connection from Seward through Anchorage and into Fairbanks was completed.

The onset of World War II changed everything. An overland route to the state was deemed a matter vital to national security in order to supply war material to the campaign in the Aleutians, and to fend off a potential invasion by Japan. In a feat of amazing engineering and construction prowess, the 1,500-mi-long route was carved out of the wilderness in eight months in 1942. The original road was crude but effective, and has been undergoing constant maintenance and upgrading ever since. Today the highway is easily traversed by every form of highway vehicle imaginable, from bicycles and motorcycles to the biggest, lumbering RVs known not so affectionately by locals as "road barns."

Crossing into Interior Alaska from the Lower 48 or from the ferry terminals in Southeast requires border crossings into Canada and then into Alaska. Travelers are advised to be very certain of all the requirements for crossing an international border, including restrictions on pets, firearms, and the need for adequate personal identification for every member of the party.

After crossing into Alaska from the Yukon Territory on the Alaska Highway, the first vestiges of what passes for civilization in the Far North are found in the town of Tok. Here you'll find food, fuel, hotels, and a couple of restaurants, and the need to make a decision. Staying on the Alaska Highway and heading roughly west will take you into the Interior and to Fairbanks, whereas heading south on the Tok Cutoff will aim you toward South Central Alaska and the population center of Anchorage. Or, you can make a huge loop tour, covering most of the paved highway in the state, taking in much of the terrific variety of landscapes and terrains that the 49th state has to offer. Head down the Tok Cutoff to the Richardson Highway (no one in Alaska uses the highway route numbers), and from there go south to Valdez. From there catch the ferry to Whittier, Cordova, or Seward, explore the Kenai and Anchorage, then head north on the Seward Highway to the Parks, to Denali, Fairbanks, and beyond. Loop back to Tok and you've seen most of what can be seen from the road system.

The **Tetlin National Wildlife Refuge Visitor Center** (✉ Mile 1229, Alaska Hwy., 99780 ☎ 907/883–5312) parallels the Alaska Highway for the first 65 highway miles after leaving Canada. This 730,000 acre refuge has most of the "charismatic megafauna" that visitors travel to Alaska to see, including black and grizzly bears, moose, Dall sheep, wolves, and caribou, as well as numerous bird species. The visitor center has a large deck outfitted with spotting scopes, and inside you'll find maps, wildlife displays, books and interpretive information. It's open May 15–September 15. To help with your planning, stop in at the **Tok Main Street Visitors Center** (✉ Mile 1314, Alaska Hwy., 99780 ☎ 907/883–5775), which has travel information covering the entire state, as well as wildlife and natural-history exhibits. The staff is quite helpful.

Where to Stay & Eat

¢–$$ **Gateway Salmon Bake & RV Park.** For highway travelers, Tok is the first stop in Alaska, and the Gateway is in turn the first stop in Tok. As an introduction to informal Alaska dining, it's tough to beat, with all-you-can-eat salmon, halibut, reindeer sausage, barbecue ribs, chicken, buffalo burgers, and salmon chowder. Seating is at picnic tables, either outdoors or under a covered pavilion. There's also a full-service RV park out back, and a very clean shower facility if you need to hose off the road dust from the long drive. *Mile 1313.1, Alaska Hwy. 907/883–5555 D, MC, V.*

$–$$$$ **Fast Eddy's Restaurant and Young's Motel.** It's much better than the name would indicate: the chef makes his own noodles for chicken noodle soup, and the homemade hoagies and pizza are a welcome relief from the roadhouse hamburgers served by most Alaska Highway restaurants. It's open 6 AM–11 PM (but no soup after 5). The summer rate for the motel rooms is $81 for a double. *Mile 1313.3, Alaska Hwy. Box 482, 99780 907/883–4411 907/883–5023 www.tokalaska.com 43 rooms Restaurant, cable TV; no a/c AE, D, MC, V.*

$$ **Westmark Tok.** The spacious dining room of this reliable, comfortable, and well-appointed hotel is a welcome respite when you are traveling the long stretches between civilization outposts along the Alaska Highway. *Junction of Alaska and Glenn Hwys. Box 130, 99780 907/883–5174 or 800/544–0970 907/883–5178 www.westmarkhotels.com 92 rooms Restaurant, cable TV, bar, shop, some pets allowed; no a/c AE, D, DC, MC, V Closed Oct.–May.*

Shopping

The **Burnt Paw** (Junction of Alaska and Glenn Hwys. 907/883–4121 907/883–5680 www.burntpawcabins.com) sells jade and ivory, Alaskan ceramics, crafts, paintings, smoked salmon—even sled-dog puppies. There are also a B&B on the premises and log cabins with traditional Alaska sod roofs. In Northway, south of Tok, **Naabia Niign** (Mile 1264, Alaska Hwy. 907/778–2297 907/778–2334) is a Native-owned crafts gallery with an excellent selection of authentic, locally made birch baskets, beadwork items, and fur moccasins and gloves.

Chicken

18 *78 mi north of Tok, 109 mi west of Dawson City.*

Chicken was once in the heart of major gold-mining operations, and the remains of many of these works are visible along the highway. Here you'll find a country store, bar, liquor store, café, and gas station. Ask about tours of the old mining operations ($5) at the café, which hosts a salmon barbecue every day from 4 PM to 8 PM. Be careful not to trespass on private property. Miners rarely have a sense of humor about trespassing.

Sports & the Outdoors

CANOEING The beautiful **Fortymile River** offers everything from a 38-mi run to a lengthy journey to the Yukon and then down to Eagle. Its waters range from easy Class I to serious Class IV (possibly Class V) stretches. Only experienced canoeists should attempt boating on this river, and rapids should be scouted beforehand. Several access points can be found off the Taylor Highway.

CanoeAlaska (Box 735, Tok 99780 907/883–2628 canoealaska.net) has been conducting guided canoe and raft trips on Interior Alaska rivers for 25 years. Trips begin in mid-May and continue through Labor Day and range from two to eight days on rivers that vary in difficulty and remoteness. Evening interpretive tours in the Arctic Voyageur, a replica of a 34-foot voyageur canoe, are offered on a lake. Multiday Voyageur trips, ACA-certified canoe instruction, and rentals to qualified paddlers are also available.

Eagle

19 *95 mi north of Chicken, 144 mi northwest of Dawson City.*

Eagle was once a seat of government and commerce for the Interior. An army post (Ft. Egbert) operated here until 1911, and territorial judge James Wickersham had his headquarters in Eagle until Fairbanks began to grow from its gold strike. The population peaked at 1,700 in 1898. Today it is fewer than 200.

The **Eagle Historical Society** (1st St. 907/547–2325 www.eagleak.org) has a two- to three-hour walking tour ($5) that visits seven museum buildings while regaling participants with tales of the famous people who have passed through this historic Yukon River border town. One daily tour begins at the courthouse at 9 in the morning, from Memorial Day to Labor Day.

YUKON TERRITORY

Gold! That's what called Canada's Yukon Territory to the world's attention with the Klondike gold rush of 1897–98. Although Yukon gold mining today is mainly in the hands of a few large companies that go almost unnoticed by the visitor, the territory's history is alive and thriving.

Though the international border divides Alaska from Yukon Territory, the Yukon River tends to unify the region. Early prospectors, miners, traders, and camp followers moved readily up and down the river with little regard to national boundaries. An earlier Alaska strike preceded the Klondike find by years, yet Circle was all but abandoned in the stampede to the creeks around Dawson City. Later gold discoveries in the Alaskan Fortymile Country, Nome, and Fairbanks reversed that flow across the border into Alaska.

Dawson City

20–23 *109 mi east of Chicken.*

Dawson City today forms the heart of the Yukon's gold-rush remembrances. Since the first swell of the gold rush more than 100 years ago, many of the original buildings have disappeared, victims of fire, flood, and weathering. But enough of them have been preserved and restored to give more than a glimpse of the city's onetime grandeur. In a period of three years up to the turn of the 20th century, Dawson was transformed into the largest, most refined city north of San Francisco and west of Winnipeg. It had grand buildings with running water, telephones, and electricity. The city's population, only about 1,500 now, numbered almost 30,000 in 1899.

Regular air service to Dawson is available from Fairbanks. You can also drive the Taylor Highway route, leaving the Alaska Highway at Tetlin Junction and winding through the Fortymile Country past the little communities of Chicken and Jack Wade Camp into Canada. The border is open 8 AM to 8 PM in summer. The Canadian section of the Taylor Highway is called Top of the World Highway. Broad views of range after range of tundra-covered mountains stretch in every direction. Travelers heading north on the Alaska Highway can turn north at Whitehorse to Dawson City, then rejoin the Alaska Highway by taking the Taylor Highway south. This adds about 100 mi to the trip.

20 **Diamond Tooth Gertie's Gambling Hall** (✉ Arctic Brotherhood Hall, Queen St. ☎ 867/993–5525), for adults 19 and over only, presents live entertainment and three different cancan shows three times a night, seven days a week. It is the only authentic, legal gambling establishment operating in all of the North. Yes, there really was a Diamond Tooth Gertie—Gertie Lovejoy, a prominent dance-hall queen who had a diamond between her two front teeth.

21 The **Dawson City Museum** houses a variety of gold-rush exhibits. You'll also find numerous relics in the Train Shelter next door, including trains from the Klondike Road Railroad that operated along the gold creeks. *✉ Territorial Administration Bldg., 5th Ave. ☎ 867/993–5291 C$7 Mid-May–Labor Day, daily 10–6.*

Parks Canada leads tours of **Bonanza Creek and *Gold Dredge Number 4,*** a wooden-hull gold dredge about 10 minutes outside town. The one-hour walk-through tour takes you into what's billed as "the largest wooden hulled, bucket line gold dredge in North America." There's also a short film about the site and the restoration of the dredge, and you can visit working gold mines in the area and pan for gold in Bonanza Creek. Exit the Klondike Highway at kilometer marker 74. *✉ Mile 7.8, Bonanza Creek Rd. Parks Canada National Office, 25 Eddy St., Hull, Québec K1A 0M5 ☎ 867/993–7200 www.parkscanada.gc.ca C$5 June–mid-Sept., daily 10–4.*

Scholars still argue the precise details of the tenure of writers Robert Service (1874–1958) and Jack London (1876–1916) in Dawson City, but no one disputes that between Service's poems and London's short stories, the two did more than anyone else to popularize and romanticize the Yukon. Service lived in his Dawson cabin, but the Jack London cabin is a reproduction, using some of the wood from his original
22 wilderness home that was found south of Dawson in the 1930s. **Robert Service's cabin** (✉ 8th Ave. and Hanson St. ☎ 867/993–5566 C$5)
23 is open for visitors June through mid-September. **Jack London's cabin** (✉ 8th Ave. and Firth St. ☎ 867/993–6317 Mid-May–mid-Sept., daily 10–1

Dawson City Museum 21
Diamond Tooth Gertie's Gambling Hall 20
Jack London's cabin 23
Robert Service's cabin 22

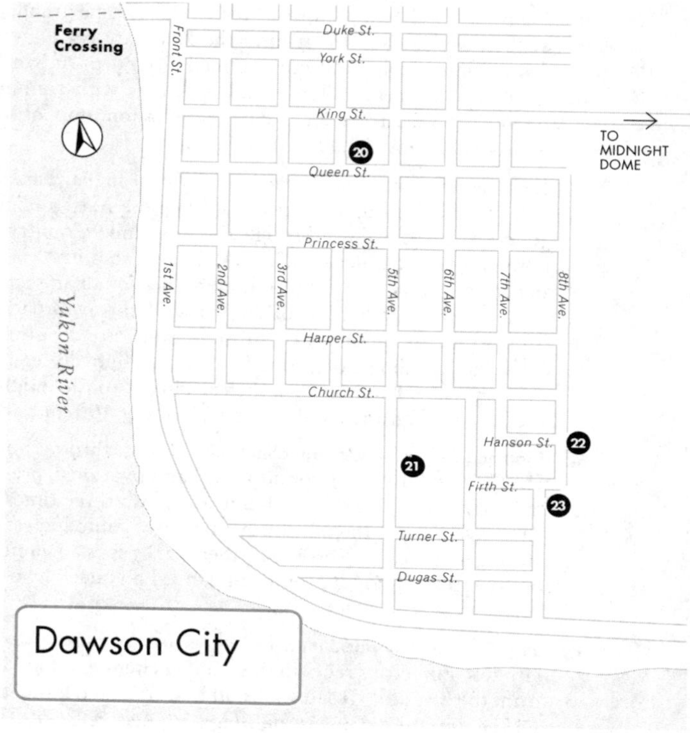

and 2–6 C$2) is literally a stone's throw from the Robert Service cabin. The small museum contains photos, documents, and letters from London's life and the gold-rush era. Half-hour talks are given at 11 and 2:15.

Where to Stay & Eat

$ **Downtown Hotel.** A large collection of artwork from area artists, including mushing scenes, accents the hotel's early-1900s decorations, and all the rooms were renovated in 2002. The Jack London Grill ($–$$) is a best bet: go for the Canadian and American regional specialties, including daily appetizer, pasta, and prime rib specials. The restaurant serves three meals a day and has an outside deck for summer dining. *2nd Ave. and Queen St., Box 780, Y0B 1G0 867/993–5346, 800/661–0514 reservations 867/993–5076 www.downtown.yk.net 59 rooms Restaurant, cable TV, hot tub, bar, Internet, meeting room, airport shuttle; no a/c AE, D, DC, MC, V.*

$–$$ **Bombay Peggy's.** Named and fashioned after one of the last of Dawson's legal madams, Peggy's is done in elaborate Victorian gold-rush style, with heavy, plush draperies and rich color schemes. Bathrooms have claw-foot tubs and pedestal sinks, and the beds have elaborate headboards. In the evening, port and sherry and savory treats are served in the parlor, and for breakfast, croissants and coffee are available. The adjoining pub serves appetizers along with a large selection of single-malt scotches, and meals can be ordered for delivery by a nearby restaurant. ✉ *2nd Ave. and Princess St., Box 411, Y0B 1G0* ☎ *867/993–6969* 📠 *867/993–6199* 🌐 *www.bombaypeggys.com* *3 rooms, 4 suites* *Fans, cable TV, in-room VCRs, Internet, airport shuttle; no smoking* 💳 *MC, V* *CP.*

$ **Eldorado Hotel.** The lobby of this hotel has gold rush–era decor. During the summer tourist season, the staff dresses up in 1898-era garb. However, the modern rooms, some with kitchenettes, are outfitted with decidedly non-1898 amenities such as cable TV and remote controls. ✉ *3rd Ave. and Princess St., Box 338, Y0B 1G0* ☎ *867/993–5451, 800/764–3536 from Alaska* 📠 *867/993–5256* 🌐 *www.eldoradohotel.ca* *52 rooms* *Dining room, some kitchenettes, cable TV, bar, laundry service, Internet, meeting room, airport shuttle; no a/c* 💳 *AE, D, DC, MC, V.*

$ **Triple "J" Hotel.** Log cabins with kitchenettes, a central hotel, and a detached annex make up this clean, quiet compound next to Diamond Tooth Gertie's. All rooms have TVs, coffeemakers, phones, and private baths. ✉ *5th Ave. and Queen St., Box 359, Y0B 1G0* ☎ *867/993–5323 or 800/764–3555* 📠 *867/993–5030* 🌐 *www.triplejhotel.com* *29 rooms, 18 cabins* *Restaurant, some kitchenettes, cable TV, bar, Internet, meeting room, airport shuttle* 💳 *AE, DC, MC, V.*

$ **Westmark Dawson City.** This downtown two-story hotel is built around a central courtyard and is convenient to the sights. With its flocked wallpaper and lace curtains, the lobby recalls the days of the gold rush. While staying at the hotel enjoy a rare opportunity to have your photo taken with a genuine RCMP Mountie in Red Serge dress uniform. Rooms are decorated in soft blues and greens. ✉ *5th Ave. and Harper St., Box 420, Y0B 1G0* ☎ *867/993–5542 or 800/544–0970* 📠 *867/993–5623* 🌐 *www.westmarkhotels.com* *133 rooms* *Dining room, bar, shop, laundry facilities, some pets allowed; no a/c* 💳 *AE, DC, MC, V* ⏲ *Closed mid-Sept.–mid-May.*

Whitehorse

24 *337 mi southeast of Dawson City, 600 mi southeast of Fairbanks.*

Near the White Horse Rapids of the Yukon River, Whitehorse began as an encampment in the late 1890s. It was a logical layover point for gold rushers heading north along the Chilkoot Trail toward Dawson to seek their fortune. The next great population boom came during World War II with the building of the Alcan—the Alaska-Canada Highway. Today this city of more than 22,000 residents is Yukon's center of commerce, communication, and transportation and the seat of the territorial government.

Besides being a great starting point for explorations of other areas of the Yukon, the town itself has plenty of diversions and recreational opportunities. You can easily spend a day exploring its museums and cultural displays—research the Yukon's mining and development history, look into the backgrounds of the town's founders, learn about its indigenous First Nations people, and gain an appreciation of the Yukon Territory from prehistoric times up to the present. You can obtain a free three-day parking permit at **City Hall** (✉2121 2nd Ave. ☎867/668–8687).

The logical place to start touring Whitehorse is the **Yukon Visitor Information Centre,** housed in the block-long, pine-sided headquarters for Yukon Tourism. Anything to do with the Yukon can be found in the reception center. *✉ 100 Hanson St. ☎ 867/667–3084 ⎙ 867/667–3546 ⊕ www.touryukon.com ⏲ May–Sept., daily 8–8; Oct.–Apr., weekdays 8:30–noon and 1–5.*

The Yukon Territorial Government Building houses the **Yukon Permanent Art Collection,** a display of works by Yukon artists depicting northern people and their culture. In addition to the collection on the premises, a brochure *Art Adventures on Yukon Time,* available at visitor reception centers throughout the Yukon, guides the way to artists' studios and provides locations of galleries and art shops. *✉2071 2nd Ave. ☎867/667–5811 ⊕ www.yukoninfo.com/whitehorse/ytg-tour 🎟 Free ⏲ Weekdays 8:30–5.*

The **MacBride Museum** is your best general introduction to the spirit and heritage of the Yukon. More than 5,000 square feet of exhibits display natural history, geology, archaeology, First Nations, Mounties in the North, the gold rush, and the city of Whitehorse. Outdoor artifacts include Sam McGee's cabin—the same Sam McGee immortalized in Robert Service's famous poem "The Cremation of Sam McGee"—the Whitehorse telegraph office, and various transportation vehicles. *✉ 1124 1st Ave. and Wood St. ☎ 867/667–2709 ⎙ 867/633–6607 ⊕ www.macbridemuseum.com 🎟 C$5 ⏲ Mid-May–Aug., daily 10–9; Sept., daily 10–5; Oct.–mid-May, Fri.–Sun. noon–5.*

The **Waterfront Walkway** along the Yukon River will take you past a few stops of interest. Your walk starts on the path along the river just east of the MacBride Museum entrance on 1st Avenue. Traveling upstream (south), you'll go by the old White Pass & Yukon Route Building, on Main Street.

The former Yukon Visitor Reception Centre at the Whitehorse Airport is the home of the **Yukon Beringia Interpretive Centre,** which presents the story of the Yukon during the Ice Age. Beringia is the name given to the large subcontinental landmass of eastern Siberia and Interior Alaska and the Yukon, which were linked by the Bering Land Bridge during the Ice Age. The center unfolds extensive information on the area's prehistoric origins and pays tribute to the First Nations people and the miners who have contributed information and exhibits to the museum. The center displays large dioramas depicting the lives of animals in Ice Age Beringia and replicas of skeletons of the animals who lived there. *✉ Mile 914, Alaska Hwy. ☎ 867/667–8855 ⊕ www.beringia.com 🎟 C$6 ⏲ May and Sept., daily 9–6; June–Aug., daily 8:30–7 and by appointment.*

★ The **SS *Klondike*,** a national historic site, is dry-docked in Rotary Park. The 210-foot stern-wheeler was built in 1929, sank in 1936, and was rebuilt in 1937. In the days when the Yukon River was the transportation link between Whitehorse and Dawson City, the *Klondike* was the largest boat plying the river. ✉ *S. Access Rd. and 2nd Ave.* ☎ *867/667–4511* 🎟 *C$5, C$15 for families* ⏲ *May–Sept., daily 9–6.*

If you're in Whitehorse during late summer, it's possible to see the chinook (king) salmon, which hold one of nature's great endurance records: the longest fish migration in the world, which is more than 1,800 mi from the ocean to Whitehorse. The **Whitehorse Rapids Dam and Fish Ladder** has interpretive exhibits, display tanks of freshwater fish, and a platform for viewing the fish ladder. The best time to visit is August, when between 150 and 2,100 salmon (average count is 800) use the ladder to bypass the dam. ✉ *End of Nisutlin Dr.* ☎ *867/633–5965* 🎟 *Free* ⏲ *June–Labor Day, daily; hrs vary, so call ahead.*

Miles Canyon, a 10-minute drive south of Whitehorse, is both scenic and historic. Although the dam below it makes the canyon seem relatively tame, it was this perilous stretch of the Yukon River that determined the location of Whitehorse as the starting point for river travel north. In 1897 Jack London won the admiration—and cash—of fellow stampeders headed north to the Klondike goldfields because of his steady hand as pilot of hand-hewn wooden boats here. You can hike on trails along the canyon or take a two-hour cruise aboard the MV *Schwatka* and experience the canyon from the waters of Lake Schwatka, which obliterated the Whitehorse Rapids when the dam creating the lake was built in 1959. ✉ *Miles Canyon Rd., 2 mi south of Whitehorse* 📫 *68 Miles Canyon Rd., Yukon Territory* ☎ *867/668–4716* 📠 *867/633–5574* 🌐 *www.yukon-wings.com/boatcruises.html* 🎟 *C$25* ⏲ *Cruises depart early to mid-June at 2 PM, mid-June to late Aug. at 2 and 4 PM, late Aug.–Sept. at 2 PM.*

At **Takhini Hot Springs,** off the Klondike Highway, there's swimming in the spring-warmed water (suits and towels are available for rent), horseback riding, areas for camping and picnicking, an outdoor climbing wall, and a "licensed" (beer and wine) restaurant. ✉ *Km 10, Takhini Hot Springs Rd., 17 mi north of Whitehorse* ☎ *867/633–2706* 🌐 *www.takhinihotsprings.yk.ca* 🎟 *C$7* ⏲ *May–Sept., daily 8 AM–10 PM; call for winter hrs.*

The **Canyon City Archaeological Dig** provides a glimpse into the past of the local First Nations people. Long before the area was developed by Western civilizations, the First Nations people used the Miles Canyon area as a seasonal fish camp. The Yukon Conservation Society conducts free tours of the area twice a day in summer; it also leads walks and hikes from short, child-friendly tours to challenging five- to six-hour scrambles on the nearby mountains. All the hikes are free and provide a great way to see the surrounding countryside with local naturalists. The society office houses a bookstore on Yukon history and wilderness and sells souvenirs, maps, and posters. ✉ *302 Hawkins St.* ☎ *867/668–5678* 🌐 *www.yukonconservation.org* 🎟 *Free* ⏲ *Tours July–late Aug., weekdays at 10 and 2.*

The **Yukon Wildlife Preserve** provides a fail-safe way of photographing rarely spotted animals in a natural setting. Animals roaming freely here include elk, caribou, mountain goats, musk ox, bison, mule deer, and Dall and Stone sheep. Two-hour tours can be arranged through Gray Line Yukon. ✉ *Gray Line Yukon, 208G Steele St.* ☎ *867/668–3225* 🖷 *867/667–4494* 🌐 *www.yukonweb.com/tourism/westours* 🎫 *C$21* ⏲ *Tours mid-May–mid-Sept., daily.*

Where to Stay & Eat

$$$–$$$$ ✕ **The Cellar.** In the Edgewater Hotel in downtown Whitehorse, this intimate two-room spot—down some stairs, as the name implies—is touted by the locals as the place to go for special occasions. The "front" room is a tad less formal, with a bar and TV, while the back room, separated by an etched glass partition, is quieter. The menu is a combination of seafood and meat dishes and a tapas selection, complemented by a large wine list. Soups, salads, and homemade desserts are also available. ✉ *101 Main St.* ☎ *867/667–2572* 💳 *AE, DC, MC, V.*

$–$$$ ✕ **Klondike Rib & Salmon BBQ.** If you're in the mood for something completely different, this is the place. It's one of the very few places where you can order arctic char, caribou, and musk ox, as well as the more common barbecue specialties such as salmon, halibut, ribs, and chicken. It's open for lunch, but the game dishes are served only at dinner. It's a very popular spot with locals and tourists, so plan on a long wait on summer weekends. ✉ *2nd Ave. and Steele St.* ☎ *867/667–7554* 💳 *MC, V* ⏲ *Closed mid-Sept.–mid-May.*

★ **¢** ✕ **The Chocolate Claim.** Choose from fresh-baked breads and pastries, homemade soups and sandwiches, salads, and quiches at this charming little deli. Artwork—ranging from paintings and pottery to rugs and quilts by local artists and artisans—is on display and for sale. On sunny days you can sit outside. ✉ *305 Strickland St.* ☎ *867/667–2202* 💳 *MC, V* ⏲ *Closed Sun.*

$$ ✕🏨 **Westmark Whitehorse Hotel and Conference Center.** You can catch a nightly Klondike vaudeville show, the Frantic Follies, in summer at this full-service, comfortable hotel in the heart of downtown. The carpeted lobby has low tables and plush chairs, an espresso bar, and a beautiful model of the Klondike riverboat. The restaurant serves pork chops, filet mignon, salmon, and low-calorie selections. ✉ *2nd Ave. and Wood St., Box 4250, Y1A 3T3* ☎ *867/393–9700 or 800/544–0970* 🖷 *867/668–2789* 🌐 *www.westmarkhotels.com* 🛏 *176 rooms, 5 suites* 👍 *Restaurant, microwaves, cable TV with movies, in-room data ports, hair salon, bar, shop, meeting rooms, travel services, some pets allowed; no a/c* 💳 *AE, MC, V.*

$–$$$ 🏨 **High Country Inn.** At this downtown inn, you'll find tastefully appointed modern rooms. Deluxe suites come with kitchenettes. Public areas are cozy, and the location is close to the SS *Klondike* and the public swimming pool. There's a tour desk to help you plan your days. ✉ *4051 4th Ave., Y1A 1H1* ☎ *867/667–4471 or 800/554–4471* 🖷 *867/667–6457* 🌐 *www.highcountryinn.yk.ca* 🛏 *86 rooms, 5 suites* 👍 *Restaurant, some kitchenettes, cable TV, bar, Internet, meeting room, some pets allowed; no a/c in some rooms* 💳 *AE, D, MC, V.*

$ 🏨 **Edgewater Hotel.** A comfortable, unpretentious bit of history in the downtown area, this corner hotel, first built during the 1898 gold rush, is in its third incarnation. The first two burned down, which might lead you to think that the place would be smoke-free, but there are some rooms for smokers. The restaurant and bar are first-rate, and the location, across the street from the Yukon River, is excellent. The small lobby is adorned with old photos of the hotel's predecessors, and give a feel for the gold-rush era. ✉ *101 Main St., Y1A 2A7* ☎ *867/667–2572 or 877/484–3334* 📠 *867/668–3014* 🌐 *www.edgewaterhotel.yk.ca* *30 rooms, 3 suites* *Restaurant, bar, meeting rooms, free parking, no-smoking rooms* 💳 *AE, DC, MC, V* 🍽 *EP.*

Sports & the Outdoors

HIKING The **Kluane National Park and Reserve** (✉ Visitor Center, 119 Logan St., Haines Junction ☎ 867/634-7207), west of Whitehorse, has millions of acres for hiking. The **Yukon Conservation Society** (☎ 867/668-5678) leads hiking expeditions of varying lengths and degrees of difficulty.

SLED-DOG RACING Whitehorse and Fairbanks organize the **Yukon Quest International Sled-Dog Race** (☎ 867/668–4711) in February. The race's starting line alternates yearly between the two cities, and in 2006 it will be in Fairbanks. This is one of the longest and toughest races in the North. See www.yukonquest.org.

INTERIOR A TO Z

To research prices, get advice from other travelers, and book travel arrangements, visit www.fodors.com.

AIR TRAVEL

Alaska Airlines and Delta Airlines fly the Anchorage–Fairbanks route. Both have connecting routes to the Lower 48 states. Air North, based in Whitehorse, has direct, scheduled air service between Alaska and Canada, flying regular runs from Fairbanks and Juneau to the Yukon Territory towns of Dawson City and Whitehorse.

In much of the Bush, federally subsidized mail runs make regular air schedules possible. From Fairbanks, you can easily catch a ride on the mail run to small, predominantly Native villages along the Yukon River or to Eskimo settlements on the Arctic coast. All of the smaller air services operate the mail runs on varying schedules. If you want to visit a particular village, or just have the desire to see a bit of Native Alaska village life, contact any one of the services. Frontier Flying Service has an extensive roster of scheduled flights that includes Anchorage, as well as many of the Bush villages in northwest Alaska, the Interior, and the North Slope of the Brooks Range. Larry's Flying Service has scheduled flights to more than a dozen Bush villages as well as charter service and flightseeing tours. Tanana Air Service flies freight and passengers to almost 30 villages along the Yukon and in the Interior and western Alaska. Wright Air Service flies from its Fairbanks base to Interior and Brooks Range villages. For commuter flights out of Anchorage, ERA Aviation flies to Cordova, Whitehorse, Homer, Iliamna, Kenai, Kodiak, and Valdez. Peninsula Airways serves the Aleutian and Pribilof Island groups and communities in Southwest Alaska from its base in Anchorage.

Air North ☎ 867/668-2228 or 800/764-0407 🌐 www.flyairnorth.com. **ERA Aviation** ☎ 907/243-6633 or 800/866-8394 🌐 www.flyera.com. **Frontier Flying Service**

☎ 907/474-0014, 800/478-6779 in Alaska 🌐 www.frontierflying.com. **Larry's Flying Service** ☎ 907/474-9169 🌐 www.larrysflying.com. **Peninsula Airways** ☎ 907/243-2485 or 800/448-4226 🌐 www.penair.com. **Tanana Air Service** ☎ 907/474-0301. **Wright Air Service** ☎ 907/474-0502, 800/478-0502 in Alaska.

BUS TRAVEL

The most common run is between Fairbanks and Anchorage by way of Denali National Park & Preserve. However, you can take side trips by bus or van into the Yukon Territory. For more information about bus service throughout the Interior, contact Princess Tours. Alaska Direct Bus Lines has year-round service. The Alaskan Express provides scheduled service between Whitehorse, Fairbanks, Valdez, Skagway, Denali National Park, Anchorage, and other communities en route. Haines is accessible from Skagway via water taxi.

The Park Connection provides regularly scheduled shuttle service between Seward, Anchorage, and Denali National Park mid-May to mid-September. Denali Overland Transportation serves Anchorage, Talkeetna, and Denali National Park with charter-bus and van service. Fairbanks has a city bus system. For information about schedules ask at the **Fairbanks Convention and Visitors Bureau** (⇨ Visitor Information).

Alaska Direct Bus Lines ☎ 907/277-6652 or 800/770-6652 has year-round service. **Alaskon Express** ☎ 907/277-5581 or 800/478-6388 🌐 www.graylineofalaska.com. **Denali Overland Transportation** ☎ 907/733-2384 📠 907/733-2385. **Park Connection** ☎ 907/245-0200 or 800/208-0200 🌐 www.alaskatravel.com. **Princess Tours** ☎ 800/426-0442 🌐 www.princesslodges.com.

CAR RENTAL

People flying into Anchorage and renting a car can reach the Interior on the Parks Highway or the Glenn and Richardson highways. All are paved, are in good condition, and offer spectacular views. The Parks Highway route is shorter by a few miles and passes by Denali National Park & Preserve, but traffic is busier.

National Agencies **Avis** ☎ 907/474-0900, 800/478-2847 in Alaska, 800/331-1212. **Budget Car and Truck Rental** ☎ 907/474-0855, 800/248-0150 in Alaska. **Hertz** ☎ 907/452-4444, 907/456-4004, or 800/654-3131. **Payless Car Rental** ☎ 907/474-0177.

CAR TRAVEL

In the Interior your choices of side trips by road from Fairbanks include the Steese Highway to historic Circle on the Yukon River, with its legacy of gold mining; the Dalton Highway, across the Yukon River and along the trans-Alaska pipeline; and the Taylor Highway (closed in winter), connecting the Alaska Highway near Tok with the historic towns of Eagle on the Alaska side of the border and Dawson City, Yukon Territory, in Canada. These are mainly well-maintained gravel roads. However, summer rain can make them slick and dangerous.

Only one road connects Alaska to the Outside—the Alaska Highway. The highway starts in Dawson Creek, British Columbia, in Canada. It is paved but long, almost 1,500 mi to Fairbanks. Lots of people make this trek in the summer, so there are ample restaurants and motels along the way. Winter driving takes more planning, as many businesses and service stations shut down for the season. An alternative route through part of Canada is the Cassiar Highway, which leaves the Yellowhead Highway several miles northwest of Prince Rupert and connects to the Alaska Highway just outside Watson Lake. The Cassiar is a more scenic drive but may have long sections of gravel road. Summer road construction somewhere along the Alaska Highway is a given.

For road reports in Alaska call the State Department of Transportation in Fairbanks. For conditions in the Yukon Territory, call the Department of Community and Transportation Services.

Department of Community and Transportation Services ☎ 867/667-8215. **State Department of Transportation** ☎ 907/456-7623 in Fairbanks.

5

EMERGENCIES

Doctors & Dentists Dawson City (Yukon Territory): **Dawson City Nursing Station** ☎ 867/993-4444. Fairbanks: **Bassett Army Hospital** ☎ 907/353-5172 or 800/478-5172; **Fairbanks Memorial Hospital** ☎ 907/452-8181; **Medical Dental Arts Building** ☎ 907/452-1866 or 907/452-7007. Tok: **Public Health Clinic** ☎ 907/883-4101. Whitehorse (Yukon Territory): **General Hospital** ☎ 867/668-9444.

Emergency Services **Police, emergency assistance** ☎ 911. **Alaska State Troopers** ☎ 907/895-4344 Delta Junction, 907/451-5100 Fairbanks, 907/832-5554 Nenana, 907/883-5111 Tok. **Royal Canadian Mounted Police** ☎ 250/782-5211 Dawson Creek, 867/667-5555 Whitehorse.

TOURS

ADVENTURE TOURS Tour Operators **Northern Alaska Tour Company** Box 82991, Fairbanks 99708 ☎ 907/474-8600 Fax 907/474-4767.

CANOEING Tour Operators **CanoeAlaska** Box 735, Tok 99780 ☎ 907/883-2628.

CLIMBING Tour Operators **Alaska-Denali Guiding** ☎ 907/733-2649. **Mountain Trip** ☎ 907/345-6499.

CRUISING Tour Operators **Riverboat Discovery** ✉ Alaska Riverways, Dale Rd. Landing, near Fairbanks International Airport ☎ 907/479-6673 or 866/479-6673. **Yukon River Tours** ✉ 214 2nd Ave., Fairbanks 99701-4811 ☎ 907/452-7162 Fax 907/452-5063.

SIGHTSEEING Tour Operators **Denali Park Resorts** ☎ 907/276-7234, 800/276-7234 information. **Gray Line of Alaska** ☎ 800/478-6388. **Northern Alaska Tour Company** ☎ 907/474-8600. **Princess Tours** ☎ 907/479-9660 or 800/426-0442. **Trans Arctic Circle Treks** ☎ 907/479-5451. **Westours** ☎ 907/456-7741 or 800/478-6388.

TRAIN TRAVEL

Between late May and early September, daily passenger service runs between Anchorage and Fairbanks by way of Talkeetna and Denali National Park & Preserve. Standard railroad coach cars have access to dining, lounge, and dome cars, operated by the Alaska Railroad. There is no such thing as a poor seat. A panorama will unfold beyond your window, with scenes of alpine meadows and snowcapped peaks and the muddy rivers and taiga forests of the Interior. If you're looking for a bit more luxury in your rail experience, ride in one of the window-dome cars with luxury seating, an outdoor viewing platform, and fine dining operated by Princess Tours. Holland America/Westours also runs rail trips in special cars that cater to their clients with a bit more personal attention and a more sumptuous menu than you'll find on the Alaska Railroad cars. However, all the Princess and Holland America cars are part of the same train and are pulled by the same engines as the "standard" AKRR cars.

Alaska Railroad ☎ 907/456-4155 or 800/544-0552. **Holland America/Westours** ☎ 907/456-7741 or 800/478-6388. **Princess Tours** ☎ 206/336-6000 or 800/426-0442.

VISITOR INFORMATION

Tourist Information **Alaska Public Lands Information Center** ✉ 250 Cushman St., Suite 1A, Fairbanks 99701 ☎ 907/456-0527 📠 907/456-0514. **Alaska Department of Fish and Game** ✉ 1300 College Rd., Fairbanks 99701 ☎ 907/459-7207. **Delta Chamber of Commerce** ✉ Mile 1422, Alaska Hwy., 99737 ☎ 907/895-5068 📠 907/895-5141. **Fairbanks Convention and Visitors Bureau** ✉ 550 1st Ave., 99701 ☎ 907/456-5774 or 800/327-5774 📠 907/452-4190. **Klondike Visitors Association** ✉ Front and King Sts. 📫 Box 389F, Dawson City, Yukon Territory, Canada Y0B 1G0 ☎ 867/993-5575 📠 867/993-6415. **Nenana Visitor Center** ☎ 907/832-5435. **Tok Main Street Visitors Center** ✉ Mile 1314, Alaska Hwy., 99780 ☎ 907/883-5775 📠 907/883-5773. **Whitehorse Visitor Reception Centre** ✉ 100 Hanson St., Box 2703, Whitehorse, Yukon Territory, Canada Y1A 2C6 ☎ 867/667-3084 📠 867/393-6351.

The Bush

Including Nome, Barrow, Prudhoe Bay & the Aleutian Islands

6

WORD OF MOUTH

"If you want off-the-beaten-path Alaska, and if you can afford the time and airfare, I strongly suggest you investigate the Aleutian and Pribilof islands. Scenery, history, great people, and heaven on earth if you're a birder."

—John

"The more I think about it, the more I liked Nome. I think the attraction is that it's so different. I love looking off in the distance and knowing there's nothing but wilderness for hundreds of miles. I've never been anywhere with such a sense of the vast and the remote. The town is funky and friendly. It seems to have a real sense of humor about itself."

—Julie304

www.fodors.com/forums

By Stanton H. Patty

Updated by Bill Sherwonit

ALASKANS CALL IT THE BUSH—those wild and lonely expanses of territory beyond cities, towns, highways, and railroad corridors stretching from the Kodiak Archipelago, Alaska Peninsula, and Aleutian Islands in the south through the Yukon-Kuskokwim Delta and into the northern High Arctic. It is a land where caribou roam and, in its northern regions, the sun really does shine at midnight; in fact it remains in the sky for several weeks in summer—and disappears altogether for weeks in winter. It is a land that knows the soft footsteps of the Eskimos and the Aleuts, the scratchings of those who search for oil and gold, and the ghosts of almost-forgotten battlefields of World War II.

It is a vast, misunderstood wonderland—bleak yet beautiful, harsh yet bountiful. A look across the Arctic tundra in summer yields the miracle of bright wildflowers growing from a sponge of permafrost ice water. In the long, dark Arctic winter, a painter's-blue kind of twilight rises from the ice and snowscapes at midday. Spring and fall are fleeting moments when the tundra awakens from its winter slumber or turns briefly brilliant with autumn colors.

The Arctic is separated by the Brooks Range from the rest of the state, and the Brooks Range itself is so grand that it contains several mountain systems. Each has its own particular character, ranging from pale, softly rounded limestone mountains in the east and west to the towering granite spires and faces of the Arrigetch Peaks in the heart of the range. Large portions of the Brooks Range's middle and western sections are preserved within Gates of the Arctic National Park and neighboring Noatak National Preserve and its eastern reaches within the Arctic National Wildlife Refuge.

North of the Brooks Range, a great apron of land called the North Slope tilts gently until it slides under the Beaufort Sea and the Arctic Ocean. The vast sweep of this frozen tundra brightens each summer with yellow Arctic poppies and dozens of other wildflower species that seem to stretch into infinite distances. Permafrost has worked over this land for centuries and fragmented it into giant polygons that make a fascinating pattern when viewed from the sky.

Great herds of caribou—hundreds of thousands of them—move in slow waves across the tundra, feeding and fattening for the next winter and attempting to stay clear of wolves and grizzlies. And out on the Arctic Ocean's Beaufort Sea, polar bears, stained a light gold from the oil of seals they have killed, pose like monarchs on ice floes, swinging their heads as if warning humans to keep their distance. One of Alaska's premier wildlands, the Arctic National Wildlife Refuge protects mountain and tundra landscape important to caribou, polar bears, grizzlies, wolves, musk ox, and other Arctic wildlife.

The rivers that drain the Brooks Range have names such as Kongakut, Kobuk, and Sheenjek. These speak of the Native peoples who have lived here for thousands of years. The great Noatak River defies the Arctic's north–south drainage pattern and runs east–west, making a right-angle turn before emptying into Kotzebue (*kots*-eh-bew) Sound.

The colorful Eskimo town of Kotzebue, the largest Native village in the state, is the jumping-off point to much of this area. Eskimo ceremonial

Because of its immense size—the Bush comprises a third of the state—and the expense of transportation, it's best to give yourself at least a week and preferably more when exploring Alaska's rural regions. But even with a week or two, you'll see no more than a small slice of Alaska's wildest and most remote parts. The easiest way to go, of course, is through a package tour. For those with shorter amounts of time, many companies offer one-, two-, or three-day tours to Arctic communities.

Numbers in the text correspond to numbers in the margin and on the Bush and Alaska Peninsula, Aleutians & Pribilofs maps.

If you have 3 days

Visit **Katmai National Park & Preserve**'s 4 Brooks Falls and Camp, where brown bears can be seen fishing for salmon, and take the bus tour to the Valley of Ten Thousand Smokes, formed in 1912 by a giant volcanic eruption. Or visit **Dutch Harbor** 9 and Unalaska in the Aleutian Islands, where guided fishing and wildlife-watching trips can be arranged. If you're visiting in winter, consider **Bethel** 1, which hosts one of the state's premier dogsled races, the Kuskokwim 300, each January and the Camai Dance Festival in late March.

If you have 5 days

On guided wildlife tours, visit **St. Paul Island** 10, one of the Pribilof Islands in the Bering Sea. Or if fishing is your thing, stay at one of the region's many lodges; you'll find several in and around **Katmai National Park & Preserve** 4 and **Wood-Tikchik State Park** 3.

If you have 7 days or more

Take a kayaking trip on **Shuyak Island State Park** 8 while staying in comfortable public-use cabins, or go with guides on a river-floating trip through the **Arctic National Wildlife Refuge** 20, where you're likely to see caribou, grizzlies, lots of birds, and perhaps even musk ox or wolves. In late winter or early spring, consider a mushing expedition through **Gates of the Arctic National Park & Preserve** 17, but be prepared for harsh weather and rustic tent camping.

---

dances are demonstrated at Kotzebue's Living Museum of the Arctic, as is the Eskimo blanket toss, a traditional activity dating to prehistoric times, when Eskimo hunters were bounced high in the air so they could see across ice ridges in their search for seals and other wildlife.

Another coastal community, this one first settled by prospectors, is the former gold-rush boomtown of Nome, where you can still pan for gold. In the spring, the going gets wild when Nome hosts a zany golf tournament with "greens" painted on the ice of the Bering Sea coast. Nome also serves as the end of the 1,049-mi Iditarod Trail Sled Dog Race, which begins in Anchorage the first Saturday in March.

Within Southwest Alaska are the biologically productive wetlands of the Yukon-Kuskokwim Delta. Sloughs, ponds, marshes, mud, streams, and puddles in these flat regions near sea level can slow water travel to a standstill. Birds thrive here, and the waters teem with life. Farther south,

Bristol Bay is the site of the largest salmon runs in the world. Nearby Wood-Tikchik encompasses huge lake systems within the nation's largest state park. And on the upper Alaska Peninsula, the brown bears of Katmai rule a vast national park, sharing salmon and trout streams with wary sportfishermen and always receiving the right-of-way. Also in the Southwest, the lower Alaska Peninsula and the Aleutian Islands reach well into the Pacific Ocean toward Alaska's closest point to Japan. This chain beckoned Russian explorers to Alaska in the 18th century. Along the islands, weathered onion-dome Russian Orthodox churches in Aleut villages brace against the fierce Pacific winds.

Dutch Harbor, in the Aleutians, a former U.S. Navy base pounded by Japanese bombs in 1942, is one of America's busiest commercial-fishing ports. Deep-sea trawlers and factory ships venture from here into the stormy north Pacific Ocean and the Bering Sea for harvests of bottom fish, crab, and other catches. Unalaska, an ancient Aleut village, is Dutch Harbor's across-the-bay neighbor and home to one of the oldest Russian Orthodox churches in Alaska. North of the Aleutian chain in the Bering Sea, the remote volcanic islands called the Pribilofs support immense populations of birds and sea mammals as well as two small Aleut communities, St. George and St. Paul.

The Bush also is where America's largest oil field, Prudhoe Bay, was discovered in 1968. At its peak, more than 2 million barrels a day of North Slope crude from Prudhoe and neighboring lesser basins flowed southward via the 800-mi pipeline to the port of Valdez, on Prince William Sound in South Central Alaska, to help fuel the Lower 48 states. Now the flow has diminished to about 1 million barrels per day.

Roads in the Bush are few, so airplanes—from jetliners to small Bush planes—are the lifelines. Throughout Alaska you'll hear about the legendary pilots of the Far North—Noel and Sig Wien, Bob Reeve, Ben Eielson, Harold Gillam, Joe Crosson, Jack Jefford, and the others—who won their wings in the early years. They are Alaska's counterparts to the cowboy heroes of the Wild West. The Bush is where America's favorite humorist, Will Rogers, died in a crash with famed aviator Wiley Post in 1935.

Be aware that many of the Bush communities have voted to be dry areas in order to fight alcohol-abuse problems affecting Alaska's Native peoples. The sale and possession of alcohol is prohibited. Enforcement is strict, and bootlegging is a felony. Nome, of course, remains wet, with numerous lively saloons.

Bush Alaskans have a deep affection for their often-raw land, which is difficult to explain to strangers. They talk of living "close to nature," a cliché, perhaps, until you realize that these Alaskans reside in the Bush all year long, adapting to brutal winter weather and isolation. They have accepted the Bush for what it is: dramatic and unforgiving.

Exploring the Bush

Philosophically speaking, the Bush is more of a lifestyle than a location. Technically, it's a place in Alaska that can't be reached by road. A tour of the state's southwestern region can begin in Bethel, an important Bush

Fishing Alaska's Bush regions offer some of the state's premier sportfishing. Southwest Alaska is especially well known around the world for its remarkable salmon migrations and healthy populations of native rainbow trout. The easiest way to find the fish is to arrange for a guided trip—many sportfishing guides combine fishing and river-floating adventures—or visit a lodge. The Alaska Department of Fish and Game, National Park Service, and U.S. Fish and Wildlife Service can provide lists of guides and outfitters who operate in the region's parks and refuges.

Native Culture More and more Native communities throughout Alaska are reconnecting with and celebrating their cultural traditions. Nowhere is this movement stronger than in the Bush. At the same time, many rural communities are recognizing the value of tourism to local economies, and a growing number of cultural tours and activities are being offered in rural villages—from drumming and dancing to arts-and-crafts exhibits and potlatches, which are traditional Native gatherings with songs, food, and gift giving.

Shopping Alaska's Arctic is known for Eskimo arts, and Southwest communities such as Bethel feature the artwork of the Athabascan, Cup'ik, and Yup'ik Eskimo cultures. Artwork ranges from wildlife or human figures carved from walrus ivory, baleen, and whalebone to grass baskets and bracelets and other jewelry fashioned from ivory, gold, Alaska jade, and other local materials. The Marine Mammals Protection Act permits the purchase of walrus-ivory goods from Native Alaskans. Bethel, Nome, Kotzebue, and Barrow all have reputable gift shops. Prices range from less than $20 for tiny earrings to hundreds of dollars for ceremonial masks and other major pieces.

Wildlife Viewing From the brown bears of Katmai National Park to the seals and seabirds of the Pribilofs and the caribou herds and wolf packs of the Arctic, the Bush in spring and summer is a place of great activity. The Alaska Peninsula has the world's largest gathering of brown bears, which congregate at clear-water streams to feed on the huge runs of salmon that return each summer. Millions of sea- and shorebirds breed in the Aleutian and Pribilof islands annually, and all sorts of marine mammals—sea lions, seals, sea otters, porpoises, and whales—inhabit coastal waters. Two of the continent's largest caribou herds, the Western Arctic and Porcupine, roam across the Arctic's mountains, valleys, and coastal plains. By far the easiest way for most travelers to see wildlife is to participate in guided tours, though independent travelers can also expect to see abundant animals if they do their homework before visiting Alaska and plan trips well in advance.

---

outpost on the Yukon-Kuskokwim Delta, surrounded by the Yukon Delta National Wildlife Refuge; off the mainland coast is the undeveloped wilderness of Nunivak Island. Next is the Alaska Peninsula, which juts out between the Pacific Ocean and the Bering Sea; here are Katmai National Park and Preserve, Aniakchak National Monument and Preserve, and

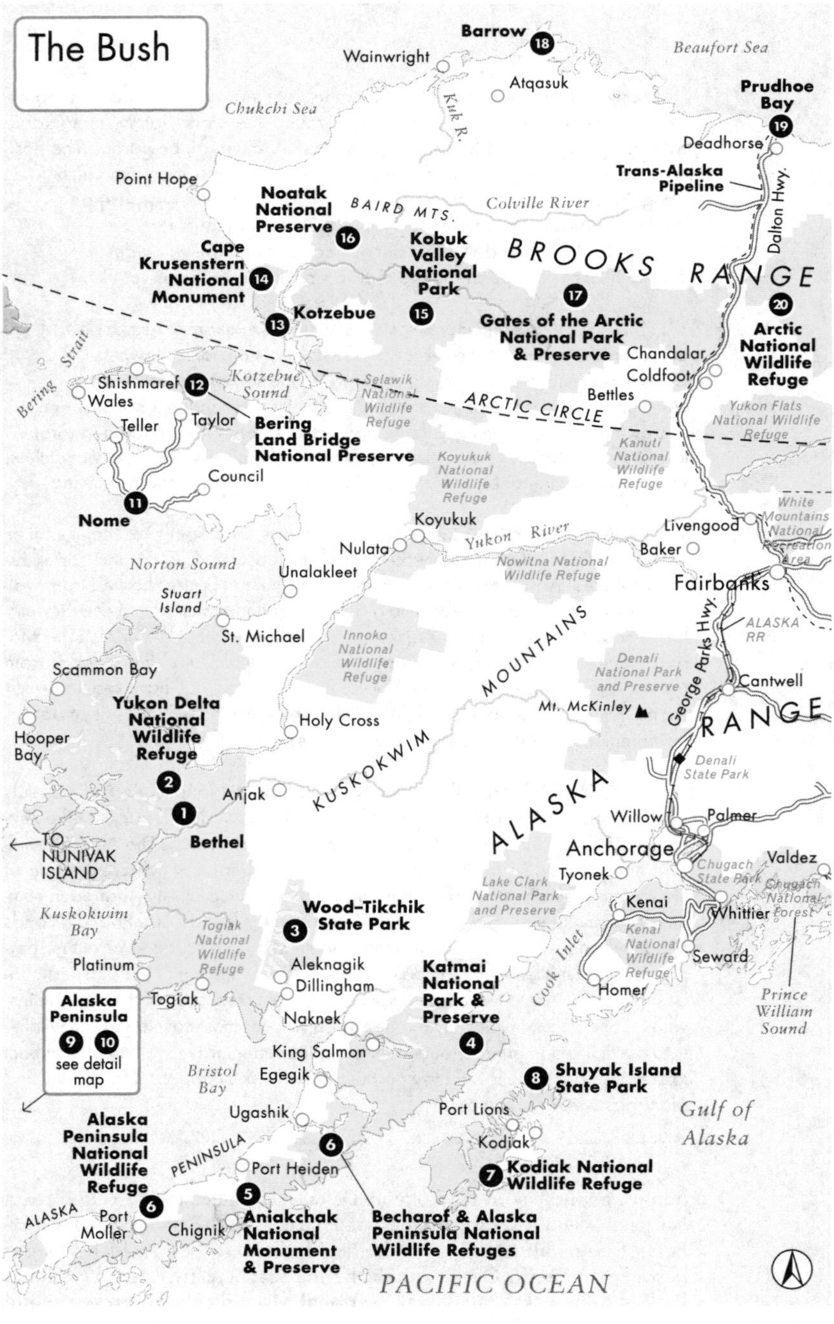
The Bush
Barrow
18
Beaufort Sea
Wainwright
Atqasuk
Kuk R.
Chukchi Sea
Prudhoe Bay
19
Deadhorse
Trans-Alaska Pipeline
Dalton Hwy.
Point Hope
Noatak National Preserve
16
BAIRD MTS.
Colville River
Cape Krusenstern National Monument
14
Kobuk Valley National Park
15
BROOKS RANGE
17
20
Kotzebue
13
Gates of the Arctic National Park & Preserve
Arctic National Wildlife Refuge
Bering Strait
Kotzebue Sound
Selawik National Wildlife Refuge
Chandalar
Coldfoot
Shishmaref
12
Wales
Bettles
ARCTIC CIRCLE
Teller
Taylor
Bering Land Bridge National Preserve
Yukon Flats National Wildlife Refuge
Kanuti National Wildlife Refuge
Koyukuk National Wildlife Refuge
Council
Nome
11
White Mountains National Recreation Area
Koyukuk
Livengood
Nulata
Yukon River
Baker
Norton Sound
Nowitna National Wildlife Refuge
Unalakleet
Fairbanks
Stuart Island
St. Michael
ALASKA RR
Innoko National Wildlife Refuge
MOUNTAINS
George Parks Hwy.
Denali National Park and Preserve
Scammon Bay
Cantwell
Yukon Delta National Wildlife Refuge
Mt. McKinley
RANGE
Hooper Bay
Holy Cross
KUSKOKWIM
Denali State Park
2
Anjak
ALASKA
1
Willow
Palmer
TO NUNIVAK ISLAND
Bethel
Anchorage
Valdez
Tyonek
Chugach State Park
Lake Clark National Park and Preserve
Chugach National Forest
Kuskokwim Bay
Wood-Tikchik State Park
3
Kenai
Whittier
Togiak National Wildlife Refuge
Kenai National Wildlife Refuge
Seward
Platinum
Aleknagik
Katmai National Park & Preserve
Cook Inlet
Dillingham
Homer
Prince William Sound
Alaska Peninsula
9
10
see detail map
Togiak
Naknek
4
King Salmon
Bristol Bay
Egegik
8
Shuyak Island State Park
Ugashik
Port Lions
Gulf of Alaska
Alaska Peninsula National Wildlife Refuge
6
Kodiak
PENINSULA
Port Heiden
7
Kodiak National Wildlife Refuge
5
ALASKA
Port Moller
6
Chignik
Aniakchak National Monument & Preserve
Becharof & Alaska Peninsula National Wildlife Refuges
PACIFIC OCEAN

the Becharof and Alaska Peninsula National Wildlife refuges. To the south of the Alaska Peninsula is the Kodiak Archipelago, where you'll find the Kodiak National Wildlife Refuge and Shuyak Island State Park; the Aleutian Islands start where the peninsula ends and sweep southwest toward Japan.

The Pribilof Islands lie north of the Aleutians, 200 mi off Alaska's coast. Head north along the Bering Sea coast and you come to Nome, just below the Arctic Circle. North of Nome is the Bering Land Bridge National Preserve. Kotzebue, just above the circle, is a coastal Eskimo town surrounded by sea and tundra and a jumping-off place for several parklands: Kobuk Valley, Noatak, Cape Krusenstern, and Gates of the Arctic (though the last is more easily reached from the town of Bettles). Barrow, another Eskimo community, sits at the very top of the state, the northernmost town in the United States. Follow the Arctic coastline eastward and you reach Deadhorse, on Prudhoe Bay, the custodian to the region's important oil and gas reserves. And east of Prudhoe Bay is the Arctic National Wildlife Refuge.

About the Restaurants

The dining options are few when traveling through Alaska's Bush; smaller communities may have only one or two eateries. Some have no restaurants at all, so be sure to check ahead of time. Restaurants are busiest during the summer peak season, from June through August, but in most cases, reservations are not needed. Many places serve Alaskan seafood and locally grown vegetables, but you can find Mexican and Asian fare even in Alaska's remotest corners—from Barrow in the far north to the Aleutian Island chain in the North Pacific.

About the Hotels

As with the restaurants, lodging choices in the Bush are few. Some communities have a single hotel; the smallest have none. Others have a mix of hotels and bed-and-breakfasts. As a rule, rooms are simply furnished, with few of the "extras" that you expect in urban hotels. You may have to share bathroom or kitchen facilities. Rooms go fast during the summer season, so be sure to book several months ahead. Seasoned Alaska travelers sometimes make reservations up to a year in advance.

WHAT IT COSTS

	$$$$	$$$	$$	$	¢
RESTAURANTS	over $25	$20–$25	$15–$20	$10–$15	under $10
HOTELS	over $225	$175–$225	$125–$175	$75–$125	under $75

Restaurant prices are for a main course at dinner. Hotel prices are for two people in a standard double room in high season, excluding service charges and tax.

Timing

The best time to visit is from June through August, when the weather is mildest (though you should still anticipate cool, wet, and sometimes stormy weather), daylight hours are longest, and the wildlife is most abundant.

SOUTHWEST

The Southwest region encompasses some of Alaska's most remote, inaccessible, and rugged land- and seascapes. Reaching from the Alaska Peninsula down through the Aleutian chain, it also includes many islands within the Bering Sea, among them the Pribilof Islands, as well as the Bristol Bay watershed, the Kodiak Archipelago, and the Yukon-Kuskokwim Delta. A place of enormous biological richness, it harbors many of North America's largest breeding populations of seabirds and waterfowl and also supports the world's densest population of brown bears and the world's greatest salmon runs. Given all this richness, it's no surprise to learn that Southwest Alaska has some of Alaska's premier parklands and refuges, from Katmai National Park to Aniakchak National Monument and the Kodiak National Wildlife Refuge. Here, too, are dozens of rural communities, most of them small, remote Native villages whose residents continue to engage in subsistence gathering.

Bethel

❶ *400 mi west of Anchorage.*

Spread out on the tundra along the Kuskokwim River, Bethel is a frontier town with about 6,400 residents, originally established by Moravian missionaries in the late 1800s. One of rural Alaska's most important trading centers, it is a hub for more than 50 Native villages in a region roughly the size of the state of Oregon. The surrounding lowland tundra is a rich green in summer and turns fiery shades of red, orange, and yellow in autumn, when plants burst with blueberries, cranberries, blackberries, and salmonberries. Salmon, arctic grayling, and Dolly Varden trout fill the area's many lakes, ponds, and streams, providing excellent fishing just a few miles outside town. The wetlands are also important breeding grounds for many varieties of birds.

The town is also the northernmost freshwater port for oceangoing vessels. Among its businesses are radio and television stations, a theater, credit union, auto repair shop, car-rental agency, beauty/barber shop, video/DVD rental store, newspaper, two colleges (including a newly founded tribal college), and the largest Alaska Native Health Service field hospital in the state, which is contracted to the tribally owned Yukon-Kuskokwim Health Corporation.

Each year, on the last weekend in March, Bethel hosts a regional celebration called the Camai Dance Festival (in Yup'ik, *camai* means "hello"). Held in the local high school's gym, which is filled to capacity for the three-day event, this festival draws dance groups from dozens of villages.

★ The **Yupiit Piciryarait (the People's way of living) Museum** emphasizes cultural education through Native elders, while also showcasing artifacts and artwork of three Native cultures: Dene Athabascan, Cup'ik, and Yup'ik. In its three galleries you'll find historic and prehistoric treasures: masks, statues, and carvings in ivory, baleen, and whalebone. Two permanent collections include past and present clothing styles plus numerous implements and tools used in traditional subsistence lifestyles. A small gift shop has locally made Native artwork for sale, including water-grass baskets, wooden spirit masks, ivory-handle knives, grass and reindeer-beard dance fans, yo-yos, dolls, and seal-gut raincoats. ✉ *Museum, 420 Eddie Hoffman Hwy.* ☎ *907/543–1819 or 800/478–3521* 🌐 *www.avcp.org* 🎫 *Free (donations requested)* ⏱ *Weekdays 1–5.*

Where to Stay & Eat

$–$$ ✕ **Shogun.** This rural café-style restaurant specializes in Chinese food, with daily lunch and dinner specials. It also serves Japanese and Italian dishes, plus American-style steaks and seafood. ✉ *320 Tundra Ave.* ☎ *907/543–2272* 💳 *MC, V.*

$$–$$$ 🏨 **Pacifica Guest House.** Three detached buildings make up this inn, which provides a quiet stay and Bush-savvy owners who provide insightful tips. Alaskan crafts and artwork adorn the modern rooms, some of which share a bath. Next door in a solarium, Diane's Café serves Alaska salmon, halibut, steaks, roasts, and a variety of vegetarian and heart-healthy meals. ✉ *1220 Hoffman Hwy.* 📫 *Box 1208, 99559* ☎ *907/543–4305* 📠 *907/543–3403 or 907/543–5715* *30 rooms, 14 with bath* *Restaurant, cable TV, library, meeting room; no a/c, no smoking* 💳 *AE, D, DC, MC, V.*

$–$$ 🏨 **Bentley's Porter House B&B.** Hospitality is never in short supply at this two-story B&B in downtown Bethel. Rooms are decorated according to theme, including African, Southwestern United States, and English countryside. Several overlook the Kuskokwim River. Besides those in the main inn, rooms are available in a nearby duplex and cottage. ✉ *624 1st Ave.* 📫 *Box 529, 99559* ☎ *907/543–3552* 📠 *907/543–3230* *35 rooms share 14 baths* *Cable TV, Internet, some pets allowed; no a/c, no smoking* 💳 *AE, D, DC, MC, V* *BP.*

off the beaten path

NUNIVAK ISLAND – Due west of Bethel, and separated from the Yukon-Kuskokwim Delta by Etolin Strait, Nunivak Island is an important wildlife refuge. Part of the **Yukon Delta National Wildlife Refuge,** this site is noted for its large herd of reindeer, a transplanted herd of musk ox, and the Eskimo settlement of Mekoryuk.

For information on the island, contact the **U.S. Fish and Wildlife Service** (☎ 907/543–3151 🌐 www.r7.fws.gov) in Bethel. Visitors, lured by fine ivory carvings, masks, and items knit from qiviut (musk-ox) wool, should check with **ERA Aviation** (☎ 800/866–8394 🌐 www.flyera.com) about accommodations, which are limited and far from deluxe.

Yukon Delta National Wildlife Refuge

❷ *Surrounds Bethel.*

At 20 million acres, Yukon Delta is the nation's largest wildlife refuge; nearly one-third of that acreage is water, in the form of lakes, sloughs, bogs, creeks, and rivers. The two most significant of these waters are the **Yukon** and **Kuskokwim** rivers, Alaska's two largest. As they flow toward the Bering Sea, these rivers carry huge amounts of sediment; over the millennia, the sediments have formed an immense delta that serves as critical breeding and rearing grounds for an estimated 100 million shorebirds and waterfowl. More than 100 species of birds nest here, traveling from nearly every state and province in North America and from all of the continents that border the Pacific Ocean. All of North America's cackling Canada geese and more than half the continent's population of black brant are born here. Other birds making the annual pilgrimage to the Yukon Delta refuge include emperor geese, tundra swans, gulls, jaegers, cranes, loons, snipe, sandpipers, and the rare bristle-thighed curlew.

Not all of the refuge is flat wetlands. North of the Yukon River are the Nulato Hills, site of the 1.3-million-acre **Andreafsky Wilderness area,** which includes both forks of the Andreafsky River, one of Alaska's specially designated Wild and Scenic Rivers. Rainbow trout, arctic char, and grayling flourish in upland rivers and creeks; pike, sheefish, and burbot thrive in lowland waters. These abundant waters are also spawning grounds to five species of Pacific salmon. Several species of mammals, ranging from black and grizzly bears to moose, beaver, mink, and arctic foxes, inhabit the refuge's lands. Occasionally, wolves venture into the delta's flats from neighboring uplands.

Given the abundance of fish and wildlife, it's not surprising that the delta holds special importance to residents of Bethel and other villages in the region. Yup'ik Eskimos have lived here for thousands of years; despite modern encroachment, the Eskimos continue their centuries-old subsistence lifestyle.

Recreation at the refuge includes observing wildlife, hiking, boating, and fishing. Access is by boat or aircraft only, and, as in most of Alaska's other remote wildlands, visitor facilities are minimal. Refuge staff can provide tips on recreational opportunities and guides and outfitters who operate in the refuge. ✉ *Box 346, Bethel 99559* ☎ *907/543–3151* 🌐 *www.r7.fws.gov.*

Wood-Tikchik State Park

★ ❸ *150 mi southeast of Bethel, 300 mi southwest of Anchorage.*

In the Bristol Bay region, Wood-Tikchik State Park—the nation's largest state park—is a water-based wildland despite its inland setting. Two separate groups of large, idyllic, interconnected lakes, some of which are up to 45 mi long, dominate the park. Besides the many large lakes and clear-water streams that fill its 1.55 million acres, the park's landscape includes rugged mountains, remnant glaciers, forested foothills, and vast expanses of lowland tundra. Everything from grizzlies and caribou to porcupines, eagles, and loons inhabits the park's forests and tundra, but Wood-Tikchik is best known for its fish. Its lakes and streams are critical spawning habitat for five species of Pacific salmon; they also support healthy populations of rainbow trout, arctic char, arctic grayling, and northern pike. The abundance of fish attracts anglers from around the world. Boaters, including rafters and kayakers, also come to explore its expansive and pristine waterways.

Managed as a wild area, Wood-Tikchik has no maintained trails and few other visitor amenities. Most of its campsites are primitive, and those who plan to explore the park should be experienced in backcountry travel and camping. Access is by either boat or air. *Mid-May–Sept.* *Box 3022, Dillingham 99576* *907/842–2375* *Oct.–mid-May* *550 W. 7th Ave., Suite 1380, Anchorage 99501* *907/269–8698* *www.alaskastateparks.org.*

You can also travel from Dillingham, the town closest to Wood-Tikchik, by boat or by air to view the walruses offshore on Round Island within **Walrus Islands State Game Sanctuary.** *Box 1030, Dillingham 99576-1030* *907/842–2334* *907/842–5514* *wildlife.alaska.gov/refuge/rnd-isl.cfm.*

Katmai National Park & Preserve

★ 4 *100 mi southeast of Wood-Tikchik, 290 mi southwest of Anchorage.*

For an extraordinary perspective on the awesome power of volcanoes, visit the 4-million-acre Katmai National Park & Preserve. In this wild, remote area at the northern end of the Alaska Peninsula, moose and almost 30 other species of mammals, including foxes, lynx, and wolves, share the landscape with bears fishing for salmon from stream banks, rivers, and along the coast. At the immensely popular **Brooks Falls and Camp,** you can see brown bears when the salmon are running in July. No special permits are required here, though there is a $10 day-use fee at Brooks. Ducks are common to see along the park's rivers, lakes, and outer coast, as are whistling swans, loons, grebes, gulls, and shorebirds. Bald eagles perch on rocky pinnacles by the sea. More than 40 species of songbirds alone can be seen during the short spring and summer season. Marine life abounds in the coastal area, with Steller's sea lions and hair seals often observed on rock outcroppings.

Compared with Denali National Park, Katmai is much more remote and its visitor facilities are fewer and more rustic (except for those able to afford to stay at wilderness lodges), but therein lies part of the park's appeal. The first visitors to the Katmai area arrived more than 4,000 years ago. Some evidence exists, in fact, that Native Alaskan people inhabited Katmai's eastern edge for at least 6,000 years. On the morning of June 1, 1912, a 2,700-foot mountain called **Novarupta** erupted. The earth shook in violent tremors for five straight days. When the quakes subsided, rivers of white-hot ash poured into the valley. A foot of ash fell on Kodiak Island, 100 mi away. Winds carried the ash to eastern Canada and as far as Texas. While Novarupta was belching pumice and scorching ash, another explosion occurred 6 mi east. The mountaintop peak of **Mt. Katmai** collapsed, creating a chasm almost 3 mi long and 2 mi wide. The molten andesite that held up Mt. Katmai had rushed through newly created fissures to Novarupta and was spewed out. Sixty hours after the first thunderous blast, more than 7 cubic mi of volcanic material had been ejected, and the green valley lay under 700 feet of ash. Everyone fled from Katmai and other villages; no one was killed.

By 1916 things had cooled off sufficiently to allow scientists to explore the area. A National Geographic expedition led by Dr. Robert F. Griggs reached the valley and found it full of steaming fumaroles, creating a moonlike landscape. The report on what Griggs dubbed the **Valley of Ten Thousand Smokes** inspired Congress in 1918 to declare the valley and the surrounding wilderness a national monument. Steam spouted in thousands of fountains from the smothered streams and springs beneath the ash and gave the valley its name. Although the steam has virtually stopped, an eerie sense of earth forces at work remains, and several nearby volcanoes still smolder.

The Native peoples never returned to their traditional village sites, though many now live in other nearby communities. They are joined by sightseers, anglers, hikers, and other outdoors enthusiasts who migrate to the Katmai region each summer. Fish and wildlife are plentiful, and a few "smokes" still drift through the volcano-sculpted valley.

No roads lead to the national park, at the base of the Alaska Peninsula. Planes wing from Anchorage along Cook Inlet, rimmed by the lofty, snowy peaks of the Alaska Range. They land at **King Salmon,** near fish-famous Bristol Bay, where passengers transfer to smaller floatplanes for the 20-minute hop to **Naknek Lake** and Brooks Camp. Travel to Brooks from King Salmon is also possible by boat. You are required to check into the park ranger station, next to Brooks Lodge, for a mandatory bear talk.

From Brooks Lodge, a daily tour bus with a naturalist aboard makes the 23-mi trip through the park to the **Valley Overlook.** Hikers can walk the 1½-mi trail for a closer look at the pumice-covered valley floor. (Some consider the return climb strenuous.)

The Katmai area is one of Alaska's premier sportfishing regions. It's possible to fish for rainbow trout and salmon at the **Brooks River,** though seasonal closures have been put in place to prevent conflicts with bears, and only fly-fishing is permitted. For those who would like to venture farther into the park, seek out the two other backcountry lodges, Grosvenor and Kulik, set in prime sportfishing territory, or contact fishing-guide services based in King Salmon. A short walk up the Brooks River brings you to Brooks Falls, where salmon can be seen from two viewing platforms, one at the falls and another a short way below it (an access trail and boardwalk are separated from the river to avoid confrontations with bears), as they leap a 6-foot-high cascade. *National Park Service, Box 7, King Salmon 99613* ☎ *907/246–3305* 🌐 *www.nps.gov/katm.*

Fodor's Choice ★

At the northern end of the Alaska Peninsula, 200 mi southwest of Anchorage, **McNeil River State Game Sanctuary** was established in 1967 to protect the world's largest gathering of brown bears. The main focus is **McNeil Falls,** where bears come to feed on chum salmon returning to spawn. During the peak of the chum run (July to mid-August) dozens of brown bears congregate at the falls. As many as 70 bears, including cubs, have been observed along the river in a single day. No more than 10 people a day, always accompanied by one or two state biologists, are allowed to visit bear-viewing sites from June 7 through August 25. Because demand is so high, an annual drawing is held in mid-March to determine permit winners. Applications must be received by March 1 to be eligible. Nearly all visitors fly into McNeil sanctuary on floatplanes. Most arrange for air-taxi flights out of Homer, on the Kenai Peninsula. Once you are in the sanctuary, all travel is on foot. ✉ *Alaska Department of Fish and Game, Division of Wildlife Conservation, 333 Raspberry Rd., Anchorage 99518-1599* ☎ *907/267–2182* 🌐 *www.wc.adfg.state.ak.us/mcneil.*

Where to Stay

All of the four lodges below are on inholdings within Katmai National Park. Three are inland, and Katmai Wilderness Lodge is on the remote outer coast.

6

$$$$ Fodor's Choice ★ **Brooks Lodge.** All the attractions of Katmai National Park are at this lodge's doorstep: fly-fishing for rainbow trout, lake trout, arctic grayling, and salmon; brown-bear viewing; and tours to the Valley of Ten Thousand Smokes. Accommodations are in detached modern cabins adorned with Alaskan artwork; they accommodate two to four people. All cabins have heat, electricity, and private toilet facilities. The cabins surround the main lodge, which has a spectacular view of aquamarine Naknek Lake; it has a circular stone fireplace and dining area where buffet-style meals are served three times daily. Price includes airfare from Anchorage. ✉ *Katmailand, 4125 Aircraft Dr., Anchorage 99502* ☎ *907/243–5448 or 800/544–0551* 🖷 *907/243–0649* 🌐 *www.katmainationalpark.com* *16 cabins* *Dining room, lake, boating, fishing, hiking, bar; no a/c, no room phones, no room TVs* *MC, V* *Closed mid-Sept.–May.*

$$$$ **Grosvenor Lodge.** Once you've arrived at this remote Katmai National Park lodge, reachable only by floatplane, you have access by motorboat to numerous rivers and streams filled with sport fish. The lodge can accommodate six people in three cabins; heated, with electricity, they share a separate bathhouse. The main lodge houses a kitchen, lounging area, and bar and has an excellent view of Grosvenor Lake. Three-, four-, and seven-night price packages include airfare from Anchorage, meals, lodging, and guiding. ✉ *Katmailand, 4125 Aircraft Dr., Anchorage 99502* ☎ *907/243–5448 or 800/544–0551* 🖷 *907/243–0649* 🌐 *www.katmailand.com* *3 cabins with shared baths* *Dining room, lake, boating, fishing, bar, travel services; no a/c, no room phones, no room TVs* *MC, V* *Closed Oct.–May* *FAP.*

★ $$$$ **Katmai Wilderness Lodge.** Built on land owned by the Russian Orthodox Church, this rustic lodge straddles the rugged outer coast of Katmai National Park, along the shores of Kukak Bay. Mountains, coastal flats, and the waters of Shelikof Strait surround the modern log cabin–style lodge, where guests stay in private bedrooms with baths and gather to eat gourmet meals in the dining room or, if the weather is right, on outdoor decks. Recreational activities include bear viewing, sea kayaking, and fishing for halibut and salmon. You may stay from three nights to a week or more. Price includes a round-trip flight from Kodiak, meals, lodging, and guide services. *Box 4332, Kodiak 99615* ☎ *800/488–8767* 🖷 *907/486–6798* 🌐 *www.katmaiwilderness.com* *7 rooms* *Dining room, boating, fishing, travel services; no a/c, no room phones, no room TVs* *No credit cards* *Closed Oct.–mid-May* *FAP.*

$$$$ **Kulik Lodge.** Positioned along the gin-clear Kulik River, between Nonvianuk and Kulik lakes, this remote wilderness lodge is reachable only by floatplane. It accommodates up to 28 anglers and is popular as a base for fly-out fishing to hot spots in the surrounding Katmai wilderness. Guests stay in two- or four-person cabins with electricity and private baths. In the evening, when fishing's done for the day, you gather in the spruce lodge, which has a large stone fireplace, dining area, and bar. Three-, four-, or seven-night packages include airfare from Anchorage, meals, lodging, and guiding. ✉ *Katmailand, 4125 Aircraft Dr., Anchorage 99502* ☎ *907/243–5448 or 800/544–0551* 🖷 *907/243–0649* 🌐 *www.kuliklodge.com* *12 cabins* *Dining room, lake, boating, fishing, bar, travel services; no a/c, no room phones, no room TVs* *MC, V* *Closed mid-Oct.–May* *FAP.*

¢ **Brooks Campground.** This National Park Service campground is a short walk from Brooks Lodge, where campers can pay to eat and shower. Designated cooking and eating shelters, latrines, well water, and a storage cache to protect food from the ever-present brown bears are available. Reservations are required. *Portable toilets, drinking water, bear boxes, picnic tables, ranger station.* *60 sites* *Katmai National Park, Box 7, King Salmon 99613* ☎ *907/246–3305, 800/365–2267 reservations* 🌐 *www.nps.gov/katm* *D, MC, V* *Closed mid-Sept.–May.*

Guided Tours

Katmai Air Services (☎ 907/246–3079 in King Salmon summer only, 800/544–0551 in Anchorage 🌐 www.katmailand.com) can arrange flightseeing tours of the park. **Katmailand** (✉ 4125 Aircraft Dr., Anchorage 99502 ☎ 907/243–5448 or 800/544–0551 🖷 907/243–0649 🌐 www.katmailand.com) assembles packages to Katmai National Park.

Aniakchak National Monument & Preserve

5 *100 mi southwest of Katmai National Park.*

Aniakchak, an extraordinary living volcano, rises to the south of Katmai. It has one of the largest calderas in the world, with a diameter averaging 6 mi across, and the small **Surprise Lake** is contained within it. Although Aniakchak last erupted in 1931, the explosion that formed the enormous crater occurred before history was written. Because the area is not glaciated, geologists place the blowup after the last Ice Age. It was literally a world-shaking event. To mark the volcano's significance, Congress established the 586,000-acre Aniakchak National Monument and Preserve in 1980.

This is wild and forbidding country, with a climate that brews mist, clouds, and winds of great force much of the year. Although the **Aniakchak River** (which drains Surprise Lake) is floatable, it has stretches of Class III and IV white water navigable only by expert river runners, and you must travel through open ocean waters to reach the nearest community, Chignik Bay (or get picked up by plane, along the coast); this makes the run an ambitious undertaking. An alternate way to enjoy Aniakchak is to wait for a clear day and fly to it in a small plane that will land you on the caldera floor or on Surprise Lake. However you choose to see it, it's an unforgettable experience. But be aware that there are no trails, campgrounds, ranger stations, or other visitor facilities here; you must be prepared to be self-sufficient.

Aniakchak is remote and expensive to reach. The only easy access is by air, usually from the town of King Salmon. Thus, few people visit this spectacular place—and those who do are likely to have the caldera all to themselves. *Aniakchak National Monument and Preserve, Box 7, King Salmon 99613 907/246–3305 www.nps.gov/ania.*

Becharof & Alaska Peninsula National Wildlife Refuges

★ 6 *Adjacent to Aniakchak National Monument and Preserve, 250 to 450 mi southwest of Anchorage.*

Stretching along the southern edge of the Alaska Peninsula, these two refuges encompass nearly 6 million acres of towering mountains, glacial lakes, broad tundra valleys, and coastal fjords. Volcanoes dominate the landscape—14 in all, of which 9 are considered active. **Mt. Veniaminov** last erupted in 1993. Other glimpses of volcanic activity include **Gas Rocks,** where gases continually seep through cracks in granitic rocks, and **Ukrinek Marrs,** a crater that bears the marks of a violent eruption in 1977.

Aside from their rugged volcanic landscapes, these two refuges are best known for abundant wildlife. More than 220 species of resident and migratory wildlife seasonally inhabit the region, including 30 land and 11 marine mammals, nearly 150 varieties of birds, and 35 species of fish. Caribou, wolves, and moose roam the region's tundra; sea lions, seals, seabirds, and waterfowl thrive along the rocky shores; bald eagles and falcons nest on craggy cliffs above the coast. You'll find brown bears nearly everywhere, from coastal lowlands to high mountain ridges.

Becharof Lake, at 35 mi long and up to 15 mi wide, is the second-largest lake in Alaska (behind Lake Iliamna). Fed by two rivers and 14 major creeks, it serves as a nursery to the world's second-biggest run of salmon. **Ugashik Lakes** are known for their salmon and trophy grayling. The world-record grayling, nearly 5 pounds (most grayling weigh a pound or less), was caught at Ugashik Narrows in 1981.

Remote and rugged, with weather that is frequently stormy, the Becharof and Alaska Peninsula refuges draw mostly anglers and hunters; however, backpackers, river runners, and mountain climbers also occasionally visit. No visitor facilities are available here, and access is only by boat or plane. Most visitors begin their trips in King Salmon and use guides or outfitters. *Box 277, King Salmon 99613 907/246–3339 www.r7.fws.gov.*

Kodiak National Wildlife Refuge

7 *50 mi south of Katmai National Park, 300 mi southwest of Anchorage.*

The 1.9-million-acre Kodiak National Wildlife Refuge lies mostly on Kodiak Island and partly on neighboring Afognak and Uganik islands, in the Gulf of Alaska. All are part of the Kodiak Archipelago, separated from Alaska's mainland by the often stormy Shelikof Strait. Within the refuge are rugged mountains, tundra meadows and lowlands, thickly forested hills, lakes, marshes, and hundreds of miles of pristine coastland. No place in the refuge is more than 15 mi from the ocean. The weather here is generally wet and cool, and storms born in the North Pacific often bring heavy rains.

Dozens of species of birds inhabit the refuge each spring and summer, including Aleutian terns, horned puffins, black oystercatchers, ravens, ptarmigan, and chickadees. At least 200 pairs of bald eagles live on the islands year-round, nesting on shoreline cliffs and in tall trees. Seeing the Kodiak brown bears alone is worth the trip to this rugged country. The world's largest carnivores (along with polar bears), Kodiak brown bears weigh only 1 pound at birth, but up to 1,500 pounds when full grown. When they emerge from their dens in spring, the bears feed on sedges and grasses, become fish eaters when salmon return in early summer, and depend heavily on Kodiak's berries in fall. Kodiak brown bears share the refuge with only a few other land mammals native to the archipelago: red fox, river otter, short-tailed weasel, and tundra vole.

All five species of Pacific salmon—chums, kings, pinks, silvers, and sockeyes—return to Kodiak's waters each year in a series of runs that begin in May and last into October. Other resident species include rainbow trout, steelhead, Dolly Varden, and arctic char. The abundance of fish and bears makes the refuge popular with anglers, hunters, and wildlife watchers. Access is only by boat or plane. Refuge staff will provide lists of guides, outfitters, and air taxis. ✉ *1390 Buskin River Rd., Kodiak 99615* ☎ *907/487–2600* 🌐 *www.r7.fws.gov.*

Where to Stay

¢ **Kodiak Refuge Public-Use Cabins.** It's possible to rent one of seven recreation cabins (accessible by floatplane or boat) within the refuge for up to seven days (longer in the off-season). Set along the coast and on inland lakes, the cabins include bunks with mattresses, kerosene heaters, tables, and benches. Reservations are awarded through quarterly lotteries, held on the first of January, April, July, and October. The cabins on inland lakes are usually not accessible in winter. ✉ *1390 Buskin River Rd., Kodiak 99615* ☎ *907/487–2600* 🌐 *www.r7.fws.gov or kodiak.fws.gov* *7 cabins* *Reservations essential* *No credit cards.*

Shuyak Island State Park

8 *50 mi north of Kodiak Island.*

The 46,000-acre Shuyak Island State Park is one of the newest (and most overlooked) units in the state parks system. The park, at the northern end of the Kodiak Archipelago, is accessible only by plane or boat. Its rugged outer coastline is balanced by a more protected system of interconnected bays, channels, and passages that make the park a favorite with sea kayakers. It also has excellent wildlife viewing, especially for seabirds and sea mammals, and top-notch sportfishing for salmon. Wildlife ranges from Sitka black-tailed deer and brown bears to sea otters, sea lions, bald eagles, puffins, and whales. The park has four public-use cabins but no developed campgrounds; limited hiking trails pass through old-growth coastal rain forest. ✉ *Alaska State Parks, Kodiak District Office, 1400 Abercrombie Dr., Kodiak 99615* ☎ *907/486–6339* 🌐 *www.alaskastateparks.org.*

Where to Stay

¢ **Alaska State Parks Cabins.** Alaska State Parks maintains four recreational public-use cabins on Shuyak Island. All are accessible by boat or plane only. The cabins may be rented for up to seven days and hold up to eight people. Each has a woodstove, propane lights, hot plate, four bunks, outside shower and wash area, cooking utensils, and pit toilets. You can make reservations up to six months in advance. ✉ *Alaska State Parks, Kodiak District Office, 1400 Abercrombie Dr., Kodiak 99615* ☎ *907/486–6339, 907/269–8400 DNR* 📠 *907/486–3320* *DNR Public Information Center, 550 W. 7th Ave., Suite 1260, Anchorage 99501* 🌐 *www.alaskastateparks.org* *4 cabins* 💳 *MC, V.*

¢ **Alaska State Parks Campgrounds.** The state has three road-accessible campgrounds (Ft. Abercrombie, Buskin River, and Pasagshak) on Kodiak Island, with a total of 48 tent sites. All have toilets, drinking water, and fishing, and two have nearby hiking trails. Camping at Pasagshak is free; the campgrounds at Fort Abercrombie and Buskin River charge $10 a night. Camping limits are 15 consecutive nights at Buskin River and Pasagshak, 7 nights at Fort Abercrombie. *Portable toilets, drinking water, bear boxes, picnic tables or shelters.* *48 tent sites* ✉ *Alaska State Parks, Kodiak District Office, 1400 Abercrombie Dr., Kodiak 99615* ☎ *907/486–6339* 📠 *907/486–3320* *Reservations not accepted* 💳 *No credit cards.*

Sports & the Outdoors

KAYAKING Contact Alaska State Parks in Kodiak for the names of companies leading guided trips in Shuyak State Park.

Aleutian Islands

The Aleutians begin 540 mi southwest of Anchorage and stretch more than 1,000 mi.

Separating the North Pacific Ocean from the Bering Sea, the Aleutian Islands (also called the Chain) stretch from the Alaska Peninsula in a southwesterly arc toward Japan. The distance from the point nearest the Alaska mainland, Unimak Island, to the most distant island, Attu, is more than 1,000 mi. This volcanic, treeless archipelago consists of about 20 large islands and several hundred smaller ones. The Aleutian Islands and surrounding coastal waters make up one of the most biologically rich areas in Alaska, harboring abundant seabird, marine mammal, and fish populations.

Before the Russians arrived in the mid 1700's, the islands were dotted with Aleut villages. Today's communities include **Nikolski,** on Umnak Island; **Unalaska,** on Unalaska Island; **Atka,** on Atka Island; and **Cold Bay,** at the peninsula's tip. The hardy Aleuts work at commercial fishing or in canneries and as expert guides for those who hunt and fish. The settlements are quite small, and accommodations are scarce.

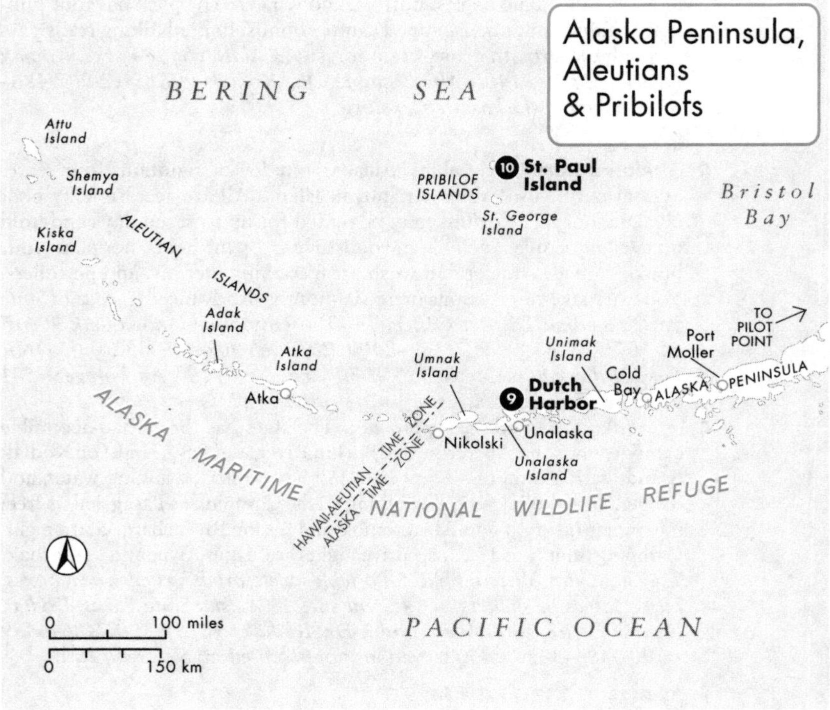

You are not allowed to visit Shemya Island, which has a remote U.S. Air Force base, without special permission. Because of downsizing, the military has closed its Adak operation, and the base's infrastructure provides the core infrastructure for what now is a small coastal community and commercial fishing port.

9 **Dutch Harbor,** on Unalaska Island, is by far the most populous destination in the Aleutian Islands. Traditionally a fishing port, it is also the region's tourism center. The Japanese bombed Dutch Harbor during World War II, and you can still see concrete bunkers, gun batteries, and a partially sunken ship left over from the war. In addition to historic military sites, you'll find a hotel and restaurants that rival those on Alaska's mainland, and guided adventure tours.

Where to Stay & Eat

★ $$$ **Grand Aleutian Hotel.** An airy three-story atrium lobby with a large stone fireplace conjures images of a Swiss chalet. Rooms have views of either Margaret Bay or Unalaska Bay. Each lushly carpeted, brightly lighted room is decorated with Alaskan artwork and is equipped with full bath, built-in hair dryer, extra vanity and sink, and in-room coffeemaker. The Chart Room Restaurant and Lounge ($$–$$$$) specializes in Pacific Rim cuisine with locally caught seafood and features a seafood buffet every

Wednesday night, year-round. Barbecues are scheduled on Friday nights in summer, on the deck overlooking Margaret Bay. Guided activities include bird-watching, cultural tours, archaeological digs, marine wildlife tours, photography, and halibut and salmon fishing. ✉ *498 Salmon Way* *Box 921169, Dutch Harbor 99692-1169* ☎ *907/581–3844 or 866/581–3844* *907/581–7150* 🌐 *www.grandaleutian.com* *112 rooms, 2 suites* *2 restaurants, cable TV, fishing, bar, Internet, meeting rooms, airport shuttle, travel services, some pets allowed, no-smoking rooms; no a/c* *AE, D, DC, MC, V.*

$ **Grand Aleutian Hotel and Unisea Inn.** For travelers on a budget, this hotel on the water has clean, spartan rooms; try to book a room with a view of the small-boat harbor. Pizza, burgers, and sandwiches are served in the Unisea Inn Sports Bar and Grill ($–$$). Sit back and watch satellite broadcasts of spectator sports or try your hand at darts, pool, or video games. Local bands play Top 40 or country music. ✉ *185 Gilman Rd.* *Box 921169, Dutch Harbor 99692* ☎ *907/581–1325, 866/581–3844 reservations* *907/581–1633* *25 rooms* *Restaurant, cable TV, hair salon, sports bar, Internet, airport shuttle, travel services, no-smoking rooms; no a/c* *AE, D, DC, MC, V.*

Pribilof Islands

200 mi north of the Aleutian Islands, 800 mi southwest of Anchorage.

The Pribilof Islands are misty, fog-bound breeding grounds of seabirds and northern fur seals. Five islets make up the Pribilof group, a tiny, green, treeless oasis with rippling belts of lush grass contrasting with red volcanic soil. In early summer seals come home from far Pacific waters to mate, and the larger islands, St. Paul and St. George, are overwhelmed with scenes of frenzied activity. The seals' barks and growls can roll out several miles to sea.

The islands are a 1,600-mi round-trip from Anchorage, over the massive snowy peaks of the Alaska Peninsula and past the rocky islands of the Aleutian chain. This was the supply route for U.S. forces during World War II, when Japan invaded Attu and Kiska islands toward the tip of the chain. During the Bering Sea leg of the flight, a playful pod of whales may be lurking below.

Wildlife watching is what brings nearly all visitors to the Pribilof Islands. Together, St. Paul and St. George islands are seasonal homes to nearly 1 million fur seals (about 80% of them on St. Paul) and 200 species of birds. Some birds migrate here from as far away as Argentina, whereas others are year-round residents. Of special interest to birders are the rare vagrant birds of native Asian species, such as the Siberian Rubythroat and Eurasian Skylark, sometimes blown here by strong western winds. Most spectacular of all is the islands' seabird population: each summer more than 2 million seabirds gather at traditional Pribilof nesting grounds; about 90% of them breed on St. George. The Pribilofs are also home to foxes, and sea lions and whales are occasionally spotted off their shores.

For most travelers, it is much easier and more cost-efficient to participate in package tours that arrange air travel from Anchorage, lodging, ground transportation on the islands, and guided activities. If you are planning to visit here, be aware that guest accommodations in the Pribilofs are very limited.

10 Fodor's Choice ★ At **St. Paul Island,** nature lovers can watch members of the largest northern fur-seal herd in the world and more than 180 varieties of birds. In town, you can visit with local residents; about 500 descendants of Aleut-Russians live here now, in the shadow of the old Russian Orthodox church and the vestiges of Aleut culture. **St. George Island** is home to nearly 2 million nesting seabirds, but it is much less frequently visited, because no organized tours go there and accommodations are limited.

Where to Stay & Eat

$$ **Trident Sea Foods.** This cafeteria-style eatery—the island's only restaurant—serves fish processors as well as visitors to St. Paul Island. Plan your day carefully, because meals are served according to a strict schedule: breakfast 5–6:30, lunch noon–1, and dinner 5–6. *Downtown St. Paul, 2 blocks from King Eider Hotel 907/546–2377 No credit cards.*

$$$$ **King Eider Hotel.** More functional than luxurious, this rustic three-story clapboard hotel is filled in summer by tour groups. The original part of this historic landmark dates to the late 1800s; it's been expanded four times since. The hotel has simply furnished rooms, a TV room, reading lounge, and gift shop. If you are traveling on your own, make reservations months in advance. *523 Tolstoi St. Box 88, St. Paul 99660 907/546–2477 or 907/278–2312, or 877/424–5637 to make tour reservations 907/546–5026 www.alaskabirding.com 26 rooms, 5 shared baths Travel services; no a/c, no room phones, no room TVs, no smoking AE, MC, V.*

$$$ **St. George Tanaq Hotel.** A national historic landmark, St. George Island's only hotel is a small, rustic building with a dark-wood interior and a mix of modern and vintage furniture. Originally built by the government to house visiting officials, the hotel can accommodate up to 18 guests and is within easy walking distance of fur-seal rookeries. Rooms are sparsely furnished with shared baths. The hotel's shared kitchen includes a stove, a refrigerator, and cooking utensils—necessary, since the island has no restaurant. *Downtown Box 939, St. George 99591 907/272–9886 or 907/859–2255 907/859–2230 www.stgeorgetanaq.com 10 rooms share 4 baths Dining room, cable TV; no a/c, no smoking MC, V.*

Guided Tours

Contact **Tanadgusix Village Corporation of St. Paul Island** (4300 B St., Suite 402, Anchorage 99503 907/278–2312 or 877/424–5637 www.alaskabirding.com) for St. Paul Island tour information.

NORTHWEST & THE ARCTIC

This is a largely roadless region of long, dark, sunless winters and short, bright summers, when the sun provides nearly three months of perpetual daylight in places like Barrow, but only shines for one or two days on points much farther south, just north of the Arctic Circle. It's the land of Eskimos and huge caribou herds and polar bears, a place where people still lead subsistence lifestyles and where Native cultural traditions are making a strong comeback. It's also a place of gold rushes past and America's largest oil field as well as a region with many of Alaska's wildest and most remote parklands and one of the country's grandest refuges, the Arctic National Wildlife Refuge.

Nome

11 *540 mi northwest of Anchorage.*

More than a century has passed since a great stampede for gold put a speck of wilderness now called Nome on the Alaska map, but gold mining and noisy saloons are still mainstays in this frontier community of 3,700 people on the icy Bering Sea. Mainly a collection of ramshackle houses and low-slung commercial buildings, Nome looks like a vintage gold-mining camp or the neglected set of a western movie—rawboned, rugged, and somewhat shabby. Cheerful hospitality and colorful history balance the town's somewhat unkempt appearance.

Only 165 mi from the coast of Siberia, Nome is considerably closer to Russia than to either Anchorage or Fairbanks. And though you'll find a local road system, to get to Nome you must either fly or mush a team of sled dogs.

For centuries before Nome gained fame as a gold-boom town, Inupiat Eskimos seasonally inhabited the area in hunting and fishing camps. The Inupiat traditionally led a nomadic lifestyle, moving with the seasons, so no permanent settlement was established at the site until gold was found by white Euro-American prospectors in the late 1890s, though Christian missionaries had introduced church missions to the region earlier in the century.

Nome's golden years began in 1898, when three prospectors—known as the Lucky Swedes—struck rich deposits on Anvil Creek, about 4 mi from what became Nome. Their discovery was followed by the formation of the Cape Nome Mining District. The following summer, even more gold was found on the beaches of Nome. Word spread quickly to the south, and when the Bering Sea ice parted the next spring, ships from Puget Sound (near Seattle) arrived in Nome with eager stampeders. An estimated 15,000 people landed in Nome between June and October of 1900, bringing the area's population to more than 20,000. Dozens of gold dredges were hauled into the region to extract the metal from Seward Peninsula sands and gravels; more than 40 are still standing, though most are no longer operable. Among the gold-rush luminaries were Wyatt Earp, the old gunfighter from the O.K. Corral, who mined the gold of Nome by opening a posh saloon; Tex Rickard, the boxing promoter, who operated another Nome saloon; and Rex Beach, the novelist.

The city of Nome was incorporated in 1901, making it Alaska's oldest first-class city, with the oldest continuous school district. The community's heyday lasted only two decades; by the early 1920s the bulk of the region's gold had been mined and only 820 or so people continued to live in Nome. Though the city's boom times ended long ago, gold mining has continued to the present, though nowadays the existing operations are small ones. Visitors are welcome to try their own luck; they can pick up a gold pan at one of Nome's stores and sift through the beach sands along a 2-mi stretch of shoreline east of Nome. Visitors can also contact the **Nome Convention and Visitors Bureau** (see below) for information on tours that feature gold panning.

Besides being known for its gold-mining origins, Nome's fame is closely tied to the **historic Iditarod Trail.** Some portions of that route were used for centuries by Eskimos and Athabascan Indians residing in Alaska's northwest region. But the Iditarod Trail's heyday was during the Territory's gold-rush era, from the late 1800s through the mid-1920s. Primarily a winter pathway, the trail acted as a transportation and communication corridor that connected mining camps and other settlements that were built during the gold rush. Actually a network of trails, the Iditarod (derived from the Athabascan Indian word *haiditarod,* meaning "a far, distant place") began at the ice-free port of Seward and ended at Nome. Including all its branches, the entire system measured more than 2,000 mi. Through the 1920s, thousands of people traveled the Iditarod Trail; most drove dog teams, but some rode on horse-drawn sleds. Others walked, snowshoed, or even bicycled, usually because they couldn't afford to own or rent a dog team.

Though Nome today is most closely associated with the Iditarod Trail Sled Dog Race, in the early 1900s it was also the site of Alaska's first organized mushing event, the All-Alaska Sweepstakes. From 1908 through 1917, the Nome Kennel Club annually staged a 408-mi sled dog race from Nome to Candle and back. The race established the reputations of several early-20th-century mushers, including three-time winners Scotty Allan and Leonhard Seppala. Seppala, a Norwegian, would race dogs over a career that spanned 45 years; he would also be a heroic figure in the 1925 "Great Race of Mercy," in which a relay of mushers and their dog teams transported diphtheria anti-toxin serum to Nome to stop what could have been a disastrous outbreak of the disease, then commonly known as the "black death." The 1925 serum run is annually celebrated as part of the Iditarod race.

Besides its gold-discovering founders and famous mushers, Nome is also proud to be the hometown of General James H. Doolittle, the Tokyo raider of World War II. When Doolittle's bombers hit Japan in a daring raid in 1942, the headline in the *Nome Nugget* proudly announced: "NOME TOWN BOY MAKES GOOD!"

A network of 250 mi or so of gravel roads around the town leads to creeks and rivers for gold panning or fishing for trout, salmon, and arctic grayling. You can also see reindeer, bears, foxes, and moose in the wild on the back roads that once connected early mining camps and hamlets. Independent travelers with hardy vehicles should go exploring. **Alaska Cab Garage** (☎ 907/443–2335 or 907/443–2939) rents pickup trucks, suburbans, minibuses, and vans, both two- and four-wheel drive. **Stampede Car Rentals** (☎ 907/443–3838 or 800/354–4606 🌐 www.

aurorainnome.com) rents vans, pickup trucks, and SUVs. Since the sun stays up late in the summer months, drive to the top of **Anvil Mountain,** near Nome, for a panoramic view of the old gold town and the Bering Sea. Be sure to carry mosquito repellent.

For exploring downtown, stop at the **Nome Convention and Visitors Bureau** (✉ 301 Front St. ☎ 907/443–6624, 800/478–1901 in Alaska 📠 907/443–5832 🌐 www.nomealaska.org/vc) for a historic-walking-tour map, a city map, and information on local activities from flightseeing to bird-watching.

Nome's only museum, the **Carrie M. McClain Memorial Museum** showcases the history of the Nome gold rush, from the "Lucky Swedes' " discovery in 1898 to Wyatt Earp's arrival in 1899 and the stampede of thousands of people into Nome in 1900. The museum also has exhibits on the lifestyles and art of the Bering Strait Inupiat Eskimos, plus historic photos and stories about the Nome Kennel Club and its All-Alaska Sweepstakes of the early 1900s. ✉ *223 Front St.* ☎ *907/443–6630* 📠 *907/443–7955* 🎟 *Free.* 🕓 *June–early Sept., daily 9–5:30; early Sept.–May, Tues.–Fri. noon–6.*

Where to Stay & Eat

★ $–$$$ ✕ **Fat Freddie's.** This popular café-style eatery overlooking the Bering Sea serves New York steak and prime rib, plus its notable burgers and seafood. During the Iditarod, many mushers hang out here after completing their grueling trips across Alaska. If you're staying at the Nome Nugget Inn, you can enter directly from the hotel. ✉ *50 Front St.* ☎ *907/443–5899* 💳 *AE, D, MC, V.*

$–$$$ ✕ **Polar Cub.** American diner food, from omelets to steak, fills the menu here. Locals like to linger over coffee, making it a good place to eavesdrop on residents discussing area issues, or just to gaze out at the Bering Sea. With its sea views, good prices, and friendly service, the Cub is a great place for early-morning breakfast. ✉ *Next to seawall, off Front St., Downtown* ☎ *907/443–5191* 💳 *AE, MC, V.*

$$$$ 🏨 **John Elmore's Grayling on a Fly.** At the site of an early 1900s gold-mining camp, this lodge sits along the clear-water Niukluk River, about 75 mi northeast of Nome. You can fish for arctic char, grayling, and four species of salmon; other outdoor activities include bird-watching and wildlife photography. Packages include transportation between the lodge and Nome. There is a three-night minimum. *In summer:* 📫 *Box 1045, Nome 99762* 📫 *In winter:* ✉ *12110 Woodward Dr., Anchorage 99516* ☎📠 *907/522–6663* 🌐 *www.grayling-on-a-fly.com* 🛏 *3 rooms* 👍 *Dining room, fishing; no a/c, no room phones, no room TVs* 💳 *No credit cards* 🕓 *Closed Oct.–May.*

$$ 🏨 **Nome Nugget Inn.** The architecture and decor of the Nugget Inn combine every cliché of the Victorian gold-rush era. Authentic it's not, but fun it is. Outside, a signpost marks the mileage to various points, serious and silly, around the globe. Inside, frontier memorabilia abounds in the lobby and lounge. Rooms are small and clean but not nearly as atmospheric. Arctic tour groups stay here. Fat Freddie's restaurant is conveniently attached to the hotel. ✉ *Front St.* 📫 *Box 1470, 99762*

907/443–4189 or 877/443–2323 907/443–5966 www.nomenuggetinn.com 47 rooms Restaurant, cable TV, bar, Internet, laundry service, some pets allowed, no-smoking rooms; no a/c AE, MC, V.

¢ **Bureau of Land Management Campground.** BLM manages a free campground at Mile 40 of the Nome-Taylor Highway. The campground, which is a short walk from the highway, has six tent sites, toilet facilities, and nearby fishing. The maximum length of stay is 14 days. The campground has a pit toilet and fire rings for cooking, but the only water is in nearby Salmon Lake and Pilgrim River; it must be boiled or otherwise treated. *Portable toilets, fire pits, swimming (lake), fishing 6 tent sites Bureau of Land Management, Nome Field Office, Box 925, 99762 907/443–2177 in Nome, 907/474–2231 in Anchorage, 800/478–1263 aurora.ak.blm.gov Reservations not accepted No credit cards Closed Oct.–Apr.*

Sports & the Outdoors

The famed 1,049-mi **Iditarod Trail Sled Dog Race**—the Olympics of sled-dog racing—reaches its culmination in Nome in mid-March. Racers start in Anchorage for a trip of nine days to two weeks. The arrival of the mushers heralds a winter carnival. For dates, starting times, and other information, contact the **Iditarod Trail Committee** (Box 870800, Wasilla 99687 907/376–5155 www.iditarod.com).

Shopping

Nome is one of the best places to buy ivory, because many of the Eskimo carvers from outlying villages come to Nome first to sell their wares to dealers. The **Arctic Trading Post** (Bering and Front Sts. 907/443–2686) has an extensive stock of authentic Eskimo ivory carvings and other Alaskan artwork, jewelry, and books. The **Board of Trade Ivory Shop** (907/443–2611) on Front Street specializes in ivory carvings but also sells Native Alaskan artwork and handicrafts. **Chukotka–Alaska** (514 Lomen 907/443–4128) sells both Native Alaskan and Russian artwork and handicrafts as well as books, beads, and furs.

Guided Tours

Visitors seeking to learn more about Nome and the surrounding region can join former Broadway showman Richard Beneville, who emphasizes Nome's gold rush and Inupiat history of the region in his **Nome Discovery Tours** (Box 2024, Nome 99762 907/443–2814).

Bering Land Bridge National Preserve

12 *100 mi north of Nome.*

The frozen ash and lava of the 2.8-million-acre Bering Land Bridge National Preserve lie between Nome and Kotzebue, immediately south of the Arctic Circle. The Imuruk lava flow is the northernmost flow of major size in the United States, and the paired *maars* (clear volcanic lakes) are a geological rarity.

Of equal interest are the paleontological features of this preserve. Sealed into the permafrost are flora and fauna—bits of twigs and leaves, tiny

VISITING IN WINTER

ALTHOUGH MANY PEOPLE THINK VISITING ALASKA IN THE WINTER IS INSANE, *there are plenty of good reasons for doing so. It just takes a bit of attitude adjustment, an adventurous spirit, and proper clothing. The advantages and opportunities for adventure are manifold.*

The northern lights *(aurora borealis) are active all year long, but it has to get dark before you can enjoy them. On a clear night, away from city lights, these shimmering curtains of color in the sky are absolutely breathtaking. Weather and solar activity have to cooperate in order to make the aurora performances happen, but when they do, the results are astounding.*

There are ***fewer bugs*** *in the winter months; if you've visited Alaska during the summer and been subjected to hordes of mosquitoes, no-see-ums, and white socks, this alone might be enough to entice you to visit.*

For a real Alaska winter experience, ***dog mushing*** *is the ultimate. Spectators can watch sprint and long distance races all over the state, capped off by the Yukon Quest and Iditarod races in February and March. There are numerous outfits in the Interior and South Central that will train you to mush your own team for a day, an overnight, or an extended trip. Fodor's discusses dog mushing and surrounding competitions with the expectation and hope that all the animals are treated with care and respect.*

Numerous opportunities exist in Alaska for both ***downhill and cross-country skiing*** *adventures. You can charter a helicopter to go backcountry skiing in the Valdez area or visit one of the downhill areas near Anchorage, Fairbanks, or Juneau. You can also ski in the winter or summer by chartering a plane to a glacier in Denali National Park.*

At Juneau, Eaglecrest is across from the city on the slopes of Douglas Island. Skiing is also done on the glaciers of the Juneau Ice Field, reached by helicopter. Turnagain Pass, 59 mi from Anchorage on the Seward Highway, is often trafficked with backcountry skiers and snowmobilers. Hilltop Ski Area and Alpenglow are small alpine ski areas within 10 mi of downtown Anchorage.

The ***World Extreme Skiing Championships*** *are held at Valdez every April. Cross-country skiers will find many miles of groomed trails in Anchorage. Additional cross-country ski trails can be found around Fairbanks, Homer, and Palmer. Snowboarding has more than caught on in South Central Alaska, and boarders are welcome at all three Anchorage ski areas. Rentals are available at the various ski areas and outdoor equipment shops.*

insects, small mammals, even remnants of woolly mammoths—that flourished here when the Bering Land Bridge linked North America to what is now Russia. Early peoples wandered through this treeless landscape, perhaps following the musk ox, whose descendants still occupy this terrain. A remarkable 250 species of flowering plants thrive in this seemingly barren region, and there are tens of thousands of migrating birds. More than 100 species, including ducks, geese, swans, sandhill cranes, and various shorebirds and songbirds, come here from around the world each spring. You may hear the haunting call of loons on the many clear lakes and lagoons.

The Bering Land Bridge National Preserve has no trails, campgrounds, or other visitor facilities. Access is largely by air taxi, although there is a road north of Nome that passes within walking distance. *National Park Service, Box 220, Nome 99762* ☎ *907/443–2522 or 907/442–3890* *www.nps.gov/bela.*

Kotzebue

13 *170 mi northeast of Nome.*

Kotzebue, Alaska's largest Eskimo community, is home to around 3,000 residents. The large majority of its people are Inupiats, who have lived at this site for at least 600 years. Their ties to the region go back much further, thousands of years into the past. For most of that time, the Inupiat were a semi-nomadic people who followed caribou and other wildlife across the landscape. In addition to caribou, they depended on whales, seals, fish, moose, and a variety of berries and other plants. Besides being talented hunters, the Inupiat were—and still are—skilled craftsmen and artists, known for their rugged gear, ceremonial parkas, Eskimo dolls, caribou skin masks, birch-bark baskets, and whalebone and walrus-ivory carvings.

Built on a 3-mi-long spit of land that juts into Kotzebue Sound, this village lies 33 mi above the Arctic Circle, on Alaska's Northwest coast. Before Europeans arrived in the region, the Inupiat name for this locale was Kikiktagruk; that was changed to Kotzebue after German explorer Otto von Kotezbue "discovered" the area in 1818 while sailing for Russia. Nowadays Kotzebue is the region's economic and political hub and headquarters for both the Northwest Arctic Borough and the NANA corporation, one of the 13 regional Native corporations formed when Congress settled the Alaskan Natives' aboriginal land claims in 1971. The region's other Eskimo villages are much smaller, with populations of 90 to 700 people.

Just as their ancestors did, modern Inupiats depend heavily on subsistence harvesting; household economies are generally a mix of hunting, fishing, gathering, and part-time seasonal jobs. Some residents also fish commercially. This region of the state has few employment opportunities outside of the government and corporation. The biggest private employer is the Red Dog Mine. Located on NANA land, Red Dog has the world's largest deposit of zinc and is expected to produce ore for at least 50 years. Local government here, as in many Bush villages, is a blend of tribal government and a more modern borough system. Other facilities and programs include the Maniilaq Health Center, the Northwest Arctic District Correspondence Program, and the University of Alaska Chukchi Campus.

Kotzebue has long, cold winters and short, cool summers. The average low temperature in January is -12 degrees (Fahrenheit), and midsummer highs rarely go much higher than the 60s. "We have four seasons—June, July, August, and winter," a tour guide jests. But don't worry about the sometimes chilly weather—the local sightseeing company has snug, bright loaner parkas for visitors on package tours. And there's plenty of light to take in the village and surrounding landscape: the sun doesn't set for 36 days, from June into July. One of summer's highlights is the annual **Northwest Native Trade Fair**; held each year after the July Fourth celebration, it features traditional Native games, a muktuk (whale meat) eating contest, seal-hook throwing contest, and Eskimo buggy race.

Strung out in clusters of weather-bleached little houses and a few public buildings on the gravelly shore of Kotzebue Sound, Kotzebue provides you with a glimpse of the way Alaska's Eskimos live today. It was an ancient Eskimo trading center; now it is an example of the modern spirit nudging Alaska's Natives into the state's mainstream culture without leaving their traditions behind.

Fodor'sChoice ★

The **NANA Regional Corporation** (Northwest Alaska Native Association; ☎ 907/442–3301 or 800/478–3301 🌐 www.nana.com) has its headquarters in Kotzebue. It was NANA that built the **Living Museum of the Arctic** (☎ 907/265–4100 or 907/442–3301 🌐 www.nana.com) in 1977 and turned it into one of Alaska's top-rated museums. The museum features cultural and natural-history displays, as well as presentations by local residents. Bleachers face a stage where stories are told, and after the storytelling, a cultural slide show relates the wisdom of the elders, followed by traditional Eskimo singing and dancing and blanket tossing, in which audience members are invited to participate. It may look like a game, but the blanket toss was serious business in the early days, when Eskimo hunters were launched high in the air from blankets of walrus or seal hide to scan the seas for game. You may even be urged to take a turn on the bouncing blanket. The museum is open when tour groups are in town or by special arrangement. Admission to the museum is free, but a fee is charged for cultural programs. After attending programs at the museum, stop at the **Gift Shop** in the Northwest Arctic Borough building (☎ 907/442–2500, 800/478–1110). The store features Native arts and crafts from throughout the Arctic region.

Additional information about Kotzebue and the surrounding region can be obtained through the **Northwest Arctic Borough** (📫 Box 110, Kotzebue 99752 ☎ 907/442–2500 or 800/478–1110 🌐 www.northwestarcticborough.org). Tours of the museum can be arranged through NANA's program **Tour Arctic** (☎ 907/265–4180 or 907/442–3341 🌐 www.tour-arctic.com).

Through Tour Arctic, visitors can also sample village life, explore the surrounding landscape, and get a sense of the Inupiats' past, present, and changing lifeways. At the **Culture Camp,** village elders demonstrate traditional life skills. During the summer fishing season, they show how salmon is prepared for smoking and drying. Or they may demonstrate techniques for making birch-bark baskets, ivory carvings, ulu knives, parkas, and a style of boot known as mukluks.

On the **city tour,** local guides introduce visitors to Inupiat culture and modern Eskimo life, while those who take the **tundra walk** will have a chance to hike across the rolling tundra outside the village and learn about the diverse plant and animal life that inhabit this northern landscape.

Tour participants will have a chance to purchase local arts and crafts while visiting Kotzebue. Depending on the tour (five options are possible), they may also stay overnight in the Nullagvik Hotel. Some tours combine overnight stays in both Kotzebue and Nome. Prices vary considerably; more details can be obtained through the Tour Arctic Web site or by contacting NANA.

If you're hiking the wildflower-carpeted tundra around Kotzebue, you are entering a "living museum" dedicated to **permafrost,** the permanently frozen ground that lies just a few inches below the spongy tundra. Even Kotzebue's 6,000-foot airport runway is built on permafrost—with a 6-inch insulating layer between the frozen ground and the airfield surface to ensure that landings are smooth, not slippery or bumpy.

Kotzebue serves as a gateway for three exceptional national **wilderness areas**: Cape Krusenstern National Monument, Kobuk Valley National Park, and Noatak National Preserve. North and east of Kotzebue is the **Brooks Range,** one of Alaska's great mountain ranges. Stretching across the state, much of the range is protected by Gates of the Arctic National Park and Preserve and the Arctic National Wildlife Refuge.

Where to Stay & Eat

¢–$$$$ ✕ **Kotzebue Pizza House.** Although this cozy pizza parlor serves pizza and Chinese food, locals especially tout the burgers, which are said to be among the best in the state. ✉ *2nd Ave. and Bison St., Downtown* ☎ *907/442–3432* ▭ *MC, V.*

$$ ✕🏨 **Nullagvik Hotel.** This hotel overlooking Kotzebue Sound is built on pilings driven into the ground because the heat of the building would melt the underlying permafrost and cause the hotel to sink. Images of Eskimo life adorn the spacious, modern rooms. Public areas on the second and third floors provide picture-window views of the bay. Usually open only in the summer, the hotel's Niggivik Restaurant ($–$$$$) serves a variety of dishes, from reindeer sausage and sourdough pancakes to New York steak and fresh, locally harvested Arctic fish. ✉ *308 Shore Ave.* 📫 *Box 336, 99752* ☎ *907/442–3331* 📠 *907/442–3340* 🌐 *www.nullagvik.com* 🛏 *75 rooms* 👍 *Restaurant, cable TV, meeting room, travel services, some pets allowed, no-smoking rooms; no a/c* ▭ *AE, D, DC, MC, V.*

Cape Krusenstern National Monument

14 *10 mi north of Kotzebue.*

Just north of Kotzebue, the 560,000-acre Cape Krusenstern National Monument has important cultural and archaeological value. This is a coastal parkland, with an extraordinary series of beach ridges built up by storms over a period of at least 5,000 years. Almost every ridge—more than 100 in all—contains artifacts of different human occupants, representing every known Arctic Eskimo culture in North America. The present Eskimo occupants, whose culture dates back some 1,400 years, use the fish, seals, caribou, and birds of this region for food and raw materials much as their ancestors did. They are also closely involved in the archaeological digs in the park that are unearthing part of their own history.

Cape Krusenstern is a starkly beautiful Arctic land shaped by ice, wind, and sea. Its low, rolling gray-white hills scalloped with light-green tundra attract hikers and backpackers, and kayakers sometimes paddle its coastline. The monument is valuable also for human and historical reasons, and it should be experienced as a marvelous living museum. It's possible to camp in the park, but be mindful, as are the Native people when they rig their big white canvas tents for summer fishing, that any tent pitched along the shore is subject to fierce winds. Further, both grizzlies and polar bears patrol the beaches in search of food, so clean camping is a must.

Check with the National Park Service in Kotzebue about hiring a local guide to interpret this unusual scene. The monument, which has no visitor facilities, is accessible by air taxi and by boat from Kotzebue. *National Park Service, Box 1029, Kotzebue 99752* ☎ *907/442–3890* *www.nps.gov/cakr.*

Kobuk Valley National Park

15 *65 mi east of Kotzebue.*

Kobuk Valley National Park lies entirely north of the Arctic Circle, along the southern edge of the Brooks Range. Its 1.14 million acres contain remarkable inland deserts and the **Great Kobuk Sand Dunes** and are home to interesting relict (remnants of otherwise extinct) flora. The park is bisected by the west-flowing **Kobuk River,** a 347-mi-long stream born in the foothills of the western Brooks Range. The Kobuk, whose Native name means "big river," has been a major transportation and trade route for centuries. Besides the Kobuk, this park contains two smaller streams that provide delightful river running, the Ambler and the Salmon. These brilliantly clear rivers are accessible by wheeled plane, and each provides a good week's worth of pleasure (if the weather cooperates).

Another place of special interest is the **Onion Portage.** Human occupation here dates back 12,500 years; herds of caribou that fed the Woodland Eskimo centuries ago are still hunted at Onion Portage by present-day Eskimo residents of the region.

Kobuk Valley National Park is, like most other Alaska parks, undeveloped wilderness with no visitor facilities. It's a good place for backpacking and river trips. In nearby Kotzebue, the National Park Service has a visitor center where staff can provide tips for travel into the park. The villages of Kobuk and Kiana both provide immediate take-off points and have air service. *National Park Service, Box 1029, Kotzebue 99752 907/442–3890 www.nps.gov/kova.*

Noatak National Preserve

16 *20 mi northeast of Kotzebue.*

Adjacent to Gates of the Arctic National Park and Preserve, the 6.5-million-acre Noatak National Preserve encompasses much of the basin of the **Noatak River.** This is the largest mountain-ringed river basin in the United States that is still relatively undeveloped; part of it is designated by the National Park Service as a Wild and Scenic River. Along its 425-mi course, this river carves out the "Grand Canyon of the Noatak," so-called by the NPS, which serves as a migration route between Arctic and sub-Arctic ecosystems. Its importance to wildlife and plants has resulted in this parkland's designation as an International Biosphere Reserve.

The Noatak River also serves as a natural highway for humans and offers particular pleasures to river runners, with inviting tundra to camp on and the Poktovik Mountains and the Igichuk Hills nearby for good hiking. Birding can be exceptional: horned grebes, gyrfalcons, golden eagles, parasitic jaegers, owls, terns, and loons are among the species you may see. You may also observe grizzly bears, Dall sheep, wolves, caribou, or lynx. As with other parks and preserves in this northwest corner of Alaska, no visitor facilities are available and you are expected to be self-sufficient. *National Park Service, Box 1029, Kotzebue 99752 907/442–3890 www.nps.gov/noat.*

Gates of the Arctic National Park & Preserve

★ 17 *180 mi east of Kotzebue.*

Gates of the Arctic National Park & Preserve is entirely north of the Arctic Circle, in the center of the Brooks Range; at 8.2 million acres, it's the size of four Yellowstones. This is parkland on a scale suitable to the country. It includes the **Endicott Mountains** to the east and the **Schwatka Mountains** to the southwest, with the **Arrigetch Peaks** in between. *Arrigetch* is an Eskimo word meaning "fingers of a hand outstretched," which aptly describes the immensely steep and smooth granite peaks that have attracted many mountaineers and backcountry explorers, past and present. To the north lies a sampling of the Arctic foothills, with their colorful tilted sediments and pale green tundra. Lovely lakes are cupped in the mountains and in the tundra.

This landscape, the ultimate wilderness, captured the heart of Arctic explorer and conservationist Robert Marshall in the 1930s. Accompanied by local residents, Marshall explored much of the region now included within Gates and named many of its features, including Frigid Crag and Boreal Mountain, two peaks on either side of the North Fork Koyukuk River. These were the original "gates" for which the park is named.

Wildlife known to inhabit the park include barren-ground caribou, grizzlies, wolves, moose, Dall sheep, wolverines, and smaller mammals and birds. The communities of Bettles and Anaktuvuk Pass are access points for Gates of the Arctic, which has no developed trails, campgrounds, or other visitor facilities (though there is a wilderness lodge on private land within the park). You can fly into Bettles commercially and charter an air taxi into the park or hike directly out of Anaktuvuk Pass. ✉ *National Park Service, 201 1st Ave., Fairbanks 99701* ☎ *907/457–5752, 907/692–5494* 🌐 *www.nps.gov/gaar.*

Where to Stay

★ $$$$ **Peace of Selby Wilderness.** On Selby/Narvak Lakes within Gates of the Arctic National Park, Peace of Selby is perfectly situated for wilderness adventures. Crafted from white spruce, the main lodge includes a kitchen, small library, bathroom, and loft. Meals, included with some rates, are cooked with fresh vegetables, fruits, and meats. If you want to rough it, you can bring along your sleeping bags and cook your own meals in one of four remote rustic log cabins, which can accommodate up to four people each. The owners also organize custom guided expeditions. Activities include hiking, fishing, wildlife viewing and photographing, river floating, and flightseeing. *Box 86, Manley Hot Springs 99756* ☎ *907/672–3206* 🌐 *www.alaskawilderness.net* *1 room in lodge, 4 cabins* *Dining room, boating, fishing, hiking, cross-country skiing, library; no a/c, no room phones, no room TVs* *No credit cards* *Closed mid-Sept.–mid-June, except for specially arranged expeditions Mar.–Apr.*

Sports & the Outdoors

Contact **Sourdough Outfitters** (Box 26066, Bettles Field 99726 ☎ 907/692–5252 907/692–5557 🌐 www.sourdoughoutfitters.com) for summer backpacking and river trips (from family float trips to wild-rapid running and fishing expeditions) and winter dogsled trips in the Brooks Range.

Barrow

18 *330 mi northeast of Kotzebue.*

The northernmost community in the United States, Barrow sits 1,300 mi south of the North Pole. The village is 10 mi south of the Beaufort Sea and Point Barrow, from which it takes its name. Point Barrow, in turn, was named in 1825 by British Capt. Beechey, who'd been ordered by the British navy to map the continent's northern coastline. Beechey wished to honor Sir John Barrow, a member of the British Admiralty. As is so often the rule, the traditional indigenous name is much more locally relevant and reflects an aspect of the landscape. The region's Inupiat Eskimos knew the site as Ukpeagvik, or "place where owls are hunted." Even today, many snowy owls nest in the tundra outside Barrow each summer, though they're not hunted as they once were as they are now protected by federal law.

Archaeological evidence from more than a dozen ancient "dwelling mounds" suggests that people have inhabited the area for at least the past 1,500 years. Described as members of the **Birnirk culture,** those early residents depended heavily on marine mammals, a tradition that continues to this day. Combining modern technology with traditional knowledge, Barrow's whaling crews annually hunt for the bowhead whales that migrate through Arctic waters each spring and fall. If the whalers are successful in their springtime hunts, they share muktuk—whale blubber—with other members of the village and celebrate their good fortune with a festival called **Nalukataq** when the whaling season ends. Besides whales, residents depend on subsistence harvests of seals, walrus, polar bears, caribou, waterfowl, grayling, and whitefish.

About 4,400 people inhabit Barrow today, making it easily the largest community on the North Slope. Nearly two-thirds of the residents are Inupiat Eskimos. Though they remain deeply rooted in their Inupiat heritage, Barrow's residents have adopted a modern lifestyle. Homes are heated by natural gas taken from nearby gas fields and the community is served by most modern conveniences, including a public-radio station and cable TV and Internet access. The community recreation center has a gymnasium, racquetball courts, weight room, and sauna and hosts a variety of social events, from dances to exercise classes and basketball tournaments. In Barrow, as in much of Bush Alaska, basketball is the favored sport, played year-round by people of all ages.

Barrow is the economic and administrative center of the **North Slope Borough,** which encompasses more than 88,000 square mi, making it the world's largest municipal government (in terms of area). The village is also headquarters of the **Arctic Slope Regional Corporation,** formed in 1971 through the Alaska Native Claims Settlement Act (ANCSA), as well as the Ukpeagvik Inupiat Corporation, which economically and politically represents the community of Barrow. Several village councils are also headquartered in the town.

Non-Natives established a presence at Barrow in the early 1880s, when the U.S. Army built a research station here. Drawn to the area by the Beaufort Sea's abundant whales, commercial whalers established the **Cape Smythe Whaling and Trading Station** in 1893; a cabin from that operation still stands, and is the oldest frame building in Alaska's Arctic. The station is now listed on the National Register of Historic Places (as are the Birnirk dwelling mounds, mentioned above).

By the early 1900s both a Presbyterian church and U.S. post office had been established. Recalling those days, an Inupiat elder named Alfred Hopson once recounted that the famed Norwegian explorer Vilhjalmur Stefansson used the Presbyterian church as a base for studies of local residents, including measurements of their head sizes. From then on, Stefansson was known locally as the "head measurer." Oil and gas exploration later brought more whites from the continental United States to the area; even more came as schools and other government agencies took root in the region. Hopson, too, played a role in the area's development, as he funneled millions of dollars in tax revenues into road building, sanitation and water services, and heath-care services.

Tourism has become an important industry in recent years, as increasing numbers of people come to Barrow to experience the local culture, wildlife, and far-north climatic extremes. This is truly the land of the midnight sun. From May 10 to August 2, the sun stays above the horizon, never setting for 82 days. Conversely, the sun disappears during the dead of winter from November 18 through January 24. Despite the season's unending daylight, even summertime temperatures can be brisk, averaging about 40 degrees. And you should be prepared for snow flurries even during the warmest months. Midsummer temperatures occasionally rise into the 60s and, on rare occasions, they'll even reach into the 70s. Despite the region's abundant wetlands, Barrow—and the North Slope in general—has a desert climate, with annual precipitation averaging less than 10 inches.

Barrow has opened its annual springtime whale festival to outsiders and there are several historic sites, including a military installation, points of native cultural importance, and a famous crash site. The Barrow airport is where you'll find the **Will Rogers and Wiley Post Monument,** which marks the 1935 crash of the American humorist and his pilot 15 mi south of town.

Drawn by both cultural and natural attractions, visitors in Barrow usually arrive on a one- or two-day tour with Alaska Airlines, the only national carrier serving the area. Packages include a bus tour of the town's dusty roads and major sights. Barrow's residents invite visitors to attend their annual whale festival in the spring, though summer is the ideal time to survey the town and its historic sites, including remnants of the Cape Smythe whaling operation, plus the Birnirk dwelling mounds, subsurface homes composed of dirt/tundra sod. A highlight of those mounds is **Mound 44,** where the frozen body of a 500-year-old Eskimo was discovered. Scientists have been studying her remains to learn more about Eskimo life and culture before encounters with outsiders.

An **early warning radar installation** (known as DEWS, for distant-early-warning-site) once watched for incoming Soviet missiles. The air force has since mothballed its big dishes, but Barrow duty must have given special meaning to the term *cold war.* The best part about visiting the top of the world is walking along the sandy beach and seeing the pack ice stretching across the horizon, even in the middle of summer.

Year-round tours are organized through **Tundra Tours** (☎ 907/852–3900 🌐 www.tundratours.com). Offered from mid-September through mid-May, the winter tours feature visits to a traditional hunting camp, the whaling station, the DEWS site, and opportunities to visit Point Barrow and watch northern lights. The summer program is highlighted by visits to local historic sites and opportunities to witness traditional cultural activities such as Eskimo dances, mask and skin-sewing demonstrations, and the blanket toss. In both winter and summer, visitors can purchase locally made Inupiat arts and crafts.

Where to Stay & Eat

★ $–$$$$ ✕ **Pepe's North of the Border.** The warmth of Pepe's will make you forget that you're in the middle of the Arctic tundra. Murals depicting Mexican village scenes highlight the Mission-style decor, and an extensive selection of Mexican dishes, from soft tacos to burritos and flautas, makes this restaurant a favorite of locals and visitors alike. The restaurant's menu is also spiced up with dishes that feature Alaskan seafood and, at the high end of things, steak and lobster. Dinner at Pepe's is surprisingly refined for being on the very fringe of civilization. ✉ *Next to Top of the World Hotel* ☎ *907/852–8200* ▭ *DC, MC, V.*

$$–$$$ ✕ **Ken's Restaurant.** Burgers, steaks, seafood, and Chinese food are the staples at this family restaurant, which has daily specials and the best prices in town. Breakfast is served throughout the day. ✉ *Above airport terminal building* ☎ *907/852–8888* ▭ *MC, V.*

★ $$–$$$ **Top of the World Hotel.** Built in 1974, this refurbished hotel on the shore of the Arctic Ocean has just about every imaginable modern convenience, including cable TV and Internet access. Still, it retains a frontier atmosphere; the lobby, for example, has one complete stuffed polar bear and the mounted head of another. You can mingle in the lobby or in front of the community television. Modern, spacious rooms have sitting areas; ask for a room with an ocean view. ✉ *1200 Agviq St.* *Box 189, 99723* ☎ *907/852–3900, 800/882–8478, 800/478–8520 in Alaska* *907/852–6752* 🌐 *www.topoftheworldhotel.com* *43 rooms* *Some in-room data ports, some refrigerators, cable TV, Internet; no a/c, no smoking* ▭ *AE, D, DC, MC, V.*

$ **Barrow Airport Inn.** As the name suggests, this modern and well-appointed property is convenient to the airport. ✉ *1815 Momegana St.* *Box 933, 99723* ☎ *907/852–2525, 808/375–2527* *907/852–2528* *15 rooms* *Some kitchenettes, microwaves, refrigerators, cable TV, Internet, travel services, no-smoking rooms; no a/c* ▭ *AE, D, MC, V* *CP.*

Shopping

The AC Value Center, or, as it's known locally, **Stuaqpak** ("Big Store"; ✉ 4725 Ahkovak St. ☎ 907/852–6711 🌐 www.alaskacommercial.com), is the largest store in town. Though it mainly sells groceries, the store also stocks Eskimo crafts made by locals, including furs, parkas, mukluks, and ceremonial masks.

Prudhoe Bay

19 *250 mi southeast of Barrow.*

Most towns have museums that chronicle local history and achievements. Deadhorse is the town anchoring life along Prudhoe Bay, but it could also serve as a museum dedicated to humankind's hunt for energy and its ability to adapt to harsh conditions.

The costly, much-publicized Arctic oil and gas project is complex and varied. One-day tours explore the tundra terrain from oil pipes to sandpipers. Along with chances to spot caribou, wildflowers, and an unusual stand of willow trees at the edge of the Arctic Ocean, the field tour surveys oil wells, stations, and oil-company residential complexes—small cities themselves. Your guide will discuss the multimillion-dollar research programs aimed at preserving the region's ecology and point out special tundra vehicles known as Rollagons, whose great weight is distributed to diminish their impact on delicate terrain.

In the past, individual travelers rarely turned up in Deadhorse and Prudhoe Bay. But now that the Dalton Highway has been opened as far north as Deadhorse, adventurous independent travelers are finding their way north. Still, most people traveling to Deadhorse either work here

THE PIPELINE HIGHWAY

STRETCHING 800 MI ACROSS THE 49TH STATE, *the trans-Alaska pipeline is both an engineering marvel and a reminder of Alaska's economic dependence on oil and gas production. It begins at Prudhoe Bay, along the Arctic Ocean, and snakes its way south to the port town of Valdez, on the shores of Prince William Sound. Along the way, the pipeline carries crude oil across three mountain ranges, 34 major rivers—including the mighty Yukon—and hundreds of smaller creeks. Though much of it is buried, more than half of the pipeline runs aboveground, where it is held aloft by 78,000 vertical supports. You can see sections of it along some of Alaska's major roadways, most notably the Dalton Highway.*

The Dalton, Alaska's northernmost highway, parallels the pipeline for more than 400 mi while connecting Interior Alaska to North Slope oil fields. It was built so that trucks could haul supplies to Prudhoe Bay and pipeline construction camps in Alaska's northern reaches, hence the fact that it's commonly referred to as the Haul Road.

Thousands of 18-wheelers continue to drive the Dalton Highway each year, but they now share the 414-mi route with recreational travelers. This doesn't mean the Dalton has become an easy drive. It's narrow as highways go, often winding, and has several steep grades, and sections may be heavily potholed or washboarded. Besides being tough on vehicles, the road has few visitor facilities. Public access ends at Deadhorse, the support town for Prudhoe Bay's industrial operations; the only way to visit the oil fields or reach the ocean is by group tour (scheduled daily in summer).

The origins of the Haul Road and trans-Alaska pipeline can be traced to 1968, when oil companies announced the discovery of a major field at Prudhoe Bay. A lawsuit by environmental groups temporarily halted work on the proposed pipeline across Alaska, but congressional legislation authorizing its construction was signed into law in November 1973. Things moved quickly after that. Work on the Haul Road began the following April and was finished in five months. Forty-eight inches wide and up to 60 feet long, the first pipes were installed in March 1975; 27 months later, oil began moving down the pipeline and reached Valdez on July 28, 1977. Four days later, the ARCO Juneau *headed south with the first tanker load of Prudhoe Bay crude.*

Since it began operation, the pipeline has transported more than 14 billion barrels (approximately 600 billion gallons) of oil across Alaska. At its peak in 1988, 2.14 million barrels of oil flowed through the pipeline in a day's time. Nowadays the daily flow is closer to 1 million barrels.

The trans-Alaska pipeline was designed and built and continues to be operated by the Alyeska Pipeline Service Company, a consortium of seven oil companies. Concerns about spills and corrosion led to the formation of a Joint Pipeline Office, composed of nine state and federal regulatory agencies. Although the pipeline has had a number of temporary shutdowns and spills, the only catastrophic event connected to the trans-Alaska pipeline project was the 1989 Exxon Valdez *oil spill, in which 270,000 barrels of oil oozed from the damaged tanker into Prince William Sound.*

or come on a tour with one of Alaska's airlines or bus-tour operators. And even those who travel here on their own must join a guided tour (arranged through the Arctic Caribou Inn) if they wish to cross the oil fields to get to the Arctic Ocean. You'll find no restaurants here, though meals can sometimes be arranged through the Prudhoe Bay Hotel.

Where to Stay

$$–$$$ **Prudhoe Bay Hotel.** Located near the end of the road at Deadhorse, this hotel is primarily intended for the workers employed in the Prudhoe Bay oilfield complex, but tourists are also welcome. Some of the rooms are bare-bones dormitory-style rooms, whereas others are slightly more upscale, with TVs and phones. All rooms share baths. The hotel includes a cafeteria/dining hall with specific hours for breakfast, lunch, and dinner; meals are buffet style. Food and drinks from vending machines can be purchased around the clock. The hotel is also just a short hop from Deadhorse's airport. ✉ *Pouch 340004, Prudhoe Bay 99734* ☎ *907/659–2449* 🖷 *907/659–2752* 🌐 *www.prudhoebayhotel.com* *170* *Cafeteria, shop, car rental; no a/c, no TV in some rooms, no phones in some rooms.* 💳 *AE, MC, V* 🍽 *EP.*

Arctic National Wildlife Refuge

★ 20 *70 mi southeast of Prudhoe Bay.*

The 18-million-acre Arctic National Wildlife Refuge, lying wholly above the Arctic Circle, is administered by the U.S. Fish and Wildlife Service and contains the only protected Arctic coastal lands in the United States (and some of the very few protected in the world), as well as millions of acres of mountains and alpine tundra, in the easternmost portion of the Brooks Range.

This is the home of one of the greatest remaining groups of caribou in the world, the **Porcupine Caribou Herd.** The herd, numbering around 123,000, is unmindful of international boundaries and migrates back and forth across Arctic lands into Canada, flowing like a wide river across the expansive coastal plain, through U-shape valleys and alpine meadows, and over high mountain passes. The refuge's coastal areas also serve as critical denning grounds for polar bears, which spend most of their year on the Arctic Ocean's pack ice. Other residents here are grizzly bears, Dall sheep, wolves, musk ox, and dozens of varieties of birds, from snowy owls to geese and tiny songbirds. The refuge's northern areas host legions of breeding waterfowl and shorebirds each summer. As in many of Alaska's more remote parks and refuges, there are no roads here, and no developed trails, campgrounds, or other visitor facilities. This is a place to experience true wilderness—and to walk with care, for the plants are fragile and the ground can be soft and wet in summer. You can expect snow to sift over the land in almost any season and should anticipate subfreezing temperatures even in summer, particularly in the mountains. Many of the refuge's clear-flowing rivers are runnable, and tundra lakes are suitable for base camps (a Kaktovik or Fort Yukon air taxi can drop you off and pick you up). The hiking, too, can be invigorating. It can also be extremely challenging for those not used to crossing wet, tussocky tundra or slippery scree deposits of rocks. But the effort is worth it; upon scrambling up a ridge, you'll look out upon wave after wave of mountains, in a wilderness that seems to stretch forever. ✉ *Refuge Manager, Arctic National Wildlife Refuge, 101 12th Ave., Room 236, Box 20, Fairbanks 99701* ☎ *907/456–0250 or 800/362–4546* 🌐 *arctic.fws.gov.*

THE BUSH A TO Z

To research prices, get advice from other travelers, and book travel arrangements, visit www.fodors.com.

6

AIR TRAVEL

Alaska Airlines is among the major carriers serving Alaska from Seattle, and it flies within Alaska to most major communities (⇨ Smart Travel Tips A to Z for airline numbers). Peninsula Airways serves the communities on the Alaskan Peninsula, the Aleutian and Pribilof islands, and parts of the Interior and Northwest.

Many Anchorage and Fairbanks air taxis serve the Bush in addition to Bush-based carriers such as Bering Air, which also offers local flightseeing tours and, weather and politics permitting, flights to Provideniya, on the Siberian coast across the Bering Strait. Cape Smythe Air Service serves the communities of the North Slope plus Kotzebue. Frontier Flying Service serves the Interior and the Bering and Arctic coasts. Wright Air Service flies throughout the Interior and Arctic Alaska.

Besides flights on those carriers, information about certified air-taxi operations is available from the Federal Aviation Administration. Individual parks and Alaska Public Lands Information centers also can supply lists of reputable air-taxi services. Make your reservations in advance, and plan for the unexpected; weather can delay a scheduled pickup for days.

Airlines & Contacts **Alaska Airlines** ☎ 800/426–0333 🌐 www.alaskaair.com. **Alaska Public Lands Information Center** ✉ 250 Cushman St., Suite 1A, Fairbanks 99701 ☎ 907/456–0527 🌐 www.nps.gov/aplic. **Bering Air** 📫 Box 1650, Nome 99762 ☎ 907/443-5464, 800/478-5422 in Alaska, 907/443-5620 Russian desk 🖷 907/443-5919 🌐 www.beringair.com. **Cape Smythe Air Service** ✉ 1707 Ahkovak St. 📫 Box 549, Barrow 99723 ☎ 907/852-8333 🖷 907/852-2509 🌐 www.capesmythe.com. **Federal Aviation Administration** ✉ Flight Standards District Office, 4510 W. International Airport Rd., Anchorage 99502-1088 ☎ 907/271-2000 🖷 907/271-4777 🌐 www.faa.gov. **Frontier Flying Service** ✉ 5245 Airport Industrial Way, Fairbanks 99709 ☎ 907/450-7250 or 800/478-6779 for reservations 🖷 907/450-7274 🌐 www.frontierflying.com. **Peninsula Airways** ✉ 6100 Boeing Ave., Anchorage 99502 ☎ 907/243-2323 or 800/448-4226 🖷 907/243-6848 🌐 www.penair.com. **Wright Air Service** ✉ 3842 University Ave. 📫 Box 60142, Fairbanks 99706 ☎ 907/474-0502, 800/478-0502 in Alaska 🖷 907/474-0375 🌐 www.wrightair.net.

BOAT & FERRY TRAVEL

The Alaska State Ferry makes monthly trips April through October to Kodiak, Dutch Harbor/Unalaska, and several other Bush communities in southwestern Alaska.

Boat & Ferry Information **Alaska State Ferry** ✉ Alaska Marine Highway System, 6858 Glacier Hwy., Juneau 99801 ☎ 800/642-0066 🖷 907/277-4829 🌐 www.alaskaferry.com.

CAR TRAVEL

The James W. Dalton Highway—formerly the construction road for the trans-Alaska pipeline—is Alaska's only highway to the High Arctic. Popularly known as the Haul Road, this 414-mi, all-gravel road begins about 73 mi north of Fairbanks, connecting with the Steese and Elliott highways to points south. Private vehicles may travel the entire length of the highway to Deadhorse. However, access to oil-company facilities and the shore of the Arctic Ocean is limited to commercial operators.

Vehicle services are limited along the highway. There are plans to add new facilities, but currently fuel, repairs, food, and lodging are available at only three places: the Yukon River crossing (Mile 56), Coldfoot (Mile 175), and Deadhorse (Mile 414). Motorists are cautioned not to expect assistance from truckers shuttling between Prudhoe Bay and Fairbanks. For Dalton Highway information, contact the Fairbanks office of the Alaska Public Lands Information Center.

Neither the Arctic and near-Arctic communities of Nome, Kotzebue, and Barrow nor Bethel, the Aleutian chain, nor the Pribilof Islands have highway connections to the rest of Alaska.

Alaska Public Lands Information Center ✉ 250 Cushman St., Suite 1A, Fairbanks 99701 ☎ 907/456-0527 🌐 www.nps.gov/aplic.

EMERGENCIES

DOCTORS & DENTISTS A statewide air-ambulance service operates through Alaska Regional Lifeflight in Anchorage.

Alaska Regional Lifeflight ☎ 800/478-9111 🌐 www.alaskaregional.com. **Maniilaq Health Center** ✉ Kotzebue ☎ 800/478-3321 🌐 www.maniilaq.org.

EMERGENCY SERVICES **Police** ☎ 907/852-0311 in Barrow, 907/442-3351 in Kotzebue, 907/443-5262 in Nome 🌐 www.kotzebuepolice.com, www.nomealaska.org in Nome. **State troopers** ☎ 907/852-3783 in Barrow, 800/789-3222 or 907/442-3222 in Kotzebue, 907/443-5525 in Nome 🌐 www.dps.state.ak.us/ast.

HOSPITALS **Norton Sound Regional Hospital** ✉ Nome ☎ 907/443-3311 🌐 www.nshcorp.org. **Samuel Simmonds Memorial Hospital** ✉ Barrow ☎ 907/852-4611.

SPORTS & THE OUTDOORS

For information about camping, hiking, and fishing, contact the following:

Alaska Department of Fish and Game Box 25526, Juneau 99802-5526 ☎ 907/465-4100 general information about fish and wildlife, 907/465-4180 sportfishing seasons and regulations, 907/465-2376 licenses 🌐 www.adfg.state.ak.us. **Alaska State Parks Information** ✉ 550 W. 7th Ave., Suite 1260, Anchorage 99501 ☎ 907/269-8400 🖷 907/269-8401 🌐 www.alaskastateparks.org. **Anchorage Alaska Public Lands Information Center** ✉ 605 W. 4th Ave., Suite 105, Anchorage 99501 ☎ 907/271-2737 🖷 907/271-2744 🌐 www.nps.gov/aplic. **Fairbanks Alaska Public Lands Information Center** ✉ 250 Cushman St., Suite 1A, Fairbanks 99701 ☎ 907/456-0527 🖷 907/456-0514 🌐 www.nps.gov/aplic. **U.S. Fish and Wildlife Service** ✉ 1011 E. Tudor Rd., Anchorage 99503 ☎ 907/786-3309 🖷 907/786-3495 🌐 www.r7.fws.gov.

TOURS

Package tours are the most common way of traveling to Bush communities, where making your flight connections and having a room to sleep in at the end of the line are no small feats. Guided trips, or stays in wilderness lodges, can be arranged in many of the Bush's remote parklands and wildlife refuges. Independent travel, particularly for campers and hikers, can be highly rewarding, but it takes careful planning. During peak season—late May through Labor Day—planes, state ferries, hotels, and sportfishing lodges are likely to be crowded with travelers on organized tours. Booking well ahead is recommended; many Alaska travelers make their reservations a year in advance.

The type of tour you choose will determine how you get there. On air tours—which include travel to most Bush communities—you will fly to and from your destination. On bus tours to Deadhorse and Prudhoe Bay, you will travel at least one way by bus. Each type of tour has its own advantages: air travel is faster and gives you an aerial perspective of the Arctic; bus tours travel at a more leisurely pace and give you a ground-level view of sweeping tundra vistas. However, most Bush locales can be reached only by plane.

Most tours to Arctic towns and villages are short—one, two, or three days. These often can be combined with visits to other regions of the state. Packages may include stays at wilderness lodges.

The Bush is home to many Native Alaskan groups, many of which are active in tourism. Often, local Native corporations act as your hosts—running the tours, hotels, and attractions. Nome Tour and Marketing in Nome (book through Alaska Airlines Vacations) provides ground transportation, accommodations, and other services for visitors. The NANA Development Corporation provides ground transportation and accommodations in Kotzebue as well as at Prudhoe Bay in conjunction with bus tours. If you visit Barrow and stay at the Top of the World Hotel, Tundra Tours (book through Alaska Airlines Vacations), another Native operation, will be your host. On Gambell Island (book through Alaska Village Tours), local residents also run all the ground operations.

Alaska Airlines Vacations Box 68900, Seattle, WA 98168 800/468-2248 alaskaair.com. **NANA Development Corporation** 800/478-3301 www.nana.com, or book through Princess Tours or Gray Line of Alaska. **Tundra Tours** 907/852-3900 www.tundratours.com.

BUS In the summer tourist season, tour operators run trips up the Dalton Highway out of Fairbanks and Anchorage. Travelers go one way by air, the other by motor coach. The route crosses the rugged Brooks Range, the Arctic Circle, and the Yukon River. It also brushes the edges of Gates of the Arctic National Park and the Arctic National Wildlife Refuge. Holland America Tours/Gray Line of Alaska operates package tours that travel the Dalton Highway to Deadhorse. Princess Tours runs tours along the Dalton Highway.

The Northern Alaska Tour Company conducts ecotours to the Arctic Circle, the Brooks Range, and Prudhoe Bay that emphasize natural and cultural history, wildlife, and geology. Groups are limited to 25 people on Arctic day tours and to 10 on Prudhoe Bay overnight trips. Some tours are completely ground-based; others include a mix of ground and air travel.

Holland American Tours/Gray Line of Alaska ✉ 1980 S. Cushman, Fairbanks 99701 ☎ 907/451-6835, 800/887-7741 in Alaska, or 800/544-2206 for reservations 🌐 www.graylineofalaska.com. **Northern Alaska Tour Company** 📪 Box 82991-W, Fairbanks 99708 ☎ 907/474-8600 or 800/474-1986 📠 907/474-4767 🌐 www.northernalaska.com. **Princess Tours** ✉ 2815 2nd Ave., Suite 400, Seattle, WA 98121 ☎ 206/336-6000 in Seattle, 907/479-9660 in Fairbanks, 800/426-0442 reservations 🌐 www.princess.com.

PLANE Alaska Airlines Vacations packages air tours to Barrow, Nome, and Kotzebue. Local arrangements are taken care of by Native ground operators. These trips are especially good for travelers who would otherwise move about independently. The Alaska Travel Industry Association can give tips on air travel and flightseeing opportunities throughout the Bush.

Alaska Airlines Vacations 📪 Box 68900, Seattle, WA 98168 ☎ 800/468-2248 🌐 alaskaair.com. **Alaska Travel Industry Association** ✉ 2600 Cordova St., Suite 201, Anchorage 99503 ☎ 907/929-2200, 800/862-5275 for vacation planner 📠 907/561-5727 🌐 www.travelalaska.com.

VISITOR INFORMATION

Alaska Travel Industry Association ✉ 2600 Cordova St., Suite 201, Anchorage 99503 ☎ 907/929-2200, 800/862-5275 for vacation planner 📠 907/561-5727 🌐 www-travelalaska.com. **City of Barrow** 📪 Box 629, Barrow 99723 ☎ 907/852-5211 📠 907/852-5871. **Bethel Chamber of Commerce** 📪 Box 329, Bethel 99559 ☎ 907/543-2911 📠 907/543-2255 🌐 www.bethelakchamber.org. **Nome Convention and Visitors Bureau** 📪 Box 240, Nome 99762 ☎ 907/443-6624, 800/478-1901 in Alaska 📠 907/443-5832 🌐 www.nomealaska.org. **Southwest Alaska Municipal Conference** ✉ 3300 Arctic Blvd., Suite 203, Anchorage 99503 ☎ 907/562-7380 📠 907/562-0438 🌐 www.swamc.org. **Unalaska–Dutch Harbor Convention and Visitors Bureau** 📪 Box 545, Unalaska 99685 ☎ 907/581-2612 or 877/581-2612 📠 907/581-2613 🌐 www.unalaska.info.

Cruising in Alaska

7

WORD OF MOUTH

"Alaska is a wonderful place to cruise, so don't let the weather dampen your fun there."

—Lydia

"I just got back from an Inside Passage cruise. Bring layers. You will need a good rain/wind jacket and a long-sleeved sweater."

—IslandGrl

"If you do decide to go on a cruise ship, consider spending the extra money for an outside cabin, preferably one with a deck."

—Orcas

"Some of my most memorable experiences have been sighting whales breaching at sunset or bears fishing off the beach in the early morning fog."

—wolfie11

www.fodors.com/forums

By M. T. Schwartzman

Updated by Sue Kernaghan

ALASKA, IT WOULD SEEM, was made for cruising. The traditional route to the state is by sea, through a 1,000-mi-long protected waterway known as the Inside Passage. From Vancouver, B.C., in the south to Skagway in the north, it winds around islands large and small, past glacier-carved fjords and hemlock-blanketed mountains. This great land is home to breaching whales, nesting eagles, spawning salmon, and calving glaciers. The towns here can be reached only by air or sea; there are no roads between them. Juneau, in fact, is the only water-locked state capital in the United States. Beyond the Inside Passage, the Gulf of Alaska leads to Prince William Sound—famous for its marine life and more fjords and glaciers—and Anchorage, Alaska's largest city.

Alaska is one of cruising's showcase destinations, and there are a wide variety of options available. Itineraries give passengers more choices than ever before—from traditional loop cruises of the Inside Passage, round-trips from Vancouver or Seattle, to one-way Inside Passage–Gulf of Alaska cruises. A number of smaller boats sail only in the Inside Passage and Prince William Sound, away from big-ship traffic.

For more detailed information on cruising in Alaska, see *Fodor's Alaska Ports of Call 2006.*

CHOOSING YOUR CRUISE

Types of Ships

The type of ship you choose is the most important factor in your Alaska cruise vacation because it will determine how you see Alaska. Ocean liners sail farther from land and visit major ports of call such as Juneau, Skagway, and Ketchikan. Small ships spend much of their time hugging the coastline, looking for wildlife, waterfalls, and other natural and scenic attractions. For more independent types, there's no better way to see Alaska than aboard the ferries of the Alaska Marine Highway System, which allow you to travel with your car or RV and explore at your own pace.

Ocean Liners

Alaska's ocean-liner fleet represents the very best that today's cruise industry has to offer. Nearly all the ships were built within the last two decades and have atrium lobbies, state-of-the-art health spas, high-tech show lounges, elaborate dining rooms, and a variety of alternative restaurants. By night they come alive with Vegas-style revues, pulsating discos, and somewhat more sedate cabaret or comedy acts. Most of the latest liners have cabins with verandas—a great bonus in Alaska for watching the scenery go by from the privacy of your own stateroom. The newest cruise ships are lined with glass throughout their corridors and public rooms, so you're never far from the sea or a great view.

Small Ships

Unlike ocean liners, the smaller vessels cruising in Alaska are designed to reach into the most remote corners of the world. Shallow drafts allow them to navigate up rivers, close to coastlines, and into shallow coves. Motorized rubber landing craft, known as Zodiacs, are usually kept on board, making it possible for passengers to go ashore almost anywhere. Alaska, not casinos or spa treatments, is the focus of these cruises. Lectures and talks—conducted daily by naturalists, Native Alaskans, and other experts in the Great Land's natural history and native cultures—are the norm. But in comparison with those on ocean liners, cabins on expedition ships can be quite small and are often less luxurious than cabins on large ships. Small ships usually have just one dining option, and entertainment is usually limited to lectures and videos, but passengers enjoy greater opportunities to see scenery and wildlife, and a better chance to get to know your fellow passengers.

Ferry Liners

The state ferry system is known as the Alaska Marine Highway because its vessels carry vehicles as well as passengers. Each ferry has a car deck that can accommodate every-size vehicle from the family car to a Winnebago. You can take your vehicle ashore, drive around, even live in it, and then transport it with you to the next port of call. From Skagway or Haines (the only Inside Passage towns connected to a road system), you can drive farther north to Fairbanks and Anchorage by way of the Alaska Highway. Each ferry also has a main, or "weather," deck to accommodate passengers, and onboard camping is allowed year-round.

Itineraries

You'll want to give some consideration to your ship's Alaskan itinerary when you are choosing your cruise. The length of the cruise will determine the variety and number of ports you visit, but so will the type of itinerary and the point of departure. **Loop cruises** start and end at the same point and usually explore ports close to one another; **one-way cruises** start at one point and end at another and range farther afield.

Ocean liners typically follow one of two itineraries: round-trip Inside Passage loops starting and finishing in Vancouver, B.C., or Seattle, and one-way Inside Passage–Gulf of Alaska cruises sailing between Vancouver or Seattle and Anchorage. Both itineraries are usually seven days, though some lines offer longer trips. A few lines also schedule one-way or round-trip sailings from San Francisco or Los Angeles. Small ships typically sail within Alaska, setting out from Juneau, Sitka, or other Alaskan ports.

Whether you sail through the Inside Passage or along it will depend on the size of your vessel. Smaller ships can navigate narrow channels, straits, and fjords. Larger vessels must sail farther from land, so don't expect to see much wildlife from the deck of a megaship.

Cruise Tours

Most cruise lines give you the option of an independent, hosted, or fully escorted land tour before or after your cruise. Independent tours allow maximum flexibility. You have a preplanned itinerary with confirmed hotel reservations and transportation arrangements, but you're free to follow your interests and whims in each town. A hosted tour is similar, but tour-company representatives are available along the route to help out should you need assistance. On fully escorted tours, you travel with a group, led by a tour director. Activities are preplanned (and typically prepaid), so you have a good idea of how much your trip will cost (not counting incidentals) before you depart.

Most cruise-tour itineraries include a ride aboard the Alaska Railroad in a glass-dome railcar. Running between Anchorage, Denali National Park and Preserve, and Fairbanks are Holland America Westours' *McKinley Explorer,* Princess Tours' *Midnight Sun Express,* and the Royal Caribbean *Wilderness Express,* which offer unobstructed views of the passing land and wildlife from private railcars. Princess Tours' "Direct to the Wilderness" rail program has private trains waiting at the Whittier dock, eliminating the need for a transfer in Anchorage. If you choose to travel by rail independently, the Alaska Railroad cars are clean and comfortable and make the trip between Anchorage and Fairbanks hooked up to the same engines as the cruise-line cars.

Of the ocean-liner fleets, only Crystal Cruises and Norwegian Cruise Lines are currently not offering cruise-tour packages with land segments in Alaska; they may, however, have tours in the Canadian Rockies. In addition to full-length cruise tours, many cruise lines have pre- or post-cruise hotel and sightseeing packages in Vancouver, B.C., Seattle, or Anchorage lasting one to three days.

Independent travel by rental car or RV before or after the cruise segment is another popular option. Generally passengers will plan to begin or end their cruise in Anchorage, the most practical port city to use as a base for exploring the state. Almost any type of car or recreational vehicle, from a small, two-person RV to a large, luxurious motor home, can be rented.

Shore Excursions

Shore excursions arranged by the cruise line are a convenient way to see the sights, although you pay extra for this convenience. Before your cruise, you'll receive a booklet describing the shore excursions your cruise line offers. A few lines let you book excursions in advance; all sell them on board during the cruise. If you cancel your excursion, you may incur penalties, the amount varying with the number of days remaining until the tour. Because these trips are specialized, many have limited capacity and are sold on a first-come, first-served basis.

Among the many options available, some are "musts." At least once during your cruise, try flightseeing—it's the only way you'll grasp the grandeur of the land. Go to an evening salmon feast, where you can savor freshly caught fish cooked over an open fire. And experience an outdoor adventure—you don't have to be athletically inclined to raft down a river or paddle a sea kayak along the coastline.

When to Go

Cruise season runs from mid-May to late September; the most popular sailing dates are from late June through August. May and June are the driest months to cruise. Daytime temperatures along the cruise routes in May, June, and September are in the 50s and 60s. July and August averages are in the 60s and 70s, with occasional days in the 80s. Bargains can be found both early and late in the season. Cruising in the low seasons provides plenty of advantages besides discounted fares. Availability of ships and particular cabins is greater in the low and shoulder seasons, and the ports are almost completely free of tourists.

November is the best month for off-season ferry travel, after the stormy month of October and while it's still relatively warm on the Inside Passage (temperatures will average about 40°F). It's a good month for wildlife watching as well. Some animals show themselves in greater numbers during November. In particular, humpback whales are abundant off Sitka, and bald eagles congregate by the thousands near Haines.

Cruise Costs

Cruise costs can vary enormously. If you shop around and book early, you will undoubtedly pay less. Your cruise fare typically includes accommodation and all onboard meals, snacks, and activities. It does not normally include airfare to the port city, shore excursions, tips, alcoholic drinks, or spa treatments. Only the most expensive Alaska cruises include airfare. Virtually all lines offer air add-ons, which may or may not be less expensive than the latest discounted fare from the airlines.

Shore excursions can be a substantial expense; the best in Alaska are not cheap. But if you skimp too much on your excursion budget, you may deprive yourself of an important part of the Alaska experience.

Tipping is another extra. At the end of the cruise, it's customary to tip your room steward, server, and the person who buses your table, though some lines include the tips in the fare. If tips are not included, expect to pay an average of $10 per day in tips. Each ship provides guidelines.

Single travelers should be aware that there are few single cabins on most ships; taking a double cabin for yourself can cost as much as twice the advertised per-person rates (which are based on two people sharing a room). Some cruise lines will find roommates of the same sex for singles so that each can travel at the regular per-person, double-occupancy rate.

BEFORE YOU GO

Once you have chosen your cruise and signed on to go, it's time to get ready. Preparations for a cruise may involve many distinct tasks, but none of them are difficult, especially if broken down into manageable steps. Most important, allow plenty of time to get ready so you don't get harried in the last couple of weeks.

Tickets & Vouchers

After you make the final payment to your travel agent, the cruise line will issue your cruise tickets and vouchers for airport–ship transfers. Depending on the airline, and whether you have purchased an air-sea package, you may receive your plane tickets or charter-flight vouchers at the same time; you may also receive vouchers for any shore excursions, although most cruise lines issue these aboard ship. Should your travel documents not arrive when promised, contact your travel agent or cruise line. If you book late, tickets may be delivered directly to the ship.

Passports & Visas

For Alaska cruises, whether they begin in the United States or in Canada, American and Canadian citizens require proof of citizenship. A valid passport, though not required, is the best document to carry. If you do not have a passport, take a certified copy of your birth certificate, which must have a raised seal, and some form of photo identification. Permanent residents of the United States who are not citizens should carry their green card.

If you are a citizen of another country, you may be required to obtain visas in advance. It is always the responsibility of the person traveling to obtain the necessary travel documents, including visas. Check with your travel agent or cruise line about specific requirements. If you do need a visa for your cruise, your travel agent should be able to help you obtain it, but there may be a charge for this service, in addition to the visa charge. Read your cruise documents carefully to see what documents you'll need for embarkation. You don't want to be turned away at the pier.

Immigration regulations require every passenger boarding a cruise ship from a U.S. port to provide additional personal data, such as your current mailing address and telephone number, to the cruise operator in advance of embarkation. Failure to provide this information required by the U.S. government may result in denial of boarding.

Disabilities & Accessibility

The latest cruise ships have been built with the needs of travelers with disabilities in mind, and many older ships have been modified to accommodate them. But several cruise lines operate older ships that have not been modified or do not have elevators: explorer-type vessels are not the easiest ships to navigate if you are in a wheelchair. The key areas to be concerned about are public rooms, outer decks, and, of course, your cabin.

If you need a specially equipped cabin, book as far in advance as possible and ask questions of your travel agent or a cruise-line representative. Specifically, ask how your cabin is configured and equipped. Is the entrance level or ramped? Are all doorways at least 30″ wide (wider if your wheelchair is not standard)? Are pathways to beds, closets, and bathrooms at least 36″ wide and unobstructed? In the bathroom, is there 42″ of clear space in front of the toilet and are there grab bars behind and on one side of it and in the bathtub and shower? Are elevators wide enough to accommodate wheelchairs?

The best cruise ship for passengers who use wheelchairs is one that ties up right at the dock at every port, at which time a ramp or even an elevator is always made available. Unfortunately, it's hard to ascertain this in advance, since a ship may tie up at the dock at one port on one voyage and, on the next, anchor in the harbor and have passengers transported to shore via tender. Ask your travel agent to find out which ships are capable of docking. If a tender is used, some ships will have crew members carry the wheelchair and passenger from the ship to the tender. Unfortunately, other ships will refuse to take wheelchairs on tenders, especially if the water is choppy.

What to Pack

Certain packing rules apply to all cruises. Always take along a sweater to counter cool evening ocean breezes or overactive air-conditioning. A rain slicker is essential—many travelers who plan on indulging in some of the more active shore excursions pack a complete rain suit. Be prepared to dress in layers, since temperatures can vary considerably during the day. Make sure you take at least one pair of comfortable walking shoes for exploring port towns, and waterproof footwear will be useful as well. Ankle-high rubber boots are ideal for many shore trips.

Generally speaking, plan on one outfit for every two days of cruising, especially if your wardrobe contains many interchangeable pieces. Ships often have laundry facilities. Don't forget your toiletries and sundry items, but if you do, these are readily available in port shops or the ship's gift shop (though usually at a premium price). Cabin amenities typically include soap and often shampoo, conditioner, and other lotions and potions.

Outlets in cabin bathrooms are usually compatible with U.S.-purchased appliances. This may not be the case on older ships or those with European registries; call ahead if this is a concern for you. Most cabin bathrooms are equipped with low-voltage outlets for electric shavers, and many newer ships have built-in hair dryers.

Take an extra pair of eyeglasses or contact lenses in your carry-on luggage. If you use a prescription drug, pack enough to last the duration of the trip or have your doctor write a prescription using the drug's generic name, because brand names vary from country to country. Always carry medications in their original packaging to avoid problems with customs officials. Don't pack them in luggage that you plan to check, in case your bags go astray. Pack a list of the offices that supply refunds for lost or stolen traveler's checks. Make a copy of your passport and keep it separate from your actual passport. If you should lose your passport or it is stolen, having a copy of it can greatly facilitate replacement. Make copies, or write down the numbers, of your credit cards in case those should be lost or stolen.

Formal/Semiformal/Casual

Although no two cruises are quite the same, evening dress tends to fall into three categories.

Formal cruises celebrate the ceremony of cruising. Jackets and ties for men are the rule for dinner, tuxedos are not uncommon, and the dress code is observed faithfully throughout the evening.

Semiformal cruises are a bit more relaxed than their formal counterparts. Men wear jackets and ties most nights.

Casual cruises are the most popular. Shipboard dress and lifestyle are informal. Men wear sport shirts and slacks to dinner most nights and don jackets and ties only two or three evenings of a typical seven-day sailing.

In today's casual-Friday world, most cruise lines have reduced the focus on formal and semiformal dining and offer multiple dining options, including room service. However, it would be wise to ask the cruise line about its dining dress code so you know what to expect and what to pack.

ARRIVING & DEPARTING

If you have purchased an air-sea package, you will be met by a cruise-company representative when your plane lands at the port city and then shuttled directly to the ship in a bus or minivan. Some cruise lines arrange to transport luggage between airport and ship so passengers don't have to deal with baggage claim at the start of your cruise or with baggage check-in at the end. If you decide not to buy the air-sea package but still plan to fly, ask your travel agent if you can use the ship's transfer bus. Otherwise, you will have to take a taxi to the ship.

If you live close to the port of embarkation, bus transportation may be available. If you are part of a group that has booked a cruise together, this transportation may be part of your package. Another option for those who live close to their point of departure is to drive to the ship, an increasingly popular option. Major U.S. and Canadian cruise ports all have parking facilities.

Embarkation

Check-In

On arrival at the dock, you must check in before boarding your ship. An officer will collect or stamp your ticket, inspect or even retain your passport or other official identification, ask you to fill out a tourist card, check that you have the correct visas, and collect any unpaid port or departure tax.

Seating assignments for the dining room are often handed out at this time, too, although most cruise ships are now offering you the opportunity to dine when and with whom you like in any of several restaurants aboard. You may also register your credit card to open a shipboard account, or that may be done later at the purser's office.

After this, you will be required to go through a security check and to pass your hand baggage through an X-ray inspection. These are the same machines in use at airports, so ask to have your photographic film inspected by hand.

Although it takes only 5 or 10 minutes per family to check in, lines are often long, so aim for off-peak hours. The worst time tends to be immediately after the ship begins boarding; the later it is, the less crowded. For example, if boarding is from 2 to 4:30, lines are shorter after 3:30.

Boarding the Ship

Before you walk up the gangway, the ship's photographer will probably take your picture; there's no charge unless you buy the picture (usually $7 to $8). On board, stewards may serve welcome drinks in souvenir glasses—for which you're usually charged between $3 and $5.

You will either be escorted to your cabin by a steward or, on a smaller ship, given your key—now usually a plastic card—by a ship's officer and directed to your cabin. Some elevators are unavailable to passengers during boarding, since they are used to transport luggage. You may arrive to find your luggage outside your cabin or just inside the door; if it hasn't arrived a half hour before sailing, contact the purser. If your luggage doesn't make it to the ship in time, the purser will have it flown to the next port.

Disembarkation

The last night of your cruise is full of business. On most ships you must place everything except your hand luggage outside your door, ready to be picked up by midnight or early in the morning. Color-coded tags, distributed to your cabin in a debarkation packet, should be placed on your luggage before the crew collects it. The color of your tag will determine when you leave the ship and help you retrieve your luggage on the pier.

Your shipboard bill is left in your room during the last day of a cruise or on the morning of your departure from the ship; to pay the bill (if you haven't already put it on your credit card) or to settle any questions, you must stand in line at the purser's office. Tips to the cabin steward and dining staff are distributed on the last night of the cruise or are automatically added to your onboard account. On many ships, you can review your account on your in-cabin television and change those tips in any way you like, up or down. You may also make changes to or discuss your bill at the purser's office at any time during the cruise. Some ships will deliver your account to your room the morning of your departure. If you have not already paid it by credit card or wish to dispute any charges on it, go to the purser immediately to settle or discuss your account. Do not wait until you're ready to get off the ship, as lines may be long and the wait could delay your departure and fray your nerves. Some lines close down their computer files for the cruise by 9 AM or 10 AM to prepare for the next cruise and may be unable to credit your account with any disputed charges, requiring you to contact your credit-card company or the cruise line later for a refund.

On the morning the cruise ends, in-room breakfast service may not be available because stewards are too busy, but you will usually find breakfast being served in both the formal dining room and at the ship's buffet dining area. Most passengers clear out of their cabins as soon as possible, gather their hand luggage, and stake out a chair in one of the public lounges to await the ship's clearance through customs. Be patient—it takes a long time to unload and sort thousands of pieces of luggage.

Passengers are disembarked in groups according to color-coded luggage tags; those with the earliest flights get off first. If you have a tight connection, notify the purser before the last day, and he or she may be able to arrange faster pre-clearing and debarkation.

ON BOARD

Shipboard Accounts

Virtually all cruise ships operate as cashless societies. Passengers charge onboard purchases and settle their accounts at the end of the cruise with a credit card, traveler's checks, or cash. You can sign for wine at dinner, drinks at the bar, shore excursions, gifts in the shop—virtually any expense you may incur aboard ship. On some lines, an imprint from a major credit card is necessary to open an account. Otherwise, a cash deposit may be required and a positive balance maintained to keep the shipboard account open. Either way, you will want to open a line of credit soon after settling in, if an account was not opened for you at embarkation. This can easily be arranged by visiting the purser's office, in the central atrium or main lobby. On most ships, you can now view your account at any time on your in-cabin television. To make your stay aboard as seamless—and as cashless—as possible, many cruise lines now add dining-room gratuities at a set rate to your onboard account. Some lines offer access to personal records via Internet; you can alter automatic tips, for example, before your cruise begins.

Tipping

For better or worse, tipping is an integral part of the cruise experience. Most companies pay their cruise staff nominal wages and expect tips to make up the difference between this nominal amount and a living wage. Most cruise lines have recommended tipping guidelines, and on many ships "voluntary" tipping for beverage service has been replaced with a mandatory 15% service charge, which is added to every bar bill. On the other hand, the most expensive luxury lines include tips in the cruise fare and may prohibit crew members from accepting additional gratuities. On many small adventure ships, a collection box is placed in the dining room or lounge on the last full day of the cruise, and passengers contribute anonymously.

Some large cruise lines now add dining-room tips of $10 to $12 per person per day directly to your bill. That sum is intended to cover all your dining-room service, other than the wine steward and the maître d' if he provides special service to you (although both those may also be included in the daily tip that is automatically added to your account); it may also include your room steward. Ask the purser if tips are being added to your bill and which personnel will receive them—waiter, busboy, and room steward are all expecting tips. You may adjust tips up or down.

Dining

Ocean liners serve food nearly around the clock. There may be as many as four breakfast options: early-morning coffee and pastries on deck, breakfast in bed through room service, buffet-style dining in the cafeteria, and a more formal breakfast in the dining room. There may also be several lunch choices, mid-afternoon hors d'oeuvres, teatime, and late-night buffets. You may eat whatever is on the menu, in any quantity, at any meal. Room service is traditionally, but not always, free (⇨ Shipboard Services, *below*).

Restaurants

The chief meals of the day are served in the main dining room, which on most ships can accommodate only half the passengers at once. Meals are therefore usually served in early (or main) and late (or second) seatings. Early seating for dinner is generally between 6 and 6:30, late seating between 8 and 8:30.

Most cruise ships have a buffet-style restaurant, usually near the swimming pool, where you can eat breakfast and lunch. On many of the newer ships, that room, nearly always on the Lido Deck near the swimming pool, becomes a casual, waiter-service dining room at dinner. Those dining rooms, often featuring grilled specialties, are popular on nights when the ship has been in port all day. Many ships provide self-serve coffee or tea in their cafeteria around the clock, as well as midnight buffets.

Some ships, particularly newer ones, also have alternative specialty restaurants for which a reservation must be made. You might have to pay a fee for grilled steak or Asian cuisine. On-demand food shops may include pizzerias, ice cream parlors, and caviar or cappuccino bars; there may be an extra charge at these facilities, too.

Smoking is often banned in main dining rooms. Smoking policies vary and change; contact your cruise line to find out what the situation will be on your cruise.

Seatings

When it comes to your dining-table assignment, you should have options on four important points: early or late seating; smoking or no-smoking section (if smoking is allowed in the dining room); a table for two, four, six, or eight; and special dietary needs. When you receive your cruise documents, you will usually receive a card asking for your dining preferences. Fill this out and return it to the cruise line, but remember that you will not get your seating assignment until you board the ship. Check it out immediately, and if your request was not met, see the maître d'—usually there is a time and place set up for changes in dining assignments.

On some ships, seating times are strictly observed. Ten to 15 minutes after the scheduled mealtime, the dining-room doors are closed, although this policy is increasingly rare. On other ships, passengers may enter the dining room at their leisure, but they must be out by the end of the seating. When a ship has just one seating, passengers may enter any time the kitchen is open.

Seating assignments often apply only to dinner. Most ships have open seating for breakfast or lunch, which means you may sit anywhere at any time the meal is served. Smaller or more luxurious ships offer open seating for all meals.

Several large cruise lines now offer several restaurant and dining options and have eliminated preassigned seating, so you can dine with whom you like at any table that's available and at any time the dining room is open.

Cuisine

Most ships serve food geared to the American palate, but there are also theme dinners featuring the cuisine of a particular country. Some European ships, especially smaller vessels, may offer a particular cuisine throughout the cruise—Scandinavian, German, Italian, or Greek, perhaps—depending on the ship's or the crew's nationality. The quality of cruise-ship cooking is generally good, but even a skilled chef is hard put to serve 500 or more extraordinary dinners per hour. Presentation is often spectacular, especially at gala midnight buffets.

There is often a direct relationship between the cost of a cruise and the quality of its cuisine. The food is very sophisticated on some (mostly expensive) lines, such as Crystal Cruises. In the more moderate price range, Celebrity Cruises has gained renown for the culinary stylings of French chef Michel Roux, who acts as a consultant to the line.

Special Diets

With notification well in advance, many ships can provide a kosher, low-salt, low-cholesterol, sugar-free, vegetarian, or other special menu. However, there's always a chance that the wrong dish will somehow be handed to you. Especially when it comes to soups and desserts, it's a good idea to ask about the ingredients.

Large ships usually offer an alternative "light" or "spa" menu based upon American Heart Association guidelines, using less fat, leaner cuts of meat, low-cholesterol or low-sodium preparations, smaller portions, salads, fresh-fruit desserts, and healthful garnishes. Some smaller ships may not be able to accommodate special dietary needs. Vegetarians generally have no trouble finding appropriate selections.

Wine

Wine at meals costs extra on most ships; prices are usually comparable to those in shoreside restaurants and are charged to your shipboard account. A handful of luxury vessels include both wine and liquor. On some lines, you can also select the wines you might like for dinner before leaving home and they will appear at your table and on your bill at the end of the cruise.

SAFETY AT SEA

Once you've settled into your cabin, locate the life vests and review the emergency instructions inside the cabin door or near the life vests. Let the ship's purser know if you have a disability that may hamper a speedy exit from your cabin. In case of a real emergency, the purser can quickly dispatch a crew member to assist you. Learn to secure the vests properly. If you are traveling with children, be sure that child-size life jackets are placed in your cabin.

Within 24 hours of embarkation, you will be asked to attend a mandatory lifeboat drill. Do so and listen carefully. If you have any questions, ask them. Only in the most extreme circumstances will you need to abandon ship—but it has happened. The time you spend learning the right procedure may serve you well in a mishap.

Fire Safety

The greatest danger facing cruise-ship passengers is fire. All of the ships reviewed in this book must meet certain international fire-safety standards requiring that ships have sprinkler systems, smoke detectors, and other safety features. These rules are designed to protect against loss of life, but they do not guarantee that a fire will not happen; in fact, fire is relatively common on cruise ships. The point here is not to alarm but to emphasize the importance of taking fire safety seriously.

Health Care

Quality medical care at sea is another important safety issue. All big ships are equipped with medical infirmaries to handle minor emergencies. However, these should not be confused with hospitals. There are no international standards governing medical facilities or personnel aboard cruise ships, although the American Medical Association has recommended that such standards be adopted. If you have a preexisting medical condition, discuss your upcoming cruise with your doctor. Pack an extra supply of any medicines you might need. Once aboard, see the ship's doctor and alert him or her to your condition, and discuss treatments or emergency procedures before any problem arises. Passengers with potentially life-threatening conditions should consider signing up with a medical evacuation service, and all passengers should review their health insurance to make sure they are covered while on a cruise.

If you become seriously ill or injured and happen to be near a major city, you may be taken to a medical facility shoreside. But if you're farther afield, you may have to be airlifted off the ship by helicopter and flown either to the nearest American territory or to an airport where you can be taken by charter jet to the United States. Many standard health insurance policies, including Medicare plans, do not cover these or other medical expenses incurred outside the United States. You can, however, buy supplemental health insurance that is in effect only when you travel.

The most common minor medical problems confronting cruise passengers are seasickness and gastrointestinal distress. Modern cruise ships, unlike their transatlantic predecessors, are relatively motion-free vessels outfitted with computer-controlled stabilizers, and they usually sail in relatively calm waters. If you do feel queasy, you can get seasickness pills aboard ship. (Many ships give them out free at the front desk.)

Outbreaks of food poisoning and viruses occasionally occur aboard cruise ships. Episodes are random; they can occur on ships old and new, big and small, budget and luxury. The Centers for Disease Control and Prevention (CDC) monitors cruise-ship hygiene and sanitation procedures, conducting voluntary inspections twice a year of all ships that sail regularly from U.S. ports (this program does not include ships that never visit the United States). A high score on the CDC report doesn't mean you won't get sick. Outbreaks have taken place on ships that consistently score very highly; conversely, some ships score very poorly yet passengers never get sick.

The latest cruise-ship sanitation scores (known as the "Green Sheet") are posted on the CDC's Web site: www.cdc.gov. A copy of the most recent sanitation inspection report on an individual vessel may be obtained by writing to **National Center for Environmental Health** (Vessel Sanitation Program, 4770 Buford Hwy., NE, Mailstop F-16 Atlanta, GA 30341-3724).

Crime on Ships

Crime aboard cruise ships has occasionally become headline news, thanks in large part to a few well-publicized cases. Most people never have any type of problem, but you should exercise the same precautions aboard ship that you would at home. Keep your valuables out of sight—on big ships virtually every cabin has a small safe in the closet. Don't carry too much cash ashore, use your credit card whenever possible, and keep your money in a secure place, such as a front pocket that's harder to pick. Single women traveling with friends should stick together, especially when returning to their cabins late at night. Be careful about whom you befriend, as you would anywhere, whether it's a fellow passenger or a member of the crew. Don't be paranoid, but do be prudent.

GOING ASHORE

Traveling by cruise ship presents an opportunity to visit many places in a short time. The flip side is that your stay in each port of call will be brief. For this reason cruise lines offer shore excursions, which maximize passengers' time. There are a number of advantages to shore excursions arranged by your ship: in some destinations, transportation may be unreliable, and a ship-packaged tour is the best way to see distant sights. Also, you don't have to worry about missing the ship. The disadvantage of a shore excursion is the cost—you pay more for the convenience of having the ship do the legwork for you. Of course, you can always book a tour independently, hire a taxi, or use foot power to explore on your own. Most of the towns have hiking trails easily accessible to port areas, and a stop at the local visitor center can help you plan a walking tour within your time limit. However, be sure to carry along rain gear and drinking water, even for the most leisurely stroll. The weather in Alaska is very fickle and subject to rapid changes.

Many of the busier port cities tend to have several ships in port at a time, and the more popular shore trips can fill up quickly. If your heart is set on a particular experience, book it before your cruise or on board as soon as you can. Some excursions, such as flightseeing trips and the Skagway narrow-gauge rail trip, are in very high demand. Information on local tours is available at the visitor-information counter usually close to the pier in each port.

Arriving in Port

When your ship arrives in a port, it will either tie up alongside a dock or anchor out in a harbor. If the ship is docked, passengers walk down the gangway to go ashore. Docking makes it easy to go back and forth between the shore and the ship.

Tendering

If your ship anchors in the harbor, you will have to take a small boat—called a launch or tender—to get ashore. Tendering is a nuisance. Passengers wishing to disembark may be required to gather in a public room, get sequenced boarding passes, and wait until their numbers are called. The ride to shore may take as long as 20 minutes. If you don't like waiting, plan to go ashore an hour or so after the ship drops its anchor.

Because tenders can be difficult to board, passengers with mobility problems may not be able to visit certain ports. The larger ships are more likely to use tenders. It is usually possible to learn before booking a cruise whether the ship will dock or anchor at its ports of call.

Before anyone is allowed to walk down the gangway or board a tender, the ship must be cleared for landing. Immigration and customs officials board the vessel to examine passports and sort through red tape. It may be more than an hour before you're allowed ashore. You will be issued a boarding pass, which you'll need to get back on board.

Returning to the Ship

Cruise lines are strict about sailing times, which are posted at the gangway and elsewhere and announced in the daily schedule of activities. Be sure to be back on board at least a half hour before the announced sailing time or you may be stranded. If you are on a shore excursion that was sold by the cruise line, however, the captain will wait for your group before casting off. That is one reason many passengers prefer ship-packaged tours.

If you're not on one of the ship's tours and the ship sails without you, immediately contact the cruise line's port representative, whose phone number is often listed on the daily schedule of activities. You may be able to hitch a ride on a pilot boat, although that is unlikely. Passengers who miss the boat must pay their own way to the next port.

THE CRUISE FLEET

For each cruise line, we list only the ships (grouped by similar configurations) that regularly cruise in Alaska. When two or more ships are substantially similar, their names are given at the beginning of a review and separated by commas. Within each cruise line, ships are listed from largest to smallest.

Passenger-capacity figures are given on the basis of two people sharing a cabin (basis-2); however, many of the larger ships have 3- and 4-berth cabins, which can increase the total number of passengers tremendously when all berths are occupied. When total occupancy figures differ from basis-2 occupancy, we give them in parentheses.

Ocean Liners

Carnival Cruise Lines

Carnival Cruise Lines is the largest and most successful cruise line in the world, carrying more passengers than any other. Brash and sometimes rowdy, Carnival throws a great party. Activities and entertainment are nonstop, beginning just after sunrise and continuing well into the night. Under Carnival's "Total Choice Dining" plan, passengers are assigned seatings in the dining room, but pizza and room service are available at all hours and most ships have an alternative restaurant as well. Carnival cruises are popular with young, single cruisers as well as with those older than 55. The line's offerings also appeal to parents cruising with their children.

In 2006, Carnival will offer seven-day, one-way cruises between Vancouver and Whittier and round-trip loop cruises from Vancouver.

Gratuities of $10 per passenger, per day are automatically added to onboard accounts and are distributed to stewards and waitstaff. Passengers may adjust the amount based on the level of service experienced. A 15% gratuity is automatically added to bar and beverage tabs.

Carnival Cruise Lines, 3655 N.W. 87th Ave., Miami, FL 33178-2428 ☎ 305/599–2600, 800/438–6744, or 800/327–9501 www.carnival.com.

THE SHIP **Carnival Spirit.** The first of Carnival's Spirit-class ships entered service in 2001 with notable design improvements over previous lines. For example, all staterooms aboard these superliners are above ocean level, making for a more comfortable cruise. Cabins have ample drawer and closet space, and in-cabin TVs show first-run films. Other innovations include eye-popping, 11-story atriums, two-level promenades (partially glass enclosed to create a protected viewing perch), wide decks, shopping malls, and reservations-only supper clubs. Greater speed allows Spirit-class ships to visit destinations in a week that would take other ships 10 days or more. Most staterooms have ocean views, and of those, 80% have balconies. This is a great ship for kids, with a 2,400-square-foot enclosed play area, plus outdoor play areas, a video wall, and an arcade. The pool, open to all ages, has a retractable roof, so you can enjoy a swim even in Alaska. *1,062 cabins, 2,124 passengers (2,667 at full occupancy), 12 passenger decks Restaurant, café, dining room, ice-cream parlor, pizzeria, in-room safes, minibars, in-room VCRs, 4 pools (1 indoor), fitness classes, gym, hair salon, outdoor hot tubs, sauna, spa, steam room, 18 bars, casino, dance club, showroom, video game room, children's pro-*

grams (ages 2–15), dry cleaning, laundry facilities, laundry service, Internet, no-smoking rooms; no kids under 4 months 💳 *AE, D, MC, V.*

Celebrity Cruises

Celebrity Cruises has made a name for itself based on sleek ships and superior food. Celebrity has risen above typical mass-market cruise cuisine by hiring Chef Michel Roux as a consultant. All food is prepared from scratch, using only fresh produce and herbs, aged beef, and fresh fish—even the ice cream on board is homemade. Celebrity provides traditional assigned seating in the dining room, with a variety of casual and specialty dining options. In just a short time Celebrity has won the admiration of its passengers, and its competitors—who have copied its nouvelle cuisine, occasional adults-only cruises, and cigar clubs, and hired its personnel (a true compliment). Celebrity attracts everyone from older couples to honeymooners.

In 2006, *Summit* will make seven-day, one-way Gulf of Alaska cruises between Vancouver and Seward; the *Infinity* will sail the Inside Passage round-trip from Vancouver; and the *Mercury* will cruise the Inside Passage from Seattle.

Tip your cabin steward/butlers $3.50 per day; chief housekeeper 50¢ per day; dining-room waiter $3.50 per day; assistant waiter $2 per day; and restaurant manager 75¢ per day, for a total of $10.25 per day. A 15% service charge is added to all beverage checks. Gratuities are typically handed out on the last night of the cruise, or they may be charged to your shipboard account.

Celebrity Cruises, 1050 Caribbean Way, Miami, FL 33132-2096 ☎ *305/539–6000 or 800/646–1456* 📠 *800/437–5111* 🌐 *www.celebrity.com.*

THE SHIPS ★ ***Infinity, Summit.*** Dramatic, exterior glass elevators, a glass-dome pool area, and a window-wrapped ship-top observation lounge keep the magnificence of Alaska well within the passenger's view. These are the newest and largest in Celebrity's fleet, and each stocks plenty of premium amenities, including a flower-filled conservatory, music library, Internet café with 18 workstations, golf simulator, brand-name boutiques, and an expansive spa with both a seawater thalassotherapy pool and a resistance swimming pool. Cabins are bright, spacious, and well appointed, and 80% have an ocean view (74% of those have private verandas). There is also in-cabin Internet access. With a staff member for every two passengers, service is especially attentive. *975 cabins, 1,950 passengers, 11 passenger decks* *Restaurant, café, dining room, food court, ice-cream parlor, pizzeria, in-room safes, minibars, in-room VCRs, 3 pools (1 indoor), fitness classes, gym, hair salon, hot tubs (indoor and outdoor), sauna, spa, steam room, 6 bars, casino, cinema, dance club, showroom, video game room, children's programs (ages 3–17), dry cleaning, laundry service, Internet* 💳 *AE, D, DC, MC, V.*

Mercury. With features such as a golf simulator, video walls, and interactive television systems in cabins, this ship is a high-tech pioneer, yet it is elegant and warm. Many large windows—including a dramatic two-story wall of glass in the dining room and wraparound windows in the Stratosphere Lounge, in the gym, and in the beauty salon—bathe the ship in natural light and afford excellent views of Alaska's natural beauty. Plus there are retractable glass sunroofs over the pools. The elaborate Elemis spas have enormous thalassotherapy pools and the latest in treatments. Standard cabins are intelligently appointed and apportioned, with few frills; space is well used, making for maximum elbow room in the bathrooms and good storage space in the closets. *935 cabins, 1,870 passengers, 10 passenger decks* *Dining room, food court, ice-cream parlor, pizzeria, in-room safes, minibars, 4 pools (1 indoors), fitness classes, gym, hair salon, outdoor hot tubs, sauna, spa, steam room, 6 bars, casino, cinema, dance club, showroom, video game room, children's programs (ages 3–17), dry cleaning, laundry service, Internet* *AE, D, DC, MC, V.*

Holland America Line

Founded in 1873, Holland America (HAL) is one of the oldest names in cruising. Steeped in the traditions of the transatlantic crossing, its cruises are classic, conservative affairs renowned for their grace and gentility. Service is taken seriously: the line maintains a school in Indonesia to train staff members, rather than hiring out of a union hall. The staff on the line's Alaska cruises includes a naturalist and a Native artist-in-residence. HAL passengers tend to be older and less active than those traveling on the ships of its parent line, Carnival, although the age difference is getting narrower. As its ships attract a more youthful clientele, HAL has taken steps to shed its "old folks" image, such as offering trendier cuisine and a "Club Hal" children's program.

Holland America's Alaska-bound ships have open seating for breakfast and lunch and four seatings for dinner. Most HAL ships also have specialty restaurants, and all provide 24-hour room service. HAL has a no-tips-required policy. For convenience, $10 per passenger, per day is automatically added to onboard accounts for stewards and waitstaff. Passengers may adjust the amount based on the level of service experienced. Tips for room service delivery are at passengers' discretion. A 15% gratuity is added to bar service tabs.

Holland America Line, 300 Elliott Ave. W, Seattle, WA 98119 *206/281–3535 or 877/932–4259* *206/281–7110* *www.hollandamerica.com.*

THE SHIPS **_Oosterdam, Westerdam, Zuiderdam._** With the highest space-to-passenger ratio in the fleet, HAL's Vista-class ships—forward-looking both in design and spirit—launched in December 2002. Exterior panorama elevators, providing expansive sea views, link 10 passenger decks. All the HAL trademarks, including a covered promenade deck encircling the entire ship, two interior promenades, and white-gloved stewards, are here, as are such up-to-date touches as in-cabin Internet access, a golf simulator, extensive spa facilities, and an alternative Pacific Northwest restaurant. A retractable dome over the pool means you can enjoy a swim even in Alaska. These ships also offer a range of understated, spacious accommodation categories, 85% of which have ocean views, most with private verandas. In 2006, the *Oosterdam* and *Westerdam* will be based in Seattle, while the *Zuiderdam* will sail from Vancouver. *924 cabins, 1,848 passengers, 11 passenger decks Specialty restaurant, dining room, buffet, pizzeria, in-cabin safes, refrigerators, in-cabin DVDs, in-cabin data ports, Wi-Fi, 2 pools (1 indoors), children's pool, fitness classes, gym, hair salon, 5 hot tubs, sauna, spa, steam room, 9 bars, casino, cinema, 2 dance clubs, library, showroom, video game room, children's programs (ages 3–18), dry cleaning, laundry service, computer room AE, D, MC, V.*

Volendam, Zaandam. These ships are structurally similar to HAL's other vessels, with signature two-tier dining rooms and a retractable roof over the main pool, but they are newer, and their themed interior design inject elements of youthfulness. They are also slightly larger and have Internet cafés and practice-size tennis courts. Huge bouquets of fresh, fragrant flowers are everywhere (a Holland America trademark); and each ship has a teak promenade completely encircling the ship, which means there will always be room for you at the rail to watch the sunset. All standard outside cabins come with a bathtub, and all suites and minisuites have private verandas. The "Passport to Fitness" program encourages a healthy diet and exercise. In 2006, the *Zaandam* will homeport in Seattle, while the *Volendam* will sail from Vancouver. *720 cabins, 1,440 passengers (1,848 at full occupancy), 10 passenger decks Specialty restaurant, dining room, buffet, in-cabin safes, refrigerators, in-cabin DVDs, Wi-Fi, 2 pools (1 indoors), children's pool, fitness classes, gym, hair salon, 2 hot tubs, sauna, spa, steam room, 6 bars, casino, cinema, dance club, library, showroom, video game room, children's programs (ages 3–18), dry cleaning, laundry facilities, laundry service, computer room AE, D, MC, V.*

Ryndam, Statendam, Veendam. An abundance of glass, outdoor deck space, and a retractable roof over the main pool make these good ships for Alaska cruising. Great views can be found along the wraparound promenade. From bow to stern, these ships are full of lounges and restaurants—14 in all—some cozy, some grand, and most with expansive floor-to-ceiling windows. The Crow's Nest, redesigned on the Ryndam with hip banquettes and an underlighted bar, is a combined observation lounge and nightclub overlooking the bow; the view-blessed Explorations Café, a combined coffee bar, Internet café, library, and card room, is a popular hangout. A three-deck atrium and a two-tier dining room, replete with dual grand staircases framing an orchestra balcony, are among the welcoming public spaces. Staterooms are comfortable, with an understated elegance. In 2006, the *Ryndam, Statendam,* and *Veendam* will cruise between Vancouver and Seward, via Glacier Bay or Hubbard Glacier. *633 cabins, 1,266 passengers (1,590 at full occupancy), 10 passenger decks Specialty restaurant, dining room, buffet, in-cabin safes, refrigerators, in-cabin DVDs, Wi-Fi, indoor pool, fitness classes, gym, hair salon, 2 hot tubs, sauna, spa, steam room, 9 bars, casino, cinema, dance club, library, showroom, video game room, children's programs (ages 3–18), dry cleaning, laundry facilities, laundry service, computer room AE, D, MC, V.*

Norwegian Cruise Line

In 1966, Norwegian Cruise Line (NCL) launched a new concept in cruising: regularly scheduled cruises on a single-class ship. No longer simply a means of transportation, the ship became a destination unto itself. NCL continues to innovate. It offers "Freestyle Cruising," which eliminates dinner table and time assignments and dress codes, and the widest choice of restaurants afloat. The line has even loosened the rules on disembarkation, which means passengers can relax in their cabins until it's time to leave the ship (instead of gathering in a lounge to wait for their numbers to be called). Most of NCL's Alaska fleet is based in Seattle rather than Vancouver, B.C., which can be a more convenient departure point for many U.S.-based passengers. The line's passenger list usually includes seniors, families, and younger couples, mostly from the United States and Canada.

NCL applies a service charge to passengers' shipboard accounts: $10 per passenger per day for those 13 and older, and $5 per day for children (ages 3–12). These automatic tips can be increased, decreased, or removed. A 15% gratuity is added to bar tabs and spa bills.

Norwegian Cruise Line, 7665 Corporate Center Dr., Miami, FL 33126 ☎ 305/436–4000 or 800/327–7030 www.ncl.com.

THE SHIPS

Norwegian Jewel. One of the line's newest and largest ships, the *Norwegian Jewel* is the "next generation" of Freestyle Cruising vessels. An extensive health club, impressive children's facilities (including a children's pool), and separate teen disco are definite pluses, as is wireless Internet access throughout the ship. Cabins are reasonably large, with stylish decor and attractive cherry-veneer cabinetry; minisuites with private verandas are especially nice. Most accommodations have compartmentalized bathrooms with toilet, sink, and showers separated by sliding glass doors and all cabins have coffeemakers. Unique to this ship are 10 Courtyard Villas sporting private courtyards and sundecks. *1,200 cabins, 2,400 passengers, 11 passenger decks 4 restaurants, 3 dining rooms, buffet, ice-cream parlor, pizzeria, in-cabin safes, refrigerators, some in-cabin DVDs, in-cabin data ports, Wi-Fi, 3 pools (1 indoors), children's pool, fitness classes, gym, hair salon, 6 hot tubs, sauna, spa, steam room, 9 bars, casino, cinema, 2 dance clubs, library, showroom, video game room, children's programs (ages 2–17), dry cleaning, laundry facilities, laundry service, computer room AE, D, MC, V.*

Fodor's Choice ★

Norwegian Star. Built specifically to accommodate Freestyle Cruising, this is one of NCL's largest and fastest ships. Offering more dining choices than any other ship in Alaska, *Star* has 10 different eateries, with everything from French, Italian, contemporary, and spa cuisine to tapas and sushi. The ship also has a 24-hour fitness center, a Balinese-theme spa, a golf driving range, and an indoor jet-current exercise pool. Garden Villas, the top-of-the-line staterooms, have private rooftop terraces. Standard cabins take their cue from high-end hotel rooms, with rich cherrywood, tea- and coffeemakers, and large bathrooms. Most staterooms can accommodate a third guest, and many cabins can be linked to create suites for larger groups. *1,120 cabins, 2,240 passengers, 11 passenger decks 8 restaurants, 2 dining rooms, ice-cream parlor, in-cabin safes, refrig-*

erators, Wi-Fi, 3 pools (1 indoors), fitness classes, gym, hair salon, 2 hot tubs, sauna, spa, steam room, 9 bars, casino, cinema, 2 dance clubs, showroom, video game room, children's programs (ages 2–17), dry cleaning, laundry service, computer room ▭ *AE, D, DC, MC, V.*

Norwegian Sun. The *Sun* comes with all the bells and whistles, including a variety of dining options, specialty bars, and Internet access—both in a café and in cabins. The 24-hour health club has expansive ocean views, and the presence of the full-service Mandara Spa means you can turn your cruise into a spa vacation. Cabins are adequately laid out, with large circular windows and sitting areas, sufficient (but not generous) shelf and drawer space, and two lower beds that convert to a queen. *1,001 cabins, 2,002 passengers (2,400 at full occupancy), 11 passenger decks* *8 restaurants, 2 dining rooms, in-cabin safes, refrigerators, 2 pools, fitness classes, gym, hair salon, 4 hot tubs, sauna, spa, steam room, 13 bars, casino, cinema, dance club, showroom, video game room, children's programs (ages 2–17), dry cleaning, laundry facilities, Internet room* ▭ *AE, D, DC, MC, V.*

Norwegian Wind. Floor-to-ceiling windows, abundant picture windows, terraced decks, and a wraparound promenade make this an ideal ship for taking in Alaska's gorgeous views. Instead of one big dining room, it has three smaller dining rooms, a bistro, a sports bar, an outdoor café, and a pizzeria. Convertible sofas in the cabins, connecting staterooms, and activity-filled children's and teens' programs make this a good choice for family cruising. *874 cabins, 1,748 passengers, 10 passenger decks* *Restaurant, 3 dining rooms, pizzeria, 2 pools, fitness classes, gym, hair salon, 2 hot tubs, spa, 9 bars, casino, dance club, showroom, video game room, children's programs (ages 2–17), dry cleaning, laundry service* ▭ *AE, MC, V.*

Princess Cruise Line

Princess was catapulted to stardom in 1977, when it became the star of *The Love Boat* television series, which introduced millions of viewers to the still-new concept of a seagoing vacation. The name and famous "seawitch" logo have remained synonymous with cruising ever since. Nearly everything about Princess is big, but the line doesn't sacrifice quality for quantity when it comes to building beautiful vessels. Service, especially in the dining rooms, is of a high standard. In short, Princess is refined without being pretentious. All Princess ships offer the line's innovative "Personal Choice Cruising" program, an individualized, unstructured style of cruising that gives passengers choice and flexibility in customizing their cruise experience, including a choice between traditional fixed seating in the dining room or open seating in any of the onboard restaurants. Princess passengers' average age is 45; you see a mix of younger and older couples on board.

Princess suggests tipping $10 per person, per day. Gratuities are automatically added to accounts, which passengers can adjust at the purser's desk; 15% is added to bar bills.

Princess Cruises, 24844 Avenue Rockefeller, Santa Clarita, CA 91355-4999 *661/753–0000 or 800/774–6237* *www.princess.com.*

THE SHIPS

Sun Princess, Dawn Princess. Four-story atriums with circular marble floors, stained-glass domes, and magnificent floating staircases are ideal settings for relaxation, people-watching, and making a grand entrance. Each subtly decorated vessel has two main showrooms and several dining rooms and restaurants (some with extra charges), from large to intimate. More than 60% of outside cabins in these sister ships have private balconies. All standard cabins are decorated in light colors and have a queen-size bed convertible to two doubles, and ample closet and bath space (with shower only). Several cabins on each ship are deemed fully accessible. A wraparound teak promenade lined with canopied steamer chairs provides a peaceful setting for reading, napping, or daydreaming, and a pool with a retractable glass roof allows for all-weather swimming. *975 cabins, 1,950 passengers, 10 passenger decks Restaurant, 2 dining rooms, ice-cream parlor, pizzeria, in-cabin safes, refrigerators, 4 pools, fitness classes, gym, hair salon, hot tubs, sauna, spa, 7 bars, casino, dance club, 2 showrooms, video game room, children's programs (ages 3–17), dry cleaning, laundry facilities, laundry service, computer room; no kids under 6 months AE, D, MC, V.*

Regal Princess. A ship-top entertainment-and-observation center brings in the scenery on this San Francisco–based ship. A little smaller than Princess's other Alaska-bound vessels, the *Regal* still has plenty of amenities, including a coffee-and-pastry café, 24-hour casual dining, teak decks, a lavish art collection, and 180 staterooms with private balconies. *795 cabins, 1,590 passengers, 11 passenger decks Dining room, pizzeria, in-cabin safes, refrigerators, 2 pools, fitness classes, gym, hair salon, outdoor hot tubs, sauna, spa, steam room, 7 bars, casino, cinema, dance club, showroom, children's programs (ages 3–17), dry cleaning, laundry facilities, laundry service, computer room; no kids under 6 months AE, D, MC, V.*

Radisson Seven Seas Cruises

The only luxury-class cruise line in Alaska, Radisson Seven Seas Cruises is part of Carlson Hospitality Worldwide, one of the world's major hotel and travel companies. The cruise line was formed in December 1994 with the merger of the one-ship Diamond Cruises and Seven Seas Cruises lines. From these modest beginnings, RSSC has grown into a major luxury player in the cruise industry.

Radisson Seven Seas Cruises manages to provide a high level of personal service and sense of intimacy on small to midsize ships, which have the stability of larger vessels. Onboard activities are oriented toward enrichment programs, socializing, and exploring the destinations on the itinerary. Although passengers tend to be older and affluent, they are still active. You'll always find open seating at dinner (which includes complimentary wine) and tips are included in the fare.

Radisson Seven Seas Cruises, 600 Corporate Dr., Suite 410, Fort Lauderdale, FL 33334 954/776–6123, 800/477–7500, or 800/285–1835 954/772–3763 www.rssc.com.

THE SHIP
Fodor's Choice
★

Seven Seas Mariner. This all-suites, all-balcony ship, in service since 2003, is also one of Radisson Seven Seas' largest, with the highest space-per-passenger ratio in the fleet. All cabins are outside suites ranging from 301 square feet to 2,002 square feet, including the verandas. Butler service is available to all but the least-expensive Deluxe Suite categories. The ship's dining rooms include Signatures, the only restaurant at sea staffed by chefs wearing the Blue Riband of Le Cordon Bleu of Paris, the famed culinary institute. Spa and salon services are provided by the high-end Carita of Paris and an outdoor pool remains open on Alaska voyages. *328 cabins, 700 passengers, 8 passenger decks* *2 specialty restaurants, dining room, buffet, in-cabin safes, refrigerators, in-cabin DVDs, Wi-Fi, pool, fitness classes, gym, hair salon, 2 hot tubs, sauna, spa, steam room, 5 bars, casino, dance club, library, showroom, children's programs (ages 6–17), dry cleaning, laundry facilities, laundry service, computer room* *AE, D, MC, V.*

Royal Caribbean Cruise Line

Imagine if the Mall of America were sent to sea. That's a fair approximation of what the megaships of Royal Caribbean Cruise Line (RCL) are all about. These mammoth vessels are indoor/outdoor wonders, with every conceivable activity in a resortlike atmosphere, including atrium lobbies, shopping arcades, large spas, and expansive sundecks. The main problem with these otherwise well-conceived vessels is that the line packs too many people aboard, making for an exasperating experience at embarkation, while tendering, and at disembarkation. Nevertheless, Royal Caribbean is one of the best-run and most popular cruise lines. Although the line competes directly with Carnival for passengers—active couples and singles in their thirties to fifties, as well as a large family contingent—there are distinct differences of ambience and energy. Royal Caribbean is a bit more sophisticated and subdued than Carnival, even while delivering a good time on a grand scale.

Royal Caribbean suggests the following tips per passenger: dining-room waiter, $3.50 a day; stateroom attendant, $3.50 a day; assistant waiter, $2 a day; headwaiter, 75¢ a day. Gratuities for other service personnel are at your discretion. A 15% gratuity is automatically added to beverage and bar bills. All gratuities may be prepaid when you book, charged to your onboard account, or paid in cash at the end of the cruise.

Royal Caribbean International, Box 25511, 1050 Caribbean Way, Miami, FL 33132 *305/539–6000 or 800/327–6700* *800/722–5329* *www.royalcaribbean.com.*

THE SHIPS
★

Radiance of the Seas, Serenade of the Seas. Royal Caribbean's Radiance-class ships aren't the largest in the fleet, but they offer great speed—allowing for longer itineraries to far-flung ports of call—and the line's highest percentage of outside cabins. They are also considered by many to be the fleet's most beautiful vessels, and include sea-facing elevators that offer panoramic ocean views while you move from deck to deck. The coffeehouse-bookstore is a novel touch. The solarium, filled with lush foliage and cascading waterfalls, has a retractable roof to convert it from an indoor pool to an outdoor pool. All cabins have two twin beds that can convert into a queen, a computer jack, a vanity table with an extendable working surface, and bedside reading lights. *1,050/1,055 cabins, 2,100/2110 passengers (both 2,501 at full occupancy), 12 passenger decks* *2 specialty restaurants, buffet, pizzeria, in-cabin safes, refrigerators, some in-cabin VCRs, in-cabin data ports, Wi-Fi, 2 pools (1 indoors), children's pool, fitness classes, gym, hair salon, 3 hot tubs, sauna, spa, steam room, 11 bars, casino, cinema, dance club, library, showroom, video game room, children's programs (ages 3–17), dry cleaning, laundry service, computer room* *AE, D, DC, MC, V.*

Vision of the Seas. Launched in 1998, *Vision of the Seas* is a few years older than Royal Caribbean's other Alaska-bound vessels, but still boasts such up-to-date amenities as a rock-climbing wall, a miniature golf course, and a broad menu of fitness classes, including yoga and Pilates. Large windows throughout and, on the uppermost deck, a viewing lounge with wraparound glass make the most of the passing scenery. The covered pool and indoor-outdoor deck area of the Solarium Spa are especially well suited to cruising in often rainy Alaska. Among the bright spacious cabins are connecting staterooms, cabins with private balconies, and family suites with separate bedrooms for parents and children. The main dining room has open seating at breakfast and lunch, and assigned seating at dinner. *999 cabins 1,998 passengers (2,435 at full occupancy), 11 passenger decks* *Dining room, buffet, in-cabin safes, some refrigerators, 2 pools (1 indoors), fitness classes, gym, hair salon, 2 indoor hot tubs, 4 outdoor hot tubs, sauna, spa, 6 bars, casino, dance club, library, showroom, video game room, children's programs (ages 3–17), dry cleaning, laundry service, computer room* *AE, D, DC, MC, V.*

Small Ships

American Safari Cruises

Unlike most yachts, which have to be chartered, American Safari's vessels sail on a regular schedule and sell tickets to individuals: there's no need to charter the whole boat, though that is an option. With just 12 to 21 passengers and such decadent amenities as ocean-view hot tubs, American Safari's yachts are among the most comfortable small ships cruising Alaska. The chefs serve a choice of creative dinner entrées, highlighting fresh local ingredients and plenty of seafood. Itineraries are usually flexible; there's no rush to move on if the group spots a pod of whales or a family of bears. All sailing is in daylight, with nights spent at anchor in secluded coves, and the yachts stop daily to let you kayak, hike, or beachcomb. An onboard naturalist gives informal lectures and guides you on shore expeditions. All three ships carry exercise equipment, kayaks, mountain bikes, Zodiac landing crafts, and insulated Mustang suits for Zodiac excursions. All shore excursions and alcoholic drinks are included in the fare.

Tips are discretionary, but 5%–10% of the fare is suggested. A lump sum is pooled among the crew at the end of the cruise.

American Safari Cruises, 19221 36th Ave. W, Suite 208, Lynnwood, WA 98036 *425/776–4700 or 888/862–8881* *425/776–8889* *www.amsafari.com.*

THE SHIPS ★ **Safari Quest.** American Safari's largest vessel, this luxurious yacht has warm wood trim throughout. Four cabins have small balconies accessed by sliding glass doors, and a single cabin is available. There's plenty of outer deck space for taking in the views, and a reading lounge on the top deck is a pleasant hideaway. *11 cabins, 21 passengers, 4 passenger decks* *Dining room, in-room VCRs, outdoor hot tub, bar; no smoking.*

Safari Escape. Although *Escape* is one of Alaska's smallest cruise ships, it comes with all kinds of creature comforts usually associated with bigger ships, including exercise equipment, mountain bikes, and, in one cabin, a private sauna. Everyone dines together at one grand table; lunch might be a gourmet picnic on a secluded beach. Standard staterooms have queen or twin beds, and port lights rather than windows. The higher-end staterooms have a king-size bed and a window. All have rich fabrics and wood paneling. *6 cabins, 12 passengers, 3 passenger decks* *Dining room, in-room VCRs, outdoor hot tub, bar; no smoking.*

Safari Spirit. Completely remodeled in 2005 with cherry woodwork, the *Safari Spirit* is one of Alaska's most luxurious yachts. A forward-facing library with a 180-degree view, covered outside deck space, an on-deck hot tub, and even a sauna/steam bath are part of the pampering. Excellent meals are served at one grand table. The bright, cheerful cabins, all with plush bedding, jetted bathtubs, and heated bathroom floors, are among the roomiest in the American Safari fleet. *6 cabins, 12 passengers, 4 decks* *Dining room, in cabin DVDs, in-cabin VCRs, gym, outdoor hot tub, sauna, bar; no smoking.*

American West Steamboat Company

In the 19th century, paddle wheelers were a key part of Alaska's coastal transport, taking adventurers and gold seekers north. In 2003 American West Steamboat Company launched the *Empress of the North,* the first overnight stern-wheeler to ply these waters in 100 years. A naturalist and historian gives lectures on local history and culture, and gold-rush follies, Russian-American dances, and Native American songs and dances bring the region's past to life. A shore excursion is included at each port of call, including a trip on the White Pass & Yukon Railroad. This novel small ship attracts primarily North American passengers, with an average age of about 55.

As with most small ships, tips are pooled by the crew at the end of cruise. A tip of $12 to $14 per person per night is suggested.

American West Steamboat Company, 2101 4th Ave., Suite 1150, Seattle, WA 98121 *206/621–0913 or 800/434–1232* *206/340–0975* *www.americanweststeamboat.com.*

THE SHIP **Empress of the North.** Alaskan art and historical artifacts enrich the public areas, and the staterooms mimic Victorian opulence, with lush fabrics and rich colors. All cabins have big picture windows, and most have balconies. Lavish two-room suites, as well as single, triple, and wheelchair-accessible cabins are available. The chandelier-lighted dining room looks formal, but it is actually small-ship casual, with open seating and no need to dress up. Variety shows, ranging from golden oldies and big band to country and western, play nightly. ➬ *112 cabins, 235 passengers, 4 passenger decks ○ Café, dining room, minibars, in-room DVDs, 3 bars, showroom; no smoking.*

Clipper Cruise Lines

Clipper Cruise Lines keeps the focus on fully experiencing each destination. A fleet of motorized Zodiacs is on hand to take passengers to isolated beaches, and on every voyage, onboard experts share their knowledge of the region's cultures, wildlife, history, and geography. Clipper chefs take pride in their healthful American cuisine. Each dish is made to order, and almost everything served is made from scratch on board. There's little formality on board these relaxed yacht-size cruisers. Casual attire is the norm, and sport coats and dresses don't usually appear until the captain's farewell party. Passengers are typically active and well-traveled older adults.

Tips are pooled together at the end of the cruise. Ten dollars per day per passenger is suggested.

⌂ *Clipper Cruise Lines, 11969 Westline Industrial Dr., St. Louis, MO 63146-3220* ☎ *314/655–6700 or 800/325–0010* ⊕ *www.clippercruise.com.*

THE SHIPS **Yorktown Clipper.** Although deck space is limited on this coastal cruiser, floor-to-ceiling windows in the forward observation lounge and large windows in the dining room allow sightseeing in all weather. Cabins are all outside, with twin lower berths and a private bathroom with a shower. Most have large windows. ➬ *69 cabins, 138 passengers, 4 passenger decks ○ Dining room, in-room safes, bar; no TV, no smoking.*

★ **Clipper Odyssey.** The *Odyssey* brings elements of a luxury yacht experience to small-ship cruising in Alaska. A window-lined dining room and lounges keep the scenery in sight. Each cabin also has an ocean view, as well as a sitting area with a sofa and a bathroom with a shower and tub. Other amenities include a small pool, exercise equipment, a jogging track (18 laps to a mile), and a library. ➬ *64 cabins, 128 passengers, 5 passenger decks ○ Dining room, in-room safes, refrigerators, pool, gym, hair salon, bar, laundry service; no smoking.*

Cruise West

A big player in small ships, Seattle-based Cruise West sends seven coastal cruisers to Alaska each summer. As with other smaller vessels, Alaskan wilderness, wildlife, and culture take precedence over shipboard diversions. An exploration leader, who is both naturalist and cruise coordinator, hosts evening lectures and joins passengers on many of the shore excursions—at least one of which is included at each port of call. Binoculars in every cabin, a library stocked with books of local interest, and crew members as keen to explore Alaska as the passengers all enhance the experience. A living room that feels like a lounge, wholesome meals with bread baked on board, open seating, and jeans are as formal as it gets. The passengers, who inevitably get to know one another during the cruise, are typically active, well-traveled, over-fifties. They come from all regions of the United States, as well as from Australia, Canada, and the United Kingdom.

Suggested tips are $12 per person per day; these are pooled for all the crew and staff at the end of the cruise.

Cruise West, 2301 5th Ave., Suite 401, Seattle, WA 98121 ☎ *206/441–8687 or 800/888–9378* *www.cruisewest.com.*

THE SHIPS

Fodor's Choice ★

Spirit of Oceanus. Cruise West's largest and only oceangoing vessel is also its most luxurious, with marble and polished wood in the dining room, lounges, library, and cabins. All staterooms are outside suites and 14 of them have teak-floor private balconies. Four of the five decks have outside viewing areas and there's an elevator on board. The ship, equipped with stabilizers for open ocean cruising, also carries a fleet of inflatable excursion crafts for close-up visits to glaciers, waterfalls, and icebergs. Breakfast and lunch are served on deck when the weather permits. *59 cabins, 118 passengers, 5 decks* *Dining room, in-cabin safes, refrigerators, in-cabin VCRs, Wi-Fi, gym, outdoor hot tub, bar, laundry service, no smoking.*

Spirit of Endeavour. One of Cruise West's largest and fastest ships, the *Endeavour* provides ample deck space and a roomy lounge with large picture windows for superb views. Most of the cabins also have picture windows, and some have connecting doors, which make them convenient for families traveling together. As with Cruise West's other ships, itineraries are flexible: the captain can linger to let passengers watch a group of whales, and still make the next stop on time. *51 cabins, 102 passengers, 4 passenger decks* *Dining room, some refrigerators, in-cabin VCRs, Wi-Fi, bar; no smoking.*

Spirit of '98. With rounded stern and wheelhouse, old-fashioned smokestack, and Victorian decor, the *Spirit of '98* evokes a turn-of-the-20th-century steamer, although she is actually a modern ship, built in 1984. Mahogany trim inside and out, overstuffed chairs with plush floral upholstery, and an old-world bar in the grand salon add to the gold-rush-era motif. For private moments, you'll find plenty of nooks and crannies aboard the ship, including the cozy Soapy's Parlor bar at the stern. All cabins, including the two single cabins on board, have picture windows. The Owner's Suite has a living room and a whirlpool tub. Some of the cabins are wheelchair accessible and there's an elevator between the main and upper decks. *48 cabins, 96 passengers, 4 passenger decks* *Dining room, some refrigerators, in-cabin VCRs, Wi-Fi, bar; no smoking.*

Spirit of Discovery. Floor-to-ceiling windows in the main lounge provide stunning views aboard this snazzy cruiser. From here, passengers have direct access to a large outdoor viewing deck, one of two aboard. Every cabin has windows and two cabins are reserved for single travelers. *43 cabins, 84 passengers, 3 decks* *Dining room, some refrigerators, some in-cabin VCRs, bar; no smoking.*

Spirit of Alaska. The sleek *Spirit of Alaska* carries a fleet of inflatable excursion craft for impromptu stops at isolated beaches and close-up looks at glaciers. She's also able to do bow landings, enabling passengers to go ashore at isolated spots without docks. Most cabins are small but cheerfully decorated. Toilets and showers are a combined unit (the toilet is inside the shower). Top-deck cabins have windows on two sides, so you can sample both port and starboard views. Solo travelers can book a lower-deck cabin with no single supplement. *39 cabins, 78 passengers, 4 passenger decks* *Dining room, some refrigerators, some in-cabin VCRs, bar; no TV in some cabins, no smoking.*

Spirit of Columbia. The *Columbia*'s interior is inspired by the national park lodges of the American West, with muted shades of evergreen, rust, and sand. Cabins range from windowless inside units (which solo travelers can book with no single supplement) to comfortable staterooms with chairs and picture windows. The Columbia Deluxe cabin stretches the width of the vessel; just under the bridge, its row of forward-facing windows gives a captain's-eye view of the ship's progress. Like the *Spirit of Alaska,* the *Columbia* can land at isolated spots without docks. *38 cabins, 78 passengers, 4 passenger decks* *Dining room, some refrigerators, some in-cabin VCRs, bar; no TV in some cabins, no smoking.*

Sheltered Seas. Passengers on this daylight touring yacht cruise the Inside Passage by day and spend each night at hotels on shore. The *Sheltered Seas* has all the amenities of other small ships, including full meal service, an onboard naturalist, lounges on two levels, and large viewing decks both fore and aft. An ice-breaking hull means she can get very close to glaciers. This unique style of cruising is popular with Alaskan residents and with visitors who like a chance to see coastal towns when other visitors have returned to their ships for the night. *No cabins, 70 passengers, 2 passenger decks* *Dining room, bar; no smoking.*

Glacier Bay Cruiseline

Glacier Bay cruises focus on soft adventure cruising. Each ship has a fleet of kayaks, a floating kayak launch, and landing craft to take passengers ashore for beachcombing and hiking expeditions. Glacier Bay offers three different cruise styles: Low, Medium, and High Adventure. Low Adventure cruises focus on scenic cruising and port calls; Medium Adventure trips alternate days of cruising, landing craft excursions, and port visits with days of moderate-intensity hiking and kayaking; High Adventure voyages bypass towns altogether and take passengers on hiking and kayaking trips in remote areas each day of the cruise. Fleece and outdoor gear, not jackets and ties, are the norm on board, and food is hearty and home style. Glacier Bay cruises attract active, adventurous 30- to 60-year-olds, though, of course, the High Adventure cruises call for a greater level of physical fitness than the Low Adventure trips. Adventure gear and training are included in the fare, and single supplements are waived in May and September.

Tipping is discretionary, but $15 to $20 per person per day is suggested. Tips are pooled among the staff and crew at the end of the cruise.

Glacier Bay Cruiseline, 2101 4th Ave., Suite 2200, Seattle, WA 98121 *206/623–7110 or 800/451–5952* *www.glacierbaycruiseline.com.*

THE SHIPS **_Wilderness Discoverer._** Glacier Bay's largest ship has plenty of viewing space on two decks with unobstructed views from the top observation deck. The surroundings are simple and decorated with Alaskan art. Most cabins have picture windows, and several can accommodate three passengers. Four outside staterooms on the top deck have queen beds and large picture windows. Only the pricier cabins have TVs, but there is a communal TV and VCR in the main lounge. *41 cabins, 87 passengers, 4 passenger decks* *Dining room, some in-cabin VCRs, bar; no TV in some cabins, no smoking.*

Wilderness Adventurer. This friendly ship has the casual comforts of home. The coffee's always on and you'll never need a jacket and tie for dinner. A full wrap deck makes the most of sunny days; Alaskan art and varnished wood enhance the otherwise simple interior. One single and some triple cabins are available. A library of books and videos has a nice selection of Alaska titles. There are no TVs, but you can watch the library tapes—or your own wildlife footage—on the VCR in the main lounge. *32 cabins, 69 passengers, 3 passenger decks* *Dining room, bar; no a/c, no TV in cabins, no smoking.*

Executive Explorer. This streamlined catamaran is one of the fastest small ships in Alaska. Its appointments include a rich wood paneling throughout; deep padded armchairs in the main lounge; and a gallery-like display of nearly 100 Alaskan prints. The main lounge has forward-facing observation windows and even the stairwells have picture windows for views of the passing scenery. Outside observation areas include a partially covered sundeck which gives a lofty perspective four decks above the water—an unusually high perch for such a small ship. Cabins have more artwork, roomy closets, and two big picture windows. Unlike Glacier Bay's other vessels, the *Executive Explorer* does not carry kayaks or landing crafts; she offers eight-day cruises from Juneau to Ketchikan, with stops in some of the better-known ports of call. *24 cabins, 49 passengers, 4 passenger decks* *Dining room, some refrigerators, some in-cabin DVDs, bar; no smoking.*

Wilderness Explorer. The *Wilderness Explorer* is billed as a "floating base camp" for "active adventure," and that's no exaggeration. Sea-kayak outings may last more than three hours (a 5-mi paddle). Discovery hikes cross dense thickets and climb rocky creek beds. You'll spend most of your time off the ship—a good thing, since you wouldn't want to spend much time on it. The ship is pleasant enough, but it's strictly utilitarian. Public spaces are limited and the cabins are positively tiny; all but one have bunk beds. One single cabin is available. This ship should be considered only by the serious outdoor enthusiast. *16 cabins, 31 passengers, 3 passenger decks* *Dining room, bar; no a/c, no TV in cabins, no smoking.*

Lindblad Expeditions

The ships of Lindblad Expeditions forgo port calls at larger, busier towns and instead spend time looking for wildlife, exploring out-of-the way inlets, and making Zodiac landings at isolated beaches. Each ship has a video-microphone, a hydrophone, and an underwater camera so passengers can listen to whale songs and watch live video of what's going on beneath the waves. In the evening, the ships' naturalists recap the day's sights and adventures over cocktails in the lounge. A video chronicler captures the whole cruise on tape. All shore excursions except flightseeing are included, and Lindblad charges one of the industry's lowest single supplements. Lindblad attracts active, adventurous, well-traveled over-forties, with quite a few singles. Some sailings are specially designed for families (fares are 25 percent off for kids under 21); other sailings focus on photography. Both itineraries—the 8-day Alaska Coastal Wilderness trip and the 12-day Alaska, British Columbia, and San Juan Islands cruise—offer an extension to Denali National Park.

Tips of $12 per person per day are suggested; these are pooled among the crew at journey's end.

Lindblad Expeditions, 96 Morton St., New York, NY 10014 ☎ 212/765–7740 or 800/397–3348 www.expeditions.com.

THE SHIPS **Sea Bird, Sea Lion.** These small, shallow-draft sister ships can tuck into nooks and crannies that bigger ships can't reach. An open-top sundeck, forward observation lounge, and viewing deck at the bow offer plenty of room to take in the scenery. These ships are comfortable, but public spaces and cabins are small. All staterooms are outside, and upper-category cabins have picture windows that open. Guests can e-mail from the ship, but Internet access is not available so you can't surf the Web. *36 cabins, 70 passengers, 4 passenger decks Dining room, bar; no TV in cabins, no smoking.*

Ferry Liners

Alaska Marine Highway System

Serving 32 ports of call in Alaska as well as Bellingham, Washington, and Prince Rupert, B.C., Alaskan ferries are a scenic option for getting to and around Alaska. Ferry travel is generally slow: maximum speed is 16.5 knots, compared with 21 knots or better for the typical large cruise ship. However, one fast ferry, the MV *Fairweather*, motors at twice that speed.

Ferries are a great way to take in the landscape, meet local people, and maybe see a whale or two. The ferry system also affords freedom of movement. Unlike the big cruise ships, which follow a set itinerary, ferries come and go frequently. You can get on and off whenever you wish, and stay as long as you want. Ferries serve major towns daily and call at smaller centers every two to three days, though some exotic routes, including the Cross-Gulf and Aleutian Chain ferries, see service only once or twice a month. Another advantage of ferry travel is affordable fares.

The ferries are less than luxurious, but comfortable enough. Each has a glass-lined observation lounge and all but the smallest ferries have a bar. Onboard cafeterias serve hearty, inexpensive meals. Cabins are simple and serviceable, and camping in the solarium is an option. Cabins book up almost instantly for cruises during the summer season; it's essential to book in advance if you're traveling with a vehicle. A number of tour operators sell packages that include shipboard accommodations. **Knightly Tours** (✉ Box 16366, Seattle, WA 98116 ☎ 206/938–8567 or 800/426–2123 🖷 206/938–8498 🌐 www.knightlytours.com) is one of the most established of these.

✉ Alaska Marine Highway System, 6858 Glacier Hwy., Juneau, AK 99801-7909 ☎ 907/465–3941 or 800/642–0066 🖷 907/465–2476 🌐 www.ferryalaska.com.

British Columbia Ferries

British Columbia Ferries, or BC Ferries, take vehicles and passengers between Port Hardy, on the northern tip of Vancouver Island, and Prince Rupert, B.C., where you can pick up an Alaskan ferry to continue your journey north. The ferry has cabins, a cafeteria, a bar, a children's play area, and an elevator on board, and the journey takes 15 hours in summer, somewhat longer in winter. Reservations are required for vehicles and recommended for foot passengers. BC Ferries also provide service to Vancouver Island from the British Columbia mainland.

✉ 1112 Fort St., Victoria, BC V8V 4V2 ☎ 250/386–3431, 888/223–3779 (in B.C. only) 🖷 250/381–5452 🌐 www.bcferries.com.

PORTS OF CALL

Waterfronts throughout Alaska are equipped for cruise passengers, but docking procedures, services, ground transportation, and proximity of attractions vary appreciably.

The information provided here explains how cruise passengers arrive and reach the ports. See chapters on Anchorage, Southeast Alaska, and South Central Alaska for detailed information on each Alaskan town's sights, restaurants, guided tours, and outdoor activities.

Anchorage

Cruise ships visiting the Anchorage area dock either at Whittier, about 55 mi from Anchorage on the western shore of Prince William Sound, or at the port city of Seward, 127 mi to the south on the Kenai Peninsula. Buses (three hours from Seward, 1½ hours from Whittier) and summer-only trains (four hours from Seward, 2½ hours from Whittier) take passengers into Anchorage.

The train station is a few blocks away from downtown Anchorage. The few ships that do sail directly to Anchorage dock just north of downtown. The major attractions are best accessed by taking a taxi downtown. It is only a 15- or 20-minute walk from the dock to town, but this is through an industrial area with heavy traffic. Anchorage is the starting or ending point for many Alaskan cruises, with passengers flying into (or out of) the city.

Rental Cars

To explore sites farther afield, such as Denali, Girdwood, and points south on the Kenai Peninsula, Anchorage is the ideal place to rent a car.

Denali Car Rental has a downtown office. National and Budget have airport desks; Budget provides free shuttle service to the airport to pick up cars.

Budget ☎ 907/243-0150. **Denali Car Rental** ✉ 1209 Gambell St. ☎ 907/276-1230 or 800/757-1230. **National Car Rental** ☎ 907/243-3255.

Cordova

Cruise ships dock at the boat harbor, and Cordova is just a short walk uphill from here. Ships are met by tour buses, or you can catch a cab.

Haines

In the past, Haines hasn't been a major stop for large cruise ships, but that's changing as the community warms to tourism and as travelers look for an alternative to the crowds at Skagway. Cruise ships dock in front of Ft. Seward, and downtown Haines is just a short walk away (about ½ mi). A regular shuttle service runs between the dock and downtown. Taxis are always standing by; two-hour-long taxi tours of the area cost about $15 per person; $12 per person for tours of the town. The Haines ferry terminal is 4½ mi northwest of downtown, and the airport is 4 mi west.

If your cruise ship only stops in Skagway, and you'd like to spend the day at this charming spot, you can catch a fast catamaran to Haines (around $80 round-trip) for a day away from the crowds. **Alaska Fjordlines** (☎ 907/766–3395 or 800/320–0146 🌐 www.alaskafjordlines.com) operates a high-speed catamaran between Haines and Juneau, stopping along the way to watch sea lions and other marine mammals. **Chilkat Cruises** (☎ 907/766–2100 or 888/766–2103 🌐 www.chilkatcruises.com) provides a passenger catamaran ferry between Skagway and Haines, with several runs a day in summer.

Homer

Large cruise ships do not stop in scenic Homer, but the town is visited by smaller ships, along with Alaska Marine Highway ferries. State ferries dock at the end of the Homer Spit. Fishing charters, restaurants, and shops line the Spit, or you can take a taxi to town, where local galleries and additional dining are found. In addition, Homer is easily reached by car from the town of Seward, where Gulf of Alaska cruises often start or finish. It's a five-hour drive by car from Anchorage.

Juneau

Juneau is an obligatory stop on the Inside Passage cruise and ferry circuit and a port of embarkation for many small cruise ships. Cruise ships dock or tender passengers ashore on the south edge of town near Marine Park and the Mt. Roberts Tramway. Several ships can tie up at once, and others anchor a short distance away in the protected harbor. Juneau's downtown shops are a short walk from the cruise-ship dock. Tour buses, city buses, and cabs meet the ships.

Downtown Juneau is compact enough so that most of its main attractions are within walking distance of one another. However, several sights—including Mendenhall Glacier, Glacier Gardens, and the Macaulay Salmon Hatchery—are too far to walk to. You can catch a tour bus or a taxi from Marine Park. Another option is the city bus that stops on South Franklin Street. For $1.50, it'll take you within 1.5 mi of the Mendenhall Visitor Center.

Ketchikan

This is another popular stop on the Inside Passage, and as many as six ships may call at Ketchikan every day. Ships dock or tender passengers ashore directly across from the Ketchikan Visitors Bureau on Front and Mission streets, in the center of downtown. Most of the town's sights are within easy walking distance of downtown. You can follow the walking-tour signs that lead you around the city. For panoramic vistas of the surrounding area, climb the stairs leading up several different steep hillsides.

To reach sights farther from downtown, hire a cab or ride the local buses. Metered taxis meet the ships right on the docks and also wait across the street. Local buses run along on the main route through town and south to Saxman. The fare is $1.50.

Kodiak Island

Kodiak is an out-of-the-way destination for smaller cruise ships and Alaska state ferries. Most ships dock at Pier 2, ½ mi south of downtown Kodiak. Some ships offer shuttles into town, but if yours does not, it's a 15-minute walk.

Metlakatla

Only Cruise West ships make a call to this Tsimshian community. Ships dock at the Metlakatla dock adjacent to town. Buses from Metlakatla Tours meet all ships and provide a guided tour of the village.

Misty Fiords National Monument

In the past, cruise ships bypassed Misty Fiords on their way up and down the Inside Passage. But today more and more cruise passengers are discovering its unspoiled beauty as ships big and small feature a day of scenic cruising through this protected wilderness. At the southern end of the Inside Passage, Misty Fiords usually lies just before or after a call at Ketchikan. The attraction here is the wilderness—3,500 square mi of it—highlighted by waterfalls and cliffs that rise 3,000 feet. Small boats enable close-up views of breathtaking vistas. Traveling on these waters can be an almost mystical experience, with the greens of the forest reflected in waters as still as black mirrors. You may find yourself in the company of a whale, see a bear fishing for salmon along the shore, or even pull in your own salmon for an evening meal. Park rangers may kayak out to your cruise ship to help point out wildlife and explain the geology of the area.

Nome

One of the most remote cruise ship destinations, Nome is visited by smaller exploration vessels. They dock a mile south of Nome at the city dock. Taxis are available to downtown for $5.

Petersburg

Getting to Petersburg is a heart-quickening experience. Only ferries and the smallest cruise ships can squeak through Wrangell Narrows. Ships that are small enough to visit Petersburg dock in the South Harbor, which is about a ½-mi walk from downtown. Everything in Petersburg is within easy walking distance of the harbor.

Prince Rupert, British Columbia

New to hosting cruise ships, this community of 15,000 retains a laid-back, small-town air. Note also that some cruise ships dock here, but don't stop long enough for passengers to disembark. Check before booking if this isn't clear on your cruise itinerary.

Ocean liners calling at Prince Rupert dock at the Northland Cruise Ship Terminal while smaller ships tie up at Atlin Cruise Ship Terminal next door. Both terminals are situated at the city's historic Cow Bay district, about five blocks from the central business district. The terminals for both British Columbia and Alaska ferries as well as the VIA Rail train station are grouped together about 2 km (1 mi) from town.

Seattle

Seattle is becoming an increasingly popular starting point for visitors to Alaska. Ships from Norwegian Cruise Line and Celebrity Cruises dock at the Bell Street Pier Cruise Terminal (Pier 66). Pier 66 is within walking distance of downtown attractions, and the Waterfront Streetcar provides trolley service along the shoreline to the cruise terminal. Holland America Line and Princess Cruises dock at the Terminal 30 Cruise Facility at the south end of the downtown waterfront near the baseball stadium. Terminal 30 is a taxi or city bus ride from downtown.

Seward

Cruise ships dock approximately 2 mi from downtown. The Seward Trolley stops at the cruise-ship dock every half hour when ships are in port (every hour on non–cruise ship days) and heads to Seward's various points of interest. The cost is $10 per person.

Sitka

Only the smallest excursion vessels can dock at Sitka. Ocean liners must drop anchor in the harbor and tender passengers ashore near Harrigan Centennial Hall or O'Connell Bridge. Both are just one street back from the main part of town; you'll recognize the hall by the big Tlingit war canoe out front. Sitka is hilly, but the waterfront attractions are an easy walk from the tender landing. You may, however, want to consider a taxi if you're heading all the way to the raptor center.

Skagway

Amazingly preserved Skagway is a major stop for cruise ships in Alaska, and this little town sometimes has four large ships in port at once. Ships may tender passengers ashore or dock at any of three side-by-side piers: Railroad Dock, Broadway Dock, or Ore Dock. It's a nice walk from the docks up through Broadway, but you can also take tours with horse-drawn surreys, old-fashioned buses, or modern vans.

Tracy Arm

Like Misty Fiords, Tracy Arm and its sister fjord, Endicott Arm, have become staples on many Inside Passage cruises. Ships sail into the arm just before or after a visit to Juneau, 50 mi to the north. A day of scenic cruising in Tracy Arm is a lesson in geology and the forces that shape Alaska. The fjord was carved by a glacier aeons ago, leaving behind sheer granite cliffs. Waterfalls continue the process of erosion that the glaciers began. Very small ships may nudge their bows under the waterfalls so crew members can fill pitchers full of glacial runoff. It's a uniquely Alaskan refreshment. Tracy Arm's glaciers haven't disappeared, though; they've just receded, and at the very end of Tracy Arm you'll come to two of them, known collectively as the twin Sawyer Glaciers.

Valdez

Ships tie up at the world's largest floating container dock. About 3 mi from the heart of town, the dock is used not only for cruise ships but also for cargo ships loading with timber and other products bound for markets "outside" (that's what Alaskans call the rest of the world). Ship-organized motor coaches meet you on the pier and provide transportation into town. Cabs and car-rental services will also provide transportation from the pier. Several local ground and adventure-tour operators meet passengers as well.

Once in town, you'll find that Valdez is a very compact community. Almost everything is within easy walking distance from the heart of town. Motor coaches drop passengers at the Visitor Information Center. Taxi service is available, and individualized tours of the area can be arranged with the cab dispatcher.

Vancouver, British Columbia

Most ships dock downtown at the Canada Place cruise-ship terminal—instantly recognizable by its rooftop of dramatic white sails and a few minutes' walk from the city center. A few vessels tie up at the Ballantyne cruise terminal, a 10- to 15-minute, $12 cab ride from downtown.

Many sights of interest are concentrated in the hemmed-in peninsula of downtown Vancouver. The heart of Vancouver—which includes the downtown area, Stanley Park, and the West End high-rise residential neighborhood—sits on this peninsula bordered by English Bay and the Pacific Ocean to the west; by False Creek, the inlet home to Granville Island, to the south; and by Burrard Inlet, the working port of the city, to the north, past which loom the North Shore mountains. The oldest part of the city—Gastown and Chinatown—lies at the edge of Burrard Inlet.

Victoria, British Columbia

Though Victoria isn't in Alaska, it's a port of call for many ships cruising the Inside Passage. Only the smallest excursion vessels can dock downtown in the Inner Harbour. Ocean liners must tie up at the Ogden Point Cruise Ship Terminal, a C$4–C$5 cab ride from downtown. Metered taxis meet the ship.

Wrangell

Wrangell is off the typical cruise ship track and is frequented by lines with an environmental or educational emphasis, such as Cruise West. Cruise ships calling in to Wrangell dock downtown, within walking distance of the museum and gift stores. Greeters welcome you and are available to answer questions.

Wrangell's attractions—the most notable being totem-filled Chief Shakes Island—are within walking distance of the pier. Petroglyph Beach, where you find rocks marked with mysterious prehistoric symbols, is 1 mi from the pier. Most cruise-ship visitors see it either on a guided shore excursion or by taxi.

UNDERSTANDING ALASKA

ALASKA AT A GLANCE

Fast Facts

Nicknames: Great Land, Land of the Midnight Sun, Last Frontier
Capital: Juneau
Motto: North to the Future
State song: *Alaska's Flag,* by Marie Drake
State bird: Willow Ptarmigan
State flower: Forget-Me-Not
State tree: Sitka spruce
Administrative divisions: 27 counties
Entered the Union: January 3, 1959, as the 49th state
Population: 624,252
Population density: 1.1 person per square mi
Median age: 34.2
Infant mortality rate: 6.1 deaths per 1,000 live births
Literacy: 11 percent have trouble with basic reading
Ethnic groups: White 69%; American Indian or Alaska Native 13%; other 7%; Asian 4%; Latino 4%; black 3%
Religion: Unaffiliated 66%; Protestant 18%; Catholic 9%; other 4%; Mormon 3%

The really heroic people are not the ones who travel 10,000 miles by dog sled, but those who stay 10,000 days in one place.

—William Gordon, Episcopal Bishop of Alaska

Geography & Environment

Land area: 570,373 square mi, the largest state
Coastline: 6,640 mi (33,904 mi of shoreline, including all islands) along North Pacific Ocean, Bering Sea, Chukchi Sea, Arctic Ocean
Terrain: Rough, tundra-dominated coast, with grass-covered, treeless islands along the western edge; barren, mountainous inland, carved by more than 3,000 rivers and dotted by more than 3 million lakes; icebound and permanently frozen North Slope; highest point: Mt. McKinley, 20,320 feet (the tallest mountain in North America)
Islands: 1,800 named islands, largest is Kodiak (3,588 square mi)
Natural resources: Arable land, cod, crab, forests, halibut, herring, natural gas, petroleum, salmon, seals, shrimp
Natural hazards: Earthquakes, extreme cold, flooding, tsunami
Environmental issues: The effects of the 1989 *Exxon Valdez* spill are still being felt in the ecosystem; oil accidents continue to be a problem. Fish are monitored for mercury, heavy metals, dioxins, and pesticides from runoff. Cruise ships are tightly regulated for wastewater and air pollution.

There is much to be said against the climate on the coast of British Columbia and Alaska; yet, I believe that the scenery of one good day will compensate the tourists who will go there in increasing numbers.

—Franklin D. Roosevelt

Economy

GSP: 28.8 billion
Per capita income: $33,568
Unemployment: 7.1%
Workforce: 292,286; government 27%; trade, transportation, and utilities 21%; educational and health services 10%; leisure and hospitality 10%; professional and business services 8%; construction 5%; financial 4%; natural resource and mining 4%; other 5%; manufacturing 4%; information 2%

Major industries: Fishing, mining, oil, timber, tourism
Agricultural products: Crab, cod, dairy products, halibut, herring, potatoes, salmon, shrimp
Exports: $1 billion
Major export products: Petroleum and coal products 6%; lumber and wood products 6%; food products 4%; transportation equipment 3%; industrial machinery and computers 3%

Did You Know?

- Alaska is home to Mt. McKinley, the highest peak in North America, as well as 17 of the 20 of the highest mountains in the United States.
- Once the only way to get around in many areas, dog mushing is now the state sport.
- Alaska has an estimated 100,000 glaciers, more than anywhere else in the inhabited world. Five percent of the state, or 29,000 square mi, is covered by them.
- North America's strongest earthquake was recorded in Alaska on March 27, 1964, with a magnitude of 9.2. Alaska has approximately 5,000 earthquakes each year.
- The trans-Alaska pipeline moves oil from the North Slope of Alaska to Valdez, the northernmost ice-free port. The pipeline is 48 inches in diameter and moves oil at about 5.5 mi per hour, requiring just under six days to travel from Prudhoe Bay to the sea.
- Alaska is home to both the easternmost and westernmost points in the United States, due to the 180th meridian, which is the global dividing line between all eastern and western longitudes on the globe. Amatignak Island, at 179° west, is only 70 mi away from Semisopochnoi Island at 179° east.

WILDLIFE & PLANT GLOSSARY

Despite its far northern location, Alaska is home to a surprisingly diverse community of animals and plants. Including marine species, more than 100 types of mammals inhabit the state, along with some 300 species of birds (the great majority seasonal migrants), nearly 440 species of fresh- and saltwater fish, and a handful of amphibians, most of them restricted to the Southeast region. The state's ecosytems also include more than 1,500 plants, including trees, shrubs, grasses, sedges, and wildflowers. What follows is a mix of notable animals and plants that you may glimpse during your wanderings.

Fauna

Arctic Tern (*Sterna paradisaea*): Arctic terns are the world's long-distance flying champs; some members of their species make annual migratory flights between the high Arctic and the Antarctic, a round-trip distance of nearly 25,000 mi. Sleekly beautiful, the bird has a black cap and striking blood-red bill and feet, which contrast sharply with the white cheeks, neck, and breast, and the pale gray wings and back. They often can be seen hovering above pond and coastal marshes in their hunt for small fish.

Bald Eagle (*Haliaeetus leucocephalus*): With a wingspan of 6 to 8 feet, these grand residents of Alaska's southern coastal areas are primarily fish eaters, but they'll also take birds or small mammals when the opportunity presents itself. The world's largest gathering of bald eagles occurs in Southeast Alaska each winter, when 1,000 to 4,000 of the nation's symbol congregate along the Chilkat River near Haines.

Beluga Whale (*Dephinapterus leucas*): Belugas are gray at birth, blueish gray as adolescents, and white as adults (the word *byelukha* is Russian for "white"). Among the smaller whales, they weigh up to 1½ tons. And though they seem to favor fish, belugas' diet includes more than 100 different species, from crabs and clams to squid. They range along much of Alaska's coast, from the Beaufort Sea down to the Gulf of Alaska.

Black Bear (*Ursus americanus*): The smallest and most timid of Alaska's three bears roams the state's forested areas, from the Southeast Panhandle to the southern slopes of the Brooks Range in the Arctic. Though generally shy, the black bear has learned to adapt to human company and often inhabit the edges of Alaska's villages and cities, including the state's urban center, Anchorage. Males generally range from 200 to 400 pounds, females from 120 to 175 pounds.

Black-capped chickadee (*Parus atricapillus*): The songbird known throughout much of the U.S. is also one of Alaska's most common residents, appearing throughout much of the state's woodlands. With two close relatives, the chestnut-backed and boreal chickadees, the black-cap is among the smallest birds to reside in Alaska year-round and is a common visitor to bird feeders. One way it gets through northern winters is by lowering its body temperature at night and shivering through the long hours of darkness.

Brown/Grizzly Bear (*Ursus arctos*): There's little that separates the brown and grizzly bear, except geography, and therefore, food. Residents of Alaska's coastal areas, brown bears have easy access to abundant, energy-rich foods, namely salmon. As a consequence, they are much larger animals than the interior-dwelling grizzly. The largest brown bears may weigh from 1,500 to 1,600 pounds, while the largest grizzlies weigh about half that. Both are "opportunistic omnivores"; like many humans, they'll eat just about anything.

Caribou (*Rangifer tarandus*): Sometimes called the "nomads of the north," caribou are the long-distance wanderers among Alaska's mammals. They are also the most abundant of the state's large mammals; in fact, there are more caribou in Alaska than people! The Western Arctic Caribou Herd alone numbers more than 400,000 members, while the Porcupine Caribou Herd has ranged between 120,000 and 180,000 animals over the past couple of decades. Another bit of caribou trivia: they are the only members of the deer family in which both sexes grow antlers. Those of cows are small, reaching only 12 to 18 inches, while the antlers of bulls may grow up to 5½ feet long with a span of up to 3 feet.

Common Loon (*Gavia immer*): Some sounds seem to be the essence of wilderness: the howl of the wolf, the hooting of the owl, and the cry of the loon. The common loon is one of five *Gavia* species to inhabit Alaska (the others are the Arctic, Pacific, red-throated, and yellow-billed). Like others of its kind, common loons are primarily fish eaters. Excellent swimmers, they are able to stay submerged for up to three minutes. They are not especially good at take-offs, however, and often need substantial distance to get into the air.

Dall Sheep (*Ovis dalli dalli*): One of four wild sheep to inhabit North America, the snow-white Dall is the only to reside within Alaska. A resident of high alpine areas, the sheep occur in mountain chains from the St. Elias Range to the Brooks Range. Males and females live apart except during mating season. Though both sexes grow horns, those of females are short spikes, while males grow grand curls that are "status symbols" displayed during mating season.

Golden Eagle (*Aquila chrysaetos*): Although the bald eagle frequents coastal areas, the golden eagle is primarily a bird of Alaska's inland regions. With a wingspan of up to 7½ feet, it can often be spotted spiraling high in the sky, riding thermals of warming air. The bird usually nests on mountain cliff faces and feeds upon small mammals and ptarmigan. The plumage of adult birds is entirely dark, except for a lighter, golden head, for which it is named. Migratory birds, golden eagles are known to spend their winters as far away as Kansas and New Mexico.

Great Horned Owl (*Bubo virginianus*): The best known of Alaska's several species of owls, the great horned's call is a familiar one in Alaska. It is a large owl with prominent ear tufts and a white throat with barred markings. It resides in forests from Southeast Alaska (where it's most uncommon) to the Interior. The great horned preys on a variety of small animals, including squirrels, hares, grouse, as well as other birds.

Harbor Seal (*Phoca vitulina*): Inhabiting shallow marine waters and estuaries along much of Alaska's southern coast, harbor seals may survive up to 30 years in the wild, on a diet of fish, squid, octopus, and shrimp. They, in turn, may be eaten or killed by killer whales, sea lions, or humans. Solitary in the water, harbor seals love company on land, and will gather in large colonies that number in the hundreds. They weigh up to 250 pounds and range in color from black to white.

Horned Puffin (*Fratercula corniculata*): Named for the stiff, black, fleshy projections above each eye, horned puffins are favorites among birders. Included in the group of diving seabirds known as "alcids," puffins spend most of their life on water, coming to land only for nesting. They are expert swimmers, using their wings to "fly" underwater and their webbed feet as rudders. Horned puffins have large orange-red and yellow bills that are roughly triangular in shape. A close relative, the tufted puffin (*Fratercula cirrhata*), is named for its yellow ear "tufts."

Humpback Whale (*Megaptera novaeangliae*): Humpbacks are long-distance migrants, traveling each spring from Mexico or Hawaii to the rich feeding waters off Alaska's coast. They usually travel in small pods of two to five animals, with immature whales and newly pregnant females migrating first, followed by mature males and then females with calves. Females are larger, weighing up to 35 tons or more; males, on average, weigh 25 tons. Hunting krill and small fish, they may eat up to 2 tons of food per day while inhabiting Alaska's waters.

Killer Whale (*Orcinus orca*): Also called orcas, killer whales form two different types of groups. Resident pods tend to remain in the same area year-round and feed primarily on fish; ranging from a handful of animals to several dozen, they are considered by researchers to be matriarchal "societies," dominated by females that may live to 70 years or more. Transient pods are less understood, though it's known they travel far while feeding on other marine mammals, from sea otters and seals to sea lions and even other species of whales.

Lynx (*Lynx canadensis*): The lynx is the only wild cat to inhabit Alaska, residing in forested areas throughout much of the state. It is a secretive animal that's not often seen. As a hunter, the lynx depends on stealth and quickness. It may kill birds, squirrels, mice, and other rodents, but the cat's primary prey is the snowshoe hare (*Lepus americanus*), particularly in winter, and its population numbers closely follow those of the hare's boom-bust cycles. Large feet and a light body help the lynx chase hares through winter's often deep snowpack.

Moose (*Alces alces gigas*): The moose is the largest member of the deer family, with the largest bulls standing 7 feet tall at the shoulders and weighing up to 1,600 pounds, with the only slightly smaller cows reaching 1,200 pounds or more. Females give birth to calves in late May and early June; twins is the norm, though the range is one to three offspring. The calves are cinnamon colored for the first few months, becoming the darker brown characteristic of adults by fall. Bulls enter the "rut" in September, with the most dominant males sometimes engaging in brutal fights that may leave the loser mortally wounded. The peak of breeding occurs in late September. Though most commonly residents of woodlands, some moose have adapted well to life in or just outside Alaska's cities.

Musk Ox (*Ovibos moschatus*): The musk ox is considered an Ice Age "relic" that survived into the present at least partly because of a defensive tactic: they stand side-by-side and form rings to fend off predators such as grizzlies and wolves. Unfortunately for the species, that tactic didn't work very well against humans armed with guns. Alaska's last native musk oxen were killed in 1865. However, musk oxen from Greenland were reintroduced to Alaska in 1930 and they now reside on Nunivak Island. The animal's most notable physical feature is its long guard hairs, which form "skirts" that nearly reach the ground. Inupiats called musk ox *oomingmak,* meaning "bearded one." Beneath those coarser hairs are fine underfur called qiviut, which can be woven into warm clothing.

Pacific Salmon (*Oncorhynchus*): All five species of Pacific salmon spawn in Alaska's waters, from the mighty king, which can weigh more than 100 pounds, to the smaller, humpbacked pink, sometimes called "humpie." Other species include the red or sockeye salmon; the silver or coho; and the chum or dog. Hundreds of millions of salmon return to Alaska's streams and lakes each summer and fall, after spending much of their lives in saltwater. They form the backbone of Alaska's fishing industry and also draw sportfishers from around the world.

Pacific Halibut (*Hippoglossus stenolepis*): The halibut is the largest of the flatfish to inhabit Alaska's coastal waters, with females weighing up to 500 pounds. Males, by contrast, rarely weigh more than 100 pounds. Long-lived "grandmother" halibut may survive 40 years or more, while producing millions of eggs each year. Bottom dwellers, they range from the Panhandle to Norton Sound. Young halibut generally stay near shore, but older fish have been found at depths of up to 3,600 feet. Voracious predators, they feed on fish, crabs, clams, squid, and other invertebrates.

Polar Bear (*Ursus maritimus*): It's strange, at first, to think of a bear as a marine mammal; but scientists knew what they were doing when they placed the polar bear in a group that includes whales, seals, and walrus. Also called the sea bear or ice bear, the polar bear is intimately tied to the marine environment. Members of the species spend most of their lives on the frozen ice pack, while inhabiting the Earth's circumpolar Arctic region. An estimated 3,000 to 5,000 reside along, and off, Alaska's Arctic coastline. True carnivores, their diet consists largely of ringed seals, which they hunt year-round. Unlike brown and black bears, most polar bears do not hibernate, the exception being females that are pregnant or have young cubs.

Rainbow Trout (*Salmo gairdneri*): A favorite of anglers, the rainbow trout inhabits streams and lakes in Alaska's coastal regions from the Southeast to the Kuskokwim Bay. The Bristol Bay region is best known for large "bows," perhaps because of its huge returns of salmon. Rainbows (and many other predators) feed heavily on salmon eggs as well as the deteriorating flesh of spawned-out salmon. Sea-run rainbows, or steelhead, grow even larger after years spent feeding in ocean waters. The state record for steelhead/rainbow trout is 42 pounds, 3 ounces.

Sea Otter (*Enhydra lutris*): Unlike most marine mammals, sea otters don't depend on blubber to stay warm. Instead, hair trapped in their dense, luxurious fur keeps their skin dry, insulating them from Alaska's often frigid coastal waters. Beneath the otter's coarse outer hairs, the soft underfur ranges in density from 170,000 to one million hairs per square inch. Not surprisingly, the otter takes good care of its coat, spending much of every day grooming the fur. Otters also spend a lot of time eating. In one study, researchers found that adult otters consumed 14 crabs a day, equaling about one-fourth of their body weight. Besides crabs, they dine on sea urchins, clams, mussels, and fish.

Sitka Blacktailed Deer (*Odocoileus hemionus sitkensis*): The Panhandle's lush temperate rain forest is the primary home of this deer, though it has been transplanted to Prince William Sound and the Kodiak Archipelago. With a dark gray in winter, which becomes a brighter reddish brown in summer, it is a stockier deer than the whitetails found in the Lower 48 states. Males average 120 pounds, and females 80 pounds. The deer stay at lower elevations during the snowy months of winter, then move up to alpine meadows in summer.

Snowy Owl (*Nyctea scandiaca*): Inhabiting the open coastal tundra, the snowy owl is found from the western Aleutian Islands to the Arctic. As the name suggests, adults are largely white (though females have scattered light brown spots), although immature birds have white faces but are heavily marked with brown. These owls depend heavily on lemmings, their primary prey, and their numbers rise and fall with swings in the lemming population. Rather than the "hoots" normally associated with owls, the snowy speaks in loud croaks or whistles.

Steller's Sea Lion (*Eumetopias jubatus*): It's ability—and tendency—to roar is what gives the sea lion its name. Because they can rotate their rear flippers and lift their bellies off the ground, sea lions can get around on land much easier than seals can. They are also much larger, with males reaching up to 9 feet long and weighing up to 1,500 pounds. Ranging from Southeast Alaska to the Bering Sea, they feed primarily on fish, but will also eat sea otters and seals. For reasons that are still unclear, their populations north of the Panhandle have suffered huge declines since the 1950s; they have been designated an endangered species.

Walrus (*Odobenus rosmarus*): The walrus's scientific name means "tooth walker" but there's no evidence that it uses its ivory tusks for getting around. But they can be dangerous weapons; there are stories of walruses defending themselves and even killing polar bears when attacked. They also sometimes use their tusks to haul themselves out of the water, onto ice floes. When feeding, walruses depend on their heavily bristled muzzles; it's said they can detect food as small as a marble. Not bad for an animal that can weigh up to 2 tons. The walrus's primary food includes clams, mussels, snails, crabs, shrimp, and worms.

Willow Ptarmigan (*Lagopus lagopus*): One of three species of ptarmigan (the others are the rock and the white-tailed), the willow is the most widespread. It is also Alaska's state bird, as picked by schoolchildren in a statewide vote. As its name suggests, this member of the *Phasianidae* family (which includes both ptarmigan and grouse) tends to hang out in willow thickets, where it both feeds and hides from a variety of predators, such as hawks, falcons, owls, and foxes. Aggressively protective parents, willow ptarmigan have been known to attack humans and grizzly bears to defend their young.

Wolf (*Canis lupus*): The largest and most charismatic of the far North's wild canines, wolves roam throughout all of mainland Alaskan while inhabiting every imaginable habitat, from rain forest to high mountain valleys to Arctic tundra. They form close-knit family groups, or packs, which may range from a few animals to more than 30 (6 to 12 is more the norm). Wolf packs hunt a variety of prey, from small mammals and birds to caribou, moose, deer, and Dall sheep. They communicate with each other through body language, barks, and the howls that are considered by many to be the voice of the wilderness.

Wolverine (*Gulo gulo*): Consider yourself lucky if you see a wolverine, because they are among the most secretive animals of the North. They are also fierce predators, with enormous strength and endurance. Biologists at Denali National Park once reported seeing a wolverine drag a Dall sheep carcass more than 2 mi; an impressive feat, since the sheep likely weighed three to four times what the wolverine did. They have been known to run 40 mph through snow when chased by human hunters. And they routinely walk 10 to 30 mi while hunting food. Though they look a lot like bears and have the ferocity of a grizzly, wolverines are in fact the largest members of the weasel family.

Wood Frog (*Rana sylvatica*): The wood frog is one of the few amphibians to inhabit Alaska—and the only one to live north of the Panhandle. These frogs range as far north as the Arctic, surviving winters through the help of a biochemical change that allows them to remain alive, in a sort of suspended state, while frozen. Come spring, the bodies revive after thawing. Though they mate and lay their eggs in water, wood frogs spend most of their lives on land, in moist areas. They feed on insects and in turn are eaten by a variety of fish, birds, and small mammals.

Flora

Balsam Poplar and Black Cottonwood (*Populus balsamifera and Populus trichocarpa*): These two closely related species sometimes interbreed and are difficult, if not impossible, to tell apart. They prefer moist terrain and are often found on valley bottoms, but may also grow on hillsides, in mixed spruce hardwood forests. Mature trees of both species have thick gray bark that is rough and deeply furrowed. In midsummer they produce large cottony seed pods.

They also have large shiny, arrowhead-shaped leaves that turn from green to yellow in fall.

Birch (*Betula*): Ranging from Kodiak Island to the Brooks Range, birch trees are important members of Alaska's boreal forests. Deciduous trees that prefer well-drained soils, they have white bark and green heart-to-diamond-shaped leaves with sharp points and toothed edges. In fall the leaves turn golden yellow. One species, the paper birch (*Betula papyrifera*), is easily distinguished by its white, peeling, paperlike bark.

Blueberry (*Vaccinium*): A favorite of berry pickers, blueberries are found throughout Alaska, except for the farthest northern reaches of the Arctic. They come in a variety of forms, including head-high forest bushes and sprawling tundra mats that may rise only an inch or two above the ground. Pink, bell-shape flowers bloom in spring and dark blue to almost black fruits begin to ripen in July or August, depending on the locale.

Cow Parsnip (*Heracleum lanatum*): Also known to some residents as wild celery or Indian celery, cow parsnip resides in open forests and meadows. The plant may grow several feet high, with dull green leaves the size of dinner plates, thick stalks that are hollow and hairy, and umbrella-shape clusters of white flowers. Ranging throughout southern and interior Alaska, the cow parsnip has a edible stem. But anyone who harvests—or walks among—this species must take great care. Oils on the stalks, in combination with sunlight, can produce severe blistering on the skin.

Devil's Club (*Echinopanax horridum*): This is a prickly forest shrub that may grow 4 to 8 feet high (sometimes higher) and forms dense, spiny thickets on moist forest soils. A woodland species, it ranges from the Panhandle into South Central Alaska and the Alaska Peninsula. Hikers need to be wary of this plant: its large, maple-like leaves (which can be a foot or more across) have spines on their stems and veins, with needles covering its pale brown trunk. Getting caught in a thicket of devil's club is no fun. In late summer, bright red berries grow in a bunch at the plant's top; favored by black bears, they're bitter to humans.

Salmonberry (*Rubus spectabilis*): This is a coastal berry, ranging from Southeast Alaska, throughout the South Central region, and west to the Aleutian Chain. The salmonberry "canes," on which the leaves and fruits grow, may reach 7 feet tall or higher; they grow in dense thickets. The juicy raspberry-like fruits may be either orange or red at maturity; the time of ripening varies with the region, from late June through August.

Spruce (*Picea*): Three species of spruce grow in Alaska and one or another can be found in nearly all wooded areas. Sitka spruce (*Picea sitchensis*) is an important member of coastal rain forest communities; white spruce (*Picea glauca*) prefers dry, well-drained soils in boreal forests that stretch from South Central Alaska north to the Arctic; black spruce (*Picea mariana*) thrives in wet, boggy areas with standing water and often underlain by permafrost.

Tall fireweed (*Epilobium angustifolium*): The fireweed is among the first plants to reinhabit burn areas and, in the proper conditions, it grows like a weed—hence the name. Found throughout much of Southeast, South Central, Western, and Interior Alaska, it's a beautiful plant, with showy fuchsia flowers growing on its stalks. The flowers bloom from bottom to top and it's sometimes said that the final opening of flowers is a sign that winter is only weeks away. Spring fireweed shoots can be eaten raw or steamed and its blossoms can be added to salads. A related species is dwarf fireweed (*Epilobium latifolium*); also known as "river beauty," it is shorter and bushier, and often grows along rivers and in alpine meadows.

Wild Prickly Rose (*Rosa acicularis*): A woodland plant, the wild rose stretches across much of Alaska, from the Southeast Panhandle north to the Brooks Range. Serrated leaves grow on prickly spines and fragrant, five-petaled flowers begin blooming in late spring. The flowers vary in color from light pink to dark red and at their peak send a wonderfully sweet fragrance throughout the forest. Appearing in late summer and fall, bright red rose "hips" rich in vitamin C can be harvested for jellies, wine, soups, or pie.

Willow (*Salix*): An estimated three dozen species of willow grow in Alaska. Some, like the felt-leaf willow (*Salix alaxensis*), may reach tree size; others form thickets of bushes; still others, like the Arctic willow (*Salix arctica*), hug the ground in alpine terrain. They often grow thickest in the sub-alpine zone between forest and tundra. Whatever the size, willows produce soft "catkins" (pussy willows) which are actually columns of densely packed flowers without petals. Their smooth-edged leaves come in various shades of green, turning yellow in fall. The plant is an important food for many species of animals, from moose to songbirds to ptarmigan.

— Bill Sherwonit

NATIVE ALASKANS

THE HISTORY OF ALASKA'S NATIVE peoples—Eskimos, Indians, and Aleuts—is not unlike that of aboriginal people throughout Central and North America. After they had held domain over their land for thousands of years, their elaborate societies were besieged by a rapid onslaught of white settlers. Unable to stem the tide, the Native peoples were forced into retreat.

The first European to visit Alaska—in 1728—was Vitus Bering, a Dane serving in the Russian navy. Bering died on his journey home, but survivors from that voyage returned to Russia with a rich booty of sea-otter furs, sparking a stampede that would crush the traditional lifestyles of Alaska's Native peoples. The way was open for eager Russian fur traders who plundered Aleut territory along the Aleutian Islands.

Records indicate that the Native population of the Aleutian chain dropped from perhaps 20,000 to about 2,500 in the first 50 years of Russian rule. Diseases took a heavy toll, but the more ruthless among the Russian frontiersmen were also responsible—killing Aleut leaders to discourage uprisings. Stories of brutality are common. One trader, Feodor Solovief, reportedly tied together 12 Aleuts and fired a musket ball through them to see how far it would penetrate. It stopped in the body of the ninth man.

In 1867 when the United States purchased Alaska, the Natives were classified in the Treaty of Cession as "uncivilized tribes." To early tourists, they were little more than "those charming folk you take pictures of in their quaint villages."

Early missionaries and government teachers in Southeast Alaska ordered Indian totem poles destroyed, mistakenly believing them to be pagan symbols. Important works of art were lost. The totem poles of the Tlingit and Haida Indians were—and still are—simply the decorative record of outstanding events in the life of a family or clan.

The plight of the Natives improved little as Alaska grew more prosperous by exploiting its great natural resources. A painful split between traditional and modern living developed—public health experts call it "a syndrome of grief." Under increasing pressure from this clash of cultures, alcoholism grew to epidemic levels, and the suicide rate of Alaskan Natives climbed to twice that of Native Americans living on reservations in the continental United States. Still, by the 1960s, Native groups were making major strides toward claiming overdue political clout. In 1966 Native leaders from across the state gathered and organized the present Alaska Foundation of Natives. It was a fragile coalition of differing cultures, but the meeting was a significant move. With 16% of the state's population, a unified Native voice was suddenly a political force to be reckoned with.

At the same time, Eskimo leaders founded the *Tundra Times* and selected Howard Rock, a quiet, articulate man from Point Hope village, as its editor. Rock, whose background was in art rather than journalism, quickly prodded Natives to press their aboriginal land claims.

"The natives are reticent by nature, and time was passing them by," the Eskimo editor said. "At first, it was kind of discouraging. Nothing happened. And then, one by one, the Native leaders started speaking up."

The *Tundra Times* helped file the first suit for Native land claims. More lawsuits followed, and soon the whole state was tied up in litigation. Oil companies, hungry to build a pipeline from the newly discovered giant oil field at Prudhoe Bay to Valdez, on Alaska's southern coast, soon realized they could not get federal construction permits until the Native land claims were settled.

In 1971 the Natives won a spectacular settlement in Congress: 40 million acres of land and almost $1 billion in cash. The settlement has not been a cure-all for the many problems of Alaska's Natives. Poverty is still widespread, as little of the land-claims money (allocated mostly to 13 regional, for-profit Native corporations by Congress) has trickled down to the village level. But the settlement has given many a sense of dignity and purpose. Several villages in the Arctic have voted themselves "dry" (prohibiting alcohol) to combat drinking problems.

Today, the fundamental issue is whether the Natives will be allowed by the larger Alaskan society to pursue their own future, says Byron Mallott, former chief operating officer of Sealaska Corp., the regional Native corporation for Southeast Alaska.

"In one way, Alaska is truly the last frontier," Mallott says. "Will the final chapter of the total and unremitting decimation of our nation's Native American people be written in Alaska—or will, with the benefit of the lesson of history, Alaska be the place where Native peoples finally are able to become a part of the overall society with their pride, strength, and ethnicity intact?" There are, he adds, few guideposts to suggest the answer.

Most of Alaska's Natives still reside in widely scattered communities spread across the ½-million square mi of Alaska. Unlike the Native Americans of the Lower 48 states, the Alaskan Natives have never been restricted to reservations. Many villages remain isolated, the preference of traditional villagers; others have plunged into modern life with mixed results. Recently, Alaska's Native peoples have become more enterprising in the tourist business. No longer content to let out-of-state tour operators have all the business, they are now starting to take charge of tours in their communities.

The various Native peoples tend to group in well-defined regions. Here is a brief look at the different Native cultures and their locations.

Eskimos. Most of Alaska's more than 40,000 Eskimos are found in scattered settlements along the Bering Sea and Arctic Ocean coasts, the deltas of the lower Yukon and Kuskokwim rivers in western Alaska, and on remote islands in the Bering Sea such as St. Lawrence, Nunivak, and Little Diomede. The principal Arctic and sub-Arctic Eskimo communities include Barrow, Kotzebue, Nome, Gambell, Savoonga, Point Hope, Wainwright, and Shishmaref.

The Eskimos are divided into two linguistic groups: the Inupiat of the Far North and the Yup'ik, who reside mostly along the coastal regions of the west. The Yup'ik share the same dialect as the Eskimos of Siberia. Both groups are famed for their hunting and fishing skills. They are also noted craftspeople, carving animals and creating jewelry from Native materials.

Indians. Alaska has four major Indian cultures: Tlingit, Haida, Athabascan, and Tsimshian.

Once among North America's most powerful tribes, the **Tlingits** (pronounced *klink*-its) are found mostly throughout coastal Southeast Alaska. They number about 13,000 and live in cities such as Juneau, Ketchikan, and Sitka and in villages from Hoonah, near Juneau, to Klukwan, near Haines.

The Tlingits developed a highly sophisticated culture and fought hard against Russian incursions. Social status among early Tlingits depended on elaborate feasts called potlatches. Heads of families and clans vied in giving away vast quantities of valuable goods, their generosity so extravagant at times that the hosts fell into a form of ancient bankruptcy. There are still potlatches for important occasions, such as funerals, but they are greatly scaled down from earlier times.

Haidas are also found mainly in Southeast Alaska, as well as in British Columbia. They number only about 1,000 in Alaska. Their principal community is Hydaburg on Prince of Wales Island, near Ketchikan. The Queen Charlotte Islands of British Columbia are another Haida center. Historically, the Haidas were far-ranging voyagers and traders. Some historians credit the artistic Haidas with originating totem carving among Alaska's Natives.

Most of Alaska's 7,000 or so **Athabascan** Indians are found in the villages of Alaska's vast Interior, including Fort Yukon, Stevens Village, Beaver, Chalkyitsik, and Minto, near Fairbanks. Other Athabascans are scattered from the Kenai Peninsula–Cook Inlet area, near Anchorage, to the Copper River area near Cordova. Linguistically, the Athabascans are related to the Navajo and Apache of the American Southwest. They were driven out of Canada by Cree tribes more than 700 years ago.

The ancestral home of the **Tsimshian** (pronounced *sim*-shee-ann) Indians was British Columbia, but Tsimshian historians say their forebears roamed through much of southeastern Alaska fishing, hunting, and trading long before the arrival of the white man. The 1,000 or so Tsimshians of Alaska settled in 1887 on Annette Island, near Ketchikan, when a dissident Church of England lay missionary, William Duncan, led them out of British Columbia to escape religious persecution. The town of Metlakatla on Annette Island is their principal community. Their artwork includes wood carvings, from totem poles to ceremonial masks.

Aleuts. With their villages on the Aleutian Islands, curving between Siberia and Alaska like broken beads, the Aleuts (pronounced al-ee-*oots*) were first in the path of early explorers and ruthless fur traders. There are about 7,000 Aleuts in Alaska today, their principal communities being Dutch Harbor/Unalaska, Akutan, Nikolski, and Atka in the Aleutians and St. Paul and St. George in the Pribilof Islands. Grass basketry, classed by museums as some of the best in the world, is the principal art of the Aleuts. Finely woven baskets from Attu, at the tip of the Aleutian chain—where villages were destroyed in American–Japanese combat during World War II and never rebuilt—are difficult-to-obtain treasures.

— Stanton H. Patty

THE CHARACTER OF ALASKA

If you're considering a cruise to Alaska, chances are you're already enchanted by the imagery associated with the 49th American state. After all, "The Great Land," a loose translation of the Aleut word *Alyeska,* boasts the highest mountain in North America—Mt. McKinley (also called Denali)—as well as 17 of the 20 highest peaks in the United States. There are more bald eagles here than anywhere else, more totem poles, thousands of glaciers, king-size salmon, and humongous halibut.

There is nothing ordinary about this land—or the people who call it home. The people of Alaska embody a spirit of adventure, self-sufficiency, and independence. Status in Alaska is measured by longevity. The greatest honor, and the title of "sourdough," is reserved for those who have spent the most time in Alaska. In the gold-rush days, prospectors and pioneers carried a stash of sourdough starter so that they could always whip up a batch of bread in short order. The old-timers became known as sourdoughs, beginning the tradition.

If your mountains are skyscrapers and wildlife means mostly pigeons, Alaska is the place to satisfy your craving for space. Room to roam is something Alaska has in abundance. Alaska is the largest state in the Union; its 570,373 square mi equal one-fifth the land mass of the Lower 48. A popular postcard shows Alaska superimposed on a map of the United States: it stretches nearly from sea to shining sea.

Geography alone makes Alaska an ideal cruise destination. Except for those in and around Haines and Skagway in the north, there are no roads linking the towns along the Panhandle. In fact, Juneau is the only state capital in the United States that cannot be reached over land. You fly in or you sail in, but you don't drive in. On a typical seven-day itinerary you'll visit up to four ports of call and one or two scenic bays or fjords. And the nature of ship travel is perfectly suited to discovering what Alaska is all about. From the deck of a cruise ship, you can come face to face with a glacier. From the dining room, you can watch a full moon rise over a snow-striped mountain. And you can enjoy it all in the lap of luxury.

The natural beauty of Alaska is hard to overstate. As you prepare for your cruise, consider these facts about Alaska's grandeur: the Inside Passage, the traditional route north to Alaska, stretches 1,000 mi from Puget Sound, Washington, in the south, to Skagway, Alaska, in the north. From there, the Gulf of Alaska arcs for another 500 mi from east to west. Alaska has thousands of glaciers. Among the most famous ones that cruise passengers visit are LeConte outside Petersburg, the southernmost calving glacier in North America, and Hubbard at Yakutat Bay in the Gulf of Alaska, 6 mi wide and 76 mi long to its source. There are 12 tidewater glaciers in Glacier Bay National Park and Preserve and another 16 glaciers in College Fjord off Prince William Sound. The Malaspina Glacier, at the entrance to Yakutat Bay, is bigger than the state of Rhode Island. Tongass National Forest, which spans great stretches of the Inside Passage, is the largest national forest in the United States. Wrangell–St. Elias National Park, a UNESCO World Heritage Site east of Anchorage and bordering the Gulf of Alaska, is the largest national park in the United States—six times the size of Yellowstone.

In such broad expanses of land, airplanes have become as common as taxis in New York. The Bush plane in particular holds a special place in Alaskan folklore: this was the machine that opened the wilderness and that provides the only access to remote communities to this day. Lake Hood, near the airport in Anchorage, is the world's largest and busiest seaplane base; if you have time, be sure to stop by to watch the brightly painted Cessnas and De Havilland Beavers coming and going hourly. Anchorage pays special tribute to the Bush pilots of the past in two museums, the Alaska Aviation Heritage Museum and the Reeve Aviation Picture Museum. Even today, the Bush pilot is a revered figure, and many Alaskans agree that there are few better ways to appreciate the wonder of the land than from the window of a Cessna.

Mere numbers cannot capture the effect of Alaska on the human spirit. First-time visitors will catch their breath at first sight of a glacier and gawk at Anchorage's Salmon Creek during the annual salmon run, when the water is so thick with fish it seems you could wade in and pluck one out.

Wildlife is everywhere in Alaska. Southeast Alaska has more brown bears than the rest of the United States combined. And Alaska ranks number one in bald eagles. Bird-watchers will have a field day looking for them perched high in the treetops—or atop telephone poles—all along the Inside Passage. In fact, eagles are so numerous here you'll have to remind yourself that they remain a threatened species. There's even an eagle hospital, the Alaska Raptor Rehabilitation Center in Sitka, where injured eagles and other birds of prey are nursed back to health.

You may also come across whales during your cruise. If so, your captain may cut the ship's engines so as not to disturb them and to allow you some time to observe them. The state has 15 species of whales. On a small-ship cruise, you may find yourself close enough to a gushing waterfall to fill a pitcher with the cool, mineral-rich glacial runoff. And don't be surprised if you see a bear foraging on the shoreline. Such are the simple pleasures of an Alaskan cruise: calving glaciers, sea lions and seals, and sensational sunsets—at midnight.

In addition to glaciers and wildlife, there's an exciting frontier history to discover. Scientists estimate that the first people arrived in Alaska some 15,000 years ago, when they migrated across the Bering Land Bridge from Asia. (Some expedition ships sail from Alaska to the Russian Far East, allowing you to follow the migration pattern in reverse.) The earliest evidence of human habitation along the Inside Passage can be found in Wrangell, where petroglyphs—mysterious markings carved into rocks and boulders on the beach—are thought to be at least 8,000 years old.

Alaska's indigenous people belong to one of four groups: Aleuts, Athabascans, Eskimos, and Northwest Coast Indians. The Aleuts live on the Aleutian Islands. Athabascans populate the Interior, and Eskimos inhabit the Arctic regions of the Far North. The Native Alaskans you are most likely to meet during your cruise are the Tlingit, Haida, or Tsimshian people of the Inside Passage.

The Tlingit are responsible for Alaska's famous totem carvings. Totem poles tell the story of a great event, identify members of the same clan, and honor great leaders. The best place to see totem poles is Saxman Native Village in Ketchikan. The original totems at the Totem Heritage Center are the oldest authentic poles in Alaska, some dating back about 200 years. Today you can still see Native artisans at work on totem poles in Ketchikan, Haines, and Sitka. Miniature totem reproductions are among the most popular souvenirs in Alaska, but ceremonial masks, decorative paddles, and woven baskets also make great gifts. These and other Native crafts are sold throughout the Inside Passage. Before you buy, look for the silver hand label, which guarantees authenticity.

Buying local crafts is just one way for cruise passengers to appreciate the local culture. Native Alaskans are often happy to show you around. In Juneau, Ketchikan, and Sitka, you can book a sightseeing tour with a Native point of view. Performances of Native dance and traditional storytelling entertain visitors in Juneau, Sitka, and Haines. Ask about these aboard your ship or at the visitor information office near the pier.

In the footsteps of Native Alaskans came European explorers. The first was Vitus Bering, who "discovered" Alaska and claimed it for Russia in 1741. The Russians made Kodiak their capital before moving the seat of government to Sitka in 1808. Next came British and Spanish explorers. Cook Inlet in Anchorage is named for British explorer Captain Cook. One member of Cook's expedition was George Vancouver, namesake of the Canadian port city where most Alaska cruises begin or end. Ketchikan sits on an island named after a Spaniard, the Count of Revillagigedo, viceroy of New Spain and a proponent of Spanish exploration of Alaska. Wrangell Island, at the southern end of the Inside Passage, is the only Alaskan port of call to have flown three flags—Russian, British, and finally American.

The connection with Europe is echoed in the nicknames given to some of Alaska's port cities. Valdez is often referred to as Alaska's Little Switzerland for the mountains that ring the city. Petersburg is Alaska's Little Norway. The town's residents still celebrate their Scandinavian heritage every May in a festival of Norwegian song and dance. If you are lucky enough to visit Petersburg on your cruise (only the smallest ships and ferries call here), you may be treated to a performance at the Sons of Norway Hall—followed by a Norwegian smorgasbord.

Russia sold Alaska to the United States in 1867 for $7.2 million, or about 2¢ an acre. Secretary of State William H. Seward, who orchestrated the purchase, was publicly ridiculed for his "folly." But opinions changed when word got out that gold had been discovered in the Far North; the news set off a stampede of legendary proportion. The gold rush, perhaps the most colorful episode in Alaska's storied history, reached a fever pitch during the winter of 1897–98. Some say up to 100,000 men headed for the goldfields. More conservative estimates put the number as low as 30,000. In either case, the Klondike gold rush put Alaska on the map, as gold-crazed prospectors, con men, and assorted other characters headed up the Inside Passage.

Anyone cruising Alaska should pick up a copy of *The Call of the Wild,* Jack London's classic novel based on his personal experiences in the Yukon. And if you're wondering what to watch, make it the Walt Disney adaptation of London's *White Fang*; it was filmed on location in Haines.

If you're an aficionado of gold-rush history, choose a cruise that includes a call at Skagway, the gateway to the Klondike of a century ago. As you sail the Lynn Canal, the natural channel that connects Skagway with the rest of the Inside Passage, keep in mind that you are following the same route and traveling in the same manner (albeit a bit more luxuriously) as the original prospectors. Once ashore, you'll hear the story of Frank Reid (the good guy) and Jefferson Randolph "Soapy" Smith (the bad guy), who shot it out for control of Skagway. You'll hear how Superintendent Samuel Steele of the Canadian Mounted Police called Skagway "the roughest place on earth." And you'll learn how, after the gold rush died down, Skagway became the birthplace of Alaska's tourism industry. Today the town looks much as it did in the early 1900s. The entire downtown area is a National Historic District, part of Klondike Gold Rush National Historic Park. Be sure to take a ride on the vintage parlor cars of the White Pass & Yukon Railway. It's one of the few chances cruise passengers have to venture deep into the mountains—just as prospectors traveled over the treacherous White Pass. From the cars of the train, you can still see the "Trail of '98," a footpath worn permanently into the mountainside.

Few establishments evoke the spirit of the frontier like the local saloon, and, depending on your itinerary, you'll have the opportunity to visit two of Alaska's most famous ones. Near the cruise-ship docks in Skagway is the Red Onion Saloon. To step inside is to return to 1898, when the saloon was founded; the bartender still serves drinks on the original mahogany bar. In Juneau, the Red Dog Saloon has been a favorite local watering hole since early in the last century. In fact, Wyatt Earp's six-shooter still hangs on the wall. It's said he left it here while just passing through.

Like Wyatt Earp, you, too, will just be passing through. But, as you are about to discover, cruising is a great way to see "The Great Land." Spend as much time as you can in Alaska. Bring plenty of film or videotape, don't forget a rain slicker, and do try everything. Go hiking and fishing. Ride the railroads, book a salmon bake, scope for eagles. Think big—and be sure to buy a souvenir totem pole.

ALASKA: A GEOLOGIC STORY

MOST PEOPLE know about Alaska's oil and gold. But did you know that the state has a desert? That camels once roamed here? That there's a fault line nearly twice as long as the San Andreas Fault? That the largest earthquake ever to hit North America struck Alaska in 1964 and affected the entire planet? That the state has 80 potentially active volcanoes and approximately 100,000 glaciers?

All these physical wonders are geological in origin and are in addition to a North Slope oil supply that accounts for 25% of U.S. production and more than 10% of U.S. consumption as well as caches of gold that fueled more than 20 rushes.

Nearly all visitors will have at least one encounter with a glacier (with 29,000 square mi of them, they're hard to miss). Courtesy of the Pleistocene Ice Age, high-latitude location, and abundant moisture from the North Pacific, Alaska has approximately 100,000 of these large sheets of ice. The vast majority are in the southern and southeastern parts of the state, as these are the areas with the most moisture. How much moisture? Portions of the Chugach Mountains can gather 600 inches of snow each year, an amount that is comparable, in rain, to the annual precipitation in Seattle. In north-central Alaska, the Brooks Range contains a glacial field of approximately 280 square mi. Although small by Alaskan standards, it is larger than all the glacial fields in the rest of the United States combined, which comprise approximately 230 square mi.

There are alpine or valley glaciers, those that form high in mountain valleys and travel to lower elevations. Alaska harbors several of the great alpine glaciers in the world, found in the high country of the Alaska Range, the Talkeetna, Wrangell, Chugach, St. Elias, and Coast mountains. Some, such as the Bering Glacier, come tantalizingly close to the water. At more than 100 mi in length, and with an area of more than 2,250 square mi, the Bering is the longest and largest Alaskan glacier, its seclusion guarded by Cape St. Elias and the stormy waters of the Gulf of Alaska. Also impressive are the Hubbard, its imposing terminus dominating the head of isolated Yakutat Bay; and the Columbia, foreboding and threatening, calving icebergs that tack in line like Nelson's fleet across the mouth of Valdez Arm.

The Malaspina Glacier is an unusual piedmont glacier. Formed by the coalescence of several glaciers, this 850-square-mi mass is lobate, or fan-shape, and occupies a benchland on the northwest side of Yakutat Bay. So much of the Alaska Range, Wrangell, Chugach, St. Elias, and Coast mountains are covered by glacial ice that it is often more appropriate to talk about ice fields than individual glaciers.

Then there are the great tidewater glaciers of Prince William Sound and southeastern Alaska. Alpine glaciers that come right to the water's edge, they creak, moan, thunder, and calve off great bergs and little bergeys. The world's longest is the previously mentioned Hubbard Glacier, which, because it stretches more than 70 mi from its head in Canada to its terminus in Yakutat Bay, is both an alpine and a tidewater glacier. Sixteen tidewater glaciers can be found in Glacier Bay National Park, 20 in Prince William Sound. Some are advancing, some retreating. Hubbard has not only advanced in recent years but has surged. In 1986, a surge by Hubbard blocked the Russell Fjord at the upper end of Yakutat Bay, turning it into Russell Lake. Later that year, the portion of the glacier acting as a dam in front of Russell Lake gave way, violently releasing the backed-up water to an elevation of 83 feet above sea level. That's pretty impressive when you stop to think that the Russell Fjord is normally at sea level. Surging glaciers can move downhill hundreds of feet per day. The Hubbard's greatest surge was in September 1899, when it advanced ½ mi into the bay in just five minutes, courtesy of an earthquake.

Glaciologists are interested in knowing more about how glaciers, especially tidewater glaciers, advance and retreat. The Columbia Glacier, both an alpine and a tidewater glacier like the Hubbard, in Prince William Sound is approximately 40 mi long, covers more than 400 square mi, and flows to sea level from 10,000- to 12,000-foot peaks in the Chugach Range. Its width at the terminus can be as much as 4 mi; its ice thickness can reach 900 feet (on average 300 feet above the water and 600 feet below). It is also only 8 mi from the shipping lanes traveled by oil tankers leaving the Alaska pipeline terminal at Valdez. Columbia has been receding since the early 1980s, sending berg after berg into Prince William Sound and into the shipping lanes to Valdez, and now that it's receding, it has the potential to calve even more bergs. Although a shallow sill, or shoal, of underwater glacial deposits keeps icebergs more than 100 feet thick from entering Prince William Sound, some big bergs still make it to the shipping lanes. Columbia's calving took its toll just after midnight on March 29, 1989, when Captain Hazlewood of the *Exxon Valdez* steered too far east while trying to avoid bergs in Valdez Arm and ran aground on Bligh Reef.

You can see many glaciers from the Alaska Marine Highway. The tidewater glaciers of Glacier Bay and the Malaspina and Hubbard glaciers in Yakutat Bay are best seen by boat or ship. Sailing into Valdez Arm, you may see more of the Columbia Glacier than you want—it's often coming to see you in the form of scores of bergs and bergeys, forcing you east toward Bligh Reef. Once you are safely ashore in Valdez it's time to look at valley glaciers. You can access either the Valdez or Worthington Glacier by road. If in the Matanuska Valley, go see the Matanuska Glacier. If on the Kenai Peninsula, try either the Exit or Portage Glacier. If you are visiting Juneau, the Mendenhall Glacier is on the outskirts of town.

More than 80 volcanoes in Alaska are potentially active. Novarupta, Pavlof, Augustine, Redoubt, and Spurr are Alaskan volcanoes that are part of the "Ring of Fire," the volcanic rim of the Pacific. From Mt. Wrangell at 144° west longitude in Southeast Alaska to Cape Wrangell at 173° east longitude at the tip of the Aleutian archipelago, southern Alaska exists, to paraphrase historian Will Durant, by volcanic decree . . . subject to change.

Anchorage (and the greater Cook Inlet area) is a great place to watch volcanoes erupt. Augustine, Redoubt, and Spurr volcanoes have put on shows up and down the Cook Inlet; the Mt. Spurr eruption of August 1992 temporarily stopped air travel into and out of Anchorage. The most violent Alaskan eruption? The 2½-day eruption of Novarupta in 1912 in what is now Katmai National Park. The 2.5 cubic mi of ash deposited there has left an Alaskan legacy: the surreal Valley of Ten Thousand Smokes.

The length of a fault system and whether or not the fault is straight over great distances are of interest to geologists. Fault length is related to earthquake magnitude. Generally speaking, the longer a fault, the greater the potential magnitude. Impressed by the 600-mi length of California's San Andreas? The onshore portion of the Denali Fault System is more than 1,000 mi long. Numerous long faults around the world move horizontally. This produces some interesting results if the fault trace is not straight. A fault system such as the Denali has a large component of horizontal movement (called strike-slip motion): crustal blocks on either side move past each other, rather than up or down. If a strike-slip fault bends, one of two situations results: a gap or hole in the crust (usually filled by volcanic outbreaks and/or sediments sloughing into the hole) or a compression of the bend, resulting in vertical uplift (mountains). Which condition occurs is a function of fault motion, whether into or out of the bend. South of Fairbanks, the Denali Fault System changes trend, from northwest–southeast to northeast–southwest. The sense of horizontal motion is into the bend, resulting in vertical uplift. What mountain just happens to be in the vicinity? Mt. McKinley, at 20,320 feet the tallest mountain in North America. Moreover, its relief (difference in elevation between the base and top of the mountain), at 18,000 feet, is unsurpassed. Mt. Everest is more than 29,000 feet, but "only" 11,000 feet above the Tibetan Plateau, which forms its base.

With such big faults, it's no wonder geologists look at Alaska as big earthquake country. Seward, Valdez, Whittier, and Anchorage are just some of the more prominent names associated with the Good Friday Earthquake of 1964. Upgraded in 1977 to magnitude 9.2, the Good Friday quake is the largest on record for North America. Fifteen to thirty seconds is not unusual for ground motion in a big, destructive earthquake; Alaskans shook for three to four minutes during the Good Friday quake. The epicenter was about 6 mi east of College Fjord in Prince William Sound, some 70 mi east of Anchorage. Vertical deformation (uplift or down-dropping of the land) affected an area of 100,000 square mi. By the time the shaking had stopped, the area of Latouche Island had moved 60 feet to the southeast and portions of the Montague Island area were uplifted by as much as 30 feet. The area of Portage was down-dropped by approximately 10 feet. The largest tsunami (often misnamed a tidal wave) that hit Hilo, Hawaii, checked in at 12½ feet; the largest at Crescent City, California, was 13 feet; and in Chenega, Alaska, Native residents were never sure what rose from the sea to smite them . . . just that it was 90 feet tall. The entire planet was affected: the area in which the quake was felt by people is estimated at 500,000 square mi—South Africa checked in to report that groundwater was sloshing around in wells.

Geologists generally describe tsunamis with respect to displacement on a fault underwater. They use the more general term "seismic sea wave" when other things, such as submarine landslides, cause enormous waves. The 90-foot seismic sea wave that hit Chenega was topped by the 220-foot wave reported from the Valdez Arm area. But a few years earlier in southeastern Alaska, on the evening of July 9, 1958, an earthquake in the Yakutat area dumped an enormous landslide into the head of Lituya Bay. The result was a seiche, or splash wave, that traveled 1,740 feet up the opposite mountainside.

Impressed yet? In the last century the average recurrence interval for Alaskan earthquakes in excess of 8.0 on the Richter Scale was 10 years. The recurrence interval for earthquakes over 7.0 is just over a year. Never mind California—Alaska is the most seismically active state in the Union. Volcanic hazard? Well, Pavlof has averaged an eruption every 6 years over the last 240.

Earthquakes, volcanoes—it's not called the Ring of Fire for nothing. The North American and Pacific tectonic plates are battling all the way from California to Japan. The two battle awfully hard in Alaska.

And now about that desert. The North Slope of Alaska is 80,000 square mi of frozen, windswept desert where Inupiat Eskimos live. It's a desert from the climatological perspective that the North Slope receives less than 10 inches of precipitation each year. If you go around the west end of the Brooks Range, you can even find sand dunes—Great Kobuk, Little Kobuk, and Hunt River sand-dune fields. Temperatures during the short, cool summers are usually between 30°F and 40°F. Temperatures during the winter can average –20°F. In winter, the Arctic Ocean moderates temperatures on the North Slope . . . but there is nothing to moderate the wind.

The first people to "come into the country" came across the Bering Land Bridge from Asia, between 10,000 and 40,000 years ago. The Bering Land Bridge was a product of the Pleistocene epoch—the "Great Ice Age"—which lowered the sea level enough for the bridge to form. At the start of the Mesozoic era (beginning about 245 million years before the present), sandstones and conglomerates deposited in a warm, shallow sea marked the beginning of Prudhoe Bay. That abundant organic matter is now abundant oil under the North Slope. Also during the Mesozoic era, oil-bearing shales were deposited in the Cook Inlet, home of Alaska's first oil boom; copper and silver deposits were formed in what is now the Copper River country; Cretaceous swamps in South Central Alaska became the Matanuska coalfield; and gold was emplaced around present-day Fairbanks and near Nome on the Seward Peninsula.

The oldest rocks in Alaska are of Precambrian age (the "Time Before Life") and are in southwestern Alaska. They have been dated at 2 billion years of age, nearly half the age of the earth. Rocks 1 billion years old have been identified in the area of the Brooks Range south to the Yukon River. Interestingly, the 1-billion-year-old rocks are native; the 2-billion-year-old rocks are expatriates. In fact, southern and southeastern Alaska are composed of a mosaic or quilt of microplates, all much smaller than continent size. Some terranes (blocks or fragments of the Earth's crust that may vary in age, geologic character, or site of origin) arrived in Alaska from as far south as the equator.

Certain Alaskan rocks tell a tale of warm climates and seas. Evidence? Hike the Holitna River basin in Southwest Alaska and look for fossil remains of the many trilobites (those now-extinct three-lobe marine arthropods that scavenged the bottoms of warm, shallow, Cambrian seas—parents, if you don't know what they look like, ask your children). The central interior of Alaska evidently was never covered by ice but was instead a cool steppe land roamed by mammoths, bison, horses, saber-toothed cats, and camels. Yes, camels.

Alaska's stunning expanse incorporates fire and ice, wind and rain, volcano, glacier, windswept tundra, towering rain forest, and mist-shrouded island. Its geologic story covers a great deal of time and distance and has produced (and is producing) some of the most exquisite land anywhere. In the north, the rocks tell a story of relative stability—geological homebodies born and raised. In the south, the patchwork terrains tell a tale of far-traveled immigrants coming into the country. Geological processes that have produced, and are still producing, both homebodies and expatriates create a land in constant flux. But the majesty of the land . . . that is the unchanging legacy of Alaska.

— Dr. Charles Lane

BOOKS & MOVIES

Books

Alaska has long been a setting for tales of heroes, great journeys, and people's epic struggle with nature. Novels with rich descriptions of the state's people, wildlife, and landscapes include Ivan Doig's *The Sea Runners* (Penguin), an adventure set in 1853, when Alaska still belonged to Russia; *Athabasca* (out of print), an Alistair MacLean thriller set around the trans-Alaska pipeline; and *Sitka* (Signet), by the popular chronicler of the American frontier, Louis L'Amour. *Alaska* (Random House), by James Michener, is a weighty historical novel about the state from prehistoric to modern times.

Alaskan authors have written a number of mystery novels about their state. Among the best are Sue Henry's *Murder on the Iditarod Trail* (Avon); John Straley's *The Woman Who Married a Bear* (Signet), about the adventures of private eye Cecil Younger; and Dana Stabenow's *A Cold-Blooded Business* (Berkley Publishing Group), whose hero is Aleut private investigator Kate Shugak.

Alaska has produced an even more significant collection of high-quality nonfiction literature. John McPhee's *Coming into the Country* (Noonday Press) is considered by some to be the most insightful book ever written about Alaska. Joe McGinniss, in *Going to Extremes* (Plume), presents a provocative "outsider's" portrait of Alaska's varied communities, people, and landscapes. Velma Wallis's best-selling *Two Old Women: An Alaska Legend of Betrayal, Courage and Survival* (Epicenter Press) recounts a traditional Native Alaskan story.

For lovers of adventure, Art Davidson's *Minus 148 Degrees: The First Winter Ascent of Mt. McKinley* (The Mountaineers Books) describes the harrowing survival story of mountaineers caught in a ferocious storm on North America's highest peak. John Krakauer's *Into the Wild* (Anchor) wonderfully constructs the life and death of a young man who died in the Alaskan wilderness while on a personal vision quest. *Fish Camp: Life on an Alaskan Shore* (Counterpoint Press), by Nancy Lord, describes the natural and cultural history of the place where she and her partner have fished for salmon for the past two decades. Former Alaska poet laureate John Haines has written several books of poetry and essays. Among his best is the essay collection *The Stars, the Snow, the Fire* (Graywolf Press), which recounts 25 years in Alaska's wilderness. Another compelling collection of essays with natural-history themes is Sherry Simpson's *The Way Winter Comes: Alaska Stories* (Sasquatch Books). One anthology of special note is Wayne Mergler's *The Last New Land: Stories of Alaska Past and Present* (Alaska Northwest Books), a wide-ranging collection of poems, short stories, and essays about Alaska; another is Bill Sherwonit's *Denali: A Literary Anthology* (The Mountaineers Books), which presents a century's worth of published stories about Mt. McKinley, North America's highest mountain, and the surrounding wilderness.

Movies

The Last Frontier has also inspired a number of filmmakers, many offering family fare. *White Fang* (1991), based on the Jack London novel, is a Walt Disney production about the life of a wild wolf dog and the hardships prospectors faced during the Klondike gold rush. The movie set is now a tourist destination in Haines. The animated family film *Balto* (1995) tells the story of one of the canine heroes in Alaska's 1925 Great Race of Mercy, in which mushers and dog teams carry diphtheria serum to Nome to stop an outbreak of the deadly disease. More pooches star in the family comedy *Snow Dogs* (2002), in which Cuba Gooding Jr. plays a Miami dentist who inherits a team of huskies. Another popular family flick is

Alaska (1996) in which two teens set out to rescue their Bush pilot dad from the wilderness.

A number of action-adventure pictures have also taken place in Alaska. *Runaway Train* (1985), a thriller starring Jon Voight, was filmed south of Anchorage; the scenery and ending are equally dramatic. *On Deadly Ground* (1994) stars Steven Seagal as an oil-company troubleshooter who rebels after discovering his employers are exploiting the land and its Native peoples. A portion of *Star Trek VI* (1991) was filmed on the Knik Glacier, northeast of Anchorage. *Limbo* (1999), set in Southeast Alaska, is a frontier drama that centers on a commercial fisherman who has become afraid of the sea. In *The Edge* (1997) Anthony Hopkins and Alec Baldwin have a great deal to be afraid of while lost in the Alaskan wilderness. *Insomnia* (2002), starring Al Pacino and Robin Williams, sees two Los Angeles detectives sent to Alaska to investigate a murder.

In August 2005,Werner Herzog's highly anticipated movie *Grizzly Man* opened in theaters, telling the fascinating and ultimately sordid story of Timothy Treadwell, a zany nature lover and actor who lived among Alaska's grizzly bears (and who was found, along with his girlfriend, mauled to death in 2003). Herzog uses Treadwell's original footage of bears as well as dozens of interviews with family members and friends.

INDEX

A

B

PHOTO CREDITS

Cover Photo (Denali National Park): *Larry Ulrich Stock Photography*. F7, *Photodisc*. F10, *Mark Newman/age fotostock*. F11 (left), *Frank Lukasseck/age fotostock*. F11 (right), *Morales/age fotostock*. F12, *True North Images/age fotostock*. F13, *Richard Cummins/viestiphoto.com*. F16, *Photodisc*. F17 (left), *Stuart Westmorland/age fotostock*. F17 (right), *Bill Terry/viestiphoto.com*. F19, *Liane Cary/age fotostock*. F20, *Robert Winslow/viestiphoto.com*. F21 (left), *Photodisc*. F21 (right), *John W. Warden/age fotostock*.

Color Section: Self-propelled exploration in the waters of Prince William Sound: *True North Images/age fotostock*. Hiking in Glacier Bay National Park & Preserve: *Larry Carver/viestiphoto.com*. Colorful autumn tundra in Denali National Park & Preserve: *Joe Englander/viestiphoto.com*. A bull moose enjoying Alaskan waters: *Bill Terry/viestiphoto.com*. Bald Eagle, Alaska Raptor Center in Sitka: *Glenn W. Swan/viestiphoto.com*. Mt. McKinley: *Photodisc*. Grizzly bear: *Steve Kaufman/age fotostock*. Prince William Sound: *Larry Carver/viestiphoto.com*. Prince William Sound's Steller's sea lions: *Photodisc*. Humpback whale: *Michael S. Nolan/age fotostock*. Hiker, Chugach State Park: *True North Images/age fotostock*. Caribou: *Frank Krahmer/age fotostock*. Totem pole, Alaska Native Heritage Center in Anchorage: *Richard Cummins/viestiphoto.com*. Bald eagle: *Bill Terry/viestiphoto.com*.

NOTES

NOTES

ABOUT OUR WRITERS

Vancouver-born freelance writer **Sue Kernaghan** is a fourth-generation British Columbian. Between Fodor's assignments, Sue writes travel feature articles and management books.

Brian Kluepfel is a New Yorker who happens to reside in California. He has lived and worked in the Bronx, Bolivia, and Berkeley and is a proud graduate of the University of San Francisco's writing program. He is a *fútbol* fanatic and a huge fan of the San Jose Earthquakes, Barcelona of Spain, and Real Potosí of Bolivia. He sometimes strums his guitar in Bay Area pubs for grins, tips, and free pisco sours.

A resident of Homer, Alaska, **Don Pitcher**'s knowledge of the state comes from many seasons spent guiding visitors to brown-bear viewing areas, counting salmon at fish weirs, studying fires in Wrangell-St. Elias National Park, and building trails in rainy Southeast Alaska. He is the author of guidebooks on Alaska, Wyoming, Yellowstone, and the San Juan Islands, and his photos are available in galleries throughout Alaska. Learn more from his Web site, www.donpitcher.com.

A midwesterner who moved to Alaska in 1984, **Tom Reale** has traveled extensively throughout the state, writing about it and about wilderness adventures for a variety of publications. He and his wife hunt, fish, camp, backpack, ski, and hike at every opportunity.

An Anchorage resident since 1982, writer **Bill Sherwonit** has contributed stories about Alaska to a variety of newspapers, magazines, and books and is the author of four books on Alaska. He also teaches a class on wilderness writing at the University of Alaska.